PRAISE FOR a taste for chaos

A Taste for Chaos is a stunner of a book—smart, jarring, innovative, witty, provocative, wise, and beautifully written. As a sustained and unified work of literary analysis, this book is nothing short of dazzling, both in its meticulously structured central argument and in its intricate exploration of the artistic tensions between order and disorder, reason and intuition, design and improvisation. Not only is this a book about the artistic endeavor, but it is also a work of art in its own right.
—Tim O'Brien, author of *The Things They Carried*

An inquisitive examination of the impulse that yields literary improvisation—which is to say, literature itself...A smart blend of psychology, philosophy and literary history... A tour de force of reading in the fields of literary theory and history befitting a George Steiner or Erich Auerbach.
—*Kirkus Review*

A Taste for Chaos provides a sweeping view of the complex history of the notion of artistic spontaneity. Packed with erudition and references ranging from Lucretius to James Brown, and written with reader-friendly clarity, Fertel's book is a lively examination of the centuries-old debate between the improvisers and the deliberators. This detailed labor of love deserves its place on any serious bookshelf devoted to literary study or the history of ideas.
—Billy Collins, Poet Laureate; author of *Aimless Love*

Fertel has Erasmus jamming with Jung and Louis Armstrong, and you can almost tap your foot to it.
—Roy Blount, Jr., author of *Alphabet Juice*

The magnificent chapter on Hermes and Odysseus is alone worth the price of the entire volume.
—Stanley Lombardo, University of Kansas; translator of the *Iliad* and the *Odyssey*

Randy Fertel leads us on a brilliant literary exploration of improvisation and the art of appearing spontaneous. From Louis Armstrong to Derrida, Twain to Jung to Joyce, he shows how order emerges from chaos. It's a delightful and fascinating book, written with a jazz-like enthusiasm.
—Walter Isaacson, CEO, Aspen Institute; author of *The Innovators*, *Steve Jobs,* and *Leonardo da Vinci*

A Taste for chaos

What Randy Fertel says in his opus on improvisation in the arts, *A Taste for Chaos,* is both important and rich with a perceptive imagination; it is a good match to Isaacson's *The Innovators,* and stands tall as another huge and hand-carved broom that removes so much dust from the floors of the academy. Fertel is about stepping up to the issue and using his head for much more than a hat rack.

—Stanley Crouch, author of *Kansas City Lightning* and *Considering Genius: Writings on Jazz*

A Taste for Chaos is a work of love: a monument to erudition, with the kind of analytical depth and expanse of reading behind its arguments—and the kind of wit and elegance in its presentation—that come only with craft and time. This book was worth every minute of the wait.

—Fred Anderson, author of *The Dominion of War*

There's nothing quite like *A Taste for Chaos*: a cool, analytic, and deeply insightful book...about improvisation and chaos. Fertel argues that craft and "reason's click clack" lead nowhere without spontaneity. Through intriguing examples gleaned from literature and literary criticism, he lead us to the heart of creativity.

—Fred Starr, author of *Lost Enlightenment* and *Bamboula!*

An inspiring book, as eccentric as its subject. It answers the questions of why some people are wonderfully, surprisingly creative (and why the rest of us are ploddingly predictable trudgers). Bravo, Fertel!

—Bill Buford, author of *Heat* and *Among the Thugs*

I love this book. *A Taste for Chaos* had me at: "evaluation is one of the least interesting things we can do with spontaneity." Fertel opens the mysterious doorway of "spontaneous creation" and shows me something clear, new, and useful on every page. Fertel is learned and light, reliable and readable, provocative and pleasurable. Even in his writing style he has caught the vitality of spontaneous creation, including some dazzling forays, yet with the authoritative voice academics demand."

—Eric Booth, author of *The Everyday Work of Art* and *The Music Teaching Artist's Bible*

I started reading New Orleanian Randy Fertel's journey through the landscape of literary improvisation with a CD of Louis Armstrong's trumpet playing softly. Gradually I realized that Louis was Fertel's exemplar rather than simple accompanist, and that all those intimidating, august, marble-busted great men of letters—Rabelais, Milton, Joyce, Jung, and so on—had also been sitting up too late, smoking, working out their riffs. Who knew? There's a new and unanticipated note on every page of Fertel's exciting book.

—Richard Rabinowitz, author of *Revolution!*

A Taste for Chaos impressive and a delight to read. As a work that is wide ranging, bringing together both insight and illumination of the disparate, it's the kind of scholarship I most admire.

—David Lynn, Editor, *The Kenyon Review*

If jazz, like love, has its own inner logic, why shouldn't it have taken Randy Fertel four decades to riff through all our notions—and then some—of what it means to be an improvisational literary artist? Seeming contradictions are anywhere you find them, and serious work always has its own timetable.

—Paul Hendrickson, National Book Critics Circle winner; authr of *Hemingway's Boat*

In *A Taste for Chaos* Randy Fertel takes us deep into the substrata of the literary imagination and the creative process, linking such seemingly disparate minds as James Joyce's and Louis Armstrong's. It's a fascinating exposition of the mysteries and benefits of improvisation.

—Bruce Boyd Raeburn, Curator of the Hogan Jazz Archive, Tulane University;
       author of *New Orleans Style and the Writing of American Jazz History*

Fertel's writing is elegant and his undertaking impressive in scope and ambition, an interesting blend of close reading and panoramic vision.

—Amy Ziering, director/producer of the film *Derrida*

A highly personal tour de force of literary criticism that got me thinking in totally new ways about improvisation, spontaneity, and invention—the tools of the trade for any jazz musician.

—Tom Sancton, author of *Song for My Fathers*

A Taste for Chaos

The Art of Literary Improvisation

Second, revised edition

Randy Fertel

SPRING PUBLICATIONS

THOMPSON, CONN.

Published by Spring Publications
Thompson, Conn.

www.springpublications.com

Second, revised edition 2023 (2.1)

First published in 2015 by Spring Journal Books, New Orleans

Cover art:
Carpe Vitam
© 1999 Alan Gerson
Used with permission

Library of Congress Control Number: 2023930074

ISBN: 978-0-88214-987-5

CONTENTS

for

James Hillman

ferocious Trickster

and for

Diana Pinckley

mistress of her own "unpremeditated verse"

both much missed

ACKNOWLEDGMENTS

Over forty years, off and on, in the making, I fear I have forgotten more people who helped me along the way than I have managed to remember. Had I been less an improviser I would have kept better notes but it would be a lesser book. I hope they will forgive my negligence, which unlike many of my improvisers is not entirely a cultivated affectation.

First thanks go to Walter Kaiser who first accidently inspired my quest to understand how improvisations were *like* and to Robert Kiely and the late Morton Bloomfield who supported my dissertation long ago when no one in my field thought writing about spontaneity made any sense. The late Lilian Furst was an early supporter of my effort to make sense of Stendhal's "'lyrical' outpouring" (as Giuseppe di Lampedusa called it). I regret that I did not get to share the more mature development of my ideas before her passing. The late Don Taylor, who taught me more about reading than anyone, did read an early version. Richard Lanham read an early version and gave me a well-placed, if impatient, kick in the pants that kept me going. My colleagues Cynthia Lewis in English, and Fred Anderson in History and Lit helped me believe in the project. I learned more about writing while team-teaching with Fred than I learned anywhere else.

Investigative reporter, the late Ron Ridenhour damned an early version with faint but helpful praise when he responded, "you sure like big words." I've done my level best to take his implicit advice. Jungians Del McNeely, Marilyn Marshall, and Susan Rowland offered helpful direction when I ventured into their field. Colleagues in Vietnam Studies Wayne Karlin and Eric Schroeder (as well as Eric's wife Susan Palo) helped me give my argument shape and point. Former colleague at Tulane, Molly Rothenberg helpfully read pieces, as did Jim Miller at the New School for Social Research. Bruce Raeburn of Tulane Hogan Jazz Archive helped with the argument's jazz related material. Amy Ziering, co-director/producer of the documentary *Derrida,* helped with my discussion of the slippery French deconstructionist. Lynn Bell cast my chart and fatefully steered me toward Trickster and the Shadow. Joseph Wittreich in a summer NEH seminar spurred me to the Milton chapter, which Stanley Fish read and made suggestions for improving. Lawrence Weschler made helpful suggestions about the Robert Irwin discussion. David Lynn, David Baker, and Anna Duke Reach, all of the *Kenyon Review,* made helpful suggestions. Many thanks to Rebecca McClanahan and my colleagues in the Kenyon Review Summer Workshop, Patricia O'Hara especially, for helping me find a more accessible, less academic voice. Special thanks to Peter White for coaxing me there. Jan Rieveschl and André Stern listened long and deeply. Fred Starr and Richard Rabinowitz both read the manuscript in the late stages and both gave me a huge boost in morale. My two favorite students from all my years of teaching, Tony Gentry and Suzanne Farrell Smith, made key suggestions. Tony was there at the beginning when he was finishing his senior thesis on Whitman and Lawrence and I my dissertation. He brought Lawrence's "Man Alive"—who would have an important role here—to my attention. Suzanne urged me to tell more about why I personally found improv so compelling. Conrad Martin and Ham Fish, colleagues at the Ridenhour Prizes for Courageous Truth-telling, made helpful suggestions at the end. Tom Howorth traded in his AutoCad for a very helpful blue pencil. Favorite nephew Rien Fertel was among my keenest readers as was editor extraordinaire, Didi Goldenhaar. Steve Kupperman and Dan Kornstein gave counsel. Kimberly Corbett understood. Susan McLean Welsh, Ron Caron, and Rick Permutt, my oldest friends, all far more musical than I, were my most persistent and supportive readers. Tripp Friedler and the staff of Free Gulliver, Deborah Bradbury especially, gave me the freedom to explore my improvisers' freedom. Susan Beninati, Susie Penman, and Siobhan Drummond did yeoman's service in helping bring the manuscript home.

My late friends Diana Pinckley and James Hillman, to whom this book is jointly dedicated, both tricksters and improvisers of the first water, read early versions and lent moral support.

While my improvisers were rubbing my nose in the value and necessity of presence, my sons Matt and Owen made do in ways I may never understand with my being so often absent. They deserved better. Matt gave me just the right book at the right moment to spur me to my conclusion— for that much thanks.

Special thanks to Nancy Cater of Spring Journal Books for embracing the project and to Alan Gerson for permission to reprint his painting *Carpe Vitam*.

My sincere thanks to Klaus Ottmann of Spring Publications for his careful and expert preparation of this revised second edition.

A line will take us hours maybe;
Yet if it does not seem a moment's thought.
Our stitching and unstitching has been naught.
—W.B. Yeats, "Adam's Curse"

When either the political or the scientific discourse
announces itself as the voice of reason, it is playing God,
and should be spanked and stood in the corner.
—Ursula K. Le Guin, *Dancing at the Edge of the World*

To find a form that accommodates the mess, that is the
task of the artist now.
—Samuel Beckett, *Conversation with John Driver*

The greatest mystery is in unsheathed reality itself.
—Eudora Welty, *The Eye of the Story*

Everything changes but the avant-garde.
—Paul Valéry

Is chaos also a foundation?
—C.G. Jung, *Red Book*

Spontaneity remains outside explanation.
—James Hillman, *Pan and the Nightmare*

Writing in the New Paradigm

Writing this book has been an adventure and an education. Forty plus years in the making, this book is anything but an improvisation in the sense we usually mean: off the cuff, impromptu, and careless. It is *not,* or so I'd like to think, unmediated by reason and logic, as *improvisers* like to claim. Nonetheless it was an adventure because just as "my" improvisers, as I'd begun to call them, follow any notion that pops into their heads, so too I let them lead me, pursuing any link to other self-styled improvisers or to any related concept.

The one rule in contemporary, Second City-type comic improvisation is that players *must say yes.* If I start a sketch saying I met a green alien, you must build on that premise. Keith Johnstone, creator of Theatresports, a form of improvisational theatre, offers this scenario:

> [...] the first player to kill an idea loses; for example:
> —'You seem out of breath. Been running?'
> —'It's my asthma...'
> This asthma attack loses because it rejects the idea about running.[1]

"There are people who prefer to say 'Yes,'" Johnstone sums up, "and there are people who prefer to say 'No.' Those who say 'Yes' are rewarded by the adventures they have, and those that say 'No' are rewarded by the safety they attain."[2]

I said yes a lot and this book is a record of the adventures that ensued. To mention just one adventure chosen at random: Emerson's celebration in his *Essays* of "that source, at once the essence of genius, of virtue, and of life,

---

1. Kenneth Johnstone, *Impro for Storytellers: Theatresports and the Art of Making Things Happen* (New York: Routledge, 1999), 7.

2. Kenneth Johnstone, *Impro: Improvisation and the Theatre* (New York: Routledge, 1987), 92.

which we call Spontaneity or Instinct"[3] led me to Montaigne's. The *Essais* of Montaigne, that "unpremeditated and accidental philosopher" as he called himself, led me to Bacon's. Bacon's *Essays* led me to his *Advancement of Learning* and *Of the Wisdom of the Ancients* where I was surprised to find in the birth of the new science the same longing for unmediated experience that I'd found in "improvised" literary texts. My newfound interest in the history of science ensured that when it came out I glommed onto James Gleick's *Chaos: Making a New Science.*[4] Gleick's book recounted the slow emergence beginning in the early 1960s but gathering steam in the 1970s and 1980s in a number of fields—from meteorology to nonlinear mathematics to economics, to name just a few—of a science that found hidden order within turbulence. Chaotics articulated for me what I was finding in "chaotic" literary texts, how order emerges without apparent guidance. Soon I was tracking French philosopher Jacques Derrida's pursuit of "différance," one aspect of which is its "soliciting...in the sense that *solicitare,* in old Latin, means to shake as a whole, to make tremble in entirety."[5] Improvised texts were not only turbulent but disruptive. What they disrupted were the reigning notions of systematic order and rationality. Cognitive neuroscientist Iain McGilchrist helped explain how that disruption was hard-wired into the bi-cameral structure of the brain.

The adventure of following this and many other threads has thus been an education. When I was an undergraduate in the late 1960s, many of my English professors had gone to school in T.S. Eliot's *The Waste Land*. A tissue of "fragments...shored against [his] ruins," Eliot's poem taught us that to achieve whatever individual talent we aspired to as artists or as critics we had to marinate ourselves in the Great Tradition. Eliot's poem promoted a syllabus: Homer, Virgil, Dante, Chaucer, Spenser, Shakespeare, Milton—these were the eminences, the great and the near great that surrounded them, whose work we had to master.

---

3. "Self-Reliance," in Ralph Waldo Emerson, *Essays, First and Second Series* (New York: Macmillan, 1926), 46.

4. James Gleick, *Chaos: Making a New Science* (New York: Penguin Books, 2008 [1987].

5. Jacques Derrida, *Margins of Philosophy,* translated, with additional notes, by Alan Bass (Chicago: The University of Chicago Press, 1985), 21.

The present book is both a continuation of Eliot's educational model and a departure. Trying to get to the bottom of this meta-tradition or meta-genre improvisation took my liberal arts education in directions I never imagined pursuing. Improv was my *vade mecum*, a boon companion, and this book an *omnium gatherum*, a place to store everything I learned along the way. Whenever I got intensely interested in some new author or field, eventually I realized it fit into my effort to understand improvisation. As a friend said (with a smile), *it can't be right, Randy, everything fits.* Goethe tells Eckermann in their *Conversations* that you must use what you study if you want to retain it. That's how this book functioned for me. For that I will always be grateful.

Certainly it began as an improvisation since the original idea had come to me in an intuitive flash during a graduate seminar. The seminar leader began with a throwaway line regarding that week's reading, an obscure Renaissance pamphlet (Thomas Nashe's *Pierce Pennylesse*) the likes of which, he claimed, we had surely never before seen. Suddenly doors started opening in my mind, and I saw Sterne's *Tristram Shandy* and Erasmus's *Praise of Folly* and Byron's *Don Juan* and Stendhal's *The Red and the Black* and numerous other texts. Books that claim spontaneous composition seemed, according to this flash of insight, to have much in common, to be *like*. The results of that moment are worked out in my first chapters, which explore the complex and, frankly, quite slippery nature of the spontaneous gesture (Chapters 1 and 2). Chapter 3 offers a taxonomy or grammar of the persistent formal and thematic conventions that "improvisations" employ to support or enforce the claim that the work before us was created without effort. Chapter 4 explores spontaneity in light of intellectual history while Chapter 5 examines the epistemological argument in seminal texts from the eighteenth and twentieth century.

Others eurekas were to follow. One crucial insight concerned where, as it were, improvisations came from. It was clear to me that, once perceived, improvisations littered the literary landscape. But I had no explanation for what caused them, nor for the phenomenon of clumping, as they seemed to gather in certain periodic clumps. One day, playing tennis of all things, it hit me: the periodic peaks were moments of historic upheaval when our way of knowing the world was changing; improvisations were articulations of those paradigm shifts, expressing the inevitable tensions such upheavals engender. Improvisers *write in* the new paradigm in this double sense. Improvisation is the form artists employ in response to a new paradigm; improvisations make up much of a new paradigm's literary output. But at the same time, deeply entwined with epistemological issues—how we know the world—and with the birth of modern science, improvisation is the mode of discourse used to create—to write in—the new paradigm. Fearing that I would lose the thought, I finished that game of tennis chanting this odd mantra: "paradigm shift, paradigm shift." Be forewarned: you are in the hands of someone who thinks about these matters while playing tennis. I got it on paper. The insight proved sounder than my backhand and is articulated in Chapter 6.

A related insight also finds expression in that chapter, that much of the postmodern project can also be understood in terms of the aesthetics of improvisation and its program to shift paradigms. Understanding Derrida's connection to improvisation—I take him as my principal example—helps disclose an expressive tension central to the deconstructive project and helps give context to both his stylistic oddities, so often challenged, and the radical nature of his prophetic vision, so difficult to understand. The point is not that the aesthetics of improvisation anticipates postmodernism or that the tradition of improvisation directly influences it. Rather, my point is more radical and probably one that would make postmodernists uncomfortable. Though vocally anti-humanistic and insistently new, Derrida's project participates in the age-old human (and often humanist) quest for immediacy, for an unmediated experience that cannot be achieved. The aesthetics of improvisation, and the persistent and archetypal locus of consciousness it expresses, is the trace that is *always already there,* anticipating and in part belying Derrida's profound originality. The coincidence in time and space of chaos science and deconstruction, so wildly different and yet extensively and deeply similar, suggests that they both spring from the same local, time-bound historical-cultural matrix, that they are twinned inflections of the same paradigm shift. Nonetheless, that the aesthetics of improvisation anticipates *both* suggests that they participate in something out-of-time and essential to our humanity, a structure of thought immutable and universal wherein are explored the polarities and the limits of reason, order, and freedom. Articulations of the same paradigm shift, they employ an aesthetics intrinsic to *paradigm shifting* whenever it occurs.

Another revelation came after being led to the Homeric "Hymn to Hermes." It was clear to me that, fully to understand improvisation, I had to take it back before the Renaissance, and that the Homeric tradition of oral-formulaic was an important locus. In the Homeric "Hymn to Hermes" I found not only a exquisite example of improvisation—a text wholly imbricated in style, form, and theme with the issue of unmediated experience—I found also what I now take to be improvisation's tutelary deity: Hermes. Hermes, or Mercury as the Romans called him, is the god of quickness who oversees borders, the fortuitous, the aleatory—all the province of improvisation, the art of the *unforeseen*. I explore the Homeric "Hymn to Hermes" as well as the near contemporary poets Sappho and Pindar in Chapter 7.

Having worked out a methodology for talking about spontaneity in Part I, I apply that methodology in Part II to major texts of the Western tradition: Milton's *Paradise Lost*, Sterne's *Tristram Shandy*, Wordsworth's "Tintern Abbey," Tennyson's *Idylls of the King*, Mark Twain's *Adventures of Huckleberry Finn*, Jung's *Red Book*, Joyce's *Ulysses*, Mann's *Dr. Faustus*, and finally, McEwan's *Saturday*.

Pursuing the adventure, it became clear that, while many of its examples are from the mainstream of the Great Tradition, improvisation is nevertheless its own tradition and one that interweaves with and shadows the Great Tradition. Improvisation is a kind of dark disruptive version ever in dialogue with the mainstream. I started out to define a kind of literature. Before I was done, or before improv was done with me, I seemed to have defined an archetype, a state of being where fundamental polarities of our being contend. Eventually the adventure led to the recognition that what I was looking at was an alternative narrative of western culture, less linear or periodic than we usually see, more cyclical or spiral in nature. Hidden in plain sight largely because all claim, like *Pierce Pennylesse*, to be unlike anything you've ever seen, improvisations are a countercurrent that "spins against," in Melville's words, the way Western culture "drives," that is, spins against the drive toward more and more objective, positivistic rationality. Improv's spin is to urge us instead to embrace subjectivity and some version of the irrational, depending on what cultural moment it inhabits. In sum, the gesture of spontaneity leads to the effort to dismantle the entire edifice of authority: how we make and judge value, how we determine what is good and bad, and how we know the world.

Like my improvisers I had no fixed agenda except to know and to understand. Of course, like everyone, improvisers especially, I had a subjective agenda, a predilection for a certain kind of out-of-the-mainstream, carnivalesque voice and text. Letting my improvisers dictate the directions I took ensured that the texts I use as examples and explore in depth are in part arbitrary, matters of personal taste, theirs and mine. There are plenty of texts I love that didn't make the cut, Virginia Woolf's *Mrs. Dalloway* to name just one. The principle criterion of selection was that they be central texts of the western tradition. Not yet tested by time, McEwan's *Saturday* is the sole exception, but will I think have a long life. In any case, in my experience readers often suggest other texts I "ought to consider." Such suggestions always seemed to me evidence that my interlocutors were seeing through my lens. I hope future readers will consider that the texts they feel I left out are not disproof of my argument; I invite them to examine such texts on their own using the methodology I here develop for examining that slippery, delightful, and rich phenomenon, spontaneity.

Following the improvisers' lead I have ventured widely and anything but safely. Improvisers rarely accept the boundaries the mainstream usually hems us in with, and it should be obvious that I followed my improvisers also in becoming an interloper beyond the English and American nineteenth century and the discipline of literary criticism that I was trained in. I'm sure readers will note the blunders I make in their fields and that they will urge other disciplines that could in the future be applied. I acknowledge the former and I look forward to reading any application of the latter.

Part I (Chapters 1 to 7) develops a methodology to explore the claim of spontaneity and the discourse of improvisation. These chapters are cumulative and are best read as a unit. In Part II (Chapters 8 to 14), readers may follow their interests among my close readings of major Western texts. If they do, I recommend they then jump to the conclusion where I offer my final statement regarding how improvisation fits in the big picture of Western art and civilization.

PART I

METHODOLOGICAL GROUNDWORK

CHAPTER ONE

"Winged by an Unconscious Will":
How to Do Things with Spontaneity

The poem refreshes life so that we share,
For a moment, the first idea...It satisfies
Belief in an immaculate beginning

And sends us, winged by an unconscious will,
To an immaculate end.
—Wallace Stevens, "Notes Toward a Supreme Fiction"

W riter Annie Dillard wants to live like a weasel. She has exchanged a long startled glance with one at Hollins Pond near her beloved Tinker Creek. Although she makes it clear she is just minutes away from suburbia and the highway, Dillard presents her encounter with the weasel as an unmediated experience of unbridled wildness. She has "been in that weasel's brain for sixty seconds, and he was in mine."[1] Directly confronted with wildness, she longs to embrace the weasel's life of instinctual purity. She wishes she "might learn something of mindlessness, something of the purity of living in the physical senses and the dignity of living without bias or motive."[2] This longing leads her to her next wild vision where she is prepared to embrace not only the weasel's wildness but also its irrationality:

> I could very calmly go wild. I could live two days in the den, curled, leaning on mouse fur, sniffing bird bones, blinking, licking, breathing musk, my hair tangled in the roots of grasses. Down is a good place to go, where the mind is single. Down is out, out of your ever-loving mind and back to your careless senses...Time and events are merely poured, unremarked, and ingested directly, like blood pulsed into my gut through a jugular vein.[3]

---

1. "Living Like a Weasel," in Annie Dillard, *Teaching a Stone to Talk* (New York: Harper Perennial, 1988), 14.

2. Ibid., 15.

3. Ibid., 15-16.

From the moment she imagines "calmly go[ing] wild," the passage is a tissue of exquisite paradoxes. Dillard longs for "mindless" experience ("Time and events…merely poured, unremarked, and ingested directly") and seems willing even to go "out of [her] ever loving mind." But getting there comes paradoxically with a plan that involves the mediation of care and skill. We learn that "the weasel lives in necessity and we live in choice, hating necessity and dying at the last ignobly in its talons." Dillard wants "to live as [she] should, as the weasel lives as he should," a life imbued with instinct and the "careless senses."[4] Yet Dillard's wish to embrace this instinctive life is a matter of will. "Could two live that way?" she asks, then exults, "We can live any way we want":

> People *take vows* of poverty, chastity, and obedience—even of silence—by choice. The thing is *to stalk your calling in a certain skilled and supple way,* to locate the most tender and live spot and plug into that pulse. This is yielding, not fighting. A weasel doesn't "attack" anything; a weasel lives as he is meant to, yielding at every moment to *the perfect freedom of single necessity.*[5]

The freedom of necessity: that is the paradox to which Annie Dillard's yearning for simplicity leads her, a kind of willed will-lessness. Indeed, most paradoxical of all, necessity is achieved by *choice,* the thing she most longs to forgo. Fraught with so many contradictions, no wonder she longs for a "place…where the mind is single."

Are these unthinking contradictions or, are they expressive tensions? Assuming the latter can tell us much about what it means to be human. We may not share the degree of Dillard's longing, but many of us, myself included, are aware of like moments. Sometimes they don't amount to more than passing thoughts, the urge to flee some Hamlet-like choice where a "single mind" would prove just the thing. If only instinct, a flash of insight, inspiration, some answer in a dream would come to our rescue. Then, usually, our longing unanswered, our choices uninspired, we return to what's needed of us, the hard work of life's hard choices.

---

4. Ibid., 15.
5. Ibid., 16; emphases added.

In her longing for wildness Dillard shows herself heir to Thoreau who sought to "remember well his ignorance" and who believed that "in Wildness is the preservation of the World."[6] But embedded in the notion of instinctive spontaneity—a notion that was around long before the Romantics and Transcendentalists brought it into vogue—are fundamental issues: What is the source of our best efforts? What are the origins of our deeds and works, of our deepest and best selves? What is the ground of being, of knowing? Can we come into the presence of the transcendent? Where? How? Through which of our faculties? The higher? Or as Dillard suggests, "[D]own is a good place to go." Can the transcendent bring us to knowing, to truth? Can we become better than, can we go or be taken beyond ourselves? If the answer is yes to any of these questions, then how, by which faculties of the self?

Self-styled spontaneous writers—improvisers I will call them here—often reveal that the quest for unmediated experience is not as easy as they would like at first to make it seem. Improvisations—writing, or art in whatever medium, that claims to be improvised—are arguments *from* Nature—where "nature" and "natural" do much of the arguments' heavy lifting. But improvisations are not always finally arguments *for* Nature. Thoreau urges "the tonic of wildness," but he would not, he says, have us follow him into the woods.[7] He goes there to get away from civilization ("Men labor under a mistake"), but he has journeyed to the woods "to live deliberately" (from *de-liberare*, to weigh carefully).[8] Improvisers like Dillard and Thoreau loudly challenge conventional, received definitions of rationality, but at the same time they subtly qualify their unconventional embrace and celebration of spontaneity and irrationality. Annie Dillard would like to have more weasel in her, but she doesn't seek to be any less Annie Dillard. Improvisers know that to achieve instinctive freedom can be, as Keats said of becoming the longed-for nightingale, to "become a sod." Worse, improvisers know that the quest for unmediated experience is not just our glory but also our curse: our glory because it is the source of much of the achieved sympathy in the world; our curse because

---

6. Henry David Thoreau, *Walden, Civil Disobedience, and Other Writings*, edited by William Rossi (New York and London: W.W. Norton, 2008), 273.

7. Ibid., 213.

8. Ibid., 7, 65.

it can be used to rationalize, even be the agency of self-centered thought and behavior. An improvisation often, in Melville's words, "spins *against* the way it drives."[9] Having a taste for chaos, as my title suggests improvisations do, doesn't necessarily mean making a full commitment to chaos.

We are all the Ancient Mariner: now killing the albatross in a moment of thoughtlessness, now blessing the water snakes with "A spring of love, gushed from my heart." How can the latter be his unequivocal redemption when the former is equally spontaneous? The improviser's final word is sympathy, all ultimately embracing Coleridge's favorite line from the Roman poet Terence, that "nothing human is foreign to me"—nothing, even our yearning to forsake, or to reach beyond, our humanity.

1. *The Rhetoric of Unmediated Spontaneity*

Improvising, then, is not just a style of composition. The claim of spontaneity sets up a conceptual field where large issues often contend. Bringing an idea to your boss you may choose one of two gambits. You can say: "I have thought long and hard about this, I have brought my best to bear on this problem" (hard work, skill, research, rational thinking, whatever the analytic tools *du jour*). Or you can begin: "this came to me this morning in the shower where I do all my best thinking." The latter gesture is at once self-protective *and* self-assertive: don't blame me if this idea doesn't pan out; but perhaps it deserves special attention because it came to me in an intuitive moment. Both gestures—though*tful* and thought*less*—authorize and validate: value my idea because I've worked hard in creating it; or, value my idea precisely because I haven't worked hard at all. The mystery, a mystery I seek here to analyze, is how the latter ploy could earn any credence at all. But it does and we deploy it all the time. How? What is the logic that shores up such a tacit argument? And at least as interesting: why? Why might I choose thoughtlessness as a persuasive device—a rhetorical gesture—rather than the more reasonable persuasions of care and craft and rationality?

---

9. "The Conflict of Convictions," in *The Poems of Herman Melville,* edited by Douglas Robillard (Kent, Ohio, and London: Kent State University Press, 2000), 55; emphasis in text.

The literary equivalent of this rhetorical gesture is the claim of spontaneous composition, improvisation: I wrote this in a dream, when inspired,
instinctively, off the top of my head, when drunk, but in any case without
thinking, without effort, without plan, and even perhaps without purpose.
Almost an accident. It just happened.

Once you go looking, texts that claim to be spontaneously composed
abound in literary history. From Homer's sung epics to Milton's *Paradise
Lost* ("this my unpremeditated verse," he calls it), from Mark Twain's pseudo-
naïf *Adventures of Huckleberry Finn* ("persons attempting to find a plot will be
shot") to Ginsberg's drug-inspired rant, *Howl*—they are everywhere.[10] Many
self-styled improvisations merit the attention of none but the most rigorous
scholars. The endless, 40,000 line verse narratives of the nineteenth century
Spasmodic School, who believed they should compose in a "spasm"—and it
shows—come to mind.

My parenthetic "and it shows" indulges in evaluation, one of the least
interesting things we can do with spontaneity. Spontaneity has evoked not
only hair-splitting but also much sword-crossing. The critical reception of
Kerouac's "kickwriting" can serve as example. On the one hand, Beat novelist
John Clellon Holmes enthuses over his friend's achievement: "The words are
no longer words, but had become things. Somehow an open circuit of feeling
had been established between his awareness and its object of the moment,
and the result was as startling as being trapped in another man's eyes."[11] On
the other, Truman Capote famously judges, "That's not writing, that's typing." John Ciardi sums Kerouac up from the hostile camp: "a high school
athlete who went from Lowell, Massachusetts to Skid Row, *losing his eraser
en route.*"[12]

---

10. *Paradise Lost,* in *The Poems of John Milton,* edited by John Carey and Alastair
Fowler (New York: W.W. Norton, 1972), bk. 9, lines 23-24; Mark Twain, *Adventures of
Huckleberry Finn,* edited by Sculley Bradley, 2nd ed. (New York: W.W. Norton, 1977),
no pagination.

11. Howard Cunnell, "Fast this Time: Jack Kerouac and the Writing of *On the Road,*"
in Jack Kerouac, *On the Road: The Original Scroll* (New York: Penguin, 2008), 36.

12. Quoted in Daniel Belgrad, *The Culture of Spontaneity: Improvisation and the Arts
in Postwar America* (Chicago: The University of Chicago Press, 1999), 239; emphasis
added.

Capote and Ciardi challenge the aesthetic value of spontaneity in the arch, confident voice of urbane craftsmen. A challenge of another sort came from the exciting work of the followers of Homeric scholar Milman Parry. Harvard scholars Parry and Lord solved the "Homeric Problem": how could such a long, complex poem have been composed in the ninth century BC, before the invention of writing?[13] But their explanation—that Homer and the epic poets of modern (former) Yugoslavia did truly improvise, did compose and sing simultaneously using the oral-formulaic method—created new critical problems. If singers of tales improvised using oral-formulaic patterns, then perhaps, as Walter Ong put it, "[i]nstead of a creator, you had an assembly-line worker"[14]—a far cry from the Romantic ideal of spontaneity that our idea of the rhapsode Homer had done much to inspire. ("Rhapsode" comes from roots meaning to stitch or weave a song, an apt description of the oral-formulaic method Parry and Lord describe.) "How could a poetry that was so unabashedly formulary," Ong continued, "so constituted of prefabricated parts, still be so good?"[15]

This line of inquiry led however not to a challenge to spontaneity, but rather to a better understanding of improvisation in an oral tradition that placed value not in the Romantic ideal of original genius but rather in "fixed, formulaic thought patterns [that] were essential for wisdom and effective administration."[16] Homer's spontaneity was valuable; it just didn't share the assumptions of the Renaissance and beyond, the Romantics especially. Its value was in creating the weft and warp that contained and preserved the ethos of Hellenic culture. It was not about change but continuance. "The epic," writes Ong's mentor Eric Havelock, is "to be considered in the first instance not as an act of creation but as an act of reminder and recall. Its patron muse is indeed Mnemosyne in whom is symbolized not just the mem-

---

13. See, among others, Milman Parry, *The Making of Homeric Verse: The Collected Papers,* edited by Adam Parry (New York: Oxford University Press, 1987); Albert Lord, *The Singer of Tales* (New York: Atheneum, 1970 [1960]); and Gregory Nagy, *Poetry as Performance: Homer and Beyond* (London: Cambridge University Press, 1996).

14. Walter J. Ong, *Orality and Literacy: The Technologizing of the Word* (New York: Routledge, 2000 [1982]), 22.

15. Ibid., 23.

16. Ibid., 22–23.

ory considered as a mental phenomenon but rather the total act of reminding, recalling, memorializing, and memorizing, which is achieved in epic verse."[17] This is a poetry "of preserved communication and what is preserved has to be typical."[18]

This solution, that Homer improvised but formulaically and in a tradition that valued continuance rather than originality or uniqueness, would seem to be a solution available only to archaic, traditional cultures that have not seen the light of day for centuries, or if so, only remotely. We find another example in *Commedia dell'Arte,* the theater of street improvisation that emerges in the Renaissance at the moment when capitalism and post-Gutenberg literate culture together threaten traditional cultures. About that emergence Robert Henke writes:

> The oral performer tends to identify with the material, not merely offered as an aesthetic object or a mimetic fiction, but as part of a patrimony or tradition. In the hands of oral performers such as the medieval *giullare* [Provençal for jester, fool], that patrimony constitutes an encyclopedic body of knowledge passed on from generation to generation.[19]

And yet improvising based on these values continues closer to home. Jazz neo-traditionalists like Wynton Marsalis are criticized for their lack of originality, denigrated as producing mere *museum* jazz. But when we make gumbo in New Orleans, to use a metaphor Marsalis would appreciate, continuance is a primary value. When continuance is a primary value, artists feel no pressure to begin anew or to create out of the void.[20] They know they will leave their mark on the piece in renewing it; instead they place primacy on the vitality and grace in the traditional melodies they improvise upon and the traditional charts they improvise with. When Wynton has composed, the accent has been upon tradition: he explores jazz's Gospel roots in *In This House, On This*

---

17. Eric Havelock, *Preface to Plato* (Cambridge, Mass.: Harvard University Press, 1963), 91.

18. Ibid., 86.

19. Robert Henke, *Performance and Literature in the Commedia dell'Arte* (New York: Cambridge University Press, 2002), 35.

20. Thanks to Brett Anderson for this insight offered at the Southern Foodways Conference on Food and Music, Oxford, Missisippi, 31 October 2009.

Morning, and *Abyssinian: A Gospel Celebration*; and with Ghanaian drummer Yacub Addy he explores its African roots in *Congo Square,* a testament to the birthplace of jazz where slaves were allowed to play their traditional drums. We think of spontaneity as pegged to originality, but the nature of spontaneity's value—as of originality—is contextual.

One of the more vehement challenges to the privileging of spontaneous creation came from the Frankfurt School's Theodor W. Adorno, whose attack on jazz improvisation was thorough and unrelenting:

> Even though jazz musicians still improvise in practice, their improvisations have become so "normalized" as to enable a whole terminology to be developed to express the standard devices of individualization...In a great many cases, such as the "break" of pre-swing jazz, the musical function of the improvised detail is determined completely by the scheme: the break can be nothing other than a disguised cadenza. Hence very few possibilities for actual improvisation remain.[21]

"Toujours déjà"—nothing is original, nothing truly un-fore-seen. And yet many texts absolutely central to the western tradition employ this gesture, insisting that they are improvised. Must we condemn, or worse, ignore the text because we suspect the claim's complete truth-value?

"Absolutely central" is my way of saying not only that these texts are excellent and worth our attention for the pleasure they give, but also that they have been crucial in how we have articulated and shaped our experience and crucial now as we look back in trying to understand the past, to understand how we got here. We cross swords over spontaneity's value or we debate the Goldilocks' question: has the improviser's spontaneity been too much, too little, or just right? Yet we sometimes misunderstand such texts, mistaking

---

21. "On Popular Music," in Theodor W. Adorno, *Essays on Music,* edited by Richard Leppert; translated by Susan H. Gillespie (Berkeley, Los Angeles, and London: University of California Press, 2002), 445. J. Bradford Robinson points out that Adorno's attack on jazz was based on very bad post-war German imitators of jazz. American jazz records were inaccessible and American jazz bands avoided Germany because of rampant inflation. See his "The Jazz Essays of Theodor Adorno: Some Thoughts on Jazz Reception in Weimar Germany," *Popular Music* 13, no. 1 (January 1994): 1–25. Thanks to Tony Gentry for this reference.

the gesture of spontaneity as a gauge of its unqualified commitment to spontaneity's value. Either lionizing or condemning such texts for their achieved (or unachieved) spontaneity, readers often miss the expressive tensions that the theme introduces.

Ironically, Adorno's idea of "immanent criticism" articulates the kind of approach I find necessary and fruitful:

> Immanent criticism of intellectual and artistic phenomena seeks to grasp, through the analysis of their form and meaning, the contradiction between their objective idea and that pretension...A successful work, according to immanent criticism, is not one which resolves objectives in a spurious harmony, but one which expresses the idea of harmony negatively by embodying the contradictions, pure and uncompromised, in its inner structure.[22]

Improvisations may all fail ultimately in their claim of pure, unmediated spontaneity. But far more interesting than their failure are the internal contradictions between an improvisation's longing for spontaneity and its recognition of that impossibility, our longing for freedom and the inherent constraints on freedom we inevitably face. These are "the contradictions, pure and uncompromised, in [improvisation's] inner structure."

Poet laureate Robert Pinsky remarks that "There are literally improvisatory poets, that is, people who compose very quickly and don't revise much. Frank O'Hara,...says that he likes to sit down and play the typewriter for an hour or two after breakfast. Very few people have that kind of ease."[23] Pinsky may be right and O'Hara may be describing his mode of composition accurately, but for the purposes of this study, I demur. I underscore from the start that I do not know for certain whether such self-styled "improvisations" are improvised in fact; I am only sure that they so declare themselves. Henceforth I shall rarely bother with the scare quotes but, given my

---

22. Theodor W. Adorno, *Prisms: Essays on Veblen, Huxley, Benjamin, Bach, Proust, Schoenberg, Spengler, Jazz, Kafka,* translated by Samuel and Shierry Weber (Cambridge, Mass.: The MIT Press, 1983), 32.

23. Quoted in Ken Gordon, "Improvisers and Revisers: An Experiment in Spontaneity," *Poets & Writers* (May/June 2006; online at *https://www.pw.org/content/improvisers_and_revisers_experiment_spontaneity*)

skepticism, you should assume they are always implied. A text's spontaneity may be a fact, to some degree the real thing. Nonetheless, for my purposes, the claim of spontaneity is a cultivated affectation. As Stephen Greenblatt says with brilliant succinctness of the Renaissance ideal of *sprezzatura,* cultivated carelessness, "We cannot locate a point of pure premeditation or pure randomness."[24] Improv theorist and practitioner Whitney Balliett captures this in-between-ness describing jazz great Thelonious Monk: "His improvisations were molten Monk compositions, and his compositions were frozen Monk improvisations."[25] Even the Homeric problem speaks to this. The epic rhapsodes truly improvised *on the spot.* And yet Homer does so using, in Ong's words, "devastatingly predictable formulas."[26] Homer's improvisations too are both molten and frozen.

In sum, *I don't care* how spontaneous or premeditated the text is or should be. "How spontaneous?" is the wrong question. Rather than split hairs over a text's degree of *achieved spontaneity,* or to get lost in the labyrinth of *that* oxymoron, let us instead bracket the questions of "if" and "how much." My interest is instead, why so-called improvisers are so insistent about their texts' improvised provenance. Blind Milton may have composed *Paradise Lost* in his head and dictated it to his daughters but what makes that unpremeditatedly inspired? And did he not have his daughters read each highly wrought verse paragraph back to him for his inner, sightless blue pencil? Why does Jack Kerouac always talk about the spontaneous composition of *On the Road*—composed at one long Benzedrine-fueled sitting and on one long, 120-foot scroll of paper—rather than the six long years of careful editing he took to get it to press?[27] Far more interesting than calibrating the novel's supposed spontaneity is the way Kerouac and fellow improvisers explore the tensions between spontaneity and craft, artlessness and art. And far more interest-

---

24. Stephen Greenblatt, *Renaissance Self-Fashioning: From More to Shakespeare* (Chicago: The University of Chicago Press, 1980), 227.

25. Whitney Balliett, "Monk," online at *http://www.monkzone.com/Balliet%20Obit. htm*

26. Ong, *Orality and Literacy,* 23.

27. So goes the legend. But Kerouac himself insisted to Neal Cassady: "I wrote that book on COFFEE, remember said rule. Benny, tea, anything I KNOW none as good as coffee for real mental power kicks" (his emphases), quoted in Cunnell, "Fast this Time," 24.

ing than scrutinizing the degree of Homer's improvisation is recognizing that his "devastatingly predictable" formulaic wingèd words (*epea pteroenta*)[28]— at once constrained and free—delineate the formal and thematic tension at the heart of improvisations throughout the ages. The heroes of Homer's improvised epic songs—the Western Tradition's foundational texts[29]—face this very conflict. Achilles is constrained by fate and free to choose (long life and no fame, or eternal fame and short life). Odysseus is ever-crafty, many-turning: *polytropos*, an epithet he shares in the ancient Greek canon only with wing-heeled Hermes, in legend his great grandfather who is often his guide. Odysseus improvises his way into and out of trouble, his men often paying the price. What interests me is not either side of these polarities, freedom and necessity, spontaneity and care and craft. What sets up improvisation's conceptual field, and what inhabits it, is their conflict.

Odysseus is known not only as *polytropos,* many turning, but also *polymetis,* the man of many tricks. *Mētis,* the classical Greek word for cunning intelligence, embodies both sides of the polarities. As Marcel Detienne and Jean-Pierre Vernant write discussing the word's "semantic field":

> Metis—intelligence which operates in the world of becoming, in circumstances of conflict—takes the form of an ability to deal with whatever comes up, drawing on certain intellectual qualities: forethought[,] perspicacity, quickness and acuteness of understanding, trickery, and even deceit…A being of *metis* slips through its adversary's fingers like running water. It is so supple as to be polymorphic; like a trap, it is the opposite of what it seems to be.[30]

Little surprise then that spontaneity should prove so slippery. Odysseus's *mētis* is everywhere on display in the *Odyssey,* the many tricks and stratagems for which he is famous. Homer describes the Trojan horse—Odysseus's most famous trick at Troy—in his eponymous epic. But there is a moment in the

---

28. For more on this subject, see John Miles Foley, *The Theory of Oral Composition: History and Methodology* (Bloomington: Indiana University Press, 1988).

29. Though Father Ong would remind us, they are not written texts but voiced songs.

30. Marcel Detienne and Jean-Pierre Vernant, *Cunning Intelligence in Greek Culture and Society,* translated by Janet Lloyd (Chicago: The University of Chicago Press, 1991), 44.

Iliad where the polarities central to improvisation—the craft of spontaneity—are shown at work. Menelaus, who has just spoken, passes the speaker's staff, symbol of authority, to Odysseus:

> But when that other drove to his feet, resourceful Odysseus,
> he would just stand and stare down, eyes fixed on the ground
>   beneath him,
> nor would he gesture with the staff backward and forward, but hold it
> clutched hard in front of him, like any man who knows nothing.
> Yes, you would call him a sullen man, and a fool likewise.
> But when he let the great voice go from his chest, and the words came
> drifting down like the winter snows, then no other mortal
> man beside could stand up against Odysseus.[31]

As Detienne and Vernant remark, "The magician of words pretends to have lost his tongue, as if he were unskilled in the rudiments of oratory."[32] His trick is as Detienne and Vernant say, "a trap [that] is the opposite of what it seems to be." His lack of craft doesn't authorize directly, as the gesture of spontaneity sometimes does—"unpremeditated but all the truer for that," as Erasmus's Folly will claim—but serves as a setup and contrast to his godlike flurry of eloquence, an eloquence that drifts, like the snows, from above. But of course, once it flows, Odysseus's eloquence is on the one hand based on craft but on the other hand is spontaneous: in the rhetorical tradition the orator's ability to improvise, his or her mastery of extempore fluency, is, in the great Roman rhetorician Quintilian's words, "The greatest fruit of our studies, the richest harvest of our long labours."[33] Odysseus uses the craft of craftlessness to underscore the craft of his spontaneous but crafted eloquence—a hall of mirrors.

---

31. Homer, *The Iliad,* translated by Richard Lattimore (Chicago: The University of Chicago Press, 1951), 106.

32. Detienne and Vernant, *Cunning Intelligence,* 22-23.

33. Quintilian, *Institutio Oratoria,* translated by Donald A. Russell (Cambridge, Mass.: Harvard University Press, 2001), bk. 10, vii. See Terence Cave, *The Cornucopian Text: Problems of Writing in the French Renaissance* (Oxford: Clarendon Press, 1979), 125ff. and Richard Lanham, *The Motives of Eloquence* (New Haven: Yale University Press, 1976).

2. *Getting our Arms around the Art of Spontaneity*

Douglas R. Hofstadter, in his brilliant *Gödel, Escher, Bach: An Eternal Golden Braid*, speaks to the paradox that lies at the heart of texts that traffic in spontaneity:

> How, then, can intelligent behavior be programmed? Isn't this then the most blatant of contradictions in terms? One of the major purposes of this book [says Hofstadter] is to urge the reader to confront the apparent contradiction head on, to savor it, to turn it over, to take it apart, to wallow in it, so that in the end the reader might emerge with new insights into the seemingly unbreachable gulf between the formal and the informal, the animate and the inanimate, the flexible and the inflexible.[34]

Hofstadter here speaks eloquently for me. He is of course, with his dialogic intermezzi and very personal, quirky voice, very much an improviser helping us to see more of the world—the improviser's ultimate goal, as we shall see.

The philosopher Ernst Cassirer once said that a philosophic concept is "rather a problem than a solution of a problem—and the full significance of this problem cannot be understood so long as it is still in its first implicit state."[35] Spontaneity is such a concept. Often presented as a solution (this idea/text is valid because it springs from inspiration or some other non-rational source), in fact, claims of spontaneous composition often signal problems artists are trying to solve. If this spontaneous composition is so good, then what is the value of craft and care and rationality? Or, on the other hand, if this spontaneous composition is so good, what is this thing "spontaneity" and how or where can I get more of it?

Further compounding the critical problem, spontaneity as an idea exists rather on the margins of philosophy than at its center and thus goes doubly unanalyzed. It resists analysis in part because it is in its nature to be hostile to analysis, thumbing its nose at the frame of mind that analyzes. That it thumbs its nose my way, determined as I am to *analyze* spontaneity deploying all the rational paraphernalia of chapter headings and footnotes, does not

---

34. Douglas R. Hofstadter, *Gödel, Escher, Bach: An Eternal Golden Braid* (New York: Basic Books, 1979), 26.

35. Ernst Cassirer, *An Essay on Man: An Introduction to a Philosophy of Human Culture* (New Haven: Yale University Press, 2021 [1944]), 180.

escape me. Likewise, spontaneous texts assert they are effortless, the product of *no* study and *no* rhetoric. Such a gesture hardly invites rhetorical study. Rhetoric is the art and study of devices of persuasion, and self-styled improvisations claim to be free not only of devices but even a desire to persuade, free of the "palpable design upon us" that Keats decried in art, what Dillard longed for: "the dignity of living without bias or motive."[36] With all these feints implicit in the gesture, little wonder that readers tend to misread the theme and gesture of spontaneity, missing the complexity in the gesture of simplicity.

Yet such texts exploit instead a less obvious, even a hidden rhetoric that generates an impression of their fortuitous, uncontrolled, spontaneous, and often playful character. The great and central texts of the Western tradition offer us a rich opportunity to explore the contours and the underpinnings and effects of these gestures. That is what I propose to do here: to study rhetorically literary texts that claim to be the product of no rhetoric and no study. To do so is to apply the *art* of analysis to what the Dutch mathematician and poet, Piet Hein, in his little poem "Ars Brevis" calls the

> one art,
> no more,
> no less:
> to do
> all things
> with art-
> lessness.[37]

Here Hein's final line break and the double stresses of "lessness" together insist upon the absence of art. At the same time those same devices invite us to note the artifice of his artlessness.

Surely the complex and problematic concept of spontaneity deserves more careful attention than we usually pay it. Seeing spontaneity as a device of persuasion, a rhetorical gesture and not necessarily a fact of artistic composition, can begin—as Cassirer would have us do—to open it up for us, critically demystify it, and make its complex meanings explicit. Such demysti-

36. John Keats, *Selected Letters,* edited by Robert Gittings (Oxford: Oxford University Press, 2002), 58.
37. "Ars Brevis," in Piet Hein, *Grooks* (Cambridge, Mass: The MIT Press, 1971), 1.

fication is all the more important because critical treatment of spontaneity and spontaneous texts has so often merited the charge literary critic Jerome McGann levels against our "uncritical absorption in romanticism's own self-representations."[38] The Romantics—Blake, Wordsworth, Coleridge, Thoreau, Emerson, *et al.*—took spontaneity as one of their key postures but that does not necessarily mean the great Romantics and their descendants did not critically explore its nature or its value. And yet this is not how Romanticism—a watershed moment in the emergence of modernity that did much to shape how we see the world today—is often seen and taught. A distinguished Harvard Romanticist once suggested in a graduate independent study that "if we really listened to Wordsworth, we would leave the university." I was tempted to take his advice, but not on its merits. The present study seeks to rebut that misreading.

I will admit with some embarrassment that I have been thinking of these matters since that moment in the late 1970s. The seed was planted by that Wordsworthian, but what spurred its germination was an incident in my second year of graduate school.

My father came to visit me out of the blue and as we drove together in Cambridge, suddenly he announced: "Cows have it so easy. Don't you wish you could just graze all day and have no worries?"

The remark must have come in response to some context because it was not its off-the-wall-ness that gave me pause. It was the substance of the wish. Here I was, trying to educate myself in a field that I cherished, English and American literature, where the great achievements came from long study and hard work, from the mastery of a craft and the long thought that gave great artists the power to speak truthfully and perhaps profoundly of life. And yet here was my father wishing for a life of effortlessness, willing to sacrifice any hope of achievement, of progress, of civilization, in favor of the simpler joys of chewing his cud.

Why do we long to lead effortless lives even though so much of what makes life worth living is the fruit of effort?

----

38. Jerome McGann, *The Romantic Ideology: A Critical Introduction* (Chicago: The University of Chicago Press, 1983), 1.

It was then that I knew that I had to see my dissertation through even though finding support for such an ambitious project had not been easy and even though writing about spontaneity at Harvard was the closest thing I've known to living an oxymoron. Somehow that incident has continued to fuel my desire to make the dissertation's first rather callow effort take flight.

Our "uncritical absorption in romanticism's own self-representations" has largely blinded us to the fact that self-proclaimed spontaneous texts—improvisations—are often internalized debates about the problematic value of spontaneity. Is spontaneity possible? Is there such a thing as immediacy? as inspiration? What is the value of reason? care? craft? judgment? will? What is the true and viable source of authenticity, of knowledge of the world, of truth? These are the sorts of questions—big questions to be sure—that spontaneous texts embed beneath a surface that seems unequivocally to celebrate the value of spontaneity and, professing a carefree air to match its apparent technical carelessness, to harbor hardly any questions at all. Often celebrations of the texture of the world around us, improvisations, the literature of apparent chaos, at their heart explore questions about the nature of reason, order, and freedom. If as the great jazz musician Charles Mingus suggests, "You got to improvise on somethin'," then at bottom these are questions that improvisers improvise on.[39] Paradoxically it is not in philosophy or criticism but in literary texts themselves that the philosophical assumptions of spontaneity have been most thoroughly analyzed, if often with poetic indirectness. So I hope to show here.

Blinders of another kind have obscured the internal debates that are the mainspring that drive most improvisations. Edward Said's cogent comments on the formalism that dominated twentieth century criticism help pinpoint why improvisation has escaped the kind of notice I wish to pay it. He writes:

> One can discern a trend in much of great Western criticism of the early twentieth century that draws readers away from experience and pushes them instead toward form and formalism. What seems guarded against in this trend is *immediacy,* that untreated bolus of direct experience, experience that can only be reflected whole or as replicable, dogmatically insistent items called facts...When we...look at the criticism fostered by some

---

39. Janet Coleman and Al Young, *Mingus/Mingus: Two Memoirs* (New York: Limelight, 2004), 36.

of the modernists, the wish to escape from experience perceived as futile panorama is central. T.S. Eliot is unintelligible without this emphasis on art opposed in some way to life, to the historical experience of the middle class, and to the disorder and dislocation of urban existence.[40]

One can hear in Said's "untreated bolus of direct experience" William James's idea of the infant's experience: "One great blooming, buzzing confusion."[41] Said is saying that formalism is a way to keep such experience at arm's length if not avoid it altogether. The improviser's opening gambit by contrast is to say, "'Blooming, buzzing confusion'?—*How do I get some?*" Our "uncritical absorption in romanticism's own self-representations" blinds us to the improvisers' ambivalence, but a refined scholarly distaste for *"immediacy, that untreated bolus of direct experience,"* can keep us from even entertaining the improviser's embrace of the world around and before us. Improvisers usually nuance that carefree embrace, but we must take the impulse seriously before we can appreciate its careful modulation.

The matter of spontaneity, then, is not just a matter of abstract philosophy. As a literary scholar, I find it exciting to offer a fresh approach to the central texts of the Western tradition as I hope to do here. But there is something more at stake. The rhetorical gesture of spontaneity is exceedingly familiar in everyday life ("it came to me in the shower"), though we employ it for the most part intuitively, without thinking, and hardly noticing. To my mind this gives us all the more reason to analyze the gesture of spontaneity, and the ideas behind it, if we seek either to deploy them well or not to be manipulated by those who do. The "rhetoric of spontaneity" is the basis for half the salesmanship of modern consumerism, from Coke's selling "The Real Thing" to all the soap sold by means of hand-held-camera, *cinema verité,* slice-of-life mini-narratives of simple people doing simple things—all based on an artifice of the inartificial and the appeal of simplicity and the primitive or unsophisticated. Whether we are selling our idea to our boss direct from the shower or our company is hawking commodities in the larger market-

---

40. "Reflections on Exile," in Edward Said, *Reflections on Exile and Other Essays* (Cambridge, Mass.: Harvard University Press, 2002), xvii-xviii; emphasis in original.

41. William James, *The Principles of Psychology,* 2 vols. (New York: Henry Holt and Company, 1890), 1:488.

place; whether a poet is convincing his audience of the authenticity of his lyric voice or an epic poet or novelist is ushering in a new paradigm—at whatever register of the spectrum or point on the continuum—the rhetoric of spontaneity is a powerful figure or topos or conceptual field that permeates human discourse. Rather like Rousseau who knew his heart and so knew mankind ("Je sens mon cœur et je connais les hommes"), President Bush, the Decider, doesn't need State Department analyses. He looks in Russian Premier Putin's eyes and sees directly into his soul. On the basis of this unmediated experience, we, Bush's constituency, should therefore trust Putin—an example that goes far to demonstrating how completely this rhetoric can be deployed to mislead us (and perhaps, in this case, its perpetrator). Thus, it is not too much to say that the gesture can be instrumental in matters of state, as well as in matters of life and death. In this case it served us ill, doing little to prepare us for Putin's power grab and culture of oligarchy, or his invasion of Georgia. At least as important: it is a matter of life, how we live it, how we conduct it, what we take its meaning to be, and how we come to know that meaning. How we best do things and with what tools matters. Improvisation is a way to work through the twists and turns as mankind develops new tools of rationality and irrationality. Many of the central texts of the Western literary tradition are about these life issues.

Why Western? Non-Western philosophy and literature are shot through with the same tensions between art and artlessness. A cultivated artlessness is central, for example, to much of Japanese aesthetics. Embracing a "strident antirationalism," writes Leonard Koren, "Zen stresses direct, intuitive insight into transcendental truth beyond all intellectual conception."[42] The Taoist sage achieves *wu-wei*, effortless action.[43] *Wabi-sabi*, defined as "the beauty of things imperfect, impermanent and incomplete," lies at the heart of the Zen-inspired tea ceremony, gardens, and *haiku*.[44] In African art and culture, *itutu*—mystic coolness—is, in Robert Farris Thompson's words, the

---

42. Leonard Koren, *Wabi-Sabi for Artists, Designers, Poets & Philosophers* (Point Reyes, California: Imperfect Publishing, 2008), 76.

43. Edward Slingerland, *Effortless Action: Wu-Wei as Conceptual Metaphor and Spiritual Ideal in Early China* (New York: Oxford University Press, 2003).

44. Koren, *Wabi-Sabi*, 7.

"sovereign concept."[45] To demonstrate the accord of these issues and rhetorical gestures in the East and West would not be difficult.[46] But I have to limit myself somewhere, don't I? I wish to bracket the Non-west while suggesting in passing that the conceptual field I seek to explore is *essentially* human and hence universal.

At first blush, then, self-proclaimed spontaneous texts appear to shout apocalyptically that, conducting life as *they* do, we will see not "through a glass darkly" but rather, as Paul promised, "face to face" (1 Corinthians 13:12). More careful study, however, reveals their persistent doubts about what it would mean to have unmediated experience or if, after all, it is even achievable.

In the poem "Notes Toward a Supreme Fiction," from which I take this chapter's title, Wallace Stevens perfectly captures the tension between many improvisations' idealized, apocalyptic visions and their inevitable frustration. Improvisation's (here, "the poem['s]") "supreme fiction" is that it

> refreshes life so that we share,
> For a moment, the first idea...It satisfies
> Belief in an immaculate beginning
>
> And sends us, winged by an unconscious will,
> To an immaculate end.[47]

---

45. Robert Farris Thompson, *Flash of the Spirit: African and Afro-American Art and Philosophy* (New York: Vintage, 1984) and *Aesthetics of the Cool: Afro-Atlantic Art and Music* (Pittsburgh and New York: Periscope, 2011).

46. For a cogent analysis of the role of spontaneity in Zen and in the work of Zhuang Zhou, see A.C. Graham, *Reason and Spontaneity: A New Solution to the Problem of Fact and Value* (London and Dublin: Curzon Press; Totowa, N.J.: Barnes & Noble Books, 1985), 184-92. See also François Cheng, *Chinese Poetic Writing: With an Anthology of T'ang Poetry,* translated by Donald A. Riggs and Jerome Seaton (Bloomington: University of Indiana Press, 1982). For examinations of improvisatory music traditions in a variety of cultures, see Derek Bailey, *Improvisation: Its Nature and Practice in Music* (Boston: Da Capo Press, 1993 [1980]). See also Bruno Nettl and Melinda Russell, *In the Course of Performance: Studies in the World of Musical Improvisation* (Chicago: The University of Chicago Press, 1998).

47. "Notes Toward a Supreme Fiction," in Wallace Stevens, *Collected Poetry and Prose* (New York: Library of America, 1997), 330-31.

Stevens here suggests that great poetry takes us back to Eden ("the first idea," "an immaculate beginning") when we communed with God face to face. And it "sends us…To an immaculate end," to the apocalypse (or "re-velation") when the veils are removed along with our sins and we face God once again. For Stevens the poetic imagination, characterized by spontaneity and "winged by an unconscious will," summons the innocence of our beginning and the purification and redemption of our end.

The poem achieves all this not by actually returning to the world's beginning or traveling forward to the world's end, but by invoking and achieving a holy present, holy because at once innocent and redeemed of sin, here, now:

> the strong exhilaration
> Of what we feel from what we think, of thought
> Beating in the heart, as if blood newly came,
>
> An elixir, an excitation, a pure power.
> The poem, through candor, brings back a power again
> That gives a candid kind to everything.[48]

Stevens's vision of "thought/Beating in the heart" and feeling "coming from what we think" answers T. S. Eliot's idea of modernity's curse, "the dissociation of sensibility," the division of mind and heart that according to Eliot set in after the Renaissance.[49] The transfusion ("as if blood newly came") is alchemical and divine: "An elixir, an excitation, a pure power." Spontaneity's immediacy in the act of composition is agent and proof of these transformations, turning the lead of experience into the gold of imagination. In this optimistic and visionary mode, Stevens continues, improvisations move us "between these points," from the Edenic innocence, "the ever early candor," to "its late plural" when head and heart are one, immediate, unmediated.[50] Thus improvisation in its exalted, optative mood claims to retrieve for us our "Belief in an immaculate beginning": an Edenic, originary self, untainted by the fall into experience. Stevens states that this "Belief" is "satisfie[d]"—as one might satisfy a longing. "Through *candor*"—a word rooted both in "set afire" and in "purity"—the world is made "candid," purified in the alembic of

48. Ibid. 331.

49. "The Metaphysical Poets" in T. S. Eliot, *Selected Essays* (London: Faber and Faber, 1932), 287-88.

50. Stevens, "Notes Toward a Supreme Fiction," 331.

unmediated experience, the union of head and heart, of will and deed. So says the improviser as vatic, or prophetic, idealist.

But driving and counterbalancing the longing for this "supreme fiction" is the supreme and poignant reality that Stevens and most improvisers also know: that such immediacy is not, in the final analysis, of this world or within the grasp of human kind when we are being merely human (which realists like myself and Stevens in a certain mood assume is most of, if not all, the time). Hence, after all, the need for and Stevens's call for the redemptive power—"an elixir, an excitation"—of poetry. And hence, Stevens hedges his visionary longing for unmediated experience with subtle qualifications. "The poem refreshes life so that we share /…the first idea," Stevens asserts optimistically and by an act of will (what Emerson called "the optative mood," his favorite).[51] But the refreshment comes, Stevens equivocates, *only* "For a moment." And, as Stevens insists, poetry retrieves for us *not the fact of* but rather our *"Belief in* an immaculate beginning."[52]

For Stevens here (and everywhere in his poetic program), poetry creates a redemptive world. The accent for Stevens, however, always falls on "creates": redemption and the ideal world or the heaven from which it descends—or which heaven represents—are man-made things, artifacts of the imagination, an "idea," however primal. The poem may be *like* a return to Eden, *like* an entrance into the ideal world, or *like* bringing on the apocalypse, but Stevens never loses sight of the *created* status of these wished-for, metaphoric states. Such goals, modeled on idealized visions (Eden) are worthy goals for Stevens, but we must never forget that they are the mind and the heart's creation, never the thing itself. Spontaneity ("winged by an unconscious will") is the agent of this creation but its status is equally tentative, hypothetical, metaphoric, metonymic, one thing standing for another, but not the thing itself. Ever the craftsman, Stevens always is shaping (mediating) the unmediated upwellings of the imagination, giving them language, giving them form. The spontaneous imagination creates *a kind of* divinity, or an experience of something that is *like* the divine, but for Stevens the divine is ever *man-made*.

---

51. Ibid., 330; "The Transcendentalist," in Ralph Waldo Emerson, *Essays and Lectures* (New York: Library of America, 1983), 199.

52. Stevens, "Notes Toward a Supreme Fiction," 330; emphasis added.

Had I brought to the poem the vulgar Romantic notion that spontaneity was of unquestioned value, then I would have missed the poem's drama and conflict. Seeing spontaneity as a problem rather than an answer, opens up this text and many others.

Those who know Stevens will recognize these as his central themes: the imagination's redemptive role, the mind's centrality to experience. Nothing new here. My reading then does not pretend to be a great interpretive revelation, though I hope I have helped reveal how much is lucidly going on in his at-first-glance impenetrable lines. What my reading makes clear, however, is that focusing on the issue of spontaneity takes us to the heart of Stevens's poetic and intellectual program. My point is that spontaneity and improvisation are an exceedingly rich vein. Opening that vein leads to many of the core issues and tensions of the literary imagination. Improvisation explores the nature and value of creativity, of artifice and its opponent artlessness, of reason and its opponents, which vary through the centuries: grace, instinct, imagination, or the unconscious, to mention but a few. Mining this vein can lead to rich close readings of individual texts and to a better understanding of these core issues, issues which I believe lie at the core of our humanity.

Thus in Stevens we see the negotiation by one "improviser" (those scare quotes one last time) of the multiform tensions central to most works that claim to be improvised. The longing for effortless, unmediated spontaneity can be univocal, without complexity or shadow. I think of such unmodulated gestures or texts as the inheritance of a vulgarized Romanticism, essentially a misreading of Romanticism's core values that have so influenced our own, both in their vulgar and more rigorous forms. But I have found that literary improvisations that have staying power, the power to keep our attention over years, decades, centuries, are not as simple as we sometimes make them. In this book I hope to recover that complexity, the kind we saw in Annie Dillard and here in Wallace Stevens.

Of course Stevens is never patently simple and the dense and refined texture of his poetry (like Dillard's prose) never invites us to rest with a simple reading. While displaying the mind at play, Stevens and Dillard tax us always, demanding a thoughtful, effortful reading. My readers will no doubt have to pore over his obscure poem and Dillard's gnarled prose more than once to follow their arguments. This is telling. Stevens and Dillard overtly celebrate spontaneity and immediacy and yet force us to work hard to get their tension-and conundrum-filled meanings that Dillard's prized "mindlessness" surely could not readily resolve. If, as I believe, the meaning of a text lies in part in the kind of reading and response the text invites or demands, what then is valued: effortlessness or the effort it takes to apprehend it? instinct or the conscious choice needed to embrace it?[53] For me, most improvisers usually finally answer the latter: conscious effort.

Almost always, the real lesson is our alertness to the tensions that the longing for immediacy creates. Sometimes the tensions are formulated as simply a matter of contrasting the everyday, primitivist longing for an effortless life against the recognition that life's joys are most often the fruit of hard work. Sometimes, as in Stevens and in Dillard, the longing and its limits are fraught with a heavy freight of religious and philosophic significance: how can humanity reach beyond itself and redeem itself; how can we know truth; how can we pierce what Walter Pater called the "thick wall of personality;" how can we reach beyond ourselves to touch the holy?[54] But in either case, simple or complex, I will argue that improvisations inhabit much the same fallen world that Stevens knowingly and willingly embraces. He, and other improvisers like him, long for Eden and for apocalypse, for a return to innocence or for the consummation of the end of time; yet they know that neither innocence nor consummation are humanly possible without forgoing or overcoming our humanness. With him they whisper concurrently in a more conservative voice: how can we cleanse our doors of perception? how can we purify our fallen reason? how can we enlarge our faculties and, ultimately, our humanness? Or, conversely, if the limits of reason cannot be stretched, or stretched enough to fit life's teeming chaos, then how can we learn best to live within those limits? Spontaneity, as we shall see, is their will-o'-the-wisp answer that momentarily promises fulfillment of all that longing, a promise and a fulfillment that are inevitably just out of reach. Sometimes, as Browning taught us, reaching beyond our grasp is our proper goal.

---

53. I am influenced here and throughout by Wolfgang Iser's *The Act of Reading: A Theory of Aesthetic Response* (Baltimore: Johns Hopkins University Press, 1978).

54. "Conclusion," in Walter Pater, *The Renaissance: Studies in Art and Poetry* (London: Macmillan and Co., 1917 [1873]), 248.

CHAPTER TWO

"Great Disorder" vs. "Violent Order": The Rhetoric of Spontaneity vs. The Rhetoric of Craft

A. A violent order is disorder; and
B. A great disorder is an order. These
Two things are one.
—Wallace Stevens, "Connoisseur of Chaos"

Whether or not there is such a thing as absolute spontaneity is, again, a hair I choose not to split. The point here, however, is that an "improvised" text is usually implicitly or explicitly shadowed by a craftsmanly, more staidly rational kind of text that it seeks to debunk and replace. Improvisations are always half of a binary, explicit or implicit. Stevens's "Notes toward a Supreme Fiction" is shadowed by and answers the decadent, highly crafted *fin de siècle* poets that Stevens had taken as his first models and here largely rejects (that lion of craft and allusion T. S. Eliot along with them). *"Notes"*—unfinished, off the top of his head, even mere doodles—is his implicit answer to their finely honed, chiseled but dead-end perfection. His muscular, enjambed, unrhymed, loosely iambic pentameter answers the Edwardians' formal, sonorous, and lilting lines given to arcane rhyme schemes and meters. In sum, gnarly as it is, this is a "more natural" Stevens than the mellifluous poetry of his aesthete masters.

Similarly, the discourses that dominate our culture shadow Dillard's first person subjective essay. Dillard's essay implicitly rejects the world of scientific positivism and commercial materialism that is too much with us, a world busy objectively reasoning and counting, measuring and selling—just beyond her beloved Tinker Creek—that surely would have little time for and less truck with embracing instinctual life, let alone weasels. Participating in the long tradition founded by Montaigne, Dillard's fluid, stream-of-thought essay (to "essay" is merely "to assay": "to try," "to test") suggests, like Stevens's "notes," that it is unfinished, perhaps with little or no purpose, and

48

all the better for that. Improvisations are spontaneous and natural (etc.) in relation to the more labored and artificial models they have come to replace. Improvisers in whatever era come to release us from the bonds of whatever formal systems the system-mongers would shackle us with. The gesture of spontaneity is almost always transgressive, seeking to break or extend the boundaries of craft and rationality. (The exceptions will be examined below). In the terms of literary critic Mikhail Bakhtin, whom we will also meet below, the gesture of spontaneity is dialogic, always in dialogue with a form more rigid, less spontaneous. By its nature, according to Bakhtin, a dialogic gesture is presented implicitly in scare quotes. Improvisation is in scare quotes not just for me but also for the improviser.

1. *Erasmus and Ecstasy, Rabelais and Rabelaisian*

In Montaigne's Renaissance, the great wellspring of this rhetoric of spontaneity is Erasmus, the Dutch humanist and theologian who flourished at the beginning of the sixteenth century. A Catholic priest and then monk who, for the sake of his scholarship, received dispensation not to practice his vocation, Erasmus dedicated his life to trying to purify the Church while fending off Luther's Reformation. The target of his scholarship and of his theology was consistently the rigidity and formalism of medieval traditions: the logic chopping of scholastic schoolmen, church authorities, monks and prelates who, rigid followers of Aristotle and Aquinas, seemed more interested in displaying their command of logic than in using logic to discover truths about the world. Ever true to the Church but always ready to attack abuses and corrupt practices, these, along with his hostility to outward forms, led to the charge that Erasmus "laid the egg that Luther hatched."

Erasmus's most popular work, *Moriae Encomium* or *The Praise of Folly,* published in Latin in 1509 and quickly translated into English, French, and German, cut both these ways. Meaning to purify the Church, Erasmus did it some harm. His title cuts two ways also: it is the person of Folly (*stultitia*) who offers the praise (*encomium*) of follies (*moriae*). *Moriae* is related to the self-referential name for paradox, oxymoron (from *oxus,* "sharp," plus *moros,* "dull") of which the *encomium* will be full. Appearing before us in cap and bells and the motley garb of the clown and fool, Folly offers a mock oration in praise of herself. She announces that she was the last born of the gods, offspring of Pluto, god of the underworld, and Freshness. Her wet-nurses were Inebriation and Ignorance. Her faithful companions were Philautia (self-love), Kolakia (flattery), Lethe (oblivion), Misoponia (laziness), Hedone (pleasure), Anoia (Madness), Tryphe (wantonness), Komos (intemperance) and Eegretos Hypnos (dead sleep).[1] Her point: everyone in their deeds worships her and her friends through imitation, but hypocritically, no one gives them credit.

Like Montaigne, who writes from the country and not the sophisticated city (of which he had been mayor), Erasmus in an introductory epistle claims he wrote the *Encomium* while riding a humble mule across the Alps. The echo of Christ's humble entry into Jerusalem is not accidental, but the first point of the gesture is that he writes far from his library. In fact he wrote the *Encomium* in his friend Sir Thomas More's library, one of the best in Europe. Nonetheless, Folly's speech is a tissue of erudition drawn from Erasmus's own *Adagia,* an annotated collection of Greek and Latin adages.[2] But Folly's (and Erasmus's) touch is light. Like Montaigne later, Erasmus writes a prose that implicitly revokes the then stylish model of Cicero's rolling, ornately rhetorical periods in favor of the clipped, "more natural" Senecan or Attic style.[3] Thus Erasmus's Folly is presented not just as spontaneous in the absolute, but pointedly as relatively *more* spontaneous, *less* artificial—dialogic.

An early moment in Folly's speech will exemplify Erasmus's light touch and help clarify this dual status of the claim of spontaneity as both absolute member of a binary and relative point on a continuum. I must quote at some length. Folly speaks:

> Here I might add that I am amazed at the...ingratitude should I say, or is it rather the laziness?...of mankind: they all cultivate me [that is, Folly] avidly and are very glad to benefit from my goodwill, but in all these cen-

---

1. Desiderius Erasmus, *The Praise of Folly,* translated by Clarence H. Miller (New Haven: Yale University Press, 1979), 17.

2. *Adagia,* in Desiderius Erasmus, *Opera Omnia,* vol. 20 (North-Holland: Elsevier, 1993 [1703-6]).

3. On this key distinction, see George Williamson, *The Senecan Amble: A Study in Prose Form from Bacon to Collier* (Chicago: The University of Chicago Press, 1951); and *"Attic" and Baroque Prose Style: The Anti-Ciceronian Movement. Essays by Morris W. Croll,* edited by J. Max Patrick and Robert O. Evans, with John M. Wallace (Princeton, N.J.: Princeton University Press, 1996).

turies there has never been a single soul who has celebrated the praises of Folly in a thankful oration—though there has been no lack of speech-writers who have spent sleepless nights burning the midnight oil to work out elaborate encomia of Busiris [a mythical Egyptian tyrant], Phalaris [a Sicilian tyrant], the quartan fever, flies, baldness, and other dangerous nuisances. From me, therefore, you will hear an extemporaneous speech, unpremeditated but all the truer for that. I say this because I wouldn't want you to think that I made it up just to show my cleverness, as ordinary speechmakers generally do. For you know that such orators even though they have labored over a speech for thirty whole years (and plagiarized some of it at that), will still swear that they dashed it off in a couple of days, or even dictated it, as a mere exercise. As for me, the method I like best of all is simply *"to blurt out whatever pops into my head."*[4]

Here we enter Erasmus's carefully calculated hall of mirrors, rather like that presented by Odysseus's speech in the *Iliad*. The speechwriters to whom he refers—Polycrates, Isocrates, and Erasmus's great model, Lucian—are all false when they "swear that they dashed it off in a couple days." In fact they labored late into the night and for thirty years to produce their mock encomia (these praisings of people and things obviously not worthy of praise, like tyrants, fevers, and flies). They do so only to show off their cleverness. Meanwhile Folly, Erasmus's persona, is making exactly the same claim: "You will hear an extemporaneous speech, unpremeditated" and "As for me, the method I like best of all is simply *'to blurt out whatever pops into my head.'"* They are falsely spontaneous; Folly and Erasmus behind her are so truly. There's our dialogic binary.

But are we meant truly to believe this absolute opposition, especially given the careful scholarship that suffuses the speech? The passage is a tissue of complex literary allusion and smells of the lamp at least as much as Folly complains her opponents' orations do. The final tag line, for example, is a quotation from Erasmus's own literary compendium (*"Quicquid in buccam venerit,"*[5]) where he lists at least a dozen classical sources for the gesture of spontaneity. And Erasmus of course writes Folly not in the vernacular but in Latin, the *lingua franca* of refined Europe in his day. Claiming carelessness, in

---

4. Erasmus, *Folly,* 12; emphasis in original.

5. Erasmus, *Adagia,* par. 472.

fact Erasmus invites the *cognoscenti* who appreciate his erudition to apprehend the relative skill and charm when he exploits the by-this-time tired *topos* of spontaneity. Her opponents pour new wine in old bottles. Folly does the same but polishes the bottle to the finest luster with erudite legerdemain and, by all accounts, in very fine Latin.

Erasmus's refined readers would readily have caught the pun in his title— *Moriae Encomium*—the first invitation into his hall of mirrors. Erasmus's praise of folly is also a praise of his friend Thomas More (*Moriae*), one of the age's most erudite scholars. More claimed of his own *Utopia* that it was "hurried and impromptu [*subitarius, atque extemporalis*]" and that "the nearer my style came to…careless simplicity [*neglectam simplicitatem*] the closer it would be to the truth."[6] More's claim of spontaneity links him to Erasmus and to the classical tradition they both admired. In praising folly Erasmus is paradoxically also praising More and the rigorous scholarship and moral stature he embodied.

The Praise of Folly is great fun, but Erasmus's deployment of the gesture of spontaneity is not just a game. At the heart of the *Encomium*, Erasmus argues for the centrality of ecstasy to Christian experience. To the reader's surprise, the value of *whatever pops into one's head* takes on new meaning when we realize that sometimes such inspirations are a matter of God's grace. Here we stumble on a critical crux in the *Encomium*: just how ecstatic is the ecstasy this Christian humanist recommends? Is this monk and scholar urging profligate wildness? Worse, is he urging an experiential inner-light theology that circumvents the authority of the apostolic Church and anticipates its opponents, Luther and Calvin? There are Renaissance scholars who would flay those who consider Erasmus's ecstasy in any other context than its very complex Christian theological underpinnings, anything more than a matter of rigorous Christian spiritual discipline, and well short of the Church's evangelical opponents.

I know this to be so from personal experience. I was once flayed in a graduate seminar, told that "anyone who would apply the term *Rabelaisian* to Rabelais *hasn't read him*." Erasmus's near contemporary, Rabelais was another

---

6. *The Yale Edition of The Complete Works of St. Thomas More*, vol. 4: *Utopia*, edited by Edward Surtz S.J. and J.H. Hexter (New Haven: Yale University Press, 1965), 39.

former monk and Christian humanist. His books, written in his vernacular French, are filled with the low humor and sensuality for which he has become known, hence *Rabelaisian.* But as with Erasmus, modern scholars spar over how low Rabelais would have us go. On one side, Mikhail Bakhtin, who celebrated Rabelais's carnivalesque world;[7] on the other, my Harvard professor, chair of the French department at the time.

Rabelais is, of course, another of my improvisers. His books (*Pantagruel,* 1532, and *Gargantua,* 1534) are saturated in the gesture of thoughtless spontaneity. Almost literally saturated: Rabelais addresses his works to "illustrious drinkers and you, precious syphilitics [*Buveurs très illustres, et vous vérolés très précieux*]."[8] He hopes his readers will think no more and drink as much as he did in writing:

> Yes, even though I, writing them, gave the matter no more thought than you, who were probably also drinking. I may add that in composing this masterpiece I have not spent or wasted more leisure than is required for my bodily refection—food and drink to you! Is that not the right time to commit to the page such sublime themes and such profound wisdom?[9]

Rabelais's hope is that his work will "smell more of wine than oil [*sentoyent plus le vin que l'huile*]."[10] Though Rabelais cribs this figure from the Latin poet Horace, he would have us believe his books are the product of lived life, and life lived to the hilt, rather that the product of scholarly lucubrations. This word, which has come to mean pedantic, refers to the oil-fueled lamps (*lux* = light) that the scholar or pedant must use as he pores over his books late into the night. Inspired by more reliable (or more unreliable!) means, improvisers have better things to do with their nights. So inspired, they seek in Rabelais's words "to suck the essential marrow [of life] [*sucer la substantifique moelle*)." But for some Renaissance scholars, one may find the essential marrow in the low but only through God's grace, for which wine is the metaphoric stand-in.

---

7. Mikhail Bakhtin, *Rabelais and his World,* translated by Hélène Iswolsky (Bloomington: Indiana University Press, 1984).

8. My translation.

9. François Rabelais, *The Five Books of Gargantua and Pantagruel,* translated by Jacques Le Clercq (New York: The Modern Library, 1936), 5.

10. Ibid.

At his first book's center—again spontaneity takes us to the center—Rabelais portrays a utopian monastic world, the Abbey of Thélème, where over the door all who enter are urged to "do as thou wilt [*Fais ce que voudras*]":

> Their whole life was ordered not by law, statute, or rule, but according to their free will and pleasure. They arose when they pleased. They ate, drank, worked, and slept when the the spirit moved them...Gargantua's plan called for perfect liberty. The only rule of the house was
> DO AS THOU WILT.[11]

Rabelais was a former monk who had left monastic life to become a doctor and scholar. The passage reads at first as a satire of monastic excesses. The monks of the Abbey of Thélème enjoy the use of a swimming pool, chambermaids, and unctuous cuisine. And yet Rabelais is also dead serious about this portrait of an ideal society. "Do as thou wilt" works only for those properly inspired because, as Rabelais continues, "men that are free, of gentle birth, well-bred, and at home in civilized company possess a natural instinct and spur that inclines them to virtue and saves them from vice. This instinct they name their honor"[12] Rabelais's monks are near kin to Blake's Jesus in *The Marriage of Heaven and Hell*: "Jesus was all virtue, and acted from impulse, not from rules."[13] Free will works from instinct but only if your free will is not debased—"all virtue." Rabelais the humanist says that a gentleman's honor makes the difference; the Christian behind the gentleman would have spoken of grace. Blake will speak of vision.

The vulgarian *Rabelaisian* notion, which the head of the Harvard French department took me to be invoking, misses the refinement and discipline that Rabelais would have us employ as we embrace the world. Hence my flaying. Recommending drunkenness is an odd way to begin a journey that ends in the goal of refinement and discipline, but that is sometimes how

---

11. Thélème is the English transliteration of the Ancient Greek noun *qšlhma* (will), from the verb *qšlw*, to will, wish, purpose. Early Christian writings use the word to refer to the will of the Christian God, the human will. Rabelais himself explains, "Thélème in Greek means free will," Rabelais, *Gargantua and Pantagruel*, 144; ibid., 154; emphasis in original.

12. Ibid.

13. William Blake, *The Poetry and Prose of William Blake*, edited by David Erdman (Garden City, N.Y.: Doubleday, 1970), 43.

the *topos* of spontaneity works, as an extreme metaphor. What "Rabelaisian" captures, however, is that Rabelais envisions that, *if* properly inspired, we would embrace *all* the world, and *all* of our humanity, the low included: to the improviser, as to the Roman poet Terence, nothing human is foreign. To my mind, my professor missed this inclusiveness, Rabelais's deepest point. Grace may come from above, but one of its effects is that it enables us to embrace the fallen world and redeem it. This is the grand gesture of the Christian humanist and the beginning of the modern world, the epistemological corollary of the age of exploration Rabelais inhabited and, by dissecting corpses, participated in.

My professor's target was not really me, after all, but Mikhail Bakhtin, who had launched a veritable industry of scholarship exploring the Rabelaisian carnivalesque throughout literary history. Now recognized by many as one of the greatest literary and philosophical minds in the twentieth century, Bakhtin was the kind of theoretical critic back in the 1970s that Keepers-of-the-Tradition worked hard to dismiss. I do not merely wish here to settle old (and petty) debts. Our teapot tempest is instructive and serves as an example of many others.[14] The terms that improvisation invokes are loaded and meant to be. Missing the nuances, their readers have generated tempest after

---

14. Perhaps citing two of the critical debates from widely disparate periods will serve to convey their persistent flavor and shape. Timothy Hampton summarizes the debate in Rabelais studies that pits the pro-humanist readers, Gérard Defaux and Michael Screech, who see Rabelais as embracing "Erasmian humanism and Pauline Christianity" against the supra- or anti-humanists, Terence Cave and François Rigolot, for whom Rabelais's "books are about the…the impossibility of moral messages," in "'Turkish Dogs': Rabelais, Erasmus, and the Rhetoric of Alterity," *Representations* 41 (Winter 1993): 59. The issue plays itself out more recently in Daniel Belgrad's *The Culture of Spontaneity* where he finds that the embrace by artists like the Abstract Expressionists of "primitivism, myth and subjectivity" was a challenge to "the dominant postwar culture." Belgrad finds fault with Michael Leja's interpretation of the same school: "Leja identifies the cultural work of abstract expressionism as…'a refurbishing of the culture's prevailing model of self as essentially autonomous, integral, rational and effectual…The relation between New York School art and the dominant culture was one of deep interdependence obscured by superficial antagonism,'" *The Culture of Spontaneity: Improvisation and the Arts in Postwar America* (Chicago: The University of Chicago Press, 1999), 264n. *Plus ça change…*

tempest as they over-and underrespond to Erasmus's ecstasy, Rabelais's libertinage, or other improvisers' extreme tropes. Critical readers not only disagree but cannot hear one another. The problem snowballs. Michael Holquist,
Bakhtin's greatest translator and champion, feels compelled in Bakhtin's last
collection in English to urge "a note of caution…Bakhtin's call to liberation
is everywhere informed by a stern awareness of necessity's central place in
the biological limits of our perception, the structure of language, and the laws
of society."[15] The topos of spontaneity, its embrace of freedom, and improvisation itself are each in their own way almost always part of a binary. What
improvisers in the end propose that we embrace almost always lies somewhere in the middle.

The tempests and misprisions called forth by the rhetorical embrace of
spontaneity are not just for the teapots of Renaissance scholars. In Sigmund
Freud's *General Introduction to Psychoanalysis,* first given orally as lectures,
the founder of the free-associative talking method feels called upon, like
Holquist, to warn with apparent anxiety that "it is out of the question that
part of the analytic treatment should consist of advice to 'live freely.'"[16] A
rather humorous moment: rod-straight Herr Doktor Professor having to
explain that he didn't mean *that* at all. The invitation to free-associate, or
to improvise, may seem an invitation to the libertine. But, often, like a full-
blooded version of Prufrock, the improviser feels compelled to add, "That is
not what [they] meant at all/That is not it, at all."

U-topia means "no place," and I am claiming that spontaneity is a *topos,*
a place in the mind. I'll return in a moment to this important term from
classical rhetoric. But to underscore the careful craft (and craftiness) of these
improvisers' hall of mirrors, let's consider a perfect analogue (and, possibly,
a direct descendent) some two centuries later. In Laurence Sterne's *Tristram Shandy,* the narrator and eponymous hero vows to throw his library key
from his coach window because mankind seems to "ever make new books,
as apothecaries make new mixtures, by pouring only out of one vessel into
another." With such bookish plagiarisms—such "pitiful,—pimping,—pettifog-

---

15. Mikhail Bakhtin, *Speech Genres and Other Late Essays,* translated by Caryl Emerson and Michael Holquist (Austin: University of Texas Press, 1986), xix.

16. Sigmund Freud, *A General Introduction to Psychoanalysis,* translated by Joan
Riviere (Garden City, N.Y.: Garden City Publishing, 1943), 375.

ging," as he calls it—Tristram will have nothing to do.[17] Not smelling of the lamp, his book will be more natural, more real, fuller of life than mere bookish books. Fine. Except that, as every annotated edition makes clear and as Sterne's contemporary readers probably easily recognized, the entire oath is a pastiche cribbed from Burton's *Anatomy of Melancholy.* Sterne's artless cry for artlessness is an artful ploy, all the more so because he means to be caught in the act, seen for the skillful, pettifogging—but crafty—plagiarist that he is. Did he plagiarize the whole gesture itself—the erudite disclaimer of erudition—from *The Praise of Folly?* He may have.

2. Art vs. Artlessness in Montaigne

Montaigne's *Essays* (first published 1580 and several times revised) offer another early Renaissance example of the gesture where Montaigne places these rhetorical gestures—art vs. artlessness—in opposition:

> But is it reasonable...that I should set forth to the world, where fashioning and art have so much credit and authority, some crude and simple products of nature, and of a feeble nature at that? Is it not making a wall without stone, or something like that, to construct books without knowledge and without art? Musical fancies are guided by art, mine by chance.[18]

Claims of careless, unpremeditated, uninformed, uneducated, unpolished spontaneity are legion in Montaigne's *Essays,* a title that in its very name, as I've pointed out above, asserts its tentative and unassuming character.[19] Recall Stevens's analogous gesture: his are merely *"Notes* toward a Supreme Fiction,"

---

17. *The Life and Opinions of Tristram Shandy, Gent.,* in *The Works of Laurence Sterne,* 4 vols. (London: Sharpe and Son, 1819), 1: 408.

18. *The Complete Essays of Montaigne,* translated by Donald M. Frame (Stanford: Stanford University Press, 1958), 611 ["Of Repentance," III: 2].

19. E.g., "These are my fancies, by which I try to give knowledge not of things, but of myself," *The Complete Essays of Montaigne,* 296 ["Of the Books," II: 10]; "It seems to be more peculiar to the mind to be prompt and sudden in its operation, and more peculiar to the judgment to be slow and deliberate...I know by experience this sort of nature that cannot bear vehement and laborious premeditation. If it doesn't go along gaily and freely, it goes nowhere worth going...I have little control over myself and my moods. Chance has more power here than I," ibid., 26 ["Of Prompt or Slow Speech," I: 10].

just as Folly's complaint against the speechwriters who falsely claim that their labor of "thirty years" is a *mere exercise*." Montaigne's passage serves us especially well because it points to the implicit opposition with artifice that lies behind most claims of spontaneity. Why claim crudeness and simplicity when fashioning and art, as he says, have so much credit and authority in the world? His appraisal is of course dead on target. We credit, we esteem, we lend authority, and we are convinced by those forms of discourse that display craft, care, and thoughtfulness. The scholar's footnotes or the lawyer's citations lend authority by their mere presence, a message they carry over and above their authority-laden content. They say: I have researched this; I have thought long and hard; I have burnt the candle at both ends—believe me! The very presence of footnotes rhetorically underscores the "fashioning and art" such texts everywhere reflect in their effort to persuade.

Montaigne's program is perhaps best summed up by one of his many self-definitions, "A new figure: an unpremeditated and accidental philosopher."[20] He thus exploits a contrary rhetoric, a rhetoric founded on "some crude and simple products of nature...guided...by chance." It is as if, anticipating his future countryman, he were asserting in contradiction of Descartes, *non cogito, ergo melior sum!* (I do not think, therefore I am the better for it)—though the self-effacing Montaigne would never boast so overtly). This opposition, between studied and artificial ornament and the simple, natural, and fortuitous, is absolutely central to Montaigne's program embodied in his free-associative style and often underscored thematically. He employs it at the very start of his *Essays,* in his advice "To the Reader": "If I had written to seek the world's favor, I should have bedecked myself better, and should present myself in a studied posture. I want to be seen here in my simple, natural, ordinary fashion, without straining or artifice; for it is myself that I portray."[21] Not seeking the world's favor or assent, Montaigne eschews the decoration ("bedecked") and "studied posture" that would convince the reader that his essays should be taken seriously. Indeed, he insists the reader "would be unreasonable to spend leisure time on so frivolous and vain a subject."

---

20. *The Complete Essays of Montaigne,* 409 ["Apology for Raymond Sebond," II: 12].
21. Ibid., 2 ["To the Reader"].

Of course the point is that, despite appearances, and despite common sense, the claim of artlessness also authorizes. Scholars often explain away the gesture of spontaneity as the "topos of affected modesty," or as the convention of anticipatory self-defense: I'm not worth attacking because either I'm not worth your trouble or, if I am worthy, this is not my best effort (a gesture every underachieving schoolchild has mastered).[22] Another scholarly response to the gesture of artlessness, and most *reasonable* of all, is to prove by careful textual and manuscript analysis that, in fact, the author was *careful*, blotting and emending many a line.[23] Even so, the gesture of spontaneity haunts us still, refusing to be explained away. There it stands in all the unreasonableness and absurdity of its self-definition: this is a *text* unmediated by artifice or effort or thought, "an extemporaneous speech, unpremeditated" as Erasmus's Folly says, *"but all the truer for that."*

"But all the truer for that"! What these scholarly dismissals and explanations miss is the positive force of the disclaimer. Yes, such claims of artlessness have been used to cover many a backside. But they often have an aggressive, in-your-face power and effect as well. And of course, as we saw in the example of Rabelais, sometimes the gesture serves as an extreme vehicle in a metaphor, the tenor of which is far more restrained. Perhaps we attempt to explain spontaneity away for the very reason that this implicit claim makes us uncomfortable, cutting as it patently does across the grain of our everyday, conscious assumptions about what commands authority in the world. But that is just what it means to do: it means to make us uncomfortable, for, "we need to be provoked,—goaded like oxen," as Thoreau puts it.[24] What it goads us toward is a reconsideration of the value of craft and rationality.

Spontaneity authorizes but does so by undermining the normal terms of authorization: this text is valuable and persuasive not because it is the product of long thought and labor, but exactly because it is not. Indeed, Mon-

---

22. Ernst Robert Curtius, *European Literature and the Latin Middle Ages*, translated by. Willard R. Trask (Princeton, N.J.: Princeton University Press, 1973 [1953]), 63; on the convention of anticipatory self-defense, see "Appendix B: Vocabulary and Diction in *Utopia*," in *The Complete Works of St. Thomas More*, 4: 580.

23. See for example *Byron's* Don Juan: *A Variorum Edition*, 5 vols., edited by Truman Guy Steffan and William W. Pratt (Austin: University of Texas Press, 1957-71).

24. Thoreau, *Walden, Civil Disobedience, and Other Writings*, 77.

taigne subtly introduces the issue of reason's value at the outset: "But is it reasonable? [*Mais est-ce raison que...*]" he asks. His opposition of the rhetorics of art and of artlessness says in effect: this is what you usually consider right and reasonable; do you still? Here is my wonderful, delectable book, suffused with life and experience, not authorities, and the mere product of thoughtless effusion. Which do you prefer? Which is truer to life? Which procedure has a better chance of getting at truth? Montaigne's image of the wall ("Is it not making a wall without stone, or something like that, to construct books without knowledge and without art?"[25]), in a sense a mere throwaway metaphor, also has this indirect and suggestive sense: to proceed this way is as absurd as constructing a wall without stones. But, he seems to ask, who wants to construct walls? We are here to engage experience, not to wall ourselves off from life. He writes of his intramural program in his key essay "Of Experience," "I would rather be an authority on myself than on Cicero."[26] So, as his rhetoric enforces, would he have us be. That he seems like Erasmus to quote so effortlessly, to be such a master of the classical canon, makes his disdain of bookishness and his embrace of carelessness the more persuasive. Having exclusively spoken Latin at home until he was six, Montaigne scorns bookishness out of desire, not out of necessity. If he scorns it at all.

Once again, Montaigne's gesture of spontaneity and craftlessness takes us to the heart of his project. Montaigne's opposition of rhetorics here and elsewhere—it begins on his first page in his "To the Reader" as noted above—telegraphs a question that permeates his book and anticipates the keynote of what is agreed by most to be the *Essais'* most seminal statement, the "Apology for Raymond Sebond."[27] There, his subject is the impotence and vanity of unaided human reason. Montaigne is no irrationalist, as more careful study than can be attempted here would make clear. Nor is he the primitivist that many of the terms he privileges—natural, simple, crude—might suggest. Like many Renaissance improvisers, Erasmus, More, and Rabelais especially, Montaigne's rhetoric of spontaneity is commissioned in the service of divine grace, employed to enforce our recognition of the limits of human reason.

---

25. *The Complete Essays of Montaigne,* 611 ["Of Repentance," III: 2].

26. Ibid., 822 ["Of Experience," III: 13].

27. Ibid., 318–457 ["Apology for Raymond Sebond," II: 12].

This recognition was central to the Renaissance humanists' program. Like poet and Anglican priest John Donne they sought "to trouble the understanding, to displace, and to discompose, and disorder the judgment."[28] While articulating with newfound pride the glories of being human in an age that discovered (or rediscovered) both classical antiquity and the new world, their purpose was ever to remind us of man's limits and his dependence on God's grace, to warn against pride becoming *hubris*. We are likely to associate the improvised with the vanguard, with poets who explore the edges of consciousness and society: Romantics, Dadaists, Surrealists, or the Beat Generation. But conservatives employ it as well, at least since Pindar (as we will see in a chapter to follow). Whatever the improvisers' politics, religious morality, or aesthetic position, the issue of rationality under various guises and permutations characterizes self-styled improvisations. This is my central point: while usually argued away, or subjected to pointless scrutiny, in fact the figure of spontaneous composition—the rhetoric of spontaneity—subtly channels the "spontaneous" texts' central issue, whether we notice it or not: the nature and value of rationality.

What is at stake in reevaluating rationality is not just epistemology and religious doctrine but also politics. As philosopher Stephen Toulmin reminds us,

> The humanists has special reasons to deplore, condemn, and try to head off the religious warfare that was picking up intensity throughout the sixteenth century, as antagonism between the two branches of Western Christianity deepened. Human modesty alone (they argued) should teach reflective Christians how limited is their ability to reach unquestioned Truth or unqualified Certainty over all matters of doctrine...[T]he risk was that, pressed into the service of worldly political interests, doctrinal issues would become fighting matters.[29]

And these became fighting matters with a vengeance, witness the burning of heretics on both sides and the onslaught of the Thirty Years War (1618-1648). The paradox of the humanist improvisations of the sixteenth and seventeenth

---

28. *The Sermons of John Donne*, 10 vols., edited by George R. Potter and Evelyn Simpson (Berkeley: University of California Press, 1962), 2:282.

29. Stephen Toulmin, *Cosmopolis: The Hidden Agenda of Modernity* (Chicago: The University of Chicago Press, 1990), 25.

centuries is that they urge nonrational faculties as a reminder of Reason's limits, *in order to promote more reasonableness amongst doctrinal opponents.*

It is easy now to think of the scholiasts as straw men, hardly worthy of Erasmus's rebuttal. But as Toulmin explains, speaking of Erasmus and Montaigne, "they regarded human affairs in a clear-eyed, non-judgmental light that led to honest practical doubt about the value of 'theory' for human experience—whether in theology, natural philosophy, metaphysics, or ethics."[30] The problem is not just the kind of system scholiasts used, it is their commitment to system itself, to knowing the world through theory and doctrine not experience. This is the great shift the humanists like Erasmus, Montaigne, Thomas More, and Rabelais effected and they effected it in part through their brilliant improvisations. If the schoolmen still seem straw men, or at least the humanists' combativeness hardly meriting our attention, Toulmin reminds us that the schoolmen's commitment to abstract theory and absolute system, to what Alfred North Whitehead calls "the rationalistic orgy of the Middle Ages," is revived by Descartes.[31] Toulmin argues that the "Quest for Certainty" Descartes pursues, the foundation of modern philosophy which "(as [John] Dewey and [Richard] Rorty argue) lead philosophy into a dead end," is in part a response to the religious upheaval of the Thirty Years War, and in part a response to Renaissance humanists, our improvisers—Erasmus, Montaigne, Rabelais, and Bacon—whose urbane and tolerant skepticism could not prevent that upheaval.[32]

3. *The Rhetoric of Rationality and Craft*

If the tension between spontaneity and craft is so central to human experience, and if so-called spontaneous texts explore a tension with their binary opposite, craft, then a logical expectation would be that the obverse would also be true, that overtly and self-styled "crafted" texts could be shown to explore the tension between spontaneity and irrationality on the one hand and craftsmanship and rationality on the other. The nineteenth century American Edgar Allan Poe is a case in point.

---

30. Ibid.

31. Alfred North Whitehead, *Science and the Modern World: Lowell Lectures, 1925* (New York: The Free Press, 1967), 20.

32. Toulmin, *Cosmopolis*, 80, 75.

As is especially Poe's "The Philosophy of Composition," which describes how he composed "The Raven." I do not know of any more vociferous paean to deliberate artistry, nor one conducted in such a ratiocinative fashion, almost like a recipe for baking a cake with Cartesian theoretical certainty: here are the ingredients and here the manner and order in which they are combined. We should not be surprised to learn that his bugbear is this:

> Most writers—poets in especial—prefer having it understood that they compose by a species of fine frenzy—an ecstatic intuition—and would positively shudder at letting the public take a peep behind the scenes, at the elaborate and vacillating crudities of thought—at the true purposes seized only at the last moment—at the innumerable glimpses of idea that arrived not at the maturity of full view—at the fully matured fancies discarded in despair as unmanageable—at the cautious selections and rejections—at the painful erasures and interpolations—in a word, at the wheels and pinions—the tackle for scene-shifting the step-ladders and demon traps—the cock's feathers, the red paint and the black patches, which, in ninety-nine cases out of a hundred, constitute the properties of the literary *histrio* [actor].[33]

If im-pro-visation is the art of the un-fore-seen, Poe's hostile view anticipates Adorno's toward jazz, and then some. For Poe the artist hides the hard work and the tissue of barely averted blunders that lie behind his/her smooth surface, hidden in part by the protestation "that they compose by a species of fine frenzy—an ecstatic intuition." Worse, Poe hints, these writers, like Erasmus's satirized speechwriters, are really frauds whose compositions are labored and constitute mere theatrical greasepaint and machinations and props.

In opposition to this chaotic, ineffective, and false artistic labor that ends in still birth, Poe offers his remedy: labor that is as orderly and steel-trap-certain as a logical syllogism. He offers up the composition of his poem "The Raven" to the surgeon's knife for dissection. It underwent just such a ratiocinative process, he says. He seeks to show that "no point in its composition is referrible [*sic*] either to accident or intuition—that the work proceeded, step

---

33. *The Selected Writings of Edgar Allan Poe: Authoritative Texts, Backgrounds and Contexts, Criticism,* edited by G.R. Thompson (New York and London: W.W. Norton, 2004), 676.

by step, to its completion with the precision and rigid consequence of a mathematical problem."[34]

The steps in Poe's syllogism are well known: poems are by his definition short, about beauty ("the work *universally* appreciable"), and sad (the "highest manifestation" of tone). "Ordinary induction"—remember Poe invented the detective story—now leads him to seek out the best possible "key-note in the construction of his poem" and he determines it is the refrain, the shorter the better, and that the most "sonorous and susceptible" sound "of protracted emphasis, admitted no doubt: and these considerations inevitably led me to the long *o* as the most sonorous vowel, in connection with *r* as the most producible consonant. "'Nevermore'...was the very first which presented itself."[35]

How nice. And so on to the choice of the most melancholy theme, death, especially the death of a beautiful woman mourned by her bereaved lover, to the choice of the raven to repeat the refrain, of the stanza and prosodic form and rhyme scheme and the locale and the weather, *tout*, all the product of his working back from effects to the poetic causes that will produce them.

This last is one of his main thrusts against the "frenzied intuitions" of his brother poets. He emphasizes that, "Here then [with the word 'Nevermore'] the poem may be said to have its beginning—at the end, where all works of art should begin—for it was here, at this point of my preconsiderations, that I first put pen to paper..." and he composes the climax of the poem, the third to last stanza.[36]

One can believe or not that Poe actually went through such a ratiocinative, backward-step-by-backward-step, deductive process. What is more interesting is how the whole house of cards seems to cave in on itself when one considers all the irrational aspects of the process which he glibly elides. For what does his theoretical assertion mean that Beauty and the longing for a lost beauty by a bereaved lover is the most universal subject for poetry? What does it mean that as Poe explains, the whole plot hinges on the narrator's "human thirst for self-torture" "to propound such queries to the bird as will bring him, the lover, the most of the luxury of sorrow, through the antici-

---

34. Ibid., 677.
35. Ibid., 679.
36. Ibid., 680.

pated answer "'Nevermore'"?[37] At the heart of all Poe's explanations lies the heart, the unexplainable: impulses on the one hand to self-injury and on the other to control through repetition compulsion that will take another century at least to begin to understand.[38] Thus it seems right that, just as Hermes oversees improvisations (as we shall see in Chapter 7) so here the ruling deity of Poe's crafted masterpiece, hovering on the mantel above the action, is Pallas Athena, known for her wisdom and for her skill in artifice [*mētis*] in constructing carefully tooled devices. She helps Hephaestus, for example, create the net that traps Mars and Aphrodite (Hermes's sister) in their amours. Poe catches doomed love in the net of his reason, but the tell-tale heart, of which his reason knows nothing, beats on. No one better bears out Stevens's point that "A violent order is disorder."[39] At the center then of Poe's celebration of deliberate artistry (and I mean both the poem and its explanation) is a subject matter beyond deliberation and beyond art. This tension is the same that we found in improvisation's celebration of the spontaneous. Like the mythic ouroboros, the snake that devours its own tail, crafted and uncrafted texts circle back on one another.

To be human is to feel this dual tug toward mastery and toward being mastered. Mastering or mastered, we achieve the state Dillard longs for, "where the mind is single." Mastering or mastered, we come to know this world or the transcendent, and to do the world's or the transcendent's will. In the middle of these two extreme states lay a third, where having mastered our instrument—perhaps ourselves—we can *let go*, certain like Rabelais's gentlemanly monks, that we will do the right thing. "This is yielding," says Dillard, "not fighting"—though we can add, it can be yielding to external inspiration or internal. That middle state, from whichever source, is the state that improvisers both limn and ambivalently long for.

Although we may classify Poe as a Romantic writer, and we usually do, nonetheless in his effort to debunk composition made "by a fine frenzy" he

---

37. Ibid., 683.

38. Compare Poe's twin heirs, Sir Arthur Conan Doyle and Sherlock Holmes: at the heart of their celebrations of ratiocinative deductions lie Holmes's cocaine addiction and evil doppelgänger Moriarty.

39. Stevens, *Collected Poetry and Prose*, 194.

seems to be the first anti-Romantic. For in literary history we tend to think of spontaneity as a Romantic and post-Romantic gesture and theme. And yet, we all agree, even Homer not only nods but improvises.[40] The claim of extemporaneous composition is evident throughout the course of literary history: in the formulaic improvisations of the archaic epic poets like Homer and the *Beowulf* poet; in the *sprezzatura*, or carelessness, of the Renaissance courtier; in the Aeolian vibrations of the Romantic lyric; in the outrageous free associations of the Dadaists; in the "kickwriting" and "wild form" of the Beat Generation. Is there a connection among the many texts in Western Literature that claim to be improvised? My answer is emphatically in the affirmative. There *are* meaningful similarities, for example, among Sappho's gestures of lyric immediacy; Milton's epic "unpremeditated verse"; Pope's Horatian "grace beyond the reach of art"; even Henry Miller's claim in *Tropic of Cancer* that he "will sing for you, a little off key perhaps, but I will sing"; or even, still again, Derrida's opening gambit in *Dissemination* that "This (therefore) will not have been a book."[41] Self-styled "spontaneous" texts bear fruitful comparison despite the yawning gulfs that may separate their cultural moments and the cultural matrices from which their spontaneous gestures spring. Spontaneity can mean many things but, more often than not, instances pertain to the same conceptual field where issues regarding the value of craft and rationality contend. Despite cultural shifts of tectonic proportions then, there is an essential point of contact when Erasmus declares in the voice of Folly that she tells an extemporaneous tale that is perforce the truer; when Wordsworth defines poetic truth as "the spontaneous overflow of powerful feelings"; when the Dadaist Tristan Tzara urges that "Thought is *produced* in the mouth"; and when the Beat Generation's muse, Neal Cassidy, recommends writing that should be read as "a continuous chain of undisciplined thought," or when his

---

40. On Homer's oral-formulaic art, see Lord's groundbreaking *The Singer of Tales*; and Michel N. Nagler's *Spontaneity and Tradition: A Study in the Oral Art of Homer* (Berkeley and Los Angeles: University of California Press, 1974).

41. Henry Miller, *Tropic of Cancer* (New York: Grove Press, 1961), 2; Jacques Derrida, *Dissemination*, translated by Barbara Johnson (Chicago: The University of Chicago Press, 1981), 3. This is from Derrida's preface, "*Hors Livre*," whose title is one of Derrida's many puns: not only "outside the book [proper]" but also "[properly] outside books."

associate, Allen Ginsberg, proclaims: "First Thought, Best Thought."[42] Yes, their tones are decidedly different: Erasmus speaks, as ever, with well-crafted irony; Wordsworth with high seriousness; and Tzara and his offspring in a tone of scandal, attempting, as ever, to *épater les bourgeois,* to shock the middle-class. Never seeking to ignore or obscure such important differences, the present study will explore the deep and essential connections among these and other artists who employ the notion of spontaneous composition. My goal is to investigate the timeless human issue that often lies embedded in gestures of spontaneity and to show how those gestures effect improvised texts and their readers.

Understanding this timeless essence, the argument that lies at the heart of spontaneous texts, can help us better understand individual spontaneous texts in their historical setting. As I've noted, such texts are notoriously problematic, often the subject of critical debates where "critics disagree," writes one Renaissance scholar, "about the extent to which such writers participate in and reproduce the rhetorical conventions, interpretive strategies and moral precepts of humanism" and whether they embrace instead some form of mysticism or libertinage.[43] Covering so much ground as I do here it is important not to get lost in academic debates and footnotes. What is instructive is that the structure of the academic debates is repeated again and again regardless of the text or author or period. Again and again scholars do battle over whether Erasmus or Rabelais or Wordsworth or Thoreau (or whoever) seeks to overturn or to maintain the existing order and what their attitude is to the agent of that change. In each case the agency in question is the author's embrace of some form of the non-rational, whichever form it has taken in the improviser's epoch. What is Erasmus's attitude toward ecstasy in *The Praise of Folly?* Just how much license does Rabelais really recommend when he urges "Do what you will [*Fais ce que voudras*]" in Gar-

---

42. William Wordsworth and S.T. Coleridge, *Lyrical Ballads 1798,* edited by W.J.B. Owen, 2nd ed. (Oxford: Oxford University Press, 1969), 157, 173; quoted in Hans Richter, *Dada: Art and Anti-Art* (London: Thames and Hudson, 1997), 35; quoted in Belgrad, *Spontaneity,* 204; Allen Ginsberg, *Spontaneous Mind: Selected Interviews 1958–1996* (New York: Perennial, 2002).

43. Timothy Hampton, "'Turkish Dogs': Rabelais, Erasmus, and the Rhetoric of Alterity," *Representations* 41 (Winter 1993): 59.

gantua's Temple de Thélème? What is Wordsworth's attitude toward the "dizzy raptures" of youth in "Tintern Abbey" and what is their relationship to "the philosophic mind"? What is Thoreau's attitude toward Nature? Can the same man who wrote that "Wildness is the preservation of the world," also have written, "Nature is hard to be overcome, but she must be overcome"?[44] Is the improviser's retreat from privileging spontaneity to more conservative stances mere lip service? Are all improvisers, like Blake's Milton, of the devil's party? Such critical problems in such profound texts are never fully resolved. Debates will inevitably continue and I am not here to resolve them. But the figure of spontaneous composition is a powerful thematic catalyst; understanding better our acculturated response to that catalyst, making its implicit meaning explicit, as Cassirer would have us do, can help to advance new approaches to long standing debates, shedding new light on these and other "spontaneous" texts.

Thus, whatever scholarly dangers may lurk on the less familiar ground I must tread, it is important that we *not* lock the study of spontaneity into a single literary period or single national literature. The rhetoric of spontaneity had a great flowering during the Romantic period, my own area of expertise, but truly to understand that rhetoric we must see that the Romantics were participating in something timeless. Still, an ahistorical method will not serve: it is imperative to understand spontaneity in each historical and cultural context.

Thus, spontaneity means one thing to a Puritan or other nonconformist who worships in a tradition of ejaculatory prayer that charges the preacher to mount the pulpit without notes of any kind.[45] It means something decidedly different to modern iconoclast Henry Miller when he writes in *Tropic of Cancer*:

> A year ago, six months ago, I thought that I was an artist. I no longer think about it, I *am*. Everything that was literature has fallen from me. There are no more books to be written thank God.

---

44. Thoreau, *Walden, Civil Disobedience, and Other Writings*, 150.

45. Lori Branch, *Rituals of Spontaneity: Sentiment and Secularism from Free Prayer to Wordsworth* (Waco, Texas: Baylor University Press, 2006).

> This then? This is not a book. This is libel, slander, defamation of char-
> acter. This is not a book in the ordinary sense of the word. No, this is a
> prolonged insult, a gob of spit in the face of Art, a kick in the pants to God,
> Man, Destiny, Time, Love, Beauty...that you will. I am going to sing for
> you, a little off key perhaps, but I will sing...
> This then is a song. I am singing.[46]

A world of difference divides the two. Yet our challenge is to see the essential similarities that bridge the divide. Puritan preacher and anti-Puritan Miller share an imperative alertness toward life and the motions of the heart. They share a distrust of art: of the authority, conventions, and artifice that complacent rationality creates. They both establish a special, intimate relationship with their audience. Both invoke not submission to their own authority, but rather an attitude of openness harmonious and congruent with their own. The Puritan seeks an openness to grace; the Modern seeks an openness to subconscious urges. Between the two lies a world of difference to be sure, but not necessarily a difference in kind. The Puritan avoids the ritual of "Papist" and Anglican and asks his auditors to open themselves to God's provenient grace; the disciple of Freud (misguided disciple according to Freud's note in *A General Introduction*) spits in the face of all that is superego and challenges his cultured readers to immolate their libraries upon the altars of Eros and the Id. The differences between those rhetorical postures, incomparable on their faces, are manifest and noteworthy. So too at bottom and much to our surprise are their *deep* similarities. Jonathan Edwards *and* Henry Miller? "Sinners in the Hands of an Angry God" and *Tropic of Cancer*? Yes, that's what I'm talking about.

4. *Literary Improvisation as a Timeless Aesthetic*

Observing these similarities, one begins to perceive a deep family resemblance among such texts. Improvisations are *polytropic,* many turning, like Odysseus, who as we shall see embodies the form. But they are nonetheless of a piece. The persistent aesthetic has been elusive first because improvisations insist that they are self-generated. Each is *sui generis,* its own kind and like no other. These are texts that at least lay claim to a freedom from intertextuality,

---

46. Miller, *Tropic of Cancer,* 1–2; emphasis in original.

speaking whatever comes into the mouth, not what comes from another book. Improvisation is a kind of non-genre genre. "In genre," the science fiction novelist William Gibson remarks, "you're sort of buying a guarantee that you are going to have essentially the same experience again and again."[47] A non-genre genre like improvisation would work by indulging in the polite fiction that it has no expectations to satisfy: having none, or keeping them covert, is the expectation it fills. The novel—which has its roots in the carnivalesque world of improvisation—promises something new, extracanonical: novel. Once it becomes canonical, the novel will have to work harder to convince us that each of its exemplars is in fact novel.

Another reason it is difficult to see the family resemblance among improvisations is that, protestations to the contrary notwithstanding, they do each belong to some genre, but wildly different genres: epideictic (or display) oratory (like Erasmus's *Praise of Folly*) and its heirs; personal essay (like Montaigne's); dialogue (like Valéry's *Idée Fixe* discussed below); epic (*Odyssey, Paradise Lost, The Prelude*); lyric forms of many varieties (ode, etc.); and both fiction and non-fiction forms of many kinds.

Improvisation is a non-genre genre insofar as examples claim or pretend to be without precedent. It is a metagenre—an overarching genre—insofar as, in fact pertaining to those genres or subgenres, it also pertains to this larger, umbrella mode of discourse. An ode is an ode insofar as it fulfills the expectations of ode: a more or less ecstatic lyric statement in three parts. An ode pertains to the improv metagenre insofar as it fulfills the expectations of improv: claiming to be more or less spontaneous and inspired, formally affecting to be unmediated by rationality and craft, while exploring the problematics of rationality, order, and freedom.

Though they may work in different genres, one can find direct lines of influence among improvisers. There is, for example, a clear line of descent from the Greek satirist Lucian (*A True History,* second century CE) to Erasmus (Folly, 1511), Sir Thomas More (*Utopia,* 1516), Rabelais (*Gargantua et Pantagruel,* 1532-64), Montaigne (*Essais,* 1580-92), Thomas Nashe (*Pierce Penniless,* 1592), Robert Burton (*The Anatomy of Melancholy,* 1621), Sir Thomas Browne (*Religio Medici,* 1643), Laurence Sterne (*Tristram Shandy,* 1761-67),

47. William Gibson, "Back From the Future," *The New York Times Magazine,* August 2007: 13.

and Lord Byron (*Don Juan,* 1817–24). But whether Montaigne, say, got his rhetoric of spontaneity from Erasmus, or Byron from Sterne who got it from Erasmus, is not the point. Improvisations are of a piece *not* because they draw from one another but because they draw from the same well. They are of a piece because they respond to the same human problems.

I should clarify, also, that when I speak of *literary* aesthetic, I do not mean to limit myself from or exclude the extra-or subliterary or from uncanonical genres, genres that do not fit into the conventional mainstream like lyric, epic, etc. It is characteristic of improvisations, as we just saw in Henry Miller, that they often overtly eschew the literary and instead cultivate the extraliterary or subliterary, what is beyond the canon or beneath it. Nor do I mean to exclude other arts, music, or painting, examples of which will be discussed in passing below.

Readers familiar with Renaissance scholarship may have noticed that a number of the writers I have brought to the table—Erasmus, Rabelais, More— are associated with the tradition of another metagenre, Menippean satire. A form developed by the Greek Cynic Menippus, whose work does not survive, Menippean satire had a resurgence in the Renaissance when humanists modeled their works on the mock encomia, dialogues, and ironic narratives of Menippus's Greek and Roman followers, Lucian, Petronius, Apuleius, Seneca, Varro, and others. In defining this "most elusive of genres," recent scholars all but delineate improvisation. "Assuming manifold shapes," writes W. Scott Blanchard, "one of " Menippean satire's

> defining features is its very rejection of aesthetic norms...; its authors
> intentions seem, in nearly every case to demonstrate the disabling and
> limiting conditions under which the human intellect operates. By suggesting that the categories and structures we impose upon our experience
> of the world are mere stays against the confusion and disorder that are
> the real conditions of human knowledge, the Menippean satirist—though
> nearly always an immensely learned author—poses uneasily between the
> role of sage and anti-intellectual iconoclast, a wise fool who is one of literature's most endearing pests.[48]

---

48. W. Scott Blanchard, *Scholars Bedlam: Menippean Satire in the Renaissance* (Lewisburg: Bucknell University Press, 1995), 11-12.

And, we can add, one of the most *enduring* pests. For Blanchard the form "challenges its readers to question the validity of conventional literary categories." Fellow Menippean scholar Howard Weinbrot sums up the form as "the genre that ate the world."[49] So, too, improvisation affects to embrace all of life.

Are improvisers just poaching on the Menippean tradition? More worrying for me, am I just poaching on Renaissance scholarship? I must admit my discovery of this recent scholarship has led to a few wakeful nights. If I am laying claim to new territory, I'd hate to think I was just, like Erasmus's faux improvisers, rebottling old wine.

But my claim holds. Menippean satire—"the genre that ate the world"—is but one of the many traditions gobbled up in turn by improvisation. Menippean satire helps explain the deep similarities between *Praise of Folly* and *Pantagruel,* one a mock encomium, the other a send up of law books. Erasmus and Rabelais both modeled themselves on Lucian, who is associated with the Menippean tradition. But *Paradise Lost? Walden? On the Road?* The question goes to matters larger than my scholarly ego. If I can demonstrate deep formal and thematic similarities amongst such disparate and unrelated works that claim to be improvised, what does that mean? What are the timeless human issues that shape a formless form that is born and reborn in countless ages and cultures? What if "the disabling and limiting conditions under which the human intellect operates" was not just a matter for satire?

Does the tradition of Menippean Satire explain the contours of Keith Johnstone's work on theater improvisation? Founder of the highly successful improv group Theatre Machine and Theatresports in the 1950s, Johnstone was instrumental in the development of improv comedy as we know it (Second City, *Whose Line Is It Anyway?*). His work reflects the tensions of the improvisation tradition. While "all his work has been to encourage the rediscovery of the imaginative response in the adult, [his] refinding of the power of the child's creativity," writes Irving Wardle, nonetheless,

> Like all great advocates of the unconscious, Johnstone is a sturdy rationalist. He brings a keen intellect, nourished on anthropology and psychology,

---

49. Howard D. Weinbrot, *Menippean Satire Reconsidered: From Antiquity to the Eighteenth Century* (Baltimore: The Johns Hopkins University Press, 2005), 1.

> to the task of demolishing intellectualism in the theatre…In rediscovering the imaginative world of childhood, he has re-examined the structural elements that bind that world together.[50]

Embracing the child's spontaneous world to demolish intellectualism and The Method while he "re-examined the structural elements that bind that world together," Johnstone could have been directly influenced by improvisation's tensions, its forces and counterforces, imbibing them for example from the Menippean satirist Molière, whom he often quotes.[51] Or he could have developed them in response to the problem faced by other improvisers: the challenge to develop an art that more truthfully reflects life's deep challenges. First among those challenges in Johnstone's terms: how to approach the world, through the adult's intellect or the child's playful imagination?

"To find laws of the spontaneous would be a contradiction in terms," writes neo-Jungian James Hillman, "for these events are irregular, lawless."[52] Nonetheless, that is exactly what I seek to do, to find the laws that make the irregular and lawless so regular and consistent in form and theme. In the next chapter I will offer a typology or grammar of the conventions of improvisation.

---

50. Irving Wardle, "Preface," in Johnstone, *Impro: Improvisation and the Theatre*, 11.

51. Ibid., ii.

52. James Hillman, *Pan and the Nightmare* (Thompson, Conn.: Spring Publications, 2020 [1972]), 74.

CHAPTER THREE

"Through Candor...A Candid Kind":
The Conventions of Literary Improvisation

The poem, through candor, brings back a power again
That gives a candid kind to everything.
—Wallace Stevens, "Notes Toward a Supreme Fiction"

W here is the Einstein to develop a unified field theory that describes this slippery "candid kind," improvisation? Like Einstein we face a number of elements, none of which are unfamiliar but which no one has yet made sense of together. Einstein had his gravity, electromagnetic fields, relativity theory, and quantum physics to harmonize and we, a number of persistent themes, styles, and formal conventions. I am not he. Like String Theorists, I offer here my interim report, a taxonomy of those elements.

Scholars are long familiar with the elements of improvisation and these elements have been widely analyzed by many hands—too many exhaustively to note—and from these I have of course benefited. But oftentimes scholars working in their period or authorial niche declare proudly that their author or text is the first of its kind, the first spontaneous, careless, open-ended, cornucopian text and hence *sui generis,* a thing unto itself. But what if what seems unique is part of a long, unspoken, unselfconscious, and unheralded tradition? What then?

One example will clarify how what I'm doing here fits in with what others have done with "improvised" texts and how I differ. Ruth Fox, writing in *The Tangled Chain: The Structure of Disorder in* The Anatomy of Melancholy, argues that Robert Burton "forged the *Anatomy* out of ... examples of numerous literary genres yet [the *Anatomy*] remains *sui generis,* the singular expression of its author's humane knowledge."[1] This no doubt captures the

---

1. Ruth A. Fox, *The Tangled Chain: The Structure of Disorder in the* Anatomy of Melancholy (Berkeley, Los Angeles, and London: University of California Press, 1976), 1.

flavor of Burton's *Anatomy*: he certainly means it to seem quirky and idio-syncratic and it is all that in spades. But I am arguing that it is also true that what intrigues Fox about the *Anatomy*, its structured disorder, its mixing of genres, even the impression it gives of being idiosyncratic, *"sui generis,"* are conventional elements in a coherent aesthetic of long date. No doubt the *Anatomy* is a "singular expression of its author's humane knowledge," but it is also an expression *like many another* of a persistent form—a metagenre—with persistent conventions and themes, where the issue of rationality is in play.

I am, again, *not* arguing that Burton "forged" the Anatomy conscious of the improvisatory tradition I seek to describe. Of course he knew many of the improvisers that preceded him (Erasmus and More to mention only his direct antecedents whom we have considered above). My goal is not to establish a self-conscious line of improvisers or to pursue their sources. The shape of their argument and the conventions they each employ rise out of an eternal human problem, the limits of reason and craft, and the ambivalent longing to go beyond them. Improvisation is a literary form that responds to this problem. Facing such a problem, artists have sometimes imitated earlier improvisers, sometimes re-created the answerable form on their own.

An analogy will help clarify. Hunger is an eternal human problem that we have everywhere and have, at all times, invented tools to address at differ-ent levels of scale, from "digging utensils" to "agriculture." We have also cre-ated certain conceptual fields that answer. "Community" helps us negotiate our sometimes conflicting desires, on the one hand to nurture those related to us and, sometimes on the other, to satisfy our own hunger, perhaps at the expense of others. "Trickster" is another conceptual field that answers: mythic stories that help us address our hunger's shame (we are insatiable; we must kill to feed ourselves) and hunger's glory (satisfying hunger delights us, nurtures those we love, and turns matter into mind or spirit). Trick-ster we will see again in these pages. Here the point is this: the Trickster tradition in some measure reinvents itself wherever humans are found in response to the human condition's antinomies. And in some measure it is self-conscious, one Trickster influencing another within a culture or, more and more in our global mass-media society, between cultures. Improvisation works both ways too.

What is new in the present study is in part my effort to synthesize, an effort to get critics working in different fields and periods to hear one another, and to harmonize their findings when they argue that their self-styled "spontaneous" texts are *sui generis*. But still more central—and which I believe has added claim to freshness—is my effort to offer a vision of a *Gestalt*: that these conventions are of a piece with other conventions and that together they form a harmonic and synergistic whole larger than the sum of their parts. I must of necessity analyze the discrete conventions here *seriatim*. But it is their synergy that is important. We might consider synergistic one worker's approaching his boss with, "Hey, boss, guess what great idea I cooked up in the shower this morning." Less synergistic is another worker's approach: "As you know, Sir, we human beings—as Chicago psychologist Mihaly Csikszentmihalyi demonstrates—often obtain our most incisive intuitions while bathing. This morning I had such a one." A master of the rhetoric of spontaneity and the form of which it is a part, the first might get his idea tried, and if it's good, perhaps a promotion. The latter just doesn't get it.

The insistence upon spontaneous creation alone then is insufficient to make a text an improvisation. What makes a coherent aesthetic and a true family resemblance is not the mere presence of a certain number of conventions but rather their mutually informing synergy. An invocation of the muse and catalog of ships or devils are conventions of epic but do not an epic make. Nor does the mere claim of careless spontaneity, or the presence of any of its other persistent conventions, make an improvisation. There are, after all, legions of disclaimers of affected modesty, and most are just that. The claim must in some way inform all levels of a work—in the texture of style, form, and theme. In other words, other rhetorical and formal features must join the improvisatory gesture, each affecting to convince the audience that this work proceeds not from the mind but from some pre-or suprarational faculty. Without support from other conventions of improvisation, the claim of spontaneity is just a gesture and usually an empty one. *With* their synergistic support, the gesture becomes a clue we follow into the special world of improvisation.

A comparison will clarify this crucial distinction. In Sir Philip Sidney's 15th sonnet to Stella, the familiar Renaissance convention of disclaiming artifice functions all by itself without the support of other conventions from the improviser's quiver:

> You that do search for every purling spring,
> Which from the ribs of old Parnassus flows,
> And every flower, not sweet perhaps, which grows
> Near thereabouts, into your poesy wring;
> You that do dictionary's method bring
> Into your rimes, running in rattling rows;
> You that poor Petrarch's long deceased woes,
> With new-born sighs and denizened wit do sing:
> You take wrong ways: those far-fet helps be such
> As do bewray a want of inward touch,
> And sure at length stol'n goods do come to light;
> But if (both for your love and skill) your name
> You seek to nurse at fullest breasts of Fame,
> Stella behold, and then begin to indite.[2]

Here, to my eye and ear, the attack on artifice remains an idea, a mere trope or figure of speech. The "rattling rows" of other poets, according to Sidney, are all derivative and *recherché*, "far-fet"—fetched from far. They are mediated by "dictionary's method" and by Petrarch, who initiated the love-sonnet tradition. (In a letter to Boccaccio, Petrarch explains that he "prefer[red] that my own style be my own, uncultivated and rude, but, made to fit, as a garment, to the measure of my mind, rather than to someone else's which may be more elegant, ambitious, and adorned, but one that, deriving from a greater genius, continually slips off, unfitted to the humble proportions of my intellect.")[3] In Petrarch's spirit, Sidney recommends that poetry be inspired with "inward touch" and directly and spontaneously: "Stella behold, and then begin to indite."

---

2. Sir Philip Sidney, *Astrophel and Stella,* XV, in *The Oxford Anthology of English Literature,* 2 vols., edited by Frank Kermode and John Hollander (New York: Oxford University Press, 1973), 1: 633.

3. Quoted in Ronald Witt, *In the Footsteps of the Ancients: The Origins of Humanism from Lovato to Bruni. Studies in Medieval and Reformation Thought* (Leiden: Brill Academic Publishers, 2003), 263.

The whole poem, however, embodies what it condemns: excessive and calculated refinement. The use of enjambment between lines and the sentiment of the final line both lend, it is true, a certain simplicity that counterpoints Sidney's classical and literary allusions and the windy turns of phrase (periphrases). But the tight final rhymes (light-indite, name-Fame) that finally clang shut with the poetic diction of "indite"—meaning "write" or "compose"—make it clear that this line is just more of the same. That Sidney does not question the poetasters' quest for fame ("if, both for your love and *skill*, your *name* / You seek to nurse at fullest breasts of *Fame*") is symptomatic. Sidney's goal too is to gain fame by the display of his skill, his wit. As in the Renaissance courtly custom of capping lines where courtiers extemporized back and forth until one outshone the other, the display of wit demands the most polished verse possible, even if spontaneous. Their goals are to hide the mind's rough workings—Poe's "wheels and pinions"—and to display the poet's polished craft, both contrary to the goal of true improvisation (by which I mean truly fitting the metagenre, not truly improvised). Sidney's perfect sonnet never *embodies* its rhetoric of immediacy and freedom from courtly sophistication. With his eye on Petrarch and poetic tradition rather than on Stella, Sidney is an improviser wannabe.

By contrast, consider these final lines from George Herbert's sonnet "Grief" (1633):

> Verses, ye are too fine a thing, too wise
> For my rough sorrows: cease, be dumbe and mute,
> Give up your feet and running to mine eyes
> And keep your measures for some lovers lute,
> Whose grief allows him musick and a ryme:
> For mine excludes both measure, tune, and time.
>   Alas, my God![4]

Herbert here takes the idea of the special veracity of spontaneous, artless expression a step further, enacting it in the dramatic texture of his verse. His rhymes are no less tight than Sidney's, but the final coda line breaks the sonnet's frame and rhyme scheme, enacting rhetorically and performatively the

---

4. *The Works of George Herbert,* edited by F.E. Hutchinson (Oxford: Clarendon Press, 1941), 164.

breakdown of the artifice he condemns as "too fine a thing." Also at work is an implicit parody of, or swerve from, the polished disclaimers of secular verse like Sidney's. Improvisations, always shadowed by their binary, usually improve on a known genre, all the while claiming to be originary, without precedent and without relationship to known genres. Herbert's artlessness is the more powerful because it is a sonnet until it gives up the sonnet form (like Montaigne's disdain of his own bookishness). Herbert's rhetoric takes much of its force from this synergistic treatment of gesture, theme, and generic form.

The criterion of synergy would exclude Sidney's *artificial* attack on artifice but include Herbert's achieving a moment where artifice seems truly to break down. Of course it is largely a matter of "seeming," of more or less successful rhetorical effect, which of course is dependent on the cultural moment.

On this continuum between Sidney and Herbert we might place Robert Herrick's "Delight in Disorder":

> A sweet disorder in the dress
> Kindles in clothes a wantonness:
> A lawn about the shoulders thrown
> Into a fine distraction:
> An erring lace, which here and there
> Enthralls the crimson stomacher:
> A cuff neglectful, and thereby
> Ribbands to flow confusedly:
> A winning wave (deserving note)
> In the tempestuous petticoat:
> A careless shoestring, in whose tie
> I see a wild civility:
> Do more bewitch me than when art
> Is too precise in every part.[5]

Here Herrick's off rhymes (thrown/distraction, there/stomacher, thereby/confusedly, tie/civility) mimic the disorder he celebrates, but his sure-handed Jonsonian craftsmanship is never far from view. And yet his themes explore the value of order and chaos.

---

5. *The Oxford Anthology of English Literature,* 1: 1117.

Such "artlessness" in Herbert and Herrick represents "a decorum of imperfection," as one critic, speaking of the Puritan poet Edward Taylor, has called such breakdowns.[6] The tension between craftsmanship and the defeat or overthrow of craft introduces an important thematic nuance in Herbert's poetry (as it will in Milton's—see Chapter 8). On the one hand, Herbert's broken verse represents his submission to God, his forsaking the pride of this-worldly self-sufficiency; on the other the restrained and subdued craftsmanship represents the Christian—at least non-ascetic Christian—imperative to employ all one's faculties to God's glorification. The poem implicitly attacks the rationality that lies behind craftsmanly choices, but it is a proud rationality that is the problem, not Reason, Judgment, Will, or their poetic agent, craftsmanship *per se*. Like Milton no mystic or ascetic, Herbert, an Anglican priest, does not forsake the secular world of verse, but tries to transform it. No Church Scholastic or "Papist," Herbert, like Milton, knows that his own efforts, his own "good works"—his craft—are futile, yet he practices them. Herbert's "crafted spontaneity" reflects these tensions so important to the theology of his day, and nuances his representation of his poetry's true subject, the proper relationship between himself and God.

1. *The Topos of Spontaneity*

The profession or suggestion of spontaneity—implicit or explicit—is all-important in improvisation. It triggers the conceptual field that improvisation explores.

In here offering a taxonomy of such claims, I do not seek to be exhaustive—a compendium of spontaneous gestures might alone fill a book. I seek rather to understand the main directions the figure takes. These directions can be adumbrated as follows, where the work of art is said to be artless because its author:

    a. is careless or effortless

    b. directly and dramatically transcribes experience

    c. writes by chance

---

6. Karl Keller, "The Example of Edward Taylor," in *The American Puritan Imagination: Essays in Revaluation,* edited by Sacvan Bercovitch (New York: Cambridge University Press, 1974), 123.

d. offers a found object

e. writes in an intimate, unthreatening situation

f. writes in an inconvenient situation, or

g. is inspired, drunk, drugged or otherwise affected by some external power

These aspects of the gesture of spontaneous composition will be considered in turn.

a. Carelessness

Improvisers convince us that hands did not shape what we experience at their hands, or at least certainly that the caretaking mind did not carefully direct those hands. One of the crucial tropes, a favorite in the Renaissance, meriting two of Erasmus's *Adagia* and quoted variously by his *Folly,* by Nashe, More, Rabelais, Burton et al., is the idea of saying whatever came into the mouth, *quicquid in buccam* [or *linguam*] *venerit*—whatever comes to the mouth or tongue. Erasmus points to sources in Aeschylus, Plato, and Lucian. Let's look at some of the ways this carelessness is expressed.

Improvisers are careless not only because they don't think before they speak but also because they haven't made the effort, as Burton says, "to lick it into shape."[7] It may come to us as "a confused company of notes" like Burton's *Anatomy,* Swift's *Tale of the Tub,* or Carlyle's *Sartor Resartus.*[8] The improvisers may not have bothered to finish and many an improvisation comes to us as a fragment (Petronius's *Satyricon,* Coleridge's "Kubla Khan"), or as a farrago, a jumble or pastiche of different genres or themes that the artist has not bothered to coordinate or to make chime. Juvenal, who takes as his subject "whatever men do," calls his satires farragoes.[9] "Satire" stems from satyr, meaning

---

7. Robert Burton, *The Anatomy of Melancholy* (East Lansing: Michigan State University Press, 1965), 24.

8. Ibid.

9. "Quidquid agunt homines, votum, timor, ira, voluptas, gaudia, discursus, nostri farrago libelli est (all the doings of mankind, their vows, their fears, their angers and their pleasures, their joys, and goings to and fro, shall form the motley subject of my page)," *Satire* 1.85-86. In *Juvenal and Persius,* translated G.G. Ramsay (Cambridge Mass: Harvard University Press, 1969), 8-9.

"full" and in the phrase "lanx satura"—literally "a full dish of various kinds of fruits"—comes to mean "miscellany" or "medley."[10] (Hence "satire" is a kind of cornucopia). Satire, farrago, medley, or miscellany of course all chime by not chiming. The fragment challenges received notions of formal order and completion and opens a window into new possibilities. So too, the farrago challenges the genre system it can't be bothered to respect, or the rationality that the decorum of genres reflects. T.S. Eliot's *The Waste Land* combines all of these. "Just a piece of rhythmical grumbling," according to Eliot, all "fragments…shored against [his] ruins," it is apparently genreless or a mixing of genres (epic and lyric among others); it is both satire of modern life and farrago, a medley of many voices.[11]

An improvisation's lack of polish and orderliness does much to underscore the artist's carelessness, but as in all things, "freedom" is a matter of degree and of context, part of a binary as I have argued above. Stuffy besides William Carlos Williams's prose poems entitled *Kora in Hell: Improvisations,* Wordsworth's iambic pentameter in *Tintern Abbey* or *The Prelude* has the force of effortlessness by comparison to the heroic couplets of the Augustan age. No one could mistake Pope's honed couplets for carelessness, yet Pope's heroic couplets breathe an immediacy that brings his live voice into the room by comparison with the bookish stuffiness of the bathetic poetasters he is ever lampooning. The dramatic immediacy of the opening of "The Epistle to Arbuthnot" makes us feel that we are overhearing a voice that is burdened by life's cares, but not by the petty cares that attend the craft of writing heroic couplets, which in Pope's hands seem effortless, unlabored. His eye, he convinces us, is on experience in the dramatic present, not on the tradition of Menippean satire in which he quite self-consciously works:

> Shut, shut the door, good John! fatigued, I said,
> Tie up the knocker, say I'm sick, I'm dead.
> The Dog-star rages! nay 'tis past a doubt,

---

10. Theodore D. Kharpertian, *A Hand to Turn the Time: The Menippean Satires of Thomas Pynchon* (Rutherford: Fairleigh Dickinson University Press; London and Toronto: Associated University Presses, 1990), 25–27.

11. T.S. Eliot, *The Waste Land: A Facsimile and Transcript of the Original Drafts Including the Annotations of Ezra Pound,* edited by Valerie Eliot (New York: Harcourt, 1974), 1, 70.

All Bedlam, or Parnassus, is let out:
Fire in each eye, and papers in each hand,
They rave, recite, and madden round the land.[12]

Dazzled by an achieved artifice that may seem like it comes to us from another order (and it does since it comes from the other side of the Romantic watershed), we may miss that no one took more seriously than Pope the Horatian commandment: *summa ars celarit artem,* the highest art hides its art. The careless, immediate voice demands his most careful art. As Yeats puts it in "Adam's Curse":

A line will take us hours maybe;
Yet if it does not seem a moment's thought.
Our stitching and unstitching has been naught.[13]

The gesture of carelessness is not always overt and explicit. Sometimes it is inscribed in the form itself. Lyric poetry—including Pope's epistles—however carefully and overtly shaped (rhyme, meter, structure of conceit, and argument) conveys some degree of "carelessness" by means of the immediacy of its voice. The same is true of music, jazz especially. This immediacy is largely a matter of the performance character of the art but it is also inscribed in the content. In musical improvisation, whether Bach or Coltrane, not constricted by the melodic line, the improviser surprises us with each next note. Of course, behind the performance lies the constraint of chord progressions. Musical improvisation is, like chaos science as we will see below, apparently carefree and random and yet it is both deterministic and free.

b. Directly and Dramatically Transcribes Experience

Closely related to the figure of carelessness is the figure of a dramatic voice that is merely recording or transcribing experience. Sometimes what we experience is "careless" because, as More suggests, no care was needed: the improviser is just reality's amanuensis in so far as it is happening here, now.

---

12. Alexander Pope, "Epistle to Dr. Arbuthnot," in *The Oxford Anthology of English Literature,* 1: 1911.

13. *Yeats's Poetry, Drama, and Prose,* edited by James Pethica (New York and London: W.W. Norton, 2000), 32.

As Lewis Hyde writes of Whitman's lyrics, "Whitman seems to feel no distance between his senses and their objects, as if perception in the gifted state were mediated not by air or skin but by some wholly conductive element that permits immediate contact with the palpable substance of things."[14] Such a speaker is Lawrence's man thinking who achieves "the direct utterance from the instant, whole man."[15] Such an improviser is "instant" (from Latin, *instare*, "to stand in" or "on") in more ways than one. He *stands* before us, made immediate to us by the dramatic presence of his voice. What he performs is *in the instant*, flowing from moment to moment, each moment *un-fore-seen*.

The improviser skates on the thin ice of the present moment, a balancing act whose breathlessness and danger can both convey the aliveness of the performer and put the audience in a similar state. Anyone who has experienced live performance with any unscripted element will know what I mean. Such performance is performative. It makes something happen: it makes us all performers. Experiencing it, one better understands all the religious and philosophic freight loaded upon the shoulders of a simple trope: this is especially valuable because I have taken no care with it.

Which is of course exactly what the Romantics did to the gesture—douse it with what critic T. E. Hulme a century later will call "spilt religion."[16] Remember Coleridge's famous dictum in the thirteenth chapter of the *Biographia Literaria* that the "primary Imagination" is "a repetition in the finite mind of the eternal act of creation of the infinite I AM." Whatever else he means here, Coleridge's echo of *Genesis* suggests that the poet creating recreates or echoes divinity ("I AM THAT I AM"). This performative nature of art is absolutely central to the Romantic program and that of its heirs. William Carlos Williams could not write of the red wheelbarrow without Wordsworth's breathy "I Wandered Lonely as a Cloud."

---

14. Lewis Hyde, *The Gift: Imagination and the Erotic Life of Property* (New York: Random House, 1983), 172.

15. "Poetry of the Present," in *The Complete Poems of D. H. Lawrence,* edited by Vivian de Sola Pinto and F. Warren Roberts, 2 vols. (New York: The Viking Press, 1964), 184.

16. T. E. Hulme, *Speculations: Essays on Humanism and the Philosophy of Art* (London: Routledge, 2010), 1:184.

I wandered lonely as a cloud
That floats on high o'er vales and hills,
When all at once I saw a crowd,
A host, of golden daffodils;
Beside the lake, beneath the trees
Fluttering and dancing in the breeze.

Continuous as the stars that shine
And twinkle on the milky way,
They stretched in never-ending line
Along the margin of a bay:
Ten thousand saw I at a glance,
Tossing their heads in sprightly dance.

The waves beside them danced; but they
Out-did the sparkling waves in glee:
A poet could not but be gay,
In such a jocund company:
I gazed—and gazed—but little thought
What wealth the show to me had brought:

For oft, when on my couch I lie
In vacant or in pensive mood,
They flash upon that inward eye
Which is the bliss of solitude;
And then my heart with pleasure fills,
And dances with the daffodils.[17]

so much depends

upon

a red wheel

barrow

glazed with rain

water

beside the

white chickens[18]

Neither poem seeks to say anything orderly or cogent about the world—nothing one could take to the bank, as we say today. Neither seeks to instruct. Wordsworth is not urging us to leave the university, nor would Williams have us move to the farm. I differ from Daniel Belgrad, who reads Williams's poem as an example of his principle of immediacy, "no ideas but in things," that the poem "is a materialist observation" whose "presence evokes the whole worldview of agrarian society."[19] Nor is giving pleasure focally their goal. In

---

17. *The Oxford Anthology of English Literature*, 2:174.

18. *Spring and All*, XXII, in *The Collected Poems of William Carlos Williams*, vol 1: 1909-1939, edited by A. Walton Litz and Christopher MacGowan (New York: New Directions, 1986), 224.

19. Belgrad, *The Culture of Spontaneity*, 32.

some measure, neither poet seeks to create an artifact—at least that is the rhetorical thrust of their art. Wordsworth anticipates and Williams fulfills what avant-garde performance artist Yves Klein expresses: "My paintings are only the ashes of my art."[20] They are what Stanley Fish describes as "self-consuming artifacts."[21] Both seek instead not only to express but to transcribe, as it were, a state of mind, neither orderly nor cogent, that could experience such odd thoughts: hosts of daffodils and red wheelbarrows are breathlessly important. Williams's follower Allen Ginsberg seeks "to transcribe...my own mind...in a form most nearly representing its actual 'occurrence.' "[22] Fellow improviser Paul Valéry is even more explicit: "A poet's function—do not be startled by this remark—is not to experience the poetic state: that is a private affair. His function is to create it in others. The poet is recognized—or at least everyone recognizes his own poet—by the simple fact that he causes his reader to become 'inspired.' "[23] What each poem (and each poet) means to entertain and instruct us by and to is to recognize such states in ourselves and to embrace rather than reject them. This is an interior world, unsophisticated and visionary, that we lose because "the world is too much with us."

Like much war literature, W. D. Ehrhart's deceptively slight poem from the Vietnam War, his most anthologized, works in much the same way, offering a rough, unpoetic formal exterior and a very intense interior state:

Hunting

Sighting down the long black barrel,
I wait till front and rear sights
form a perfect line on his body,
then slowly squeeze the trigger.

---

20. "Lecture at the Sorbonne," in *Overcoming the Problematics of Art: The Writings of Yves Klein,* translated by Klaus Ottmann (Putnam, Conn.: Spring Publications, 2014 [2007]), 82.

21. Stanley Fish, *Self-Consuming Artifacts: The Experience of Seventeenth Century Literature* (Berkeley and Los Angeles: University of California Press, 1972).

22. "When the Mode of the Music Changes, the Walls of the City Shake," in Allen Ginsberg, *Deliberate Prose* (New York: Harper Perennial, 2001), 247.

23. "Poetry and Abstract Thought," quoted in Edward Hirsch, *How to Read a Poem: And Fall in Love with Poetry* (New York: Harvest, 1999), 115.

The thought occurs
that I have never hunted anything in my whole life
except other men.

But I have learned by now
where such thoughts lead,
and soon pass on
to chow, and sleep,
and how much longer till I change my socks.[24]

The poem does not ask us to celebrate the rough and callow—but lethal—youth who is to some extent Ehrhart's exhausted alter-ego. If there is meaning here it is in Ehrhart's invitation to the reader to join him in this polarized mental place that holds in suspension his elegiac longing for the innocence the action of the poem has by now negated. The poem is a tragic miniature: a fall from a high place, innocence, because of our tragic flaw, innocence, despite the apparent innocence of the poetic surface. Ehrhart's grunt is Graham Green's Alden Pyle from *The Quiet American* writ small.

So apparently slight, these lyrics convey all that freight by performatively creating like states in us. Poets create the taste by which they are enjoyed, according to Wordsworth, but do so not discursively or even cognitively, through rhetorical means, but in this near and strict, experiential, phenomenological sense: these poems are nonsense—witness the proliferation of daffodil and wheelbarrow parodies—unless you enter into their state of mind. Though we may bring to bear on the poem the biographical fact that Dr. Williams wrote after attending a young patient through the night—outside the window, a farm scene—surely his medical practice and his patient's health do not depend upon the red wheelbarrow and its attendants. The poem's inflation bespeaks the poet's deflation. Wordsworth's sophisticated contemporaries in London couldn't care less about daffodils. More's the pity perhaps. Ehrhart's audience, who treated returning American vets as the Other, are asked to listen for once and to enter the dark place the poet remembers in what tranquility is left him. In each case the poet's point is edgier than mere sentiment. Williams has waked the night. He is Thoreau's man awake, his

---

24. W. D. Ehrhart, "Hunting," in *Winning Hearts and Minds: War Poems by Vietnam Vets,* edited by Larry Rottman, et al. (New York: McGraw-Hill, 1972), 33.

eyes wide open taking in the scene. So too, Wordsworth amongst the daffodils. So too, finally, Ehrhart's grunt who is learning "How cold steel is, and
keen with hunger of blood" in the words of Wilfred Owen, who used rough
off-rhymes, discordant rhythms, and disturbing images and actions to convey
the raw horror of war.[25]

All this comes out of their creation of a dramatic presence in the poems.
The dramatic arts, film included, can work this way. The hand-held cameras
of Italian Neorealists and Robert Altman—one of Hollywood's great improvisers—mean to convince us (with some degree of irony of course) that we
witness real experience in the dramatic present, unshaped by caretaking
human hands. The realism of much drama where the proscenium acts as a
translucent fourth wall has a similar effect.

The work of David Mamet—both on stage and in film—is the counterex-
ample that helps prove my point. Mamet's proscenium never is quite invisible,
always present to call attention to the artistic framing of the action. Mamet
never lets us forget that he stands with an Olympian grin—I would say Apollonian—behind the overtly artificial staccato dialogue that characterizes and
dominates his work. It is telling that, famously for Mamet, the actor is a mere
puppet in his directorial hands. He insists that his dialogue be just as wooden.
As if to say: this is not transcription of a present moment but the work of an
artist whose effort is everywhere on display. Mamet's ego is large but this is
an aesthetic and rhetorical choice. Like Kubrick, another artist who everywhere insists upon the artificiality of his art,[26] Mamet's goal is not to move us
emotionally but rather to reflection. The world of Method acting, by contrast,
is the world of improvisation. This is paradoxical in a way familiar to us here,
since it is a freedom entered into and achieved through *method*. Anathema
to Mamet and only a little less so to Kubrick, The Method invites the actor
through the hard work of improvising in rehearsal to explore and make pres-

---

25. "Arms and the Boy," in *The Collected Poems of Wilfred Owen*, edited by Cecil Day
Lewis and Edmund Blunden (New York: New Directions, 1965), 43.

26. Michael Herr states that he "could not explain that strange irresistible require-
ment [Kubrick] had for pushing his actors as far beyond a 'naturalistic' style as he
could get them to go, and often selecting their most extreme, awkward, emotionally
confusing work for his final cut," in Michael Herr, *Kubrick* (New York: Grove Press,
2000), 60.

ent the dark recesses of the unconscious self. The Method (like John Wesley's Methodists) uses method to go beyond method. But where eighteenth-century Methodists access an inner light that bespeaks and is the conduit of divine truth, Marlon Brando retrieves the higher truths of Stanley Kowalski's animal appeal from the depths of his gut. Such performance moves us in part because it invites us to experience similar recesses in ourselves. Even though the hard work of the method lies behind it, Brando's acting is like the lyric poet or the jazz musician in conveying an utterly in-the-moment and present animal emotionalism and sexuality.[27] Improvisation has been missing not only its Einstein but also its Lee Strasburg: the persistent conventions we are describing are improvisation's "method."

Years of careful craft may lie behind such performance. Consider James McNeill Whistler's answer when charged by Ruskin with, basically, *improvising*: for "ask[ing] two hundred guineas for throwing a pot of paint in the public's face." The painting in question was *Nocturne in Black and Gold: The Falling Rocket*. Whistler's explanation of the thrown pot was this: "I did it in 15 minutes with the experience of a lifetime." That Whistler says this in such a context goes perfectly to the point of the gesture. Such art is "careless" in the sense that it does not have its eye cast over its shoulder on tradition and other paintings or texts, about which it professes not to care but against which it is in fact in dialogue. Rather, its eye is on the moment that passes, on the rocket that falls sputtering from the sky and the folds of the coat of the woman beneath, and the light that catches its fur lining. Odd as it may seem, Jackson Pollock's Action Painting is but a half-step away: a measure of the aesthetic value of his paintings comes not from the inherent beauty of his swirls, but from the sense that in viewing a Pollock one is experiencing the wild state of mind that would swirl the paint so. Ed Harris, who directed as well as starred in the *Pollock* biopic, captured this not only narratively, but also cinematographically, as his steady-cam swirls around Pollock swirling paint on the canvas.

---

27. That such a performance invites and even enforces empathy, not ironic disdain, perhaps helps to explain why the American Film Board demanded the expurgation of the rape scene only recently restored.

Thus, while it might be argued that in considering improvisation we should distinguish between improvised performance and improvised text, I think the operative and more telling distinction is between performances that present themselves as complete and authoritative texts (Mamet, Kubrick) and those that insist they are performances in process. Bernarda Shahn describes this quality in her husband Ben Shahn's "palimpsest paintings":

> He had found in the markings and tracings that were left upon a picture,...as he might wash out and rework an image, an effective pictorial element. He called such an accumulation of traces a "palimpsest": he had, at an earlier time, expunged such marks, but now he studied their qualities, preserving the effect as part of the completed work. He commented, "The feeling about the form is a vital part of the picture; it has a dimension, almost a time dimension."[28]

Such improvisations anticipate postmodernism's "'epistemology' of performance—knowing as making, producing, doing, acting."[29] Eschewing the authority of the completed text, improvisation's insistence on its performance nature draws the audience into the process of completing the text. The improviser's attitude to himself, to the world, and to the audience are all one: open, direct, and yet dialogic.

c. Chance

Saying whatever comes to mind gives a large role to chance and leads to the free-associative flow that is the improviser's stock-in-trade.

The modern composer John Cage achieves a careful carelessness by means of chance and accidents. Cage achieved utterly formless music in one instance by casting the *I Ching* over and over again, each hexagram denoting a note. It took months. As Lewis Hyde relates, "It took so much time, he would toss coins as he rode the New York subway." Hyde adds, "He *worked hard* at chance...One famous piece less than five minutes long took him four

---

28. Bernarda Bryson Shahn, *Ben Shahn* (New York: Abrams, 1972), 184; quoted in Belgrad, *Spontaneity*, 34-35.

29. Gregory L. Ulmer, "The Object of Post-Criticism," in *The Anti-Aesthetic: Essays on Postmodern Culture*, edited by Hal Foster (Seattle: Bay Press, 1983), 94.

years to write."[30] Another method Cage made famous exploits not chance but accident, whatever noise comes his way during the act of composition or performance. One piece, *4'33"*, consists of silence punctuated by the pianist opening and shutting the keyboard, an invitation not only to listen to the silence but to the accidental sounds that inevitably break the silence—the audience's coughing and rustling—"to hear," as Lewis Hyde writes, "the plenitude of what happens."[31]

These methods of composition reflect Cage's effort performatively to represent and to provoke a state of mind. His is a Romantic gesture but studiously avoids the emphasis on Romantic ego. You do not experience his music through his consciousness, as Wordsworth invited us to experience his daffodils through his (as an inducement to become open to like visionary states). Cage seeks a kind of Zen state of absence or absent-mindedness, what the Buddhist calls "apprentice mind." Cage seeks not to express the grand Romantic ego but its opposite, an egolessness. "Personality is a flimsy thing on which to build an art," he writes.[32] Still, this kind of carelessness, taking care not to take care, minimizing intentionality, paradoxically has the same effect as the Romantics' heightened states of visionary consciousness. The point is to create a state of mind that *opens* the mind, and the ear, to the world around us. Hyde appreciatively applies to Cage Mark Twain's witticism about Richard Wagner: "His music is better than it sounds."[33] It may not be to our taste, but if we hear it, it makes us taste—and gobble up—more of the world.

"More" is of course the operative word, and "open" here means "more open." Dialogic binaries are at work. This performative gesture rejects those normative states of mind that consider noise not worth hearing or attending to, and that allow no room for chance and accident to break into our lives, though of course they inevitably will. Does life's meaning reside only in the expected and the controlled? Improvisers emphatically say no. Who could

---

30. Lewis Hyde, *Trickster Makes This World: Mischief, Myth and Art* (New York: Farrar, Straus and Giroux, 1997), 143; emphasis in original. My treatment of Cage here relies extensively on Hyde's insightful discussion.

31. Hyde, *Trickster*, 150.

32. Ibid., 147.

33. Ibid., 149n.

expect or anticipate any of the notes in Louis Armstrong's cascading opening cadenza in *West End Blues*? However we make sense of the world through the lives that we live or the art we create, life and art must encompass not only what we foresee but what is unforeseen. We can do so only by means of "the mind that contingency demands."[34] When we do, in Wallace Stevens's words, "Life's nonsense pierces us with strange relation."

Emphasizing the Romantics, Moderns, and Postmoderns in this discussion should not obscure my main point. We may never learn *not* to see the gesture of spontaneity as a product of the Romantic Period, but the fact is that it is not. Created carelessly, "whatever comes into the mouth," Erasmus's *Praise of Folly* forces us to acknowledge that while we may go about our lives convinced that we (and our rational, willful minds) are running the show, in fact Folly and her minions (Self-Love, Flattery, Oblivion, Laziness, Pleasure, Madness, Wantonness, Intemperance, and Dead Sleep) hold the reins and often provide the spurs. We may think rational decisions shape our lives and livelihoods, but in fact instincts and appetites and accidents have an equal role. We may marry for prudential reasons, but lust or greed, or hopefully that most irrational emotion, love, rarely trail far behind. John Cage might have urged Erasmus to include Chance as one of Folly's cronies. Why marry this woman and not another? Yes, her dowry was attractive but who put her in your way on the street that day? What of that woman with a still larger dowry that inhabits the next street but whom you did not meet? Erasmus's point is not that we should abjure the God-given use of our higher faculties. His point is that we should open our awareness to the huge role of our lower faculties and faculties or agencies not ours at all: relying not on man's most divine attribute, his will, but his more human faculties; not on life's order but rather on its accidents; and of course on God's grace. The surprising paradox that Erasmus exploits both for the sake of humor and of dead seriousness is that a churchman would recommend an openness to carelessness and accident as a way of coming to know God's grace and will. And yet mankind has trusted to sorts and to oracles since the dawn of time to know what will happen next. Romanticism is a spilt version of such religious faith.

---

34. Ibid., 141.

Im-pro-vis-ations from whatever age—or cage/Cage—call attention to the power of the un-fore-seen and fortuitous in our lives.

d. Found Objects

Embracing chance as a part of life, improvisations inevitably privilege found objects. Thomas More's *Utopia* is authentic because it is in effect a found object, free of the mediation of More's intrusive editorial hand: it really happened, a conversation that took place at his country estate between identifiably real people. The novel tradition will favor this trope of the found document's special authenticity. The trope is central to the many more or less thinly veiled "found" documents in fiction's history, all the journals, diaries, and epistolary novels that always seem to be found by some ingenuous editor who is unable or unwilling artfully to shape them. What you get is what I found, no more, no less, but all the better for that. The improviser is a *bricoleur* who tinkers together found objects of no intrinsic value.

Modern art will push the gesture to the extreme, making art of non-art (urinals, bicycle seats and handlebars and glass uncarefully broken and carefully preserved), hence debunking received artistic codes and making very fuzzy the distinction between realism (an art made of the life's *faits divers*) and visionary imagination. Marcel Duchamp explained simply that his readymades were meant to shift the focus of art from physical craft, which produced mere "retinal art"—art experienced merely by the eye—to intellectual interpretation.[35] Cage defines modern art "as art that cannot be interrupted by non-art."[36] Both definitions function by asserting that the art is not mediated by the editor/artist's hand but illuminated by the artist's vision, that we can best capture life by being open to it, being its captive, not its captor. Picasso's notion of found art, "I do not seek, I find," takes us back to our beginning to the trope of carelessness. For Picasso, the effort of seeking is beneath him. He achieves Kant's "purposefulness without purpose [*Zweckmässigkeit ohne Zweck*]." Only by such means will we truly see the world. As the medieval mystic Meister Eckhart remarks: "We are made perfect by what happens to

---

35. Marjorie Perloff, *Unoriginal Genius: Poetry by Other Means in the New Century* (Chicago: The University of Chicago Press, 2012), 163.

36. Quoted in Hyde, *Trickster,* 98.

us rather than by what we do."[37] To allow this into one's value system is to reject the mainstream values of modern Western culture which center upon achievement and goal-oriented performance. For the improviser the going— what is found in the journey of performance—is the goal.

e. The Trope of Intimacy

Quoting Martial in the *Adagia*, Erasmus underscores why the tag "whatever comes into the mouth" has taken on associations of authenticity and sincerity. Saying whatever by chance shall have come to mind is something "we are accustomed to do among trusted friends, among whom we are frivolous and chatter about anything we please with impunity."[38] Martial—the first-century Roman poet who wrote "off-the-cuff" epigrams—praises a two-man chaise that affords him and his patron a special solitude: "Here at my side, here may you, Jubatus, say whatever rises to your lips."[39] Knowing that the world is a dangerous and political place, we can wisely speak truly only in a friendly setting. Improvisation shoehorns its audience into community by positing a community: if you are hearing me, we must be of like minds. This gesture becomes central to the "culture of spontaneity" Daniel Belgrad describes in the postwar American avant-garde where across many arts "a subjective epistemology privileges dialogue over logical exposition as a means of communication."[40]

This creation of an intimate relationship with the audience is crucial, even if it is sometimes second-hand, voyeuristic. The consonance of the intimacy trope both with the gesture of spontaneity and the theme of freedom is suggested by Friedrich Schiller's seminal Romantic improvisation *On the Aesthetic Education of Man in a Series of Letters* (1795).[41] The *Aesthetic Letters*

37. Ibid., 142.

38. "Quemadmodum apud fidos amiculos facere solemus, apud quos impune quiduis nugamur atque effutimus," Erasmus, *Adagia*, 472.

39. "Hic mecum licet, hic, Iubate, quidquid in buccam tibi venerit loquaris," in Martial, *Epigrams*, 2 vols., translated by Walter C.A. Ker (London: William Heinemann; New York: G.P. Putnam's Sons), 2:334-35 (bk. 12, epigram 24).

40. Belgrad, *Spontaneity*, 111.

41. Friedrich Schiller, *The Aesthetic Letters, Essays, and the Philosophical Letters*, translated by John Weiss (Boston: Little and Brown, 1845).

celebrate the *Spieltrieb,* the spirit of play in art. In his preface Schiller avers that he could not have written his theories except in letters. Being about the value of play, of course Schiller's discourse must contain the element of freedom or play that we associate with intimate letters.

Writers may, like Martial, dramatize a second party, a listener or inter-locutor, usually silent. We as audience enjoy the added pleasure of overhear-ing: we listen in on the intimate converse of lovers addressing their lovers; poets (like Sappho), their muse (Aphrodite); Dryden in the *Essay on Dramatic Poesy,* his fellow city dwellers (as will Conrad's Marlowe awaiting the tide on the same river); Pope, his manservant; Wordsworth, his sister in "Tin-tern Abbey" or his friend Coleridge in the *Prelude*; or Coleridge, his infant son in "Dejection: An Ode." Jack Kerouac will write *On the Road* to explain Neal Cassidy to his new wife. In *Visions of Cody,* Kerouac promises readers he will draw them into his Beat community: "Now what I'm going to do is this—think things over one by one, blowing on the visions of them and *also* excitedly discussing them as if with friends."[42] Allen Ginsberg captures the connection between the intimacy trope and the trope of inspiration when he explains in an interview:

> We all talk among ourselves and we have common understandings, and we say anything we want to say...So then—what happens if you make a distinction between what you tell your friends and what you tell your Muse? The problem is to break down that distinction: when you approach the Muse to talk as frankly as you would talk with yourself or with your friends...That meant...a complete revision of what literature was sup-posed to be...It's the ability to commit to writing, to *write,* the same way that you are![43]

As always, Ginsberg's take is extreme, but in the main what he says is true of literature far older than his own: improvisers seek to represent or to create that state of intimacy which inspires immediacy, freedom from mediation—"to *write,* the same way that you are"—writing as pure presence, the equivalent

---

42. Jack Kerouac, *Visions of Cody* (New York: Penguin, 1993), 98.

43. *Paris Review* interview with Tom Clark (1965); quoted in Marjorie Perloff, *Poetic License: Essays on Modernist and Postmodernist Lyric* (Evanston, Ill.: Northwestern University Press, 1990), 201-2.

of Wynton Marsalis's take on Louis Armstrong: "There's no barrier between the horn and his soul."[44]

The conversation is not always lyric—first person—as it is in most of these examples. Dryden's *An Essay of Dramatick Poesie* and More's *Utopia* exemplify the dialogue, unmediated by narrative intervention, which is a form improvisers since Lucian have exploited. The intimacy is not always one on one. Folly addresses a half-dramatized crowd but achieves intimacy with her good humor and by forgoing the logic-chopping of the scholiasts, meeting the carnivalesque groundlings on their level and not, despite her elevation on the stage, from on high. The intimacy she creates is an intimacy of mind not body, though her many hints of bodily intimacy contribute to the letting-loose her voice represents. Always the intimacy we are allowed to eavesdrop on is a token of sincerity and authenticity achieved not only between the friends but *within* the speaker(s): just as the friends can be freer with one another, the speaker is freer to journey within to find the truth in him-or herself. And we are freer to believe it because we overhear intimate converse that has no rhetorical purpose: free of "palpable design" (Keats), "bias or motive" (Dillard). Like Huck's first person narrative, intimately addressed to the reader, they are free of "purpose…or moral…or plot"—and don't you mistake it or you'll be shot! Many first person novels, from *David Copperfield* to *Catcher in the Rye,* exploit this rhetoric. The heroes of these last three first person novels relate their narratives to undramatized audiences. All hate phonies whose self-presentation is corrupted by their palpable design upon us.

Likewise, intimacy and its consequent freedom are sometimes achieved because there is no audience at all. Many an improvisation comes to us characterized as a diary that anticipates no audience, mere musings that have no audience for the author to have designs upon. We eavesdrop on self-communing. Browne's *Religio Medici* is no diary but it is diary-like, "a private exercise directed to my selfe…rather a memoriall unto me then an example or rule unto any other."[45] Burton writes his "confused company of notes"

---

44. Stephanie Bennett, producer "Let the Good Times Role: A Film about the Roots of American Music," DVD, Delilah Music Pictures in Association with Island Visual Arts, 1992; emphasis added.

45. "To the Reader," in *The Prose of Sir Thomas Browne,* edited by Norman J. Endicott (New York: New York University Press, 1968), 6.

in part because he has "no...benefactors" nor can he afford "six or seven *amanuenses.*"[46] Thus he need please no one but himself and nothing need come between him and his subject. He is free of rhetorical purpose or moral or plot. With his "miscellaneous masses of Sheets, and oftener Shreds and Snips," Carlyle's Diogenes Teufelsdröckh self-communes high in his tower in *Sartor Resartus* because he is above the commonwealth. His Eternal Yea is the more sincere because he affirms it for himself alone. Or like Montaigne and Burton, the improviser recommends the reader find better occupation than to read his pages. Having read that, we read on partly as voyeurs witnessing the improviser's own converse with him or herself. The improviser's dramatized audience, however large or small or absent, is surrogate to us as readers. In all of these instances, intimacy assures the absence of mediation.

f. Locale—The Pastoral Trope

The improviser's authenticity is a product not only of intimacy but also of locale. Kindred to the trope of intimacy and the spontaneity it generates is what we may call a scenic or pastoral trope, what Walter Kaiser calls "the *en voyage* excuse."[47] The speaker is able to free himself of the constraints and masks that society forces upon us not only because more numerous society is absent but also because the city, the court, and the study have been left behind. The solitude that Martial and his intimate, Jubatus, enjoy is due in part to their being in the simplicity of a chaise, not a "traveling-coach and curricle": "no black driver of Libyan steed, nor runner with upgirt loins goes before; nowhere is any muleteer; the nags will be silent." Martial rejoices here not only in being free of company but of the trappings of civilization. Of course "civilized" is all a matter of degree: what's unsophisticated to a modern ear about a chaise, carried, I imagine, by slaves? But context makes clear that a chaise is more rustic than "traveling-coach and curricle."

---

46. Burton, *The Anatomy of Melancholy*, 16.

47. Walter Kaiser, *Praisers of Folly: Erasmus, Rabelais, Shakespeare* (Cambridge, Mass.: Harvard University Press, 1963), 33. See also Kaiser's excellent discussion of the use of "en voyage" topos in Petrarch's book on folly (*De sui ipsius et multorum ignorantia*).

Improvisers exploited this pastoral locus long before Rousseau rejected the imprisoning sophistication of the city. Examples are legion. The fifteenth-century churchman, philosopher, and mystic Nicolas of Cusa, known as Cusanus, claimed that his philosophy of "learned ignorance"—which proposed that we could know God through our "divine human mind"—came to him "at sea while returning from Greece."[48] Erasmus writes the *Encomium*, he claims, while riding a mule across the Alps. Having been long immersed in the affairs of city and court as mayor of Bordeaux, Montaigne writes his Essays from his rural seat. Wordsworth, who will make the pastoral trope central to his poetic program, writes "Tintern Abbey" while walking the Wye Valley. The tradition of celebrating walking as the avenue to truth is a long one and relies in part on this pastoral trope: *solvitur ambulando*— "the solution comes through walking." In "Notes Toward a Supreme Fiction," Stevens offers:

> Perhaps
> The truth depends on a walk around a lake,
>
> A composing as the body tires, a stop
> To see hepatica, a stop to watch
> A definition growing certain and
>
> A wait within that certainty, a rest
> In the swags of pine-trees bordering the lake.[49]

And Thoreau in his *Journal* offers, "The moment my legs begin to move, my thoughts begin to flow," and "A man thinks as well through his legs and arms as through his brain."[50] Logic stems from *logos* meaning path, but here legs are a replacement for the rational road to truth.

Swift, in *A Tale of the Tub*, with ironic point turns the pastoral trope on its head, situating the anti-heroic improviser in the heat and mire of the city, in Grub Street: "The shrewdest Pieces of this Treatise, were conceived in Bed, in a Garret: At other times (for a Reason best known to my self) I thought

---

48. Nicolas of Cusa, *On Learned Ignorance,* translated by Jasper Hopkins (Minneapolis: Banning Press, 1981), 158.

49. Stevens, "Notes Toward a Supreme Fiction," 333-34.

50. *The Heart of Thoreau's Journals,* edited by Odell Shepard (New York: Dover, 1961), 212; Henry David Thoureau, *A Writer's Journal,* edited by Laurence Stapleton (London: Heinemann, 1961), 64.

fit to sharpen my Invention with Hunger; and in general, the whole Work was begun, continued, and ended, under a long Course of Physic, and a great want of Money."[51] Oddly (and of course ironically), Swift's persona's "want of Money" is further proof of authenticity: proof that he has no rhetorical purpose or "palpable design," driven not by the will with an agenda—something important to say—but only by the desire to fill the page in order to fill his purse and hungry belly.

Carlyle also turns the trope upside-down but with less irony than his master Swift. More underground man than anti-hero, Carlyle's Teufelsdröckh composes his bag of notes in a world free of the city because in his aerie he is high above it. Modern jazz has it both ways. First it pushes the pastoral topos to its furthest extreme, intimating its African origins. At the same time it plays upon the Swiftian urban setting, identifying itself with the decaying inner city, now a source of raw passion and energy. Jazz by this ambiguity celebrates the city's chaotic energy but cries out for society's renewal through the renovative influence of music, that art Goethe called the most daemonic. The noise Cage's postmodernism embraces is the city's, not the country's. He relates how he "was standing on a corner of Madison Avenue waiting for a bus and I happened to look at the pavement, and I noticed that the experience of looking at the pavement was the same as the experience of looking" at the exhibit he had just left. He adds without a trace of irony: "The aesthetic enjoyment was just as high."[52] They are for Cage equally high because both art exhibit and urban experience are untainted by the sophistications of aesthetic taste and expectation. To the extent possible, Cage returns, and returns us, to unmediated hearing when a cough can serve as a musical event.

It is clear then that, like the topos of spontaneity itself, the rural topos (and its dark, urban mirror image) authenticates by claiming immediacy, a freedom from mediation. Writing from the country, the improviser has no taint of courtly sycophancy, pulpit moralizing, university formalism, Grub Street self-promotion, or the sophistications of London or Paris or New York. Because removed from their books, they do not smell of the study's lamp. Just as spontaneity raises issues about the nature, value, and use of Reason,

---

51. Jonathan Swift, *A Tale of the Tub,* edited by A.C. Guthkelch and D. Nichol Smith (Oxford: Clarendon Press, 1958), 44.

52. Quoted in Hyde, *Trickster,* 144.

"provinciality" questions the worth of Reason's most important product: civilization. In Swift's ultra-conservative hands the pastoral trope turned upside down fends off the pretensions of the new urban bottom feeder—Grub Street denizens—while celebrating the new urban energy. Through his pose of urbanity Cage rejects art's exclusionary pretentions. The pose of *amateur*—adopted, for example, by Montaigne, Burton, Browne, Sterne, Byron, and, in a sense, Cage—frees the improviser of the taint of the professions and professionalism and the careerism that surely follows. Free of books, civilization, and the competitive marketplace, they are free to experience *and to love* all that remains: in a word, life, naked and primary in all its diversity and contingency. Of course like most pastoral, most improvisations will in the end seek not to forsake the city entirely, but rather to enliven the city, civilization, and art by infusing it with the spirit of the pastoral green world that lies beyond the city walls.

g. Freedom of expression or candor

Parrhesia, the rhetorical figure for "free-spokenness" or candid speech, is a rhetorical figure or trope often deployed in improvisation.[53] As I've noted, candor has roots both in "set afire" and in "purity." Free of care, direction by our rational faculties, purpose or motive, the pressure of society's or the genre system's codes of decorum, and enjoying the freedoms allowed by intimacy among friends and by being away from the city and court, improvisers are free to express what they will. Freed in these ways, they push the envelope regarding what can be said or what can properly be the subject for art.

It would be incongruous or anachronistic to speak of "freedom of expression" as we come to know it under the American Constitution's First Amendment and yet that is where improvisation is headed from the start. Improvisation throbs with a democratic impulse that will be discussed below.

h. Inspiration

Sometimes, however, the source of inspiration is not the Edenic green world but its antetype: heaven itself. Divine inspiration is the ultimate *author-*

---

53. Richard Lanham, *A Handlist of Rhetorical Terms: A Guide for Students of English Literature* (Berkeley, Los Angeles, and London: University of California Press, 1991), 110.

ization of artless authenticity. The tradition of divine inspiration is of course long and complex and need not be anatomized here. Blake offers a typical example in a letter to Butts:

> I have written this poem [*Milton* and/or *The Four Zoas*—Blake is ambiguous] from immediate Dictation, twelve or sometimes twenty or thirty lines at a time, without Premeditation and even against my Will; the Time it has taken in writing was thus rendered Non Existent, and an immense Poem Exists which seems to be the Labor of a long Life, all produced without Labor or Study.[54]

Blake's *"immediate* Dictation" has, it should be noted, not only its temporal but its etymological force: unmediated. His "the Labor of a long Life" seems to anticipate Whistler's "with the experience of a lifetime," but Blake dismisses it: it only "seems to be" so, but is instead "produced without Labor or Study." This poem was dictated during a "three years' Slumber" without the mediation of his own, let alone his higher, faculties ("even against my Will"). Writing so, Blake rises above the clock-time of man's fallen perception into a visionary perception of Eternity ("Time...was thus rendered Non Existent"). To make such a claim is to authenticate his poetic utterance for "the Eternal...is always present to the wise."[55] The fruit of such visionary immediacy is a poem "without Labor or Study," but all the wiser for that.

Where Blake receives dictation from angels, other improvisers are inspired through various forms of trance, variously induced. Sometimes inspiration comes not from above but from a bottle. *In vino veritas,* of course. When Faulkner says that he needs only tobacco, bourbon, and an empty room to write, it becomes almost inevitable that his churning, baroque prose will be associated with spontaneity even by his finest critics, as when Irving Howe claims that Faulkner's "central subject has remained constant, but each return to it has an air of improvisation as if he were forever seeing his world in a new way."[56] As always what is in question here are not Faulkner's work habits, how much he revised, but rather the "air of improvisation" which not

---

54. 25 April 1803, in *The Poetry and Prose of William Blake,* 697.

55. "Night the Ninth," in *The Poetry and Prose of William Blake,* 375.

56. Irving Howe, *William Faulkner: A Critical Study* (Chicago: The University of Chicago Press, 1975), 3.

only his emotionally supercharged style but also such authorial remarks as these about "tobacco and bourbon" help to create.

This trope of the special authority of induced heightened states of consciousness—to varying degrees a secular travesty of religious doctrines of inspiration—becomes central to the Romantic program for poetry. Taken to an extreme it becomes Coleridge and De Quincey's opium-eating and Rimbaud's "deréglement des sens." Our century finds the even greater extremes of the Dadaists, Surrealists, and Beats, the cultivation of automatic writing, exquisite corpse, and other pointed offenses against the cult of craft, skill, and mastery. Yet the trope is of long date. Remember Rabelais's promise that he gave his book "no more thought than you, who were probably also drinking."

A century before the Romantics deployed with high seriousness the rhetorical gestures I have here itemized, Swift devastatingly lampooned them. Swift's persona in *A Mechanical Operation of the Spirit,* his satire of religious enthusiasts who believe they can have unmediated experience of God, offers a veritable catalog of the professions of carelessness, all parodic:

> Now, Sir, to proceed after the Method in present Wear…I desire you will be my Witness to the World, how careless and sudden a Scribble it has been; That it was but Yesterday, when You and I began accidently to fall into Discourse on this Matter: That I was not very well, when we parted; That the Post is in such haste, I have had no manner of Time to digest it into Order, or correct the Style; And if any other Modern Excuses, for Haste and Negligence, shall occur to you in Reading, I beg you to insert them, faithfully promising they shall be thankfully acknowledged.[57]

Swift here anticipates Poe's satire of writers' pride in their fine frenzy. His discourse is "careless and sudden," inspired "accidentally" by an intimate conversation. The author is impaired by ill health (impairment being a characteristic of the improviser's persona as we will see in the next section). To make the post he has had no time to revise. Finally, most devastatingly, he asks that his interlocutor fill in the blanks if there are any newly fashionable protestations of "Haste and Negligence." By means of these superb parodies

---

57. "The Mechanical Operation of the Spirit," in *The Writings of Jonathan Swift,* edited by Robert A. Greenberg and William Bowman Piper (New York: W.W. Norton, 1979), 399.

of the rhetoric of spontaneity, Swift makes his improvisations outcries for the mediation of Anglican and Augustan moderation and culture even as he exults in the city's new-found energy. One wonders how the Romantics following in the wake of such withering ironies could have employed the rhetoric so deadpan. Byron's brilliant ironies in *Don Juan*—where he "rattle[s] on exactly as I talk / With any body in a ride or walk"—are the legacy of Swift.

But what strikes me most in Swift's ironic sendup of the spontaneous gesture—"to proceed after the Method in present Wear"—is not that the rhetoric of spontaneity has by 1710 become old hat enough to merit his satire. Rather it is that it so perfectly echoes Erasmus's opening gambit two centuries earlier: "I wouldn't want you to think that I made it up just to show off my cleverness, as ordinary speechmakers generally do. For you know that such orators, even though they have labored over a speech for thirty years (and plagiarized some of it at that), will still swear that they dashed it off in a couple of days, or even dictated it as a mere exercise."[58] And the figure used ironically goes still further back. The lineage—Lucian, Erasmus, Swift—is clear-cut and unquestionable; no one can doubt Erasmus's knowledge of Lucian or Swift's knowledge of both. But is it a matter of quotation or of men dealing with the same human problem? If your opponents set themselves up as having a special relationship to truth and to divinity, one way to take them down a peg is to challenge their pretention to being inspired and their inspiration's source. This is the age-old problem of inspiration: is the source god or the devil? Erasmus directs his *avant*-garde, humanist ironies against the scholiasts' hair-splitting logic; Swift aims his *arrière*-garde ironies against evangelicals' logic-forsaking enthusiasm. Both suggest the source is daemonic rather than divine.

2. *Persona: Fools and Tricksters*

The improviser's mask enables him or her to embrace life's plenitude, diversity, and richness. Fools, naturals, madmen, clowns, jesters, libertines, amateurs, charlatans, confidence men—improvisers' personae all inhabit the margins and embrace what the sensible and prudential usually leave out, the ethically, socially, or psychologically marginal. They explore the underside or

---

58. Erasmus, *The Praise of Folly*, 12.

outside or, paradoxically, an inside deeper than the staid usually go. The classical tradition of Menippean satire, which serves as a source for much improvisation (if there are sources), assumed the false etymology that "satyr"—half beast—lay behind the satirist's persona. In some measure all improvisations offer this conundrum, that the reprobate, taking advantage of their disadvantage, should instruct the self-righteous.

If, as Aristotle argues, the speaker's "character may almost be called the most effective means of persuasion he possesses," then the improviser at first glance is disconcertingly unauthoritative.[59] The claim of spontaneity is partly explained away by Curtius's "topos of affected modesty" and the figure of "anticipatory self-defense" and yet many of our improvisers are anything but modest and are clearly on the offense. Indeed, some seek to give offense (as we saw Rabelais and Henry Miller do). There is, too, an all-important note in these disclaimers that scholarly explanations do little to explain. For all their folly of the head, we forgive improvisers and come to trust them as we do because they convince us that they are moved and motivated instead by the folly of the heart (or "blood consciousness" as Lawrence would say—whatever term the writer privileges in opposition to received notions of systematic rationality). Unmediated by rationality, his artless effort will therefore be true and worthy of our attention. The improviser's character is, despite appearances, a device of persuasion: it challenges us to re-evaluate our attitude toward rationality and judgment and the personae who rigidly embody them.

Most familiar and recognizable is the fool or natural, traditionally thought to be God's or Nature's child, touched by a special grace: Erasmus's Folly incarnate; More's narrator Hythlodaeus, who is "expert in trifles"; Burton's Democritus Jr., the laughing philosopher *redux*; or the more or less provincial and libertine personae of Montaigne, Nashe, Browne, and Sterne. Swift's personae inhabit that urbane but equally constricted "province" called Grub Street. The improviser represents himself as a bit out of the box, even a bit mad, like Pope outraged at some poetaster or Swift, whose modest proposals would ironically have us embrace infanticide, or worse, religious enthusiasm.

---

59. *The Basic Works of Aristotle*, edited by Richard McKeon (New York: Random House, 1941), 1329.

Pantalon and Dottore, the two *senex* or *vecchi* of *Commedia dell'Arte,* serve as comic Faust figures who boast in ridiculous fashion, lampooning the scholastics' pretense to contain all human knowledge.[60] At the furthest extreme, the improviser is the Wild Man of the green world, utterly free of civilization's constraints. In less extreme versions, the voice of improvisation is temporarily made a fool by drink, or madness, or some other impairment. Are they the narrative tradition's first unreliable narrators? Unreliable and yet, as in the fool tradition, improvisations are saturated in the Pauline injunction to be "a fool for Christ."

We need not linger long in describing these many masks of the improvisers' personae, which have been variously studied by diverse hands.[61] Rather, what is important first of all is, once again, to urge their isomorphism, their structural or functional similarity: fools, naturals, madmen, clowns, libertines, amateurs, charlatans, and confidence men are all functionally one, all situated beyond civilization's pall, all placed there in order to provide commentary on civilization's and reason's limits and to urge our getting beyond them. Second, it is important to insist on the links between these masks and Romanticism's and post-Romanticism's characteristic personae. The links are obscured in part by the Romantics themselves, whose personae tend not to wear the cap and bells so obviously as their Renaissance and Enlightenment counterparts. But the links are also in part obscured by our own vision, filtered as it is by the notion of traditionlessness, novelty, and individual genius implicit in the Romantic ideology: *jamais déjà* (never before). Yet Romantics, too, speak to their urban and urbane audiences with an analogous mixture of naïveté, unworldliness, and cultivated provinciality that places them below

---

60. Henke, *Performance and Literature in the Commedia dell'Arte,* 137ff.

61. On the fool tradition, see Johan Huizinga, *Homo Ludens: A Study of the Play Element in Culture* (Boston: Beacon Press, 1955 [1950]) and Walter Kaiser, *Praisers of Folly.* On the "geneology of the Wildman myth," see Hayden White, "The Forms of Wildness: The Archeology of an Idea," in *The Wildman Within: An Image in Western Thought from the Renaissance to Romanticism,* edited by Edward Dudley and Maximilian Novak (Pittsburgh: University of Pittsburgh Press, 1972), 3-38. On madmen, see Michel Foucault, *Madness and Civilization: A History of Insanity in the Age of Reason* (New York: Vintage, 1973 [1965]) and Lilian Feder, *Madness in Literature* (Princeton, N.J.: Princeton University Press, 1980).

their audiences in respectability, and yet perforce above them. The more ironic the Romantic narrative poem, the more overtly fool-like the persona becomes. Byron sets the extreme benchmark in *Don Juan* with his eponymous hero and playful narrative voice. Wordsworth more subtly exploits the mad and the beggarly in the *Lyrical Ballads* (as, e.g., "We Are Seven" and "The Thorn"); more overtly exploits the traditional fool in "Peter Bell"; and in "Resolution and Independence" appears before us foolishly in his own person. The Romantic persona, even when dead serious (as is Coleridge in "Dejection: An Ode," "Ancient Mariner," or "Kubla Khan,"), is more or less a fool or madman ("weave a circle round him thrice") like his Renaissance counterpart, but rarely draws attention overtly to the tradition to which he or she belongs. All these voices suggest to their audience that their foolishness is more fruitful than the respectable sanity of the citizen.

The desire to *épater* or shock *le bon bourgeois* figures in the improviser's persona ever more overtly in the aftermath of the Romantic period. Carlyle's Bohemian Teufelsdröckh, in his tower cut off from the world at his feet, anticipates the many nineteenth and twentieth century "fools" who know better than the prudential world what the world is all about. Primitives within the city walls, they are the brothers of those primitives without, like Thoreau, who cultivate the artlessness and wildness of nature. Rimbaud quests for a radical dissolution (*déreglement*) of the senses in dark Africa; Baudelaire back home in Paris submerges himself in the flowing wildness of the city crowd (*la foule*). Artaud and the Surrealists and Beats after him embrace madness. The history of improvisation takes us from Folly to *folie,* or just plain crazy. The avant-garde's flirtation with or embrace of madness is an effort to reveal the more pathological craziness of mainstream society.

Sane or mad, the improviser is marginal. Daniel Belgrad calls attention to

> the social dynamic (or at times social fiction) that recurred persistently among the avant-garde of the 1940s and 1950s. The pattern is that of the creative artist seeking the means to cultural authority ("looking for a voice" or "coming to authorship"), who, because of class or ethnic background begins this search from the disadvantaged position of the cultural outsider…Significantly, a great majority of the producers of spontaneous art in the 1940s and 1950s were first-or second-generation Americans, or

hailed from positions socially or geographically remote from the institutional centers of cultural authority.[62]

Improvisers want to include more of life in part so that they might be included.

All these gestures are one: a breaking free of civilization's constraints in order to embrace, to gobble up, more of life. The improviser's foolish, barrier-breaking persona is instrumental in setting the banquet's table.

3. *Key Stylistic Conventions*

Improvisation debunks reason's power to comprehend life because of its pressing awareness of all that reason cannot accommodate or make sense of: life's (and the mind's) multiplicity, its ever-random surprises. But what the rational mind cannot accommodate, *im-pro-visation's* art of the *un-fore-seen* emphatically can. This principle of the apparently unforeseen nature of its art is articulated in each of the stylistic conventions that dominate the form:

  a. simplicity

  b. free-association

  c. digression

  d. catalog or encyclopedic enumeration

  e. formlessness, fragmentation, imperfection

  f. swerve from generic tradition, or

  g. biographical realism

Employing these stylistic conventions, and setting their art in a special relation to tradition that I will describe below, the improviser achieves an encyclopedic art that is perfectly cast to haul into the net of its improvised discourse as much of life as possible, or, in any case, *more* than its more rational and reasonable rival discourses.

a. Simplicity

Removed from the centers of power and iconoclastic, the improviser ever employs a style that gives the appearance of being free from current fashion, of following no model, of being in a style, as it were, never-before-seen. And yet at the same time the improviser's style, in part covertly, in part quite

---

62. Belgrad, *Spontaneity*, 40–41.

pointedly, swerves from the style privileged by the dominant culture, and thus mirrors as antitype the model it refuses to acknowledge. Like pastoral, improvisation affects a naive, innocent, simple style, but its simplicity is decidedly relative, a matter of contrast to the reigning style: again our binary. As Terry Eagleton remarks, "Cervantes assures us that he will give us this history 'neat and naked,' without the usual paraphernalia of [romantic] literature. But a naked and neat style is just as much a style as any other."[63] The improviser's simplicity may have the complexity of Burton's baroque exploding periods, an effort to upstage the Ciceronian fashion, as Morris Croll and Stanley Fish, working on sixteenth-and seventeenth-century prose writers, have shown; or it may have the elevation of the Romantics' "natural" diction—elevated but pointedly un-Augustan and so "a man speaking to men"; or it may have the apparent naïveté of Huck's polysyndeton-rich ("and...and...and") sentences—rhetorically complex and sophisticated but less overtly so and, thus, pointedly un-Victorian, the source, according to Hemingway in *Green Hills of Africa,* of "all modern American literature."[64] In each and every case improvisation's style is pointedly "indecorous": refusing to follow, and debunking the style of the day. The target is now the nascent rationality of classical Greece (as it is in the Homeric "Hymn to Hermes," and the poetry of Pindar and Sappho treated below); now the logic-chopping of the Schoolmen (as in Erasmus, More, and Rabelais, Bacon, Burton, and Browne); now the self-satisfied rationality of the Royal Academy (as in Swift and Sterne) or of Locke (Sterne's other target); now the mechanical associationalism, the positivism, or the Newtonian physics of the Enlightenment (diversely targeted by the Romantics). After the Romantics, scientific positivism and the bourgeois and technological culture that thrives on it become improvisation's opportunistic targets.

b. Free-Association

Claiming that their speech is spontaneous, that they will say *quicquid in buccam venerit,* whatever comes into the mouth, improvisers proceed not along

---

63. Terry Eagleton, *The English Novel: An Introduction* (London: Wiley-Blackwell, 2013), 4.

64. *"Attic" and Baroque Prose Style: The Anti-Ciceronian Movement. Essays by Morris W. Croll*; Stanley E. Fish, *Seventeenth-Century Prose: Modern Essays in Criticism* (New York: Oxford University Press, 1971).

logical lines but according to the association of ideas or emotions or sounds or sensations in the free-flow of their unforeseen occurrence. Meant to appear the creature of whimsy and mood, the improviser's style captures with whim just what logic would chop out as beyond or beneath its purview. This convention of freedom is subject to many permutations, from the clipped and exploded periods of Renaissance prose writers, to Wordsworth's "natural diction," to the hand-held cameras, available-lighting techniques, and muddy sound tracks of Robert Altman or Bernardo Bertolucci.

Free association bodies forth a mind at work upon the world. Of course all writing presents in some fashion the impression of a mind at work. But the improviser insistently and self-reflexively calls attention to processes of mind. And it is the kind, the nature, of the mental processes that distinguishes improvisation. Improvisers place themselves in opposition to the mental processes and style of their satiric target. The scholastic mind proceeds within rigid logical categories and distinctions; the Ciceronian mind proceeds by pre-ordained rhetorical (grammatical and tropic) categories and schemes; the Lockean-Hartlean mind proceeds according to a mechanical process of association (so the post-Lockean improviser claims at least); the modern scientific positivist proceeds according to his or her self-sufficient, self-satisfied scientific method.

Each of these targets embodies the supposition that knowledge or the means to obtain it is somehow pre-ordained, fore-known. Expression for the scholastics, for the Renaissance Ciceronian, for the Enlightenment associationalists, or for the scientific positivists is a matter of encapsulating in language (or experiment) what is already known. Striking a classical stance, they express, or re-express, received truths, truths authorized elsewhere and by others. Improvisers by contrast are always discovering knowledge and truth. They either become their own authority or throw the very notion of authority out the window: "We must each," they are saying, "make our own truth—*watch!*" They do so through their style and their characterization of a mind at work and its openness to what comes. Always at issue is the vitality or breadth that the targeted style or philosophy purportedly lacks. Improvisers pretend to greater liveliness and scope, and thereby to greater truth, and underline their achievement in the immediate and unmediated texture of their style. By jumping from subject to subject, by mixing their metaphors, by using ellipsis (...), anacholuthon (broken syntax), catachresis (improper use of words or logic), polysyndeton (and...and...and), parataxis (no conjunctions: *veni*; *vidi*; *vici*), shifts in prosody, hand-held cameras that seem to wander through a scene, and other devices of analogous effect, improvisers coax new truths from the sensible world that they affect to embrace in all its multiplicity and fullness.

c. Digression

One extension of this free-associative style is the digression, an association so full-blown that it disrupts the normal progression of narrative or discourse. One effect of digression in improvisational writing is to make its narratives episodic rather than linear and consecutive, for the details of each event overpower the consciousness of the free-associating persona, retarding or exploding the narrative flow. In the extreme the digressive quality also has a tendency to make its narratives anti-narratives (Sterne, Byron) and of its orations anti-orations (e.g. Erasmus's *Folly*, Thomas Nashe's *Pierce Pennylesse*) or its films anti-Hollywood (e.g., Altman's entire corpus, but especially and most pointedly *The Player*). It also lends to its lyrics and narratives both an epiphanic quality (for each moment and each detail is a revelation) and to flatten, if at a high pitch, their emotional curve: each moment and each action is equally important. As Lewis Hyde says, "Perception, in the gifted state, is a constant hierophany."[65] Digression is the Blakean visionary moment that opens up eternity.

d. Catalog or encyclopedic enumeration

Another result of the associative impulse is the catalog or enumeration, where one item calls forth another and another paratactically ("and then... and then"). Rhetoricians Quintilian, Cicero, and Erasmus each recommend free-association and digression as methods for achieving *copia*, copiousness or verbal amplification.[66] What Eric Havelock, writing of the Homeric tradition, says of oral poetry applies more generally to improvisation, that its "law of narrative syntax...takes the form of parataxis: the language is additive,

---

65. Hyde, *The Gift*, 173.

66. See Quintilian, *Institutio Oratoria* 10.7; and Terence Cave, *The Cornucopian Text*, 3-34.

as image is connected to image by 'and' rather than subordinated in some thoughtful relationship."[67] For Havelock, Homer "act[s] as a kind of versified encyclopedia."[68] Again, for Havelock, what Plato objects to in mimesis is that "it is polymorphous and...exhibits the characteristics of a rich and unpredictable flux of experience."[69]

Proceeding by association, the improviser garners all aspects of life that come to mind or eye. The "quickness"—both its aliveness and its speed—of the improviser's voice fosters the encyclopedic texture of the mode. Of the *Commedia dell'Arte,* the improvisatory theatre of Renaissance Italy, Robert Henke writes, as noted above, that the impulse to "copiousness became more than just a stylistic or formal enterprise, but one that aimed at encyclopedic knowledge."[70] A texture of totality may be conveyed by the illogic or lack of obvious logic of the catalog. What the improviser offers is whatever comes before the persona's eye. William Carlos Williams in *Paterson* explains his poetry's "one answer: write carelessly so that nothing that is not green will survive,"[71] a visionary remark hard to parse outside the locus of improvisation with its pastoral trope. What unites the catalog is its polymorphous aliveness, both of the eye that sees and of what it sees. The improviser embraces the persona of the primitive mind, and for Claude Lévi-Strauss "the primitive mind totalizes."[72] Lewis Hyde best captures the catalog's effect on the reader:

> One of the effects of reading Whitman's famous catalogs is to induce his own equanimity in the reader. Each element of creation seems equally fascinating. The poet's eye focuses with unqualified attention on such a wide range of creation that our sense of discrimination soon withdraws

---

67. Eric A. Havelock, *The Muse Learns to Write: Reflections on Orality and Literacy from Antiquity to the Present* (New Haven: Yale University Press, 1986), 76.

68. Ibid., 29.

69. Eric A. Havelock, *Preface to Plato* (Cambridge, Mass.: Harvard University Press, 1963), 23.

70. Henke, *Performance and Literature in the Commedia dell'Arte,* 43.

71. William Carlos Williams, *Paterson,* rev. ed. prepared by Christopher MacGowan (New York: New Directions, 1992), 129.

72. Claude Lévi-Strauss, *The Savage Mind* (Chicago: The University of Chicago Press, 1966), 245.

for lack of use, and that part of us which can sense the underlying coherence comes forward…Whitman puts hierarchy to sleep.[73]

As does jazz. Composer, musician, and scholar Gunther Schuller describes the "'democratization' of rhythmic values" in jazz:

> So-called weak beats (or weak parts of rhythmic units) are *not* underplayed as in "classical" music. Instead, they are brought up to the level of strong beats, and very often even emphasized *beyond* the strong beat. The jazz musician does this not only by maintaining an equality of dynamics among "weak" and "strong" elements, but also by preserving the full sonority of notes, even though they may happen to fall on weak parts of a measure.[74]

"What a far cry from the 1-2-3-4, 1-2-3-4 of military marches!" he adds parenthetically.[75] Schuller argues that this "'democratization' of rhythmic values" "gives an Armstrong solo that peculiar sense of inner drive and forward momentum," each note fighting for its moment in the sun:

> Armstrong was incapable of not swinging. Even if we isolate a single quarter note from the context of a phrase, we can clearly hear the forward thrust of that note, and in it we recognize the unmistakable Armstrong personality. It is as if such notes wish to burst out of the confines of their rhythmic placement. They wish to do more than a single note can do; they wish to express the exuberance of an entire phrase.[76]

Satchmo—a nickname he earned with his huge, satchel-sized mouth—gobbles up his "wonderful world" note by note.

Another way the improviser conveys encyclopedic totality is by means of what might be called an alpha-omega, or all-encompassing, structure or trope. Nashe's pamphlet-oration *Pierce Pennylesse* relates all of Elizabethan life to a catalog of the seven deadly sins. Folly's oration adds to the catalog of sins a parade of all professions, all foolish. The encyclopedic impulse surfaces in Rabelais's catalogs of *torches-culs* (ass-wipes) and of other equally absurd things that go on for pages; in Burton's catalog of melancholies; and in

---

73. Hyde, *The Gift*, 163.

74. Gunther Schuller, *Early Jazz: Its Roots and Musical Development* (New York and Oxford: Oxford University Press, 1968), 8. Emphasis in original.

75. Ibid., 10.

76. Ibid., 91–92.

Browne's catalogs of quincunxes (five-sided objects) and *pseudodoxiae* (false ideas). Sterne writes an unfinishable autobiography with catalogs of militariana, curses, and orthographic squiggles. Wordsworth's epic on the growth of the poet's mind catalogs sensations and spots of time. Whitman is here master among masters, his *Song of Myself* a catalog of catalogs.

The alpha-omega structure may be geographical, a structural articulation, as it were, of "the *en voyage* excuse" discussed above. As in many improvisations, Wordsworth's epic cannot stay put, flowing like its dominant image, the river, across France, from London to Grasmere, and throughout the Lake District. The seventh volume of *Tristram Shandy* begins an endless sentimental journey through the continent, which spins off into the equally improvised *Sentimental Journey. Don Juan* is an imaginative encyclopedia of European history and culture. The Ancient Mariner, whose ballad is compulsively told, goes from here to the South Pole and back, presenting before us repeatedly the wide sweep of the horizon. Melville's encyclopedia of cytology explores the encyclopedic microcosm of diverse sailors on the Pequod as the whaler journeys the macrocosm of the seven seas. (Yes, *Moby Dick* is an improvisation and we know it from the first sentence, "Call me Ishmael," which establishes an intimate conversation between an outsider and his audience). Thoreau—for whom "the traveler must be born again on the road" (*Week on the Concord and Merrimack*)—explores eternity in one year at Walden Pond, seeking an encyclopedic knowledge of the pond and its environs. The goal of Rimbaud's ceaseless *voyage* is a vision of *l'infinie,* while for the Beats the goal of their ceaseless road trips is that "IT" that encompasses all.

The alpha-omega, or all-encompassing, structure is sometimes writ small in a kind of alpha-omega trope or figure of speech. Folly likes categorical statement that lets no one escape from her vision of universal folly: "Is anything at all done among mortals that is not full of folly? Isn't everything done by fools, among fools?" No one is left out. Similarly, she relishes the images of gods when "they take their seats at the place where heaven juts farthest out, and lean forward to watch what mankind is about…Good lord, what a theatre, how manifold the feverish fretting of fools!"[77] In the preface to *Have with You Saffron Walden,* Thomas Nashe recommends to the appreciation of

---

77. Erasmus, *The Praise of Folly,* 39.

his reader "the melodious God of Gamut" and reminds him that there is "life and sinnewes in everie thing."[78] Byron associates Erasmus's heavenly birds-eye viewpoint figure with the *"improvvisatore"* style:

> I perch upon an humbler promontory
> Amidst life's infinite variety:
> With no greater care for what is nicknamed glory,
> But speculating as I cast mine eye
> On what may suit or may not suit my story,
> And never straining hard to versify
> I rattle on exactly as I talk
> With any body in a ride or walk.[79]

The figure is subtly handled in Wordsworth's treatment of landscape, where the foreground is always situated within a sweeping horizon. It is treated overtly by Coleridge in "This Lime Tree Bower My Prison" and by Wordsworth in the Mount Snowden episode of *The Prelude*. In these poets, the high promontory from which all can be seen is associated with the Romantic Imagination and with the sympathy and empathy for all life, for the vision of the One Life, which the spontaneous agency of the Imagination elicits. Thoreau, characteristically, finds in his chapter "Spring" what has been called the central demonstration of *Walden* on the least high of promontories, the railroad cut near Walden Pond. There he experiences a vision that encapsulates— gobbles up—all life (discussed below in Chapter 6).

e. Formlessness, fragmentation, imperfection

Because of his or her foolishness, the persona of improvisation either cannot stick to the point or cannot finish it. Like Burton's *Anatomy*, Teufelsdröckh's autobiography in *Sartor Resartus* comes to his troubled redactor's hands in "Six considerable PAPER-BAGS, carefully sealed,...in the inside of which...lie miscellaneous masses of Sheets, and oftener Shreds and Snips, written in Professor Teufelsdröckh's scarce legible *cursiv-schrift*"[80]—and is

---

78. *The Works of Thomas Nashe*, 3 vols., edited by Ronald B. McKerrow (London: A. H. Bullen, 1904), 3:23.

79. *Byron's Don Juan: A Variorum Edition*, canto 15, st. 19.

80. [Thomas] Carlyle, *Sartor Resartus*, edited by Archibald MacMechan (Boston and London: The Atheneum Press, 1902), 69.

all the truer for its messiness. Their form is formless—so they claim. Creatures of impulse, whimsy, and mood, improvisations sometimes end as fragments (as the inspiration, which is sometimes just a highfalutin word for "whim," passes) or become miscellanies or farragoes (as the mood shifts). Of course my point is not that the improviser's mood literally changes or breaks off in the act of creation—this we usually cannot know—but rather that it makes rhetorical sense for the improviser to create the appearance of a shift or breakdown.

As with improvisation's other features, its rhetoric of formlessness conveys presence, immediacy, authenticity. Formlessness offers not empty form but instead the overflowing fullness of lived life. The miscellany or farrago avoids the mediation of the received, orderly form. The fragment paradoxically captures more of life than completed forms can, for the completed form has at least one eye cast on its formal model that mediates what is seen and how it is shaped. The closed form shuts the door that the formless form leaves wide open pointing to the fullness beyond.

For me there was a certain pathos in discovering Allen Ginsberg's many midcentury rants reinventing these same truths about the improvisation he practices. The rants are suffused with his frustration with an audience that just doesn't grok what he is doing, as we see in this passage part of which I have quoted above and here quote at length:

> Trouble with conventional form (fixed line count and stanza form) is, it's too symmetrical, geometrical, numbered and pre-fixed—unlike to my own mind which has no beginning and end, nor fixed measure of thought (or speech—or writing) other than its own cornerless mystery—to transcribe the latter in a form most nearly representing its actual "occurrence" is my method—which requires the skill of freedom of composition—which will lead poetry to the expression of the highest moments of the mindbody—mystical illumination—and its deepest emotion (through tears—love's all)—in the forms nearest to what it actually looks like (data of mystical imagery) and feels like (rhythm of actual speech and rhythm prompted by direct transcription of visual and other mental data)—plus not to forget the sudden genius-like imagination or fabulation of unreal and out of this world verbal constructions which express the true gaiety and excess of freedom—(and also by their nature express the first cause of

the world) by means of spontaneous irrational juxtaposition of sublimely related fact, by the dentist drill singing against the piano music.[81]

The sentence goes on for another 150 words. Would his audience have understood better the "cornerless mystery" of his mind, would his tone have been different, if he had been able to point to the tradition of which he was an unwitting part, a tradition that had been shaking the city walls for two millennia at least? Probably not, which just increases the pathos. Of course if a mainstream audience did grok him, improvisation's work would be done—which can never happen. There will always be city walls to shake, just as there will always be guardians of the dying paradigm who maintain them.

For Ginsberg as for his fellow improvisers, "formless" is of course part of an implicit binary: more formless than "x" where "x" is some craftsmanly virtuoso form. The rhetoric of craft offers a mastery of form and conveys it by a number of structural means, too numerous here to adumbrate. Perhaps the most important of these are the structures that register as closed, carefully completed. You know the masters when you see them: Horace, the Renaissance sonneteers, Gustave Flaubert and Henry James, Oscar Wilde and the *fin-de-siècle* poets. Tight, closed forms from master craftsmen seem to the improviser claustrophobic. In the self-contained world of *The Ambassadors,* James's sympathetic central consciousness Strether seems to bridle at the tight reins his own creator submits his artistry to. Strether longingly recommends "more life" as life's central lesson: "I want to see more life…live all you can; it is a mistake not to." *Le maître* himself, Flaubert, embraces the open contours of improvisation in his final episodic novel, a Menippean fragment, *Bouvard et Pécuchet.* Flaubert satirizes the weaknesses of all sciences by tracing the quest of his two eponymous fools in their encyclopedic quest to know everything. The tighter Reason purports to hold the reins, the more likely is the resurgence of the Irrational.

Cut short, the fragment acknowledges life's overflowing cornucopia that it, the fragment, points to but knows it cannot contain. Affecting to look steadily upon life, when life shifts the fragment ends. Improvisers' orations, essays, dialogues, and poetic effusions end for no logical reason but because of whim: because inspiration has left them (in the comic vein, because they are

---

81. Ginsberg, *Deliberate Prose,* 247.

too drunk to continue; in the serious, as among the Romantics, because the inspiring wind has died down, or because some outside influence intercedes). Dryden's sea battle, the setting for his *Essay of Dramatick Poesie*, is over and the tide changes; *Tristram Shandy* (however complete, and I think it is) terminates open-ended with Sterne's death, and *Don Juan* with Byron's. Conveying a sense of life's flux, fragments "achieve by their inachievement," as has been said of Pascal's fragmented *Pensées*.[82] They suggestively represent life's variety and multiplicity by incompletely representing it. Again Williams: "By the brokenness of his composition the poet makes himself master of a certain weapon which he could possess himself of in no other way."[83] Like the hero of myth, by accepting his wound in the marginal world he ventures into, the improviser is ready to bring his boon back to society in order to revivify it. The improviser is likely to be in a hurry. Taking "no manner of Time to digest it into Order, or correct the Style," they ignore the master craftsman Horace's advice to publish nothing for nine years.

Acknowledging that "poetic fragments occur in periods other than the Romantic," Marjorie Levinson argues that the fragment "figures in our criticism as an *exemplary* Romantic expression. This semantic priority enormously influences our practical criticism, and at a most elementary as well as unconscious level."[84] This is exactly my point: that the fragment's status as a peculiarly or particularly Romantic phenomenon, a status belied by its many acknowledged antecedents, betrays our "uncritical absorption in romanticism's own self-representations" and reflects our failure to examine our premises as we respond to the texts' rhetoric. Unpacking the rhetoric of spontaneity, of which the fragment is but one formal piece, helps us see that the Romantics are not alone in trying to deal with the conflict between received and new forms and received and new definitions of rationality. Surely, facing the legacy of the Enlightenment, they do so with an urgency and seriousness

---

82. Lucien Goldmann's comment on Pascal's *Pensées*, quoted in Marjorie Levinson, *The Romantic Fragment Poem: A Critique of a Form* (Chapel Hill: University of North Carolina, 1986), 230n.

83. William Carlos Williams, *Kora in Hell: Improvisations* (New York: New Directions, 1957), 19.

84. Levinson, *The Romantic Fragment Poem*, 6.

peculiarly their own. Still the structure, whether the text is ironic or dead serious, is isomorphic, having the same formal shape: the incompleteness of the text always speaks to the problem of completion, which is itself a problem of reason and craft. Romantic "antecedents" do not anticipate Romanticism in a kind of Whiggish literary historiography. In their own way, improvisations work the same side of the street, exploring in each epoch the same fundamental human problem: with the whole world there before us—a world improvisations lovingly present—how do we stretch ourselves and our instruments of understanding and articulation to accommodate that world with what Milton calls an "answerable style"?[85]

In a word, suddenly it is less of a surprise, and less likely a matter of historical or textual accident, that Heraclitus, for whom the river of life flows forever onward, comes down to us in fragments.

Fragmented, free-associative and digressive, formless and without generic expectation, filled with the chaos of catalogs and the messiness of reality— improvisations anticipate John Ruskin's doctrine of imperfection, the idea that the "reach" of great art, in Browning's phrase, must "exceed [its] grasp." Browning offers this principle in the voice of Fra Lippo Lippi, a fresco painter who works in wet plaster and hence another improviser. Embracing the hit or miss, perhaps improvisers miss more often, but doing so they achieve their target, challenging our rational hierarchies of taste.

f. Swerve from Generic Tradition

The relationship of the improviser's "formless form" to known genres displays the same rhetoric of presence and authenticity. The relationship asserted may be one of two: 1) that it pertains to no known genre and hence follows no generic authority; or 2) that it pertains to a genre but swerves from it in a significant way. Improvisations thus authenticate themselves *vis à vis* generic expectations either by claiming to be uncanonical, *nova reperta* (newfound things), and therefore free of worn-out artifice, or by claiming to be renovations of the generic canon and therefore revitalizations of worn-out

---

85. *Paradise Lost,* in *The Poems of John Milton,* edited by John Carey and Alastair Fowler (New York: W.W. Norton, 1972), bk. 9, line 20.

artifice. Most improvisers have it both ways. Erasmus notes in his dedication that the tradition of mock-oration goes back to Lucian (whose *Gallus* he
and More translated together in 1505); in his oration he mocks the tradition
of scholastic oratory—this one, he insists through Folly, is *really* improvised.
What Erasmus is doing with genre is best understood in light of his general
humanist program: he wishes to hurdle Thomistic method and the authority of the Schools in order to get to the purer authority and presence of the
classics and the Gospel. Within Folly's oration proper, the influence of these
traditions is more or less obfuscated. For example, Folly does not draw attention to Lucian's mock-oration on the Sophists, crucially analogous to his own
treatment of the Schoolmen. Folly's primary claim is immediacy, the here-
and-now, though ultimately Erasmus wants our understanding of classical
and Christian antiquity to mediate contemporary life. Like other improvisers, Erasmus's attitude toward genre reflects the Renaissance maxim, *retrocedens accedit*, "look[ing] back to see forward,...advancing by retreating."[86]
More respectful of genres than they let on, improvisers nonetheless seek to
redefine and enlarge the genre tradition.

Like Erasmus, whom he claimed with characteristic hyperbole was both
father and mother to his writings, Rabelais now renovates the genre exploited,
as in Gargantua's letter to Pantagruel (Chapter VI); he now obscures generic
ties altogether, as in his prefatory claim to be composing no Homeric allegory.
Rather, he is merely a drinker speaking to drunks. Like many improvisers,
Rabelais ironically exploits many genres, making a mockery of each. Screech's
work on the legalistic matrix in Rabelais helps us understand what are perhaps his largest generic coordinates and target, the tradition of law books.
Rabelais mocks legal systems by writing an anatomy *qua* law book, making it
clear that the mediation of systematized law cannot deal with the Rabelaisian
vision of life's variety. A new genre and new order are needed, not radically
to change but to purify the *status quo*. Iconoclasts though they present themselves, rather than to break the forms, many improvisers' efforts finally are
to remove the encrustations from received forms and so to renew them. Such

---

86. James Hillman, "Hermetic Intoxication," in *Uniform Edition of the Writings of
James Hillman*, vol. 6: *Mythic Figures* (Thompson, Conn.: Spring Publications, 2021
[2007]), 268.

encrustations or impurities keep us from the thing itself, filter out the diversity of life that such genres were originally meant to reflect and capture but now seem incomplete.

Like Rabelais, Sterne creates a compendium of genres and mocks them all for their insufficiency. The overriding generic tradition at work is autobiography, itself in a sense a recent invention. Sterne's full title is pointedly chosen, *The Life and Opinions of Tristram Shandy, Gentleman.* Sterne pushes the conventions of autobiography far beyond their limits: the conventional day of birth is stretched backward to the moment of conception; the convention of "key incidents" expands *ad nauseum* as Tristram lingers over every incident but gets nowhere; the convention of mixing present opinions and reflections with past occurrences explodes into Sterne's inexhaustible effusion of sensibility. Managing to describe only four early incidents (conception, birth, christening, Bobby's death—a fifth, Tristram's first breeches, is promised but never arrives), Sterne spends more time explaining their contextual background than the events themselves. Sterne's point: that life is far too complex to be rendered in the conventional form of autobiography. Not only Tristram's ever-rambling mind, but also this formal feature of generic burlesque provides the shape of the apparently shapeless novel.

Wordsworth's treatment of genre is likewise tacit, not to say obfuscatory. As I argue below, in "Tintern Abbey" he transforms the conventions of the ode to conform to his Romantic program for poetry. The ode is a lyric, though public effusion, and Wordsworth will make it more intimate, addressing it to his sister; the ode is sublime, and Wordsworth transvaluates the concept by finding sublimity not in the heroic but in the everyday. Coleridge does much the same in the Conversation Poems, a series that climaxes with "Dejection: An Ode." *The Prelude* is an improvised Miltonic epic, but where Milton is inspired by the Holy Spirit to write "this my unpremeditated verse," Wordsworth increases the texture of spontaneity, inspired by the "divine ventriloquist," the Imagination, writing with greater intimacy and immediacy. His epic concerns not arms and the man, but nature and the mind; he justifies himself not to an unseen Muse, or to an unseen generalized audience of Man, but to the more intimate, and hence authenticating, audience of his friend Coleridge. Together they will write the "experiment," *Lyrical Ballads,* conflating in a new way these two genres (lyric and ballad) and many more besides (inscription, pastoral, ode, loco-descriptive elegy).

In generalizing about improvisation's treatment of genre, we must note that the claim of being experimental or traditionless, *nova reperta*, boils down to the same thing as the claim of being a renovation of tradition. To invent a new genre is simply to renovate the entire genre system, the canon or *paideia* of humanistic letters. Harold Bloom's idea of the swerve or *clinamen* as a psychological impulse in strong poets has also this rhetorical motivation: it authenticates as more sincere, more immediate, more applicable to the flux of lived life.

What is essential, then, is that improvisations swerve from a particular genre or from the genre system as a whole. Those cast as essays or dialogues are less emphatic in their anti-generic boasts, and yet both, if not swerves, are humanistic renovations of classical forms, the epistle and dialogue that had fallen from use. All improvisations swerve from their generic model by emphasizing the here-and-now, performance character of their discourse. Oral-formulaic, lyric, dialogue, first person narrative and non-narrative (essay, anatomy)—all privilege not only the orality of the first person, but also its dramatic presentness. Thus improvisation in part validates Derrida's point that western metaphysics privileges the oral over the written. Free-associating, creating structure and form as they go, improvisers make meaning, find truth on the move, as they go. Substance—experience—precedes essence almost as much for the Renaissance improviser as for the twentieth century existentialist. The conversation poems and odes of the Romantics are homeopathic, discovering their illness in the process of performing their cure. The cure lies in the texture of the performance no less for Renaissance improvisers than in the more extreme articulations of the Action Painters or the Beats' "kickwriting" and "wild form." It is true that for the Renaissance improviser the whole body of Christian doctrine is in a sense a given and that, by contrast, the whole point of the twentieth century is that there are no *données* or givens. But then, the whole point of the Renaissance humanist is not to treat his *données* as given at all—this had been the fatal mistake of the Schoolmen. The Christian logos is *there* only when embodied in a lived life. Christ's truth must be won again and again through performance: *imitatio Christi*. In this their task and technique is isomorphic with that of the twentieth century surrealist, modern, Beat, and postmodern: shoring "these fragments...against [the] ruins" of the modern world.

Improvisation's complex relation to genre helps explain philosopher Gary Peters's counterintuitive perception that this art of the un-fore-seen, with its "valorization of originality, novelty, innovation, and unpredictability," and its commitment to "interrupt...the continuity of history with the mark of the new,"[87] is more backward-than forward-looking. Drawing on Walter Benjamin's reading of Paul Klee's *Angelus Novus,* who "faces backwards into the future," Peters sees this as the "tragic predicament of the improviser."[88] Peters calls this problem the "scrap yard challenge":

> The artist...is thrown into a situation piled high with the discarded waste products of cultural history. These are the defunct, clapped-out, disintegrating remnants of past times on the edge of an oblivion that promise, at best, a faint but continuing resonance as nostalgia and the cliché or, at worse, as universal forgetfulness. Improvisation, in the celebratory sense, conceives of itself as transcending these outmoded structures and threadbare pathways through acts of spontaneity that inhabit the moment, the instant, the pure futurity of the "now," without history's "spirit of gravity" (Nietzsche) weighing upon the shoulders of the creative artist.[89]

Perhaps this "tragic predicament" is true of the belated, twentieth century *avant-garde* improvisers who mostly concern Peters. But for many of their predecessors, the improvisers' predicament—shaping a discourse in and by the present moment and yet always glancing backward at the genres—*retrocedens accedit,* advancing by retreating—becomes an opportunity, a fortunate fall if you will.

g. Biographical Realism

The improviser's voice is emphatically a spoken voice and its lifelikeness and liveliness engenders the impression of biographical realism in the form. The identification between author and persona is rarely exact or complete, but improvisers almost always invite some measure of identification. Although

---

87. Gary Peters, *The Philosophy of Improvisation* (Chicago: The University of Chicago Press, 2009), 103-4.

88. Ibid., 2.

89. Ibid., 17-18.

New Criticism once enjoined us not to confuse the author with his/her narrator, we need not always bemoan the confusion as unsophisticated reading. The personae of Rabelais, Nashe, Sterne, Diderot, Byron, and Joyce, for example, will always be inseparable from their creators. The autobiographical element helps to make credible the vitality of the persona: s/he does not only seem alive, s/he is so. As historians of narrative Scholes and Kellogg argue, the tendency of narrators to assert themselves "into narrative is not a romantic tendency so much as a realistic one."[90] The details of the improviser's often well-known biography make but one of the many allusive *faits divers* with which s/he improvises his tale. Autobiography, in short, contributes to the mimetic texture of improvisation. Often loveable in spite of or because of his/her many flaws, the improviser invites us to gobble him/her up as s/he gobbles up the world.

4. *Key Themes*

The claim of spontaneity or the presence of any of the persistent conventions we have adumbrated is no guarantee that we are entering the world of improvisation. Stanley Fish is surely right to warn us against the idea

> that there is a fixed relationship between the presence of certain rhetorical and stylistic devices and either intention or meaning. What the *Anatomy [of Melancholy]* shows is that the same descriptively observable techniques, in the service of different visions, may mean differently, and that only the analysis in time of the total reading experience will prevent the drawing of premature and facile conclusions.[91]

Nonetheless, working together synergistically, the conventions and devices of a form tend to give rise to meanings that we rightly associate with that form. What Joseph Wittreich writes of the prophetic tradition in literature applies equally to improvisation, that "like any other genre, prophecy, for all its variables, contains a set of thematic constants."[92] Pastoral expresses

90. Robert Scholes and Robert Kellogg, *The Nature of Narrative* (New York: Oxford University Press, 1966), 191–92.

91. Fish, *Self-Consuming Artifacts,* 352.

92. "A Poet Amongst Poets: Milton and the Tradition of Prophecy," in *Milton and the Line of Vision,* edited by Joseph Anthony Wittreich (Madison: University of Wis-

ambivalent and complex longings for the *locus amoenus,* and epic, ambivalent, and complex longings for the heroic and for heroic community. So, too, the aesthetic of improvisation expresses its own complex longing, the longing for unmediated experience, for incarnate freedom. Though improvised texts "may [and do] mean differently" and only close analysis can discern the all-important differences among them, still they manifest a matrix of themes, "a set of thematic constants," related to this longing for freedom and unmediated experience.

Embracing the fool and attacking systematic and positivistic rationality— "reason's click-clack" in Stevens's lovely phrase[93]—improvisations enforce the view that, as Victor Frankl puts it, *"Logos* is deeper than logic," or as Lenin says, "Reality is slyer than any theory."[94] Improvisers hate closed systems that claim to explain everything while suffering from a systemic myopia that ensures that much goes unseen, unexplained. The hierophantic and apocalyptic ecstasy improvisers invoke and evoke is ambitious to say the least. Thoreau packs it all into an epigram: "The unconsciousness of man is the consciousness of God, the end of the world.[95] For, the claim of spontaneity not only authorizes and validates. It also, as we have seen, brings on the apocalypse, both goal and completion of the world. All improvisations wing us "by an unconscious will,/To an immaculate end" (Stevens), returning us to Eden, omega united in the end with alpha. In pagan terms, improvisations by "Enwrap[ing] our fancy" try to do what Orpheus did in Thrace (employing the lyre Hermes invented), "where woods and rocks had ears/To rapture."[96] In Christian-humanist terms, improvisations seek, like Wordsworth, to make "Paradise, and groves/Elysian, Fortunate Fields.../A simple produce of the

---

consin Press, 1975), 104.

93. Stevens, "Notes toward a Supreme Fiction," 335.

94. Quoted in Joseph Campbell, *Creative Mythology: The Masks of God* (New York: Viking, 1968), 424; quoted in John Berger, *The Success and Failure of Picasso* (New York: Pantheon, 1989), 120.

95. Quoted in Gordon V. Boudreau, *The Roots of Walden and the Tree of Life* (Nashville: Vanderbilt University Press, 1991), 155.

96. John Milton, *Paradise Lost,* bk. 7, lines 35–36. Also see Chapter 7 below for Hermes's importance to improvisation.

common day.[97] However apocalyptic, they are nonetheless emphatically of this world, "come," to quote the Gospel of John (whom James's Strether echoes), "that [we] might have life, and that [we] might have it more abundantly" (John 10:10).

Though rationality is the thematic crux of most improvisations, examples of the form will differ in the degree to which they reject Reason and embrace Unreason, and, depending on the historical moment, the kind of Unreason (be it divine inspiration, the unconscious, madness, instinct, chance, etc.) they embrace. But on a deeper thematic level, improvisations, perhaps each and all of them, share the persistent theme of sympathy. It is not by accident that improvisations are read and loved for their details: in their catalogs and with their associative style, improvisers shower love upon the minutiae of life. Derek Bailey, himself a practitioner of "total improvisation" or "free music," finds this quality in musical improvisation. Speaking of Indian raga, Bailey generalizes that "something common to most improvised music, is that different constituents do not have obvious hierarchical values. Anything which can be considered as decoration, for instance, is not in some way subservient to that which it decorates. The most powerful expression of the identity of a piece might be in the smallest details."[98] It is this loving embrace of detail that motivates and charges Louis Armstrong's famed minimalism to which Gunther Schuller attributes a "'democratization' of rhythmic values."[99] For early aficionado of hot jazz Hugues Panassié, whom Bailey quotes, "As [Armstrong] went on, his improvisations grew hotter, his style became more and more simple—until at the end there was nothing *but the endless repetition of one fragment of melody—or even a single note insistently sounded and executed with cataclysmic intonations.*"[100]

---

97. "Prospectus" to *The Excursion*, in *The Poetical Works of William Wordsworth*, edited by Ernest De Selincourt, 5 vols. (Oxford: Clarendon Press, 1940-49), vol. 4, lines 47-48, 55.

98. Derek Bailey, *Improvisation: Its Nature and Practice in Music* (Boston: Da Capo Press, 1993), 5.

99. Schuller, *Early Jazz*, 8.

100. Ibid., 50; emphasis added.

The texture of encyclopedic realism brings before the reader the whole sweep of experience and opens both text and self to life's messiness. In the twentieth century this becomes the "heterogeneous matter" that French philosopher Georges Bataille and the Surrealists force us to embrace; it is what German critic Walter Benjamin calls *"profane illumination,* a materialistic, anthropological inspiration."[101] "'Abstract art,'" it has been remarked of Jackson Pollock's action paintings, "is an unfortunate misnomer—it is actually the most concrete of styles."[102] Daniel Belgrad adds: "Indeed, its insistent materiality was intended as a radical counterstatement to the 'abstract' quality of the scientific method." The same is said of Kerouac's "body of fiction": "The representation of the magical nature of entrancing and life-affirming fleeting detail is the outstanding feature."[103]

This convention of embracing all of life has both a rhetorical and a thematic effect. Like Terence, the improviser says, "Nothing human is foreign to me." In the midst of its often satiric or burlesque texture, improvisation presents the imperative of sympathy and kinetically shows us how: through an openness to all the experience it bodies forth. At the heart of their satire, blindness and constriction persist as the essential targets. The improviser sees the world not like Spinoza *sub specie aeternitatis* but, rather, *sub specie encyclopediae.* Spinoza's religious gesture places experience in the context of the afterlife and God's providential plan; improvisation's gesture places experience in the context of *this* world's infinite variety and flux. Spinoza helps us to judge our folly in terms of the Final Judgment and solicits our perception of God's infinite love. The improviser helps us empathically to judge our follies in terms of all the world's follies and solicits our love for one another (and oneself) in the here-and-now. Emphatically a poetics of presence, improvisation would have us embrace the presence all around us, if only, they say, we would open our eyes to it, removing the veil placed on us by rationality and systematic logic. As philosopher Stephen Toulmin argues, speaking of Renais-

---

101. "Surrealism," in Walter Benjamin, *Reflections: Essays, Aphorisms, Autobiographical Writings,* translated by Edmund Jephcott, edited by Peter Demetz (New York: Harcourt Brace Jovanovich, 1978), 179; emphasis in text.

102. George McNeil, "American Abstractionists Venerable at Twenty," *ArtNews* 55, no. 3 (May 1956): 65, as quoted in Belgrad, *Spontaneity,* 114.

103. Cunnell, "Fast this Time: Jack Kerouac and the Writing of *On the Road,*" 16.

sance humanists we have been discussing, "All the varieties of fallibility, formerly ignored, began to be celebrated as charmingly limitless consequences of human character and personality. Rather than deploring these failings, as moral casuists might do, lay [as opposed to clerical] readers were interested in recognizing what made human conduct admirable or deplorable, noble or selfish, inspiring or laughable."[104] The cataloguing impulse expresses, according to poet Richard Wilbur, "a longing to possess the world, and to praise it."[105] The improviser's poetics of presence is nowhere more evident than in its tendency to digression and to the episodic handling of narrative. Improvisation presses toward apocalypse with every event, almost every paragraph. Each is epiphanic, a revelation of, an opening up to, the transcendent in the present moment.[106]

And yet, as we shall see, each of these solutions is optative at best and ultimately for most improvisers problematic. Inevitably mediated by language, convention, and form, improvisations often finally question the inspiration, ecstasy, or unmediated experience that promised to usher in the longed-for epiphanies and apocalypses. Unmediated experience is a will-o'the-wisp. We might glimpse it. We might feel its presence. Then it is gone.

Inveterate stance-takers, improvisers preach the acceptance of human frailty even as they satirize human follies. But the last word, *sub specie encyclopediae,* is sympathy, or, to use a term associated with the Romantics, empathy. In a passage in Milton's "Nativity Ode" that Coleridge will echo in "Kubla Khan," the great Puritan poet imagines recreating the celestial song the angelic choir sang at the creation. He imagines, as Wallace Stevens will later, that hearing this primordial improvisation will at once take us back to Eden and usher in apocalypse:

---

104. Toulmin, *Cosmopolis,* 27.

105. Quoted in Edward Hirsch, *How to Read a Poem: And Fall in Love with Poetry* (New York: Harcourt, 1999), 75.

106. M. H. Abrams's *Natural Supernaturalism: Tradition and Revolution in Romantic Literature* (New York: W. W. Norton, 1971) is a profound study of the many moments in literary history starting with Augustine's confessions and especially among Romantics and their heirs when "an instant of consciousness, or else an ordinary object or event, suddenly blazes into revelation" (385).

> For if such holy Song
> Enwrap our fancy long,
>   Time will run back and fetch the age of gold,
> And speckl'd vanity
> Will sicken soon and die,
>   And leprous sin will melt from earthly mold,
> And Hell itself will pass away,
> And leave her dolorous mansions to the peering day.[107]

At the center of the vision Mercy holds sway:

> Yea Truth, and Justice then
> Will down return to men,
>   Th'enamel'd Arras of the Rainbow wearing,
> And Mercy sit between,
> Thron'd in Celestial sheen,
>   With radiant feet the tissued clouds down steering,
> And Heav'n as at some festival
> Will open wide the Gates of her high Palace Hall.[108]

Improvisation's central human paradox is that if we forgo the comforting but quite limited and usually hierarchical order that systematic reason can win from experience, and if we instead loosen up—to the chaotic primacy of our emotions, instincts, impulses, and even our frailties—we can regain a lost, richer egalitarian order. Improvisation is shot through with the spirit of democracy, especially the shared sense that we will get to what's right by allowing what's flawed to play itself out. Improvisation's ultimate message is that the results of our fall from grace offer a way back: passion and the instinctual life that feeds it; knowledge of good and evil; alertness to the fallen world itself. The inspiration of spontaneity and the conventions that express it together try kinetically and performatively to get us there.

Improvisations may seem to adopt what was known as the Pelagian heresy, the belief that original sin did not taint human nature, as cited by Augustine in his attack on the *heresy*, that "God has conferred upon men liberty of their own will, in order that by purity and sinlessness of life [that is, not by God's

---

107. "On the Morning of Christ's Nativity," *The Poems of John Milton*, lines 133-40.
108. Ibid., lines 141-48.

grace] they may become like unto God."[109] But improvisers rarely in the end forget our flawed nature. Wishing to espouse the limitlessness and perfection of unmediated vision, they rarely finally forget human limitation or imperfection. The moral code improvisers offer their readers does not simplistically or indifferently accept the evil in human nature. Moral realists as much as they are literary realists, improvisers are clear on the question of evil: though they attribute to man the divine property of bringing good out of the Fall's evils, they know too that the results of our fall have an equal capacity to produce evil. Among those results is spontaneity itself: impulsiveness, thoughtlessness, carelessness. Natural instinct, like nature, may be "red in tooth and claw." Flirting with that danger, indeed embracing it, the improviser teaches us nevertheless how to have, like Dryden's Shakespeare, "a comprehensive soul," a soul encyclopedic, oceanic, and all-embracing (see Chapter 5 below).

Such complete and insistent commitments as the improviser's to seize all of life usually call forth its opposite, and it is true that death—the ineluctable human limit—haunts the tradition of improvisation. Exploring the nature of that marginal character, the hipster, whom he calls the "White Negro," Norman Mailer captures the close connection between the commitment to "the enormous present" and the specter of death:

> The real argument which the mystic must always advance is the very intensity of his private vision—his argument depends from the vision precisely because what was felt in the vision is so extraordinary that no rational argument, no hypotheses of "oceanic feelings" and certainly no skeptical reductions can explain away what has become for him the reality more real than the reality of closely reasoned logic. His inner experience of the possibilities within death is his logic. So, too, for the existentialist. And the psychopath. And the saint and the bullfighter and the lover. The common denominator for all of them is their burning consciousness of the present, exactly that incandescent consciousness which the possibilities within death has opened for them.[110]

---

109. Augustine, *De natura et gratia, contra Pelagium* LXIV, as quoted in James Miller, *Examined Lives: From Socrates to Nietzsche* (New York: Farrar Straus and Giroux, 2011), 248.

110. "The White Negro: Superficial Remarks on the Hipster," in Norman Mailer, *Advertisements for Myself and Other Writings* (New York: Putnam, 1959), 341-42.

Mailer is himself an eloquent spokesman for and practitioner of the aesthetics of improvisation, both in writing and in film.[111] Death overtly haunts improvisers like Montaigne, Burton, Browne, Sterne, Coleridge, Byron, and Huck Finn ("I heard an owl, away off, who-whooing about somebody that was dead, and a whippowill and a dog crying about somebody that was going to die"[112]), to name just a few, as much as it will the modern hipsters, Ginsberg and Kerouac. It haunts that greatest of improvisers, *polytropos* Odysseus, who visits Hades in his improvised epic. His great grandfather is Hermes, *psychopompos*, guide of souls to the underworld. Inspiring a "burning consciousness of the present" that is the improviser's greatest gift, death, the great leveler, also enforces the imperative of empathy. For, though like Walter Pater we seek "to burn always with this hard, gem-like flame, to maintain this ecstasy, [that] is success in life," nevertheless we must *all* in the end burn out.

5. *Improv Synergy I: Burton's Anatomy of Melancholy*

Our purpose must ever be, while analyzing the separate conventions of the form, to glimpse the synergistic relationship of those conventions whether at the micro level of stylistic and rhetorical features or at the macro level of form and theme.

Thus, at the micro stylistic level, when Robert Burton, speaking in *The Anatomy of Melancholy* behind the mask of Democritus Junior, makes what may be the most complete disclaimer of careful craftsmanship in literary history, part of the point is to note the exploding grammar of his anacholuthon-riddled style:

> And for those other faults of barbarism, *Dorick* dialect, extemporanean style, tautologies, apish imitation, a rhapsody of rags gathered together from several dung-hills, excrements of authors, toys and fopperies confusedly tumbled out, without art, invention, judgement, wit, learning,

---

111. For an account of Mailer's many writings on film improvisation and his three improvised films, including one which included an unscripted but bloody fistfight between Rip Torn and Mailer, see Richard Brody, "Norman Mailer at the Movies," *The New Yorker*, October 30, 2013 (online at *https://www.newyorker.com/culture/richard-brody/norman-mailer-at-the-movies*).

112. Twain, *Adventures of Huckleberry Finn*, ed. Sculley Bradley, 9.

harsh, raw, rude, phantastical, absurd, insolent, indiscreet, ill-composed, indigested, vain, scurrile, idle, dull and dry, I confess all ('tis partly affected) thou canst not think worse of me than I do myself. 'Tis not worth the reading, I yield it, I desire thee not to lose time in perusing so vain a subject...I had not time to lick it into form, as [a Bear] doth her young ones, but even so to publish it, as it was first written, *quicquid in buccam venit* [whatever comes into the mouth], in an extemporean [*sic*] style, as I do commonly other exercises, *effudi quicquid dictavit genius meus* [effusions which my genius dictates], out of a confused company of notes, and writ with as small deliberation as I do ordinarily speak, without all affectation of big words, fustian phrases, jingling terms, tropes, strong lines, that like *Acestes'* arrows caught fire as they flew, strains of wit, brave heats, elogies [eulogies], hyperbolical exornations [embellishments], elegancies, &c. which so many affect. I am...a loose, plain, rude writer.[113]

Burton here epitomizes the rhetoric of spontaneity, writing that is "loose, plain, [and] rude." Claiming to write without thought and without art, Burton, like other improvisers, writes in a turbulent, libertine, associative style that thumbs its nose at accepted canons of beauty and craftsmanship. Pointedly indecorous, his prose lacks the sense of proportion of mainstream, classical kinds, here the Ciceronian period. Exemplifying improvisation's encyclopedic impulse, Burton layers catalog upon catalog: [layer 1:] "other faults of barbarism, *Dorick* dialect, extemporanean style, tautologies, apish imitation, a rhapsody of rags gathered together from [layer 2:] several dung-hills, excrements of authors, toys and fopperies confusedly tumbled out, without [layer 3:] art, invention, judgement, wit, learning, harsh, raw, rude, phantastical, absurd, insolent, indiscreet, ill-composed, indigested, vain, scurrile, idle, dull and dry."

Presenting himself as Democritus Jr., spiritual offspring of the Laughing Philosopher (for laughing at human follies), Burton exemplifies, too, the form's characteristic voice, characterized by foolishness, iconoclasm, and unconventionality. Often in the unmediated first person or in a dialogue unmediated by narrative intrusion, the metagenre's spokesman or "hero" is like Burton's an "antihero," a culturally marginal persona, someone out of the mainstream

---

113. Burton, *The Anatomy of Melancholy*, 24.

of society and power. The kind's form is formless or fragmented, or apparently so, or it is so claimed, as Burton does here ("I had not time to lick it into form...but even so to publish it...out of a confused company of notes"). This feature of apparent amorphousness has helped to obscure the existence of improvisation as a persistent aesthetic. Often in a form declaredly without precedent, improvisations are often a hybrid form (from *hibrida, hubris*— unnatural, lawless) raiding other kinds, and often standing in a parodic or burlesque relationship to them if they are ironic texts. In the serious vein, improvisations are not parodies but rather "renovations" of existing genres.

The genre Burton is renewing is of course the "anatomy." The fact that many of improvisation's conventions largely coincide with Northrop Frye's description of the anatomy form in his own *Anatomy of Criticism* helps underscore the persistence of the improv aesthetic. Frye's own *Anatomy* shares with improvisation many of these same conventions, and most importantly, the same urge to freedom and openness characteristic of the kind. Although overtly in favor of a *systematic* approach to literature, Frye's *Anatomy*, like other improvisations, is more deeply motivated by the incorporative impulse that Frank Lentricchia astutely describes: "The real desideratum of Northrop Frye's world is freedom, the shedding of all constraints, and the pecking order of the modes is structured according to the fullness of freedom each mode is thought to image forth."[114]

Burton's magnificent disclaimer packs into it hints of all of improvisation's stylistic and formal conventions. His encyclopedic text, about all the melancholies man has suffered, shares improvisation's dominant themes: iconoclasm, irrationalism, unmediated experience, and sympathy. Improvisation's practitioners flirt with or betray—and are often accused of—heretical tendencies like Gnosticism (experiential rather than doctrine-driven religion which reveals spirit or divinity in matter and in man's acts); Palladianism (the belief that Adam's fall was a happy fall leading to the present world and/or to the opportunity for Christ's redemption); and antinomianism (the challenge to systematic laws).

---

114. Frank Lentricchia, *After the New Criticism* (Chicago: The University of Chicago Press, 1981), 22.

6. *Improv Synergy II: Improvisation's Predictability in "Kubla Khan"*

Coleridge's "Kubla Khan" manages to exemplify just about every convention and theme in the improviser's bag of tricks. Exploring its unheralded connection to this unheralded form will exemplify how improvisations exploit the persistent conventions and themes I have adumbrated. Tracing how the poem works as an improvisation will help make my case for the unacknowledged life of this perennial form.

Like many improvisations, "Kubla Khan" establishes its spontaneous credentials even before the poem properly starts. Its title has three parts:

> Kubla Khan
> Or, A Vision in a Dream.
> A Fragment.

Its first subtitle sets the scene and genre—sort of. The poem is "A *Vision* in a Dream." Thus, it is *sui-generis,* shaped by a vision, an intrinsically idiosyncratic form. Are any two visions alike? Or, it is a throwback to an antiquated form—the medieval dream vision—that it is at best marginal, if not completely outside, and a challenge to, the canon of Coleridge's day. William Blake and later, Francis Thompson, will exploit the genre and be thought crazy. The Pre-Raphaelites, in part inspired by "Kubla Khan" and fueled by the Gothic or medieval movement, will gentrify the form and dream visions will run rampant through the century. But "Kubla Khan" is also "A Vision in a *Dream*," the product of the dark unconscious forces that the poem ambivalently celebrates. So conceived, a vision dreamt, it is not the result of mere craftsmanship.

The second subtitle confirms these generic signposts—sort of. The poem is all the more authentic (and improvised) because "A Fragment": his dream, we learn in the poem's prefatory note, is interrupted by an unexpected guest—which, as in many improvisations, we are asked by an overabundance of realistic details, to believe really happened. The fragment is again authentic because inspired by a mind-altering drug, in this case opium ("an anodyne had been prescribed"). The result is a poem—"all the images rose up before him as *things,* with a parallel production of the correspondent expressions, without any sensation or consciousness of effort"—that is, effortless and unmediated, a mere transcription of a dream—figural rather than verbal—and therefore, once more, authentic.

Meanwhile, Coleridge has it both ways on the genre front. It is authentic because *sui generis,* free of the constrictions of the poetic canon, but, like improvisations, it bears an uncomfortable relationship to a known genre. Although he does not identify it as an ode (as he did his conversation poem, "Dejection: An Ode"), "Kubla Khan" is widely agreed to have been shaped by the generic expectations of the tripartite Pindaric ode tradition, a genre identified with wild effusions and hence with the authenticity of sublime emotion. Famously deeply read, Coleridge is so erudite that he dreams in odes. As Ginsberg will often say, bucking the demands of formalist critics, "Mind is shapely, art is shapely." Coleridge writes an ode not with his eye on the generic expectations of ode, but, more authentically, because of his innate dialectical cast of mind. The poem is a veritable orgy of authentications.

And yet authenticity and the visionary imagination—the two values the poem overtly prizes—are issues the poem finally will ambivalently explore. For being authentic is not without its dangers. The poem describes Kubla Khan's "pleasure-dome," a pastoral place ("gardens bright"), perhaps originary and Edenic ("Alph, the sacred river, ran"). But therein lies a "savage place" where a "mighty fountain" seethes. At the heart of this unmediated vision of this man-made paradise lies a dark force:

> And from this chasm, with ceaseless turmoil seething,
> As if this earth in fast thick pants were breathing,
> A mighty fountain momently [every moment] was forced:
> Amid whose swift half-intermitted burst
> Huge fragments vaulted like rebounding hail,
> Or chaffy grain beneath the thresher's flail:
> And 'mid these dancing rocks at once and ever
> It flung up momently the sacred river.[115]

The force is uncontrollable. "A *savage* place!" it is "as holy and enchanted/As e'er beneath a waning moon was *haunted/By woman wailing for her demon-lover!*"[116] It comes of its own will and goes we know not where and without positive effect: it "sank in tumult to a lifeless ocean." Many readers identify

---

115. *The Oxford Anthology of English Literature,* 2: 256.
116. Emphasis added.

the tumultuous fountain with the visionary imagination, which Coleridge, it is thought, means to celebrate here as he does elsewhere, as in the *Biographia Literaria.* Of that literary life Byron spoofed, "Coleridge explains metaphysics to the nation./I wish he would explain his explanation"—but the elder poet's celebratory tone there is clear:

> The IMAGINATION, then, I consider either as primary, or secondary. The primary IMAGINATION I hold to be the living power and prime agent of all human perception, and as a repetition in the finite mind of the eternal act of creation in the infinite I AM. The secondary I consider as an echo of the former, co-existing with the conscious will, yet still as identical with the primary in the *kind* of its agency, and differing only in *degree,* and in the *mode* of its operation. It dissolves, diffuses, dissipates, in order to recreate; or where this process is rendered impossible, yet still, at all events, it struggles to idealize and to unify. It is essentially vital, even as all objects (as objects) are essentially fixed and dead.[117]

"Kubla Khan" in part supports the celebratory reading: the visionary persona inspired by the dream, having fed on "honey-dew/And drunk the milk of Paradise" and been inspired, reenacts this life force, writing the poem we read.

And yet again, there are things to make us uncomfortable, as many other readers note. The fountain's creative force is associated with violence: "'mid this tumult Kubla heard from far/Ancestral voices prophesying war." The pleasure-dome and the creative imagination that built it seem endangered and, perhaps soon to be a victim of war, fleeting. Like the improviser's persona, the visionary speaker of the poem is marginal, even dangerous to society exactly because he is an inspired visionary:

> And all [who heard him] should cry, Beware! Beware!
> His flashing eyes, his floating hair!
> Weave a circle round him thrice,
> And close your eyes with holy dread,
> For he on honey-dew hath fed,
> And drunk the milk of Paradise.

---

117. Samuel Taylor Coleridge, *Biographia Literaria, or Biographical Sketches of My Literary Life and Opinions,* edited by J. Shawcross, 2 vols. (Oxford: Oxford University Press, 1907), 1: 202; emphasis in original.

Having been enlarged by his unmediated experience of the vision, the poet within the poem would, though ostracized, improve society by recreating the pleasure-dome. But clearly, vision and the imagination has its dangers.

Still worse, this authentic, dream-inspired, originary effusion that, if heard, would bring on ostracism and yet would renew society is, we finally learn, actually one full step short of unmediated. Like most improvisers, Coleridge takes one step back from an apocalyptic face-to-face with unmediated vision. He still sees through a glass darkly, for the vision doesn't even exist: even though we have just witnessed it, it suddenly has a new reality, or non-reality. The vision of the pleasure dome is posited again: "It was a miracle of rare device,/A sunny pleasure-dome with caves of ice!" But just as quickly we learn that the reality of the vision is contingent, still conditionally awaiting inspiration:

> A damsel with a dulcimer
>   In a vision once I saw:
> It was an Abyssinian maid,
> And on her dulcimer she played,
> Singing of Mount Abora.
> Could I revive within me
> Her symphony and song,
> To such a deep delight 'twould win me,
> That with music loud and long,
> I would build that dome in air,
> That sunny dome! those caves of ice![118]

Either the pleasure dome has indeed been fleeting and needs to be rebuilt, or the poet's vision of it was an airy nothing. Like a dream, it's there, and then it's not. Echoing the angelic "holy song" in Milton's "Nativity Ode" where the elder poet offers a similar contingent hypothesis ("For if such holy Song/Enwrap our fancy long"), Coleridge longs to recapture the dream, the inspiration, the vision—even though one fears it too. There's Coleridge's literary life in a nutshell: longing for a return of inspiration but fearing it.

Coleridge, the great celebrator of the creative imagination, "a repetition in the finite mind of the eternal act of creation of the infinite I AM," is also

---

118. Emphasis added..

aware of its dark side and its contingent nature. His deepest explorations of the problematic value of the creative imagination are performed in improvisations, "Kubla Khan" and "Dejection: An Ode." The creative imagination has the power to enlarge our humanness, *if* it exists, *if* it can be recaptured, and *at what cost?*

Reading "Kubla Khan" as an improvisation does not take us to a brand new reading of the poem or its poet. Coleridge's and the poem's ambivalence to the visionary imagination is familiar territory. What is new here is a deeper reading of how its form, style, and theme deeply cohere in expressing that ambivalence. Pure *lagniappe,* as we say in New Orleans, the something extra, is the perception that in his ambivalence Coleridge participates in an old and deeply human predicament. Seeing the poem as participating in this long line of improvisers increases our sense of the poignancy of the poem—and of the poet's state of mind. Writing in loneliness about longing for a vision that he imagines would complete him, Coleridge also imagines that if he were to succeed in attaining that vision, it would make him lonelier—"weave a circle round him thrice." And yet in articulating the longing for unmediated vision, Coleridge in fact joins a long line of improvisers with a similar ambivalence. Improvisation still awaits its Einstein fully to grasp its complex laws, and yet what I have laid out in this chapter about the conventions and the dynamics of improvisation seems to offer in some measure the power to predict, that key ambition of the scientific method. Once you have detected the claim of unmediated spontaneity, if the synergy among the thematic and formal conventions is there, then many of the other conventions and themes seem to fall into place. Before improvisations are done, these apparent celebrations of the unmediated will ask hard questions about immediacy: Is it possible? How can I get some? Do I really want any? But having asked those questions, the improvisation has redefined or enlarged what it means to be a rich and full human being, less constricted by normal modes of rationality. Like the shapely self-ordering forms that chaos science has discovered by looking at the world with a new form of rationality, a new way of measuring and perceiving reality, once seen by means of the anatomy I have offered, this unconventional, protean literature of chaos seems conventional, orderly, and shapely.

Wallace Stevens's Zen-koan-like lines help define the kind of order improvisers offer:

A. A violent order is disorder; and
B. A great disorder is an order. These
Two things are one.[119]

Improvisers claim that the received order, leaving too much out of its purview, is mere disorder. As Kenneth Burke calls to our attention, "A way of seeing involves a way of not seeing."[120] The violence of the old order, the way that it forcefully excludes and forcefully will have its way and no other, confirms and worsens that disorder. The improvisers' loving, inclusive disorder is the new, higher order they offer us.

7. *Improv Synergy III:* The Great Gatsby

The Great Gatsby exhibits in a surprising degree many of these formal conventions and thematic features and serves to demonstrate their synergistic relationship.

In what seems at first a throwaway moment in *The Great Gatsby,* Fitzgerald tellingly conflates jazz's improvisational quality with its kinetic power and encyclopedic impulse:

> "Ladies and gentlemen," [the conductor] cried. At the request of Mr.
> Gatsby we are going to play for you Mr. Vladimir Tostoff's latest work,
> which attracted so much attention at Carnegie Hall last May. If you
> read the papers, you know there was a big sensation." He smiled with
> jovial condescension, and added: "Some sensation!" Whereupon every-
> body laughed.
>   "The piece is known," he concluded lustily, "as Vladimir Tostoff's Jazz
> History of the World..."[121]

The passage is rife with subtle jokes. The composer's mock-Russian name plays upon jazz's trope of careless spontaneity: Tostoff = "tossed off." His "jovial condescension" is directed at the absurdity of the idea that a Carn-

---

119. "Connoisseur of Chaos," Stevens, *Collected Poetry and Prose,* 194.

120. Kenneth Burke, *Permanence and Change: An Anatomy of Purpose* (Los Altos, California: Hermes, 1954), 49.

121. F. Scott Fitzgerald, *The Great Gatsby* (New York: Charles Scribner's Sons, 1925), 3.

egie Hall, uptown audience could respond with enthusiasm, let alone the appropriate "sensation." Stuffed shirts, they have no sensuality at all: "Some sensation!" By contrast, the young ladies of the Jazz Age respond on Gatsby's suburban lawn just as the music would have them respond: with a careless, libertine sensuousness, an openness to experience equal to the music's own. The narrator continues: "When the Jazz History of the World was over, girls were putting their heads on men's shoulders in a puppyish, convivial way, girls were swooning backward playfully into men's arms, even into groups, knowing that someone would arrest their falls..."[122] An odd response to a "History of" anything, it is kinetic and empathic. Like the Romantics' Eolian Harp, they take on the spirit of the vibrations that pass through them. Most telling, they respond as if they could, like the music, sum up human history in their dance. Their summation lies in their gesture: a willingness to fall, "swooning backward playfully into men's arms...knowing that someone would arrest their falls." Such is the Jazz Age's carefree version of the notion of *felix culpa,* not that it is happy that we fell, but that it can't or won't hurt, so why not? Certainly the taste of *that* apple—the experience of *this* world—is worth a go. Pagans though they be, Fitzgerald's Jazz Age dancers act as if the Christian promise of first and last things, our delivery into God's merciful hands, is fulfilled. They act as if, giving themselves up, they will not be taken advantage of, as if in the political and musical democracy that America represents, the disenfranchised are not exploited. But of course they are wrong: the novel explodes with demonstrations that, in fact, "speckl'd vanity" and "leprous sin" still thrive (as in the Valley of Ashes) and Hell's (and East Egg's) "dolorous mansions" remain intact and closed.

Thus, though a minor character who does not reappear, the conductor is sympathetic and something of a moral conveyor. We feel he has, in his good-humored way, the right to mock the stuffed shirts of Carnegie Hall and even mockingly to manipulate the sensuous crowds on the lawn. Even so, the carelessness he so values is highly and centrally problematic in the novel as a whole. In *The Great Gatsby,* spontaneity is not only careless. It is also feckless. It does harm. As usual, the text's invocation of spontaneity leads us directly to the heart of the matter. Nick says, "They were careless people, Tom and

---

122. Ibid., 33.

Daisy—they smashed up things and creatures and then retreated back into their money or their vast carelessness, or whatever it was that kept them together, and let other people clean up the mess they had made."[123]

Jay Gatsby, though he strives for the requisite high-toned *sprezzatura* of East Egg, is finally anything but "careless," and he alone is in the end "exempt from [Nick Carraway's] reaction."[124] Gatsby's every act—from silk shirts to mansions in West Egg—is calculated toward a single end, winning Daisy. Even his requesting the jazz piece—if that is not one of the conductor's jokes, for Gatsby seems to have a deaf ear for music—is another of his calculated efforts to "fit in" to a world in which he has no place: if this is what is popular now, this is how I will attract the drones that will eventually attract my queen bee. The queen bee and her entourage are of course a brilliant study in a carelessness that at first enchants but inevitably leads to disaster.

For, of course, what Nick learns from experiencing these people is the real lyric heart of the book, and his name's symbolic overtones suggest the centrality of the issue of care and carelessness to him and to the novel. Much of the novel involves Nick Carraway's attempt, exhausted by the war, to do "away" with "cares" by being "carried away" by the Jazz Age. The "lesson" he learns is that we cannot do away with our cares, and that those who seem to, do so at their own moral peril. He learns that the allure of carelessness to the earnest, like Jay Gatsby and himself, is veritably Satanic. The "casual," moneyed East is attractive because in "the West...an evening was hurried from phase to phase toward its close, in a continually disappointed anticipation or in sheer nervous dread of the moment itself."[125] Fitzgerald's careless Easterners share with the improviser the ability to embrace the moment. They fulfill Walter Pater's injunction "to burn always with a hard gemlike flame." The novel asks the question: which way of life is finally more open to what Nick in his breathy, exhausted voice calls "the inexhaustible variety of life"?[126] After the central action of the novel, Nick returns to his staid Midwestern roots. Perhaps he overreacts, but the nature of his choice is clear: "I wanted

---

123. Ibid., 153.
124. Ibid., 1.
125. Ibid., 9.
126. Ibid., 24.

the world to be in uniform and at a sort of moral attention forever."[127] "In uniform" and "at...attention" hint that he prefers the chaos of warfare to the moral corruption of the carefree but hollow harmonies of the home front. At least in war comrades take care of one another.

Nick's name, presumably Nicholas, means *victory of the people* (*nike* + *laus*), ironic insofar as it points back to the war that we may have won but clearly at great public and personal cost. Though suffused with Fitzgerald's masterful craftsmanship, the novel is Nick's narrative, and he seems to tell it like the Ancient Mariner out of a deep compulsion to be heard. His voice has the intimacy and free-flowing grace of the improviser. But he speaks to us from the other side of the novel's debacle, and the easy flow is chastened, cautious, precise—the voice of a man who has stayed too long on spontaneity's dark side. In the end Nick learns also that Gatsby's yearning for the innocent green light on the dock is as ennobling as it is wrongheaded. While it signifies his naïve striving to emulate an innocence that is all pretend, even so it is a striving. We are all fallen, our innocence gone; even so we must strive to regain our innocence, hoping that what we achieve, if we achieve anything, is not some mockery of the term, but rather a Blakean "higher innocence." This for Carraway is what Gatsby achieves, expressed by his "extraordinary gift for hope, a romantic readiness." Thus for Fitzgerald we have all fallen, we all live west of Eden in our version of West Egg. We must strive to regain Paradise but can only hope that when we get there we find the solid rock of Jerusalem, not the false fronts of East Egg (or Hollywood). Accent on *strive*: "boats against the current," we won't get there carelessly.

Jazz offers a momentary exception. As a prophetic and apocalyptic improvised art, jazz can bring Eden back momentarily and individually, but no longer can it cleanse an entire society. Jerusalem weeps. Like the Romantics before him, prophet of the Jazz Age Fitzgerald longs for the revolution that will renew society but settles for an interior, personal apocalypse. His Wordsworth's "Paradise, and groves/Elysian, Fortunate Fields" are available even to a Jay Gatsby; but there is finally nothing simple and nothing common about them. The democracy that America promised and that Jazz invokes is individually accessible but mocked by the powers that be, the well-heeled but

---

127. Ibid., 1.

spiritually sleazy inhabitants of East Egg. Filled with paradox, the novel celebrates in Nick's measured voice the craftsmanly improvisations of the Jazz Age's musicians and condemns the slapdash and empty imitations that piggyback on their loose-limbed brilliance.

Perhaps the reader is not as smitten with my reading of *The Great Gatsby* as I, but personally I find it striking that a text that I have known virtually all my reading life should yield up so much when seen through the lens of spontaneity and improvisation. Taking spontaneity as my "god-term," as Kenneth Burke would say, I find the novel saturated in the terms that usually litter improvisation's conceptual field: care, carelessness, craft, the improvisation of jazz.

I have a memory of my first reading of *Gatsby* that has accumulated some ironies with the years. When in high school I first read the novel, I remember sitting at the kitchen table and remarking to my mother, "Listen to this last sentence. Fitzgerald must have rewritten it a hundred times: 'So we beat on, boats against the current, borne back ceaselessly into the past.'" She listened and replied, "Oh, he probably just tossed it off."

My mother was a life-long reader too but never one to give a book a second thought. She was at the time a budding businesswoman. She had bought Chris Steak House in New Orleans a few years before which she would build into an empire deploying her incredible analytic skills and her keen intuition: Ruth's Chris Steak House. She was a math-science wiz, but her quick judgment could have made a chapter in Malcolm Gladwell's *Blink*.

The moment was something of a nascent turning point in my life as a reader. It was pointless to argue—it was always pointless with her—but I silently stood by my guns: the sentence had been carefully crafted. It began to dawn on me at that moment, if unconsciously, that there was something about me and reading that I needed to pay attention to. In graduate school it would be confirmed that the sentence was prized, one of the dazzlers of American literature. But what interests me is not one-upping my mother, who has now passed, but rather to savor the delicious ironies that come cascading down the years.

There is of course the irony that my mother, a hard worker like no other, knew for sure it was just "tossed off" (like Fitzgerald's composer perhaps). And I, I would spend thirty years fascinated with spontaneity and working hard to prove that those who seem to toss things off work very hard to give the appearance of having done so.

Then there are the ironies of the sentence itself, the suggestions that however much we long to live in the present, the past stays with us and we must *"beat on...against the current."* The past, like the present east of Eden, demands of us care, craft, and hard work.

As Stevens has it, "Through candor...a candid kind." What genre is untouched by the gesture of spontaneity? The epic is inspired by the muses and improvised by the bard. The foundational epics of our culture, the *Iliad* and the *Odyssey,* are the one about a warrior of immense skill who loses control, and the other about an adventurer who improvises with great craft *and* great carelessness. The lyric is "the spontaneous overflow of powerful feelings...from emotion recollected in tranquility."[128] Pastoral records the simple pleadings of simple shepherds, Corydon to Philomela, whom we overhear. That Pastoral is among the most obviously artificial of genres, invented by Theocritus, the sophisticated librarian of Alexandria, does not gainsay my point. All of these genres and more—epideictic oration, essay, Menippean satire, novel—seem to have at their heart an expressive tension between art and artlessness, reason and unreason, determinism and freedom.

---

128. Wordsworth and Coleridge, *Lyrical Ballads*, 173.

CHAPTER FOUR

"Perceiving the Idea of This Invention":
Spontaneity in Literary and Intellectual History

> Begin, ephebe, by perceiving the idea
> Of this invention, this invented world,
> The inconceivable idea of the sun.
> You must become an ignorant man again
> And see the sun again with an ignorant eye
> And see it clearly in the idea of it.
> —Wallace Stevens, "Notes Toward a Supreme Fiction"

I mprovisations are, then, of a piece for a reason. Improvisations claim by design to be in some way without design. Unshaped by human reason or craft, they transcend what mere craft or reason could achieve. But improvisations in their deep structure often finally call such transcendence in question. Positing a state of mind where to will *is* to create, but rarely in the end certain if such a state can or should be achieved, improvisation is perfectly fitted by its persistent figures, conventions, and themes to explore the boundaries of human will, reason, and freedom. At work in such texts is a kind of primitivist or naturalistic argument—an argument from nature—that relies on the equation of the natural and spontaneous with the authentic and true. There is, we must agree, something fundamentally true about man's nature in the equation. As A.C. Graham points out in his excellent study, *Reason and Spontaneity*:

> There are activities in which [man] is most intelligent when he is most spontaneous, in which to think may even be dangerous; the ski jumper or the tightrope walker cannot afford to hesitate and reflect. While still learning to swim or drive a car or speak a foreign language, he does have to think what to do next, but it is when he comes to trust his own reflexes that he will have mastered the skill.[1]

---

1. Graham, *Reason and Spontaneity*, 8.

Furthermore, even a quick glance at the history of modern psychology suggests that spontaneity holds important clues about the self and self-development. For Freud the process of free-association is the foundation of his talking cure, a clue to the source of our neuroses. For Piaget spontaneous play has a crucial role in the dynamic movement between developmental stages.[2] And for developmental psychologists such as Abraham Maslow, spontaneity is characteristic of peak experiences and the upper reaches of human development, moments of Being rather than Becoming, which appear to achieve what Kant called "purposefulness without purpose (*Zweckmässigkeit ohne Zweck*)" or Schopenhauer, "willed will-lessness."[3]

Such yearnings now permeate pop culture. University of Chicago psychologist Mihaly Csikszentmihalyi's bestselling books on "flow" have brought analyses of this kind of "optimal experience," as he calls it, to the attention of a wide audience.[4] Malcolm Gladwell teaches us how to deploy our "adaptive unconscious" in the *blink* of an eye.[5] Jonah Lehrer urges us to solve complex problems using "the processing powers of the emotional brain, the supercomputer of the mind."[6] Nobel laureate Daniel Kahneman, in work that underpins Gladwell's and Lehrer's more pop versions, describes the strengths and the many biases that weaken both the intuitive brain and the logical, deliberative

2. Jean Piaget, *Play, Dreams, and Imitation in Childhood* (New York: W.W. Norton, 1962).

3. Abraham Maslow, *Toward a Psychology of Being* (Princeton, N.J.: Van Nostrand, 1968); also see Jane Loevinger and Augusto Blasi's *Ego Development* (San Francisco: Jossey-Bass, 1977) who find spontaneity to characterize the sixth and final stage of human development, a stage peopled by the likes of Jesus, Buddha, and Gandhi; Immanuel Kant, *Critique of Judgment,* translated by J.H. Bernard (New York: Hafner Press, 1951), 55; Arthur Schopenhauer, *World as Will and Representation,* translated by Judith Norman and Alistair Welchman; edited by Christopher Janaway (Cambridge: Cambridge University Press, 2010).

4. See Mihaly Csikszentmihalyi, *Flow: The Psychology of Optimal Experience* (New York: Harper & Row, 1990) and *Creativity: Flow and the Psychology of Discovery and Invention* (New York: HarperCollins, 1996).

5. Malcolm Gladwell, *Blink: The Power of Thinking without Thinking* (New York: Little, Brown and Company, 2005).

6. Jonah Lehrer, *How We Decide* (New York: Houghton Mifflin, 2009), 238.

brain.[7] Drama coach Keith Johnstone gives us lessons in "impro." Improvisation is offered as the key to Christian ethics (*Improvisation: The Drama of
Christian Ethics* by Samuel Wells) and to business organizations (*Organizational Improvisation* by Ken N. Kamoche). In these many fields, improvisation
is, as composer Alec Wilder puts it, "the lightning mystery…*the* creative mystery of our age."[8] In a sense, improvisers throughout the centuries anticipate
these peak experiences, offering representations of what D. H. Lawrence calls
"Man Thinking": "the direct utterance of the instant, whole man."[9]

This quick survey of modern psychological and popular thought, obviously
inadequate, helps me to acknowledge the value of achieved spontaneity in life
and in the arts. I am arguing, however, for the need here to bracket spontane-
ity-in-the-world, whose value must remain, in a sense, unquestioned. Doing
so will help us to discuss on the one hand the rhetoric of spontaneity, on the
other the poet's thematic treatment of spontaneity—both of which are deeply
problematical.

My scare quotes, then, do not extend from the question of spontaneous
composition to the value of spontaneity itself. For decades I've used the
example of the moment of insight in the shower. *What makes such moments
so authoritative?* I've skeptically asked. Yet, trying to learn where in the brain
flashes of insight occur and under what conditions, Mark Jung-Beeman, a cognitive neuroscientist at Northwestern, has determined that "if you want to
encourage insights, then you've got to encourage people to relax." He explains:
"The relaxation phase is critical…That's why so many insights happen during
warm showers."[10] *Gestalt* psychologist Wolfgang Köhler adds: "After periods
during which one has actively tried to solve a problem," solutions "tend to
occur at moments of extreme mental passivity…A well-known physicist in
Scotland once told me that this kind of thing is generally recognized by physi-
cists in Britain. 'We often talk about the three B's,' he said, "the Bus, the Bath,

---

7. Daniel Kahneman, *Thinking, Fast and Slow* (New York: Farrar Straus and Giroux,
2011).

8. Quoted in Whitney Balliett, *Improvising: Sixteen Musicians and Their Art* (New
York: Oxford University Press, 1977), vi.

9. "Poetry of the Present," in *D. H. Lawrence: The Complete Poems*, 184.

10. Quoted in Jonah Lehrer, "The Eureka Hunt," *The New Yorker* (28 July 2008): 43.

and the Bed. That's where the great discoveries are made in our science."[11] Archimedes set the pattern when he had his *Eureka!* moment in the tub. So much for my skepticism.

And yet, while many instances of spontaneous experience may be of the highest value, all spontaneous behavior need not be so. There is much to be skeptical of—the modern horrors done in the name of intuition and instinct and the heart. Malcolm Gladwell wants to teach us how to deploy the "thin slicing" of "the adaptive unconscious" to tap the resources of our unconscious mind."[12] He is also equally concerned to convey thin slicing's dangers, the split-second decisions of four police officers in the Bronx that make them dead certain that Amadou Diallo was proffering a gun rather than his wallet, and that made Amadou Diallo dead from forty-one rounds. Though we may lend to spontaneity a certain sanctity, spontaneity is no proof against hellish results.

Nor can we ignore that there is something fundamentally false in the pat equation of the natural and spontaneous with the veracious and true. Let us remember what the great Oxford critic, novelist, and Christian apologist C. S. Lewis said of such "naturalistic" talk, that it was "a scandal of philosophy."[13] Indeed the thrust of much of post-Cartesian philosophy is to show that spontaneous immediacy is impossible. Thus, it is surprising that literary criticism—so influenced by philosophy of late—has so seldom calmly examined literature's innumerable claims of spontaneity. For Descartes the originary act is the *cogito*: by definition no experience—and no being—can antecede the moment of self-awareness. For Kant, spontaneity, the ability to act according to one's own self-determination, is the key to transcendent freedom. But for Kant it is also true that the unmediated experience of the world that spontaneity promises is impossible: "Perceptions without concepts are blind." The *Ding an sich* (thing-in-itself) can never be experienced because the world is always mediated by innate categories of mind: time and space. For Hegel

---

11. Wolfgang Köhler, "The Task of Gestalt Psychology," quoted in Stephen Nachmanovitch, *Free Play: The Power of Improvisation in Life and Art* (New York: Penguin Putnam, 1990), 152.

12. Gladwell, *Blink,* 14 and passim.

13. C. S. Lewis, *Studies in Words,* 2nd ed. (London: Cambridge University Press, 1967), 46.

the goal of life is to overcome immediacy, to process it with the Will. The unmediated in Hegel's system is lifeless and without value because it does not *participate* in the realization of the world's goal, Historical Consciousness. To Hegel, for example, Africa "is no historical part of the World; it has no move-ment or development to exhibit...What we properly understand by Africa, is the Unhistorical, Undeveloped Spirit, still involved in the conditions of mere nature..."[14] Here we meet with not only political incorrectness but also an irony of cultural history that offers an intriguing window into the intellectual history of spontaneity. For this culture that Hegel distains with such hauteur becomes in the twentieth century not only a major influence on High Mod-ernism, but also the fountainhead of that art, jazz, which by embracing its "Unhistorical, Undeveloped Spirit" and its involvement "in the conditions of mere nature" takes the *art* of immediacy to new heights.

Phenomenology, which Hegel helped to inspire, is by contrast about the fundamental importance of a pre-reflective *cogito*—a kind of *precogito*—that informs our experience of phenomena. At the same time, however, phenom-enology teaches that all perception is intentional—shaped by the human eye, what Gombrich of the Constance School calls "The Beholder's Share."[15] In Ricoeur's hermeneutic phenomenology, for example, perception always comes through the structure of consciousness; we constitute every object in the act of consciousness intentionally directed toward it. Ricoeur nostalgi-cally laments the union of thought and deed that athletes and dancers embody (that we saw Graham celebrate above), their *"gracious* freedom whose bodily spontaneity [is] allied with the initiative which moves it without resistance."[16] Admitting his longing for such "incarnate freedom," Ricoeur ultimately throws his considerable philosophic weight behind celebrating rather "a free-dom which is human and *not* divine,...a freedom which does not posit itself absolutely, because it is not Transcendence. To will," he concedes in the mov-

---

14. Quoted in Lewis Hyde, *Trickster Makes This World,* 229.

15. See E.H. Gombrich, "Evidence of Images," in *Interpretation : Theory and Prac-tice,* edited by Charles S. Singleton (Baltimore: John Hopkins University Press, 1969), 43; and *Art and Illusion: A Study in the Psychology of Pictorial Representation,* 2nd ed. (Princeton, N.J.: Princeton University Press, 1961), 208–11.

16. Paul Ricoeur, *Freedom and Nature: The Voluntary and the Involuntary,* translated by Erazim V. Kohák (Evanston, Ill.: Northwestern University Press, 1966), 485.

ing final words of his lengthy and weighty tome, "is not to create."[17] Thus, for Ricoeur, despite our longing for immediacy, we can recover an approximation of this lost immediacy only through the act of interpretation: "For the second immediacy that we seek and the second naïveté that we await are no longer accessible to us anywhere else than in a hermeneutics; we can believe only by interpreting."[18] Such interpretation, however, is clearly an act of will, and the approximation only that. Ricoeur here seems to dodge at the last minute his "longing for Paradise," which as Milan Kundera points out "is man's longing not to be man."[19] It is an exquisitely humanistic moment where Ricoeur simultaneously embraces man's longing for transcendence and its impossibility.[20] Like his countryman Camus would have Sisyphus do, Ricoeur seems to manage to smile as he accepts the absurdity of his longing.

Finally, for Derrida, "toujours déjà": there is always something before, something that antecedes the apparently originary, spontaneous act. Appealing to the authority of Freud, he writes: "That the present in general is not primal but reconstituted, that it is not the absolute wholly living form which constitutes experience, that there is no purity of the living present, such is the theme, formidable for metaphysics, which Freud in a conceptual scheme unequal to the thing itself, would have us pursue."[21] The extensive links between Derrida's project of deconstruction and the aesthetic form improvisation will be discussed in Chapter 6. Meanwhile, this quick survey suggests that claims for the special veracity of spontaneity cannot stand up to the close scrutiny of serious philosophy. Yet, in another sense, what philosophy teaches us is that improvisers, in their quest to draw a bead on

---

17. Ibid., 486. Ricoeur's emphases throughout.

18. Paul Ricoeur, *The Symbolism of Evil,* translated by Emerson Buchanan (New York: Harper and Row, 1967), 352.

19. Milan Kundera, *The Unbearable Lightness of Being* (New York: Harper and Row, 1987 [1984]), 296.

20. Note that Ricoeur's gesture in effect invokes Hermes who rules hermeneutics and, as we shall see in Chapter 6, improvisation. In the Homeric "Hymn to Hermes" the messenger of the gods, like Ricoeur, expresses the same longing for transcendence and acknowledges its impossibility.

21. Jacques Derrida, *Writing and Difference,* translated by Alan Bass (Chicago: The University of Chicago Press, 1978), 212.

self-transcendent experience, are trying to say the unsayable. For, one way or another, such peak experiences—St. Teresa's ecstasy or the phenomenologist's *precogito*—are beyond, or before, words. In so doing, improvisers perform what Wittgenstein, who taught us to be silent before the unsayable, considered "reconnaissance expeditions," dangerous but sometimes a source of knowledge (*connaissance*) we cannot do without.[22] The philosophical paradox of improvisations is that, while affecting to embody spontaneous immediacy, most improvisations are about its impossibility. Improvisers embody Zeno's paradox of the tortoise and the hare: coming by half-measures ever closer to the overt goal of unmediated experience, they never arrive, and most know it. Largely a reaction to systematic and positivistic rationality, such a pursuit meanwhile reaches its covert, and far more cautious, objective: to expose the limits of rationality and to extend them by whatever means available.

Nietzsche's attack on reason and his celebration of the Dionysian spirit perhaps go furthest amongst modern philosophers in trying to surmount the paradox. In *The Birth of Tragedy* his embrace of undifferentiated instinctual impulse, of the "Dionysian flood and excess" and his contempt for Apollonian reason seem complete.[23] Thomas Mann objected to Nietzsche's "complete, we must assume,...deliberate, misperception of the power relationship between instinct and intellect," his "corybantic overestimation" of the instinctual, and his irresponsibility in not recognizing the necessity of fostering "the weak little flame of reason, of spirit, of justice" in the modern world.[24] And yet perhaps Mann's reading of Nietzsche is wrong. As Lilian Feder has argued, Nietzsche's vision of the Dionysian includes an element of Apollonian control: "In fact, his very recreation of Dionysiac ritual describes a control of impulses by releasing them symbolically into consciousness. The very words, dance, and music of ritual observance channel instinctual aims into harmo-

---

22. Quoted in Lawrence Weschler, *Seeing is Forgetting the Name of the Thing One Sees: A Life of Contemporary Artist Robert Irwin* (Berkeley and Los Angeles: University of California Press, 1982), 118.

23. Friedrich Nietzsche, *The Birth of Tragedy* and *The Genealogy of Morals,* translated by Francis Golffing (Garden City, N.Y.: Doubleday, 1956), 129.

24. *Thomas Mann's Addresses Delivered at the Library of Congress, 1942-1949* (Rockville, Maryland: Wildside Press, 2008), 88.

nious social rather than highly individual and anarchic expression."[25] Even with Nietzsche, to summon again Stephen Greenblatt's remark, "We cannot locate a point of pure premeditation or pure randomness."

John Stuart Mill's attack on the rhetoric of spontaneity in "Nature," an essay written about the time of and published posthumously two years after *The Birth of Tragedy*, is here instructive, helping to draw a finer bead on the rhetoric of spontaneity by describing its polar opposite, the rhetoric of craft. Made, he reports in the *Autobiography*, a "mere reasoning machine" by Jeremy Bentham, and saved from depression by Wordsworth's lyrics, Mill in *On Liberty* hailed spontaneity as a better agent of the greatest good than Utilitarianism's quantitative rationality. Nonetheless, at the end of his life, Mill attacked the authenticating function of "spontaneity," condemning,

> the vein of sentiment so common in the modern world (though unknown to the philosophic ancients) which exalts instinct at the expense of reason; an aberration rendered still more mischievous by the opinion commonly held in conjunction with it, that every, or amost every feeling or impulse which acts promptly without waiting to ask questions, is an instinct. Thus almost every variety of unreflecting and uncalculating impulse receives a kind of consecration.[26]

Mill's appeal to the authority of the ancients, arguing that the naturalistic argument was "unknown to the philosophic ancients," is itself specious. Intellectual historians have traced the classical roots of the primitivist and naturalist line of thinking, a line of thinking exploited of course by our improvisers.[27] Even so, Mill perfectly captures the imperfect reasoning behind the frame of mind that consecrates the impulsive and spontaneous:

> This reasoning, followed out consistently, would lead to the conclusion that the Deity intended, and approves, whatever human beings do; since all that they do being the consequence of some of the impulses with which

25. Feder, *Madness in Literature*, 209.

26. "Three Essays on Religion: Nature," in *The Collected Works of John Stuart Mill*, vol. 10: *Essays on Ethics, Religion, and Society*, edited by J.M. Robson (Toronto: University of Toronto Press and Routledge & Kegan Paul, 1969 [1833]), 392.

27. See Arthur O. Lovejoy and George Boas, *Primitivism and Related Ideas in Antiquity* (New York: Octagon Books, 1965 [1935]).

their Creator must have endowed them, all must equally be considered as done in obedience to his will...[But] since what is done with deliberation seems more the man's own act, and he is held more completely responsible for it than for what he does from sudden impulse, the considerate part of human conduct is apt to be set down as man's share in the business, and the inconsiderate as God's.[28]

Mill pinpoints the distrust of reason and deliberation ("the considerate part of human conduct") as well as the Gnosticism implicit in the celebration of "spontaneous" behavior: inspired perhaps by immanent deity, "spontaneity" sanctifies any and all individual acts. Mill thus foresees the notion's inherent potential for self-serving and self-righteous absolutism, of a world beset by sectarian and individualist, indeed solipsist, confusion: who is to judge anyone's spontaneity or where it leads? Almost reeling back into a Benthamite, Mill sums up his position emphatically: "the ways of Nature are to be conquered, not obeyed."[29]

Mill helps clarify what is implicit in claims of spontaneity, that at bottom they are arguments from nature. Clearly my father's primitivist longing to embrace bovine simplicity is a far cry from such complex and sophisticated arguments as those that Mill attacks. Nonetheless the impulses are of a kind, all expressive, in Kundera's words, of "a longing not to be a man." It is important to place the everyday primitivism on the same continuum with philosophical primitivism so that we can understand just how widespread is this human longing and the rhetorical figure that often expresses it. The fundamental idea is that we can get to truth or to a better life not by employing the higher orders of human effort but rather by the lower orders, by our instinctual or animal natures, or by no employment at all. This is what Mill attacks, and with some reason.

"Reason" is of course the crucial term. For the point is also to recognize that Mill not only appeals to but also embodies a contrary rhetoric or manner of persuasion, which cognitive neuroscientist Iain McGilchrist calls "the rhetoric of reason" which "[m]ost people are completely and unreflectively

---

28. Mill, "Three Essays on Religion: Nature," 392.
29. Ibid., 381.

seduced by."[30] For instrumental in his attack upon naturalism is his tacit presentation of a more attractive vision and mode of discourse. In a manner exactly contrary to that displayed by Montaigne in the *Essays* (or by us when we approach our boss fresh from the shower), Mill's opposite rhetoric is implicit in his densely-reasoned, hard-nosed style. "How," he seems to be saying, "could you be of that party when being of my party means thinking as clearly, carefully, and rationally as this?" "Let us reason this out," he invites, and no sooner have we heard the invitation that we have accepted: merely reading his difficult, cautious, painstaking prose, laden with what Coleridge called the "hooks and eyes" of logical connection ("Thus...since...Since"), makes us of his party. Mill's prose is an initiation in rationality and in civilization, at least in party name. For what matters to Mill as he carries his argument forward is that we agree to join him against the "irrational" opposition. Hence the ill-founded but nonetheless effective allusion to the ancients: they, he claims, the foundation of our civilization, knew better. So should we.

Thus, like those he opposes, Mill plays emotional, rhetorical cards. The crucial difference is that where Mill works hard to keep the emotional aspects of his prose unnoticed, improvisers highlight the passionate, sometimes irrational nature of their work. Of the two, it may be said, Mill's rhetoric of rationality has the stronger appeal to common sense, which is a nice sense to have on your side, rhetorically speaking. But by appealing to our *uncommon* senses—the unconscious, the irrational, the divine in us or inspiring us—the rhetoric of spontaneity gets its own game started. Where Mill appeals to us by means of the clarity and dignity of his well-wrought prose, improvisers claim to say and think whatever comes to mind, and invite us like them to be careless, impulsive, and to indulge our instinctual natures, to embrace the undignified—a drinker speaking to "Buveurs très illustres, et vous vérolés très précieux." Where Mill invites at every point the mediation of the mind at work, Nietzsche (in legend a *vérolé* or syphilitic himself) begins on the contrary note, insisting that direct apprehension, not intellectual perception, is the goal: "Much will have been gained for esthetics once we have succeeded

---

30. Iain McGilchrist, *The Divided Brain and the Search for Meaning: Why Are We So Unhappy?* (New Haven: Yale University Press, 2012), Kindle edition, loc. 373.

in apprehending directly—rather than merely *ascertaining*—that art owes its continuous evolution to the Apollonian-Dionysiac duality."[31] By emphatically denigrating "ascertaining," Nietzsche overthrows rationality in favor of the experiential and phenomenological: I don't need to *know* this duality but to *experience* it ("apprehending"—from *prehendere* "to seize"—apparently not with the mind, or perhaps not only with the mind). Where Mill's rhetoric of care and craft relies on an overt patina of rationality, the improviser exploits a contrary rhetoric based on a patina of irrationality (or the like). Claiming to write without thought and without art and "proving" it in the turbulent, often formless, fragmented, and ungrammatical texture of his prose, and masked in a persona characterized by foolishness and unconventionality, the improviser writes in a libertine, associative style that thumbs its nose at accepted canons of beauty and craftsmanship. His foolishness disqualifies him from our trust and yet, in practice, gains our trust all the more.

Crucial to a complete understanding of the rhetoric of spontaneity, then, is our recognition of its dialectical opposite: the rhetoric of care, craft, and rationality. Mill certainly did not invent it. It is as old as Aristotle, and the opposition of these two rhetorics as old as Plato and Aristotle. The rhetoric of craft is represented not by Emerson's *Man Thinking*,[32] but rather by *Man Having Thought*. It is characterized by a logical, reasoned style articulated in the persona of the calm, reasonable man (here the patriarchal gender seems appropriate). Its conventions are the dialectical opposite of those of the rhetoric of spontaneity. If in John Ciardi's joke Kerouac's jejune improvising is symbolized by his having lost his eraser, then the rhetoric of craftsmanship may be summed up by that great self-conscious craftsman Nabokov's acknowledgment of his dependence on them: "Spontaneous eloquence seems to me a miracle. I have rewritten—often several times—every word I have ever published. My pencils outlast their erasers."[33] Ever arch, Nabo-

---

31. Nietzsche, *The Birth of Tragedy* and *The Genealogy of Morals,* 19; emphasis in original.

32. "The American Scholar," in *The Collected Works of Ralph Waldo Emerson,* 5 vols., edited by Robert E. Spiller (Cambridge, Mass.: The Belknap Press of Harvard University Press, 1971), 1: 53.

33. Vladimir Nabokov, *Strong Opinions* (New York: Vintage, 1990), 4.

kov refuses to display his rough drafts because, "Only ambitious nonentities and hearty mediocrities exhibit their rough drafts. It is like passing around samples of one's sputum."[34] Take that, you Beats!

It is important, then, to recognize the inherent decorum, or set of conventions, implicit in these rhetorics, and, further, to recognize that these competing decorums are not value-neutral, but convey competing visions of man and the world. To take the present study as an example: I myself here choose the rhetoric I do to fit my attitude toward my audience and my theme. My theme is not the glories of spontaneous, unmediated behavior—though I admit there are plenty—but rather spontaneity's complexities and problematics. My object is not to have you affected by the rhetoric of spontaneity, but rather calmly to consider it. In speaking of a rhetoric of spontaneity and a literary kind called improvisation, I am finally striving to illuminate a decorum, an indecorous one, but a decorum nonetheless, where style, form, and theme are *fitted* to one another. Understanding that decorum means not only adumbrating its conventions and rules but the themes and issues that they trigger.

---

34. Ibid.

CHAPTER FIVE

"The First Idea":
Unpacking Spontaneity

The poem refreshes life so that we share,
For a moment, the first idea...
—Wallace Stevens, "Notes Toward a Supreme Fiction"

1. *The Many Masks of Spontaneity*

Even in its etymology the concept of spontaneity stores a host of contradictions. "Spontaneity" paradoxically invokes both man's free will and also its opposite, man's dependence on powerful, external forces. On the one hand the word is rooted in *sua sponte,* "of one's own accord." Emerson has this aspect of the word in mind when he writes of spontaneity as "our instinctual, our true self" and inquires:

> What is the aboriginal Self, on which a universal reliance may be grounded? What is the nature and power of that science-baffling star, without parallax, without calculable elements, which shoots a ray of beauty even into trivial and impure actions, if the least mark of independence appear? The inquiry leads us to that source, at once the essence of genius, of virtue, and of life, which we call Spontaneity or Instinct.[1]

Here, the true self is marked by independence and is achieved through spontaneity and instinct which, found out and achieved of one's own accord, are unadulterated by cultural overlays. As in Rousseau, the eighteenth-century Enlightenment primitivist who fueled the fires of Romanticism, spontaneity here represents a way back to our pre-civilized selves, before we were enchained and corrupted by society and by art. Spontaneity is a way to insure that our words and deeds originate in us, in our best selves, not in some external, social, or literary convention.

On the other hand, however, spontaneity is related also to *spons, spondere,* meaning "to promise or to bind oneself" and the root of our "*respon*sibility." Its

---

1. "Self-Reliance," in Emerson, *Essays,* 46.

Greek root *spendein* means "to pour a libation." Spontaneity is thus associated with the poet's submission to his or her daemon, relinquishing freedom in order to experience or partake in the transcendent. Thus, conversely, spontaneity may originate not in the self at all, but from some impulse from the gods, from what Spenser, relying on the heritage of Plato's *Ion* and *Timaeus,* calls *enthusiasmos*: Poetry is "no arte, but a diuine gift and heauenly instinct not to bee gotten by laboure and learning, but adorned with both: and poured into the witte by a certain ἐνθουσιἄσμός [*enthusiasmós*] and celestiall inspiration."[2] Here "arte" has its etymological force: poetry is not *a made or fashioned thing.* It is not the product of the human hand. Infused by a presence beyond and larger than our own, we achieve our full destiny as creatures made in the likeness of our creator.

Thus, on the one hand, employing their free will, poets express their individuality and achieve their full humanity. On the other, submitting to a Will larger than their own, poets achieve more than mere humanity can hope to. Both extremes seem to have coexisted simultaneously in the western mind from the start: Plato embraces the poet's divine afflatus at the same time that the Greek Sophists embrace the rhetors' (orators') achieved mastery through the cultivation of the craft of *inventio* (invention) and *copia* (abundance). (Plato attacked the Sophists for practicing the art of epideictic oratory, oration for the sake of competition and display—akin to what we would now call *mere rhetoric*—not for the sake of finding out truth.) In fact the two ideas coexist here in Spenser, who has it both ways though he gives divine inspiration priority: poetry is "no arte, but a diuine gift and heauenly instinct not to bee gotten by laboure and learning, *but adorned with both*." Creation is "gotten" through the divine; man's "laboure and learning" comes afterward as adornment. Such, at a glance and in a nutshell, are spontaneity's more extreme resonances—ambiguous and contradictory as they are.[3]

---

2. Edmund Spenser's "Argument to October," in his "Shepheardes Calendar," in *Spenser's Minor Poems,* vol. 1 of *The Poetical Works of Edmund Spenser,* edited by Ernest de Sélincourt (Oxford: Clarendon Press, 1909), x.

3. For accounts of the intertwining of poetry and inspired prophecy see the collection of essays edited by James L. Kugel, *Poetry and Prophecy: The Beginning of a Literary Tradition* (Ithaca: Cornell University Press, 1990); and Norman O. Brown, *Apocalypse and/or Metamorphosis* (Berkeley and Los Angeles: University of California Press, 1991).

What is not ambiguous is that spontaneity—in both its strains—tacitly equates the Unmediated with the True and thus serves as an authenticating device. In either case what poets achieve is authenticated by the divine within or without.

We have seen this authenticating gesture above, but will here explore it further. For example, consider how, in the dedicatory epistle to *Utopia*, Thomas More complexly asserts his freedom from mediation and craft:

> I am almost ashamed, my dear Peter Giles, to send you this little book about the state of Utopia after almost a year, when I am sure you looked for it within a month and a half. Certainly you know that I was relieved of all the labor of gathering materials for the work and that I had to give no thought at all to their arrangement. I had only to repeat what in your company I heard Raphael [Hythlodaeus] relate. Hence there was no reason for me to take trouble about the style of the narrative, seeing that his language could not be polished. It was, first of all, hurried and impromptu [*subitarius, atque extemporalis*], secondly, the product of a person who, as you know, was not so well acquainted with Latin as with Greek. Therefore the nearer my style came to his careless simplicity [*neglectam simplicitatem*] the closer it would be to the truth.[4]

More here folds the rhetoric of carelessness in with a rhetoric of realism. I was there, the mimetic artist declares, *this, unadulterated, unshaped by human hands, is what really happened.* As in Hamlet's speech to the players, More's apparent "purpose...is, to hold, as 'twere, the mirror up to nature." Of course it could be argued that More's gesture of realism is motivated by the need to protect himself amidst the considerable intrigues of court (which later killed him): *although this may seem to be my satire of England, these are in fact the opinions of a real man other than myself; I am but a neutral transcriber of our conversation about his adventure.*

But there is much else at work. More wishes us to believe that what follows is true not only because it is a transcription of Hythlodaeus's account, but also because Hythlodaeus's style is unspoiled by art, is just unmediated, real experience. But of course we are meant not to miss the irony that after all "Hythlodaeus," the Raphael whose narration he "transcribes," means "expert

---

4. *The Yale Edition of The Complete Works of St. Thomas More*, vol. 4: *Utopia*, 39.

in trifles," or "peddler of nonsense," perhaps homage to his friend Erasmus and his Folly. "Raphael Hythlodaeus," as his translator Robert M. Adams points out, could be a "fantastic trilingual pun" meaning "God heals [Heb., *Raphael*] through the nonsense [Gr., *huthlos*] of God"[5]—Erasmian indeed! More addresses his epistle to Giles—a real person—because fictively Giles too was there and thus more proof of the third party account. The carelessness of Hythlodaeus's Latin and of More's redaction is the final touch in this process of authentication. The "language could not be polished" because "hurried and impromptu" and thus untainted by bookishness and learning. *If it looks like satire, surely this bumpkin can't have meant that.* By means of these gestures More is claiming, again ironically, that this is the real thing, worthy of our careful consideration. Here at the last the ironies evaporate: what More does want is a *careful* reading. *Utopia's* complex ironies will demand it.

Indeed, careless reading is the charge one group of More's critics level against the other. The problem in More's text upon which critics break their lances, as with other Renaissance improvisations, is the question of Reason. What is More's attitude to the exceedingly rational Utopians and, for example, the communism they practiced? The great *Beowulf* scholar and More biographer R.W. Chambers points out that for some, "no treatise is better calculated to nourish the heart of a radical" and, indeed, *Utopia* "did more to make William Morris a Socialist than ever Karl Marx did." But for Chambers, himself a Catholic, Morris missed More's irony: "The underlying thought of *Utopia* always is, *With nothing save Reason to guide them, the Utopians do this; and yet we Christian Englishmen, we Christian Europeans...!* [...] More did not mean that Heathendom is better than Christianity. He meant that some Christians are worse than heathens."[6]

More's authentication by means of the gestures of spontaneity and of realism finds a near perfect echo in a more modern dialogue where Reason is again the crux, French poet and polymath Paul Valéry's *Idée Fixe, ou deux hommes à la mer.* Valéry's preface contains in a nutshell the same rhetorical flourishes, and must be quoted at length:

---

5. Sir Thomas More, *Utopia*, edited and translated by Robert M. Adams (New York: W.W. Norton, 1992), 5n.9.

6. R. W. Chambers, "The Meaning of *Utopia*," in ibid., 139-40; emphasis in original.

This book is the child of haste. It should be taken for what it is: an occa-sional work, improvised from start to finish. Though it was intended for a highly critical audience—the medical profession—it had to be done quickly, thus taking on all that hurried work involves in the way of risks, rashness, and impurities. When the mind is pressed for time, that outer compulsion prevents it from applying those within. Its own ideal stan-dards are put aside: it relaxes its rigor, finds the quickest way out, by way of its least resistances, and relies for results on its own chance responses.

But that is just what happens in familiar talk...The same applies in this instance. What is offered for the reader's consideration is not the "ideas" which our two men by the sea happen to be exchanging, but the exchange itself: the 'ideas' are simply the pieces in a game where rapidity is the essential thing. Our two men are wasting their time at a great rate: what they say amounts only to the elementary forms of what they could say, and such terms as "Implex" and "Omnivalence" are not to be taken for more than a kind of harmless amusement. True, most of the terms actually current in Psychology are hardly more 'convenient' or precise than these.[7]

Valéry's ostensible disclaimer of polish subtly morphs into a claim of verisi-militude: to write a dialogue hastily is consonant with the nature of dialogue. His claims of mere playfulness and inconsequence resolve into the suggestion that the speakers are closer to the truth than systematic psychologists (or phy-sicians, it is also more gently suggested, for, on his own account, they make up his ostensible audience and the butt of his gentle ironies). What follows, he is claiming by disclaiming it, is more consequential, truer and more real, than what system-and jargon-mongering scientists achieve. Because of its careless, hasty, spontaneous freedom this "duologue," as Valéry calls the piece, is more authentic. But its authenticity is not merely a matter of verisimilitude, a mat-ter of crafting carelessness. The subtitle's "deux hommes à la mer" is a pun that means not only "at the sea" but also "(lost) at sea": "*overboard.*" So, too, the main title means not only "fixed ideas" but of course "obsessions." These men have crossed the bounds of reason; they are lost because they err (not only "make mistakes" but "wander," a favorite pun of Thoreau). Like Tho-

---

7. *The Collected Works of Paul Valéry,* vol. 5: *Idée Fixe,* translated by David Paul (Princeton, N.J.: Princeton University Press, 1971), 5.

reau they are willing to err on the side of obscurity and excess. "I fear chiefly," writes Thoreau, "lest my expression not be *extra vagrant* enough, may not wander far enough outside the narrow limits of my daily experience...I desire to speak somewhere without bounds; like a man in awaking moment, to men in their waking moments."[8] By wandering *à la mer,* "without bounds," we become Thoreau's "man in a waking moment" or D. H. Lawrence's "Man Alive." "What is offered for the reader's consideration," says Valéry, "is not the 'ideas' which our two men by the sea happen to be exchanging, but the exchange itself." In these gestures Valéry promotes quickness, the aliveness of process, of community (their warm connection), and of the unconscious ("at sea") over the death-in-life of bloodless ideas (*idées fixes*) exchanged by two minds of a scientific bent. Valéry also wrote the satiric *Monsieur Teste* (=*tête*, head), the man of pure intellect. What began as a simple and modest disclaimer ushers us into the world of improvisation, where not only is irrationality (of some sort) *at play*, but also the value of rationality is *in play.*

By means of this overdetermined use of the rhetoric of spontaneity, Valéry prepares us for his central theme: the Bergsonian opposition between *élan vital* and *raideur,* vitality and rigidity or stiffness.

French philosopher and Nobel Laureate Henri Bergson, Valéry's contemporary, was famous for his notion of duration, or lived time (*le temps duré*), as opposed to clock time. Bergson also elaborated "process philosophy," which privileged motion and change over static values, and intuition over intellect. *Idée Fixe* is a Bergsonian celebration of an openness to life's inevitable flux. Our embrace of *élan* (from *élancer,* to throw a lance) over *raideur* (stiffness) is determined from the start as Valéry invites us to enjoy these *overboard* men and their freewheeling, spontaneous dialogue and Valéry's own effortless achievement. The lesson Valéry offers lies not in their ideas—so marred throughout the "duologue" by the scientific positivism of their professions—but in their hell-bent pursuit of those ideas. The going is the goal: process, not product.

But let us not miss here the other paradox of the spontaneity figure embodied in Valéry's text: that it functions in certain contexts as a token of craft,

---

8. Thoreau, *Walden, Civil Disobedience, and Other Writings,* 218.

not carelessness. Likewise, when Bach plays completely off the cuff a six-part fugue at the King of Prussia's request, we feel we are witnessing the work of the head and not the heart, Montaigne's "[m]usical fancies...guided by art," the culmination of the Enlightenment, not the birth of Romanticism.[9] Bach's early biographer makes the "message" of Bach's improvising perfectly clear:

> The musicians went with [Bach] from room to room, and Bach was invited everywhere to try [different instruments] and to play unpremeditated compositions. After he had gone on for some time, he asked the King to give him a subject for a Fugue, in order to execute it immediately without any preparation. The King admired the *learned manner* in which his subject was thus executed extempore; and, probably to see *how far an art could be carried,* expressed a wish to hear a Fugue with six Obligato parts. But as it was not every subject that is fit for such full harmony, Bach chose one himself, and immediately executed it to the astonishment of all present in the same magnificent and *learned manner* as he had done that of the King.[10]

The genius that inspires Bach here is apparently his own; its "transcendence" is apparently only metaphoric and entirely of this world, an inflated, courtly word for "excellence."[11] By contrast, we seem to have crossed the Romantic divide when Beethoven says, "You ask me where I get my ideas? That I can't say with any certainty. They come unbidden, directly, I could grasp them with my hands."[12] Beethoven's spontaneous genius seems to have an otherworldly source, the Romantic Imagination, Coleridge's "eternal I AM" perhaps, not craftsmanship. The Renaissance courtier (like Sir Philip Sidney) seems to be in Bach's court, not Beethoven's, when he displays the achieved *sprezzatura* the codebooks of his day require.

---

9. See Hofstadter's dazzling analysis of the fugue's formal and thematic complexity in *Gödel, Escher, Bach,* 4-10.

10. Johann Nikolaus Forkel, quoted ibid., 4; emphases added.

11. This terrestrial reading is confirmed by Nachmanovitch's story of Bach's student who asked, "'Papa, how do you think of so many tunes?' to which Bach replied, 'My dear boy, my greatest difficulty is to avoid stepping on them when I get up in the morning,'" in Nachmanovitch, *Free Play,* 4.

12. Quoted in Johnstone, *Impro: Improvisation and the Theatre,* 88.

Thus spontaneity can fulfill and maintain received codes as well as break or challenge them. Certain jazz musicians improvise in a cool manner that shows off their skill and intellect. Others, by contrast, fire their riffs with the soul of city streets and, such is the rhetorical subtext, the primitivism of darkest Africa. New Orleans jazz great Danny Barker says "if you can't dance to this music, there's something wrong with you," especially true of the traditional jazz of which he was a master, for jazz began as dance hall music. But it is also true that there is that jazz you *can't* dance to (e.g., Chick Corea) but which makes your soul dance. Cool jazz offers aesthetic, intellective pleasure, appreciation of that art which hides art (*summa ars celare artem*). Hot jazz, as it was first called by its creators, never pointing to or lowering a mask whose nature it is to claim no mask exists, offers momentary freedom from the straitjacket of urban life. Cool jazz expresses mastery and invites our admiration; hot jazz embodies being mastered and paradoxically also invites our admiration. Distinct and unmistakable, these rhetorical effects nevertheless go by the same name: improvisation. Cool, craftsmanly jazz is more about the mediation of intellect than soul. Hot jazz aspires to that state of immediacy Wynton Marsalis, a cool musician himself, describes when he says of Louis Armstrong, "As a musician, technically, he's on the highest possible level, because *there's no barrier between the horn and his soul.*"[13] Unmediated, Louis Armstrong, arguably the greatest artist of the twentieth century, surpasses what mere art can achieve.

Louis Armstrong was the catalyst for the union of heart and head that was essential to the birth of jazz as we know it. New Orleans musicians in the 1890s were distinguished by those who could read music and those who could not. Readers—those who played by reading scores—were likely to be French Creoles, descendants of the free men of color (*gens de couleur libres*) who were offspring of plantation owners and their slaves and likely to have been schooled in European culture and religion, i.e., Catholicism. They lived downtown across Canal Street, a cultural dividing line, in or near the French Quarter. Non-readers were more likely to live uptown—just blocks away—and to

---

13. Stephanie Bennett, producer, *Let the Good Times Role: A Film about the Roots of American Music*, DVD, Delilah Music Pictures in Association with Island Visual Arts, 1992; emphasis added.

be descendants of plantation slaves who came to New Orleans during Reconstruction to escape the brutality of White Councils—called the KKK elsewhere. Many, like Armstrong, were influenced by the spiritualist churches deeply imbued with African rhythms, their call and response improvised patterns, and their spirituality. Paradoxically called "head" musicians because what they played came from their head not the page, these darker skinned musicians and their hot, wild "raggedy" music were at first disdained by the lighter skinned Creoles. Only the virtuosity of the young, unschooled Louis Armstrong was able to break down the barrier. Jazz as we know it—virtuoso *and* improvised—is a result of the wedding of those forces, hot and cool, intellective and soulful.

The rhetoric of the performances of one distant relative of the jazz tradition, James Brown, in bandleader Paul Shaffer's words, "the most ferocious barbarian of all," demonstrates how intertwined these two effects can be.[14] In a *New Yorker* profile, Philip Gourevitch describes how his performances were at once literally spontaneous and "orchestrated according to the most rigorous discipline":

> Although no two nights are the same, and much of what you see and hear when he's onstage is truly spontaneous, the dazzle of these unpredictable moments is grounded in his ensemble's dazzling tightness. He proceeds without song lists, conducting fiercely drilled sidemen and sidewomen through each split-second transition with an elaborate vocabulary of hand signals. "It's like a quarterback—I call the songs as we go," he says.[15]

"Even in his earliest, wildest days," Gourevitch continues,

> his outrageousness was carefully calculated to convey that, while he cannot be contained, he is always in control. In contrast to the effortlessness that so many performers strive for in their quest to exhibit mastery, James Brown makes the display of effort one of the most striking features of his art...He is the image of abandon, yet his precision remains absolute, his equilibrium is never shaken, there is no abandon.[16]

---

14. Paul Shaffer, *We'll Be Here for the Rest of Our Lives* (New York: Doubleday, 2009), 80-84.

15. Philip Gourevitch, "Mr. Brown," in *The New Yorker* (29 July 2002): 51.

16. Ibid., 54.

James Brown shares with Bach this insistence on effort*ful* spontaneity, effortful effortlessness, as it were. Though both were prodigies and child performers, surely it's a surprise that Bach and James Brown should share *anything*. Were artists so heterogeneous ever yoked? Bach conveys his magisterial effort by choosing "a Fugue with six Obligato parts" which as Hofstadter remarks is like "playing...sixty simultaneous blindfold games of chess, and winning them all," or we might now add, like doing flying splits from the theatre balcony.[17] But what Gourevitch says about Brown's "outrageousness" applies to them both, that it was "carefully calculated to convey that, while he cannot be contained, he is always totally in control."[18]

Why? What motivates this insistence on effortful effortlessness? Clearly with Bach it is a way to display his extraordinary genius, his total mastery. Brown certainly shares Bach's well-earned grandiosity. He explains the sacrosanctity of his improvised performances this way in talking about the recording and remixing process: "I mean, he [the producer] not really understanding that when it comes from me, it's the real thing...It's God." Compare Kerouac, who complained to Robert Giroux, who wanted to cut up the scroll to revise *On the Road*, "This manuscript has been dictated by the Holy Ghost."[19] Kerouac doesn't mention which member of the Trinity helped him edit for six years.Too, Brown's motivation seems to be at least in part political, an expression of his particular version of black pride. As Gourevitch writes, "This was the man whose ultimate civil-rights-era message song was 'I Don't Want Nobody to Give Me Nothing (Open Up the Door, I'll Get it Myself).'"[20] And perhaps for both there is a religious dimension to their embrace of this "image of abandon, yet his precision remains absolute, his equilibrium is never shaken, there is no abandon."

So, paradoxically, the gesture of spontaneity contains its own dialectical opposite, the rhetoric of craft. Sometimes the opposites are inextricable. Such complexity—and downright slipperiness—makes the attempt to ana-

---

17. Hofstadter, *Gödel, Escher, Bach*, 7.

18. Gourevitch, "Mr. Brown," 51.

19. Quoted in Howard Cunnell, "Fast this Time: Jack Kerouac and the Writing of *On the Road*," 52.

20. Gourevitch, "Mr. Brown," 57-58.

lyze spontaneity challenging and has given this analyst sweaty palms more than once. Sometimes gestures of spontaneity contain expressive elements of both head and heart, both reason and unreason, both Apollo and Dionysus. In Erasmus's *Praise of Folly* one motive behind Folly's claim of spontaneity is to show off the skill with which she turns the trope of carelessness, in part one-upping the orators at their own game, turning their conventional figure of carelessness in such a new and artful way that we admire her rhetorical skill. Her one-upmanship is crowned by employing a classical allusion to assert her carelessness. It takes wit to follow such wit and to appreciate it. As Erasmus states in his dedicatory epistle to More, his "jeu d'esprit" deserves More's attention because it "is not utterly deficient in wit." We must have a certain measure of classical learning (or at least know Erasmus's *Adagia*) to appreciate the playful irony of the allusions. Such play and displays of wit are self-regarding; they work by appealing to that elect group or coterie that, by appreciating, is affirmed and authenticated. Through his letter and through Folly's claim of spontaneity Erasmus demands the intellectual assessment demanded by all epideictic, or display, literature: is this witty? is the skill displayed here worthy of admiration?

At the same time, however, Erasmus and his persona make claims that cut the other way. In the *Adagia* citation mentioned above ("quicquid in linguam venerit"), more than half the quotations listed by Erasmus have a negative import: Erasmus stresses not the impromptu but the ill-timed.[21] In the dedicatory letter Erasmus emphasizes the opposite: he asks More to consider the paradoxical proposition that his "praise of Folly is not altogether foolish." Folly says her "extemporaneous speech, unpremeditated" is "all the truer for that." As in Thomas More's trilingual pun, Raphael Hythlodaeus, we are invited to consider what it means to claim that through folly and carelessness we can arrive at truth, and divine truth at that.[22] The oxymoronic construction, like the many dense ironies of the larger oration, involves us not only in rational, but also intuitive processes of mind.[23] Folly teaches us—indeed

---

21. The same proportions are true in the *Adagia*'s next entry, "quicquid in buccam venerit," whatever comes into the mouth.

22. See note 5 above.

23. Rosalie Colie makes this point regarding the nature of paradox in *Paradoxia*

kinetically forces us—by means of her clipped Senecan style, her a-logical transitions, and her ironies and paradoxes, to accept her propositions not on authority as the hated Schoolmen would have us do, but on the basis of experience. She would have us test them on our pulse. Quickness, meaning both speed and aliveness, is all.

Although in the study of post-Romantic spontaneous gestures we are mainly concerned with the rhetoric of the heart, we must be alert to recognize elements of its paradoxical alter-image that can co-exist in improvised texts of any epoch. The fundamental opposition embedded in the topos of spontaneity, however, remains between the rhetoric of heart and of head, carelessness and of craft, will-lessness and will, freedom and constraint. These most basic of rhetorical postures are so familiar that they go unseen, so common that we use them day in and day out to impress or persuade our fellows (or our bosses), to defeat our opponents, or, like the "Godfather of Soul," to give pleasure to our audiences while politically empowering them.

2. The Naturalistic Argument in Dryden's "An Essay of Dramatick Poesie"

James Brown to the contrary notwithstanding, I may seem thus far to be suggesting that improvisations are all weighty philosophical tracts. Rather, my point is that the rhetoric of spontaneity introduces epistemological matters that improvisers can turn to in conducting their poetic argument, whether the issues of Reason and Freedom and Nature lie at the argument's center or its periphery. John Dryden's "An Essay of Dramatick Poesie" (1668) helps make my point.

Yet another Essay! Dryden chooses "essay" rather than Sir Philip Sidney's more rational, forensic "A *Defense* of Poetry." Noting that the essay is a form in which the matter is "problematical," Dryden reminds us of the word's Montaignean roots, "attempt," not a final or authoritative solution. Like Valéry's, Dryden's dialogue is fraught with the rhetoric of spontaneity. Dryden's Hora-

---

Epidemica: The Renaissance Tradition of Paradox (Princeton, N.J.: Princeton University Press, 1966), 3-40. See also Lanham, *The Motives of Eloquence* where he argues that Castiglione's *The Courtier* works not to purvey a hypostatized idea of *sprezzatura* but rather conveys the process of thought behind the idea. Lanham writes: "Castiglione tries to teach us a skill, an intuition, not a conscious, considered response" (149).

tian epigraph modestly calls attention to his being a mere "whetstone," which "makes steel sharp, but of itself cannot cut."[24] Dryden appeals to the reader to accept "this incorrect Essay, written in the Country [like Erasmus's *Praise of Folly*] without the help of Books, or advice of Friends." The dedicatory letter to Lord Buckhurst characterizes his dialogue in the following self-deprecating manner:

> As I was lately reviewing *my loose Papers,* amongst the rest I found this Essay, the writing of which in *this rude and indigested manner* wherein your Lord now sees it, serv'd as *an amusement* to me *in the Country,* when the violence of the last Plague had driven me from Town. Seeing then our Theatres shut up, I was engag'd in these kind of thoughts with the same delight with which men think upon their absent Mistresses.[25]

The thoughts which follow, then, have as their object not truth but delight and an odd, extramural species of pleasure at that: "the same delight with which men think upon their absent Mistresses." Like Thomas More's dialogue in *Utopia,* however, this one "really," "authentically" happened. The dialogue takes place on a barge at the mouth of the Thames where Dryden and his friends have gone to witness the British sea battle with the Dutch. Other realistic *faits divers* or actual incidents (e.g., the recent plague and closing of the theaters) reinforce this gesture of verisimilitude. Just as More and Peter Giles are of flesh and blood, so Dryden's contemporaries (and we, with the help of footnotes) can perceive recognizable people behind the transparent guise of the dialogue's personae: Crites is Sir Robert Howard; Eugenius is Charles Sackville, Lord Buckhurst; Lisideius is Sir Charles Sedley—all familiar courtiers. Lastly, Dryden stands grinning behind Neander, whose name—meaning the new man—at once confidently hints that he is the rising playwright of his day and, more important for our purposes, places him in the fool tradition: a newborn, a mere infant, and a fool—a *parvenu*—at that.

Noting these gestures, we should not be surprised by the conduct of the argument that follows. Writing during the heyday of classic French theater—

---

24. *The Works of John Dryden,* vol. 17: *Prose, 1668–1691, An Essay of Dramatick Poesie and Shorter Works,* edited by Samuel Holt Monk and A. E. Wallace Maurer (Berkeley, Los Angeles, and London: University of California Press, 1971), 2.

25. Ibid., 3; emphases added.

Corneille, Molière; Racine would soon follow—Dryden seeks to "vindicate the honor of our *English Writers*, from the censure of those who unjustly prefer the *French* before them."[26] To do so he makes this the issue: do the French dramatists' adherence to Aristotelian rules make them superior to the irregular English? In our terms: is careful, rule-bound rationalism and artifice superior to a careless disregard for the rational? On the face of things it would seem an easy choice, but Dryden makes it still easier. He lines up his firepower against the French, as the British fleet did against the Dutch, so there can be no doubt.

In the shootout, "nature" and "natural" are Dryden's secret weapons. Neander's vindication of the English stage proceeds from the following definition of drama: "the lively imitation of Nature."[27] Since the English dramatists, he argues, are more vigorous, "more quick and fuller of spirit," and display more "variety and copiousness," they are more "lively."[28] Since they are more natural in speech, characterization, and plotting, they are "truer to nature." The "regular" (according to rule) perfections French rationality can achieve are, by contrast, "the Beauties of a Statue, but not a Man, because not animated with the Soul of Poesie."[29] Systematic rules cannot help us to present life in all its variety or quickness.

Like the argument as a whole, the most famous passage of the dialogue is based on the "naturalistic" moral and aesthetic norms that are typical of improvisations ("naturalistic" here in the sense we saw Mill employ: "from nature"). Shakespeare, Neander says,

> was the man who of all Modern, and perhaps Ancient Poets, had the largest and most comprehensive soul. All the Images of Nature were still present to him, and he drew them, not laboriously, but luckily: when he describes any thing, you more than see it, you feel it too. Those who accuse him to have wanted learning, give him the greatest commendation; he was naturally learn'd; he needed not the spectacles of Books to read Nature; he look'd inwards, and found her there.[30]

---

26. Ibid., 7.
27. Ibid., 44.
28. Ibid., 7, 44, 53.
29. Ibid., 44.
30. Ibid., 55.

Dryden captures and exploits many of improvisation's central traits and gestures. Shakespeare represents the modern, the new. With his "comprehensive soul" he achieves the incorporative, encyclopedic quality of improvisation. Of course Shakespeare does not labor but proceeds "luckily" (i.e., by chance, not purposefully). Dryden celebrates the dramatist's achieved immediacy: what he describes is "still [i.e., always] present to him"; free of bookish "spectacles,"—or any spectacles for that matter—he "look[s] inward" to find nature. Unmediated. That Shakespeare is describing his own heart when he describes Nature suggests improvisation's passionate, affective quality. The ultimate criterion of judgment is not the head but the heart: "you more than see it, you feel it too."

Where Sidney's *Defence* is tasked with proving dramatic poetry equal to history and philosophy, Dryden's "Essay" seeks only to prove its worthy liveliness. Dryden's "Essay" is not an epistemological tract even though his argument proceeds from an epistemological stance: the high value placed on Nature, variety, "quickness," knowing the world without the mediation of books like Aristotle's *Poetics,* as opposed to French bookish, rule-mongering rationality. These terms enable him to load the dice from the first roll: the considerable achievement of French classical drama will clearly not get a hearing once Dryden has set these criteria. But it is important to recognize that Dryden sets his priorities *even before* the crucial definition of drama as the "lively imitation of Nature." They are set in his title, in the "freedom of his Discourse," in his choice of dialogue form, in his exploitation of the gestures of spontaneity and carelessness. These several features of Dryden's voice implicitly privilege "naturalness," "quickness," and variety. They leave us no choice but to bestow the laurels upon Shakespeare and the English stage, and upon those newcomers, like Dryden, who follow in his lively footsteps.

3. *Diderot's* Le Neveu de Rameau

Like the mistress of Dryden's dedicatory epistle, the point of departure for Denis Diderot's *Le Neveu de Rameau* (Rameau's Nephew) are the fugitive thoughts the narrator (a stand-in for Diderot) indulges in and likens to "my little flirts."[31] Like Dryden's "Essay," *Le Neveu* is filled with recognizable

---

31. Diderot writes, "I give my mind license to wander wherever it fancies. I leave it

events and personages including Diderot himself (named *Moi* in the dialogue) and his interlocutor (*Lui*), the nephew of composer Jean-Philippe Rameau. A dialogue like Dryden's "Essay," its argument is based on naturalistic arguments, i.e., arguments from nature, though in this case more problematic and laced with slippery ironies. One of Diderot's finest readers, Lester Crocker, calls attention to the tension we have seen in other improvisations: "In *Le Neveu de Rameau* we have an artfully concealed order underlying the appearance of reckless confusion."[32] Like most improvisations, central to its critical reception has been that it is "in every way unique."[33]

As co-editor of the *Encyclopédie* and a principal figure of the French Enlightenment, Diderot was a *philosophe* or public intellectual bent on knowing the world through systematic rationality. Immanuel Kant would later argue that *Sapere aude*—dare to know—should serve as motto for the Enlightenment's program of applying reason and science to areas long dominated by the authority of tradition and faith. *Daring to know* represented for Kant a maturation of Western culture. Building upon the Scientific Revolution of Bacon, Galileo, Kepler, and Newton, the Enlightenment philosophers sought, to use Kant's metaphor, to bring Western civilization into adulthood. For Peter France, "The history of [Diderot's] thinking can be seen as a series of attempts to formulate rational systems of explanation—of the physical world, of moral, social and political behavior, of aesthetics."[34]

But that word "systems" is often a cue for an improviser to appear and to take aim. In Diderot's case the attack against the systematic, rational order he sought to create with the *Encyclopédie* came from within, from himself. As

---

completely free to pursue the first wise or foolish idea that it encounters, just as, on the Allée de Foy, you see our young rakes pursuing a flighty, smiling, sharp-eyed, snub-nosed little tart, abandoning this one to follow that one, trying them all but not settling on any. In my case, my thoughts are my little flirts," in Denis Diderot, *Rameau's Nephew and First Satire,* translated by Margaret Mauldon (New York: Oxford World's Classics, 2006), 3. All quotations are from this translation unless otherwise noted.

32. Lester Crocker, *Diderot's Chaotic Order: Approach to Synthesis* (Princeton, N.J.: Princeton University Press, 1974), 104-5.

33. Nicholas Cronk, "Introduction," in Diderot, *Rameau's Nephew and First Satire,* vii.

34. Peter France, *Diderot* (New York: Oxford University Press, 1983), 50.

France adds, "In *Rameau's Nephew,* more than in any other of Diderot's writings, we see the *philosophe*'s awareness of a reality which refuses to be encompassed by the orderly schemes of philosophy." System mongers are always the improvisers' target, in this case Diderot's own program.

The dialogue's Horatian epigraph anticipates the narrator's fugitive thoughts: "Born under the baleful sign of Vertumnis." Vertumnis, the god of the seasons and hence of change and flux, may refer to the narrator's state of mind, to the flow of the dialogue (anticipating Valéry in *Idée Fixe*), or in general to humanity and the universe. Diderot sought an orderly world but was cursed to be constantly aware of the flux and disorder we are heir to. Or blessed, since it is that awareness that has given his posthumous works, *Le Neveu* and *Jacques le Fataliste,* their ability to move us still. Alfred North Whitehead speaks of the "age of reason" having but a "one-eyed reason, deficient in its vision of depth."[35] Diderot was blessed and cursed with two eyes.

The narrator's smug self-satisfaction at the dialogue's beginning is a cue for Jung's Shadow, those parts of ourselves that we prefer to deny, to raise its head: enter *Lui* (himself), a dissolute and parasitic music teacher who feeds upon his rich patrons.[36] Rameau's self-defense (or boast) is, not unlike Dryden's defense of Shakespeare, that his evil character was what nature gave him:

> Since I can secure my happiness by means of vices which come naturally to me, that I've acquired without labour and preserved without effort, which suit the ways of my country, conform to the tastes of my protectors, and are more appropriate to their special little needs than virtues which would embarrass them by making them feel ashamed all day long; it would be extremely odd were I to torment myself like a soul in hell, to become something other than what I am, and develop a character quite alien to my own; highly estimable qualities, I admit, to avoid argument, but which I'd find exceedingly difficult to acquire and to practice, which would get me nowhere, perhaps worse than nowhere, by continually

---

35. Whitehead, *Science and the Modern World,* 74.

36. Jung writes, "By shadow I mean the 'negative' side of the personality, the sum of all those unpleasant qualities we like to hide, together with the insufficiently developed functions and the contents of the personal unconscious." *Collected Works of C. G. Jung,* vol. 7: *Two Essays on Analytic Psychology,* edited and translated by Gerhard Adler and R. F. C. Hull (Princeton, N.J.: Princeton University Press, 1970), 66n.5.

showing up the rich from whom beggars like myself seek to earn their livelihood. The world praises virtue, but loathes it and flees from it; virtue is left out in the cold, and in this world one must keep one's feet warm.[37]

Vice here takes the high moral ground because it is natural, "acquired without labour and preserved without effort." Sincere evil. Satan couldn't have argued it better.

Care and carelessness, craft and the grace beyond the reach of craft are in constant tension in the dialogue. Rameau dismisses musicians who have merely "mastered everything that can be learnt about their respective playing" but are unable to reach beyond art.[38] He prides himself in "how little importance [he] attach[es] to method and precepts. He who must follow instructions will never get far. Geniuses read little, do a lot, and create themselves."[39] "All that matters," we learn, "is keeping your eyes open."[40] Rameau's appeal is in part that he is Thoreau's "man in a waking moment" or D. H. Lawrence's "Man Alive."

Rameau displays how alert he is when throughout the dialogue he breaks into improvised musical and dramatic pantomimes, now imitating violin or piano, now imitating this or that character in high society. When he does, *Moi* remarks, he is "transported by a passion, an enthusiasm so akin to madness that it wasn't clear whether he'd ever recover from it, or whether he shouldn't be flung into a carriage and taken straight to the madhouse."[41] As Foucault remarks in his discussion of *Le Neveu*, "the rationality of the Enlightenment found in [the insane] a sort of darkened mirror, an inoffensive caricature."[42] Certainly Vertumnis, the god of flux of the dialogue's epigraph, could serve as Rameau's tutelary deity. The Diderot figure remarks on how Rameau's "tone varies; sometimes it's high-flown, sometimes familiar and low."[43]

---

37. Diderot, *Rameau's Nephew and First Satire*, 36.

38. Ibid., 6

39. Ibid., 43.

40. Denis Diderot, *Rameau's Nephew* and *D'Alembert's Dream*, translated by Leonard Tancock (London: Penguin, 1966), 63. Mauldon translates: "the only thing that matters is to see clearly," Diderot, *Rameau's Nephew and First Satire*, 31.

41. Diderot, *Rameau's Nephew and First Satire*, 68.

42. Michel *Foucault, Madness and Civilization*, 199.

43. Diderot, *Rameau's Nephew and First Satire*, 60.

A ready improviser with eyes open, Rameau seeks to achieve a wickedness so complete that he will pass beyond good and evil:

> HIM: If there's any area in which it really matters to be sublime, it is, above all else, in wickedness. People spit upon a petty thief, but cannot refuse a kind of respect to a great criminal. His courage astounds, his cruelty terrifies. People value unity of character in everything.

> ME: But you have not yet developed this prized unity of character. At times you seem to vacillate in your principles. It isn't clear whether your wickedness comes naturally or through study; or whether study has taken you as far as it can.[44]

Rameau's vote would seem to be for nature, but in a manner hardly as high-minded as Dryden's. He deploys his reputation for thought-free carelessness as a kind of get-out-of-jail card:

> I say whatever comes into my head, if it's sensible, so much the better, but if it's pointless, no one pays attention. I make good use of my freedom of speech. Never once in my life have I thought before speaking, while speaking, or after speaking. So I never offend anyone.[45]

His only care is to hide his Shadow while acting it out. He finds in great literature

> a digest of everything one ought to do, and everything one ought not to say. Thus, when I read *L'Avare*, [Molière's *The Miser*] I tell myself: be miserly, if you wish, but take care not to talk like the miser. When I read *Tartuffe*, I tell myself: be a hypocrite, if you wish, but don't talk like a hypocrite. Keep those vices which serve you well, but beware of the tone and the air that go with them, and would make you appear ridiculous. To be sure of avoiding that tone and air, one must know what they are; now, those authors have portrayed them superbly.[46]

If we tend to associate spontaneity with good-heartedness and good acts (The Ancient Mariner's blessing the water snakes with "A spring of love, gushed from my heart"), *Le Neveu* reminds us rather of the Ancient Mariner as albatross marksman.

---

44. Ibid., 58–59.
45. Ibid., 46.
46. Ibid., 49.

While the narrator often takes offense, Diderot's achievement in *Le Neveu* is in part that he invites us to take Rameau's challenge to the philosophe seriously, much more so than those of the interlocutors in Dryden's "Essay." *Moi* may start the dialogue in the driver's seat but Rameau presents challenges to his smugness that wrest the reins from him. Rameau anticipates his later countrymen, the surrealists, who seek to *épater les bourgeois*. Like many of improvisation's personae, "Rameau," in Peter France's words, "plays the part of the fool, but in doing so, like the traditional jester he turns the tables by casting doubts on the sanity of those who patronize him."[47] *Le Neveu* is striking and admirable in part because the author himself as "the figure of the respectable normality" leads the way in being shocked into partial submission.[48]

Rameau's ultimate trump card, the reason we have to weigh him carefully, is that the narrator cannot in the end dismiss his sincerity. If Rameau is Diderot and the Enlightenment's Shadow, what both the *philosophes* and polite but corrupt society would prefer to ignore or repress, at least he doesn't pretend otherwise. The narrator remarks:

> He is a composite of nobility and baseness, good sense and irrationality. The concepts of honour and dishonour must surely be strangely jumbled in his head, for he makes no parade of the good qualities which nature has given him, and, for the bad, evinces no shame.[49]

Spontaneity may not originate in Rameau's best self but at least it's not derived from the utterly corrupt, equally shameless high society on which he feeds. *Le Neveu* is no epistemological tract but it comes in response to an epistemological program that helped shape the modern world. Rameau casts a dark but vibrant shadow on the century of lights, the Age of Reason, and looks ahead to a time when others of his impish ilk will challenge the scientific positivism that is the Enlightenment's heir.

As I write in the fall of 2013, the third centenary of Diderot's birth, the French government is considering reinterring Diderot in the Paris Pantheon. Built as a church to St. Geneviève by Louis XV, who had sworn to honor her

---

47. France, *Diderot*, 81.

48. Ibid.

49. Diderot, *Rameau's Nephew and First Satire*, 3.

should he recover from a grave illness, and newly renamed by French revolutionaries, the Pantheon was turned into a site for burial and commemoration. Because of exorbitant cost the church was not finished until 1791, two years after the king's beheading. Now, Diderot would join there his fellow *lumières*, Rousseau and Voltaire, none of whom survived to witness the Revolution.

As a student nearby at the Sorbonne, in 1971, 180 years later, I visited the crypt. A new revolution, *soixante-huit*, still rumbled intermittently in the streets nearby. Alongside the Pantheon, busses held gendarmes in full riot gear awaiting the next *manif* when paving stones might again be unearthed and hurled. The day's best-known slogan was *enlève un pavé, la liberté est en-dessous* (pick up a paving stone, freedom lies beneath). Derrida, whose impish improvising we will consider below, who would do much to deconstruct the Enlightenment, published his first book during that epochal year three years previous (1968).

What has stayed with me from my visit to the Pantheon crypt are the tombs of Rousseau and Voltaire, enemies in life, neighbors in eternity. What I remember best is a bas-relief on Rousseau's tomb portraying a hand reaching through the doors and brandishing a torch. The legend, his last words: "encore de la lumière." More light. To a young man struggling to soak up French culture, the words struck me as heroic and poetic in the French grand manner. Now I see the allusion to Rousseau's most important, perhaps truly heroic contribution: the Enlightenment and the French Revolution it helped to foment, the reason a million mourners are said to have attended his Pantheon re-interment in 1794.

On the strength of *Le Neveu de Rameau*, perhaps the legend on Diderot's tomb should be the even more heroic and more modern *encore de l'ombre: more shadow.*

4. *Ginsberg's Ambivalent* Howl

In pre-Romantic texts we tend critically to under-react to the way the rhetoric of spontaneity subtly works upon us. We may miss Diderot's invocation of his "little flirts," the dialogue's flux and flow, and the way both prepare us to embrace a character we would normally hold at arm's length. We expect to find a rhetoric of craft and so dismiss the gesture of spontaneity as white noise or affected modesty at most. In post-Romantic texts the opposite expectation sometimes equally blinds us. For example, many of Beat poet Allen Ginsberg's readers miss the profound ambivalence about the quest for ecstatic vision at the heart of *Howl*, another text where epistemological questions are at issue.[50]

As with most odes, at the center of Ginsberg's *Howl* lies his vision of the presence now absent. The ode is traditionally structured in three sections, strophe, antistrophe, and epode ("turn, counterturn, and stand," language that reflected both the way the Greek chorus recited the speech before the audience, but also the thematic structure). The climactic moment of the strophe, which precipitates the antistrophe, is an almost literal *turn* to the elegized Carl Solomon ("ah, Carl").[51] What enables the moment of direct vision is Ginsberg's achievement of images that, despite their relative simplicity and directness, sum up the main concerns of the strophe. The strophe—a single sentence, 2,000-word enumeration of frustrations, of separations, of *coiti interrupti* (*co-itus* = going, or coming, together)—expresses the problem that the antistrophe's turn will try to explain:

> with mother finally ******, and the last fantastic book
> flung out of the tenement window, and the last
> door closed at 4 A.M. and the last telephone
> slammed at the wall in reply and the last fur-
> nished room emptied down to the last piece
> of mental furniture, a yellow paper rose twisted
> on a wire hanger in the closet, and even that
> imaginary, nothing but a hopeful little bit of
> hallucination—[52]

---

50. Marjorie Perloff is decidedly one who does not miss these ambivalences. See her fine essay on the Collected Poems, "A Lion in the Living Room," in *Poetic License*, 199–230.

51. Allen Ginsberg, *Howl and Other Poems* (San Francisco: City Lights, 1956), 19.

52. Ibid. In the annotated *Howl: Original Draft Facsimile*, edited by Barry Miles (New York: Harper Perennial, 1995), Ginsberg confirms this identification, admitting that "The unworldly love hypostatized as comradeship through thick and thin with Carl Solomon rose of primordial filial loyalty to my mother, then in distress," xi.

First his mother is slammed like Carl into the insane asylum, now so "******,"
that, Oedipal object of course, she cannot be ******. If there is any doubt that
Ginsberg's asterisks represent the slang for coition, the pressure of the series
of "f" sounds erases it: "finally [fucked]…fantastic…flung." It is right that the
image of Ginsberg's mother ushers in this enumeration of frustrations, since
he has identified her from the beginning with Carl, both insane.[53] Next "the
last fantastic book" is "flung" out the tenement window, *separated* from its
reader who longs for a kind of vision that is not mere fantasy, and a reader
who, living in a tenement, is *separated* from the seats of comfort and of power.
"The last door" is "closed" behind a frustrated lover and another, rejected by
his "angel" lover no doubt, slams the telephone "at the wall in reply." The
imagery frustratingly echoes the imagery of Revelations, where the opening
of the last seal brings on apocalypse. Instead, a room/brain is *separated* from
its furniture ("the last furnished room emptied down to the last piece of mental furniture"): the effort to make a home/vision is given up. It appears there
will be no New Jerusalem in this fallen New World.

At the heart of *Howl* is this effort to find a vision the poet can live with
and live within, and to determine the means to achieve it. This quest is the
subject of the poem's long opening which this climaxes. The strophe is about
the quest by "my generation" for vision, for "the ancient heavenly connection
to the starry dynamo in the machinery of night."[54] His generation's quest for
this enabling vision, with God absconded and grace gone, is reduced now to
the agency of drugs and of life on the margins. The quest has been disastrous
to say the least—"I saw the best minds of my generation destroyed by madness / starving, hysterical, naked"[55]—and the long strophe is an enumeration
of that disaster. The disaster is summed up here in the image of "yellow paper
[which] rose twisted on a wire hanger in the closet." The yellow paper suggests
at once a false housel or Eucharist, a pseudo Holy Spirit, *and* a visionary text
manqué. Nothing is raised on high in a holy place by an inner spirit; instead,
all we get is something "twisted on a wire hanger in the closet," the wire
hanger perhaps a hint at a 1950s-style backstreet abortion. The climax of this

---

53. Ginsberg, *Howl,* 9.
54. Ibid.
55. Ibid.

anticlimax is even more devastating: "and even *that* [is] imaginary, nothing but a hopeful little bit of hallucination."[56] This defines their quest for inspiration through the end of a needle. It is apparently as difficult to enter into the Kingdom of Vision using the point of a needle as to enter the Kingdom of Heaven through the needle's eye. While the Blakean doors of perception beckon through doors opened by William Burroughs and Aldous Huxley, they are condemned always to doubt the sordid means, and the merely imaginary, merely hallucinatory ends achieved. Not the eye, but rather the point of the needle altering all, alters nothing.

In contrast to all this comes Carl at the end of the strophe, whose vision was the real thing and whose achievement represents the Adamic birth of the Beat Generation:

> ah, Carl, while you are not safe I am not safe, and
>   now you're really in the total animal soup of
>   time—
> and who therefore ran through the icy streets obsessed
>   with a sudden flash of the alchemy of the use
>   of the ellipsis the catalog the measure & the vibrat-
>   ing plane,
> who dreamt and made incarnate gaps in Time & Space
>   through images juxtaposed, and trapped the
>   archangel of the soul between 2 visual images
>   and joined the elemental verbs and set the
>   noun and dash of consciousness together jumping
>   with sensation of Pater Omnipotens Aeterna
>   Deus
> to recreate the syntax and measure of poor human
>   prose and stand before you speechless and intel-
>   ligent and shaking with shame, rejecting yet con-
>   fessing out the soul to conform to the rhythm
>   of thought in his naked and endless head,...[57]

---

56. Emphases added.
57. Ibid., 19-20.

Inspired by "the sudden flash of the alchemy," Carl Solomon achieves the breakthrough in poetic form that will characterize the Beat Generation's poetic line.[58] Where through artificial means "my generation" gets everything wrong, Solomon through Hermetic, alchemical art here gets everything right. Describing point by point the achieved spontaneity that will dominate the technique of the Beats and particularly that of *Howl*, Ginsberg recounts how Solomon creates "the ellipsis catalog, a variable measure & the vibrating plane"; the "juxtaposed...images" that make "incarnate gaps in Time and Space"; the concatenation of "visual images" that "trap[s] the archangel of the soul...and joined the elemental verbs and set the noun and dash of consciousness together jumping with sensation of Pater Omnipotens Aeterna Deus." This is religion spilling into poetry (or vice versa, poetry spilling into religion) in great crashing waves. Ginsberg's claim is that Solomon's achievement, and by extension that of the Beats, is the incarnate, originary Word. Ginsberg catalogs the *techniques* that bring this state of grace into being, yet his emphasis nonetheless is on its unmediated achievement. Carl "*ran* through the icy streets"; the "flash" is "sudden" with sources in the unconscious and irrational ("dreamt"). Its effect is beyond the mediation of language: "speechless and intelligent and shaking with shame." Ginsberg presents us a madman, Carl Solomon, Ur-Beat, as Lear on a cityscape heath, unaccommodated man, "*but*" as Folly would add, "*all the truer for that!*"

By contrast, their generation's quest for inspiration is but a pale and sordid effort to recreate this *echt* inspiration. It is doomed to frustration and fruitlessness. By contrast, Solomon's achievement, like many improvisations, brings on apocalypse:

> the madman bum and angel beat in Time, unknown,
>> yet putting down here what might be left to say
>> in time come after death,
> and rose reincarnate in the ghostly clothes of jazz in
>> the goldhorn shadow of the band and blew the
>> suffering of America's naked mind for love into

---

58. This passage echoes Kerouac's "Essentials of Spontaneous Prose," which Ginsberg kept pinned to his wall. See Ginsberg's "Improvised Poetics," in *Composed on the Tongue* (Mechanicsville, Virginia: Grey Fox Press, 2001), 42.

> an eli eli lamma lamma sabacthani saxophone
> cry that shivered the cities down to the last radio
> with the absolute heart of the poem of life butchered
> out of their own bodies good to eat a thousand
> years.[59]

Ginsberg here conflates Christ's Greek lament on the cross—"Lord, Lord, why hast thou forsaken me?"—with images of the jazz saxophonist that echo Joshua, antetype of Christ as martial commander, who brings down the walls of those who would keep the chosen from the Promised Land and New Jerusalem. Echoed too are the trumpets of doom sounded by Christ's angels that bring on Apocalypse. Joined (not *separated* from—finally *coitus* is attained), the Beats and their jazz brethren bring down Jericho, "shiver[ing] the cities down to the last radio" and create manna in the wilderness—"good to eat a thousand years"—out of "the poem of life butchered out of their own bodies."

"Butchered" sounds like something is amiss here, but not so. The dismembered Fisher King arises reborn. Ginsberg's program is redemption through the body, making it spirit but leaving it body at the same time, for as the "Footnote to *Howl*" makes clear, "Everything is holy!"[60] The antistrophe that follows begins with this question: "What sphinx of cement and aluminum bashed open their skulls and ate up their brains and imagination?" Ginsberg's answer: "Moloch! Solitude! Filth! Ugliness!" Moloch, whose name in Hebrew means *king* and who is a devil associated with human sacrifice, represents the city and corporate culture that have destroyed the best minds of the generation. At the heart of Ginsberg's long catalog of Moloch's villainies lies this split between mind and body: "Moloch in whom I am a consciousness without a body!"[61] Hence the utter appropriateness of the sustenance image: the food we eat becomes us, remaining material, but, sustaining our life, it becomes spirit also.

So, too, Ginsberg's ideal relationship with time. Carl, insane and institutionalized, is at present "really in the total animal soup of time—." A hard place, but just where he wants to be, *in time.* For at his best Ginsberg, like his

---

59. Ginsberg, *Howl*, 20.

60. Ibid., 27.

61. Ibid., 22.

model Blake, found visionary windows in time where all Eternity could be seen. "The eye altering alters all"; by contrast, "Moloch['s] eyes are a thousand blind windows!" "Incarnate gaps in Time & Space" are the result of this true vision: through the windows of vision, all Eternity can be experienced in an hour.[62] Just so, Carl in his insane asylum and Ginsberg in his poem make manna out of human detritus. *Howl* is the apocalyptic last book that answers the false prophecy of "the last fantastic book flung out of the tenement window." Inspired by Carl, who has taught him to knit together mind and body, Ginsberg creates a new gospel in which nothing human is foreign. Like all improvisations, *Howl* gobbles up the world.

Dean Moriarty's version of the Beat poetics in *On the Road,* though less precise about the techniques involved, is consonant with Ginsberg's. Both stop and open up time:

> "Now, man, that alto man last night had IT—he held it once he found it; I've never seen a guy who could hold it so long." I wanted to know what 'IT' meant. "Ah well"—Dean laughed—"now you're asking me impon-de-rables—ahem! Here's a guy and everybody's there, right? Up to him to put down what's on everybody's mind. He starts the first chorus, then lines up his ideas, people, yeah, yeah, but get it, a sudden somewhere in the middle of the chorus he gets it—everybody looks up and knows; they listen; he picks it up and carries. Time stops. He's filling empty space with the sub-stance of our lives, confessions of his bellybottom strain, remembrance of ideas, rehashes of old blowing. He has to blow across bridges and come back and do it with such infinite feeling soul-exploratory for the tune of the moment that everybody knows it's not the tune that counts but IT—" Dean could go no further; he was sweating telling about it.[63]

IT, too, would seem to gobble up the world.

Dryden, Diderot, James Brown, and Ginsberg? Spenser, Thomas More, and Valéry? Were ever opposites more violently yoked together? Compared to Ginsberg's, Dryden's use of the rhetoric of spontaneity is subtle to the point of being invisible, and never perhaps goes beyond rhetoric: a device of persuasion. Compared to Dryden's, Ginsberg's apparent commitment to his long breathed line, to "the dash of consciousness," and to visionary poet-

---

62. Ibid., 20.
63. Jack Kerouac, *On the Road* (New York: Penguin, 1976), 207.

ics is so complete that we are likely to miss the many ways that the poem celebrates a vision whose source lies in craft. "The Bum's as holy as the seraphim!"[64] But the bum's inspiration from a bottle or needle cannot match the *crafted* source of inspiration the poem celebrates: the "sudden flash of the alchemy" achieved through the techniques of the new Beat poetics ("the use of the ellipsis catalog..." etc.). Though Ginsberg may seem in every way to celebrate a poetry achieved without art, this *ars poetica* is the poem's heart. Accent on *ars*. (Doubly!)

This then is what is truly compelling: texts that hold in suspension and explore the tensions involved in the competing rhetorics, of craft and of spontaneity. They are compelling because they are true to human experience. We yearn ever, often at the same time, to master and to be mastered. On the one hand we yearn to be authoritative, authentic, worthy of praise; on the other there is an impulse in us to acknowledge our frailty, our incompleteness, our recognition that as Martha Carson's gospel hymn announces, "you can't stand up alone."[65] We are all, like Neander, new men and women, longing for the life-bringing, incoming tide that will float us home and back to health. The question is which will best get us there: *floating* or *navigating*? On a tidal river like Dryden's Thames, of course, the answer, as in most improvisations, is *both*. The tide will take you back to London but as on Mark Twain's Mississippi, there are shoals that the pilot must avoid with great care and skill. Like Joseph Campbell's hero, the improviser knows (or rather intuits) that true mastery lies the way of suffering the wound, the wound of our insufficiency and limitations, the inadequacy of our mind and art. As William Carlos Williams writes in his "Prologue" to *Kora in Hell: Improvisations*: "By the brokenness of his composition the poet makes himself master of a certain weapon which he could possess himself of in no other way."[66]

"Floating or navigating?"—the question takes us to another central Western text where the image is more ominous. Conrad's *Heart of Darkness* also records a conversation that takes place as men wait for the Thames' tide to float a ship up to the civilized bright glow of London. While they wait in the

---

64. Ginsberg, *Howl*, 27.

65. See, for example, Jessie Winchester, "I Can't Stand Up Alone" on *Learn to Love It*, Bearsville Records, 1974.

66. Williams, *Kora in Hell*, 19.

offing, Marlowe tells the tale of his steamer churning up the Congo River where Kurtz has preceded him, following his heart's instincts to "the horror" of colonial power and conquest and exploitation. In the telling Marlowe makes clear that while we might be tempted to condemn Kurtz's behavior as individual corruption, in fact Kurtz, "a universal genius," and even colonialism itself, represent the very flower of civilization and rationality. Just as improvisation would gobble up the world, so too Marlowe has a vision of Kurtz just before his last moment ("The horror! The horror!") "on the stretcher opening his mouth voraciously as if to devour all the earth with all its mankind."[67] Gobbling up the world is not always a good thing.

Floating or navigating? Neither is proof against the darkness of the voracious human heart. Improvisation's sunny world would have us forget that momentarily. But before it is done, improvisation reminds us of the damage sometimes done in spontaneity's name.

---

67. Joseph Conrad, *Heart of Darkness*, edited by Richard Kimbrough (New York: W.W. Norton, 1988), 72.

CHAPTER SIX

"Strange Relation":
Chaos Science <-> Improvisation <-> Postmodernism

Life's nonsense pierces us with strange relation.
—Wallace Stevens, "Notes Toward a Supreme Fiction"

"Now that science is looking," writes James Gleick in *Chaos: Making a New Science*, "chaos seems to be everywhere."[1] So, too, with the literature of chaos. Once perceived, improvisations seem ubiquitous, not just in the Romantic Period and not just in literature. Understanding the aesthetics of improvisation can help us get our minds around two important recent phenomena: chaos or dynamic systems science, and postmodernism. Both share with improvisation not only formal conventions, but also these deeper concerns: the effort to violate and to extend the boundaries of our rationality, and the effort to reconcile the deterministic and the free. Like Katherine Hayles, *doyenne* of chaotics and literature, I am not arguing for a causal connection in either direction between chaos science and improv.[2] That improvisation's conventions and central issues coincide with recent developments in science, philosophy, criticism, and the plastic arts serves to clarify what is at stake in recognizing improvisation as a coherent aesthetic form with a morphology that persists over time and across disciplines. Improvisation is not only older than we like to think, it is also newer, ever renewing itself in the endless play of paradigm shifts.

---

1. James Gleick, *Chaos: Making a New Science* (New York: Viking, 1987), 7.

2. See N. Katherine Hayles, *Chaos and Order: Complex Dynamics in Literature and Science* (Chicago: The University of Chicago Press, 1991), 7. Hayles in that anthology of essays and in her earlier *Chaos Bound: Orderly Disorder in Contemporary Literature and Science* (Chicago: The University of Chicago Press, 1990) is concerned with poststructuralism and with contemporary narrative, as is Alexander J. Argyros, *Blessed Rage for Order: Deconstruction, Evolution, and Chaos* (Ann Arbor: University of Michigan Press, 1991).

1. *Chaos Science and Improvisation*

Modern science since its foundation has longed for an unmediated experience of Nature, what one-time surrealist turned physicist Wolfgang Paalen eloquently describes as science's "pretended Zero-point of observation...like a chaste sword tip inserted between perception and interpretation."[3] Francis Bacon, founder of the modern scientific method, imagined Nature as the god Pan, whose spouse, the scientist, is Echo: "For that is in fact the true philosophy which echoes most faithfully the voice of the world itself, and is written as it were from the world's own dictation; being indeed nothing else than the image and reflection of it, which it only repeats and echoes, but adds nothing of its own."[4] Bacon's vision of the empirical scientist as nature's unmediated echo, mirror, ventriloquist, or amanuensis faithfully recording nature's speech anticipates an important strain in Romanticism: the quest for Ruskin's "innocent eye" or Emerson's "transparent eye-ball."[5] The quest—in various degrees of extravagance—lies near improvisation's heart.

But the experimental method Bacon's inductive science depends on to achieve this ventriloquism relies first of all on hypotheses that inevitably shape the voice of Nature that we hear. We see light as a particle or a wave depending on the experiment we submit light to. Second, this immediacy was achieved paradoxically through the mediation of experimental tools like the microscope, telescope, and air-pump, whose "aim was the *'Inlargement of the dominion* of the Senses.'"[6] Science thus held this contradiction in suspension,

---

3. Wolfgang Paalen, "Paysage Totemique," *Dyn* 1 (Spring 1942), as quoted in and translated by Daniel Belgrad in *The Culture of Spontaneity,* 60.

4. *Of the Wisdom of the Ancients,* in *The Works of Francis Bacon,* 14 vols. (London: Longman, 1857-74), 13: 101. This is a translation of Bacon's *De sapientia veterum* (1609).

5. "The whole technical power of painting," writes Ruskin, "depends on our recovery of what might be called the innocence of the eye; that is to say, of a sort of childish perception of these flat stains of colour, merely as such, without consciousness of what they signify—as a blind man would see them if suddenly gifted with sight," in *The Elements of Drawing; in Three Letters to Beginners* (London: Smith, Elder, 1856-57), 6. Ruskin's blind man is of course hogwash. "Nature," in *The Collected Works of Ralph Waldo Emerson,* 1: 10.

6. Steven Shapin and Simon Shaffer, *Leviathan and the Air-Pump: Hobbes, Boyle, and the Experimental Life* (Princeton, N.J.: Princeton University Press, 2011), 35-36.

the longing for unmediated experience and the excitement about these new tools of mediation.

The yearning for unmediated experience is doomed to failure even more intrinsically by the "beholder's share" inherent in perception. If we want to see accurately we must acknowledge the bit of ourselves we contribute to what we see, the way that our perceptual lens shapes our world. "There is no innocent eye," says art historian E.H. Gombrich, no unmediated experience.[7] For philosopher of aesthetics Nelson Goodman,

> The eye always comes ancient to its work, obsessed by its past and by old and new insinuations of the ear, nose, tongue, fingers, heart, and brain. It functions not as an instrument self-powered and alone, but as a dutiful member of a complex and capricious organism. Not only how but what it sees is regulated by need and prejudice.[8]

Cognitive neuroscience has confirmed the truth that we shape experience not just by the software of prejudice and desire, but also the hardwiring of our brain and nervous system. In his study of nineteenth-and twentieth-century artists who anticipated the findings of neuroscience, journalist Jonah Lehrer writes of Paul Cézanne's unfinished paintings:

> Modern neuroscientific studies of the visual cortex have confirmed the intuitions of Cézanne and the Gestaltists: visual experience transcends visual sensations. Cézanne's mountain arose from the empty canvas because the brain, in a brazen attempt to make sense of the painting, filled in its details...Reality is continually refined until the original sensation—that incomplete canvas—is swallowed by our subjectivity...There is no such thing as immaculate perception.[9]

They are quoting seventeenth-century polymath Robert Hooke's *Micrographia* (1665).

7. See E.H. Gombrich, "Evidence of Images," in *Interpretation: Theory and Practice*, edited by Charles S. Singleton (Baltimore: The John Hopkins University Press, 1969), 43, and *Art and Illusion: A Study in the Psychology of Pictorial Representation* (Princeton, N.J.: Princeton University Press, 1961).

8. Nelson Goodman, *Languages of Art* (Indianapolis: Bobbs-Merrill, 1968), 7-8.

9. Jonah Lehrer, *Proust was a Neuroscientist* (New York: Houghton Mifflin, 2007), 117. See also neuroscientist Semir Zeki's explorations of "non finito art" from Michelangelo to Cézanne in *Splendours and Miseries of the Brain* (London: Wiley-Blackwell, 2009), ch. 12 and 13.

Nonetheless, we can't rid ourselves of the longing for unmediated experience any more than we can remove the lens that prevents it. Rather, what we must note, examine, and appreciate is the complexity of the human response to this dilemma: an innate longing that has no hope of fulfillment—no hope even down to the level of how our brain works. For just as post-Cartesian philosophy has called an achieved immediacy in question, so too post-Newtonian science has challenged Bacon's quest for neutral observation.

The point is not only to note this shift in the conception of the scientist's goal and method but also to realize the role of literary form in its articulation. For new forms of science are often articulated in "new" forms of expression that exploit the rhetoric of spontaneity and share the deep concern of literary improvisation with the dilemmas of freedom and constraint. The founder of modern scientific method, Bacon embodied his new empiricism in his Senecan-style *Essays,* a literary form that embodies a representation of Man Thinking. As Stanley Fish points out, Bacon's "essays advocate nothing (except perhaps a certain openness and alertness of mind)."[10] René Descartes will be the target of many of the improvisers who, following in Bacon's wake, will attempt to disrupt the Cartesian method and to break through the mind-body split Descartes advanced. Nonetheless, like his contemporary improvisers, he conceived his *Discourse on Method* as a widening of reason's powers beyond the constraints of the scholastic method. His first person autobiographical narrative, a swerve and answer to the scholiast's appeal to authority, grounds his method in experience in lived life. Maurice Blanchot celebrates not only the *Method's* "freedom of form" but that "this form is no longer that of a simple exposition (as in scholastic philosophy), but rather describes the very movement of research that joins thought and existence in a fundamental experience."[11] Improvisation's binary is always a matter of degree, improvisers leap-frogging one another time after time.

The improvisational form is crucial in John Locke's effort to take Bacon's empiricism into the realm of philosophy and psychology. He does so in an *Essay,* about which he writes:

---

10. Stanley Fish, *Self Consuming Artifacts: The Experience of Seventeenth Century Literature* (Berkeley and Los Angeles: University of California Press, 1972), 94.

11. Maurice Blanchot, *The Infinite Conversation,* as quoted in Peters, *The Philosophy of Improvisation,* 148.

Some hasty and undigested Thoughts, on a Subject I had never before considered,...gave the first entrance into this Discourse, which having been thus begun by Chance, was continued by Intreaty; written by incoherent parcels; and, after long intervals of neglect, resum'd again as my Humour or Occasion permitted; and at last, in a retirement, where an Attendance on my Health gave me leisure, it was brought into that order, thou now seest it.[12]

His psychology will on the one hand portray the mind's clean slate upon which experience directly writes, on the other the false association of ideas "either voluntarily, or by chance" that mediates simple ideas and is the source of most human error.[13] The *Essay on Human Understanding,* though just "hasty and undigested Thoughts," will be a brief for the hard work required in extricating the false associations of ideas to arrive at truth. The *Essay* advocates "hasty and undigested Thoughts" while demonstrating their peril.

Stephen Greenblatt persuasively makes the case that Bacon's scientific method, as well as modernity itself, comes out of the Renaissance rediscovery of Lucretius's *De Rerum Natura* (*On the Nature of Things*). Because of Lucretian Epicurean materialism, Greenblatt argues, in a good summary both of the birth of the Enlightenment and of what it means to be modern,

it became increasingly possible to turn away from a preoccupation with angels and demons and immaterial causes and to focus instead on things in this world; to understand that humans are made of the same stuff as everything else and are part of the natural order; to conduct experiments without fear that one is infringing on God's jealously guarded secrets; to question authorities and challenge received doctrines to legitimate the pursuit of pleasure and the avoidance of pain; to imagine that there are other worlds beside the one that we inhabit; to entertain the thought that the sun is only one star in an infinite universe; to live an ethical life without reference to postmortem rewards and punishments; to contemplate without trembling the death of the soul. In short, it became possible—in the poet Auden's phrase to find the mortal world enough.[14]

---

12. John Locke, *An Essay Concerning Human Understanding,* edited by Peter H. Nidditch (Oxford: Oxford University Press, 1975), 7.

13. Ibid., 396.

14. Stephen Greenblatt, *The Swerve: How the World Became Modern* (New York: Norton, 2012), 10–11.

In short, because of Lucretius, "the world swerved in a new direction."[15] Greenblatt himself testifies to the important role Lucretius's form and style had in galvanizing his Renaissance audience. But he misses the epic poem's links, both formal and thematic, to earlier (and later) improvised texts. Like other improvisations, Lucretius begins by invoking inspiration. In this case, even though at the center of his materialism is a denial of the gods, he seeks to be inspired by Venus. For Lucretius the universe in its endless generation and destruction is inherently sexual, hence his poem is inspired not by memory or the muses, but rather by sexual energy—about the furthest remove possible from rationality. Like other improvisations, *De Rerum Natura* swerves from known genres, a didactic epic far more supple and passionate than the classical model for *didactic* epics, Hesiod's *Works and Days,* and far more didactic than Homer's great narrative poems. Clearly an epic, it is nonetheless a newfound thing. Anticipating *The Prelude*'s intimate address to Wordsworth's friend Coleridge, Lucretius passionately addresses his epic to his patron Gaius Memmius. His philosophic goal is to overcome the superstition that keeps us from knowing the world as it is, and that fuels our fear of death. Like other paradigm shifters, Lucretius's would have us enlarge our rationality, cleanse our doors of perception. Death, as in other improvisations, haunts the poem though he asserts an answer to the haunting: "death is nothing to us". So too, the problem of free will and determinism lies at the poem's center. Where superstition inspires fatalism, Lucretian atomism explains how through the swerve or *clinamen,* which occurs *sua sponte* (of its on accord, that is, spontaneously) our free will overcomes the endless chain of deterministic causality. "Sua sponte"—the etymology of "spontaneous,"—occurs over twenty times in the poem.[16]

---

15. Ibid., 11.

16. Monte Ransome Johnson, "Nature, Spontaneity and Voluntary Action in Lucretius," in *Lucretius: Poetry, Philosophy, Science,* edited by Daryn Lehoux, A.D. Morrison, and Alison Sharrock (Oxford: Oxford University Press, 2013). Johnson makes it clear that by *sua sponte* Lucretius means neither that natural events are causeless or random nor that they have a will of their own, but rather that nature does not obey the gods or providence.

But most telling, for me the linchpin, is Lucretius's encyclopedic embrace of life, in Greenblatt's words, his "glorious affirmation of vitality."[17] Auden's "to find the mortal world enough" may not be the endpoint for the Christian humanists that Lucretius inspired—*all* my Renaissance improvisers: More, Erasmus, Montaigne, Rabelais, Burton—but it is again and again in various degrees the goal they flirt with. Like Lucretius they seek to seize all of life and invite us to do the same. If Lucretius inspired modern science and marks the beginning of modernity, the mode of discourse he deploys has ancient roots and modern and contemporary echoes. Modernity begins to seem the climactic triumph of the perennial improvisational space where the nature and value of our rational tools are always in question and the artist's ultimate expression is "a glorious affirmation of vitality." Seize not just the day but all of life is improvisation's theme: *carpe vitam.*

Leaping ahead to our own century, we can see that the psychologist Jerome Bruner also turns to the conventions of improvisation in attempting to extend the boundaries of his field. In *On Knowing: Essays for the Left Hand,* he attacks the restrictive rationality of mainstream psychology: "the topics were ones I could not cope with by the universalized methods of experiment or logical analysis alone. Hence the subtitle: 'Essays for the Left Hand.'...I don't think that psychology should enter the age-old battle to understand the nature of man with one hand tied behind his back—left *or* right."[18] Bruner plays here with the concept of right and left hemispheres of the brain. The right brain is associated with the left hand and creativity; the left brain with the analytic mind and the right hand. Working with his left hand, like our literary improvisers Bruner calls for a new genre:

> I have felt that the self-imposed fetish of objectivity has kept us from developing a needed genre of psychological writing—call it protopsychological writing if you will—the preparatory intellectual and emotional labors on which our later, more formalized, efforts are based. The genre in its very nature is literary and metaphoric, yet it is something more

---

17. Greenblatt, *The Swerve,* 9.

18. Jerome S. Bruner, *On Knowing: Essays for the Left Hand,* exp. ed. (Cambridge, Mass. and London: The Belknap Press of Harvard University Press, 1979), ix-xi.

than this. It inhabits a realm midway between the humanities and the sciences. It is the left hand trying to transmit to the right.[19]

His essays will be about such left-handed/right-hemisphere topics as creativity, the learning process, aesthetic knowledge, and subjective emotions, what his Harvard predecessor William James championed as "the 'unscientific' half of existence."[20] And yet, paradoxically, the topic at the heart of his book concerns the limits of our freedom, the brain's mediation of our sense experience:

> We know now... that the nervous system is not the one-way [read: unmediated] street we thought it was—carrying messages from the environment to the brain, there to be organized into representations of the world. Rather, the brain has a program that is its own, and monitoring orders are sent out from the brain to the sense organs and relay stations specifying priorities for different kinds of environmental messages. Selectivity is the rule and a nervous system...is as much an editorial hierarchy as it is a system for carrying signals.[21]

Thus Bruner, a working scientist, employs the aesthetics of improvisation on the one hand to urge a freeing up of the rational mind; on the other hand he employs it to acknowledge the hardwired limits of the mind's freedom—limits which neuroscientists forty years after him will confirm.[22] Such tensions are ever at the heart of improvisation.

This endless conflict between left and right brain hemispheres is what Iain McGilchrist finds at the heart of human history in his magisterial recent work on neuroscience, *The Master and the Emissary: The Divided Brain and the Making of the Western World,* a book in which neuroscience can be said to have come of age not just as a medical but also as a cultural discipline. Quick

---

19. Ibid., 5.

20. "Are We Automata?," in William James, *Essays in Psychology* (Cambridge, Mass. and London: Harvard University Press, 1983), 40.

21. Bruner, *On Knowing*, 6.

22. Semir Zeki, a professor of neurobiology at University College London, reports that although the brain employs one-third of its mass to sight, that "it distills, or abstracts, the essence of what it sees—like a caricature does—because of its limited memory system." Quoted in Marilia Duffles, "Secrets of Human Thinking," *Financial Times* (2 March 2002): 4.

to dissociate himself from the too-pat popular version of the hemisphere split, McGilchrist offers a sweeping account of cultural history since the Greeks, exploring how, meant by evolution to work in coordination but inherently in conflict, the hemispheres have through "a succession of shifts of balance" come to dysfunction: the rationalistic, analytic left brain usurping the intuitive gestalt function of the right. For McGilchrist, rationalistic, positivistic science and technology have come to rule the roost in the last 200 (or more) years: "The balance has swung too far—perhaps irretrievably far—toward the Apollonian left hemisphere, which now appears to believe that it can do anything, make anything, on its own."[23] My effort here may be seen as a granular version—down to the textual level—of McGilchrist's sweeping history of human culture. Improvisation is the right hemisphere's periodic push-back against this dysfunctional trend.

The history of chaos science further exemplifies this turn to the rhetoric and conventions of improvisation, and displays like tensions. Chaos science is full of manifestos, uncharacteristic of science's usual "self-imposed fetish of objectivity." The quirky and iconoclastic books and articles of Benoît Mandelbrot, one of the founders of chaos science, and of Ilya Prigogine, Nobel Laureate and one of its most articulate illuminators, slowed their acceptance among mainstream scientists. But this quirkiness did much to promote their deep program, an openness to the non-linear, self-organizing aspects of nature.[24]

Mandelbrot discovered these self-ordering systems by taking up the challenge "to study those forms that Euclid leaves aside as being 'formless,' to investigate the morphology of the 'amorphous.'"[25] His new science describes "a new world of plastic beauty" and the "family of shapes [he] call[s] fractals

---

23. Iain McGilchrist, *Master and the Emissary: The Divided Brain and the Making of the Western World* (New Haven: Yale University Press, 2009), 240.

24. Mandelbrot's colleagues, it should be noted, prefer now to be called dynamical systems scientists. I will use the earlier and more popular designation to signal the link to the literature of chaos, Improvisation. Both names, however, are ironic misnomers. Both the science and the literature of chaos describe apparently turbulent but in fact self-ordering systems.

25. Benoît B. Mandelbrot, *The Fractal Geometry of Nature* (New York: W.H. Freeman, 1983), 1.

which makes it up."[26] In so doing he describes the regularity of irregular and fragmented patterns. This "openness" is conveyed by Mandelbrot's eschewing, as he says in his Preface, the form of "textbook [or] treatise in mathematics" and his characterizing *The Fractal Geometry of Nature* instead as a "casebook…a compilation concerning actual cases linked by a common theme" and as "a scientific Essay because it is written from a personal point of view and without attempting completeness. Also, like many Essays, it tends to digressions and interruptions."[27]

There's that *essay* again! In his encyclopedic tendency, his digressions, and his swerve from the traditional form, Mandelbrot echoes Bacon and Locke and participates in the line of improvisation. His eccentric first-person voice, so offensive to mainstream scientists who long did their best to marginalize him, unwittingly looks toward the foolish persona of the improvisatory aesthetic and helps implicitly to debunk the scientific method that has no room for the unreasonableness of life's complexity.

Indeed, the questions chaos scientists pose are just what improvisations ask: Does the measuring device of ordered rationality answer the thing measured? Will rationality miss nothing of life's profusion? Is it enough only to measure the predetermined? What about all the fortuitous, random aspects of life? Fittingly, Mandelbrot's first manifesto challenged the very pretense of science to accurate measurement, not in the subatomic world where quantum physics had already made clear the limits of measuring, but, counterintuitively, even in the everyday world. Asking "How Long is the Coast of Britain?" Mandelbrot called attention to the fact that measurement, apparently the simplest of tasks, becomes problematic when you shift the scale you measure with. Choose a kilometer and you get one number. Choose a meter and you will see more of the coast's fragmented arcs, and get a larger, "more accurate" number. Choose a millimeter and you get a still larger, still "more accurate" number, and so on. So what does it mean to measure accurately? Each change in scale forces you to account for more of the circumference, more of the apparently random chaos of inlets and bays that a larger scale ignores as irrelevant. This scale-shifting uncovers order within apparent

---

26. Ibid., 2.
27. Ibid.

chaos. Called fractal geometry, Mandelbrot's essay was one of the crucial steps in the foundation of the new science of chaos.

Mandelbrot's choice of the "boundary" image to articulate his challenge to linear science had a poetic justice, for chaos science, like all revolutions in science, assaults and extends boundaries.[28] Chaos science is a paradigm shift that calls into question the nature of measuring, the value of our tools of measurement, and the very notion of accuracy. We might compare "fuzzy logic," another new science that stretches the boundaries of science and logic and achieves greater precision by debunking Aristotelian logic and by embracing subjectivity and intuition. (Like "Chaos" science, "Fuzzy" logic is a misnomer: "Fuzzy logic is not logic that is fuzzy, but logic that describes and tames fuzziness.")[29]

The result of these reevaluations is twofold. It changes *how* we see, broadening the tools of reason and science. Secondly, it changes *what* we see. Where Euclidean geometry and Newtonian physics before could see only mechanistic and deterministic order in the cosmos, chaos science now can see more: the hidden order in nature's non-linear profusion, in the apparently random, turbulent, and unpredictable. What was irrelevant to science, what was mere noise, is now central to our understanding of the unfolding order of nature. To broaden the scope of reason is to embrace more of life, even those shapes which scientists have, according to Mandelbrot in a catalog typical of improvisation "call[ed] *grainy, hydralike, in between, pimply, pocky, ramified, seaweedy, strange, tangled, tortuous, wiggly, wispy, wrinkled,* and the like."[30] Looking at these forms with his rigorous new mathematics, Mandelbrot finds "a world of pure plastic beauty unsuspected till now."[31] So to broaden the scope of reason is an effort to see life whole, to discover its fundamental principles, "the morphology of the amorphous."

---

28. See Thomas S. Kuhn, *The Structure of Scientific Revolutions,* 4th ed. (Chicago and London: The University of Chicago Press, 2012 [1962]).

29. Daniel McNeill and Paul Freiberger, *Fuzzy Logic: The Revolutionary Computer Technology That Is Changing Our World* (New York: Touchstone, 1993), 12.

30. Mandelbrot, *The Fractal Geometry of Nature,* 5; emphasis in text.

31. Ibid., 4.

Chaos scientists find a universality that is not just qualitative but quantitative, not just patterns and structures that are analogous, but also, like the Greek golden rectangle, maintain always the same numerical proportions. Mitchell J. Feigenbaum was the first to discover the universal constant in chaotic systems.[32] Like the spontaneity of spontaneous texts, the *randomness* or disorder of chaos is real: we can never know what the next point in a solution to a nonlinear equation will be. But like the formal system of conventions employed by improvisations, chaos is a *deterministic* system: each point in the universe of solutions will be on a predetermined, self-similar structure. Each point, randomly chosen, will be part of an order. Think improvised jazz: each note fits the system of chromatic changes but we auditors know not what the next note will be. Ultimately the revolution of chaos science lay in its double proof at once that "nature is nonlinear in its soul" and that "Nature is constrained."[33] So, too, are spontaneous texts which, as we saw in "Kubla Khan," predictably employ the same conventions to achieve roughly the same thematic ends. And so too the rhetor's art as Quintilian first described it: one is constrained to master the skills of oratory in order to become skillful; once skilled, *inventio*'s improvisatory function kicks in and one is no longer constrained. You must pass through a linear progression acquiring your skills; once the skills are acquired you enter the realm of the non-linear. It becomes clearer why the rhetorical tradition since Quintilian has placed improvisation, tapping such power, as the culmination of its art, "The greatest fruit of our studies, the richest harvest of our long labour."[34]

Chaos science's relation to *life as we experience it* is another significant feature of its revolution. "The paradigm shift of paradigm shifts," as chaos scientist Ralph Abraham calls it, chaos science implicitly condemns the reductionism and the increasing specialization of modern science.[35] The last of the twentieth-century's trio of dismantlers of Newtonian physics (after relativity and quantum mechanics), chaos science is the only one of that group, as Gleick points out, that "applies to the universe we see and touch, to objects

---

32. See Gleick's discussion in *Chaos*, 173-75.
33. Ibid., 152.
34. *Institutio Oratoria* 10.7.
35. As quoted in Gleick, *Chaos*, 52.

on a human scale."[36] And part of its deep agenda is to make us feel *At Home in the Universe,* as Stuart Kauffman's recent title tellingly suggests and as Ralph Abraham's new book makes clear (*Chaos, Gaia, Eros: A Chaos Pioneer Uncovers the Three Great Streams of History*). Both Kauffman and Abraham are Chaos science pioneers. Such an appeal explains why, despite the complexity of its mathematics, chaos science has achieved a certain broad-based popular status, spawning a virtual industry at a grass-roots level as well as in the academy. Aficionados of Chaos pursue the science through Gleick's superb history of its birth and through Mandelbrot's encyclopedic *Fractals,* the best-selling book on higher mathematics in history, and through user-friendly software products and full-color, coffee-table books. Chaos scientists bemoan this popularization and yet it is inevitable: chaos science is a science *of* the world and *for* the people.

Like the science, the literature of chaos, improvisation, is a democratic leveler with broad appeal. Improvisations debunk received truths, received ways of expressions, and received hierarchies. Like chaos science, improvisations would have us see more of life, not only what Reason can see, the categorical, but what comes to us through the visionary, the unconscious, or the intuitive. It is a literature whose ultimate theme is the admonition to embrace more of life. Terence's adage (now enlarged) could do double service as motto not only for literary improvisation but also for chaotics: "nothing human (or natural) is foreign to me."

This theme of the all-inclusive embrace is itself a transvaluation of traditional, received values. Chaos science finds meaning in every random point: every point carries new information and is therefore valuable. If I ask you to count by twos (2, 4, 6, ...), to use Katherine Hayles's example, then information does not reside in the individual integers but in the underlying pattern (counting by twos).[37] Implicit in such an operation are the following equations: predictable = understandable = meaningful = valuable. In a chaotic system, on the other hand, these contrary equations are in force: random = unpredictable = meaningful = valuable. Analogously, to embrace all of life, the fool as much as the reasonable man, the unconscious as much

36. Ibid., 6.
37. Hayles, *Chaos Bound,* 6.

as the conscious upends received hierarchies. Stephen Dedalus in that monumental improvisation *Ulysses* finds "the manifestation of God" not in church or ecclesiastical ritual but in the shouts of children on a football pitch. "That is God," he tells the schoolmaster, his boss, and is fired for the epiphany. To appreciate the found as much as the made object, the accidental as much as the expected event, or as the poet Wallace Stevens sums it up, to find the "strange relation" in "life's nonsense" and not just in its sense, is to redefine man not as *homo faber* but rather as *homo experiens*—not man the maker, but rather man experiencing; and not man as noun but as present participle, man becoming not being. Chaos scientist and Nobel laureate Ilya Prigogine has a book by that title: *From Being to Becoming*.

If man is defined by his experiencing, then the challenge is to be alert to life in the moment. To embrace these new defining characteristics of man is to go beyond seizing the day. It is to enjoin us to seize all of life: *carpe vitam*. To do so, as Stevens's carefully chosen verb suggests, will "pierce us with strange relation"—to have one's armor of sophistication and civilization and rationality, one's artificial boundaries, breached and ruptured. This imagery of a wounding that becomes a gift and a boon suggests that the improviser enacts the myth of the hero, who, as Joseph Campbell makes clear, can begin his or her journey in quest of a true, transcendent heroism only by abandoning his sense of adequacy or completeness.[38] The wound, our insufficiency, is our link to the sacred, for as Norman O. Brown writes, "A sacred act must involve violence and rupture, breaking the boundary."[39] Improvisation's foolish persona serves this archetypal function at the same time that it provides the means for the improviser to explore more of life, high and low, rational and irrational. It is by being mastered (wounded) that the hero becomes master; thus the archetype of the hero contains within it spontaneity's two poles. Embracing life's totality is ultimately, like spontaneity itself, a problematic gesture. Just as we are doomed to the mediation of mind, of language, and of perception—even, according to Bruner and to neuroscientists, to the empirical selectivity hard-wired into our nervous system—so too are we doomed to

---

38. Joseph Campbell, *The Hero with a Thousand Faces* (New York: Pantheon, 1949), 16-17.

39. "Dionysus in 1990," in Brown, *Apocalypse and/or Metamorphosis*, 197.

choices. To choose "this, not that" is, as Kenneth Burke argues, the fundamental human gesture, the gesture that separates us from other species.[40] And to choose is not only to embrace but also to exclude. "To embrace life" then has meaning only as part of a binary, as an opposition to, a rejection of more exclusive forms of being and thinking: systematic rationality, the School-men's logic, Newtonian science, Enlightenment rationalism, scientific positivism, post-industrial, corporate America. All these are *more* exclusionary than the improviser's incorporative gesture. The gesture's meaning inheres not in what's *embraced* but in the performance of *embracing more,* which is to acknowledge that the gesture is fundamentally rhetorical and performative.

But this gesture is not one classical science is able to make. Classical science attempts to become nature's ventriloquist in large part because it has forced upon modern man the recognition that nature is essentially dumb and hence isolated from man. As Prigogine points out, "the paradox of classical science" is that

> it revealed to men a dead, passive nature, a nature that behaves as an automaton which, once programmed, continues to follow the rules inscribed in the program. In this sense the dialogue with nature isolated man from nature instead of bringing him closer to it. A triumph of nature turned into a sad truth. It seemed that science debased everything it touched.[41]

This view lies at the heart of Wordsworth's "we murder to dissect" and of the Romantics' reaction against Newton's rainbow and the physical sciences. The development of the biological sciences, championed by Goethe, in the early nineteenth century was one result. Chaos science continues this Romantic trend. Nature may still be dumb but it is also noisy, full of "grainy, hydralike, in between, pimply, pocky, ramified, seaweedy, strange, tangled, tortuous, wiggly, wispy, wrinkled" aspects, so difficult for classical science even to see (or hear), let alone rationally to describe. Nature may be dumb

---

40. "Terministic Screens," in Kenneth Burke, *Language as Symbolic Action: Essays on Life, Literature, and Method* (Berkeley and Los Angeles: University of California Press, 1966), 4.

41. Ilya Prigogine, *From Being to Becoming: Time and Complexity in the Physical Sciences* (New York: W. H. Freeman & Co., 1981), 6.

but, random and non-linear, it is no automaton. It is full of surprises. Nor need we under this new paradigm feel wholly isolated from nature. For, best of all, not dumb at all, Nature speaks the same language we do. The foliations that essentially characterize natural form—microcosmic and macrocosmic—shape too the form of our blood and nervous systems. The "One Life" is after all, as Coleridge poetically argued, "within us *and* abroad."[42] As Prigogine's subtitle declares, chaotics promises a "new dialogue with nature"—a far cry from Bacon's unmediated echo.

Thoreau anticipates the universal fractal geometry of all life when, in what has been called the central demonstration of *Walden,* he describes water flowing down "a deep cut on the railroad." The form the coursing water takes is a self-ordering system that resembles all life:

> When the frost comes out in the spring, and even in a thawing day in the winter, the sand begins to flow down the slopes like lava, sometimes bursting out through the snow and overflowing it where no sand was to be seen before. Innumerable little streams overlap and interlace one with another, exhibiting a sort of hybrid product, which obeys half way the law of currents, and half way that of vegetation. As it flows it takes the forms of sappy leaves or vines, making heaps of pulpy sprays a foot or more in depth, and resembling, as you look down on them, the laciniated [fringed] lobed and imbricated [overlapping] thalluses [green shoots] of some lichens; or you are reminded of coral, of leopards' paws or birds' feet, of brains or lungs or bowels, and excrements of all kinds...You find thus in the very sands an anticipation of the vegetable leaf. No wonder that the earth expresses itself outwardly in leaves, it so labors with the idea inwardly. The atoms have already learned this law, and are pregnant by it.[43]

"What makes this sand foliage remarkable," he continues, is its spontaneity: "its springing into existence thus suddenly." Even language reflects these dynamic, self-ordering forces:

> *Internally,* whether in the globe or animal body, it is a moist thick lobe, a word especially applicable to the liver and lungs and the *leaves* of fat,

---

42. Samuel Taylor Coleridge, "The Eolian Harp," in *The Oxford Anthology of English Literature,* 2: 237, line 26; emphasis added.

43. Thoreau, *Walden, Civil Disobedience, and Other Writings,* 205.

(λείβω, *labor, lapsus,* to flow or slip downward, a lapsing; λοβος, *globus,* lobe, globe, also lap, flap, and many other words), *externally* a dry thin *leaf,* even as the *f* and *v* are a pressed and dried *b.* The radicals of lobe are *lb,* the soft mass of the *b* (single lobed, or B, double lobed), with a liquid *l* behind it pressing it forward. In globe, *glb,* the guttural *g* adds to the meaning the capacity of the throat.[44]

Linguists will tell you Thoreau here goes astray. But he is determined to see the principle everywhere, in everything:

The feathers and wings of birds are still drier and thinner leaves. Thus, also, you pass from the lumpish grub in the earth to the airy and fluttering butterfly. The very globe continually transcends and translates itself, and becomes winged in its orbit. Even ice begins with delicate crystal leaves, as if it had flowed into moulds which the fronds of water plants have impressed on the watery mirror. The whole tree itself is but one leaf and rivers are still vaster leaves whose pulp is intervening earth, and towns and cities are the ova of insects in their axils.[45]

"Thus," Thoreau concludes, "it seemed this one hillside illustrated the principle of all the operations of Nature."[46]

In a sense Thoreau's language throughout this long, complex passage indulges in pathetic fallacy, projecting human characteristics onto nature. But it is important to see just how much humanness he is attributing to nature, and to acknowledge that he does so on the basis not merely of emotion but of a unitary vision—he does not merely feel *for* nature but truly with it. For finally in concluding that "the very globe continually transcends and translates itself, and becomes winged in its orbit," Thoreau ascribes to all of nature the very same longing that is at the center of his book: the self-transcendence symbolized by the *talaria* (Hermes's winged shoes) he wishes John Field, one of his surrogates and exempla in the "Baker Farm" chapter, could get on his "wading webbed bog-trotting feet."[47] His foliage-like webfeet would become foliage-like, feathered wings, the utterly terrestrial becoming the divinely celestial. This is what Thoreau would wish upon us all: that through

---

44. Ibid., 206.
45. Ibid.
46. Ibid., 207.
47. Ibid., 143.

participation with nature we find our oneness with it and with divinity. Like chaos science, Thoreau here through a grand monist vision leaps the chasm between man and nature. This includes our most human invention, speech. His leap is associated with winged Hermes, the trickster god and mediator between gods and men, who we will see in my next chapter is the muse or tutelary deity of improvisation.[48]

In sum then, chaos science helps us to contextualize the boundary-breaking and paradigm-shifting nature of literary improvisation, and to appreciate its incorporative, encyclopedic gesture. At the heart of both the science and the literature of chaos lie questions about the nature of reason and of freedom. At its heart, the literature of apparent chaos, improvisation, shares with chaos science not only the effort to violate and extend boundaries, but also a concern with the deterministic and the free. Improvisation represents an archetypal locus of consciousness, a structure of thought immutable and universal, which takes this form whenever an artist, or scientist, finds himself in that locus—mental place—or conceptual space.

What locus? What conceptual space? Improvisation is preeminently the aesthetic of paradigm shifts when a culture questions reason's limits and, through such questioning, seeks to redefine and expand reason's tools and its scope. Improvisations appear throughout literary history, but they proliferate during periods of social and intellectual upheaval: classical Greece, the Renaissance, the Industrial Revolution (early and late), and, with quickening pace, the twentieth century. Whatever the improviser's politics, for or against the paradigm shift, the issue of rationality's constraints is central and characteristic.

In a sense, however, the issue of reason is just the thematic tip of the iceberg. Beneath the issue of reason's use lie questions about what we use reason

---

48. A former colleague believed that this central demonstration of Walden was scientifically sound. I believe I had the gall to quote at him Schiller's response to Goethe after a night of hearing about the *Urpflanze,* the "original plant" that Goethe thought had been the primordial ancestor of all life: "It is not an experience," said Schiller, "it is an idea." It seems to me now that chaos science in many ways confirms Thoreau's great unitary vision. Gordon, my apologies. See Boudreau, *The Roots of Walden and the Tree of Life.*

on and for, that is, to understand and to appreciate not only Nature, but also the fundamental polarities of our being: freedom and necessity, chaos and order, the impulses to incorporate and to exclude. The genre that tries on for size unreason—the fortuitous, the uncontrolled, the fuzzy, and the encyclopedic and oceanic—is an answerable form to deal with the limiting and controlling power of Reason, that murderous dissector and excluder.

A comparison with *fin-de-siècle* aestheticism is here telling. Aestheticism is improvisation's logical opposite in that it celebrates art, not artlessness; total control of one's materials and craft, not submission to forces beyond them; in sum, decadence, not renewal. Where aestheticism results from a cultural dead-end (however fruitful) where all past skills are at the disposal of the *fin-de-siècle* craftsman-artist, spontaneity is the stuff and the agent of cultural breakthroughs: spontaneous texts fly by the seat of their pants because the old forms and old skills no longer apply or are no longer adequate. Conversely, vatic spontaneity, as for example Pindar's, or ironic spontaneity, as for example Swift's, can be mustered in a rear-guard action to fend off the new. Either way, improvisers arise during periods of breakthrough, be they the agent of the van-or rear-guard. In the next chapter we will look at examples of both political stances, both conservative and radical.

One of the features of improvisation that helps persuade me that we are dealing here with a coherent and persistent literary aesthetic is its uncanny predictability, the fact that it is a deterministic system. Though we never know quite what an improviser will say next, we *do* know, at a certain level of scale, the directions their turbulent texts will take. My Faustian assertion here is that, just as Feigenbaum has discovered the universal mathematical constant in chaos, so too have we discovered the universal constants of improvisation. No Einstein, I will settle for being improvisation's Feigenbaum. Starting with the gesture of spontaneity and deploying the conventions described in Chapter 3, the improviser will insist that systematic rationality must be subverted/enlarged/debunked by whatever terms the dominant market least promotes: inspiration/vision/enthusiasm/intuition/heart/opium/madness.

Having insisted upon this subversion, the improviser will then backtrack, admitting that, after all, inspiration/vision/enthusiasm/intuition/heart/opium/madness and the immediacy achieved thereby are in some way problematic, not necessarily what we hoped for, or not necessarily achievable.

Finally the improviser will "settle" for the gesture of embracing life: we can't have true immediacy, but if we purify/enlarge/redefine rationality, making it more open to life, we can at least experience more of life's profusion and plenitude. *Carpe vitam!*

I qualify "settle" because, while the gesture of embracing life is often cast as a retreat from the more radical quest to experience pure presence, often too the gesture takes on a hieratic, apocalyptic quality, no retreat at all. Ralph Abraham's recent *Chaos, Gaia, Eros,* an important chaos scientist's encyclopedic study of myth, history, and the environment, demonstrates that this quasi-religious and apocalyptic impulse exists in chaos science as well.

2. Postmodernism and Improvisation I

This is the pattern of improvisation, a pattern we have seen already in these pages, finding it in such wildly diverse authors as John Dryden and Jerome Bruner, George Herbert and Henry David Thoreau, John Locke and Benoît Mandelbrot, to recall just a few. Improvisers challenge the prevailing rationality; they offer some new faculty or instrumentality that promises a deeper penetration of the world's immediacies; then, if deeper penetration becomes problematic, they settle instead for a *broader* penetration, and embrace the concrete particulars of the world. Postmodernism, like chaos science, embodies this pattern and can be better understood in light of the aesthetics of improvisation.

Postmodernism shares with improvisation many of its fundamental characteristics: the insistently oppositional nature of its discourse; its interest in borders and the liminal; its canon-breaking insistence that every artifact be treated with equal regard as text and resource; its interest in and use of the aleatory, products of chance, and mere "noise"; its forsaking, in Derrida's term, "the operation of mastery" as an object of desire. The incorporative, encyclopedic gesture is central to both. In one of the foundational texts of postmodernism, *Learning from Las Vegas,* for example, architect Robert Venturi urges us to "learn from everything"—even the architecture of Las Vegas.[49] Both display a tendency to, as Gregory Ulmer describes in writing

---

49. Robert Venturi, Dennis Scott Brown, and Steven Izenour, *Learning from Las Vegas* (Cambridge, Mass., and London: The MIT Press, 1972).

on postmodernism, "abandon the conventional book form in favor of the essay—incomplete, digressive, without proof or conclusion, in which could be juxtaposed fragments, minute details...drawn from every level of the contemporary world."[50] And both display what Ulmer calls "an epistemology of performance—knowing as making, producing, doing, acting."[51]

Derrida, a key voice of the movement, will serve here as example, for he best exhibits another crucial link between improvisation and postmodernism: the willingness to play the fool. Derrida plays the game of deconstruction with a tone of apparent dead seriousness, but it is only when one sees the fool's cap and bells he slyly but surreptitiously wears that his program begins to make a kind of sense. Only when we see his kinship to Erasmus's Folly do we see that, like all improvisers before him, he seeks to embrace life's non-sense, what had been left out (differed and deferred) by the status quo and the powers that be—literary, philosophic, economical, political—that enforce that status quo. Being an improviser he is of course encyclopedic, all-encompassing. Derrida takes everything—and everyone—on.

The foolish aspect of Derrida's persona, his antic, Jarryan "'pataphysics," as it were, is rarely remarked upon but crucial in his affecting such an all-encompassing challenge.[52] Derrida's effort is ever to provoke, to "épater les bourgeois." The old guard's angry counterattacks on deconstruction target the very weapons Derrida purposefully deploys from his fool's bag of tricks: puns, the failure to define key terms, the macaronic play of many languages and many texts. Like the fool of the Renaissance court, Derrida will just not sit still; like the alchemical metal named after improvisation's muse Mercury, he cannot be pinned down.

---

50. Ulmer, "The Object of Post-Criticism," 97.

51. Ibid., 94.

52. Burhan Tufail notes "only one reference to Jarry in Derrida," "Oulipian Grammatology: *La règle du jeu*," in *The French Connections of Jacques Derrida*, edited by Julian Wolfreys, John Brannigan, and Ruth Robbins (Albany: State University of New York, 1999), 132. Yet Jarry's pataphysics anticipates much in Derrida. Being a "science of 'laws governing exceptions,'" it also anticipates chaos science. Quoted in *Selected Works of Alfred Jarry*, edited by Roger Shattuck and Simon Watson Taylor (New York: Grove Press, 1980), 19. See Hayles's example of non-linear series where meaning comes not from an underlying pattern but from the granular detail in *Chaos Bound*, 6.

Nor can his central concepts. In "Différance" he writes:

> It is the domination of beings that *différance* everywhere comes to solicit, in the sense that *solicitare,* in old Latin, means to shake as a whole, to make tremble in entirety. Therefore, it is the determination of Being as presence or as beingness that is interrogated by the thought of *différance.* Such a question could not emerge and be understood unless the *différance* between Being and beings were somewhere to be broached. First consequence: *différance* is not. It is not a present being, however excellent, unique, principal, or transcendent. It governs nothing, reigns over nothing, and nowhere exercises any authority. It is not announced by any capital letter. Not only is there no kingdom of *différance,* but *différance* instigates the subversion of every kingdom.[53]

Derrida's insistence on the archaic definition of "solicitation"—from *sollus,* "all," and *ciere,* "to move, to shake"—is characteristic. To shake the status quo *to its foundations* is exactly the point. It is a goal shared with the fool whose carnivalesque purpose is to turn the world upside down. First presented, we must remember, in the heady days of 1968, "soixante-huit," Derrida's revolution is the more complete, not only "instigat[ing] the subversion of every kingdom," but with no one and no thing, not even the fool himself, sitting the throne.

With the overthrow of the logocentric, Derrida theoretically promises nothing, no presence. Theoretically what *différance* finally yields is a *vide,* a great emptiness: "First consequence: *différance* is not." Were Derrida to show his fool's pied colors outright here, the appropriate tag to go with the revelation would be "Gotcha!" So, in practice, by the pressure of the improvisatory conventions he deploys, Derrida offers a new immediacy and presence. The goal of his performance is not to convey a certain body of knowledge or of concepts. It is rather to produce in the audience the state of consciousness that can appreciate, if not directly experience, the *texture* (the interweaving, the touch, the enfolding) of the world. *Carpe vitam! Voilà* presence: it is not what we seize, but our act of seizing.

Like most of us, Derrida would have his cake and eat it too. He celebrates improvisation even as, echoing Adorno, he declares improvisation impossible:

---

53. Derrida, *Margins of Philosophy,* 21.

It is not easy to improvise. It's the most difficult thing to do. Even when one improvises in front of a camera or a microphone, one ventriloquizes or leaves another to speak in one's place, the schemas and languages that are already there. There are already a great number of prescriptions that are prescribed in our memory and in our culture. All the names are already preprogrammed. It's already the names that inhibit our ability to ever really improvise. One can't say whatever one wants. One is obliged, more or less, to reproduce the stereotypical discourse. And so I believe in improvisation, and I fight for improvisation. But always with the belief that it's impossible. And there, where there is improvisation, I am not able to see myself. I am blind to myself, and it's what I will see, no, I won't see it, it's for others to see. The one who is improvised here, no, I won't ever see him.[54]

Again, as Stephen Greenblatt says, "We cannot locate a point of pure premeditation or pure randomness." Just as for Adorno in jazz "the improvised detail is determined completely by the scheme," so for Derrida "the schemas and languages...are already there." He believes in improvisation despite its impossibility. It exists only in an unselfconscious state. For the moment, at least, Derrida is a Cartesian: if improvisation exists, his *cogito* and hence his *ego*, doesn't.

Derrida denies the existence of pure presence promised by logos and by the status quo, but he also affirms it, tacitly in his performative style and explicitly in at least one place. What he says elsewhere of Lévi-Strauss applies equally to himself, that he "remain[s] faithful to this double intention: to preserve as an instrument something whose truth value he criticizes."[55] Derrida is adamant that pure presence does not exist and is not available to us. *Toujours déjà*: there is always something before, something that antecedes the apparently originary or spontaneous act. Derrida nonetheless explicitly discovers pure presence in Antonin Artaud's theater of cruelty, which is "not a *representation*. It is life itself."[56] Artaud's illogical theater of cruelty is "the primordial and privileged site," the "triumph of pure mise en scène" over the logo-and

---

54. From an "unpublished interview, 1982," quoted in *Derrida*, DVD, directed by Kirby Dick and Amy Ziering (2002; Zeitgeist Films, 2004).

55. Derrida, *Writing and Difference*, 284.

56. Ibid., 234.

theocentric text.[57] "Released from the text and the author-god," Derrida adds, *"mise en scène* [is] returned to its creative and founding freedom."[58] Of course, as Derrida admits, Artaud's achievement of this affirmation depends largely upon his negation of classical theater—the *differ,* the dialogic opposition, in *différance.* Thus, like other improvisations, Artaud's art and Derrida's deconstruction achieve their originary force by opposing, shaking up, something that preceded them. Indeed, "there is always," Derrida asserts, "a murder at the origin of cruelty": "And, first of all, a parricide. The origin of theater, such as it must be restored, is the hand lifted against the abusive wielder of the logos, against the father, against the God of a stage subjugated to the power of speech and text."[59] As with improviser Robert Altman, with Derrida and with Artaud there is no proscenium. Actor and audience are performatively one. The contradiction at the heart of this project—"origin…restored" and elsewhere, "returned to its creative and founding freedom"—goes unnoticed. *Toujours déjà* indeed!

Derrida's challenge to the status quo is embodied not only in his persona and in his philosophic embrace of parricide but also in his improvisatory style. The use of abrupt openings, puns, neologisms, oxymora (e.g., "speech before words"[60]) digressions, fragments, catachreses (mixed metaphors), and anacolutha (broken syntax or grammar) convey the impression, as do other improvisations, of a mind at work. As do the clipped, Senecan periods in the quote above: "It is not easy to improvise. It's the most difficult thing to do." Certainly, like other improvisers and to the objection of many, Derrida's style has this effect, to make his readers work and think. The intertextual nature of his text promotes both effects: we witness Derrida reading, playing off texts; we ourselves perforce do the same.

And like many improvisations Derrida emphasizes the here-and-now, performance character of his discourse.[61] He claims that the "question[ing] of the

---

57. Ibid., 236.
58. Ibid., 237.
59. Ibid., 239.
60. Ibid., 240.
61. On the performative nature of Derrida's deconstruction, see Rodolphe Gasché,

here and now is explicitly enacted in dissemination," but everywhere belies the claim in his prose's texture and in the immediacy of the pleasure that it gives.[62] His performance—his *mise en scène*, as it were—*embodies* rather than *represents* deconstruction, achieving (like Artaud) the presence he denies exists. But conveying this impression also depends not only on these devices that improvisers have used since classical times, but also on the fundamental gesture and stance of displacing another more logical and discursive style. Derrida calls this gesture parricide; Harold Bloom calls it a swerve, *clinamen*, from the poetic father figure. It is, as I have shown, a gesture fundamental to improvisation: my style is newer, more alive, and truer to life than *your* style. Paradoxically Derrida must kill not only western metaphysical writing as generic father but also improvisation. Historically, improvisation is the form that through its dramatic spoken-ness most vociferously privileges orality and presence, the two key logocentric terms Derrida sets out to deconstruct in western metaphysics. Like most sons, he becomes the father while, and by, killing him.

Finally, like most improvisations, Derrida's deconstruction retreats from the extremity it apparently embraces. He writes:

> The absence of an author and his text does not abandon the stage to dereliction. The stage is not forsaken, given over to improvisatory anarchy, to "chance vaticination"...or to "the capriciousness of untrained inspiration." Everything, thus will be *prescribed* in a writing and a text whose fabric will no longer resemble the model of classical representation.[63]

In this passage Derrida struggles with one of the central expressive tensions that informs the heart of improvisations throughout literary history. Freedom does not bring "anarchy"; prophecy is not by "chance"; and inspiration is neither capricious nor "untrained." Indeed "[e]verything...will be *prescribed*"! What an odd and surprising end for our return to our "creative and *founding* freedom" invoked by such a radical voice! And how like the central paradox of chaos science, where the radical freedom of dynamic systems leads to an

---

Inventions of Difference: On Jacques Derrida (Cambridge, Mass.: Harvard University Press, 1994).

62. Derrida, *Dissemination*, 7.

63. Derrida, *Writing and Difference*, 239.

awareness of the limits of that freedom: "Nature was *constrained*."[64] Like many other improvisers, Artaud and Derrida associate this new freedom with the freedom of dreams, "but," Derrida explains, "of *cruel* dreams, that is to say, absolutely necessary and determined dreams, dreams calculated and given direction, as opposed to what Artaud believed to be the empirical disorder of spontaneous dreams."[65] Having murdered father, theatrical director, deity, text, and logos, each for representing coercive control, Artaud and Derrida here enthrone an author with control over "the *law* of dreams."[66] In fact, Derrida hastens to clarify, the theater of cruelty is not a theater of the unconscious: "Almost the contrary. Cruelty is consciousness, is exposed lucidity."[67] Where *id* was, there shall *ego* be, apparently.

Despite these qualifications to the apparent radical nature of his vision, Derrida finally moves, like other improvisations and like chaos science, toward a hieratic, apocalyptic, and all-embracing vision of *this* world. "Regression toward the unconscious," he writes, "fails if it does not reawaken the sacred, if it is not both the 'mystic' experience of 'revelation' and the manifestation of life in their first emergence…A new epiphany of the supernatural and the divine must occur within cruelty."[68] His emphasis is as much on *life* as on the *divine*. Improvisation's trope of the catalog anticipates Derrida's privileging of gesture and *mise en scène* over text. Like Stephen Dedalus at the school window in *Ulysses*—"That is god," he says, pointing to boys playing in the schoolyard—both gestures point to the world rather than to some meaning behind it; both capture in their epiphanies as much of life as possible in their ever-widening net.

Having noted the stylistic and rhetorical gambits that situate Derrida in the aesthetic of improvisation, the extent to which we can anticipate, even predict, this endgame does indeed suggest that "everything" is "prescribed." Understanding Derrida's connection to the aesthetic of improvisation helps disclose an expressive tension central to the deconstructive project and to

---

64. Gleick, *Chaos*, 152.
65. Derrida, *Writing and Difference*, 242.
66. Ibid.; emphasis in original.
67. Ibid.
68. Ibid., 243.

contextualize both the necessity of Derrida's stylistic oddities, so often challenged, and the radical nature of his prophetic vision, so often misunderstood.
The point is not that the aesthetics of improvisation anticipates postmodernism or that the tradition of improvisation directly influences it. Rather,
my point is more radical and probably one that will make postmodernists
uncomfortable. Though vocally anti-humanistic and insistently new, Derrida's project participates in the age-old human (if not necessarily humanist)
quest for immediacy, for an unmediated experience that cannot be achieved.
The aesthetics of improvisation, and the persistent and archetypal locus of
consciousness it expresses, is the trace that is *always already* there, anticipating and in part belying Derrida's profound originality.

The coincidence in time and space of chaos science and deconstruction,
so wildly different on the surface and yet extensively and deeply similar,
suggests that they both spring from the same local, time-bound historical-
cultural matrix, that they are twinned inflexions of the same synchronic
paradigm shift. Nonetheless, that the aesthetics of improvisation anticipates
both suggests that they participate in something out-of-time and essential to
our humanity, a diachronic structure of thought immutable and universal
wherein are explored the polarities and the limits of reason, order, and freedom.[69] Articulations of the same paradigm shift, they employ an aesthetic
intrinsic to *paradigm-shifting* whenever it occurs.

Improvisers, Derrida included, *write in* the new paradigm in this double
sense. Improvisation is the form artists employ when they work *within* or
during a new paradigm. Improvisations make up much of a new paradigm's
literary output. But, first and foremost and logically prior, improvisation is
the form used to *bring about* the paradigm shift. Improvisations are part and
parcel of creating—*writing in*—the new paradigm.

3. *Postmodernism and Improvisation II*

One further example, drawn from a practical rather than theoretical source,
can help clarify postmodernism's participation in the aesthetics of improvisation while serving further to exemplify improvisation's almost uncanny pre-

---

69. On the tension between global and local in chaos science and deconstruction,
see Hayles, *Chaos Bound,* 209-35.

dictability. It will demonstrate at the same time improvisation's currency not only in contemporary science and literary-philosophical discourse, but also in the current arts scene. In *Seeing is Forgetting the Name of the Thing One Sees*, about the installation artist Robert Irwin, Lawrence Weschler describes the artist's quest to embody in his art the "primacy of perception":

> Irwin has become increasingly convinced that perception precedes conception, that every thought or idea arises within the *context* of an infinite field of perceptual presence which it thereupon rushes to delimit...Irwin defines *perception* as the individual's originary, direct interface with the phenomenally given. We are speaking here of the overbrimming synesthesia of undifferentiated sensations—they are not even defined yet as sounds versus colors, and so forth—they exist as the plenum of experience.[70]

Like other improvisers, Irwin seems to long to return to William James's "one great blooming, buzzing confusion." Wechsler's title is drawn from Valéry, an improviser as we have seen, and a key modern theorist on spontaneity. Weschler traces Irwin's ideas to his experiences in Japan with Zen and his reading of the phenomenologists. Irwin's quest is to be not an artificer or maker of artifacts, but rather a passive transcriber or even a ventriloquist's dummy:

> He became convinced, [writes Weschler], that if he could give himself over to the canvas, if he devoted the time, that instead of his telling it what was correct, it would tell him. "Renaissance man tells the world what he finds interesting about it and then tries to control it. I took to waiting for the world to tell me so that I could respond. Intuition replaced logic. I just attended to the circumstances, and after weeks and weeks of observation, of hairline readjustments, the right solution would presently announce itself."[71]

These ideas find articulation in Irwin's increasing minimalism and increasing de-emphasis of the art object (mediation) in favor of the act of perception (pre-mediation). The goal of his late line paintings (that is, mere arrangements of lines on canvas) says Irwin, "is that they have no existence beyond your participation. They are not abstractable in that sense" and cannot be

---

70. Weschler, *Seeing Is Forgetting the Name of the Thing One Sees,* 180.
71. Ibid., 74

conceptualized as idea.[72] "They only 'work,'" adds Weschler, "immediately; they command an incredible presence—'a rich floating sense of energy,' as Irwin describes it—but only to one who is in fact *present.*"[73]

Proceeding from intuition, not logic, and striving for so much immediacy, Irwin's art, we will not be surprised to hear, seeks to reorganize the way we think and see. "What we're really talking about," Irwin tells Weschler,

> is changing the whole visual structure of how you look at the world. Because now when I walk down the street, I no longer at least to the same degree, bring the world into focus in the same way…So the implications of that kind of art are very rash; I mean, in time they have the ability to change every single thing in the culture itself, because all of our systems—social systems, political systems, all our institutions—are simply reasonable reflections of how our mind organizes. So we're talking about a different mental organization, which ultimately, in time, has to result in different social, political, and cultural organizations, because they're the same thing.[74]

Such ambition helps explain why his New York dealer, Arnold Glimcher, once remarked that "The avant-garde today may persist in the life and work of only one man—and that's Bob Irwin."[75] Certainly in his ambition he is heir to the postwar "culture of spontaneity" that Belgrad describes (to offer but one example among many):

> Spontaneous beat writing pursued an integration of conscious and unconscious thought processes; it thus brought to awareness the ideological contradictions normally hidden from the conscious mind. As Ginsberg explained his poetic technique to Ezra Pound: "You manifest the process of thoughts—make a model of consciousness,…with all the dramatic imperfections, fuck-ups—anyone with sense can see the crazy part." This technique of disclosing the social neurosis criticized the dominant culture from within.[76]

---

72. Ibid., 76.
73. Ibid., 76-77.
74. Ibid., 200.
75. Ibid., 201.
76. Belgrad, *The Culture of Spontaneity,* 230.

But the two parts of this dialectic, the quest for immediacy and the rejection of received forms of institutional reason, call forth their inevitable third: the retreat from the quest for pure presence. Throughout Irwin's career, Weschler finally admits,

> he has been trying to approach—and slowly getting closer and closer to his goal—that presence that would not be metaphorical. For Irwin sees presence and metaphor as polar opposites. Presence demands presence, whereas metaphor allows, indeed requires, absence—evasion…Across [his career], in calibrating presence, Irwin was still creating objects that were metaphors of presence. Even [his two most successful installations] were more about what it might be like to be present than about presences. They were however getting closer to the quarry, and in his most recent work, Irwin has gotten closer still.[77]

Characteristically "his most successful piece to date" in this approach to pure presence is "one that has never been realized"—characteristic because pure presence, after all, can never be realized. Equally symptomatic is his quest to "calibrat[e] presence"—a locution that either indulges in a Zen koan or gets caught in the inevitable paradox of immediacy, or both. To say that his Faustian pursuit is characteristic is not to denigrate Irwin's brilliant career and art, but to suggest that even if realized, this "most successful piece" would again recede, like the vanishing horizon that escapes ahead of our endless quest to reach it. Still, and predictably, Irwin settles for embracing more and more of life, as he tells his biographer:

> There are things I've undertaken as an artist that I will never accomplish in my lifetime…It's just not possible. The kind of change I'm envisioning, the ideas I'm entertaining, simply don't enter society whole. There's always a process of mediation, overlapping, intermeshing, threading into the fabric. *But we're headed there: the complexity of consciousness, its capacity to sustain being in presence in all its rich variety will be growing with each generation.* Sometimes I feel on the verge of that.[78]

The going is the goal, apparently, along with all that life one experiences along the path. "If man's reach should not exceed his grasp, / Then what's a heaven

---

77. Weschler, *Seeing Is Forgetting the Name of the Thing One Sees,* 198.
78. Ibid., 202; emphasis added.

for?" asked Browning's improviser, the fresco painter Fra Lippo Lippi. On that basis, Irwin's is a magnificent Ruskinian failure.

Like other improvisations, Irwin's endpoint is not this acceptance of mediation's inevitability, but rather the injunction to embrace the world: *carpe vitam.* Weschler's 2008 expanded edition of *Seeing* traces Irwin's trajectory from minimalist to an almost rococo embrace of the world's richness, as for example his gloriously rich garden for the Getty Museum in Los Angeles. For Irwin, Weschler explains, in modernism's

> collapse of figure and ground (...the successive compressions of the subject matter of art from God to Christ to king to servant to shawl to this mere color red...) it had never been a question of bleaching out the figure, of making the figure as undifferentiated as the ground around it. Rather, the ground was being heightened, was suddenly being attended to with all the focus previously reserved for the figure alone...It meant pumping up awareness of that object's entire surround, which is to say engaging the whole world, attending to it with all the intensity normally reserved for art objects.[79]

We might pause for a moment to appreciate the brilliance of Irwin's minimalist history of art: "from God to Christ to king to servant to shawl to this mere color red..." But in the end Irwin's focus is not on art or art history but rather on the world and our perception of it. Weschler explains that ultimately, "Turning people on to the world, in this view, means turning them on to the single most beautiful thing in the world: the human capacity, the human responsibility, for perception."[80]

In tracing the predictability of Irwin's rhetoric—from its quest for a radical presence, to its acceptance of mediation's inevitability, and finally to the encyclopedic embrace of the world—I do not mean to suggest that his quest is risible, in any way unworthy of our respect. Irwin's inadequate reach—along with his act of reaching—helps us see the limits of our sight and mind. The value of recognizing those limits is surely what Socrates was all about and also one of the things Erasmus meant when he offered that "ignorance is a part

---

79. Lawrence Weschler, *Seeing Is Forgetting the Name of the Thing One Sees: Over Thirty Years of Conversations with Robert Irwin,* exp. ed. (Berkeley and Los Angeles: University of California Press, 2008); emphasis added.

80. Ibid., 227.

of knowledge." Irwin's project traces the curve of longing for immediacy to its inevitable frustration. The longing is as old as the earliest shaman whose rituals sought to make *this* place holy with divine presence. Irwin's art participates in that ancient shamanistic rite, just as does Derrida's art and Artaud's and Kerouac's, and just as does chaos science, as Abraham's recent book makes clear.[81] Who is to say that in our perception of the improviser's hierophany we do not experience such holiness? But it is not there. If we experience it is we who bring it, we who supply the presence that he has sought to evoke in us by creating the state of mind that brings such presence into being. As Irwin points out, "the most beautiful thing in the world" is not just "the human capacity," but also "the human responsibility, for perception." This is not to express a kind of spiritual atheism but rather just to acknowledge the inevitable element of self-projection in the experience of the holy. The experience of the holy, what is beyond mediation, beyond human ken, is the product of human mediation, mankind's inevitable way of knowing.

I do not entirely agree, nor would Irwin agree, with LeRoi Jones's skepticism when he challenges the visionary ambitions of Kerouac's "Essentials of Spontaneous Prose":

> The pure power of the creative climax can never be the reader's; even though he has traced and followed frantically the writer's steps, to that final "race to the wire of time." The *actual* experience of this "race" is experienced *only* by the writer, whose entire psyche is involved and from whence the work is extracted...The reader is finished, stopped, but his mind still lingers, sometimes frantically, between the essential and the projected.[82]

But that the audience cannot share an unmediated experience of the artist's vision does not mean that the work of art can't create the conditions under which the audience might project an approximation of that state. A Zen koan Irwin might appreciate: the work of art mediates an unmediated experience, not of the artwork itself or the world it figures, but of the audience's own world.

---

81. See Ralph Abraham, *Chaos, Gaia, Eros: A Chaos Pioneer Uncovers the Three Great Streams of History* (New York: HarperCollins, 1994).

82. Quoted in Belgrad, *Spontaneity*, 254.

John Cage's music shares with Irwin's art this urge to minimalism and the embrace of the aleatory, pure chance. More importantly, the two artists share this deep rhetorical structure and purpose, the desire to create in the audience not the appreciative experience of an artifact but rather the state of mind by means of which it can be apprehended, to be present to presence. Both participate in the Romantic injunction to "create the taste by which they are appreciated." For both conceptual artists as for the Romantics, the real goal is a new attitude to the world around us, not merely to art or to artifacts. The goal in their art is not a new experience in a museum or concert hall, but rather simply to walk down the street in a different state of mind, attentive to the ever-passing world.

It would be tempting to apply to the history of improvisation, both literary and extra-literary, Irwin's idea that our "capacity to sustain being in presence in all its rich variety will be growing with each generation." In an important sense—the history of style and of artistic taste—it does apply: each generation of the avant-garde pushes back a bit further the restrictions of systematic thought and the moral and aesthetic restrictions defining what does and does not, can or cannot, make art ("God to Christ to king" etc.). We can't do without parricide. Improvisers embrace more and more of life, Blanchot's "heterogeneous matter," now the commonplace, now the subconscious, now the underclass, now the libidinous, now the random and aleatory. But it must be emphasized that, however much the barriers recede, barriers are always there. Their nature does not, perhaps cannot, change. This is true aesthetically, formalistically: to have barriers to leap, thresholds to breach, is part of the improviser's project, part of the implicit and necessary binary, dialogic structure of his discourse. Improvisation thrives on, perhaps cannot exist without, opposition. And it is true ontologically: the barriers the mind sets between us and pure presence never change in kind, be they conceived as Kant's categories, Bruner's selectivity, or Gombrich's "beholder's share." Thus the history of improvisation also tells another story, the story of each new generation confronting not only life's rich and random variety with new, ever more all-embracing tools, but also the story of each generation seeking and prophetically describing and reaching for, like Irwin, the degree zero of epiphanic presence, but hitting the wall of the mind's inevitable and ubiquitous mediation.

We will see in the next chapter that even Hermes, the Greeks' mythic embodiment of the union of will and deed, fails to surmount this wall that always has and always will haunt us all. What Hermes offers in its stead is what these postmoderns offer and what improvisers have always offered: an art that is just this side of unmediated.

CHAPTER SEVEN

"A Primitive Astronomy":
Hermes and Literary Improvisation

> We say: At night an Arabian in my room,
> With his damned hoobla-hoobla-hoobla-how,
> Inscribes a primitive astronomy
>
> Across the unscrawled foes the future casts
> And throws his stars around the floor.
> —Wallace Stevens, "Notes Toward a Supreme Fiction"

One way to look at the metagenre improvisation is through the lens of myth. For Chaos scientist Ralph Abraham, "Myth is an attractor in the realm of ideas."[1] If, as I am arguing, this tension between our longing for immediacy and its inevitable frustration is hardwired into our nature, then it is little surprise that Greek myth captures that tension in one of its most important and complex gods. As Ezra Pound writes: "a god is an eternal state of mind."[2] One way to understand myth is just so, that each mythic figure embodies a fundamental type in human experience, a state of being, or what I have called a conceptual field. Types are not just personality or character types, but also fundamental, perennial human situations. The Greeks put a name to the eternal state of mind that is improvisation's special precinct, that place where we ever long for an immediacy we cannot completely inhabit. They called it Hermes.

Nietzsche set Dionysus, the god of excess, sexuality, and fecundity, in opposition to Apollo, the god of craft and rationality. But Dionysus is not Apollo's only counterpart and antagonist on Olympus. Priority surely goes to Apollo's half-brother, Hermes, who shares much with Dionysus. They are both belated: Hermes last of the twelve Olympians; Dionysus, a minor god,

---

1. Abraham, *Chaos, Gaia, Eros,* 118.
2. Quoted in Hyde, *Trickster Makes This World,* 11.

later still. As the god of boundaries and intermediary between the divine and human, Hermes is a fitting deity to oversee literary improvisation. As his Latin name, Mercury, suggests, Hermes is the god of quickness and formlessness. Hermes guides us to the heights and depths of experience, to the glories of Olympus and the shadows of Hades, and across the boundaries of ordinary reality to experience other states of consciousness. For Jung, writing of Hermes's alchemical guise, "Mercurius" is "the arcanum, the prima materia, the 'father of metals,' the primeval chaos, the earth of paradise, the 'material upon which nature worked a little, but nevertheless left imperfect.'"[3]

Hermes is endlessly, effortlessly inventive. He invents the lyre, fire, and the rituals of sacrifice. Associated with consciousness and with that other fire bringer, the Titan Prometheus (whose name means "forethought"), Hermes represents the immediacy of a special kind of "fore" thought, more akin to imagination, to the summoning of images, or to phenomenologists' *precogito*, rather than to the categorical thinking of Apollo or Zeus.

An inflection of folklore's Trickster, Hermes rules the fortuitous, the unforeseen; he is the bringer of luck, good or ill, whatever cannot be got by study or effort. As patron of travelers and "Prince of Thieves"—Apollo's name for him in the Homeric "Hymn to Hermes"—Hermes is the breaker of limitation. He moves, writes Otto, in a "divine sphere of operation" that "is no longer delimited by human wishes but rather by the totality of existence. Hence it comes about that [his] compass contains good and evil, the desirable and the disappointing, the lofty and the base."[4] Born significantly in pastoral Arcadia, Hermes rules over a realm fecund, profuse, and innocent of death. His mother is Maia, an earth spirit akin to ever-generative Gaia (whom chaos scientist Ralph Abraham, mentioned above, celebrates). Associated with Aphrodite—their soul union provides the model for the hermaphrodite—Hermes embraces not only the world's details but also its polar energies, male and female. For Hermes, finally, life is not a tragic event culminated by death.

---

3. *Collected Works of C. G. Jung*, vol. 13: *Alchemical Studies,* edited and translated by Gerhard Adler and R.F.C. Hull (Princeton, N.J.: Princeton University Press, 1967), par. 282.

4. Walter F. Otto, *The Homeric Gods: The Spiritual Significance of Greek Religion,* translated by Moses Hadas (London: Thames and Hudson, 1954), 121.

Rather, as Kerényi points out, "Life's most obvious alternative course—its overflowing in generation and productivity, its fruitfulness and multiplication—appears...as something incalculable, as purest accident."[5]

In these many ways Hermes is a fit patron for literary improvisation: the embodiment of quickness; filled with irreverent vitality and effortless creativity; embracing the fortuitous, the unconscious, and life's nonlinear and amoral profusion; penetrating boundaries of every sort; and embracing life's totality. "Hermes permeates the whole world," Raphael López-Pedraza writes, "because of his ability to make connections."[6]   Put another way, Hermes and improvisation are what the mythographer/artist expresses to articulate life under the aspect of nonlinear vitality and profusion, life *sub specie* chaos. Such a point of view is available under any conditions but would be more prevalent during periods of upheaval—paradigm shifts—when the complexities of life press upon the artist's awareness and beyond reason's capacity to perceive and accommodate them. "Life *sub specie* chaos" is not to say—as Freud felt compelled to remind us regarding free-association—that improvisation simply celebrates the free and random. Rather it explores the ubiquitous interplay and tension of the deterministic and free and explores our complex, ambivalent longing for unmediated experience, for incarnate freedom. Who better to oversee and embody that longing than Hermes?

1. *Hermetic Improvisation*

The Homeric "Hymn to Hermes" perfectly exemplifies these longings and the recognition of their inevitable frustration. The Homeric hymns, composed in the Homeric style (hence the name) over the course of a thousand years (600 B.C. to 400 A.D.), are oral-formulaic poems meant to be sung. The term hymn stems from *hymnos,* originally a form of "woven" or "spun" speech, a commonplace in oral-formulaic self-characterization. Like Pindar's *Odes,* with which they are associated, The Homeric hymns are hymns of praise, here to the gods rather than to Pindar's athletes, and are characterized for the most part by a solemn, high seriousness. The exception is the "Hymn

---

5. Karl Kerényi, *Hermes: Guide of Souls* (Thompson, Conn.: Spring Publications, 2020 [1976]), 26.

6. Raphael López-Pedraza, *Hermes and His Children* (Einsiedeln: Daimon, 1989), 22.

to Hermes," which in many ways stands apart. Eschewing the hymns' convention of *gravitas*, the "Hymn to Hermes" exploits comedic elements at every opportunity. Its broad, low humor—as when Hermes farts in Apollo's face—should leave no question that nothing human (or divine) is foreign to Hermes or his hymn's poet. Indeed, in the Roman poet Horace, who took Mercurius, Hermes's Roman counterpart, as his protector and divine model, the god is *superis deorum gratus et imus*: "Pleasing thus the gods of the upper regions and of the lower."[7] The Hymn's lack of "depth and piety" has led one critic "to consider the *Hymn to Hermes* a spoof or some sort of an early example of mock-epyllion"[8] (or minor epic). Likewise, the "Hymn to Hermes" is the least unified of the hymns and as such has presented critical difficulties. Such difficulties are typical of improvisations, which always break generic rules and make modern critics wonder which generic cubbyhole to squeeze them into. They belong rather in the far more spacious cubbyhole—almost a cubbyhole without walls—that I call improvisation. So fixed—or allowed to flow beyond bounds as is their wont—they give up their meaning more readily.

Though finally concerned, as we shall see, with limitation, like most improvisations the hymn is rich in portraits of freedom and immediacy. After his conventional invocation of the muse and description of Hermes's lineage, the hymn poet describes the god's first day:

> Born in the morning,
> he played the lyre
> by afternoon, and
> by evening had stolen the cattle
> of the Archer Apollo—
> all on the fourth day
> of this month
> in which the lady Maia
> produced him.

For after he jumped down from
the immortal loins of his mother
he couldn't lie still very long

---

7. Kerényi, *Hermes,* 61.

8. *The Homeric Hymns,* translated by Apostolos N. Athanassakis (Baltimore: The Johns Hopkins University Press, 2004 [1976]), 76n.

in his sacred cradle,
but leaped right up
to search for the cattle of Apollo,
climbing over the threshold
of this high-roofed cave.[9]

Typically, Hermes doesn't passively suffer parturition. Rather, he jumps down from his mother's loins, then leaps right up to pull a prank on Apollo.

And just as typical, for he is the god of lucky accidents, called *hermaion* in Greek, at the very threshold of the cave Hermes stumbles on a tortoise with which he creates the first lyre and invents the first song. The hymn poet lingers over Hermes's act of originary invention, emphasizing its immediacy, its union of will and deed:

Then, just as a thought
runs quick
through the heart of a man
whose troubles pile up
and shake him, or
when you see a twinkling
spin off the eyes,
just like that
the glorious Hermes
started thinking
about words and actions.[10]

Or as another translator renders the last lines: "so quickly did honorable Hermes/Hit on the deed realized simultaneous with its conception."[11] The hymn poet builds a portrait of Hermes's quickness and immediacy by incremental repetition. This immediacy is echoed in Hermes's first song:

The god tried to improvise,
singing along beautifully,
as teen-age boys do,

---

9. *The Homeric Hymns,* translated by Charles Boer (Chicago: The Swallow Press, 1972 [1970]), 23.

10. Ibid., 25.

11. *Works of Hesiod and the Homeric Hymns,* translated by Daryl Hine (Chicago and London: The University of Chicago Press, 2005 [1972]), 136.

mockingly, at festivals,
making their smart cracks.

> He sang about Zeus,
> the son of Cronus,
> and Maia in her beautiful shoes,
> how they talked during their love affair,
> a boast about
> his own glorious origin.
> And he honored the servants
> of the nymph
> and her beautiful house.
> ...
> And when he had sung about these,
> other subjects were found
> pressing in his mind.[12]

Hermes's song is perhaps the world's first improvisation within an improvisation. (Adam's first prayer in *Paradise Lost* will be another.)[13] And it is a doubly Hermetic, self-referential art: a song about his own birth. More importantly, the song is roguish, a "mocking" improvisation "like teenage boys do"; and it is indecorous, a song about his own parents' amours, perhaps the first recorded Freudian primal scene. The other song he sings in the hymn will be a theogony, the encyclopedic, alpha-omega story of the birth of all the gods.

Having finished the world's first song, Hermes immediately turns to planning the world's first robbery:

But then,
picking up the hollow lyre,
he put it in his sacred cradle.
He was getting hungry:
he bounded out
of the fragrant room,
yet with an eye out too,
and working on a shrewd trick in his head,
like those done by robber types

---

12. *The Homeric Hymns* (Boer), 25–26.

13. *Paradise Lost*, in *The Poems of John Milton*, edited by John Carey and Alastair Fowler (New York: W.W. Norton, 1972), Bk. 5: 136–52. See Chapter 8.

who operate
at this hour
of the dark night.[14]

As always, the poet emphasizes the imp in Hermes's improvisations.

At the heart of the "Hymn to Hermes" is this opposition between impulse and rational thought. It is embodied in his prank upon and confrontation with Apollo that dominate the hymn. The theft is of course an overstepping of limits. Hermes's iconoclastic attitude is best expressed by his response to being lifted from his crib by Apollo:

Then powerful Argeiphontes,
lifted up by the god's arms,
intentionally
released an omen,
an insolent servant
of his stomach,
a reckless little messenger.[15]

So much, in Hermes's view, for the patron of high culture, the embodiment of Olympian order, golden keeper of the sun and of culture, and for the seriousness and respect he is normally granted: a fart right in the face.

Even so, it is significant that through his pranks Hermes creates culture, not anarchy. He respects limits in surprising ways. After his theft Hermes invents fire and performs the world's first ritual sacrifice.[16] The poet emphasizes the step-by-step, custom-bound nature of this act, which Hermes performs to the letter even simultaneously as he invents the letters:

Hermes,
with a happy heart,
took out the rich meats
onto a smooth rock
and cut them,

---

14. *The Homeric Hymns* (Boer), 26.

15. Ibid., 42.

16. The Titan Prometheus, in fact, invents the first sacrifice but, wishing to eat the meat himself, betrays his titanic, ungodlike nature. Hermes invents *ritual sacrifice,* whereby humans get the meat and the gods get the essence of the sacrificed animal in the form of smoke and bones.

> arbitrarily,
> into twelve parts,
> but he treated each part
> as if it were perfect for gift-offering.[17]

Significantly, Hermes is constrained not to partake even though he himself is a god, indeed *because* he is a god:

> But then glorious Hermes himself
> wanted some of the sacred meat:
> immortal or not,
> the delicious smells
> troubled him.
> His noble heart
> persuaded him, however,
> not to let them pass
> down his own divine gullet,
> though he wanted to,
> badly.[18]

By emphasizing the power of the impulse that Hermes forgoes ("he wanted to,/badly"), the poet underscores the paradox: Hermes, the lord of impulse and the broaching of limits, is limited by his own godhead ("His noble heart"). He who always acts on impulse cannot commit sacrilege against the fundamental customs upon which society is (or will be) based and from which his godhead derives power and glory. To do so, as Lewis Hyde makes clear, is to sacrifice his divinity. A poignant strange loop: the god of borders and liminality who invites us to infringe rigid human order and limitation meets here his own limits. Accepting his limits will enable him to cross the border from the dark cave of his birth to the bright fields of Olympus. For that is his aim in this sacrifice, so to apportion the lots that he, last of the twelve, will be counted among the Olympians.

Like Prometheus, that other firebringer, Hermes is a world maker. Lewis Hyde's title: *Trickster Makes This World.* He is, above all, a life bringer. But Hermes is subject to one further limitation and it is the heart of the hymn. At

---

17. *The Homeric Hymns* (Boer), 30.
18. Ibid.

the climax of his debate with Apollo, Hermes requests that Apollo share his gift of prophecy that, as lord of Delphos, lends Apollo a special role and significance among Olympians: he alone knows Zeus's will and thus the future. Apollo's reply is adamant:

> But as for oracles,
> my dearest friend,
> which you are always asking about,
> it isn't permitted for you
> to know them,
> nor any other god.
> For the mind of Zeus alone
> knows them.
> I have given my word
> and sworn a strong oath
> that nobody other than myself
> among the ever-living gods
> shall know
> the profound will of Zeus.[19]

The next part of Apollo's speech describes at length men's uncertain quest for "divine secrets" and makes clear that Hermes, in his wish for foreknowledge, is a surrogate for us, the audience.

Finally, however, Apollo offers Hermes half-measure: you cannot prophesy, but through the mediation of the "bee-maidens," you can know the future:

> Well, I give them to you.
> And if you ask them something sincerely,
> rejoice over it.
> And if you teach some mortal man,
> he will hear you—
> if he is lucky.[20]

Unlike Apollo's foreknowledge, which is based on direct contact with Zeus, Hermes's prophecy is triply conditional. Hermes must ask the bee-maidens and do so "sincerely." And, it is hinted, he may be doomed to Cassandra's fate

---

19. Ibid., 58.
20. Ibid., 60.

to go unheeded by mortals: "mortal man/...will hear you—/if he is lucky." He will be lucky only if the "bee-maidens" have eaten the honey that is the source of their prophetic gift. Unlike Apollo and Zeus, Hermes enjoys only this contingent prophetic gift: the power is not entirely in his hands.

In almost every respect Hermes embodies consciousness unmediated by thought, the union of will and deed, but even he can know Zeus's Will, the intentionality of the Universe, as it were, only through mediation. Like Hermes we long to know His Will directly, face to face, but we must settle for the world around us as His Book, "through the glass darkly." Hermes represents a celebration of life in its ever-changing variety and multeity, that life in its fullness that does not admit of dissection. But finally the hymn is about his limitations, his being cut off from pure presence: he cannot know the mind of Zeus, cannot directly prophesy. Embodying in his every action the transcendent union between thought and deed, Hermes seeks the ultimate transcendence, and thereby functions as our surrogate: the poem is as much about the audience's longing as it is about that of Hermes. We want to know the future, our fate. Like the chaos scientist and like the improviser, Hermes works within a strictly deterministic system in which, paradoxically, each and every event is random, unpredictable. The hymn's anticipation of chaotics is striking.

I also find it striking—and moving—that this rich portrait and hymn of praise to the god's gifts of incarnate freedom culminates in a portrait of that freedom's limits. A lesser poet would surely have stopped short of this humanizing of what is after all, like all the Homeric hymns, a poem of apotheosis, a poem not only that praises a god but dramatizes how he achieves his divinity. The human dimension the poet attributes to Hermes—for what is less divine and more human than limitation—suggests again that the portrait of Hermes is ultimately about the audience's own limits and our own longing to overcome them. Hermes demonstrates his originary powers with every new invention he creates: lyre, winged sandals (the talaria Thoreau will long for in *Walden*), fire, sacrifice, the Pan flute. But Hermes is finally belated—*toujours déjà!*—before Zeus's impenetrable, truly originary mind, and Apollo's more seamless and complete entrée to prophecy. The rhetorical effect is ultimately consolatory: even Hermes must suffer the humiliation of limits; why should not we?

This opposition—the mimetic representation of immediacy that hints at immediacy's limits—is typical of most improvisations. Typical too is the longing the poem expresses: since we are all belated, nothing that we do can be enough. If only we could take on transcendent power. If only…Our longing can neither cease nor be satisfied.

If Hermes is an analogue for us, then the poem hints—surprisingly—at a kind of restrained Confucian answer to the conundrum that faces us. Hermes achieves his divinity by performing customary ritual even as he creates those rites, presumably in accord with the wishes of Zeus. Likewise, we may come to know the will of the universe by fulfilling our customary duties, by doing *what's right*: *themis* in ancient Greek, named for the Titaness Themis, Zeus's second wife, as we are about to see. By doing so we conform to the will of the universe and the universe conforms to us. As Emerson put it, though with the accent more on the individual than on the customary: "If a single man plant himself indomitably on his instincts, and there abide, the huge world will come round to him."[21] It was Bobby Kennedy's favorite quote.

2. *Odysseus as Hermetic Improviser*

Wanting to become an Olympian, Hermes is on his best behavior in his Homeric hymn. But for Hermes as Trickster, instinctively "what's right"—*themis*—is not entirely to his taste. Rather than upheld, "what's right" is rather something to be overturned, messed with: like stealing Apollo's cattle, as his great-grandfather had done, an act that will get many of Odysseus's men killed. Hermes likes to stir the pot. Hermes is polytropic, as we have noted, many turning, a god of many wiles, an epithet he shares in the Greek canon uniquely with Odysseus.

Both Hermes and Odysseus are not only polytropic but also polymetic, masters of many tricks. The genealogy of the gods clarifies what's going on here and speaks to the nature of Hermes's, Odysseus's, and the improviser's cunning intelligence. *Metis*—the "cunning intelligence" we encountered above in Chapter 1—is the province of Metis, the Titaness Zeus first took to wife after defeating Kronos, Time. Learning from an augury that his son by Metis will defeat him just as he did Kronos, Zeus contrives to swallow her.

---

21. "The American Scholar," in *The Collected Works of Ralph Waldo Emerson*, 1: 69.

The daughter of Okeanos, Metis is one of those polytropic deities who shape-shifts, like water, and he must struggle with her until she assumes a form that he can swallow. She is pregnant not with a son but with the manly Athena. With the help of Hermes and Hephaestus, the only other gods who possess *metis*, Hephaestus cleaves Zeus's skull and Athena is born fully armored.

Athena too has the gift of *metis*. Thus the three gods Homer associates with Odysseus—Athena, Hermes, and Hephaestus[22]—are associated with *metis*— as is a fourth, the Titan Prometheus, another child of Metis. Odysseus's principal antagonist other than Poseidon is Apollo, who derives his prophetic gift from Metis's replacement, Zeus's second wife, Themis.

Themis, in turn, represents Moral Law, what's right. It is largely she who through her marriage to Zeus has created the cosmos's sovereign order. Themis gives birth to the cosmos's orderly parts: the Horai (Seasons), Eirene (Peace), Eunomia (Good Order), Dike (Justice), and the Moirai (the Fates: Klotho, Lakhesis, and Atropos). It is Themis who is pictured to this day blindfolded with the scales of justice (Dike). With his new sovereign order in place, Zeus is free to marry Hera, who continues Themis's oversight of the cosmic order.

As his battle with Kronos suggests, the problem newly-enthroned Zeus faces is Time. Both his Titaness wives are oracular, hence part of the solution to the problem of Time: knowing the future. Metis, the offspring of Okeanos (Ocean), "represents divination through water"; Themis, the offspring of Gaia (Earth), "is patron to the oracles of the earth."[23] Delphi, first among many earth oracles, is a gift from Themis to Apollo. Detienne and Vernant explain:

> The omniscience of Themis relates to an order conceived as already inau-gurated and henceforth definitively fixed and stable…She spells out the

---

22. Hephaestus has no active role in the *Odyssey*, but Athena compares them in *metic* terms when she prepares Odysseus for the final battle:

> As a master craftsman washes
> gold over beaten silver—a man the god of fire
> and Queen Athena trained in every fine technique—
> and finishes off his latest effort, handsome work,
> so she lavished splendor over his head and shoulders now.
>
> *Odyssey* 6.256-60 (trans. Robert Fagles)

23. Detienne and Vernant, *Cunning Intelligence*, 107.

future as if it was already written and since she expresses what will be as if it were what is, she gives no advice but rather pronounces sentence: she commands or she forbids. Metis, by contrast, relates to the future seen from the point of view of its uncertainties...[Themis's] role is to indicate what is forbidden, what frontiers must not be crossed and the hierarchy that must be respected for each individual to be kept forever within the limits of his own domain and status.[24]

Themis's forbidden, infrangible frontiers and her embrace of hierarchy are exactly the red flags that incite Trickster who, in Lewis Hyde's words, is Lord of In-Between. By swallowing Metis, Zeus takes in the cunning that will help him foresee and prevent the next usurpation. Swallowing Metis and marrying Themis, achieving a kind of Jungian syzygy or conjunction of opposites, Zeus ensures the new order he promulgates will be certain and lasting. But that doesn't mean the balance of power won't or shouldn't be challenged or upset. Metis's cunning intelligence lives on in the Titan Prometheus (Forethought), in the gods Athena, Hermes, and Hephaestus, and in Odysseus. After all, without Prometheus's cunning, man would have no fire; without Athena, no olive tree, no plough and no horse's bit; without Hermes, no ritual sacrifice and no lyre; without Hephaestus, no metal tools; without Odysseus, no fall of Troy.

Each of those *metic* gods has a key role in the *Odyssey*, the first two as the hero's allies, the last as his off-stage enemy along with Apollo, whose intelligence is anything but hermetic or Metis-like. Apollo gets his power of divination from the goddess Themis, who was present at his birth at Delos. Knowing Zeus's will, the future, Apollo doesn't need *metis*, the power of knowing what's needed in the present moment "from the point of view of [life's] uncertainties." Knowing the future, the present is certain, and from Apollo's point of view, not a problem.

With all this mythic background in place, we can see that, if the Homeric "Hymn to Hermes" invites us to experience Hermes as a surrogate to us, that other Hermes poem, Homer's *Odyssey*, can be read as an imaginative answer to the question, what would Hermes be like if he were human, in the flesh, anthropomorphized, transubstantiated? The poem sets this up first by work-

24. Ibid., 107–8.

ing overtime to link Odysseus and Hermes. They are after all related by blood: Odysseus's maternal grandfather is the thief Autolycus (=the wolf itself—a Trickster reference), son of Hermes and Chione. About him Ovid writes,

> Autolycus, clever at every kind of deception,
> Who could make black white and white black,
> A worthy successor to his father in art.[25]

And a worthy ancestor to Odysseus. Hermes guides Autolycus's grandson twice, first to get him off the island of Calypso and second to bring him the herb moly that will protect him from Circe's spell. So it can be said that Hermes gets the action of the *Odyssey* started and then restarted. He also oversees Odysseus's arrival in Ithaca. Known for their swift ships, the Phaeacians who carry him there pour their last nightly libation to Hermes:

> Here he found
> the Phaeacian lords and captains tipping out
> libations now to the guide and giant-killer Hermes,
> the god to whom they would always pour the final cup
> before they sought their beds.[26]

The Phaeacians partake of Hermes's unmediated *metis*, the craft whereby their ships "know in a flash their mates' intentions."[27]

The thematic importance of Odysseus's own *metis* becomes evident in the Cyclops episode, where Homer makes use of a complicated pun. Gregory Nagy's guidance is essential here. When the Cyclops Polyphemus imprisons him, Odysseus tricks him by giving his name as *Outis*, "no one." When the fellow Cyclopes respond, *"Perhaps someone has wronged you?,"* Nagy explains, *"mē tis,* 'perhaps someone,' which sounds like the noun *metis,* which means 'craft.'" *"Mē tis,"* Nagy argues, signals, "the verbal craft used by Odysseus in devising this stratagem." The ironic link "is made explicit later on when the narrating hero actually refers to his stratagem as a *metis* ([*Odyssey*] ix 414)."[28]

---

25. Ovid, *Metamorphoses* 11.367-69 (trans. Stanley Lombardo).

26. *Odyssey* 7.160-64 (Fagles).

27. Ibid., 8.627.

28. Gregory Nagy, *The Ancient Greek Hero in 24 Hours* (Cambridge, Mass., and London, England: The Belknap Press of Harvard University Press, 2013), 301-2.

Thus is Odysseus hoisted on the petard of his own *metis*. The blunder has far reaching consequences. Further puns ensue, as Nagy explains, as when Odysseus is described as *outidanos,* "'good-for-nothing,' derivative of the pronoun *ou tis,* 'no one': whenever this epithet is applied to a hero in the *Iliad,* it is intended to revile the name of that hero by erasing his epic identity...So, Odysseus has suffered a mental erasure. The name that the hero had heretofore achieved for himself has been reduced to nothing and must hereafter be rebuilt from nothing."[29]

This state of mental erasure occurs several times in the *Odyssey* literally as a state of disorientation of his *noos* or rational, as opposed to intuitive, thinking:

> Listen to me, my comrades, brothers in hardship,
> we can't tell east from west, the dawn from the dusk,
> nor where the sun that lights our lives goes under earth
> nor where it rises. We must think of a plan at once,
> some cunning stroke. I doubt there's one still left.[30]

Nagy explains at length what happens next:

> Despite such moments of disorientation for Odysseus, his *noos* "thinking" ultimately reorients him, steering him away from his Iliadic past and toward his ultimate Odyssean future...Odysseus must keep adapting his identity by making his *noos* fit the *noos* of the many different characters he encounters in the course of his *nostos* in progress. In order to adapt, he must master many different forms of discourse, many different kinds of ainos. That is why he is addressed as *poluainos,* "having many different kinds of *ainos*" [manners of discourse], by the Sirens when he sails past their island.[31]

Thus Odysseus is not only *polytropos* and *polymetis,* he is also *polyainos,* a master of many discourses, perhaps the first instance of what Bakhtin calls heteroglossia. We might alternatively say he is *polysemous,* a master of many signs. This is true first in the sense that as trickster he manipulates signs, like the Trojan horse or, here, his masquerading as *Outis* [No One]. It is also true

---

29. Ibid., 304.
30. *Odyssey* 10.209–11 (Fagles).
31. Nagy, *The Ancient Greek Hero,* 311.

that as exile and traveler Odysseus is like the Phaeacians, who "know all ports of call and all the rich green fields."[32] Because of his travels, master of many systems of signs, Odysseus knows that all systems are contingent. Polysemy figures crucially in Tiresias's prophecy of Odysseus's end. He must carry an oar inland until it is mistaken for a winnowing fan. Within one setting, the shaped piece of wood signifies oar; in the other, a winnowing fan. Ever adaptive to his context, Odysseus for Nagy "is the ultimate multiform."[33]

In all this, *polytropos, polymetis, polyainos,* or *polysemous,* Odysseus limns the character of the improviser. Many turning, many crafted, many discoursed: through those skills the improviser rides the present moment "seen," as Detienne and Vernant say of Metis, "from the point of view of its uncertainties."

Odysseus and the improviser are in a special sense counter-heroic in such a manner as to redefine the heroic. As Nagy explains, the classical hero is *unseasonal* until the moment of his death, when finally he becomes *timely.* "Hero" derives from "*hōrā* (plural *hōrai*) 'season, seasonality, the right time, the perfect time.'"[34] "The goddess of *hōrā* was Hera (the two forms *hōrā* and *Hera* are linguistically related to each other). She was the goddess of seasons, in charge of making everything happen on time, happen in season, and happen in a timely way."[35] Hera's oversight of the Horai, who oversee the seasonal and timely, is a role she took over from Zeus's second wife, the Horai's mother Themis. The hero fulfills his destiny in death when his hour has finally come. He meets his deterministic, fated end. His thread of life finally cut by Themis's daughter Atropos, whose name means "no turning," the hero is finally timely, his fate perfected.

That is *one* solution of Zeus's problem of Time, the solution available under the aegis of Hera, and by extension of Themis and Apollo, where life is governed by "what's right." The improviser, who does his best never to quit turning, offers another. Recalling Jung on Mercurius, "the material upon which nature worked a little, but nevertheless left imperfect," we can say

---

32. *Odyssey* 8.628.
33. Nagy, *The Ancient Greek Hero,* 312.
34. Ibid., 243.
35. Ibid., 32.

that the improviser embraces his own and life's imperfection. For him life is deterministic but only imperfectly: ever alive to the moment, he knows the network of possibilities the present moment imperfectly promises. It is his job through *metis* to shape the possibility most advantageous to his glory. Haunted by death, the improviser nonetheless does his best to thumb his nose at it—Odysseus returns from Hades—just as he thumbs his nose at Themis, she who would have us do things according to "what's right." Master of many systems of signs, the improviser knows that Themis's Moral Law is contingent upon her earthbound, hierarchical, and categorical point of view. She oversees what is fixed and certain. The improviser knows that "fixed and certain" is a figment of the left, analytic brain. Offspring of Metis, daughter of Okeanos (Ocean), the improviser is oceanic, concerned with what flows. Death is coming; in the meantime the improviser seizes with the right hemisphere not only the passing moment but life itself in all its contingencies, of which the improviser is master.

Homer does not celebrate Odysseus's improvisations univocally or unambiguously. Odysseus's *metis* causes the death of all his men.[36] His trick of calling himself "No one" backfires and, Nagy argues, erases the glory he had attained at Troy. Odysseus is disoriented, losing his trust in his *metis* and his sense of self. To regain it he must journey to Hades and tell his pack of lies to the Phaeacians, giving them what they want to hear, rebuilding his self-concept by adapting his *noos,* his rational self. Doing so, Odysseus improvises his way back to his craftiness and to Ithaca. While Odysseus is a master of intuitive thinking, it is by deployment of his more rational *noos* that he restores his character. Like other improvisations, the *Odyssey* seems to embrace intuition at the expense of rationality, but in the end it is by their union, their interweaving, that salvation and homecoming are achieved.

3. Pindar's Orphic Improvisations

If ambivalent improvisations are Hermetic, the more self-assured are Orphic. The Greek poet Pindar's self-assurance before the epiphanic provides an

---

36. On Odysseus's tragically inept leadership, see Jonathan Shay, *Odysseus in America: Combat Trauma and the Trials of Homecoming* (New York: Scribner, 2002). Shay writes, "Odysseus emerges not as a monster, but as a human like ourselves," 120.

instructive contrast to the ambivalence we have been tracing in improvisation. Indeed, his self-assurance is so thorough, so shot through his poetic stance and rhetoric, that it is difficult to represent in short quotes. But as W. R. Johnson argues, "Pindar really believed that he saw the gods and eternity...he believed in his own magic."[37] Johnson explains:

> to master the complexities that multiplied as archaic Greece was dying and classical Greece was coming into existence, Pindar recovered what was always surely the original function and meaning of lyric poethood (*vates*—"seer," "bard," "shaman," "prophet"), and so successful was this rethinking and reformulating of the vanished ideal that it is fair to say that in a sense Pindar invented the vatic personality. While his other great contemporaries, poets and nonpoets alike were rushing forward to the enlightenment, while communities were being transformed into states and states into empires, while verse was giving way to prose and faith was giving way to reason, Pindar was becoming Orpheus.[38]

For Paul Fry all odes' invocations are ironic, the poet uneasy "about having sought inspiration to describe inspiration."[39] Nevertheless Pindar is so certain of his inspiration that he hardly bothers to invoke it. As Johnson remarks, "The god (the muse) is always with him, otherwise there would be no song at all, and this is scarcely worth his mentioning."[40] Pindar's claims of spontaneity likewise are rarely explicit but everywhere implicit in his effusive free-associating voice.

Orphic improvisations do not long for, but rather, like the biblical prophet Amos, are dead certain of their transcendence. Orpheus represents the vatic poet whose inspiration is unquestioned and unquestioning. The impeccable genealogy of Orpheus's inspiration perhaps affords him this certitude. Son of the Muse Calliope, Orpheus received his lyre directly from Apollo, the god of prophecy. The lyre connects Orpheus to Hermes, its inventor. The Muses,

---

37. W. R. Johnson, *The Idea of the Lyric: Lyric Modes in Ancient and Modern Poetry* (Berkeley and Los Angeles: University of California Press, 1982), 62.

38. Ibid., 59-60.

39. Paul H. Fry, *The Poet's Calling in the English Ode* (New Haven and London: Yale University Press, 1980), 10-11.

40. Johnson, *The Idea of the Lyric*, 67.

"the Triple Mountain-Goddess of inspiration"[41] themselves, teach him to play it. In all, a pretty strong provenance. The effects of his song are equally impressive: he can enchant the wild beast and cause the trees and stones to move. Mythic founder of the lyric genre, Orpheus is associated with the worship of Apollo and of Dionysus. Pindar, taking Orpheus rather than Hermes as his model, will be known for his lawlessness (Horace), for his *beau désordre* or "beautiful disorder" (Boileau), and for his tremendous flights of passionate inspiration (Longinus).

How does Pindar create this impression of beautiful disorder that will prove so influential to Renaissance courtiers and to the Romantics? Pindar's associative transitions and arcane allusions are key, conveying the impression of a man in the heat of passionate thought. Crucial too is his shifting of meters, probably the source of Horace's view of his "lawlessness." Though employing a carefully ordered and crafted form—strophe, antistrophe, epode—Pindar nevertheless achieves the impression that form follows thought, not some predetermined structure. Finally there is the question of formal unity. Modern Pindar studies agree that the odes are unified in tone, every passage encomiastic. But as Johnson points out, this should not obscure for us the nonlinear, nonrational nature of the poems as they are experienced.[42] Again, the information theory implicit in Chaos science can help us to understand the nature of Pindaric coherence. In Pindar, as in fractals, the code is written into each element and each element is equally important. As David Young writes:

> It is impossible to travel "lineally" [*sic*] from start to finish of a Pindaric ode, dismissing what has been said the while, and not to dismiss most of what Pindar has to say, for...the coherence of Pindar's poems depends primarily upon the cross-references of one part of the poem with other parts. The unity thus created is formed by the aggregate of all passages, and the beginning is still very important at the end of the poem and, ultimately, the end is important at the beginning.[43]

---

41. Robert Graves, *The Greek Myths: Complete Edition* (New York: Penguin, 1993), 115.

42. Johnson, *The Idea of the Lyric*, 69.

43. David C. Young, "Pindaric Criticism," in *Pindaros und Bakchylides*, edited by

In Pindar all information is important because, infused with his spirit, inspired by the divine, every moment is epiphanic, suffused with eternity. One of Pindar's appeals to the Romantics must have been this epiphanic structuring of experience where every Now is an eternal Moment.

Pindar's Orphic self-assurance in embracing the epiphanic moment provides a telling contrast that speaks to our understanding of improvisation as a literary kind. For it is instructive that Pindar's vatic experience, however deep his faith, is used as a rhetorical device to answer the doubting moderns of his time. Like other improvisers, Pindar strikes his vatic stance in opposition to the emerging positivistic rationality. The Rush Limbaugh of his day (my apologies to the poet), Pindar fights a rearguard action in an effort to preserve the eternal verities and consoling myths that emerging science and rationality—Liberalism in the broadest sense—were beginning to call in doubt.

Pindar's odes are thus, in an important sense, neither a humanistic endeavor, nor a liberal one. The humanism of the Homeric "Hymn to Hermes," its effort to portray human lineaments through the divine, is what Pindar is fighting. Pindar is interested not in empathizing with the all-too-human, but rather in participating in the divine, as the heroes he celebrates do. His vatic stance is truly hierophantic in the double sense that Mircea Eliade describes: he makes the moment and the place holy, and the audience with them. The experience of Pindar's excitement and of his difficulty makes the audience originary. As Johnson argues, "he allows us, he invites us, to become the dancers who become the dance."[44] Not acknowledging the artificial status of his rhetoric, Pindar's dance is ultimately both authoritarian and decadent. It would have us toe his line even as we dance. In this he differs from what I take to be the Hermetic mainstream of the tradition of improvisation but it is an important current that the brave and religious or political fanatics sometimes travel.

What draws the line Pindar would have us toe is the aristocratic tradition of gift-giving. Like Swift who will share Pindar's aristocratic leanings, Pindar

---

William Calder and Jacob Stern (Darmstadt: Wissenschaftliche Buchgesellschaft, 1970), 87-88. Quoted in Johnson, *The Idea of the Lyric,* 69.

44. Johnson, *Idea of the Lyric,* 69.

relies on patronage to fund his poesis. Though objectionable to many modern readers, this poetry-for-hire, as Leslie Kurke has recently argued, must be understood in light of aristocratic gift-exchange, so central to the ethos of Homeric epic but something of an archaism in Pindar's day as the ideology of the polis (as opposed to the aristocratic household) began to embrace a money economy.[45] "Pindar's era," Kurke writes, "was heir to the crisis of the aristocracy, the last flowering of tyranny, the rise of the democratic polis, and the shift from a premonetary to a money economy."[46] It took not *money* but *wealth* (aristocratic self-sufficiency) to train and to compete. Thus, the athlete's victory is a gift of *kleos,* honor, to his aristocratic family and to his community. Pindar sees being paid for his odes in the same light. He may be paid in specie or in symbolic gifts, but in either case his poems are gift of *kleos* to the family and community. Thus, Kurke concluded, "the impetus behind [Pindar's victory odes] represents a kind of counterrevolution on the part of the aristocracy."[47] Pindar's is a rearguard action in this way.

At the heart of the gift-exchange system, as in improvisation, lies a tension between freedom and necessity. The act of giving is always an act of gratuitous generosity; it is also, in the gift-exchange system, always a response to the obligations created by having received gifts. Both/and, not either/or. As anthropologist Marcel Mauss, first to describe the system, writes of the Trobriand Islanders: "pains are taken to show one's freedom and autonomy as well as one's magnanimity, yet all the time one is actuated by the mechanisms of obligation which are resident in the gifts themselves."[48] Pindar's *beau désordre* navigate these crosscurrents.

4. Sappho's Classical Improvisation

By contrast, Sappho's questioning of our yearning for unmediated experience is far more typical of Greek classicism and the mainstream of the improvisatory aesthetic. Sappho's "Prayer to Aphrodite"—roughly contemporary

---

45. Leslie Kurke, *The Traffic in Praise: Pindar and the Poetics of Social Economy* (Berkeley: California Classical Studies, 2013 [1991]).

46. Ibid., 226.

47. Ibid., 224.

48. Quoted in ibid., 82.

with the Homeric hymn poet and with Pindar—is a tissue of immediacies mediated by the powerful, distancing rhetoric of Sappho's apostrophe, which begins and ends the poem, ring fashion. Sappho slowly leads us unaware into the ultimate immediacy: the divine voice of the goddess most closely associated with Hermes, Aphrodite (together they form the hermaphrodite). The poem begins with an apostrophe:

> Immortal Aphrodite, elegant daughter
> Of Zeus, goddess of guile, I pray to you:
> Do not, my lady, break my heart with sufferings,
> But come to me...

The passage slyly segues into what might be called generic or proleptic (as if) epiphanies:

> if once before you heard
> My voice from afar, and listened to my speech,
> And left your father's house and yoked your car
> And came. Beautiful, lightening-swift they were,
> The sparrows that drew you over the black earth,
> With wheeling wings, from heaven through the fiery air.

The narrative's hypothetical nature is marked by the hypothetic "if"—"*if once before*": come now, she is arguing, *if ever* you came before. This reading is overwhelmed, however, by our dawning recognition that what is being described is something that has happened often: "once" is ironic understatement, for she has come many times, every time Sappho has fallen in love. This is what I mean by generic epiphanies: these have occurred many times and have not the power of an epiphany here-and-now. Like the vision in "Kubla Khan," this one is contingent upon the next inspiration. Nevertheless Sappho lends a measure of power to this past experience of divine immanence. Her use of polysyndeton ("*and* listened to my speech,/*And* left your father's house and yoked your car/*And* came") underscores the swiftness of the action and enhances the effect of immediacy. So, too, the "lightning-swift" sparrows "with wheeling wings" convey speed and dazzling power. The same effect is achieved prosodically when Sappho (at least in translation) comes to a full stop at the end of the stanza (the first stanza not to be enjambed), then begins the next stanza with the dramatic, "Suddenly they were here."

The clipped sentence also marks a turn in the nature of the epiphany described. Now we will hear not of "generic" experiences of the divine, but something more direct. We learn of the deity's countenance and her words, though still indirectly:

> But you, my lady,
> Turned on me your immortal face and smiled,
> And asked, why was I calling you again, and what
> Was my complaint, and what did I have in mind
> For my grand passion?

Finally, suddenly, we experience the divine through direct speech:

> "Who is it now that I
> Must lure into your arms? Who is the culprit, Sappho?
> If she's avoiding you, she'll seek you out;
> If she disdains your gifts, she'll be the giver;
> If she won't kiss, she'll kiss you yet despite herself."

The poem functions like a temple to Aphrodite, admitting us slowly step by step closer and closer to the inner sanctum where the deity can be directly experienced, if not fully known. But the final stanza brings us back to ourselves, reading a poem:

> Come now again, my lady, and set me free
> From anxious troubles, and help me to achieve
> The longing of my heart: Be my ally, in person![49]

The close reminds us that the inner sanctum is not so easily breached, that the longed-for objects (both love object and transcendent deity) are not so easily attained. And they are doubly difficult, for the reprise of the apostrophe ("Come now again...") functions to remind us that these epiphanies suffer either the remoteness of the past, or the tentativeness of mere hypothesis and longing, or both.

Sappho's quest to breach the threshold is echoed in the Homeric "Hymn to Hermes" where Hermes "climb[s] over the threshold/of this high-roofed cave." It is shared by Hermes himself, who is in essence the divine embodiment of thresholds and borders. Like Foucault's madmen, who literally

---

49. Johnson, *Idea of the Lyric*, 45.

inhabit the city gate, the improviser inhabits the threshold. The improviser, like the madman, is "inversely exalted," authorized by that grace beyond the reach of reason that is experienced because s/he has been marginalized.[50] Paradoxically, improvisers marginalize and disempower themselves in order to gain the right to instruct the righteous. They "take advantage of the disadvantages," as African American culture since slavery has done. We may often be blinded by the improviser's bluff, optative mood, and fail to see that s/he presents him or herself as wounded, limited.

Like the hero of myth, the improviser ventures forth beyond civilization's bounds; like him s/he is wounded (confronted by limitation); like him s/he returns with a gift for the improvement of society. Unless we undergo the wounding we cannot pass through the *póros* [the porous doorway] to the higher Logos. Such is the rhetoric and deep mythic structure of improvisation. The critical problem—the difficulty of seeing all this—persists largely because spontaneity's supposed innocence is privileged by critics and therefore we fail to heed its rhetorical status.

Charles O. Hartman, for example, though surely among the most interesting recent commentators on improvisation and its "riddle of spontaneous art and artful spontaneity," mistakes trope for type in Robert Creeley's "I Know a Man" (here quoted in full and, I should add, accurately):

> As I sd to my
> friend, because I am
> always talking,—John, I
>
> sd, which was not his
> name, the darkness sur-
> rounds us, what
>
> can we do against
> it, or else, shall we &
> why not, buy a goddamn big car,
>
> drive, he sd, for
> christ's sake, look
> out where yr going.[51]

---

50. Michel Foucault, *Madness and Civilization*, 11.
51. Quoted in Charles O. Hartman, *Jazz Text: Voice and Improvisation in Poetry, Jazz*

Hartman rightly calls attention to the "distant echo" of the Sapphic stanzaic form and rightly points out the multi-dialogic nature of this poem, a narrator speaking both to an interlocutor and to himself. He sees it, convincingly, as a kind of Kerouacian miniature, a conversation perhaps between a loquacious and ecstatically Dionysian Dean Moriarty figure ("because I am always talking") and a more cautious Sal Paradise ("look out where yr going").

But the Sapphic echo is more complete, more deeply structural than that. As in the "Hymn to Aphrodite" just discussed, the Dionysian speaker, well aware of the absence that impends all around them, longs for presence:

> the darkness sur-
> rounds us, what
>
> can we do against
> it, or else, shall we &
> why not, buy a goddamn big car

The presence he longs for ideally is that divine radiance that will answer the "darkness [that] sur-/rounds us"; in the meantime he will settle for a pale though sensational stand-in in the American manner: "a goddamn big car." But as in Sappho, the Apollonian figure of reason is also there to set things back on the ground: "look/out where yr going." Surely Hartman overstates the identification of Dionysian speaker with the poet ("the talker in the poem speaks for the poet"[52]). For Hartman is right only on a spiritual plane when he argues that "through the play of his imagination the compulsive talker is exactly looking out where he is or might be going."[53] "Look/out where yr going" couldn't make any clearer that on the practical, quotidian plane this is exactly what the speaker does not do.

This is not to say that our sympathies are totally with the Apollonian voice either. Rather, as so often in improvisations, the point is both/and, not either/or: we are invited to experience the pull and attraction of both modes of being and seeing, just as we are drawn both to the poem's artlessness and to its art. Though for Hartman "the poem insists on the priority of speech" and

---

and Song (Princeton, N. J.: Princeton University Press, 1991), 39 (online at *https://www. poetryfoundation.org/poems/42839/i-know-a-man*).

52. Hartman, *Jazz Text,* 42.

53. Ibid., 40

"the poet seems more intent on momentum than on accomplishment," surely Creeley's poem would have us experience both, both speech and text or composition, both momentum and accomplishment, both going and goal.[54] Or as Hartman says elsewhere: "We can think of the achievement as *instantaneous* composition, or as instantaneous *composition*. Either way, it must amaze."[55] Indeed. It does.

I have crossed swords with this reader of Creeley because it is instructive that this critical problem dogs the critical history of post-Romanticism. We are more prepared to see in Sappho's lyricism a rhetorical substructure that is not hostile to rhetoric. In Romantic and post-Romantic texts, however, we are likely to make the mistake Gerald Bruns makes when he distinguishes between "rhetorical" and "Romantic" improvisation.[56] For all improvisations are rhetorical, even those like Pindar's that deny it.

5. *Hermes as* Bricoleur: *The Examples of Lévi-Strauss and Louis Armstrong*

In Chapter 3 above we were looking for an Einstein, someone to create a unified field theory for improvisation. Now that we better understand the role of Trickster in improvisation, we are better prepared to consider that the great French Structuralist Claude Lévi-Strauss perhaps fills the bill. Not that Lévi-Strauss has an analytic interest in Trickster. His Structuralist approach is interested in myth's structural dynamics rather than in the mythic gods of Edith Hamilton or Joseph Campbell. But his arch-idea of *bricolage* to explain those dynamics takes us equally into the dynamics of improvisation. Trickster is a *bricoleur*. And, *bricoleur* himself, Lévi-Strauss is a Trickster.

Bricolage is French for tinkering or collage making. In *bricolage*, working with the limited range of things that happen to be available, one creates value out of the tossed off or thrown away. Hermes stumbles over the tortoise and on the spur of the moment tinkers together the lyre. Working with what is at hand, a *bricoleur* improvises solutions to both practical and aesthetic problems. *Bricolage* is related to the African American compensatory principle since the slave era of "taking advantage of the disadvantages," and is

---

54. Ibid., 41, 44.
55. Ibid., 34; emphasis in text.
56. Ibid., 48.

also expressed as "making a way out of no way." Toni Morrison has said that "the major things Black art has to have are these: it must have the ability to use found objects, the appearance of using found things, and it must look effortless."[57] Improv has been doing the same things for a long time.

Lévi-Strauss contrasts *bricolage* to the goal-driven enterprise of engineering, a stand-in, in Lévi-Strauss's argument, for the scientific positivism that has dominated our culture at least since the nineteenth century. *Bricolage*, according to Lévi-Strauss, is the method of myth:

> The characteristic feature of mythical thought is that it expresses itself by means of a heterogeneous repertoire...[The bricoleur's] universe of instruments is closed and the rules of the his game are always to make do with "whatever is at hand," that is to say with a set of tools and materials which is always finite and is also heterogeneous because what it contains bears no relation to the current project, or indeed to any particular project, but is the contingent result of all the occasions there have been to renew or enrich the stock or to maintain it with the remains of previous constructions or destructions.[58]

That's an earful but the point is this: scientific positivism, here engineering, is characterized by being rational, instrumental, goal driven. Science has an infinite set of tools to draw upon and brings the right instruments to bear as needed to fulfill its goal. Its goal orientation is in itself a major difference: by contrast, myth—and Trickster—orient toward joy: the pleasure of knowing, experiencing, embracing the world, riding the present moment's edge. As Lévi-Strauss contends, mythical thinking—in our case improvisation— "can reach brilliant unforeseen results on the intellectual plane."[59] Un-foreseen = im-pro-visation.

As we have seen, Hermes is the god of lucky accidents, *hermaion* in Greek. His first act after parturition, tinkering the first lyre out the tortoise, is a *hermaion*. All his actions in the hymn are improvised reactions to the moment. It is striking to consider how many improvisations are *bricolages*, compendia tinkered from manifold sources: Rabelais's *Gargantua and Pantagruel*, Mon-

---

57. Quoted in Thomas Brothers, *Louis Armstrong's New Orleans* (New York: Norton, 2007), 294.

58. Lévi-Strauss, *The Savage Mind*, 17.

59. Ibid.,

taigne's *Essays*, Burton's *Anatomy of Melancholy*, and Whitman's *Leaves of Grass* come readily to mind.

And Lévi-Strauss himself is both improviser and tinkerer. With the idea of *bricolage* he creates the taste by which he is to be relished. His break-out book, the memoir-cum-travelogue *Tristes Tropiques*, like other improvisations that deny generic connection, begins by claiming not to be a travelogue, a form he detests: "I hate travelling and explorers. Yet here I am proposing to tell the story of my expeditions…[T]his kind of narrative enjoys a vogue which I, for my part, find incomprehensible."[60] It is improvised, written, he tells us elsewhere, in "a permanent state of intense exasperation, putting in whatever occurred to me without any forethought."[61] As his biographer Patrick Wilcken points out, *Tristes Tropiques* "had the fresh, slightly disorganized feel of stream-of-consciousness that still makes it an infectious read… *Tristes Tropiques* gave us…not the dry inventories found in conventional ethnographies, but a kind of immediacy—the vivid first impressions of each encounter."[62] Again his biographer: "*Tristes Tropiques* is alive to the senses. In the field he jotted down tasting notes from the tropics, including the thirteen different flavors of honey that the Nambikwara gathered, whose aromas he likened to bouquets of burgundy, and detailed appreciations of exotic fruits."[63] Like our improvisers, Lévi-Strauss gobbles up the world.

Lévi-Strauss at one point considered a career in music.[64] His *The Raw and the Cooked*, it has been argued, is symphonic in structure with a preface titled "Overture," and such chapters as "The Bird-Nester's Aria" and "The Well-Tempered 'Good Manners' Sonata," "The Opossum's Cantata" and "Well-Tempered Astronomy."[65] I don't know if Lévi-Strauss ever turned his

---

60. Claude Lévi-Strauss, *Tristes Tropiques*, translated by John Weightman and Doreen Weightman (New York: Penguin, 2012), 17.

61. Quoted by Patrick Wilcken, "Introduction," in Lévi-Strauss, *Tristes Tropiques*, 6.

62. Ibid., 7–8.

63. Ibid., 9.

64. Wilcken writes, "One way to approach Lévi-Strauss is as he saw himself—as an *artiste manqué*, a man who would have loved to have been a painter like his father, or a musician, had he had the talent." *Claude Lévi-Strauss: The Poet in the Laboratory* (New York: Penguin, 2010), 337.

65. Ibid. 281.

SWISS KRISSLY

SATCHMO-SLOGAN
(Leave It All Behind Ya)

Courtesy of the Louis Armstrong House and Museum

attention to jazz, but *bricolage* can be and has been used to help understand the emergence of jazz improvisation.

In his first known public appearance, Louis Armstrong demonstrated an early mastery of both *bricolage* and improvisation. About to appear on stage at South Rampart Street's Iroquois Theatre amateur contest, little Louis suddenly stuck his head in a flour sack, a throwaway gesture tinkered from and pushing back against minstrelsy. He won.

Laughing Louie grew to be one of the most effective Trickster figures of the twentieth century. At a concert in Memphis following an arrest for sitting with his white manager's wife, Louis dedicated "I'll Be Glad When You're

Dead, You Rascal You" to the Memphis police. His band got nervous but the police, who probably didn't hear or understand the lyrics, were thrilled by the call-out. Like Trickster—think of Hermes's fart in Apollo's face—Louis overtly embraced our lower functions. In an iconic image, Louis pictures himself in a water closet, his pants pulled down, recommending, "leave it all behind you…Swiss Krissly"—his favorite herbal laxative.

Sources for Louis's embrace of the Trickster spirit, even at so young an age, are overdetermined. First, he could have received it as an African retention or legacy from many sources. In the 1880s, the Tulane folklorist Alcée Fortier, a white Creole descendent of planters, collected the *Bouki* and *Compair Lapin* folktales at Laura Plantation in Edgard, La., the town just up-river from Louis's mother MayAnn's birthplace, a plantation in Boutte, La. They formed the basis of his friend Joel Chandler Harris's *Br'er Rabbit*. "Don't you throw me into that briar patch," says Br'er Rabbit, taking advantage of the disadvantages. So even in "Back a' Town" New Orleans Louis could have heard plantation tales of Br'er Rabbit's cunning intelligence. Or he could have received Trickster's cultivated immediacy and his disruptive vibe through the deeply-African Sanctified Churches, which as jazz historian Thomas Brothers demonstrates, were crucial to Louis's early shaping of jazz.[66] "It 'all came from the Old Sanctified Churches," Louis wrote.[67]

Trickster's principle that all value is contingent is something Louis could have learned just by intimately experiencing the alien culture of the Karnofskys, the Jewish family that befriended him. Louis grew up fatherless with a mother who probably turned tricks. His home, where City Hall now stands, was in the Battlefield, so-called because it was so violent, guns and knives always at the ready. Its other name was Black Storyville because its honky-tonks and whorehouses offered a less expensive alternative to the high-flying, better-known white Storyville across Canal Street. His home on Liberty at Perdido was three blocks from the Karnofskys at Perdido and South Rampart. The difference between those two worlds offered the lesson every stranger in a strange land learns—like learning a second language—that how we do things,

---

66. Brothers, *Louis Armstrong's New Orleans*, 31ff.

67. *Louis Armstrong in his Own Words: Selected Writings*, edited by Thomas Brothers (New York: Oxford University Press, 1999), 170.

what we value, and what things mean is not absolute and authoritative but merely contingent. Like Odysseus, such travelers in strange lands seem to be polysemous.

Perhaps Tillie Karnofsky told Louis tales of the Russian Trickster Baba Yaga as she fed him that "good Jewish" food that he would relish for the rest of his life. The Jewish festival of Purim or New Orleans's own Carnival showed the value of Trickster as holy fool.

More telling, Louis could have learned the spirit of Trickster in Jewish culture itself, which shared with African American culture the compensatory gesture of "taking advantage of the disadvantages." Barred from the guilds in the middle ages, Jews made their livings by creating value out of the value-less, the tossed-off, or thrown away: rags and bones, waste, remnants, the second hand, even interest which was marginalized by canonic law. Whence the Karnofsky rag-and-bone cart that Louis worked, along with Karnofsky's sons Alex and Morris, and whence the second-hand stores that lined South Rampart. Certainly he learned Trickster's spirited role in commerce in the streets on the Karnofsky rag-and-bone cart, bartering for the tossed-off with pennies and bits of candy. Trickster often wears a coin purse because Trickster's crossroads is also the place of commerce, the marketplace, which he also oversees. Improvisation transgresses, it crosses the line and embraces everything, sex and commerce included, as part of life. Commerce may seem like the mainstream's heartbeat but it also includes the street hawkers whose street patter I witnessed growing up visiting an eccentric paternal grandmother on South Rampart above the then-defunct Fertel Loan Office, "Best Rates in the City." At ten and twelve I first heard the voice of Trickster, that *just inside they had the perfect blue suit for you for next Sattaday night.* In sum, South Rampart Street was populated with bricoleurs who thrived on the edge of the city and of commerce, dealers in second-hand goods, pawn-brokers like my family, who make value out of the valueless.

On another rag cart, to attract customers Louis learned from a man named Larenzo, probably African American, how to play a ten-cent tin horn and how to bend notes into the blues. When the Karnofskys loaned him $2 toward a $5 cornet, Louis quickly realized he "could play '*Home* Sweet Home'—then *here* come the *Blues.*"[68]

---

68. Ibid., 12; emphasis in text.

By bending and worrying pitch the blues produces the jagged harmonies, dissonance, and blue notes that have no place in, but are in dialogue with, the rationality of Western harmony or *solfège*. Blue notes literally have no place on the *do re mi* scale. Blues creates something marginal, outside the decorous mainstream and dominant culture, but nonetheless new and lasting. In Apollo's hands the lyre is as pure and sweet as a spring on Mt. Olympus; had Hermes kept it, the lyre would have played a blues as hot and discordant as the River Styx which he crossed conducting souls to Hades.

The Louis Armstrong House and Museum in Queens has introduced us to Louis's life-long collage making, many on the boxes of his extensive reel-to-reel tape collection—so, both aural and visual bricolages. But Louis is a collage maker, a bricoleur, in more ways than those two. In Louis's hands jazz improv stitches together the "real *fancy* things [he found] among the White Folks' *throw aways*," as he says of his work on Alex Karnofsky's cart.[69] But in his hands, riffs stolen from "the big cats, Verdi and Wagner"—as he told Edward R. Murrow—aren't privileged.[70] Louis's quotations don't bring with them the high culture they elsewhere represent. Because meaning is contextual, pieces of a collage tinkered together are imported *value neutral.* The value is created in and by the new context, established by the *bricoleur.* This is part of the meaning of Louis's flattening definition of jazz to "*anything that makes you pat your foot to is good music*": if it makes you dance it's all gold.[71]

The most telling example of Louis's *bricolage* comes from the other side of the spectrum of tinkered sources: not high opera but the nonsense, meaningless syllables of scat, which if Pops didn't invent, he at least popularized. Scat brings value to the utterly valueless, meaningless syllables. The word "scat" perhaps comes across as meaningless itself, but of course it does mean something: animal excrement—shit, the utterly valueless unless it is used as

---

69. Ibid., 16; emphasis in text.

70. Edward R. Murrow and Fred W. Friendly, producers of *Satchmo the Great,* CBS-TV with United Artists, 1957.

71. On *Satchmo the Great,* Louis tells Murrow, "Jazz is a variety of all good music. And the only way to sum up music is there ain't but two things in music: good and bad. Now, if it sounds good, you don't worry what it is, just go and enjoy it. See what I mean? And anything you can pat your foot to is good music."

One of Louis Armstrong's many collages (LAHM 1987.3.45)

manure. If Pops didn't invent scat when he dropped his sheet music while recording "Heebie Jeebies," as the legend goes, it's an interesting mythic meme since Trickster, Hermes, is associated with the fortuitous, the happy accident—*hermaion.* Stumble over a tortoise, or drop your sheet music, and create the means of great art. Such is the irrational art of Trickster.

We can get at how *bricolage* works, the rhetoric of the merely tinkered together, by lingering another moment over scat. Compare for a moment Louis's singing, inspired by Tillie's Russian lullabies to sing from the heart, to Frank Sinatra's singing. "With all the smoothness of a piece of sandpaper calling for its mate," as Edward R. Murrow describes it, Louis's rasp compares unfavorably to Frank's voice.[72] The Voice, as it was called, is clear as a bell, smooth as satin, choose your favorite cliché. Louis's technique, which seems the wrong word to deploy, for it seems without technique, without craft, is so invisible that many imagined Louis's as a god-given talent, born not made: a *primitive* genius. I love Sinatra's singing and I'm not going to suggest that lonely Frank is not soulful, but where Louis is about heart, Sinatra is right-left-and-center about *craft*. Craft—his dedication to the technical aspects of breathing and phrasing, timbre and diction is what Sinatra is about. And Sinatra and scat? Google those words and what you get is "Stranger in the Night." Period. *Scooby doobie doo*: a closing that calculatedly if belatedly, half-heartedly to my ear, rides the wave of scat's popularity. And if you think "scoobie doobie doo" came from the heart rather than from sheet music, I have a bridge to Hoboken to sell you. There may be a bit of a wait crossing.

Much of Louis's output is based on "tossed off," tinkered motifs—melodic phrases, breaks, and gestures from popular songs, blues, spirituals, and opera. Joshua Barrett counts twenty or so disparate "sources" for the great "West End Blues" cadenza.[73] It is not a matter of Louis finding the nugget of gold hidden within the manure of popular songs, opera, blues, or hymns, but of his realizing that *all* manure *is* gold. This is an important point. To poet Charles Bernstein, "A professional poet throws nothing out except the eggshells and the coffee grounds,"[74] obviously spoken by someone who doesn't garden or compost. Eggshells and coffee grounds are prized for making black gold, as potent as manure. In the cadenza, "Washwoman Blues" is no more a throwaway and no less valuable than Don Jose's "Flower Song" from Bizet's *Carmen*—both quoted in the cadenza. Louis himself is a kind of throwaway, all but tossed away by the mainstream culture. His horn, and the Karnofskys, saved him from that. Arguing that Rampart Street was the perfect place to grow up, Louis turns being thrown away into gold. Writing about Buddy Bolden on South Rampart Street, Michael Ondaadji writes that Rampart Street's paving

---

72. Ibid.

73. Joshua Barrett, "Louis Armstrong and Opera," *The Musical Quarterly* 76, no. 2 (Summer 1992): 216–41.

74. Charles Bernstein, "Me and My Pharaoh…" (online at *https://www.poetryfoundation.org/poetrymagazine/poems/56905/me-and-my-pharaoh-*).

stones were "made marble by jazz."[75] Ondaadji could as well have said "made manure by jazz."

The title of Lévi-Strauss's *La Pensée Sauvage*, from which we get this critical term *bricolage*, is a pun that the English translation, *The Savage Mind*, does not begin to capture. *Sauvage* means savage, as in the dismissive *uncivilized savages*, but it also means *wild* in the appreciative sense that Rousseau used it, as in *untamed, primitive. Pensée* means *mind* or *thought* but it also refers simply enough to the flower pansy, an image that introduces a touch of the natural and the pastoral: a wild pansy. The image of a pansy on the cover of Lévi-Strauss's first French edition made this pun clear. And yet, because the pansy is a hybridized flower, hybridized from *heartsease,* a humble weed, a mere throwaway, Lévi-Strauss knew "pansy" also evokes the opposite: civilization. Thus a pansy is also a *pensée*, a product of thought, of culture. Lévi-Strauss's own suggested translation was *Mind in the Wild.* To convey the complexity of Lévi-Strauss's pun, consider this example of a *wild* pansy, a pansy gone native, re-wilded as it were, once again a mere weed. I draw these puns from Lévi-Strauss' biographer who sums up that, Lévi-Strauss's "book is not about primitive thought, but a kind of untrammeled thinking, the mind running free."[76]

A wild pansy

The "mind running free" is part of Louis's persona. Remember Aristotle's dictum, that the speaker's "character may almost be called the most effective means of persuasion he possesses."[77] Louis doesn't just avidly smoke weed. He presents himself as a weed grown wild in the cracks in Rampart Street's pavement who, taking advantage of the disadvantages, achieves in his music and his life "a kind of untrammeled thinking, the mind running free." This is the longing at the heart of improvisation, to be free of, untrammeled by, the mainstream's reigning rationality and craftsmanship.

---

75. Michael Ondaatji, *Coming Through Slaughter* (New York: Vintage, 1996), 2.

76. Wilcken, *Claude Lévi-Strauss,* 259.

77. *The Basic Works of Aristotle,* edited by Richard McKeon (New York: Random House, 1941), 1329.

Where did Little Louis of Perdido and Liberty—Lost and Freedom Streets—find this spirit? Finally, there is always the explanation of genius, that a genius such as Louis, so tuned to his daimon's voice, could have learned of Trickster from within. Among his many roles, Trickster is our shadow side, and one of the things that shapes Little Louis into the Louis Armstrong we know is his deep embrace of his shadow, all those things about our nature that the mainstream would like to deny.

To the modern mind jazz invented improvisation but in fact jazz is anticipated by and participates in this ancient discourse I call improvisation, though discourse begins to seem too stuffy a word. Describe improv, no matter what the date or provenance, and you're describing jazz. Describe jazz and you're describing improv. Seeing art of all kinds through the lens of this perennial form is to witness how the mainstream is perennially challenged. The gesture of craftslessness and irrationality—I did it on the spur of the moment without thought, or care, or craft, a way to "take advantage of the disadvantages"—is always an effort to dismantle the edifice of authority, how we make and judge value, how we determine what is good and bad, and how we know the world. All value and all knowledge is contingent; it does not, mainstream to the contrary notwithstanding, come from above from some higher authority. We *make* value, we *make* authority *as we go*. Embodied by Trickster, lord of the crossroads, lord of the in-between, this is the vision of improv, of all those bricoleurs who work in remnants, be they Louis Karnofsky, Claude Lévi-Strauss, Louis Armstrong, and all those who confect that disruptive music called jazz, or the many improvisers through the centuries we have been discussing. This vision of the value of untrammeled thought is the essence of the jazz revolution, and of the many paradigm shifts we have been tracing.

6. Improvisation's "Supreme Fiction"

Free of, untrammeled by, the mainstream's reigning rationality and craftsmanship: this is, in Wallace Stevens's words, improvisation's "supreme fiction." By qualifying their spontaneity as neither natural nor absolute and by their understanding of the world as contingent, improvisations—except again for those extreme, vatic instances like Pindar's—exemplify Roland Barthes's notion of the healthy sign, which draws attention to its arbitrariness—like

Odysseus's oar/winnowing fan—not trying, as Terry Eagleton explains, "to palm itself off as 'natural' but which, in the very moment of conveying a meaning, communicates something of its own relative, artificial status as well."[78] Eagleton adds that "the impulse behind this belief...is a political one: signs which pass themselves off as natural, which offer themselves as the only conceivable way of viewing the world, are by that token authoritarian and ideological."[79] The rhetorical gestures of improvisations, are in a sense the ultimate "natural" signs, where the scare quotes are performative, part of their ironic meaning: like Louis's famous grin and apparently "effortless" playing as he profusely sweats, they are "natural" signs of the natural. Thus improvisations acknowledge, however subtly, the artificial, mediated status of their immediacies. This keeps them from lapsing into decadence. Pindar, who has no need for scare quotes, is the exception that proves this rule.

Barthes's *aperçu* helps us better to understand the critical history, writ large, of spontaneity. The overtly rhetorical nature of pre-Romantic spontaneity, though susceptible to misreading, is manifest largely because pre-Romantic audiences (and critical readers) of Sterne, for example, or of Pope, expect a rhetorical art. The pitch of seriousness with which the Romantics profess to reject rhetoric and to embrace raw spontaneity almost loses for spontaneity its status as a rhetorical figure, obscuring the subtle qualifications of the rhetoric as neither natural nor absolute. Because of this, post-Romantic improvisations tend to take on a measure of decadence, producing some of the wilder, vatic instances of the form in the nineteenth and twentieth centuries (the 40,000 lines of Bailey's *Festus,* Yeats's automatic writings, the surrealists and the Beat Poets at their least effective). It is through the filter of this decadent understanding of spontaneity that we get the critical misreadings of both Romantic and pre-Romantic texts that miss their rhetorical nature, and overestimate their commitment to unmediated, transcendent experience. It is also this decadent reading of spontaneity that lies, I believe, at the bottom of the conflict between humanistic and suprahumanistic readers of "spontaneous" texts. The suprahumanists, who imagine some unme-

---

78. Terry Eagleton, *Literary Theory: An Introduction* (Minneapolis and London: University of Minnesota Press, 1993 [1983]), 135.

79. Ibid.

diated experience of the transcendent, consciously or unconsciously apply phenomenology's natural yearning for immediate presence but fail to register phenomenology's intellectually rigorous acknowledgment that such immediacy is fundamentally unavailable to us. Theirs is the decadent Romantic reading that Jerome McGann rightly chastises.

In part, the point then is to come down squarely on the side of the humanist reading in the critical debates often surrounding these texts. The gesture of spontaneous composition is complex, multivalent like Hermes himself, *polytropos*. It cuts more than one way. But the rhetorical strategy in which it is employed, however outlandishly, is in the mainstream of the humanist tradition. Vatic improvisations in their decadence are the exceptions that prove the rule.

Both the figure of Hermes and Barthes's notion of the healthy sign thus help explain the sense of freedom that permeates improvisations (excepting again vatic improvisations where the sense of freedom is Pindar's alone and, at least to this reader, claustrophobic). Always emphatically assuming a point of view, improvisations invite us to do the same, to assume our first-person, subjective voice as we experience and embrace this world, though longing for the ultimate presence of the next. The agency of that assumption—grace, ecstasy, inspiration, the imagination, the unconscious, blood consciousness, the id, Louis's marijuana—will depend largely on what the improviser and his or her milieu put forward as newly more incorporative, whatever embraces more of life. Whatever the agency, it will have about it a beyond-the-bounds character in some degree; hence the antinomian, lawless streak that runs through improvisation. Even so, the structure of its argument is fully determined, subject to the laws that shape improvisation, and finally less hostile to law and limit than we would expect.

In part the point here is to perceive that, despite their extensive differences, these agencies—grace, ecstasy, inspiration, the imagination, the unconscious, blood consciousness, the id—function isomorphically in improvisations from different periods. Although protean, they have the same formal shape. Furthermore, the pattern of these self-styled "chaotic" texts—established (at least for our purposes here) by the Homeric hymn poet, by Pindar, and by Sappho—is repeated again and again in literary history. Lucian's "True History," Petronius's "fragmentary" *Satyricon,* Apuleius's *Golden Ass,* Juvenal's farragoes, Horace's lyric *Odes* and *Epodes,* Martial's intimate *Epigrams*—each exploits a rhetoric of "naturalness," of a freedom from mediation. They present themselves as free of the adulterations and artifice of the dominant culture, enjoying "a grace beyond the reach of" each culture's over-sophisticated, decadent "art"—and certainly well beyond that culture's concern with the acquisition of power and money. In so doing, they suggest that the faculties of mind used to produce such crafted decadence (or decadent craft) must be replaced by or enlarged by other faculties, faculties whose value is questioned by the dominant culture, and finally questioned perhaps by the improviser.

Along the way, the improviser celebrates the life-in-its-immediacy, the bucolic green world or the wildness of Lévi-Strauss's Brazil, Louis Armstrong's African roots or, paradoxically, his urban Battlefield, what culture has lost touch with. Improvisation's relation to pastoral on the one hand and to prophecy on the other suggests first that Norman O. Brown is right when he writes that "prophecy is a critical response to the 'urban revolution,' that irreversible commitment of the human race to the city and civilization,"[80] and second that improvisation is prophecy's (and pastoral's) fullest articulation.This pattern is repeated in the turmoil of the Renaissance (Erasmus, More, Rabelais, Montaigne) and at the birth of the industrial and scientific revolution (Swift, Sterne, Pope). It comes to full flower at the height of the industrial revolution (Blake, Wordsworth, Coleridge, Keats, Byron, Browning), and at the birth of the technological age (Joyce, Woolf, Miller, Valéry, Apollinaire [and all the surrealists], Pound, Williams, Stevens, Moore, Mann [especially of *Doctor Faustus* and *Confessions of Felix Krull, Confidence Man*]). As an almost wholly decadent trope and topos it rampages in our postindustrial world, a world in which every moment is originary because history does not exist and all artistry, indeed all human effort, is thought corrupt. Even so, subtler, more complex adherents like Creeley can sometimes be found.

Decadent is a strong word but must not be shied from. It serves to remind us of the consequences of our failure to register spontaneity's dark side. The Ancient Mariner is redeemed because he blesses the water snakes gratu-

---

80. Brown, *Apocalypse and/or Metamorphosis,* 46.

itously and irrationally: "unawares." This leads to the moral that Coleridge told Mrs. Barbault the poem expressed too directly: "He prayeth best, who loveth best/All things both great and small." Meanwhile the poem hints less directly that acts equally gratuitous and irrational—like his killing the albatross—can be heinous and have dire consequences, the deaths of the entire crew and of Nature as we know it. So too we may admire Odysseus's always ready, ever polytropic improvisations. But his improvisations, like Huck Finn's two millennia later, are not only what gets him out of, but also into trouble. In Odysseus's case, the impulse to improvise costs the lives of *his* entire crew, hundreds of men. We will explore the consequences of "free and easy" Huck's going "a good deal on instinct" below.

While our post-Romantic tendency is to embrace improvisation's optative and positive themes, Swiftian satire reminds us that the mechanical operation of the spirit and other enthusiasms can lead to darker possibilities. Bill Buford, in his brilliant exploration of British football hooligans, *Among the Thugs,* offers one unexpected example. He finds in the spectator experience that part of the appeal of crowds is their "existing so intensely in the present that it is possible for an individual, briefly, to cease being an individual, to disappear into the power of numbers—the strength of them, the emotion of belonging to them..."[81] Finding the usual tensions we have found again and again in improvisation but flipping the terms of improvisation's legerdemain, Buford finds the crowd experience to be

> formlessness in a contrivance of form. Being a spectator is an insistently structured experience: there is a ticket that confers exclusivity; there are gates that govern what is possible here, inside, what is not possible there, outside...Outside, one experience; inside another; outside again, and the crowd experience, like the match which governs it, is terminated: there is an ending, closure, a point when the crowd can be designated as having ceased to exist. In every crowd, there is something—with form—to contain the inherently formless nature of the crowd itself, to control what is potentially uncontrollable.[82]

---

81. Bill Buford, *Among the Thugs* (New York: Vintage Books, 1991), 190-91.
82. Ibid., 191.

As always, this violent experience of order emerging from chaos is a liminal, threshold experience. On the far side of the threshold, the crowd experiences something larger than its individual members, something transcendent. But from the near side, those behaviors appear nothing but violence and chaos.

Surely Hitler stands as the most extreme example of the evil spontaneity can do. Jung read Hitler as a man who "listens intently to a stream of suggestions from a whispered source and then *acts upon them.*"[83] Once you have opened the doors to external forces, dampening Reason's ability to judge, you never know who will come knocking, whether the force steering you will be demonic or divine, pathological or healthy. How do you judge once you've programmatically dismissed judgment?

A Note on the Cover

The ground is now prepared to explain my cover illustration, *Carpe Vitam*, which, besides providing some comic relief from those dark thoughts, returns us to the main subject of this chapter.

Painted by New Orleans artist Alan Gerson, the cover illustrates Hermes, lord of improvisation.[84] Gerson calls his cartoonish figures "goofy guys." They seem perfectly to capture the lack of depth and piety critics find in the hymn and in Hermes himself. Gerson's *faux naïf* style captures the faux primitive spirit of improvisation while, upon more careful scrutiny, reveals itself to be well-crafted and painterly.

Hermes's small coin-purse and the cityscape above which he hovers relate to his oversight of commerce, the radio tower, his oversight of communications (which helps explain, as we shall see in Chapter 13, why James Joyce made his Odysseus/Hermes character Leopold Bloom an advertising canvasser). The setting is clearly New York where a statue of Hermes as Lord of the Crossroads, and of the road and travel as well, graces the main entrance to

---

83. *C. G. Jung Speaking: Interviews and Encounters,* edited by William McGuire and R. F. C. Hull (Princeton, N.J.: Princeton University Press, 1977), 119; emphasis in original.

84. Alan Gerson. He is represented by LeMieux Galleries in New Orleans and by others in Los Angeles, Santa Fe, and Scottsdale.

Grand Central Station. (A personal note: although I commissioned this paint-
ing before taking a place in New York, the view is almost identical to what
I see from my window—an example of the synchronicity associated with
Hermes we will explore below in the Jung, Joyce, Mann chapter).

Gerson portrays Hermes's mythic attributes: winged sandals (*talaria*),
winged cap, and the herald's staff, the Greek *kerykeion* or Latin *caduceus*. For
some reason he paints the staff with four snakes rather than Hermes's normal two. I like to think Gerson segments the snakes to suggest the turbulence of hermetic experience and the apparent fragmentedness of the literary form Hermes oversees. Since the tri-colored snake is clearly a venomous
coral snake rather than a non-venomous kingsnake—"Red on yellow, venom
fellow; red on black, safe from attack"—I suspect all four are venomous and
expressive of hermetic mischief from which, on the homeopathic principle,
health comes. Homeopathy has roots in hermetic alchemy. The homeopathic
principle *simila similibus curantur* ("like is cured by like") stems from sixteenth century Swiss physician and alchemist Paracelsus who "founds his
doctrine on Hermes."[85] (More synchronicities: Paracelsus lived part of his
nomadic career in Jung's Basel and enjoyed the patronage of Erasmus after
healing the latter's printer, Forben).

Hermes mischievously holds in his right hand the golden apple that Eris,
goddess of discord, brought to a wedding inscribed "for the most beautiful."
Hera, Athena, and Aphrodite all claimed it and Zeus asked Paris to decide.
Hermes conveyed the apple and the task to Paris. For choosing her, Aphrodite
promised Paris the most beautiful mortal, Helen, which led to the Trojan
War. Hermes is Lord of Mischief, always stirring it up. His "goofy gay" nose
here recalls Pinocchio, which perhaps alludes to Herme's role as Lord of Liars.
Pinocchio shares with Odysseus and Hermes the descent into hell.

In commissioning the painting, the only things I asked Gerson to include
are worked into the banner that surrounds the figure. *Psychopompós* (ψυχο-
πομπός), guide of souls, is an epithet attributed to Hermes for his role of con-

---

85. Whitall N. Perry, "The Alchemy in Homeopathy," *Studies in Comparative Religion* 16, no. 1/2 (Winter-Spring 1984) (online at *http://www.studiesincomparativereli-
gion.com/public/articles/The_Alchemy_in_Homeopathy-by_Whitall_N_Perry.aspx*).

ducting the dead to Hades. The other two are my additions to the Hermes myth. The mathematical formula, $Z \longrightarrow Z2 + C$, is chaos scientist Mitchell Feigenbaum's universal constant in chaotic systems.[86] *Carpe Vitam* at the top expresses the ultimate goal of improvisation.

---

86. See James Gleick's discussion in *Chaos*, 173-75.

PART II

APPLICATIONS

CHAPTER EIGHT

Milton and the Problematics of Inspiration

> What the reader must finally learn is that the analytical
> intellect, so important in the formulation of necessary
> distinctions, is itself an instrument of perversion and
> the child of corruption because it divides and contrasts
> and evaluates where there is in reality a single harmoni-
> ous unity.
> —Stanley Fish, *Surprised by Sin*

Puritan poet and polemicist John Milton, whose *Areopagitica* (1644) is among the most impassioned defenses of free speech and freedom of the press, is rarely found cheek by jowl with the often flamboyant improvisers in these pages. Yet it is still true that his lapidary epic *Paradise Lost* satisfies, though never flamboyantly, many of the conventions of improvisation. *Paradise Lost,* like many improvisations, is a *genera mista,* and not just a mixed genre but, as Barbara Lewalski argues, a consummation of all genres: epic, drama, pastoral, and many others.[1] It is nothing if not encyclopedic: writ large it is a cornucopia of human history (and pre-history), of human culture, Biblical and Classical; on a smaller scale it contains catalogs of angels, fallen and unfallen, catalogs of flora and fauna in Eden. *Copia,* "expansive richness of utterance," is one of Milton's dominant rhetorical devices, as it is for improvisation.[2] And while it is true that few would associate Milton's narrative persona with the fool tradition, it is also true that writing blind, in isolation, and as a Cromwellian outcast from the Restoration Court, he writes and presents himself as a socially marginal persona:

---

1. Barbara Lewalski, Paradise Lost *and the Rhetoric of Literary Forms* (Princeton, N.J.: Princeton University Press, 1985).

2. Lanham, *A Handlist of Rhetorical Terms,* 42.

> fall'n on evil days,
> On evil days though fall'n, and evil tongues;
> In darkness, and with dangers compast round,
> And solitude.[3]

Where improvisers almost all write studiously in the vernacular, Milton's Latinate prose is mannered and overtly artificial. Nonetheless, it is clear from his note on versification usually published with the poem that Milton intends dialogically to overleap the adulterations of modern times for the greater simplicity of "*English* Heroic Verse without Rime, as that of *Homer* in *Greek,* and of *Virgil* in *Latin*; Rime being no necessary Adjunct or true Ornament of Poem or good Verse…but the Invention of a barbarous Age, to set off wretched matter and lame Meter."[4] His epic is not *sui generis,* yet Milton insists in a number of ways familiar to criticism that it swerves significantly from the classical epic tradition, inspired by his Christian "Heavenly Muse." The famous invocations in Books 1, 3, 7, and 9 satisfy three conventions of improvisations in one fell swoop: they digress from the principle narrative; they introduce a note of biographical realism; and they insistently sound the note that Milton's highly-wrought epic is in fact not the effort of his hand or mind at all, but the inspiration of his "celestial patroness":

> who deigns
> Her nightly visitation unimplor'd,
> And dictates to me slumb'ring, or inspires
> Easy my unpremeditated Verse.[5]

Thematically speaking, Milton's heretical embrace of the Fortunate Fall is an embrace too of the overarching theme of improvisation: the embrace of this life, here, now, and all of it, our own shadows included.

Thus, as with all improvisations, so too with *Paradise Lost*: it is the poet's insistence both within and without the text upon the inspired nature of his creation that cues us that we have entered the world of improvisation. If T.S.

---

3. *Paradise Lost,* in John Milton, *Complete Poems and Major Prose,* edited by Merritt Y. Hughes (New York: The Odyssey Press, 1957), 7.25-28.

4. "The Verse," in Milton, *Complete Poems,* 210.

5. Ibid., 9.21-24.

Eliot found that the first line was always a gift, Milton's Muse—by whatever name: "the meaning, not the Name I call"[6]—seems to have been far more generous. Milton's earliest, anonymous biographer (assumed to be his nephew, Edward Philips) recorded his remark that "he waking early (as is the use of temperate men) had commonly a good stock of verses ready against his amanuensis came; which if it happened to be later than ordinary, he would complain, saying he wanted to be milked."[7] And, according to his third wife, Betty, Milton was no plagiarist but "stole from nobody but the Muse who inspired him and being asked by a lady present who the Muse was, replied that it was God's grace, and the Holy Spirit visited him nightly." Critics tend unequivocally to accept such remarks. As recent biographer A.N. Wilson writes, "There can be no doubt that the religious conviction about the celestial origins of *Paradise Lost* came from her husband."[8] And yet a close look at *Paradise Lost* suggests that for Milton inspiration in practice represents problem rather than conviction, question rather than answer.

In fact, Milton characterizes only untainted Eden and unfallen humankind in terms of unmediated spontaneity, and often questions even that. Raphael's entry into Eden is greeted by nature's "Wild[ness] above Rule or Art...for Nature here/Wanton'd as in her prime, and play'd at will/Her

---

6. *Paradise Lost*, 7.5.

7. Quoted in A.N. Wilson, *The Life of John Milton* (Oxford: Oxford University Press, 1983), 197.

8. Ibid., 222. As well, Meg Harris Williams writes of Milton's desire to "be milked": "the sensuous intensity of the passage tells us without external corroboration that Milton's description of inspiration is not mere convention, but to be taken literally," in *Inspiration in Milton and Keats* (Totowa, N.J.: Barnes & Noble Books, 1982), 87–88. One is forced to wonder what form Williams imagines such "external corroboration" might take—did Betty, like Blake's wife, set an extra place at table? Other treatments of Milton's inspiration include Robert L. Entzminger, *Divine Word: Milton and the Redemption of Language* (Pittsburgh: Duquesne University Press, 1985); E.R. Gregory, *Milton and the Muses* (Tuscaloosa: University of Alabama Press, 1989); Walter Schindler, *Voice and Crisis: Invocation in Miltons's Poetry* (Hamden, Conn.: Archon Books, 1984); and Joseph Anthony Wittreich, "'A Poet Amongst Poets': Milton and the Tradition of Prophecy."

Virgin Fancies, pouring forth more sweet."[9] Adam and Eve's first prayer—
the world's first poem, as it were—is likewise rich in immediacy:

> So all was clear'd, and to the Field they haste.
> But first from under shady arborous roof,
> Soon as they forth were come to open sight
> Of day-spring, and the Sun, who scarce up risen
> With wheels yet hov'ring o'er the Ocean brim,
> Shot parallel to the earth his dewy ray,
> Discovering in wide Lantskip all the East
> Of Paradise and *Eden*'s happy Plains,
> Lowly they bow'd adoring, and began
> Thir Orisons, each Morning duly paid
> In various style, for neither various style
> Nor holy rapture wanted they to praise
> Thir Maker, in fit strains pronounct or sung
> Unmeditated, such prompt eloquence
> Flow'd from their lips, in Prose or numerous Verse,
> More tuneable than needed Lute or Harp
> To add more sweetness, ...[10]

Milton evokes immediacy with a rhetorical power reminiscent of the Homeric
"Hymn to Hermes." The scene is temporally immediate: they "haste"; they
move "first," and "soon"; the sun at "day-spring" is "scarce up," and "sho[o]
t[s its] dewy ray." Even though it is "unmediated" and "prompt," their song
achieves a "various style"—the *copia* recommended since Cicero and Quintilian and stressed by Renaissance rhetoricians—and "fit strains": the proper
rhetorical and prosodic elements.[11] These skills—*copia*, rhetoric, and prosody—take years of effort for fallen man to acquire. Milton is demonstrating
that unfallen Adam and Eve achieve effortlessly and through holy rapture
what fallen man is doomed to achieve by the sweat of his brow, indeed what

---

9. *Paradise Lost,* 5.294-97.

10. Ibid., 5.136-52.

11. Stanley Fish reads "various style" differently, as "unpatterned," in *Surprised by Sin: The Reader in Paradise Lost* (Berkeley, Los Angeles, and London: University of California Press, 1971), 143, a passage I will take issue with below.

his master, Spenser, proclaimed "not to bee gotten by laboure and learning," is available only through inspiration.[12] In this prelapsarian felicity, Nature's quickness harmoniously answers and participates in theirs. The sweetness of their verse ("More tuneable than needed Lute or Harp/To add more sweetness"), echoes Raphael's experience of Eden whose "Virgin Fancies, pouring forth more sweet." Furthermore, unfallen man has the good, Puritan sense to avoid the mediation of musical accompaniment. "More tuneable than needed Lute or Harp/To add more sweetness" is Milton's satiric thrust against Anglican and Papist liturgy. Like many improvisations this Edenic one begins on the satiric note that the prevailing art is wrongheaded and then proceeds to imitate the offending art. For the hymn is itself liturgical. Nevertheless, in terms of its inspiration, Adam and Eve's morning hymn, the world's first improvisation, may also be the world's last unproblematic improvisation.

The allusion to contemporary church politics implicit in the description of Adam and Eve's unmediated spontaneity is symptomatic and typical of improvisation. We are ever reminded that such a world is lost, that like Adam on fallen Mount Pisgah we require angelic anointment of euphrasy and rue (symbolic of joy and sorrow respectively) to cleanse the doors of perception.[13] In *Paradise Lost*, postlapsarian inspiration, Milton's included, is fraught with problems.

Though for Milton the infusion of grace is the answer to all problems, the experience of grace for Milton raises questions as it does for all Protestants this side of the Pelagian heresy, the view that original sin did not taint human nature. Milton charges the word "infuse" with the burden of conveying many of his doubts. Its etymology (*infudere*, "to pour in") echoes in meaning the Greek root of spontaneity (*spendein*, "to pour a libation"). The word occurs only four times in *Paradise Lost*, in contexts which are among the poem's most crucial moments. Things "inspired" are no less equivocal. Regarding the serpent, for example, we learn that

> in at his Mouth
> The devil enter'd, and his brutal sense,

---

12. *The Shepheardes Calender*, in *Spenser's Minor Poems*, 456.
13. *Paradise Lost*, 9.414.

> In heart or head, possessing soon *inspir'd*
> With act intelligential...[14]

Likewise men and angels are as likely to be "inspir'd/With dev'lish machination," or with Satan's "inspiring venom,"[15] as by the One True Word. But "infuse" and its cognates appear less often and always at the most charged of moments.

"Infuse" occurs, for example, no less than at the creation of the world:

> Thus God the Heav'n created, thus the Earth,
> Matter unform'd and void: Darkness profound
> Cover'd th' Abyss: but on the watery calm
> His brooding wings the Spirit of God outspread,
> And vital virtue infus'd, and vital warmth
> Throughout the fluid Mass, but downward purg'd
> The black tartareous cold Infernal dregs
> Adverse to life: then founded, then conglob'd
> Like things to like, the rest to several place
> Disparted, and between spun out the Air.[16]

Here the word is charged with positive value, the resonant fricatives and sibilants ("vital virtue infused") all the more attractive in contrast to the frightening plosives and hard consonants which follow: "downward purg'd/The black tartareous cold Infernal dregs."

The harsh imagery of the passage's end harkens of course to Satanic regions. In fact "infuse" first occurs in a Satanic context, which precedes—both in the poem and in the narrative—the creation of the world. The speech with which Satan precipitates the war in heaven is described with these words:

> So spake the false Arch-Angel, and infus'd
> Bad influence into th' unwary breast
> Of his Associate...[17]

And so begins the fall that will precipitate our fall. "Infuse" is thus problematic, undermined by association with Satan's "bad influence" and his fall, even when in Book 7 it seems not to be.

---

14. Ibid., 9.188-90. Emphasis added.
15. Ibid., 6.503-4; 4.804.
16. Ibid., 7.232-41.
17. Ibid., 5.694-96.

It next appears in human context and rightly this occurrence is the most complex and problematic. Adam describes the creation of Eve:

> Mine eyes he clos'd, but op'n left the Cell
> Of Fancy my internal sight, by which
> Abstract as in a trace methought I saw,
> Through sleeping, where I lay, and saw the shape
> Still glorious before whom awake I stood;
> Who stooping op'n'd my left side, and took
> From thence a Rib, with cordial spirits warm,
> And Life-blood streaming fresh; wide was the wound,
> But suddenly with flesh fill'd up and heal'd:
> The Rib he formed and fashion'd with his hands;
> Under his forming hands a Creature grew,
> Manlike, but of different sex, so lovely fair,
> That what seem'd fair in all the World, seem'd now
> Mean, or in her summ'd up, in her contain'd
> And in her looks, which from that time infus'd
> Sweetness into my heart, unfelt before,
> And into all things from her Air inspired
> The spirit of love and amorous delight.[18]

I call this "infusion" the most problematic because both Adam's fall and his redemption are prefigured here. What is "infused" and "inspired" is that over-sensuousness ("amorous delight") which informs Adam's uxorious love ("Sweetness") for Eve. Even so, Adam is also inspired with "the spirit of love" which is the beginning and, insofar as it is within his power, not Christ's, the agent of his future redemption. It is a crucial passage, and the notion of infusion/inspiration is its linchpin. Infusion's negative connotations here vie on an equal footing with positive.

The word's final occurrence in *Paradise Lost* leaves Milton's ambivalence not at all in doubt. Just after Eve decides to include Adam in her fall, she is described in this manner:

> So saying, from the Tree her step she turn'd,
> But first low Reverence done, as to the power
> That dwelt within, whose presence had infus'd

---

18. Ibid., 8.460-77.

Into the plant sciential sap, deriv'd
From Nectar, drink of Gods.[19]

Milton darkly hints that Eve's genuflection—"low Reverence done," a questionable Romish ritual in itself—is part of a dark and pagan mass. The ambiguous "as to"—is it "in order to" or the preferred "as if to"?—suggests that she kneels to Satan, not the God she thinks she does. The "Nectar, drink of Gods" seals her paganism. The "presence" which "infuses" the "sciential sap" is in effect Satanic, for this is not what God intended at all. She is guilty here too, it has been argued, of both primitivism and paganism: worshipping both tree and tree's spirit. We are a far cry from the innocence and immediacy of Adam and Eve's first *aubade*.

Thus things "infused," coming crucially at the beginnings of Satan's Fall, of the world's creation, of Man's Fall, and of Man's redemption. Once we have detected this dark, narrative undercurrent concerning the value of supernatural visitations, we see that even the seeming magisterial calm of Milton's invocations is not unperturbed. Not only is there the familiar ambiguity about what his Muse should be called—"Descend from Heav'n *Urania*, by that name / If rightly thou art call'd.../ The meaning, not the Name I call..."[20]—there are also hints that the source of poetic inspiration is ambiguous. First of all, as in Eve's worshipping before the tree, Milton cannot be sure who does the inspiring. The invocation to Book 3 is loaded with well-hidden booby traps. Two of the four blind poets to whom he compares himself, Thamyris and Phineus, were known for their overreaching. Thamyris challenged the Muses to a contest and the tag *Thamyris insanit* (Thamyris rages) was proverbial. The Thracian king Phineus also offended the gods, inciting their jealousy by becoming too good a prophet. Coming after the scene in Pandemonium where we have witnessed Satan's hubris and rivalry, such references are suggestive. In Book 7's invocation Milton will compare his "presum[ing]" to describe the "Empyreal Air" to Bellerophon's presumptuous ride on Pegasus.[21] In Book 3 again, his final invocation to "Celestial Light," to

---

19. Ibid., 9.834–38.

20. Ibid., 7.1–5.

21. Stanley Fish anticipates me in finding an ambivalent subtext in these classical allusions and in those to Orpheus, which I discuss below, in his "With Mortal Voice:

> Shine inward, and the mind through all her powers
> Irradiate, there plant eyes, all mist from thence
> Purge and disperse...[22]

echoes Beelzebub's hope in Book 2 that his Satan-inspired plan will enable them to

> Dwell not unvisited of Heav'n's fair Light
> Secure, and at the bright'ning Orient beam
> Purge off this gloom...[23]

Milton put the boldest front possible on his blindness as a token of inspiration in part because his continental critics attacked it as a sign of God's vengeance for regicide. At the same time but more covertly, Milton encodes his doubts about the nature of his inspiration because his theme, the effects of Adam's fall, demands it. Fallen man will never again be sure of the source of "thoughts, that voluntary move / Harmonious numbers."[24] Even the ever-certain bravado, Milton.

Another disturbing mythic precursor whom Milton, like Pindar, invokes more than once is Orpheus. In Book 3 Milton seems certain that he sings "of *Chaos* and *Eternal Night*...With other notes than to th' *Orphean* Lyre," that is, that unlike Orpheus his music and visionary power will not fail him and leave him stranded in Hell.[25] As so often in the postlapsarian world, and despite the expression of certainty, the adequacy of inspiration is at issue. Orpheus again intrudes in Book 7. Milton wonders if his Muse will fail to protect him as Calliope did when her son, Orpheus was seized and torn apart by the Thracian maidens:

> Standing on earth, not rapt above the pole,
> More safe I sing with mortal voice, unchanged
> To hoarse or mute, though fallen on evil days,
> On evil days though fall'n, and evil tongues;
> In darkness, and with dangers compast round,

Milton Defends against the Muse," *English Literature History* 62, no. 3 (Fall 1995): 509-27. My thanks to Professor Fish for pointing me to his paper.

22. *Paradise Lost*, 3.52-54.
23. Ibid., 2.398-400.
24. Ibid., 3.37—38.
25. Ibid., 3.18, 17.

And solitude; yet not alone, while thou
Visit'st my slumbers Nightly, or when Morn
Purples the East; still govern thou my Song,
Urania, and fit audience find, though few.
But drive far off the barbarous dissonance
Of *Bacchus* and his Revellers, the Race
Of that wild Rout that tore the *Thracian* Bard
In *Rhodope,* where Woods and Rocks have Ears
To rapture, till the savage clamour drown'd
Both Harp and Voice; nor could the Muse defend
Her Son. So fail not thou, who thee implores:
For thou art Heavn'ly, shee an empty dream.[26]

Here, as elsewhere, Milton at once harmonizes classical and Christian myth and swerves from the classical prototypes to show the victory of Christian myth. And yet the calm of the Horatian "fit audience though few" should not blind us to the anxiety being expressed here. As type of the inspired poet, Orpheus is a crucial instance of the myth of inspiration and its dangers. As the son of Calliope, the heroic and epic muse who here fails to save him, and of Apollo, the god of the sun, of poetry, and of prophecy, Orpheus is especially appropriate to Milton's task and situation. If like Orpheus's Muse his is "an empty dream," his audience too will reject him. If deserted by Apollonian calm and objectivity, he will be seized by Dionysian rapture and subjectivity. That way for Milton, as for the rationalist Mill, solipsism lies.

After all, alongside the doubt that inspiration's source is Satanic lies an equally disturbing doubt: that the source of inspiration is solipsism. Book IX's invocation again proclaims the poem's freedom from mere artificial conventions of epic, that the poet is not "skilled nor studious" in martial themes. The poet's claim of inspired spontaneity is expressed with equal humility in the form of a question:

If answerable style I can obtain
Of my Celestial Patroness, who deigns
Her nightly visitations unimplor'd,
And dictates to me slumb'ring, or inspires
Easy my unpremeditated Verse...[27]

---

26. Ibid., 7.23–39.
27. Ibid., 9.20–24.

The humility here is in part conventional. Yet the invocation ends with a more dogged question. Milton lists the possible hindrances to his epic achievement:

> unless an age too late, or cold
> Climate, or Years damp my intended wing
> Deprest, and much they may, if all be mine,
> Not Hers who brings it nightly to my Ear.[28]

Death or flagging health will dampen his efforts unless they are *her* efforts. In a sense this is but an elaborate compliment to his Muse, the stuff of courtly sonneteers: I can't do without you. And yet in the context of the epic, and set here in climactic final and logically overarching position, the fear rings true: "if all be mine,/Not hers." For after all, this is the ultimate problem of the prophetic poet: not that the mantle is too heavy; nor that God's word will "make thy belly bitter"; nor that he will go unheard in his society; nor even that his vision is devil-inspired (Revelations 10:9). All these must be faced. But the worst fear, especially now in our secular age, is that, like Swift's spider in *The Battle of the Books*, the prophet just spins his vision out of his own belly. Or rather, this fear is the moral and theological equivalent of the fear that inspiration is demonic. For without grace man is doomed to solipsism, all effort tainted by his corrupt and fallen nature.

Thus Milton's "visitations unimplored," which "inspires/Easy my unpremeditated verse" borders ultimately on Satan's primal sin, his belief that he was "self-begot, self-rais'd/By our own quick'ning power..."[29] Milton's point is that the notion that our "puissance" is, in Satan's words, "our own" is always Satanic, that since Adam's fall, our puissance is *never* our own. These doubts about prevenient grace prove Milton no Arminian, the hint that he may not be justified, that he is no Calvinist. We are never self-sufficient, no artistic creation ever free of the linguistic and literary conventions it inevitably employs, if only parodically. As Isabel MacCaffrey states, "The uniqueness of *Paradise Lost* is in a sense its perfect victory over uniqueness."[30] We are all belated, all seeking originary power that we shall never have. The claim of

---

28. Ibid., 9.44–47.

29. Ibid., 5.860–61.

30. Isabel Gamble MacCaffrey, Paradise Lost *as "Myth"* (Cambridge, Mass.: Harvard University Press, 1959), 2.

spontaneity invokes such origins but, typical of improvisations, Milton's epic (like Adam and Eve's hymn) is extremely sophisticated, highly aware of the artificial conventions they claim not to employ. Disclaiming artifice, they create a system of counter-conventions that have the advantage of seeming more "natural," of not seeming conventional at all. They are finally aware, however, of the slippery nature of that word "natural."

I must hasten to respond to what the reader must be thinking, that of course there is nothing "spontaneous" or "natural" in the texture of Milton's lapidary, "builded" epic. This is in part my point. It does not matter whether, as the legends have it, he composed in bed and by whole verse paragraphs which in his blindness he recited to his daughters; what matters is that the texture of his poetry resounds with his long contemplation and craftsmanship. As in the broken artifice of Herbert's "Grief," discussed above, the tension between craftsmanship and the defeat or overthrow of craft is important because it introduces an important thematic nuance, emphasizing on the one hand a Christian's submission to God, on the other their acceptance of the burden of employing their faculties to God's glorification. The poem implicitly attacks the rationality that lies behind craftsmanly choices; but it is a *proud* rationality, a rationality that believes in its sufficiency, that is the problem, not Reason, Judgment, Will, which at their best, made in God's image, are reflections of God. Thus the tension and problematic we saw in discussing Milton's imagery is equally at work in his epic's texture. If Milton overtly speaks more loudly of inspiration and "unpremeditated verse" than he does of his mastery of his art, the quantities are reversed in the texture of his poetry, which, like Mill's "Essay on Nature," virtually shouts care and craft. Furthermore, Milton's symbology of "euphrasy and rue"—which Michael applies to clear Adam's eyes on Mt. Pisgah so that he may receive the apocalyptic vision and its promise of redemption—hints that experience (joy and sorrow), rather than some problematic source of inspiration, is the best teacher. Like all improvisers, only more so, Milton displays at every turn his mastery of the conventions he decries as artificial, what Mill calls "the considerate part of human conduct."[31] This is not to call Milton's bluff. It is simply to respond to the tensions, the contradictory texture of his poem,

---

31. Mill, "Three Essays on Religion: Nature," 392.

something we must do if we are adequately to analyze the rhetoric of spontaneity in *Paradise Lost.*

This is I think the point of Stanley Fish's study of Milton's ambivalence toward his muse. For Fish, Milton in invoking his muse at once yearns for and fears to be rapt (at once enraptured/inspired and raped/unmanned).[32] Milton longs to be authorized and to be author. Theologically Milton is in a hard spot: 1) grace must be prevenient; 2) but good works must be his own; and yet because 1), therefore not 2). This is a hard spot every Christian of Milton's ilk must negotiate. Sterne will be another as we will see in the next chapter. In *Paradise Lost* it is negotiated in part by means of the texture of ambivalence to authorship and to inspiration.

Our look at Milton's epic improvisation helps us to see the ambiguity and ambivalence at work in what appears the most unequivocal of texts. It also helps us to see what, and how much, Romantic texts are asserting when they assert their spontaneous provenience. Thoreau gets it all into an epigram: "The unconsciousness of man is the consciousness of God, the end of the world."[33] For the claim of spontaneity not only authorizes and validates ("shoots a ray of beauty into trivial and impure actions," as Emerson writes of spontaneity).[34] It also brings on the apocalypse, both goal and completion of the world. All improvisations are ultimately apocalyptic; all try to return us to Eden, as we saw the Angelic symphony is empowered to do in Milton's "Nativity Ode." In pagan terms improvisations by "Enwrap[ing] our fancy" try to do what Orpheus did in Thrace, "where Woods and Rocks had Ears/To rapture."[35] Among the many effects of this apocalyptic rapture—besides the death of vanity, sin, and Hell—is the dawning of a new regime. Literally at the center of this visionary regime, between Truth and Justice, sits Mercy. Eden of course is lost in Milton's epic, but its merciful return through Christ's redemptive death is the epic's promise.

---

32. Fish, "With Mortal Voice," 516-18.

33. He adds: "The very thrills of genius are disorganizing," 13 February 1840, in *A Writer's Journal*, 2.

34. "Self-Reliance," in Emerson, *Essays*, 46.

35. *Paradise Lost*, 7.35-36.

It is again Mercy upon which hinges the turn toward apocalypse that climaxes in the promise of Book XII. Here in Book XI, mercy is the agent of grace that *inspires* a wordless, hence, valid prayer, for Milton here invokes the rhetoric of spontaneity:

> Thus [Adam and Eve] in lowliest plight repentant stood
> Praying, for from the Mercy-seat above
> Prevenient Grace descending had remov'd
> The stony from their hearts, and made new flesh
> Regenerate grow instead, that sighs now breath'd
> Unutterable, which the Spirit of prayer
> Inspir'd, and wing'd for Heav'n with speedier flight
> Than loudest Oratory...[36]

Having followed the subtle but complex subtext regarding things infused and inspired, we are prepared to respond to this language heavily laden with the familiar terms of inspiration and spontaneous immediacy: "that *sighs* now *breath'd / Unutterable,* which the *Spirit* of prayer / *Inspir'd,* and *wing'd* for Heav'n with speedier *flight* / Than loudest Oratory" (my emphases). Milton's comparison ("Than loudest Oratory") exploits the sentiments of Plato's *Gorgias* and articulated by Pascal in the *Pensées*: "La vrai éloquence se moque de l'éloquence (True eloquence mocks eloquence)."

Still, and most important, this prayer's achieved immediacy is an immediacy with a crucial difference, for it is clearly and overarchingly mediated by "Prevenient Grace descending [that] remov[es] / The stony from th[e]ir hearts, and made new flesh." The rhetoric of immediacy Milton evokes for this prayer is equal to, but set in stark contrast to, the far more liturgical morning hymn from Book 5 discussed above. By contrast, the immediacy evoked in the aubade, though inspired by a "holy rapture," seems natural, "sprung from the heart," and seems to look ahead to Wordsworth. Nevertheless, now in contrast to these "sighs now breath'd / Unutterable" the naturalness of the morning song seems merely *recherché.* Now fallen, Adam and Eve's prayer seems to participate in the breakdown of artifice we saw exemplified by Herbert's broken coda in "Grief." George Herbert's broken coda "Alas my God" exactly anticipates their sentiment.

---

36. Ibid., 9.1–8.

As if the rhetoric of immediacy in the description of the prayers was inadequate, Milton underscores it three more times. First Milton's narrator underscores the power of this eloquence unmediated by language, again emphasizing the language of *spiritus*:

> To Heav'n their prayers
> *Flew up*, nor miss'd the way, by envious *winds*
> *Blown vagabond or frustrate*: in they *pass'd*
> *Dimensionless* through Heav'nly doors; *then clad*
> *With incense*, where the Golden Altar *fum'd,*
> By their great Intercessor, came in sight
> Before the Father's Throne...[37]

Then Milton's Christ underscores the same theme (though super-adding to the language of inspiration the conceit of generation). He promises to mediate the unmediated:

> See Father, what first fruits on Earth are sprung
> From thy implanted Grace in Man, *these Sighs*
> And Prayers, which in this Golden *Censer, mixt*
> *With Incense,* I thy Priest before thee bring,
> Fruits of more pleasing savor from thy seed
> Sown with contrition in his heart, than those
> Which his own hand manuring all the Trees
> Of Paradise could have produced, ere fall'n
> From innocence. Now therefore bend thine ear
> To supplication, hear *his sighs though mute;*
> *Unskillful with what words to pray,* let mee
> Interpret for him...[38]

Felix culpa: after tasting of the Tree of Knowledge, Adam's fall is fortunate because contrition's unmediated prayers have "more pleasing savour" than those that would have been produced by his "manuring all the Trees/Of Paradise" before he had "fallen from innocence." Finally Adam himself comments on his tacit, wordless prayer's surprising efficacy to meet the challenge despite in their disgrace in not reaching to heaven and to God:

---

37. Ibid., 9.14–20. Emphases added.
38. Ibid., 9.22–32. Emphases added.

> that from us aught should ascend to Heav'n
> So prevalent [i.e., powerful] as to concern the mind
> Of God high-blest, or to incline his will,
> Hard to belief may seem; yet this will Prayer,
> Or *one short sigh of human breath,* up-borne
> Ev'n to the Seat of God.[39]

Though surprising, its effect is confirmed by the appearance of the archangel Michael, a messenger sent by God and Christ. Identified in Cabbalistic thought with Hermes (improvisation's *genius loci* as I have argued above), Michael's explicitly hermetic associations are confirmed when Milton invokes the myth of Hermes's lulling the many-eyed Argus, "Charm'd with *Arcadian* Pipe, the Pastoral Reed/Of *Hermes,* or his opiate Rod."[40] Michael's hermetic nature is more subtly suggested when Milton describes Michael and his "cohort bright" as having "four faces each/...like a double *Janus,*"[41] an image which more subtly looks toward the cube-like "herms," archaic hermetic lingams that were set at cross-roads in the ancient world. Like Hermes, Michael is intermediary between the divine and human; he is a sort of *psychopompos* ("the spirit who shows the way"—an Hermetic epithet), a conveyor of souls to the underworld: his first duty is to disclose to Adam and Eve their future death. Like him he guides Adam to the heights and depths of experience, bringing the light of prophecy from Heaven, the gift, we learn in the Homeric hymn, Zeus and Apollo sometimes grant to Hermes. Like many improvisers Michael shares his encyclopedic vision of future history from the Olympus-like heights, here Mount Pisgah:

> So both ascend
> In the Visions of God: It was a Hill
> Of Paradise the highest, from whose top
> The Hemisphere of Earth in clearest Ken
> Stretcht out to the amplest reach of prospect lay.[42]

Finally, like Hermes Michael broaches the boundaries of ordinary reality, inspiring extraordinary states of consciousness, not only through direct

---

39. Ibid., 9.143-48. Emphasis added.
40. Ibid., 11.132-33.
41. Ibid., 11.129-30.
42. Ibid., 11.376-80.

prophecy, but also through Eve's roughly parallel and simultaneous prophetic dream.

It is the emphatic presence of these agencies—"Prevenient grace," the Hermes figure, Michael, and his eye-cleansing euphrasy and rue—along with the telling contrast between the morning prayer of Book V with that "sighs now breathed/Unutterable," that seem to me thoroughly to contradict Stanley Fish's romantic privileging of the state of unitary nature and innocence that pervades his *Surprised by Sin* and creates an unresolved tension in his argument. Fish stands as a crucial and enormously influential example of a contemporary critic whose work is suffused—and in part damaged—by the Romantic Ideology. Fish writes for example, in the passage I took for my epigraph:

> What the reader must finally learn is that the analytical intellect, so important in the formulation of necessary distinctions, is itself an instrument of perversion and the child of corruption because it divides and contrasts and evaluates where there is in reality a single harmonious unity.[43]

And:

> Choosing disunion creates the fractured vision [the critic W.C.B.] Watkins calls consciousness; to say that Adam and Eve are unconsciously good is meaningless unless it is intended as praise. The reader must understand that mindlessness—a sense of well-being because the mind knows nothing else (no *better*, we might say mistakenly)—is virtuous, and that his inability to be mindless is his punishment.[44]

In this privileging of "mindlessness," Fish's work seems to get the terms exactly wrong and in a way that betrays its provenance (like that of *Self-Consuming Artifacts*) in the post-Romantic era, circa 1967. To say so is of course to risk the appearance and charge of reaction. Not so—I believe I share in the main Professor Fish's politics. But the risk must be run, for so much is at stake. Fish's early work looms large not only in Milton and Renaissance studies, but also in the Romantic studies which his influence (most of it, of course, to the good) has more subtly pervaded. Fish taught us how to read

---

43. Fish, *Surprised by Sin,* 143.
44. Ibid., 144.

Milton and has been teaching us how to read literature in general ever since; but because of his "uncritical absorption in romanticism's own self-representations" (McGann), because in other words he reads with glasses of the wrong color, we often end up reading different books. Fish would be among the first to agree that we *always* read with filters of one sort of another: the point is not to become filterless, to read without assumptions, predilections, predispositions, contexts. The point rather is to be self-conscious of our filters, to be mindful. How? Through the very "vigilance" Fish elsewhere urges as the task with which *Paradise Lost* confronts the reader. This contradiction, Fish's recommending both mindlessness and vigilance, lies at the heart of *Surprised by Sin.*

Fish's attempt to resolve this tension fails because of the vulgarly romantic filter he sometimes sees through. He writes: "The reader labours consciously to recover a lost unity of vision, which when found, absorbs and nullifies the consciousness."[45] Fish seems wrong on both sides of the equation. For though we seek and long for "a lost unity of vision," what we find if we find it is quite another, not the one we lost at all. It's as if Fish confused Blake's state of innocence with his state of higher innocence. Yes, innocence is profoundly attractive, but Blake, like Milton, makes clear its limitations. The state of higher innocence in both Blakean and Miltonic dialectics affirms the unitary vision of innocence but also *wholly* negates it: the new unitary vision is wholly other because it also incorporates the state of experience, a state innocence knows nothing of. The paradox of vision, as of redemption, is that we achieve them by longing for an immediacy that has no part in their achievement. Thus consciousness is absorbed in vision but, despite Fish, not nullified. The state of visionary consciousness Milton both recommends and induces shoulders the burden of consciousness that our fall dooms us to and blesses us with.

In part the problem is the problem familiar among uncritical readers of improvisations: Fish mistakes Milton's attack on reason for a type rather than a trope. But Milton's point, as with most improvisers, is not to be rid of reason and consciousness, but to challenge that proud rationality uninformed by faith and by grace. Yes, Milton invites us to jump to such conclusions as Fish's: so at first glance the rhetoric of Book V's morning prayer seems to invite us.

---

45. Ibid., 328.

But the contrast with the fallen prayer of Book XI makes clear that what we prize as originary has its origins elsewhere. Fish is of course right that the question of Milton's adherence to or rejection of the idea of the fortunate fall is the lynchpin. But I stand with those whom Fish attacks, for Christ's words surely could not be clearer. They bear re-quoting:

> See Father, what first fruits on Earth are sprung
> From thy implanted Grace in Man, these Sighs
> And Prayers, which in this Golden Censer, mixt
> With Incense, I thy Priest before thee bring,
> Fruits of more pleasing savor from thy seed
> Sown with contrition in his heart, than those
> Which his own hand manuring all the Trees
> Of Paradise could have produced, ere fall'n
> From innocence. Now therefore bend thine ear
> To supplication, hear his sighs though mute;
> Unskillful with what words to pray, let mee
> Interpret for him...

The fall is perhaps not "virtuous" in the sense Fish means it (moral, ethical, excellent, noble), but it is so in the word's Miltonic, root sense, a sense cognate with the Latin for man (*vir*). The fall is the source of our power (*virtus*) to be fully human in this world.

CHAPTER NINE

Tristam Shandy:
The Raw and the Cooked

> But this, as I said above, is not the case of the inhab-
> itants of this earth;—our minds shine not through
> the body, but are wrapt up here in a dark covering of
> uncrystalized flesh and blood; so that if we would come
> to the specifick characters of them, we must go some
> other way to work.
> —Laurence Sterne, *Tristram Shandy*

1. The *"Carefree"* World of Tristram Shandy

Saturated in the rhetoric of spontaneity, *Tristram Shandy* for many modern readers seems to celebrate what Marianne Moore termed "the raw material of poetry in/all its rawness."[1] "This rhapsodical work," as its narrator calls it, is full of digressions that proceed insistently "out of all rule."[2] The narrator's "inconsiderate" (unconsidered) "way of talking" is governed by "my pen" for "I govern not it."[3] Having written the first sentence of a chapter, he assures us, he "trust[s] to Almighty God for the second."[4] The whole, he insinuates at the close, is merely "A COCK and a BULL" story[5]—not only free-wheeling but apparently pointless and with nothing to prove.

---

1. "Poetry," in *The Poems of Marianne Moore*, edited by Grace Schulman (New York: Viking, 2003), edited by Grace Schulman (New York: Viking, 2003), 135.

2. Laurence Sterne, *The Life and Opinions of Tristram Shandy, Gentleman*, 9 vols., in *The Florida Edition of the Works of Laurence Sterne*, edited by Melvyn New and Joan New (Gainesville: University of Florida Press, 1978-84), 4.10.337. Note: Sterne citations are noted by volume, chapter, and page number. The emphasis is Sterne's unless otherwise noted. I have silently removed Sterne's emphasis in proper names.

3. Ibid., 6.36,.562; 6.6.500.

4. Ibid., 8.2.656.

5. Ibid., 9.33.809. Emphasis in text.

It is, in all this and in a legion of similar self-definitions too numerous to catalog, a self-styled improvisation: "a careless kind of civil, non-sensical good humoured *Shandean* book."[6] Though like all improvisations professing to be *sui generis, Tristram Shandy's* relationship to the Renaissance improvisers who largely peopled the first part of this book—Erasmus, Rabelais, Montaigne especially—is well known. Published posthumously, Sterne's *A Fragment in the Manner of Rabelais,* was probably written in 1759, the same year the first two volumes of his famous novel were published. (The rest followed in 1761, 1762, 1765, and 1767). *Tristram Shandy* exploits many of the conventions of the form. Sterne's achieves a conversational style through his liberal use of reader-address, free-association, the colloquial and vernacular, and of course idiosyncratic punctuation, especially the dash—which critics are unanimous in praising. By means of these and by means of what Ian Watt calls "the tone of conversational abandon...the reader at once feels that he is being directly addressed in an easy and unbuttoned way, and that the units of meaning are being strung together in the most spontaneous way."[7]

Much of the novel, furthermore, seems to work by inviting us to indulge our natural yearning for the natural. Sterne lends Uncle Toby more ready-appeal than Walter Shandy on the grounds that the former is a natural, the latter an over-sophisticated pedant. With Toby, in this novel of sensibility, all comes from the heart and we like him for it; with Walter the brain mediates all and we reserve judgment. One of Toby's appeals is his heedlessness and disregard for conventionality, and Sterne directs much of the novel's humor against conventions of all sorts: social conventions, as well as those of autobiography, philosophy, printing, and the nascent novel itself. Such satire relies on the premise that conventions are "unnatural," spun like Walter's *Tristrapoedia* "every thread of it, out of his own brain."[8] Overtly Sterne explodes conventions and in their stead draws "real" life. Conventions cannot express

---

6. Ibid., 6.18.525. Emphasis in the text.

7. Ian Watt, "The Comic Syntax of *Tristram Shandy,*" in *Studies in Ciriticsm and Aesthetics, 1660-1800,* edited by Howard Anderson and John S. Shea (Minneapolis: University of Minnesota Press, 1967), 320.

8. Ibid., 5.16.445.

the raw flux of life, the premise runs, because by definition they are conventions, not life. This absurd premise—for are not the mind and its creations part of life?—permeates the novel. But it does not go unexamined.

Walter's *Tristrapoedia* is a case in point. Meant to make up for the misfortunes Tristram has already suffered, "geniture, nose, and name,"[9] the *Tristrapoedia* is never applied because Walter is too busy, and too constricted, writing it. What constricts him is a principle for writing exactly opposite to the one informing Tristram's writing. Where Tristram follows his every whim, Walter follows John de la Casse (of course he needs an authority) in believing that "his first thoughts were always the temptations of the evil one."[10] Meanwhile, Tristram is "all that time totally neglected and abandoned to my mother," and, Tristram adds, "the first part of the work, upon which my father had spent the most of his pains, was rendered entirely useless."[11]

Walter is ludicrous because he tries to keep up with life's *élan vital* not with the quickness of the heart, the feelings Sterne might have shown him feeling for his son, but rather with the idea—and authority—clogged, hobby-horsical mechanics of the brain. And the ludicrous verges on far worse when in the next chapter, left to the carelessness of Susannah, Tristram suffers the falling of the sash upon his private parts.[12] Tristram may almost suffer castration, but implicitly the novel asks us to prefer Tristram's careless yet joyful and fecund way of writing to the narrow, cold, and *impotent* manner of Walter. In all such confrontations, this novel that is as much about the immediate act of writing as it is the action it narrates, seems to prefer unmediated, unreflective, natural, inartificial, and thoughtless experience to careful and thoughtful artifice and rhetoric.

Thus at first glance, in the world of the novel, not only is there more in life than is dreamt of in philosophy, but philosophy seems downright dangerous. "The Weak part of the Sciences," Sterne wrote Dodsley, is where the novel's

---

9. Ibid.
10. Ibid. 5.16.447.
11. Ibid., 5.16.448.
12. Ibid., 5.17.449.

"true point of Ridicule lies."[13] And as the epigraph to Volume 1 points out, quoting Epictetus and invoking Locke, "it is not actions, but opinions about actions, which disturb men."[14] Sterne saturates the novel in such oppositions: between things and opinions; between immediacy and mediations of all kinds; between the real and the unreal; between the raw and the cooked. Its labyrinthine irony makes it extremely difficult to know where we finally come out.

In fact the choice the novel would have us make is finally not so simple as Tristram vs. Walter, raw vs. cooked. Raw experience, I wish to make clear, has no real—only rhetorical—existence in *Tristram Shandy*. This is true too of Marianne Moore's poem on "Poetry." Like Sterne, Moore invites a vulgar Romantic celebration of "the raw material of poetry in all its rawness" but forces us to give it a second thought:

> In the meantime, if you demand on the one hand,
> the raw material of poetry in
> all its rawness and
> that which is on the other hand
> genuine, you are interested in poetry.[15]

The prosy, overtly anti-artificial texture of her poem suggests that we treat the opposition as a both/and rather than an either/or, that is, to identify rawness with the genuine, the equation Sterne overtly makes. Subtly however, like Sterne, Moore with her footnotes (to T. S. Eliot and to Yeats's *Autobiographies*!) and with her gem-like, chiseled tone and vocabulary enforces the opposition as written ("on the one hand…on the other"). She seems to describe improvisation to a tee: "raw material" is not genuine but still we in our full humanity demand it. Moore leaves unspecified "that which is on the other hand genuine" but whatever it is, apparently it isn't "raw." Like all improvisa-

---

13. Letter to Robert Dodsley, 23 May 1759, in *The Florida Edition of the Works of Laurence Sterne*, 7: 80.

14. I rely on Work's notes for the translation: Laurence Sterne, *The Life and Opinions of Tristram Shandy, Gentleman*, edited by James Aiken Work (New York: The Odyssey Press, 1940), 1n. See also Melvyn New's discussion of the Epictetus epigraph in *Tristram Shandy: A Book for Free Spirits* (New York: Twayne Publishers, 1994), 52-53.

15. Moore, "Poetry," 135.

tions, "Poetry" flirts with the notion of the unmediated only to affirm, as her friend Wallace Stevens will do time and again, the necessity and the virtues of the mediation of its art: "that which is on the other hand / genuine."

Sterne's novel too is imbued with the tension between real and rhetorical and leans more toward the art pole and away from the natural than we sometimes assume. Characters in the novel, Tristram especially, and perhaps the novel itself, yearn for the natural, the raw.[16] And Tristram and the novel invite us to yearn with them. But it also finally contextualizes the wish for raw experience with the sobering if not melancholy recognition that all is mediated, well-stewed in mental juices, this side of Eden.

Because of *Tristram Shandy*'s insistent and brilliant rhetoric of carelessness and because of its satire of artifice it is easy to misread the novel's attitude toward raw experience, easy to make the mistake Hazlitt did about Wordsworth and the Lake School when he said that their goal was a poetry founded "on a principle of sheer humanity, on pure nature void of art."[17]

---

16. See "Sterne and the Nostalgia for Reality," in Robert Alter, *Partial Magic: The Novel as a Self-Conscious Genre* (Berkeley, Los Angeles and London: University of California Press, 1975), 30-56.

17. *Lectures of the English Poets,* in *The Complete Works of William Hazlitt,* edited by P. P. Howe, 21 vols. (London: J. M. Dent and Sons, 1932), 5: 162. For examples of critics who following Hazlitt succumb to Sterne's rhetoric of the raw and natural, see, e.g., Toby Olshin, "Genre and Tristram Shandy: the Novel of Quickness," *Genre* 4 (December 1971): 360-75; "Preface," in Laurence Sterne, *Tristram Shandy: An Authoritative Text,* edited by Howard Anderson (New York and London: W.W. Norton, 1980); William J. Farrell, "Nature versus Art as a Comic Pattern in *Tristram Shandy,*" *English Literature History* 30, no. 1 (March 1963): 16-35; Graham Petrie, "Rhetoric as Fictional Technique in *Tristram Shandy,*" *Philological Quarterly* 48, no. 4 (October 1969): 479-94; Martin Price, *To the Palace of Wisdom: Studies in Order and Energy from Dryden to Blake* (New York: Doubleday, 1964). Anticipating my approach, Richard Lanham discusses the rhetorical world of the novel in *Tristram Shandy: The Games of Pleasure* (Berkeley and Los Angeles: University of California Press, 1973). Robert Alter writes that, "Tristram Shandy abundantly illustrates…that a new 'authentic' literature liberated from conventions is a sheer impossibility," in *Partial Magic,* 33. Finally, Melvyn New's compact but magisterial *Tristram Shandy: A Book for Free Spirits* confirms my own views on how we are meant to respond to

The brilliant first sentence of *Tristram Shandy,* for the first of many times in the novel, expresses but more subtly qualifies this yearning for the raw and real. It sets up an opposition between constraint and freedom, determinism and free will, an opposition that the balance of the novel will explore:

> I wish either my father or my mother, or indeed both of them, as they were in duty equally bound to it, had minded what they were about when they begot me; had they duly consider'd how much depended upon what they were then doing;—that not only the production of a rational Being was concern'd in it, but that possibly the happy formation and tempera-ture of his body, perhaps his genius and the very cast of his mind;—and, for aught they knew to the contrary, even the fortunes of his whole house might take their turn from the humours and dispositions which were then uppermost:——Had they duly weighed and considered all this, and proceeded accordingly,——I am verily persuaded I should have made a quite different figure in the world, from that, in which the reader is likely to see me.[18]

The passage—which it takes a moment to realize is about the act of coitus that created Tristram—opposes the freedoms of desire and of the heart with the constraints of duty and the mind. Being careful was, Tristram insists, first of all emphatically a duty: they were "equally bound," they should have "duly consider'd," and "had they duly" taken thought, his whole life would have been changed. It is the Mind that would have effected this change: they should have "minded," "consider'd," "weighed and considered...and pro-ceeded accordingly." And it is Tristram's Mind that would have been affected: if they had done so "a rational Being...his genius and the very cast of his mind" would have "made a quite different figure in the world." In all, the pas-sage pleads for care and thought in a careless and thoughtless and haphazard world. Its priority is Reason's proper care and feeding.

We may quickly forget the novel begins on such a note because of course the many ironies of the passage turn the plea upside-down. Does Tristram

---

the central dichotomies of the novel: "the intuitive and instinctual versus the cal-culating; the heart versus the head; the social versus the selfish; benevolence versus self-interest" (69).

18. *Tristram Shandy,* 1.1.1.

really wish his parents to take "care" and be thoughtful during an act we think of as natural and spontaneous? It is in fact duty—his father's to wind the clock on Sunday, and his mother's to satisfy her husband's lust while apparently having no lust of her own—that precipitate the query that diffuses Tristram's humors. And does he really believe in these medieval theories of humours and homunculi? Even to his contemporary readers, how absurd. The ironies turn the passage into a plea for freedom: the freedom to enjoy life, sensual life especially, and to live free from the constraints of duty and rationality. The balance of the chapter, recounting his mother's question about the winding of the clock, adds to these self-consuming ironies a plea for the freedom from the Lockean shackles of habitual modes of thought (and of clock time). The opening of *Tristram Shandy,* then, seems to be a satire of caution and rationality and of the compulsive desire for care and thought. It seems to make clear that there is little room for rationality in the world and that what goes for Reason in this world hardly deserves the name. It seems to suggest that life is too vital for such constraints. *Carpe diem!* Life is haphazard but let us embrace it—as is!

Yet in the midst of setting up such oppositions, Sterne's opening chapter— as likewise the whole of the book—finally makes clear that in truth life offers no such pat dichotomies. His parents' taking pleasure in the act which conceived him would have been a good thing: it might have foretold, if not helped to effect, a greater intimacy in their shared lives, an intimacy clearly lacking throughout the novel. And perhaps pleasure would have forestalled the habitual associational trains of thought that led to her asking about the clock. Conversely, even though much of the book demonstrates their ill-effects, what Tristram overtly asks for, more care and thought, might indeed have benefited his upbringing (delight that he is notwithstanding). Life demands both care and carelessness, sometimes simultaneously.

The book's satire upon rationality is well-known. But Sterne does not merely in Reason's stead valorize and privilege "unaccomodated man" and the way such men presumably experience things, in unmediated fashion. He also calls such matters into question. In Sterne's vision of things, raw experience does not exist. It is largely the novel's burden to tease us out of our natural penchant for the natural, and to enforce Sterne's own far more sophisticated vision.

2. *Trim's Hat Trick*

Trim's natural eloquence, so called, upon hearing the news of brother Bobby's death—Trim's famous hat trick—complexly explores the novel's central oppositions between rationality and irrationality, artificiality and raw experience.[19] The episode both invites the reading that raw, natural experience is a good thing, and at the same time cuts the ground right out from under such naïveté.

Volume 5, wherein Trim dramatically drops his hat, also emphatically begins on such a note of raw vs. cooked. Tristram vows to throw his library's key from his coach window because mankind seems "for ever [to be] mak[ing] new books, as apothecaries make new mixtures, by pouring only out of one vessel into another." With such bookish plagiarisms—such "pitiful——pimping——pettifogging," as he calls it[20]—Tristram will have nothing to do. Not smelling of the lamp, his book will be more natural, more real. Fine. Except that, as every annotated edition makes clear and as Sterne's contemporary readers probably easily recognized, the entire oath is a pastiche "cribbed" from Burton's *Anatomy of Melancholy.*[21] Sterne's artless cry for artlessness is an artful ploy, all the more so because he means to be caught in the act, seen for the skillful, pettifogging—but crafty—plagiarist that he is.

---

19. Lanham and Swearingen have treated the episode at some length. For Lanham, as for me, the "hat trick" (the phrase is his) is "mechanical" (61-62). Swearingen demurs. Reflecting a blind spot for primitivism that phenomenologists, despite themselves, sometimes display, Swearingen sees Trim's gesture as representing the unmediated and, he adds, "It might also be observed that the more primitive and spontaneous the mode of articulation, the more convincing it is," *Reflexivity in* Tristram Shandy: *An Essay in Phenomenological Criticism* (New Haven and London: Yale University Press, 1977), 168. Swearingen's point of view is neck-deep in the Romantic ideology. Martin Price does not treat the hat trick episode but says this of Trim's response to Yorick's sermon (which reminds him of his brother Tom, imprisoned by the Inquisition): "His power of sympathy breaks through all the forms of language and achieves a terrifying immediacy," *To the Palace of Wisdom*, 323. But see New, *A Book for Free Spirit*, who is devastating on such sentimental readings of the theme of sentiment in the novel.

20. *Tristram Shandy*, 5.1.408.

21. See the notes in Work's edition, 342 n.1, and in New's edition, 3: 339 n. 408.11-18.

The same opposition between nature and art and the same undercurrent, witty by-play are at work in the series of introductions to Trim's hat trick, introductions which provide further and essential contextualizations for the trick itself. No lover of Sterne will be surprised by the number of these introductory false starts. But they are many and must be attended to closely.

The first is the long-promised chapter upon whiskers. The witty undercurrent is as usual sexual: La Fosseuse's name puns upon *le fosse*, meaning ditch or deep cavity. A *fosse* (as a military term) is first mentioned in regard to Toby's wounding in the groin.[22] A *fosse* plays a role too—again one with sexual overtones when Trim takes the tumble (again, I use the term advisedly) with Bridget that breaks the bridge that eventuates circuitously, and painfully, in the fallen sash.[23] The way Sterne lards sexual innuendo upon *fosse* and Toby's other military terms is virtuoso. "Toby" itself is eighteenth-century slang for "penis." He is often egged on to repeat the tale of the Widow Wadman by Walter Shandy, who "smil[es] mysteriously," thus ensuring we don't miss any innuendo. Toby "would cry" that "Trim's foot,...getting into the cuvette [another, smaller ditch], he tumbled full against the bridge too.—It was a thousand to one, my uncle Toby would add, that the poor fellow did not break a leg.—Ay truly! my father would say,——a limb is soon broke, brother Toby, in such encounters."[24] Foot, cuvette, broken legs and limbs, and the bridge: Sterne strews the sexual innuendoes by the armful. The play is not only fun but also calls attention to the problem of language, a key Sternean theme.

"La Fosseuse" is laden with sexual connotations not only by narrative event but also by etymology. The term *fosse* stems from the Latin verb *fodere*, meaning "to dig"; in its metaphorical usage it meant "to prick" or "to prod." The French word is of course masculine. "La Fosseuse," then, is a feminine or female ditch or cavity, or a female ditch digger, or a prodding of a female. The puns—like the narrative events—are wonderfully salacious and Sternean. Likewise, La Fosseuse's whiskers, because of his suggestive whispering, will not, just like Tristram's nose, stay put on his face. The joke is not only sexual

---

22. *Tristram Shandy*, 2.5.110.
23. Ibid., 3.24.248–50.
24. Ibid., 3.24.248.

but Lockean, calling attention to the abuses words are heir to, especially in over-sophisticated milieux like the court of Navarre.

So far, considering all these problems of language, Trim's laconic, mincing-no-words eloquence, soon to follow, is looking all the more attractive. But in fact the La Fosseuse joke's elaborate architectonics—the digression is longer than any chapter in the volume—call attention to the architect, the artificer, to sad Tristram and to the salacious Sterne behind him. This gesture of breaking the proscenium and forcing us to glimpse the characters as actors and Tristram and Sterne as artificers is familiar in this novel. Here it aligns them (Tristram and Sterne) with Walter the artificer rather than Trim the naturally eloquent, and next and last introduction to Trim's hat trick repeats the gesture with a flourish. This last introduction, at the end of Chapter 6, contextualizes the hat trick in an upstairs/downstairs kind of contrast between Walter and Trim in their respective responses to Bobby's death. While Walter upstairs indulges his pride in his own eloquence, quoting "Philosophy['s]...entire set" of "fine saying[s]" upon Death,[25] Trim in the kitchen goes "strait forwards as nature could lead him, to the heart."[26] Sterne emphasizes the contrast:

> A curious observer of nature, had he been worth the inventory of all Job's stock—though, by the bye, *your curious observers are seldom worth a groat*—would have given the half of it, to have heard Corporal Trim and my father, two orators so contrasted by nature and education, haranguing over the same bier.
>
> My father a man of deep reading—prompt memory—with Cato, and Seneca, and Epictetus, at his fingers ends.—
>
> The corporal—with nothing—to remember—of no deeper reading than his muster-roll—or greater names at his finger's end, than the contents of it.
>
> The one proceeding from period to period, by metaphor and allusion, and striking the fancy as he went along, (as men of wit and fancy do) with the entertainment and pleasantry of his pictures and images.
>
> The other, without wit or antithesis, or point, or turn, this way or that, but leaving the images on one side, and the pictures on the other, going strait forwards as nature could lead him, to the heart.[27]

---

25. Ibid., 5.3.421.

26. Ibid., 5.6.429.

27. Ibid., 5.6.428–29; emphasis in text.

Sterne so emphasizes the contrast, in fact, that in the midst of valorizing naturalness the passage becomes a set piece, an overtly framed artifact. And just when our hearts beat warmest for this raw expounder of raw emotions, Tristram adds this reflexive touch, finishing the paragraph last quoted: "O Trim! would to heaven thou had'st a better historian!—would!—thy historian had a better pair of breeches!——O ye criticks! will nothing melt you?"[28] As usual the passage cuts in more than one direction. "Historian" suggests that real events are herein recorded and are for that reason all the more worthy to move us. And yet the general tenor of the passage and the reference to the critics who had been less pleased with the artifacts, Volumes 3 and 4, call attention to the fictionality of character and action: history as storytelling. The appeal to the critics to help Sterne/Tristram buy a new pair of pants suggests the author creates the fiction not with the naked, motiveless eye, or from and for the sensitive heart, but with the calculating brain in order to fill the miserly pocketbook. The challenge to "curious observers" at the head of the set piece calls into question the nature of "objective" perception.

Such are the several layers of context to Trim's Hat Trick, all of them calling attention to the issue of mediation, the nature of language and of artifice. The trick itself is equally complex but easily retold. Assuming the pose Trim had used in reciting Yorick's sermon, Trim asks: "Are we not here now... (striking the end of his stick perpendicularly upon the floor, so as to give the idea of health and stability)—and are we not—(dropping his hat upon the ground) gone! in a moment!" " 'Twas," Tristram adds, "infinitely striking!"[29] And the response in the kitchen is as spontaneous and direct from the heart as Trim's performance: "Susannah burst into a flood of tears"; unlike the critics who have been pestering Sterne, Jonathan, Obadiah, the cook, and the chambermaid "all melted."[30] Tristram himself is roused to exclaim that the preservation of the constitution of church and state hinge "upon the right understanding of this stroke of the corporal's eloquence." And he attributes Trim's success to his trusting "more to *his hat* than to *his head*." Raw expression of raw experience has seldom been more expressively and persuasively embodied or applauded. Trim's achievement at first glance seems to echo and to be

---

28. Ibid., 5.6.429.
29. Ibid., 5.7.431.
30. Ibid.

an analogue to Yorick's "plain *English* without any periphrasis."[31] And it has never, I wager, been more fun.

And yet, as the first word of Sterne's next chapter has it: "Stay." Is that really what happens? Is Trim's eloquent gesture really so raw, natural, and direct? So it strikes us, and clearly is meant to, set as it is in contrast with Walter Shandy's pedantry. But is the corporal's gesture really so unmediated? Although Tristram says with insistence that it is without "turn" (i.e., trope, figure of speech) and leaves "images to one side," is it not in fact a metaphor or even a simile Trim constructs?—death is *like this.* His gesture is thus at least as mediated, as circuitous in procedure, abstract in tenor, and generally well-simmered in rhetorical form and purpose as any of Walter's wit and antitheses. Although it has been argued that Trim's posture earlier in reading Yorick's sermon (a posture he repeats here in the kitchen) is clumsy and unschooled in the precise gestures of the rhetor, Sterne's point there as here is that this natural, unschooled naïf is in no way naive.[32] He contorts his posture not because of nature—his ignorance of Quintilian and Cicero—but because he badly imitates what he has seen in the theater. In short, a conventional butler of the eighteenth-century stage, Trim is a dandy, ludicrous because he clumsily apes his social betters. Here the joke is compounded: his re-assuming his "unschooled" pose strikes us as pure, if clumsy, calculation. Trim hasn't, like Don Quixote, read too many romances; but he has snuck away to too much theatre. His gesture is not raw. It is literally histrionic.

Sterne's point is that ignorance, while it may be "part of knowledge" as Erasmus taught, still is no sure sign of innocence. As the sequel makes clear, *self-regard* motivates Trim's hat trick no less than it does Walter's erudite eloquence or Tristram's concocted history. For when Trim expands upon his metaphor, Sterne makes clear that Susannah's tears had not come by accident, but by Trim's concerted and skillful design. Further plucking the heart strings, Trim continues, a downstairs Marvell singing of seizing the day to his not-so-coy mistress in a passage that is difficult until we realize that, like the novel's opening sentence, its subtext is, in a word, sex. Trim through flattery seeks to bed Susannah:

---

31. Ibid., 1.11.29; emphasis in text.
32. Farrell, "Nature versus Art," 29.

And trust me, Susy, added the corporal, turning to Susannah, whose eyes were swimming in water,—before that time comes round again,—many a bright eye will be dim.—Susannah…wept—but she court'sied too.—Are we not, continued Trim, looking still at Susannah—are we not like a flower of the field—a tear of pride stole in betwixt every two tears of humiliation—else no tongue could have described Susannah's affliction—is not all flesh grass?—'Tis clay,—'tis dirt.—They all looked directly at the scullion,—the scullion had just been scouring a fish-kettle.—It was not fair.——[33]

What is unfair—and this remark is surely the narrator's intrusion—is the thought that Trim should compare the scullion to Susannah: Susannah with her "bright eye" wins hands down—she is the lily of the field who does not spin, the scullion the mere clay beneath her feet. Hence Suzannah's "tear of pride" that steals "in betwixt every two tears of humiliation." But though *we* may have difficulty at first glance discerning Trim's text and subtext, *Susannah* has none. She declares: "I could hear Trim talk so for ever."[34]

In sum, Trim's natural eloquence, direct from the heart, is no more, no less, and no better than a wooing. If "old hat" is eighteenth-century slang for "female genitalia" as Sterne's editors note, and if in this novel a nose is always a nose (except when it's a penis), then perhaps Tristram is right that Trim's success is due to his trusting "more to *his hat* than to *his head*." Alone amongst the males at Shandy Hall, Trim is able to embrace and to express his sexuality.

Thus I have called his gesture a "trick" advisedly. Its impetus derives not from the intuition or the heart but rather from the groin, with a stop-off in the calculating brain. It is not raw. It is rhetorical, a device of persuasion cunningly mustered and deployed—to use one of Trim and Toby's military metaphors. As another digressive gesture makes plain, again breaking the proscenium arch and cooling the narrative's emotional register, the hat trick chapter is not a tale of or from the heart but is "a chapter of chamber maids, green gowns and old hats" or, to translate the eighteenth-century slang, loose women, whores, and female genitalia.[35]

---

33. *Tristram Shandy*, 5.9.435.

34. Ibid.

35. I rely here on James Work's notes in his edition, 363n.1 and 549n.1, and also on Howard Anderson's in his *Autoritative Text*, 255n.5.

Recognizing that Trim's eloquence is neither so heart-felt nor so pure—a recognition that context and close attention to his hat trick both enforce—leads us to re-evaluate Walter's eloquence. If Trim's isn't so good perhaps, as Lanham has argued, Walter's isn't as bad as most critics think. Walter "was systematical, and like all systematick reasoners, he would move both heaven and earth, and twist and torture every thing in nature to support his hypothesis."[36] But the question the book asks is, do not we all "twist and torture" not only "every thing in nature" but by the very nature of things, by the very nature of the mind and heart? As Lanham argues:

> We must understand before we can feel. What we must understand, as we see it in Yorick and the Shandy brothers, is that pleasure, satisfaction, is the necessary precondition to the kind of selfless feeling for others on which a true society—rather than merely a collection of individuals—must be based...One of the lessons Tristram teaches us is that when we feel for others, we do so largely for the pleasure of the feeling...Furthermore, it is the necessary precondition of spontaneous feeling. Sentimentality must precede sentiment. We will feel for others only when we have felt enough for ourselves.[37]

Tristram Shandy initially invites us to celebrate fools and follies of the heart gladly, but Sterne's irony is finally a great leveler, enforcing the recognition that we are all fools and that follies resort all from the same springs. Walter is "a dupe to" his love of eloquence, Trim a dupe not only to his love of giving advice but to his libido.[38] Lanham only errs when he finds that Tristram's hobby-horse alone is unmechanical and liberating.[39] Everyone is a fool to his given hobby-horse and every hobby-horse is a kind of automatic drive that takes us where it will, no matter what we will. That is what hobby-horses do after all: they mediate or serve as "terministic screens," as Kenneth Burke calls them, shaping reality. Burke writes: "Even if any given terminology is a *reflection* of reality, by its very nature as a terminology it must be a *selection* of reality; and to this extent it must function also as a *deflection* of reality."[40]

---

36. *Tristram Shandy*, 1.19.61.

37. Lanham, *Tristram Shandy: The Games of Pleasure*, 100.

38. *Tristram Shandy*, 5.3.419.

39. Lanham, *Games of Pleasure*, 96.

40. See "Terministic Screens," in Burke, *Language as Symbolic Action*, 45.

Sometimes we specialize—Walter in his theories and his eloquence in expressing them, Toby in his wound and his fortifications used to talk about his wound, Trim in his martial and sexual prowess. But we also have our general hobby-horses too: our slant on things, our "prepossession[s]" as Sterne calls them; "the thick wall of personality" Pater spoke of, "which no real voice has ever pierced on its way to us, or from us to that which we can only conjecture to be without";[41] and Gombrich's "beholder's share." As Ernst Cassirer writes of Sterne's contemporary, Kant: "Experience, he says, is no doubt the first product of our understanding. But it is not a simple fact; it is a compound of two opposite factors, of matter and form"—form which we've supplied.[42]

We have also our self-regard to look after, and that is what Trim's hat trick and the whole episode regarding brother Bobby's death are finally all about. While apparently building a pat opposition between natural and sophisticated, between the raw and the artificial, the episode really works earnestly to lay bare an identity: all the characters in the episode from Walter Shandy down to the scullery maid, Trim included, respond according to their hobby-horses and according to their needs, wishes, and desires.

That death is the episode's impetus and central image is telling, indeed it is essential. For we may laugh and look down upon Walter's onanistic erudition, Trim's wooing, Toby's pained silence, and even the "foolish" scullion's overtly self-regarding response to Bobby's death, "So am not I."[43] But Sterne demonstrates in his sobering way that everyone's response to death is inevitably that homely and home response: "So am not I." Faced with death we all will do what makes us feel most alive. Thus to compare Susannah's looks to the scullion's is unfair finally because in their inner lives the two women are one. Susannah's response is equally self-regarding: she thinks immediately of his mistress's soon to be cast off "green-gown" (slang for "whore," so making Trim's lewd advances all the more apposite). In sum, Sterne says let it be: let people do whatever eases for them the dread of death. La Fosseuse's name, at

---

41. *Tristram Shandy*, 5.12.439; "Conclusion," Pater, *The Renaissance*, 187.

42. Cassirer, *An Essay on Man*, 207-8.

43. *Tristram Shandy*, 5.7.430.

the head of the episode, is in this regard again appropriate. For *fosseuse* also echoes *fossoyeur*, gravedigger; like Yorick he wears a *momento mori* as a name.

Another way to keep death at bay is to enjoy oneself. Hence the novel "if 'tis wrote against anything——'tis wrote…against the spleen."[44] And hence, as Lanham urges, to charge its characters with self-regard is misdirected. The Carnival spirit of the novel insists that we have fun. Not only does Walter indulge himself in eloquence at this moment, so too does Trim. For earlier in the novel we hear of "the only dark line in" "Trim's character," that: "The fellow lov'd to advise,—or rather to hear himself talk;…set his tongue a-going,— you had no hold of him;—he was voluble."[45]

Sterne purposefully obscures and downplays this "dark line" here, and yet makes it manifest. For despite the narrator's depiction of Trim's natural and laconic eloquence in his oration, this is a truer characterization: he "lov'd to advise,—or rather to hear himself talk." That this would apply equally to Walter is also the point. Once again the opposition between Trim and Walter breaks down.

Conversely, the end to all Walter's eloquence regarding his son Bobby's death equals Trim's in its "directness." His long peroration reaches a climax when he recalls Socrates's remarks on his "three desolate sons." Tristram's mother, who has had her ear to the keyhole for some time, mistakes this for a revelation of Walter's extra-marital paternity. When she rushes in declaring, "You have one more, Mr. Shandy, than I know of," his witty retort succeeds in banishing his distress, though surely at the expense of his wife's: "By heaven! I have one less,—said my father, getting up and walking out of the room."[46] So ends Walter Shandy's peroration and his grief just like Trim: "without wit or antithesis, or point, or turn, this way or that, but leaving the images on one side, and the pictures on the other, going strait forwards as nature could lead him, to the heart." Have ever two men, "so contrasted by nature and education," shown so much affinity? On the one hand we have the directness and simplicity of Walter's, "By heaven! I have one less." On the other we have the apparent directness and simplicity of "Are we not here now;…and

---

44. Ibid., 4.22.360.
45. Ibid., 2.5.109.
46. Ibid., 5.13.442.

are we not... ——gone in a moment?"[47] And of course in the end neither are direct or simple.

At the close of the episode, Tristram/Sterne's response to Trim's wooing applies to the novel's whole crew, upstairs and down: "—Now I love you for this—and 'tis this delicious mixture within you which makes you dear creatures what you are—and he who hates you for it —— all I can say of the matter, is—That he has either a pumkin for his head—or a pippin for his heart,—and whenever he is dissected 'twill be found so."[48] Whatever gets you by is Sterne's at once joyful and melancholy theme, a theme enlivened by the humor which his enemies the critics lack but which is essential to getting us by. The whole episode looks forward to Volume 7, that volume haunted autobiographically by Sterne's tuberculosis and narratively by the galloping specter of death.

One last point in regard to the episode, and it is an overarching one: a further implication of recognizing that Trim's natural eloquence is in fact rhetorical is that the episode flies directly in the face of Locke's perfectly naive and mistaken complaint against rhetoric at the end of the famous "Abuse of Words" chapter of the *Essay*. There he laments, like Socrates in the *Gorgias*, that mankind prefers figurative and allusive language to "dry Truth and real Knowledge," and that "Men love to deceive, and be deceived, since Rhetorick that powerful instrument of Error and Deceit...has always been had in great Reputation."[49]

But to lament the colors and figures of rhetoric, Sterne's episode replies, is to label as a problem what is in fact a solution. Rhetoric is how we get what we think we need. That what we think we need and what we really need seldom coincide should not surprise us since we have learned from Yorick's ironies in his sermon in Volume 2 that "INTEREST stood always unconcern'd whilst the cause was hearing,—and...PASSION never got into the judgment-seat, and pronounc'd sentence in the stead of reason, which is supposed

---

47. Ibid., 5.9.432.

48. Ibid., 5.9.435. Lanham reads this as Trim's speech but hints that there is some ambiguity, *Tristram Shandy: The Games of Pleasure*, 61.

49. John Locke, *An Essay Concerning Human Understanding*, 508.

always to preside and determine upon the case."[50] But instead of despairing at these limits on Reason's powers, Sterne puts the entire force of the novel behind the proposition that it all adds to the fun. Loosen up, John Locke! And as for "dry Truth and Real Knowledge," so-called—the novel demonstrates time and again that these are self-contradictory terms and that Locke should have known better. There is no "innocent eye," Gombrich reminds us, but always a "beholder's share" interceding between us and raw reality. *Toujours déjà.* All that seems raw is mediated, and probably rhetorical. But, Sterne adds, that doesn't mean it can't be fun nor a consolation before the inevitable specter of death.

One must quickly add that for Sterne it does not follow from "fun" and the avoidance of spleen that we should lay care and craft, our rationality, to rest the way the "Papists," according to the sermon, lay conscience to rest. As Yorick's sermon states without equivocation and without waver, "Reason,…is supposed always to preside and determine upon the case." Frail instrument that it is, our reason must be nurtured and honed, not forgone. For Sterne, like most improvisers, it will succeed the better the more we acknowledge Reason's frailty.

---

50. *Tristram Shandy,* 2.17.147.

CHAPTER TEN

"Tintern Abbey":
Wordsworth's Revolutionary
Expression of Love

The innocent eye is a myth.
—Gombrich, *Art and Illusion*

An art that is to be naive is thus a contradiction in
terms, but the representation of a naiveté in a ficti-
tious personage is quite a beautiful though rare art.
—Kant, *Critique of Judgment*

I yearn toward some philosophic Song
Of Truth that cherishes our daily life;
With meditations passionate from deep
Recesses in man's heart, immortal verse
Thoughtfully fitted to the Orphean lyre.
—Wordsworth, *The Prelude*

Hazlitt anticipates in large measure a major strain among modern critical views when he insisted upon Wordsworth's anti-artificial poetics:

[Wordsworth's] popular, inartificial style gets rid (at a blow) of all the trappings of verse, of all the high places of poetry...We begin *de novo*, on a *tabula rasa* of poetry...The author tramples on the pride of art with greater pride. The Ode and Epode, the Strophe and the Antistrophe, he laughs to scorn. The harp of Homer, the trump of Pindar and of Alcæus are still.[1]

But Hazlitt misses how central traditional genres were to Wordsworth's program for poetry. Wordsworth's treatment of traditional forms and of artifice is more complex than Hazlitt allows. "Tintern Abbey" more directly carries

---

1. "The Spirit of the Age," in *The Complete Works of William Hazlitt*, 11: 87.

on the pseudo-Pindaric ode tradition than critics have seen.[2] The trump of Pindar sounds not so still, so quiet, as Hazlitt assumed.

But hearing the Pindaric note in "Tintern Abbey" matters more than mere curiosity about formal generic tradition. Understanding the poem's complex relation to the ode can help us to understand, if not to solve, a long-standing critical problem that goes to the heart of how we read Wordsworth. Critics still debate whether the "central affirmation" of the poem, "the philosophic mind," is an affirmation at all. Critics argue over whether the poem affirms maturation or regressively yearns for childhood. The failure of most critics to take the poem's generic declaration seriously is symptomatic of our assumption that the poem is an artless, improvised creation. Wordsworth himself helped foster this assumption with the declaration to Isabella Fenwick that "not a line of it was altered."[3] Taking Wordsworth at his word has

---

2. I am arguing here that M.H. Abrams's definition of the "Greater Romantic Lyric" as "displacing" the greater ode does not precisely apply to "Tintern Abbey." See his "Structure and Style of the Greater Romantic Lyric," in *From Sensibility to Romanticism: Essays Presented to Frederick A. Pottle,* edited by Frederick W. Hilles and Harold Bloom (New York: Oxford University Press, 1965), 527-60.

3. In context Wordsworth's remark, "not a line of it was altered" could refer specifically to the original manuscript or even to the act of mental composition, and not to later editorial revisions in subsequent editions. Mary Moorman, however, in her important biography exemplifies the generalized effect of Wordsworth's note when she echoes, "very little of it was ever altered, and the "Tintern Abbey" that we know today is virtually that composed on the Wye's banks." *William Wordsworth: A Biography,* vol. 1: *The Early Years, 1770-1805* (London, Oxford, and New York: Oxford University Press, 1968), 402. The myth has blinded us to the many emendations Wordsworth made to the poem over the years: I count 39, the first a line deletion in the first edition of *Lyrical Ballads,* and one (lines 13-14) going through several variants. Owen argues from manuscript evidence, furthermore, that the poem was begun some months before visiting the banks of the Wye, in William Wordsworth and S.T. Coleridge, *Lyrical Ballads, 1798,* edited by W.J.B. Owen (London: Oxford University Press, 1967), 149-50n. These inaccuracies and discrepancies compel a rhetorical treatment of the profession of spontaneous redaction, even though Wordsworth was quite capable of it (see David Perkins, *Wordsworth and the Poetry of Sincerity* (Cambridge, Mass.: Harvard University Press, 1964), 61-83; and J. Bard McNulty who argues that the poem was written in "a matter of hours" in "Self-Awareness in the Making of 'Tintern Abbey,'" *The Wordsworth Circle* 12, no. 2 (1981): 97. What has not been fully

led to the kind of romantic primitivism that projects itself upon Wordsworth and his poem, and casts doubt on the poem's affirmation of the "philosophic mind." The critical irony in this situation lies in the fact that "Tintern Abbey" covertly addresses this same romantic primitivism. Wordsworth's declaration of genre can serve as a springboard to a revisionist reading of the poem. Not only is "Tintern Abbey" an ode, it is also far more positive about artifice and mediation than critics, following Hazlitt, have seen.[4]

Speaking of "symptoms" and of "romantic primitivism" is not to point a finger. The poem's rhetoric of immediacy and artlessness pervades the poem and has not unreasonably captivated the attention of the poem's finest readers. "Nature herself seems," as Arnold remarked, "to take the pen out of his hand, and to write for him."[5] From critics we may glean the impression that nature—untainted by man or by mind, unmediated, inartificial, primitive, and fluid—provides the poem's moral and aesthetic norm, premise, and principle. In "Tintern Abbey," according to these critics, Wordsworth gropes toward this ideal. It follows from this romantic reading that Wordsworth's purpose and task in the poem is to recover youth's unmediated experience of nature,

---

explored is not whether or not he improvised, but why he insistently brings it to the reader's attention.

4. My approach is anticipated by Robert Pinsky who strikes just the right note when he argues that this "strain of Romanticism" should be treated "not as a doctrine but a dilemma," in *The Situation of Poetry: Contemporary Poetry and its Traditions* (Princeton, N.J.: Princeton University Press, 1976), 47.

5. "Wordsworth," in *The Complete Prose Works of Matthew Arnold*, vol. 9: *English Literature and Irish Politics*, edited by R.H. Super (Ann Arbor: The University of Michigan Press, 1973), 53. See also Harold Bloom who remarks "the peculiar *nakedness* of Wordsworth's poetry, its strong sense of being alone with the visible universe, with no myth or figure to mediate between ego and phenomena," *The Visionary Company: A Reading of English Romantic Poetry* (Ithaca and London: Cornell University Press, 1971), 133. So, too, Albert Gérard reads the opening paragraph's final image, the "Hermit," as an example of "the highest form of contemplation and wisdom;...[of] man stripped of all inessentials, living in intimate communication with nature," which for Gérard represents "a human ideal toward which Wordsworth was groping at the time," *English Romantic Poetry: Ethos, Structure, and Symbol in Coleridge, Wordsworth, Shelley, and Keats* (Berkeley and Los Angeles: University of California Press, 1968), 102.

> That had no need of remoter charm,
> By thought supplied, or any interest
> Unborrowed from the eye.—[6]

It follows, too, that Wordsworth achieves the recovery he seeks at the poem's end when he catches,

> The language of my former heart, and read
> My former pleasures in the shooting lights
> Of [Dorothy's] wild eyes.[7]

Yet from these implications it also follows that Wordsworth's poem "celebrat[es]...nature's immediacy which has now been lost," and is characterized by a "regressive hunger" and a "reversion to primitive ways of thinking."[8] If so, then what is agreed to be the poem's primary affirmation, the "philosophic mind," must either be an affirmation plagued by doubts, or a mere rationalization of his true and greater loss: the unmediated experience of nature in his youth.[9] There's the rub.

There is thus much to support the reading that this poem, saturated in a rhetoric of immediacy, yearns for a recovery of such a mode of being. But "Tintern Abbey" is more complicated than that reading suggests. A complete reading of the poem depends upon also recognizing the poem's contrary rhetoric, its rhetoric of craft, mediation, and tradition. These two contrary rhetorics—of artlessness and of art—constitute the poem's central expressive tension. For many readers the poem is a paean to nature's benign influence, a celebration of his youth, an affirmation of continuities between his former and present selves, and at its end, an apotheosis of nature's child, his

---

6. "Lines Written a Few Miles above Tintern Abbey: On Revisiting the Banks of the Wye during a Tour. July 13, 1798," lines 82-84. (All references are to Owen's edition of the *Lyrical Ballads*; see note 3 above.)

7. Ibid., 118-20.

8. Frances Ferguson, *Wordsworth: Language as Counter-Spirit* (New Haven and London: Yale University Press, 1977), 145; Alan Grob, *The Philosophical Mind: A Study of Wordsworth's Poetry and Thought, 1797-1805* (Columbus: Ohio State University Press, 1973), 34; Raymond Dexter Havens, *The Mind of the Poet*, vol. 1: *A Study of Wordsworth's Thought* (Baltimore: The John Hopkins Press, 1941), 79.

9. Gérard, *English Romantic Poetry*, 105ff; F.W. Bateson, *Wordsworth: A Re-Interpretation* (London: Longmans, 1956 [1954]), 142.

sister Dorothy. "Tintern Abbey" by insistently claiming that it is spontaneous, unmediated expression invites this reading—but it is partial. For in more
subtle ways the poem claims also that it is a thoughtful and mediated expression, not only what some deny, an affirmation, but also an enactment of "the
philosophic mind." "Tintern Abbey" is not only "Lines" as its full title humbly
suggests, but also a careful refinement of the pseudo-Pindaric ode.

1. *"Tintern Abbey" as Revolutionary Ode*

What then are the rhetorical and thematic implications of its being, and at
once claiming to be, and not to be, an ode?[10] Wordsworth's treatment of the
pseudo-Pindaric ode is revolutionary—in both the word's older ("revolving
back to older ways") and more modern sense: "change." Such treatment places
the poem in an ambiguous relationship to poetic tradition which speaks to
the central ambiguity of the poem: is Wordsworth unconvinced and uncon-
vincing when he says he does not mourn the loss of his boyhood raptures,
and when he celebrates the philosophic mind as "abundant recompence"? Or
does he mean it? In sum, is the poem elegy or ode?

Wordsworth's complete title at first glance suggests that the poem is neither, that it is entirely uncanonical, neither ode nor elegy, and, despite the
volume's title, neither lyric nor ballad. It is just "lines." It is true that "Lines…,"
along with the poem's opening ("Five years have passed…"), places the poem
in the topographic elegy or revisit poem tradition. Critics have argued that
Coleridge's "Frost at Midnight" was his model for handling the tradition in a
new and productive fashion.[11]

---

10. It is noteworthy that, working independently, Nabholtz and I parse the poem's
three-part odic structure in the same manner: lines 1–58, 59–112, and 112–60. See John
R. Nabholtz, "The Integrity of Wordsworth's 'Tintern Abbey,'" *The Journal of English
and Germanic Philology* 73, no. 2 (April 1974): 227–38. Though obscure, once hinted at,
the poem's odic structure is readily discernible. Both seeing it as an ode, we both read
the poem as affirming "an act of progressive mind" (233). Hence, our conception of
the generic whole shapes our interpretation of the parts.

11. E.g., Mary Jacobus, *Tradition and Experiment in Wordsworth's* Lyrical Ballads
(1798) (Oxford: Clarendon Press, 1976), 105; David Bromwich, *Disowned by Memory:
Wordsworth's Poetry of the 1790s* (Chicago and London: The University of Chicago
Press, 1998), 70.

This lineage is true as far as it goes. But behind "Frost at Midnight" lies not only the topographic elegy but the ode. "Frost" is related to a group now called the Conversation Poems, which when first published in *Poems on Various Subjects, 1796* were entitled "effusions," a tag-word associated with not only the lyric but also specifically the ode tradition.[12] Coleridge's interest in

---

12. I say this despite Beer who writes that "the word 'effusion'...suggests a certain disregard for conventional poetic forms," in *Coleridge's Poems,* edited by J. B. Beer (London: Dent; New York: Dutton, 1963), 19. See by contrast Bishop Lowth who writes that "the most ancient of all poems extant...is the thanksgiving Ode of Moses on passing the Red Sea, the most perfect of its kind, and the true and genuine effusion of the joyful affections," Robert Lowth, *Lectures on the Sacred Poetry of the Hebrews,* translated from the Latin by G. Gregory; edited by Calvin E. Stowe (Boston: Crocker & Brewster; Boston: J. Leavitt, 1829 [1787]), 211. On Lowth's influence on Coleridge and the Higher Criticism, see E. S. Shaffer, *"Kubla Khan" and the Fall of Jerusalem: The Mythological School in Biblical Criticism and Secular Literature, 1770-1880* (Cambridge: Cambridge University Press, 1975). The historical link between Pindar and that central Romantic image, the Eolian harp, argues for the centrality of the ode to Coleridge and Wordsworth. "Aeolian" is Pindar's term to characterize many of his odes, an allusion to the prosodic form he sometimes employed. Thus "eolian" would have had for Coleridge connotations of Pindaric sublimity and passion. His famous treatment of the Eolian harp was first published as "Effusion XXXV" in the 1796 volume. Coleridge, who often experimented in classical meters, may have known that another name for this Aeolian meter was "logaoedic," a name whose etymology, "prose-song," suggests a rhythm "standing between the rhythm of prose and of poetry" (*OED*). "Logaoedic" seems an uncannily accurate description of the metrical effects Coleridge was striving for in the blank verse of his Conversation Poems, and Wordsworth in "Tintern Abbey." At the least, "Aeolian's" Pindaric associations nicely underscore the harp's basic symbolism: natural inspiration and passionate sublimity. Coleridge's volume's title, *Poems on Various Subjects,* acknowledges the poems' occasional nature, a characteristic feature of ode, and thus further suggests how central to their program for poetry was Coleridge and Wordsworth's effort to redeem the ode. The last poem in the volume, entitled in full, "Religious Musings: A Desultory Poem Written on the Christmas Eve of 1794," firms up the pattern "Tintern Abbey" will follow. Based directly on Milton's "Nativity Ode," it employs blank verse paragraphs rather than Milton's irregular stanzas. Its title looks forward to "Tintern Abbey" in specifying the date, in Coleridge's case even at the expense of an outright lie: it was not finished until 1796. All these reasons—Pindaric, prosodic, and Miltonic—argue that the ode provides the final overlay

the ode is reflected in a letter to Thomas Poole, dated 26 December 1796, where he writes: "If it [his own "Ode to the Departing Year"] be found to possess the impetuosity of Transition, and that Precipitation of Fancy and Feeling, which are the *essential* excellencies of the sublimer Ode, its deficiency in less important respects will be easily pardoned."[13] On the next day he laments to Southey his censure of the genre in his "Preface" to *Poems* (dated 1797), where Southey had written, "I now think the Ode the most worthless species of composition as well as the most difficult."[14]

The ode was in the air—to be despised or redeemed. Wordsworth's note to the poem, added in the 1800 second edition, surely clinches the generic argument. He writes:

> I have not ventured to call this Poem an Ode; but it was written with a hope that in the transitions, and the impassioned music of the versification would be found the principle requisites of that species of composition.[15]

Wordsworth couldn't have been more explicit. The note has often been read as dismissing or as disdaining the ode as an overused and much abused form in the contemporary popular magazines. But in fact the note looks over the heads of the Charlotte Smiths and John Wolcotts, who flooded the popular magazines with odes, to the tradition's purer mainstream. Wordsworth's language suggests anything but disdain, anything but rebelliousness: "I have not ventured," he writes, "to call this poem an ode." What hinders him, it seems, is not rebellious, Romantic iconoclasm, a distaste for traditional forms, or even for vulgarized traditional forms, but quite the opposite: a healthy respect for tradition.

Yet, as I have said, Wordsworth's treatment of the form is revolutionary, but in an ambiguous way. It is revolutionary first in the word's older sense: it seeks to revolve back to, return to, and renew the sublime ode. It affects to do what the eighteenth-century critics like Samuel Johnson had tried in

---

or mediation that shapes the structure of the Greater Romantic Lyric.

13. *Collected Letters of Samuel Taylor Coleridge,* edited by Earl Leslie Griggs, 6 vols. (Oxford: Clarendon Press, 1956-71), 1: 289; emphasis in text.

14. Ibid., 1: 290n.

15. *Lyrical Ballads,* 149n.

prose, to show how ode-writers since Cowley had deformed the ode. But Wordsworth goes Johnson one better, not only criticizing but demonstrating how to write better odes. Nonetheless, his treatment of the ode has a surprising consonance with Johnson's strictures on the late plague of ode-writers. Wordsworth's blank verse avoids Cowley's irregular measures; his morality is "natural" (i.e. sensible) like Gray's, but unlike Gray's not "too stale."[16] He avoids the allusions and stale mythology that bothered Johnson in Pope's St. Cecelia's Day ode and by cultivating the common language of men he echoes and answers Johnson's condemnation of those who think "their language more poetical as it is more remote from common use."[17] Just as Wordsworth's note to the poem echoes Johnson's Dictionary—that the "ode is characterized by sublimity, rapture and quickness of transition" (s.v. "ode")—so, too, Wordsworth's performance echoes Johnson's critical desire to perfect, not debunk, the ode.

But Wordsworth's renewal of the ode tradition was in other ways conducted in perfectly Romantic fashion—a revolution in the modern sense of radical transformation. Wordsworth advances the ode's essential characteristics according to the Romantic program for poetry. Where, firstly, the neoclassic age found the sublime in the terrible and in high state occasions, Wordsworth finds it in the humble, quiet landscape of the Wye valley, and in the humble and personal occasion of his return. "Tintern Abbey," secondly, is rapturous, but Wordsworth addresses his poetic raptures, we eventually learn, not to majesty or to nation-at-large, but to his sister in familiar conversation. Furthermore, obfuscating its relation to the ode tradition—which, despite the generic note, it does in part—"Tintern Abbey" rivals and outdoes the traditional "rapture." For if the ode is inspired utterance, it makes rhetorical sense to appear not to have its mind on earthly things—like other odes. To write extracanonically is to be free of artifice; it is to achieve inspired, unmediated expression. The poem's verse pattern, diction, and design in some ways reflect the ode's third characteristic: liberty and boldness. It is widely agreed

---

16. Samuel Johnson, *Lives of the English Poets*, edited by George Birkbeck Hill, 3 vols. (Oxford: Clarendon Press, 1905), 3:434.

17. Ibid., 4:435.

that his choice of blank verse has lofty, Miltonic implications.[18] But in Wordsworth's hands blank verse has less the "builded" and lapidary feel Milton famously achieves; instead his modulates to the cadences of the spoken voice and of felt emotion. Wordsworth's verse paragraphs of uneven length, often ending and beginning in mid-line, avoid the patent affectation of the stanzaic irregular ode where "freedoms" in measure and rhyme scheme are belied by being regularly repeated.

The only blank verse odes prior to Wordsworth's and Coleridge's are those by hymnwriter Isaac Watts in his 1706 *Horae Lyricae*.[19] In that volume's preface Watts links the ode tradition and Miltonic blank verse: "it is my opinion" he writes, "that the free and unconfined numbers of Pindar, or the noble measures of Milton without rhyme, would best maintain the dignity of the [religious] theme, as well as give loose to the devout soul, nor check the raptures of her faith and love."[20] In these several ways then, Wordsworth's treatment of the ode reflects his commitment to achieving a "natural" spontaneous immediacy of expression.

But we must be careful to place the accent as much on "achieve" as on "natural." For, "written" as Wordsworth's note declares "with the requisites of that species of composition" in mind, "Tintern Abbey" presents itself not only as extracanonical, but also as canonical, as the product of care, skill, judgment, and rationality. The language of his note is not only respectful in tone, it is also stiff, traditional, and rationalistic: "I have not ventured…; but it was written with the hope… would be found the principle requisites of

---

18. See, e.g., Geoffrey H. Hartman, *The Unmediated Vision: An Interpretation of Wordsworth, Hopkins, Rilke, and Valéry* (New York: Harcourt, Brace & World, 1966 [1954]), 177, 78n.

19. See Isaac Watts, *Horae Lyricae and Divine Songs* (Boston: Little, Brown and Company, 1854 [1706]), especially Watts's "A Sight of Christ," "True Monarchy," "True Courage," and "The Celebrated Victory." On the relation of Wordsworth to Watts (via Wesley and Methodism), see Richard E. Brantley, *Wordsworth's "Natural Methodism"* (New Haven: Yale University Press, 1975). On Coleridge's references to the *Horæ Lyricæ* in the famous Gutch Notebook, see John Livingston Lowes, *The Road to Xanadu: A Study in the Ways of Imagination* (New York: Vintage Books, 1959 [1927]), 419.

20. Watts, *Horae Lyricae*, xcviii.

that species of composition." Read in conjunction with the poem's insistent rhetoric of artlessness, Wordsworth's note reflects the tension that is the ode's fourth characteristic, the feature that lies at the very center of the tradition. Edward Young's preface to "Ocean: an Ode" enlarges upon the ode's opposition between judgment and imagination, rationality and fancy:

> Judgment, indeed, that masculine power of the mind in ode, as in all compositions, should bear supreme sway; and a beautiful imagination, as its mistress, should be subdued to its dominion...
>
> But then in ode, there is this difference from other kinds of poetry; that, there, the imagination like a beautiful mistress, is indulged in the appearance of domineering; though the judgment like an artful lover, in reality carries its point; and the less it is suspected of it, it shows the more masterly conduct, and deserves the greater commendation.[21]

Following the fashion of his day, Young personifies the opposition: wayward mistress and artful master. Such a method is echoed in the many odes to Fancy and The Poetic Character, where the neo-classical poets treat faculties of mind as allegorical figures. Wordsworth not only introduces this formal polarity of the ode by means of the note, but also makes it the theme of his poem. He does so dramatically, without resort to allegory: "Tintern Abbey" is a poem about the opposition between rapturous imagination and genius, and the art, judgment, and rapture-with-a-difference of the "philosophic mind." In this way Wordsworth perfects the ode in a peculiarly Romantic fashion, writing a more "natural" ode that furthermore takes as its subject the nature of ode writing, the nature of rapturous imagination.[22] It asks the hard question that will require a complex and somewhat ambivalent response: which is better, a "natural," innocent rapture, or a wise, cultivated rapture?

Wordsworth's two rhetorics authorize and validate the poem in two contradictory ways. He asks us to believe in the poem's expressed experience both because it is spontaneous and unmediated by artifice, and also because it carefully reworks and improves poetic tradition. Not only is this poet "a

---

21. "On Lyric Poetry," in *The Poetical Works of Edward Young,* 2 vols. (Boston: Little, Brown, and Company, 1859), 2:147.

22. Fry argues that all odes debate the nature of the rapturous imagination; but we must add to this that they always do so as if they were the first. Fry provides a fine bibliography on the ode in *The Poet's Calling,* 9, 279 n. 8.

man speaking to men," but he is also a better poet than heretofore. His is at once a poem natural and inartificial, and the demonstration of a higher, purer poetic artifice. This tension is reflected in the subject of the poem, in the subtle opposition between Wordsworth's "natural" youth and the cultivated "philosophic mind" of maturity. In defining the mature imagination, the judgment of the "philosophic mind" from one point of view subtly bears, to quote Young again, "supreme sway" and obscurely "carries its point" over the rapture of youth now lost, meriting therefore our "greater commendation." "Tintern Abbey" is not an elegy to the loss of his boyish youth. It is a joyful ode celebrating the philosophic mind and the poetic craft that have come with years, hard work, and experience, and which enable him to write his renovated ode.

What complicates the joy, as we will see, is his sister Dorothy.

2. "Philosophic Mind" and the Rhetoric of Craft

"Tintern Abbey" is a poem of cruces, but the most important crux is Wordsworth's description of his youth. The depiction of youth is almost invariably read as positive and sympathetic, indeed as an elegiac idealization of the imagination's sources. But Nabholtz catches the scent of Wordsworth's covert argument when he tentatively suggests in a note that there "seems something unclear about the language," a "suggestion of something excessive, almost unhealthy about the experience."[23] Wordsworth tells us he is "changed,"

>   no doubt, from what I was, when first
> I came among these hills; when like a roe
> I bounded o'er the mountains, by the sides
> Of the deep rivers, and the lonely streams,
> Wherever nature led; ...
>   For nature then
> (The coarser pleasures of my boyish days,
> And their glad animal movements all gone by,)
> To me was all in all.—I cannot paint
> What then I was. The sounding cataract
> Haunted me like a passion: the tall rock,
> The mountain, and the deep and gloomy wood,

---

23. Nabholtz, "The Integrity of Wordsworth's 'Tintern Abbey,' " 234n.

> Their colours and their forms, were then to me
> An appetite; a feeling and a love,
> That had no need of a remoter charm,
> By thought supplied, nor any interest
> Unborrowed from the eye.—That time is past,
> And all its aching joys are now no more,
> And all its dizzy raptures.[24]

The passage is not merely "equivocal," as Sheats too suggests.[25] It is a brilliant equivocation, intermixing positive and negative clues to interpretation and judgment. The youth's physical energy ("bounded") and his intimacy with sublime aspects of nature ("deep rivers" and "lonely streams") first attract us. The attribution of loneliness to streams, although something of a dead metaphor, suggests a union between the youth and nature, a suffusion of his emotion into the natural scene. The next clause, "Wherever nature led," caps this suggestion of intimacy and union. This youth experiences such union with nature that he follows its silent commands. Who could not but admire and yearn for such a mode of being?

It comes as something of a surprise therefore when the next clause discomforts our attraction to the youth. Now we hear that the youthful Wordsworth was,

> more like a man
> Flying from something that he dreads, than one
> Who sought the thing he loved.[26]

Later in the poem Wordsworth posits the *love* of nature as the product of the mature "philosophic mind." But even at this point in the poem, without the aid of the contrast, we sense something amiss in his youthful experience. Being moved as if by fear chimes badly with the preceding assertion that the youth "bounded...wherever nature led." Flight and fear contradict intimacy and union. If nature "led" his boundings, it did so in an authoritarian relationship, not a maternal and benign one.

---

24. "Tintern Abbey," lines 67-86.

25. See Paul D. Sheats, *The Making of Wordsworth's Poetry, 1785-1798* (Cambridge, Mass.: Harvard University Press, 1973), 237.

26. "Tintern Abbey," lines 70-72.

And yet, still more negatively, the clause suggests that the fear was produced by the youth's own psyche, not by some outside source in nature. What
is going on here is a repetition of that frenzied state of mind Wordsworth will
attribute also to his Cambridge years, when,

> To every natural form, rock, fruit or flower,
> Even to loose stones that cover the high-way,
> I gave a moral life, I saw them feel,
> Or link'd them to some feeling: the great mass
> Lay bedded in a quickening soul, and all
> That I beheld respired with inward meaning.[27]

Such emotional projection is, as Cassirer has remarked in a passage unfriendly
to Wordsworth, "but the anteroom of art."[28] And yet Wordsworth would
have agreed: such experience comes dangerously close to the subjective and
solipsistic fancy that he feared led merely to "the abyss of idealism."[29] In *The
Prelude* Wordsworth treats such modes of imaginative projection sympathetically as necessary stages in the development of the true poetic imagination. But just as necessary is his leaving such stages behind. An interfusion of
nature and man that blurs, mingles and obscures the reality of either does not
characterize the experience of nature Wordsworth ultimately seeks. Whatever their differences—and they begin to seem less and less—Wordsworth
would have appreciated Blake's commitment to the "strong, clear bounding
line" that keeps things distinct.[30] And like Blake he seeks in his experience of
nature a perception of correspondence, wherein man and nature's realities
are wedded but their separateness maintained, not "interfused." True vision
is not fuzzy.

In spite of its cultivated appearance of spontaneity, "Tintern Abbey's"
opening carefully keeps nature and man distinct even while it suggests correspondences. "Sweet" in the phrase "sweet inland murmur" has been read as

---

27. William Wordsworth, *The Prelude, or Growth of a Poet's Mind*, edited by Ernest
de Selincourt and Stephen Gill (Oxford: Oxford University Press, 1970), 37 (bk. 3, lines
130-35).

28. Cassirer, *An Essay on Man*, 154.

29. *The Poetical Works of William Wordsworth*, 4: 463.

30. Anne Kostelanetz Mellor, *Blake's Human Form Divine* (Berkeley, Los Angeles,
and London: University of California Press, 1974), xvi.

an instance of emotional projection.[31] But in fact "sweet" draws on an obsolete usage (the kind of usage that would have survived in Wales or the Lake District), "sweet water" meaning "fresh, not salt" as it does today in the Louisiana delta south of New Orleans.[32] Wordsworth's note to the phrase ("The river is not affected by the tides a few miles above Tintern") hence refers to the river's purity, and calls attention to the poet's use of language in a denotative almost scientific way. Though apparently arcane enough to his London audience that he was forced to emend to the epithet "soft," his usage does not reflect pathetic fallacy. The Wordsworth's emotions saturate the paragraph, as we have seen; but there is no evidence nonetheless that they distort the landscape. Wordsworth's frequent demonstratives ("These...cliffs," "this...sycamore," "these plots," "These orchard-tufts," "these hedge-rows," "these...farms"), typical of improvisations, simply point out the realistic details of the scene before him. Sheats characterizes such imagery as *"presentational, because it seeks to reproduce the presentation of phenomena to the mind in experience."*[33] When Wordsworth seems to speak for nature, as when he imaginatively projects unseen inhabitants into the scene, his language firmly establishes what he is doing: "as might seem"—comparative adverb, subjunctive mood, and tentative verb—introduce the hypothetical portrait of "vagrant dwellers" or "some Hermit." Such careful qualifications call attention to the fact that the Hermit owes his very existence to an act of Wordsworth's mind: hardly "unaccommodated man." Conversely Wordsworth's descriptions of the scene's influence upon *him* reflect equal caution and care. "These steep and lofty cliffs" do not simply produce emotion in the poet, but rather "on a wild secluded scene impress / Thoughts of a more deep seclusion."[34] At first it seems Wordsworth attributes thoughts to nature, as the landscape affects him by producing feelings of loneliness. Loneliness is produced, even a feeling of alienation, but the verb "impress" keeps the mind and its object distinct: the thoughts are pressed onto the landscape, but the

---

31. Sheats, *The Making of Wordsworth's Poetry*, 232.

32. For a fuller treatment of this point, see my "The Wye's 'Sweet Inland Murmur,'" *The Wordsworth Circle* 16, no. 3 (Summer 1985): 134-35.

33. Sheats, *The Making of Wordsworth's Poetry*, 87-88.

34. "Tintern Abbey," lines 6-7.

landscape remains the landscape, the thoughts remain an act of mind. Nature and man are intimately related, but not confused. The quiet of the sky and pastoral scene ("green to the very door," "pastoral farms") is reflected in the quiet figure of Wordsworth beneath the sycamore.

By contrast, the portrait of youth is anything but quiet. "Bounding o'er... mountains" and "flying [as if] from something that he dreads" suggests a frenzied self-absorption that contrasts sharply with the quiet survey of the opening paragraph. What the two selves see reflect, and indeed follow from, the difference: the youth experienced sublime terror in the Wye valley, the mature man harmonious and homely beauty. The contrast undermines our estimation of the youth and, as well, the conventions of the sublime tradition, which we begin to sense are based on the cultivation of self-absorbed and sensational emotions. The contrast thus looks ahead to the famous opposition in the *Preface of 1800* where Wordsworth states that what "distinguishes these Poems from the popular Poetry of the day...is this, that the feelings therein developed give importance to the action and situation and not the action and situation to the feeling."[35] The youth's rush through the landscape belongs in the latter category and reflects the "degrading thirst after outrageous stimulation" Wordsworth's Preface attacks.[36] Within the poem, the youth's "aching joys" and "dizzy raptures" will be compared implicitly to maturity's "tender joys" and "healing thoughts."

My point echoes the point Wordsworth emphatically makes in the *Preface*:

> The subject is indeed important! For the human mind is capable of being excited without the application of gross and violent stimulants; and...one being is elevated above another in proportion as he possesses this capability. It has therefore appeared to me that to endeavour to produce or enlarge this capability is one of the best services in which, at any period, a writer can be engaged; but this service, excellent at all times, is especially so at the present day. For a multitude of causes unknown to former times are now acting with a combined force to blunt the discriminating powers of the mind and, unfitting it for all voluntary exertion to reduce it to a state of almost savage torpor.[37]

---

35. *Lyrical Ballads*, 158.
36. Ibid., 160.
37. Ibid., 159-60.

Continuing in this prophetic vein, Wordsworth condemns "the great national events which are daily taking place," an allusion to the French Revolution and its repercussions in England. The passage is not only a brilliant gloss on his volume's seemingly underwritten ballads but also on its masterpiece. Since "Tintern Abbey" recalls 1793 when he had just returned from the French Revolution and challenges that time in his life, the poem literally turns *from* that "great [inter]national event." Its title—"July 13"—hints at the eve of that Revolution, but the poem offers a different beginning. For like the simpler ballads of the volume, "Tintern Abbey" turns upon the unsensational, even the everyday, and celebrates (and demonstrates) the mind that can appreciate them as the heart of the matter. It looks ahead to the Prospectus in the Preface to the *Excursion* where Wordsworth seeks to achieve "Paradise, and groves/Elysian, Fortunate Fields" not through political revolution; he believes them rather, "a simple produce [*sic*; read "product"] of the common day."[38] Only by avoiding "gross and violent stimulants," can we escape modern life's "savage torpor." The phrase sums up the negative strokes in the portrait of youth: violently and primitively active, and yet dull of mind.

Though the portrait does much to disturb our attraction to the youth and our high estimation of his mode of being, the point is still in part that Wordsworth makes it difficult to perceive the qualifications. It is hard, perhaps impossible to shake free of the celebratory reading. I am not waffling; I am arguing rather for the text's complexity and equivocation. The poet half lulls us into sympathetic response, half goads us to more judicious appraisal—in fact he does both at full steam. In his next complex stroke the poet raises the difficulty and equivocation again. Speaking again of a union between the youth and nature, Wordsworth interposes an ambiguous parenthesis that invites both approval and judgment and in doing so makes judgment difficult:

> For nature then
> (The coarser pleasures of my boyish days,
> And their glad animal movements all gone by,)
> To me was all in all.—[39]

---

38. "Prospectus" to *The Excursion*, in *The Poetical Works of William Wordsworth*, 5: 4 (lines 47-48, 55).

39. "Tintern Abbey," lines 73-76.

"Animal movements" echoes the bounding of the roe-like youth, and seems to reiterate the most attractive feature of the portrait, physical vitality. Yet here "animal movements" merges with "coarser pleasures." The intrusive parenthesis ("...coarser pleasures...") undermines the youth's most attractive feature: "nature...To me was all in all." Just what kind of love and union is this?—so Wordsworth would have us ask. He forces us to look elsewhere for the poem's normative values.

By now as we read the passage, we may have gotten the hint that there is something "excessively enthusiastic and even unspiritual," as one critic put it, about the emotions involved in being "Haunted...ike a passion" by nature.[40] But again Wordsworth makes the portrait attractive, intimating a union between the youth and nature so complete that we cannot tell if the emotion described is in the youth or in nature:

> The sounding cataract
> Haunted me like a passion: the tall rock,
> The mountain, and the deep and gloomy wood,
> Their colours and their forms, were then to me
> An appetite: a feeling and a love,
> That had no need of a remoter charm,
> By thought supplied, nor any interest
> Unborrowed from the eye.—[41]

We are unsure whether nature produces the "passion," "appetite," "feeling," and "love" in the youth, or whether its details and attributes simply *were* these primitive emotions. We sense that "appetite" is again too animal and sensual, but the passage climaxes in the seeming affirmation of youth's unmediated, sensuous responsiveness: "That had no need of remoter charm, / By thought supplied, or any interest / Unborrowed from the eye." The youthful experience of nature was raw and real—unmediated—and therefore it would seem of the highest value.

Later affirming the "philosophic mind," Wordsworth will glance back at this portrait of youth's unmediated experience and deem it "thoughtless." Although the word chimes well with this gloss of "unmediated," "raw," and

---

40. Brantley, *Wordsworth's "Natural Methodism,"* 126.
41. Ibid., lines 77–84.

"real," the moral stricture is unmistakable. Wordsworth sustains the portrait's ambiguous and equivocal nature in the epithets leading up to this crucial one. We do not know, for example, how to take Wordsworth's first summary overview of his youthful experience:

> That time is past,
> And all its aching joys are now no more,
> And all its dizzy raptures.[42]

"Dizzy" may have merely its physical and psychological sense, the giddiness or vertigo produced by rapid movement or heights; or it may have its figurative sense, "whirling with mad rapidity" (*OED*). In either case "dizzy" culminates the imagery of movement and of heights in the portrait. Read sympathetically, "dizzy" merely reinforces our sympathy: energetic and instinctual, the youth achieves sublime, "dizzy raptures." Nevertheless moral connotations resound in the adjective. In northern dialect "dizzy" means "foolish, stupid," and in modern usage, "wanting in moral stability." In like manner, "aching joys" both attracts us and puts us on our guard. It looks back to the youth's "haunted...passions," and suggests again that the youth's experience of nature was "sublime." To the cultivator of the Sublime, such oxymoronic emotions were not only acceptable, they were *de rigueur*. But the Burkean, sensationalistic "sublime" fares badly in Wordsworth's portrait as we have seen. Nature's ministry, we will hear in *The Prelude*, works through such dizzying terrors. But if "Tintern Abbey" succeeds in making the paradox of youth's sublimity appealing, the poem also makes the sublime quite unattractive. The implicit contrast between the youth's "aching joys" and "dizzy raptures" and the mature man's "healing thoughts" and "tender joys" makes us wonder if the pain is not just pain. At the least the portrait's ambiguous epithets have their own dizzying effect upon the reader.

The most fundamental paradox of Wordsworth's depiction of youth is surely this: that what he overtly describes as a state of immediacy, he covertly shows rife with emotional projection and shot through with mediation. Wordsworth *tells* us the youth needs not supply any thought or charm to appreciate nature, yet he also *shows* us that the youth supplied much else.

---

42. Ibid., lines 84-86.

Unlike the youth, the mature man recognizes and takes responsibility for this "beholder's share" in his experience of nature. Even though the poet half longs for the unmediated experience of youth, he also hints simultaneously that it *wasn't* unmediated in the first place. Perhaps what he longs for—but holds in check—is the illusion, the myth of immediacy. In depicting the "philosophic mind" and in his concluding address to Dorothy, Wordsworth while overtly affirming this myth, undermines it by affirming the mind's mediating powers. The ensuing portrait enforces the theme of disjunction between the two selves ("That time is past"), sketching the ways in which the "philosophic mind" represents a break with former modes of being and perception.

The break is acute but beneficial: the "other gifts" which "have followed" obviate the need to "mourn" or "murmur." Thus, where the youth found self-projected, haunting fears in nature, the mature man hears oftentimes

> The still, sad music of humanity,
> Nor harsh nor grating, though of ample power
> To chasten and subdue.[43]

His experience in youth Wordsworth implies—though it is only implicit—was harsh and grating. And what is implicitly chastened and subdued here are youth's proud self-absorption and discontent. Wordsworth learns what Elijah learns on Horeb that the

> LORD was not in the wind; and after the wind—an earthquake; but the LORD was not in the earthquake. And after the earthquake—fire; but the LORD was not in the fire. And after the fire—a soft murmuring sound.
> (1 Kings 19: 11-12)

This text would have had special potency for Wordsworth since it follows Elijah's being cast out of the household of Ahab (that false king) and his slaying the false prophets of Baal, details Wordsworth may have connected with the Bloody Terror. Most significantly the text follows Elijah's thoughts of suicide, thoughts that we know Wordsworth himself contemplated in 1793.

Like Elijah, Wordsworth's response is finally to take on the mantle of prophecy, finding sublimity no longer in the *terrible,* but now in the beautiful:

> And I have felt
> A presence that disturbs me with the joy

---

43. Ibid., lines 92-94.

Of elevated thoughts; a sense sublime
Of something far more deeply interfused,
Whose dwelling is the light of setting suns,
And the round ocean, and the living air,
And the blue sky, and in the mind of man,
A motion and a spirit, that impels
All thinking things, all objects of all thought,
And rolls through all things. Therefore am I still
A lover of the meadows and the woods,
And mountains; and of all that we behold
From this green earth; of all the mighty world
Of eye and ear, both what they half-create,
And what perceive; well pleased to recognize
In nature and the language of the sense,
The anchor of my purest thoughts, the nurse,
The guide, the guardian of my heart, and soul
Of all my moral being.[44]

Not only the quiet of "setting suns," "round ocean," "living air," and "blue sky" recall the opening paragraph's quiet harmony, but so too does the pastoral imagery: "meadows and woods," "this green earth." Wordsworth of "philosophic mind" is "disturbed" like the youth, but now by the "joy of elevated thoughts." Still a lover of nature, he is kept distinct from it, avoiding untoward unity of self with nature: something is "interfused" here, but it is interfused "more deeply" than before and equally in the objects of nature and in "the mind of man." This "presence" "impels/All thinking things, all objects of all thought,/And rolls through all things;" but the series suggests not a union between the objects of nature and the self but a correspondence among them effected by the supernatural "presence." Again Blake, despite his hostile reading of Wordsworth, provides the best gloss when he writes in his annotations to Wordsworth's 1815 Preface to *Poems*:

> Imagination is the Divine Vision not of The World nor of Man nor from Man as. [*sic*] he is a Natural Man but only as he is a Spiritual Man.[45]

---

44. Ibid., lines 94–112.

45. *The Poetry and Prose of William Blake*, 655.

For, most important, the portrait acknowledges the perceiving and imaginative role of mind in its experience of nature. "Nature" is "recognized" as "anchor," "nurse," "guide," "guardian," and even "soul" "of all my moral being." But "the language of the sense" significantly shares this august post. This difficult phrase overtly acknowledges nature's influence, the influence of direct, sensuous experience. But also, more subtly and obscurely, it insists upon the mind's responsibility for itself, its role of mediation through the human construct, language. The "language of the sense" involves, as he has just predicated, a process of mind: "all the mighty world/Of eye and ear, both what they half-create,/And what perceive." These compressed lines have been read as evidence of Wordsworth's commitment to a radical empiricism.[46] But they are also susceptible instead to the reading that Wordsworth is affirming a cautious transcendentalist epistemology, one that accepts the mind's shaping influence but avoids the "abyss of idealism."[47] The world of sense is "half-created" through the mediation of the human mind, but its objective reality is maintained ("what perceive"). According to this more persuasive reading, the depiction of the "philosophic mind" is not a description of unmediated, unreflective experience, but quite the opposite. Read this way, "the philosophic mind" is tacitly set in contrast, and tacitly answers the portrait of youth.

The point, however, is not simply to decide between the empiricist and transcendentalist Wordsworth. The point, as always in this poem, is that Wordsworth makes it difficult to see how large is the gulf between his two selves. We can easily glance over the subtle ways that the new immersion in nature differs in kind from the youth's. His experience of nature is no longer immediate and unmediated; and yet he affirms it after seeming to affirm the immediacy of youth.

Wordsworth's alienation from nature implicit in this portrait of maturity leads many to the view that Wordsworth merely rationalizes when he calls his later mode of being "abundant recompence." Not simply the primitivist,

---

46. See H.W. Garrod, *Wordsworth: Lectures and Essays* (Oxford: Clarendon Press, 1927), 105–6; and Arthur Beatty, *William Wordsworth: His Doctrine and Art in Their Historical Relations* (Madison: University of Wisconsin Press, 1960 [1922]), 108ff.

47. Melvin Rader, *Wordsworth: A Philosophical Approach* (Oxford: Clarendon Press, 1967), 154ff.

vulgarly Romantic critical assumption that Wordsworth's goal is unmediated experience leads to such a reading. Wordsworth's own equivocations and subtlety are also responsible. Why then the two arguments? And why make the covert argument so hard to discover? If attaining the "philosophical mind" is such unalloyed joy, why the ambiguity about his genre and about the loss of his boyish raptures? Why make the negation of youth's participation in nature so difficult to discern? Why does the poem seem to be about continuity and union with nature rather than discontinuity and separation?

The answer is twofold. If seeing two arguments in the poem strains the eye, that, as in the gestaltist drawing of the rabbit-duck, is in part the point. We see the rabbit when we go looking for the rabbit, the duck when we go looking for the duck. By straining the eye the poem breaks our habitual modes of perception, "awakening," as Coleridge wrote of their mutual goal in *Lyrical Ballads*, "the minds attention from the lethargy of custom."[48] It has been

Rabbit or Duck?

suggested that the poem "is hard to read,...is in some ways vague and hints at a more precise notion of human development than it really articulates."[49] But seeing two distinct and contradictory arguments in the poem clarifies that the poem is not so much about a "precise notion of human development" as it is a rumination upon and a record, an act, of developing—a process that lacks precise outlines. The poem is primarily and finally about what modern developmental psychologists term a "stage transition," wherein "development consists in structural changes, [and] any new structure constitutes *a break from the old one*."[50]

---

48. Coleridge, *Biographia Literaria*, 2: 6.

49. David Ferry, *The Limits of Mortality: An Essay on Wordsworth's Major Poems* (Middletown, Conn.: Wesleyan University Press, 1959), 109.

50. Loevinger and Blasi, *Ego Development*, 38; emphasis added.

Having two contradictory arguments in the same poem—one celebrating and yearning for youth's mode of being, one delineating the "new structure" and the consequent "break" or differences from the old—is difficult. Yet if the poem's true subject is an act of developing and the poem records a stage transition, then such a contradiction makes psychological and poetic sense. Growth is a painful experience, involving us in the trauma of venturing into the unknown, and into untested modes of being. In growing we inevitably move both forward and yearn regressively for out former state if only because we are then free of the uncertainty we now experience. Interpreting the poem in this way helps to explain the "muddle" so many tough-minded critics find in the poem—the poem is muddled but for lucidly expressive reasons.

But Wordsworth's reasons for the poem's equivocations are not only aesthetic and mimetic, nor are they only self-regarding. Another reason for all the problematics stands beside him: Dorothy. Only at the end, well past the problematic celebration of youth, do we learn that Dorothy stands by his side with all the hallmarks of youth: the wild eyes, "the language of [his] former heart," and the "wild ecstasies." Read in this way, the motivation for the earlier equivocal treatment of his youth becomes clearer. He cannot put his youthful state firmly behind him, because doing so puts Dorothy behind him, suggests that she is beneath him, that she should change. This reading chimes with Richard Fadem's convincing treatment of Dorothy's "arrested growth."[51] With great gentleness, Wordsworth subtly and obscurely urges her to give up youth and to pursue the "philosophic mind":

> Therefore let the moon
> Shine on thee in thy solitary walk;
> And let the misty mountain winds be free
> To blow against thee: and in after years,
> When these wild ecstasies shall be matured
> Into a sober pleasure, when thy mind
> Shall be a mansion of all lovely forms,
> Thy memory be as a dwelling-place

---

51. Richard Fadem, "Dorothy Wordsworth: A View from 'Tintern Abbey,'" *The Wordsworth Circle* 9, no. 1 (Winter 1978): 17-32. Though his article is more about Dorothy than the poem, his view that "Tintern Abbey" "is not, as Eliot instructed us to read *In Memoriam,* a poem of doubt" (27), agrees with my own on many points.

For all sweet sounds and harmonies; Oh! then,
If solitude, or fear, or pain, or grief,
Should be thy portion, with what healing thoughts
Of tender joy wilt thou remember me,
And these my exhortations![52]

Although these lines have often been taken as Wordsworth's final elegiac recognition that the loss of unmediated and rapturous imagination is inexorable,
Wordsworth terms them "exhortations." Wordsworth embeds his hortative
advice in his wandering period's center: give up your wild ecstasies for the
more valuable and humane pursuit of "sober pleasures." Wordsworth lovingly exhorts his sister to grow, as he has done, through reflection. Avoiding
the sublimity of the Jeremiad and choosing the gentler coaxing sometimes
employed in the New Testament, Wordsworth achieves the prophet's task of
effecting change in his community, here the community that meant the most
to him in 1798, the family.

Wordsworth's "revolutionary" ode affirms immediacy of experience, but
a higher immediacy achieved, paradoxically, by craft. The philosophic mind's
rapturous imagination, as "Tintern Abbey" suggestively portrays it in word,
gesture, and act, discerns not new and radical political and metaphysical
truths, but rather hears the old tunes, "the still sad music of humanity." As
Paul Sheats has resonantly written:

> An authentic and living spiritual illumination, Wordsworth's philoso-
> phy is private, idiosyncratic, and enthusiastic. And yet it is also the
> product of a mind that, in 1798, was deeply concerned to avoid idio-
> syncrasy and relativism, a mind that sought rest in the stability and
> permanence of truth.[53]

One of the ways Wordsworth avoids such idiosyncrasies and enthusiasms
is by participating in the age-old tradition of the ode, recovering (and yet reinventing) its stable and permanent truths. In "Tintern Abbey" Wordsworth
participates in and expresses the old truth that man seeks ever for divine
enlightenment through rapturous ecstasy, in a loss of Self in a greater Other,
only barely to approximate it through the cultivation of his own faculties.

---

52. "Tintern Abbey," lines 135-47.
53. Sheats, *The Making of Wordsworth's Poetry*, 228.

Tragically, the approximation is only that: a near copy of what we can imagine true spontaneous ecstasy to yield. The divine comedy offered in the poem's affirmation is that, not only are such pale versions of spontaneity all we have, but they suffice. As in Auden's memorable line, "The mortal world"—both nature's and man's—is "enough."[54] The 1815 title—"Lines Composed..."—reminds us to heed a theme central to the poem since 1798: the value of the reflective, "philosophic mind" whose mode of thinking is so valuable that even the loss of youth's thoughtless immediacy need not cause us to "mourn nor murmur." "Tintern Abbey" is an elegy to this tragic loss and a paean to this happy gain. Ultimately the ode to joy, however muffled by Wordsworth's loving concern for his sister, drowns out the elegy.

---

54. "Lullaby," in W. H. Auden, *Collected Poems,* edited by Edward Mendelson (New York: Random House, 1976), 132.

CHAPTER ELEVEN

Tennyson:
"Toil Cöoperant to an End"

Ah, what pitfalls are in that word *Nature*!
—Matthew Arnold

1. *Lyric Effusion or Poetic Artifact?*

Another Harvard moment: a Tennyson seminar held in the Warren House office of one of the world's foremost Tennyson scholars. *In Memoriam* is under discussion. My dissertation idea is rattling around my brain. I make the case that for all the poem's protestations of unmediated, formless grief Tennyson knew what he was doing, forming a poem about formless grief that he had every intention of publishing from the start. I can't remember the *ex cathedra* pronouncement in detail but it came down on me like a ton of bricks. It had something to do with my moral stature and sanity.

The greatest lyric poet of his age, Tennyson was at once he "most tradition-bound of English poets" and one of the most profoundly experimental.[1] Although Wordsworth—the Wordsworth of such "spontaneous" utterances as "I wandered lonely as a cloud"—was a continuing presence in Tennyson's life, Tennyson early committed himself to the influence of Keats and Byron. It is clear, furthermore, from the influences traceable in Tennyson's early poetry that his Keats was the Keats who wished "to load every rift with ore," and his Byron the craftsman who saw himself as the "last Augustan." The Laureate grew tired of the rhapsodic *"Childe Harold,"* his son tells us, preferring

---

1. Robert Pattison, *Tennyson and Tradition* (Cambridge, Mass.: Harvard University Press, 1979), 8. Although conceived independently, my reading of the rhetorical texture of Tennyson's poetry is extensively substantiated by Pattison's superb book. My debt to Pattison for ways to talk about that texture is great, as will be obvious.

the robust *Don Juan*.[2] Tennyson's spontaneity, like Byron's, is more akin to Pope's Horatian cultivation of a grace beyond the reach of art than it is to the Romantic quest (if there was one) for divine afflatus. By a number of poetic means Tennyson's poetry, whatever its lyricism, "compels the work to be studied as artifact instead of-as inspiration," as Robert Pattison, who is among his best commentators, has written.[3] As such, his poetry provides a counter-example to the mode of improvisation, an example all the more enlightening because it comes in response to the Romantic exploitation of the mode. A study of Browning's poetry or that of the Spasmodics would reveal directions, good and bad, the Romantics' rhetoric of spontaneity takes under sympathetic hands. Examining instead the poetic means by which Tennyson insistently departed from Romantic rhetorical postures, and the thematic implications of that departure—Tennyson's anti-naturalism—will shed an even bolder light on the nature of Romantic spontaneity.

For Harold Bloom, Tennyson was a failed Romantic because of his profound "distrust of his own creative powers. A god spoke in him, or a demon, and a revulsion accompanied the maturing of his voice."[4] A Bloomian reading of Tennyson's insistence upon the crafted artifice of his poetry might be mounted with success: faced with the Romantics' lyric achievement and his own belatedness, Tennyson chose self-protectively not to rival his precursors on their own ground. He shifted the ground, played at a different game that he could win. Like Pope, with whom, for Edmund Wilson, Tennyson shares "a triumph of artifice" and a failure of emotion, Tennyson seems to have decided early that he would make his mark on history by becoming a correct poet: a master of tradition and poetic craft.[5] But Bloom and Wilson both grab the right stick by the wrong end. Tennyson's insistence upon craft is not self-

---

2. Hallam Tennyson, *Alfred Lord Tennyson: A Memoir*, 2 vols. (London: Macmillan, 1924 [1897]), 2: 287 (hereafter cited as *Memoir*).

3. Pattison, *Tennyson and Tradition*, 20.

4. "Tennyson, Hallam, and Romantic Tradition," in Harold Bloom, *The Ringers in the Tower: Studies in Romantic Tradition* (Chicago: The University of Chicago Press, 1971), 147.

5. "Pope and Tennyson," in Edmund Wilson, *Shores of Light: A Literary Chronicle of the Twenties and Thirties* (New York: Farrar, Straus and Giroux, 1979 [1952]), 256.

protection, but attack; and his treatment of emotion is of a different kind than the Romantics'. His poetic posture flies in the face of Romantic professions of spontaneity: it declares the dual speciousness of the lyric conceit. For lyric is false first of all in declaring itself spontaneous. Lyric art is still always art. For Tennyson, as for many of the Victorians, as Jerome Buckley has shown, "Poetry could no longer continue to exalt pure emotion at the expense of practical reason; unpremeditated art, if indeed it ever existed, would henceforth seem a contradiction in terms."[6] Furthermore, lyric is false in declaring the inevitable benefits of its spontaneity. Sometimes natural, raw emotion is but "wild cries," as Tennyson will artfully moan in *In Memoriam.* As Ruskin remarked, expressing oneself "under the impulse of passion" might or might not lead to new truths.[7] The subtle truths which we found to be in conflict with Wordsworth's overt rhetoric in "Tintern Abbey" is insistently true for Tennyson: all poetry, all utterance worth its breath, is "formed," and all truth is "formulated." For Tennyson from the beginning: "all, as in some piece of art, / Is toil cöoperant to an end."[8]

Tennyson acknowledges, indeed enforces, our recognition of the mediation inherent in art by a number of poetic devices. Characteristic of his career is his mode of pairing poems in "two voices." In his many *débats,* the two voices are masks or extreme projections of Tennyson, neither of which are Tennyson in the flesh. We are induced to contemplate the extreme poles and the drama of their near, but never final, resolution. In the pendant portraits or monologues, Tennyson plays one character type against another: the sensuous Mariana against the intellectual Isabel, drawn from *Measure for Measure;* the disembodied, uxorious Tithonus against the full-bodied, loveless Ulysses. Wordsworth himself had employed the device in "Expostulation and Reply" and "The Tables Turned," and Paul Sheats's superb remarks on Wordsworth's pendant debates are worth keeping in mind:

---

6. Jerome Hamilton Buckley, *The Victorian Temper: A Study in Literary Culture* (New York: Vintage, 1964 [1951]), 25–26.

7. Quoted in Buckley, *Victorian Temper,* 16.

8. *In Memoriam,* CXXVIII. The text here and throughout is that of *The Poems of Tennyson,* edited by Christopher Ricks (London and Harlow: Longman's, Green and Co., 1969).

To quote these lines ["One impulse from a vernal wood," etc.] as a sober summary of Wordsworth's doctrine of nature is to ignore the fact that the speaker of this poem and its companion piece, *Expostulation and Reply,* is a dramatic character, and that his language is appropriate to the debate, a genre that sanctions hyperbole, ellipsis, and condensation, all tacitly understood as the product of the contest dramatized...Although its form is exaggerated, the point made by "William" is not, then, anti-intellectual. Wordsworth is not seeking to substitute an unthinking and instinctive communion with nature for the life of reason proper to man, but is rather pointing out the proper use of reason. The impulse of this vernal wood will teach us only if we reflect upon its spiritual and cosmo-logical implications.[9]

Not only does this passage also perfectly describe the distancing effect of Tennyson's poetic art, but it also helps make the point that my purpose in this chapter, and perhaps Tennyson's purpose, is not to fight with Word-sworth, but rather with those Sheats is here fighting against: those who read Wordsworth as anti-intellectual. Like the "real" Wordsworth, Tennyson's constant aim was to evoke, in Wordsworth's words, "the universal intellec-tual property in man,—sensations which all men have felt and feel in some degree daily and hourly."[10]

Even so, the overt rhetorical postures of their poems differ. While it might be valid to apply Wordsworth's description of his often-actionless poetry to the even less dramatic poetry of Tennyson—that "the feeling therein devel-oped gives importance to the action and situation, and not the action and situ-ation to the feeling"[11]—still Tennyson labors to make that feeling the object of contemplation rather than an agent of engendering like feeling. "I wandered lonely as a cloud" works at first, as I argued above, by evoking a sympathetic sensation of breathless awe. I say "at first" because by the end of the poem we are led, like the poet, to reflection, a movement anticipated by Wordsworth's

---

9. Sheats, *The Making of Wordsworth's Poetry,* 208-10.

10. "Upon Epitaphs," in *Wordsworth's Literary Criticism,* edited by Nowell C. Smith (London: Henry Frowde, 1905), 121.

11. William Wordsworth, "Preface to *Lyrical Ballads,*" in Wordsworth and Coleridge, *Lyrical Ballads,* 159.

use of the less dramatic and immediate past tense ("wandered," "saw"). But Wordsworth's poem begins upon the note of dramatic, personal effusion: his title, for example, which is only his first line (and it was titleless on first publication) channels us directly into the dramatic moment recounted; and the verbs which perhaps most stay with us are the eternal-present tense of "floats" and the even more dramatic present participles: "fluttering and dancing." Tennyson's "Mariana," by contrast, is lyrical, as Arthur Hallam suggested, "a...palpable transition of the poet into Mariana's feelings." But the poem's poetic epigraph from *Measure for Measure*—"Mariana in the moated grange"—distances us from the drama.[12] The past tense is used throughout. Wordsworth, like Coleridge's Mariner, seizes us by the collar, saying, in effect: this is what happened to me. Tennyson says more playfully, in effect: what if we take Shakespeare's poetic creation and imagine what she might have felt? Wordsworth, having induced sympathetic sensations, leads us to reflect on what such sensations imply; Tennyson forces us to contemplate from a distance from the outset. We experience Mariana's loneliness as object, not subject. A large part of our experience of the poem, furthermore, is our appreciation of Tennyson's poetic *tour de force* in realizing so much from such slight materials: "Mariana in the moated grange."[13] Finally, the difference between the two poets is concisely suggested by comparing the narrative action of the two poems: Wordsworth *wanders*, then lies, Mariana sits. Wordsworth depicts transition, Tennyson static emotional states. This is true except in *Maud* and *In Memoriam*, which, as we shall see, are Tennyson's closest flirtations with the Romantic tradition, but finally his most anti-Romantic poems.

---

12. Arthur Henry Hallam, "Letter to W. B. Donne" (1831), in *Memoir*, 1: 501.

13. This is by and large the terms in which contemporary criticism celebrated the poem. W. J. Fox, on *Chiefly Lyrical*, enthuses: "The whole of this poem, of eighty-four lines, is generated-by the legitimate process of poetical creation, as that process is conducted in a philosophical mind, from a half sentence in Shakespeare. These is no mere amplification; it is all production; and production from that single germ. That must be a rich intellect, in which thoughts thus take root and grow," *Westminster Review* (Jan. 1831), reprinted in *Lord Alfred Tennyson: The Critical Heritage*, edited by John Jump (London and New York: Routledge, 2002 [1967]), 28–29. See Hallam's remarks to the same effect reprinted in the same volume.

And, of course, Mariana is not Tennyson but Mariana. Both poets employed personae in their poetic careers; both struggled with a naive penchant in the reading-public for equating creations with creators. But in the case of Wordsworth, whose poetic "I" more often than not invites at least partial identification, for reasons we have explored, we feel in hindsight that he set thereby his own trap. Tennyson, on the other hand, despite many naive readings to the contrary, rarely spoke in his own voice: his poetic "I" is almost always man-representative, The Poet, or someone else entire. Tennyson's early odes reintroduce neo-classical allegory as a mode of treatment.[14] His later, "Laureate" odes are even less subjective and more public.

Apart from the occasional odes, which deal with contemporary events, Tennyson's subjects—Mariana, Isabel, Tithonus, and Ulysses—and his genres—debate, monologue, and even the ode—are drawn overtly from tradition. The traditions are native or classical, but always bookish—another distancing device. Wordsworth's overt claim is often, as we have seen, to being traditionless, or participating in the more "primitive" source of oral tradition, as in *Michael*:

> this Tale, while I was yet a Boy
> Careless of books, yet having felt the power
> Of Nature, by the gentle agency
> Of natural objects, led me on to feel
> For passions that were not my own, and think
> (At random and imperfectly indeed)
> On man, the heart of man, and human life.
> Therefore, although it be a history
> Homely and rude, I will relate the same
> For the delight of a few natural hearts;
> And, with yet fonder feeling, for the sake
> Of youthful Poets, who among these hills
> Will be my second self when I am gone.[15]

---

14. As Andrew Fichter writes, his odes are "a challenge to the aesthetics of the ode by allowing moral and political argument to displace lyricism," in "Ode and Elegy: Idea and Form in Tennyson's Early Poetry," *English Literature History* 40, no. 3 (Autumn 1973): 410.

15. William Wordsworth, *Poetical Works*, edited by Ernest De Selincourt, 5 vols. (Oxford: Clarendon Press, 1940-49), 2: 81.

Michael is subtitled "A Pastoral Poem," but the overt claim is that Wordsworth has not had his eye on the Clorises and Daphnes of the pastoral tradition, but on the inhabitants of his native land, who are "natural" counterparts to Clorise and Daphne. Likewise it is addressed to "natural hearts," those unversed in the pastoral tradition. Covertly of course the opposite claim is also meant: we are to note the ways this "pastoral" is more "natural" than its artificial predecessors. Hence to appreciate the poem fully, both artistically and thematically, knowledge of the tradition of pastoral is necessary. We must know, for example, the artificiality of pastoral's claims of artlessness to appreciate the more "natural," offhand way Wordsworth makes the claim: "(At random and imperfectly indeed)." The above lines are themselves, as Pattison remarks, a framing device typical of idyll, but in them "the self is prominent…in a way atypical of idyll. The story of Michael is given as Wordsworth felt it, and so Romantic immediacy is preserved," (though we can now add, "Romantic immediacy" is also subtly broken).[16] In any case, Tennyson's use of the framing device has, as Pattison argues, the more traditional effect of distancing poet from poetic utterance, and audience from poem.[17]

A similar frame begins and ends *In Memoriam,* Tennyson's most confessional poem, as Eliot has described it, "the concentrated diary of a man confessing himself."[18] The most Romantic of his poems, it is also his most anti-Romantic, and the ways in which it mirrors Romanticism's dual "creeds" of spontaneity and naturalness sum up the several distancing devices I have been describing.

---

16. Pattison, *Tennyson and Tradition,* 37.

17. Pattison writes: "The framing device, which reminds the reader of the artificiality of the situation, vitiates any emotional immediacy that might be conveyed by the central poetic material. But even as emotional involvement is curbed by the distance created by the poet, aesthetic reflection is encouraged, and the reader is invited to see the poetry from a vantage point beyond feeling—a vantage point purged of ephemeral emotionality that will allow him to discern the true shape or form of the poem and its subject" (ibid., 19).

18. "In Memoriam," in Eliot, *Selected Essays,* 334.

2. In Memoriam *as Counter-Improvisation*

We can better appreciate how the rhetoric of craft operates in *In Memoriam* by considering for a moment all the good reasons for such rhetoric not to have obtruded in the poem at all. A diary-like series of elegiac lyrics, concerned like most elegies more with the poet's subjective feelings than with the objective loss of Hallam, and, unlike previous elegies, concerned with the flux and change of feelings over time, *In Memoriam* finally affirms a religious faith based on intuition. The intuition is gleaned from mystical experience in a pastoral setting (lyric XCV). Thus, in its fragmentedness; its subjective interest; its implicit and explicit claims of the insufficiency of traditional forms, and by contrast its own innovativeness; and in its themes of pastoral, flux, and intuition, *In Memoriam* is an improvisation *in potentia*. These qualities lead to and support the received reading of the poem that it is "a poem in process, not of product," "virtually formless," and comparable in theme and method to Wordsworth's *Prelude* and to Coleridge's *Aids to Reflection*.[19] Unsystematic but not unmethodical, it is an attack on rationalistic system-mongering—like all improvisations.[20]

Such a reading accounts for much of our experience of In Memoriam, but Robert Pattison has, I think accounted for more when he writes as follows:

> *In Memoriam* (1850) is in many ways a master feat of legerdemain. It purports to be—and it is—a poet's disjointed confession of faith when confronted by the death of his dearest friend; yet it is also Tennyson's most highly structured and formally innovative poem up to 1850. Since its publication, biographers and critics have rightly claimed, as Tennyson himself said, that it is his own personal statement of grief and hope following the death of Hallam; yet in many aspects, *In Memoriam* is as cool and dispassionate a performance in verse as any of Tennyson's earlier dramatic monologues on classical subjects. It pretends to have—and in fact has—the spontaneity of the penitent's cry as he gropes toward faith;

---

19. A. Dwight Culler, *The Poetry of Tennyson* (New Haven: Yale University Press, 1977), 159; Jerome Hamilton Buckley, *Tennyson: The Growth of the Poet* (Cambridge, Mass.: Harvard University Press, 1960), 112, 108; Culler, *The Poetry of Tennyson*, 156–57.

20. See Culler, *The Poetry of Tennyson*, 158–59.

yet it is just as surely one of the most calculating...poems in the English language. *In Memoriam* makes an attempt to combine the immediacy of the lyric with the playful artifice of the idyll, ... in *In Memoriam* the two are wholly synthesized.[21]

Thus what is remarkable about *In Memoriam*—potentially so radical an essay in improvisation—is the extent to which it is counter-improvisation, calling in question the conventions and the themes of the form. Tempted long to entitle his poem "Fragments of an Elegy," or "The Way of the Soul," Tennyson finally settled on this more stately, object-oriented, and "monumental" title: *In Memoriam A. H. H. obiit MDCCCXXXIII.*[22] And though it will deal with the poet's changing feelings, from grief to hopefulness, from doubt to affirmation of faith—indeed will even deal with the problem that change seems to betray the sincerity of his grief—Tennyson chooses to introduce his fluxional lyrics with the "Prologue," which sums up the imagic and thematic patterns of the whole, and ensures the reader that the "wild and wandering cries" that follow will result in regained faith, hope, and, not least of all, in the stately poetic control with which the "Prologue" itself was written:

> Strong Son of God, immortal Love,
> Whom we, that have not seen thy face,
> By faith, and faith alone, embrace,
> Believing where we cannot prove.[23]

In Memoriam wins this faith in the course of its protracted progress; but as here expressed it is a faith as old as the Psalms, the Gospel of John, Paul's epistles, or Augustine's *Confessions.*[24] A true, i.e., a radical improvisation, furthermore—which claims to win its truths by unmediated experience and forces the reader to share the experience stage by stage, processes which *In Memoriam* in part embodies—would not offer its results in an overarching view from the beginning. Whitman, whose respect for Tennyson comes as something of a surprise, well exemplifies this more radical poetic structure in

---

21. Pattison, *Tennyson and Tradition,* 103.

22. *Memoir,* 1: 393 n.

23. *In Memoriam,* "Prologue."

24. See Ricks's notes in *The Poems of Tennyson,* 862-64.

the almost contemporary "Crossing Brooklyn Ferry."[25] Near the close Whitman writes:

> We understand then do we not?
> What I promised without mentioning it, have you not accepted?
> What the study could not teach—what the preaching could not
>   accomplish is accomplished, is it not?[26]

Whitman here suggests that the argument and moral upon which his poem turns—the problem, not unlike that of *In Memoriam,* of achieving unity with past, present, and future generations—has until this moment been unarticulated. Inarticulate, indirect, the poet forces the reader to create the poem he reads, finding the theme which, once found, unites him with the poet—thus satisfying the pivotal problem of the poem, of uniting poet with his audience, of seeing "face to face."[27] Again, Tennyson is more traditional in the truths he offers. Where Tennyson's "Prologue" could be a translation from John, Whitman's opening lines heretically swerve from the First Epistle to the Corinthians: for Paul we "see now through a glass, darkly; but then [after the apocalypse] face to face;" but for the vatic Whitman "I see you face to face" in the immediate present tense of the poem. Tennyson throws us back upon tradition and well-tested truths that his experience has confirmed; Whitman and his readers find new truths, or at least as new as the apocalypse-and heresy-inclined Romantic movement. Writing a poem about doubt and the process of doubting, Tennyson assures our doubts from the outset. This is not to criticize Tennyson, but to realize that his poem is as much about faith as it is about doubt—though the skeptical modern imagination would pre-

---

25. Walt Whitman, "A Word about Tennyson," in *The Collected Prose,* vol. 2 of *The Works of Walt Whitman: The Deathbed Edition,* edited by Malcolm Cowley (New York: Minerva Press, 1968 [1948]), 417-19.

26. Walt Whitman, *Leaves of Grass: Comprehensive Reader's Edition,* edited by H.W. Blodgett and Sculley Bradley (New York: W.W. Norton, 1965), 164.

27. Walt Whitman, "Crossing Brooklyn Ferry," in *The Norton Anthology of American Literature,* edited by Nina Baym and Robert S. Levine, shorter 8th ed. (New York and London: W.W. Norton, 1998), 1069.

fer it otherwise.[28] *In Memoriam* offers to its audience not only a process but a product: faith.

In his quest for fellowship with his audience, Whitman's poetic "I" is everyone who ever crosses the Brooklyn Ferry. But the "I" is first and last Whitman himself because what binds them, we learn, is the experience of the sensuous world. His own bodily "eye" and in turn the "eyes" of past, present, and future generations do the experiencing. Whitman's "I" is a persona if the modern critics insist; but he at least, for these good reasons, insists to the contrary. Whitman's "I" becomes representative and universal without passing through a mask. Tennyson does otherwise. Also wanting to speak as representative man, he insists that "'I' is not always the author speaking of himself, but the voice of the human race "speaking thro' him," and that "It must be remembered this is a poem, not an actual biography."[29] Publishing In Memoriam anonymously was historically somewhat farcical, for everyone knew its author. But as Pattison remarks, "It makes more sense to treat the poem's supposed anonymity as one of its conceits: it is a poem that could be anyone's, addressed to the public at large, like classical elegiac."[30] Tennyson's "I" is a persona from its moment of publication.

Thematically this distance between poet and persona, audience and poem, is important because as Buckley has written, "Whatever the disorder of its original composition, *In Memoriam*…is meant to escape the error of wildness, delirium, and mere subjective rhapsody."[31] Pattison has studied at length the attack on lyric that is an important undercurrent of the poem.[32] As in *Maud,* Tennyson's next major publication, we are invited to watch the spectacle of wild rhapsody, even madness, rather than participate in it. The latter poem was taken by many of its contemporaries as a celebration of the irrational; it was criticized for being in the ultra-Romantic tradition of the

---

28. T.S. Eliot, for example, writes: "It is not religious because of the quality of its faith, but because of the quality of its doubt. Its faith is a poor thing, but doubt is a very intense experience," "In Memoriam," 336.

29. *Memoir,* 1: 304-5.

30. Pattison, *Tennyson and Tradition,* 109.

31. Buckley, *Tennyson,* 119.

32. Pattison, *Tennyson and Tradition,* 111-12, 120-24.

Spasmodics (whose name, though it was given them by unfriendly critics, suggests how extreme was their commitment to spontaneity).[33] More recent criticism, however, has demonstrated the extent to which Maud is a rebuttal of Spasmodic premises along the lines of the assumptions of the "anti-Romantic" school. In the end, Maud's lover gives up his hysterical subjectivity to embrace the program of Carlyle, Newman, and Arnold: objectivity, intellectual discipline, and social commitment. In *In Memoriam,* perhaps more successfully, Tennyson mediates our experience of wild rhapsody by the foreknowledge that all will turn out well—healthy, hopeful, and wise—in the end. Most important: although the sources of wisdom are in part intuitive and extra-rational, wisdom is conceived in rational terms. Wisdom, though based on experience, is grounded in tradition.

Generically, Whitman's "Crossing Brooklyn Ferry" is perhaps his rendition of Coleridge's meditative "Lime Tree Bower My Prison" or Wordsworth's "Tintern Abbey": all are finally about the poet's attempt to bind himself to "the still sad music of humanity." But in Whitman's poem it is for the reader to make such connections to the Romantic tradition; our reading, though enriched, does not depend on our making the connections. In the precursor poems, likewise, it is for the reader to discover the traditions—odic, meditative—from which the poets are working and, to which they, in effect, bind themselves. Tennyson's allusiveness to poetic tradition, by contrast, is more explicit and has the same distancing and validating effects I have been describing. Wordsworth's "Lines: written a few miles above Tintern Abbey...," as we have seen, is either elegy or ode, we know not which. Tennyson's In Memoriam is elegy. Even so, Tennyson's poem exploits, as Pattison and others have shown, a large range of generic traditions besides elegy: lyric, amatory song, threnody, pastoral, epithalamium, epic.[34] As in most improvisations, *In Memoriam* expresses discontent with the "artificial" conventions of the genres even as it satisfies and exploits them. But the degree to which

---

33. On the Spasmodics, see Buckley's excellent essay, "The Spasmodic School," in *Victorian Temper,* 41-65.

34. See Pattison, *Tennyson and Tradition,* 103-27; *The Poetry of Tennyson,* 149-89; Buckley, *Tennyson,* 107-28; and E. D. H. Johnson, "In Memoriam: The Way of the Poet," *Victorian Studies* 2, no. 2 (December 1958): 139-48.

Tennyson satisfies the conventions of his genres is extreme. Even his verse form, which Tennyson claims to have invented, is in fact but his rendition of classical elegiac: dactylic hexameter becomes tetrameter quatrains under his hand.[35] Whether or not Tennyson was familiar with the seventeenth century poet who, we now know, first produced the quatrain is less important than the fact that his "invention" is a "renovation" of a long-established tradition. As Pattison writes, *In Memoriam* "avoids falling into the opposite [i.e. Romantic] camp of rebellion against the [elegiac] form...because it is propped up by the elegiac stanza. *In Memoriam* finally manages what Tennyson had wanted all along: it is completely traditional and completely original at the same time."[36] Our experience of the poem thus hinges in part upon our perception of the traditionally apt nature of the utterance. The formal objective of *In Memoriam*, "to evolve a new form that sacrifices nothing of the past," coincides, as Pattison argues, "to perfection with the poem's theme, which is the preservation of the dead beloved, entire and intact, in the flux of time."[37] Our experience of Tennyson's manipulation of generic conventions is intimate with and essential to our experience of his master theme.

Tennyson's treatment in *In Memoriam* of the pastoral tradition—that genre which proceeds from the notion of a static, eternal Golden Age—is of special interest here. The poem's relation to the pastoral-elegiac tradition is a complex one. Tennyson follows the conventional patterns of the pastoral elegy, calls them into question, and finally reaffirms them. For example, he follows implicitly the seasonal pattern established by Theocritus and Bion, and employed by Milton and Shelley. Yet, reflexively, the poem brings forward the scientific findings, unknown to the Romantics, let alone Theocritus, that argue against the traditional consolation offered by seasonal renewal, and against the simplistic vision of natural benevolence and harmony. Nature, he sees, is not cyclic but evolutionary, "careful of the type" but "careless of the single life" (LV). Nature is "red in tooth and claw" (LVI). Pastoral is rejected. Nevertheless, the gentle, pastoral setting of XCV is intimately

---

35. See Pattison's brilliant discussion of Tennyson's careful transformation of elegiac meters, *Tennyson and Tradition*, 103-8.

36. Ibid., 109.

37. Ibid., 115.

connected with the super-sensual, mystical trance that brings the poet union with the beloved, and consolation. Who is to say whether the agent of that trance was nature or something beyond nature? This complex treatment of pastoral conventions is comparable to Arnold's manner in "Thyrsis" or even to Wordsworth's in "Michael." Romantic and post-Romantic treatments of pastoral work by sloughing off whatever the modern mind cannot accept in a convention, personalizing the "essential" emotions that remain. Attacking the artificial convention, such treatments seek to uncover and realize the universality of the natural emotion that, they suppose, first generated the convention. Shorn of its artificiality, the tradition is restored. But the result is that *In Memoriam* affirms not the "natural" quietude of pastoral, but rather a quiescence and harmony achieved through the act of grieving and the activity of art. As such it is akin to the reading of "Tintern Abbey" offered in these pages. Nonetheless it was perhaps meant as an answer to the received reading of Wordsworth.

Wordsworth invited a radical reading of his "pastoral covenant" in such optative passages as the following, part of which I have quoted before:

> Paradise, and groves
> Elysian, Fortunate Fields—like those of old
> Sought in the Atlantic Main—why should they be
> A history of departed things,
> Or a mere fiction of what never was?
> For the discerning intellect of Man,
> When wedded to this goodly universe
> In love and holy passion, shall find these
> A simple produce of the common day.[38]

Following Virgil's Fourth Eclogue, Wordsworth conflates the pastoral idea of the *locus amoenus* with the apocalyptic Golden Age. As an emotional appeal Wordsworth's rhetoric has validity; his language stresses the *effort* involved in this apocalyptic marriage of man and nature: "discerning intellect" "wedded" (which like the verb "behold" is in Wordsworth's corpus a sentient act). Nevertheless such language conflicts with the suggestion of "natural" inevitabil-

---

38. "Prospectus" to *The Excursion,* in William Wordsworth, *Poetical Works,* 5: 4, lines 47–55.

ity and of passivity in the last lines: "shall find these / A simple produce of the common day"—though "produce" (as opposed to the more likely word choice, "product") again stresses the *activity* and *effort* involved. In any case, whatever our subtle reading, Wordsworth's hope for a marriage between nature and man is susceptible to the simpler reading that it usually got: for many, its message was the primitivist dictum, "Follow nature." Tennyson's treatment of the pastoral tradition in the *Idylls of the King* is less even-handed than in *In Memoriam* and in part reflects an attempt to rebut this "simplesse" in Wordsworth's pastoral vision.

3. *Pastoralism and the Attack on Naturalism in Tennyson's* Idylls of the King

In the *Idylls of the King* Tennyson agrees with Arnold's caveat—"Ah, what pitfalls are in that word *Nature!*"[39]—and with John Stuart Mill's even more pointed dictum that "the ways of Nature are to be conquered, not obeyed."[40] Like Arnold's discursive sonnet "In Harmony with Nature" and Mill's Essay on Nature, the *Idylls* attack philosophical naturalism, "the doctrine that man ought to follow nature."[41] In his attack, Tennyson adopts an antipastoral strategy: the subtle subversion of pastoral conventions to illuminate pastoral's false idealism, hollow sentimentality, and vicious passivity. The *Idylls* have justly been called "the subtlest anatomy of the failure of ideality in our literature."[42] Tennyson's ironic treatment of the pastoral genre is one of the

---

39. *Literature and Dogma*, in *The Complete Prose Works of Matthew Arnold*, vol. 6: *Dissent and Dogma*, edited by R.H. Super (Ann Arbor: University of Michigan Press, 1968), 389.

40. Mill, "Three Essays on Religion: Nature," 381.

41. Ibid., 401. Although published posthumously in 1874, Mill's "Essay on Nature" was written between the years 1850 and 1858, and thus coincides with the dates of the early *Idylls*. "Naturalism," a protean word, will be employed here only in the philosophical sense articulated by Mill and should not be confused with "naturalism" as employed by the followers of Zola.

42. John D. Rosenberg, *The Fall of Camelot: A Study of Tennyson's* Idylls of the King (Cambridge, Mass.: Harvard University Press, 1973), 11. Rosenberg treats Tennyson's antinaturalism at length and argues that the poem has a strong element of generic parody, especially parody of romance and pastoral (104ff.). Among other critics who have considered either the theme of naturalism or the pastoral method are Clyde de

subtlest strokes in that anatomy, and a close examination of it enables us more fully to understand his thematic treatment of philosophical naturalism. Although I will not argue here that pastoral conventions dominate Tennyson's Idylls, even the title suggests how central and important "pastoral" is to his purpose, and illustrates his manipulation of generic conventions and associations. Since Gladstone's early review, Tennyson's choice of *"Idylls"* has vexed critics trying to decipher his generic intentions. Following Gladstone, Buckley argues for an etymological interpretation. Derived from the Greek for "picture," "Idylls" was meant "to designate not a single unified narrative but a group of chivalric tableaux." Buckley is surely right that "Tennyson was far too familiar with the traditional genres ever to confuse the idyl and the epic."[43] Even so, "idyll" implies more than an allusion to the non-epic nar-

---

L. Ryals, who sees an important relationship between the *Idylls* and the Theocritan pastoral tradition, in *From the Great Deep: Essays on* Idylls of the King (Athens, Ohio: Ohio University Press, 1967); J. Philip Eggers, who traces the "pattern of nature images [by means of which] Tennyson cautioned against the many errors that arise from naturalism" and who suggests in passing that "the landscape of the Idylls [is] a deceptively pastoral ambience," in *King Arthur's Laureate: A Study of Tennyson's* Idylls of the King (New York: New York University Press, 1971), 194, 204; and Pauline Fletcher, who has surveyed Tennyson's images of the pastoral garden and finds his treatment increasingly anti-Romantic, in "Romantic and Anti-Romantic Gardens in Tennyson and Swinburne," *Studies in Romanticism* 18, no. 1 (Spring 1979): 81–97. She stops short, however, of considering the gardens and other pastoral images in the Idylls. Robert Pattison's *Tennyson and Tradition* deals with Tennyson's manipulation of the idyll tradition and thus bears on the present study; see his discussions of antipastoral method in the *Idylls* (67ff.) and in *In Memoriam* (117–25). In regard to the *Idylls of the King,* although Pattison argues that "the new genre he created out of traditional material makes fun of the old forms" (146), he does not broach Tennyson's ironic treatment of the pastoral form in that poem. General treatments of the pastoral tradition that have influenced this study are William Empson, *Some Versions of Pastoral* (New York: New Directions, 1960); Poggioli, *The Oaten Flute*; Harold E. Toliver, *Pastoral Forms and Attitudes* (Berkeley, Los Angeles, and London: University of California Press, 1971); and Raymond Williams, *The Country and the City* (New York: Oxford University Press, 1973). None of these critics, unfortunately, consider Tennyson in their surveys of pastoral writers.

43. Buckley, *Tennyson,* 172. For Gladstone's remarks, see his unsigned review of the *Idylls* in the *Quarterly Review* 106, no. 212 (October 1859): 454–85; reprinted in *Lord*

rative technique. Despite the slight difference in spelling, "idyll" obviously echoes Tennyson's *Idylls* and with them the Theocritan pastorals on which they are modeled. It is perhaps significant that although the sentiment itself is ancient, the first recorded use of the adjective "idyllic" as meaning "full of natural simple charm or picturesqueness" occurred in 1856.[44] We may miss the obvious generic and thematic associations of the title by attending too closely to its abstruse etymological undertones.

Without intending a wholly pastoral treatment in his poem, Tennyson expected his title to raise certain generic expectations. In a limited sense, his *Idylls* are "idyllic." They are set in the Golden Age of Britain when, compared to Victorian England, men were men and nature was uncluttered by factories and waste—and the need for a Second Reform Bill. However, the title takes on ironic resonance when we realize that in this preindustrial tale men are as likely to reel "back into the beast" as to be simple and natural, and that in it nature is anything but benign.[45]

The title is ironic too in linking the genre of shepherds and swains with a king. But Arthur himself is a pastoral figure, even though he is also king, warrior, city-builder, and civilizer. For one thing, he is pastoral in his simplicity: "His ways are sweet," says Bedivere, the first knighted; and as Arthur says himself, "I, being simple, thought to work His will."[46] Arthur's simplicity pervades the *Idylls,* suggested by his single-mindedness, deliberateness, and directness; and, of course, by his cuckoldry. Furthermore, just as Christian symbolism hovers always in the background of Arthur's char-

---

Alfred Tennyson: The Critical Heritage, 241-66.

44. *OED,* s.v. "idyllic." Pattison is right to attempt to dispel "the notion that idyll and pastoral are necessarily the same. A pastoral may need to be an idyll, but an idyll is definitely not of necessity a pastoral" (*Tennyson and Tradition,* 29). Still, Tennyson could exploit the vulgar notion Pattison is debunking, even while he, as classicist, kept the distinctions between the forms firmly in mind.

45. "The Passing of Arthur," line 26; hereafter lineation will be noted parenthetically using the following abbreviations: "The Coming of Arthur" (*CA*); "Gareth and Lynette" (*GL*); "The Marriage of Geraint" (*MG*); "Geraint and Enid" (*GE*); "Balin and Balan" (*BB*); "Pelleas and Ettarre" (*PE*); "The Last Tournament" (*LT*); "The Passing of Arthur" (*PA*).

46. *CA,* line 179; *PA,* line 22.

acterization, so, too, behind the symbol of Christ the King hovers the symbol of Christ the Good Shepherd.[47] As a pastoral figure, Arthur learns that things are not so simple as they had seemed when first he rang in the Golden Age, that simplicity does not suffice. Both the title of Tennyson's poem and his central character partake of pastoral associations, but they do so only to call into question the pastoral ideals of spontaneity, simplicity, innocence, and the benignity of nature.

Through these and other pastoral associations Tennyson endeavors to make us see the potential hollowness of the yearning for lost natural harmony, heroic innocence, and a perfect but static society.

"The Coming of Arthur" first depicts not a pastoral setting but quite its opposite. Nature here is unreclaimed by man, violent and fearsome:

> And so there grew great tracts of wilderness,
> Wherein the beast was ever more and more,
> But man was less and less, ...
>
> And thus the land of Cameliard was waste,
> Thick with wet woods, and many a beast therein,
> And none or few to scare or chase the beast;
> So that wild dog, and wolf and boar and bear
> Came night and day, and rooted in the fields,
> And wallowed in the gardens of the King.[48]

Tennyson describes this pre-Arthurian world in a pointedly non-pastoral manner: the beasts "rooted in the fields,/And wallowed in the gardens of the King"; "wild dog," "wolf and boar and bear" prevail, not domesticated sheep and kine. In turn, Arthur's coming makes the pastoral setting possible. He

> drave
> The heathen; after, slew the beast, and felled
> The forest, letting in the sun, and made
> Broad pathways for the hunter and the knight.[49]

---

47. Rosenberg, *The Fall of Camelot*, 39.

48. *CA*, lines 10-12, 20-25.

49. *CA*, lines 58-61.

Thus the "romance" and the "pastoral" of Arthur begin. At his marriage the time is May, that month that promises the eternal summertime associated with pastoral. In "The Coming of Arthur" nature seems tractable; but the balance of the *Idylls* portrays the swift reëncroachment of these vicious natural forces: heathen, beast, and forest.

In the next of the *Idylls*, Gareth embodies the springtime hopes of Arthur's youthful and aspiring kingdom. Related to Arthur through his mother Bellicent, Gareth is pointedly like Arthur. His speech is direct; the art of his "folktales" is "artless"—though he uses them as arguments against his mother's restraints. Compared to his brother Gawain, whom we are later to know as the jaded knight of the Round Table, he is all ingenuous naiveté. Compared to the hated Modred, his other brother, he is all innocence. Though no pastoral shepherd by birth, he assumes the garb of a "tiller of the soil." By virtue of his speaking "rough" and "sudden," Arthur dubs him "worthy to be knight."[50] In Arthur's realm, spontaneity, the expression of "natural instincts," is rewarded. Gareth's boon is granted, and he goes in quest of heroism and of love.

"Gareth and Lynette" has been called the "Edenic phase of Camelot."[51] Like the first Eden, moreover, the Camelot of "Gareth and Lynette" contains the seeds of its own fall. Gareth is as innocent as he humanly can be. But in this idyll of innocence an undercurrent of sham and deceit casts doubt on the existence of perfect innocence.

To be sure, Gareth's sham is sham at its least offensive, motivated by maternal and filial love. Speaking of his masquerade, Gareth says:

> Our one white lie sits like a little ghost
> Here on the threshold of our enterprise.
> Let love be blamed for it, not she, nor I:
> Well, we will make amends.[52]

In demanding the masquerade, his mother Bellicent means only to protect her son; in playing it out, Gareth merely expresses devotion. His discomfort

---

50. *GL,* lines 638-39.

51. Rosenberg, *The Fall of Camelot,* 107.

52. *GL,* lines 291-94.

with the deceit further argues for his innocent nature. Yet the question is repeatedly put before us: why is the sham continued? Arthur asks:

> But wherefore would ye men should wonder at you?
> Nay, rather for the sake of me, their King,
> And the deed's sake my knighthood do the deed,
> Than to be noised of.[53]

Arthur's excessively complex syntax suggests his perplexity. He rightly sees that Gareth disguises himself not merely to please his mother, but rather—like Shakespeare's Hal—to aggrandize the honor of his deeds by an element of the unexpected. In the end Arthur lets it pass as a childish ploy not worthy of a king's censure. But this seeing and not acting against an injustice involves the King in the consequences of Gareth's second "white lie": the false pretenses of his relationship with Lynette.

In the world of the *Idylls*, deception, however "innocent," always causes personal pain. If "Gareth and Lynette" were read alone, this undercurrent of deceit would go unnoticed. But Gareth's "little ghost" becomes a specter that haunts the *Idylls*. In "Lancelot and Elaine," Lancelot's assumption of false identity results in a broken heart, an unnecessary injury to Lancelot, and a few lost diamonds. Ultimately, Gareth's "white lie" is comparable to that other "innocent" sham in Arthur's realm, the illicit love of Lancelot and Guinevere. The immediate effect of Gareth's lie is Lynette's pain. She "gloried," she tells Lancelot,

> in my knave,
> Who being still rebuked, would answer still
> Courteous as any knight—but now, if knight,
> The marvel dies, and leaves me fooled and tricked,
> And only wondering wherefore played upon:
> And doubtful whether I and mine be scorned.
> Where should be truth if not in Arthur's hall,
> In Arthur's presence?[54]

Lynette's faith in the character of Arthur and of his realm is shaken. Here is the skepticism that will increasingly plague Arthur. Tennyson's telling psycho-

---

53. *GL*, lines 557-60.
54. *GL*, lines 1217-24.

logical point is that shaken faith turns in upon itself, undermining the individual. She responds "petulantly" that "for worse than being fooled/Of others, is to fool one's self," thus foreshadowing Pelleas's more violent response to disillusionment.[55] Wounds of this kind fester in the course of the Idylls.

Tennyson's fairy tale of innocence and adventure rankles. Deceit reverberates throughout the idyll in the actions of Bellicent, Gareth, Arthur, and Lancelot, and of course in the capping stroke, the deceit of the four horsemen. We are left wondering, however faintly, about the groundwork of Arthur's regency, about the terms of chivalry that demand deeds done both for their own sake and for the sake of honor. At the end we are left with the question, Who is the greater sham: the hollow specter of death who is but "a blooming boy"; or Gareth, the swainlike innocent whose shamming contains the seeds of pain and death?[56] Is he a chip off the same block as his brothers, Gawain and Modred? In sum, Gareth's idyll leaves us with uncomfortable feelings about the ideal of innocence: is it so beneficial? is it possible?

As if in response to the sinister innocence suggested in "Gareth and Lynette," the two Geraint idylls present the first serious stages in the slow decay of Arthur's kingdom. Skepticism now moves the action. In these idylls the natural forces that will eventually overwhelm the kingdom begin to manifest themselves. In "The Marriage of Geraint" the description of Yniol's decrepit castle is ominous:

> Then rode Geraint into the castle court,
> His charger trampling many a prickly star
> Of sprouted thistle on the broken stones.
> He looked and saw that all was ruinous.
> Here stood a shattered archway plumed with fern;
> And here had fallen a great part of a tower,
> Whole, like a crag that tumbles from the cliff,
> And like a crag was gay with wilding flowers:
> And high above a piece of turret stair,
> Worn by the feet that now were silent, wound
> Bare to the sun, and monstrous ivy-stems
> Claspt the gray walls with hairy-fibred arms,

---

55. *GL,* lines 1242–43.

56. *GL,* line 1373.

> And sucked the joining of the stones, and looked
> A knot, beneath, of snakes, aloft, a grove.[57]

The description is a paradigm of Tennyson's use and treatment of nature in the *Idylls*. The malignant natural details ("prickly star / Of sprouted thistle," "monstrous ivy-stems," "hairy-fibred arms" that "sucked the joining of stones, and looked / A knot...of snakes") ironically undermine their seemingly benign aspects: the "shattered archway plumed with fern," the "crag...gay with wilding flowers," and again those "monstrous ivy-stems" that looked "aloft, a grove." Nature, to say the least, has its deceptive beauties. On the other hand, nature's destructive powers are all but explicit. Tennyson's two-part epic simile comparing the fallen tower to a tumbling crag suggests that nature easily razes the artifices of man.

Geraint will weed this garden, his skepticism will be allayed, and Arthur's order will be reaffirmed. In the next idyll, however, Tennyson presents a picture of nature's even more forcefully deceptive beauties. In this case, Tennyson uses overtly pastoral imagery and conventions to make his point.

Choosing to take "To the wilds!"[58] Geraint leads, or follows, Enid through perilous wilderness and waste filled with robbers and bandits. After several such adventures in which nature has the ominous characteristics we have been describing, Geraint and Enid come upon a pastoral-like vignette:

> So through the green gloom of the wood they past,
> And issuing under open heavens beheld
> A little town with towers, upon a rock,
> And close beneath, a meadow gemlike chased
> In the brown wild, and mowers mowing in it:
> And down a rocky pathway from the place
> There came a fair-haired youth, that in his hand
> Bare victual for the mowers: and Geraint
> Had ruth again on Enid looking pale.[59]

Tennyson emphasizes the pictorial qualities of the scene by depicting the woods ("the brown wild") as a frame in which this pastoral glade is set ("gem-

---

57. *MG,* lines 312–25.

58. *GE,* line 28.

59. *GE,* lines 195–203.

like chased").[60] He enacts this framing in the first three lines: we almost see through Geraint and Enid's eyes as they issue from the trees whose branches produce the frame. The halting spondee, "green gloom," and the quickening anapestic effect "of the wood" together present mimetically their stopping at first in awe of the view, then hurrying on all the more quickly because of its allure.[61] Moved by this picture of pastoral grace and harmony, Geraint remembers his love for Enid and requests food for her.

The idyllic scene continues undisturbed as Geraint and Enid partake of the mowers' repast. The mowers are generous and properly observant of degree. They profess obedience to their Earl. The sense of pastoral harmony is so complete that, when they invite Geraint to the Earl's palace, he retorts in kind with a properly pastoral sentiment: "... into no Earl's palace will I go. / I know, God knows, too much of palaces!"[62]

The pastoral bubble is soon burst. The "gracious" Limours, Earl of the mowers, visits them in the humble quarters Geraint has requested and proves to be not only a former suitor to Enid, but a savage one. Called "the wild lord of the place," he characterizes himself in the same manner:

> I call mine own self wild,
> But keep a touch of sweet civility
> Here in the heart of waste and wilderness.[63]

As he seeks to seduce Enid, he argues that his wildness is but a mask, a name; "sweet civility" is his true self. But this is all delusion: his heart *is* "waste and wilderness." His pastoral land similarly is not a sweet haven from wilderness, differentiated from the evils of the world, as the frame has led us to expect. The frame itself, reflecting the pastoral convention of the

---

60. *OED*, s.v. "chase," sb.[2], meaning "to 'set' (a gem, etc.)," cites this line.

61. Compare Wordsworth's more affirmative exploitation of these poetic devices, both image and prosody, in *Peter Bell: A Tale* (lines 356-65). Once in his *locus amoenus*, Peter meets the humble ass that will lead him ultimately to a recognition of nature's benevolence and the need for human kindness. Geraint and Enid's experience in their pastoral glade is, by contrast, thoroughly ironic. On the use of the framing device in idylls, see Pattison, *Tennyson and Tradition*, 19. He does not call attention to any instances of Tennyson's questioning treatment of the idyllic frame.

62. *GE*, lines 235-36.

63. *GE*, lines 277; *GE*, lines 311-13.

faraway place, is part of the deception. As we witness Limours's attempted seduction of Enid we realize that even the "attractive" naïveté of the mower who introduces them into the castle takes on a vicious aspect. As he says, "I myself am his," and he must share in the wild Limours's viciousness.[64] On the other hand, the earl's name echoes the pastoral service of his vassals: Limours, the mowers. The echo is not only phonetic but semantic, for in Old French *li mours* means "turf grounds."[65] In this idyll, naïveté, "sweet civility," and rapacious wildness are all one. Limours deploys pastoral associations as a seductive mask.

In "Geraint and Enid," then, the pastoral genre itself comes under Tennyson's critical glance. We will see this again in "Pelleas and Ettarre," a closely related idyll. As David Shaw points out, Geraint is absurdly skeptical while Pelleas is absurdly credulous, and Tennyson's point is that "doubt and faith are inseparable."[66] In the idylls following "Geraint and Enid," nature becomes harsher and more malevolent until the climactic storm of "Merlin and Vivien." There is no longer time nor place for pastoral respite in these idylls, save perhaps in the gardens.

Gardens are an equivocal setting. They can be the site for either pastoral or romance. Tennyson uses them as a symbol of man's control over nature through artifice, and thus as a symbol of potential redemption of nature's otherwise malignant force. In Tennyson, the pastoral associations (which derive from the Edenic and Garden of Adonis myths) are muted. But it is worth noting that in "Balin and Balan" a garden is the setting for the adulterous scene between Lancelot and Guinevere, which Balin witnesses. Balin is the guilt-ridden knight who idealistically dedicates himself to Guinevere and,

---

64. *GE,* line 227.

65. Frederic Godefroy, *Dictionnaire de l'ancienne langue française* (Paris: F. Vieweg 1888), s.v. "mour" (i.e., "terrain à tourbe"). The earl's name derives from *Mabinogion,* but Tennyson transposes the names of Limours and Doorm. This transposition has been explained by arguing that Tennyson wished to emphasize the echo of "doom" in "Doorm" (on which see *The Poems of Tennyson,* 1558 n.); but here we see that reversing the names had this second attraction.

66. W. David Shaw, "Idylls of the King: A Dialectical Reading," *Victorian Poetry* 7, no. 3 (Autumn 1969): 181.

fighting "hard with himself," strives "to learn the graces of their Table."[67] He is the symbol of potential control, and it is ironic, yet sadly just, that it is in the garden that his models undeceive him. The stormy setting of "Merlin and Vivien," the next idyll, seems almost a logical extrapolation of this adulterous garden. The limits around the ivy-encrusted oak which Vivien creates with her spell parody the garden's man-made walls which keep out invidious natural forces: her magical walls keep them in.

The next idyll in which pastoral conventions play a central role is "Pelleas and Ettarre." Like Gareth and like Balin, Pelleas is an innocent. His naiveté is characterized in a purely pastoral vein as he enters the "hall at old Caerleon":

> the high doors
> Were softly sundered, and through these a youth,
> Pelleas, and the sweet smell of the fields
> Past, and the sunshine came along with him.[68]

The echo here of Arthur's "letting in the sun" conveys the hope of renewal, sadly needed by this time in Arthur's realm. Not only is Pelleas associated with the "sweet smell of the fields" but he speaks with the directness (and the polysyndeton) associated with pastoral figures: "'Make me thy knight, because I know, Sir King,/All that belongs to knighthood, and I love.'"[69] We learn that he is "Sir Pelleas of the isles" and almost wonder if his island is not the golden isles of pastoral or even the Sicily-like isle of Theocritus and Virgil. The flashback of the tale involves an incident right out of pastoral-romance, and repays extensive quotation. Pelleas,

> Riding at noon, a day or twain before,
> Across the forest called of Dean, to find
> Caerleon and the King, had felt the sun
> Beat like a strong knight on his helm, and reeled
> Almost to falling from his horse; but saw
> Near him a mound of even-sloping side,
> Whereon a hundred stately beeches grew,
> And here and there great hollies under them;

---

67. *BB*, lines 233–34.

68. *PE*, lines 3–6.

69. *PE*, lines, 7–8.

But for a mile all round was open space,
And fern and heath: and slowly Pelleas drew
To that dim day, then binding his good horse
To a tree, cast himself down; and as he lay
At random looking over the brown earth
Through that green-glooming twilight of the grove,
It seemed to Pelleas that the fern without
Burnt as a living fire of emeralds,
So that his eyes were dazzled looking at it.
Then o'er it crost the dimness of a cloud
Floating, and once the shadow of a bird
Flying, and then a fawn; and his eyes closed.
And since he loved all maidens, but no maid
In special, half-awake he whispered, "Where?
O where? I love thee, though I know thee not.
For fair thou are and pure as Guinevere,
And I will make thee with my spear and sword
As famous—O my Queen, my Guinevere,
For I will be thine Arthur when we meet."

    Suddenly wakened with a sound of talk
And laughter at the limit of the wood,
And glancing through the hoary boles, he saw,
Strange as to some old prophet might have seemed
A vision hovering on a sea of fire,
Damsels in divers colours like the cloud
Of sunset and sunrise, and all of them
On horses, and the horses richly trapt
Breast-high in that bright line of bracken stood:
And all the damsels talked confusedly,
And one was pointing this way, and one that,
Because the way was lost.[70]

Tennyson emphasizes the paradisiac splendor and uniqueness of the place:
the beeches are "stately"; the cloud, bird, and fawn seem to float in a timeless moment; finally, the dazzling vision creates an aura around the brightly
appareled host of damsels. Pelleas's "glancing through the hoary boles" recre-

---

70. *PE,* lines 19-57.

ates the framing device that we noted above in "Geraint and Enid." The whole episode is set off in a special time and space. Evoking the topos of the *locus amoenus,* it recalls the processional dream-visions of the pastoral-romance tradition. As Rosenberg notes, Pelleas "enters a grove which appears to be the archetype of a pastoral paradise and the antithesis of the dark wood through which he later flees."[71] But it is not just a matter of contrast: what will happen in the dark wood results inevitably from what happens in this delusively happy grove.

As Renato Poggioli writes, "The topos itself is but an idyllic prelude to a bucolic interlude, where the characters rest from their adventures or passions."[72] In Pelleas's case, however, his experience in this "happy place" is a dark interlude at best, the source of his passions rather than a rest from them. Calidore's experience on the "spacious Plaine" beneath Mount Acidale in the "Pastorella Cantos" of *The Faerie Queene* acutely points Tennyson's expressive divergences from the conventions of pastoral dream-vision.[73] Calidore witnesses concentric circles of naked nymphs, the three Graces, and a maiden named Love, all dancing harmoniously. From this vision and Colin Clout's interpretation, he learns his final lesson in courtesy. Spenser's "spacious Plaine" is truly paradisal: splendid, unique, timeless, and intrinsic to the visionary lesson Calidore learns. Before *his* vision, by contrast, Pelleas is stunned by the sun, then blinded by the dazzling "living fire" of ferns. Nature's beauty here more actively deceives than in "Geraint and Enid." Such beauty and the conventions of pastoral-romance lead Pelleas to expect a vision of beatific harmony. Pelleas sees beauty, "A vision hovering on a sea of fire"; but what is really there to see is a reverse image of pastoral grace: damsels "in divers colours" who talk "confusedly," stand amidst harsh bracken, and point in contradictory directions. At their center is Ettarre, the self-centered and uncivil woman with whom Pelleas falls in love, tainted by the skepticism of

---

71. Rosenberg, *The Fall of Camelot,* 70.

72. Poggioli, *The Oaten Flute,* 9.

73. See *The Faerie Queene,* Book VI, canto X. I suggest Spenser as an analogue rather than as a source. Ricks (*The Poems of Tennyson,* 1689n.) suggests the medieval lay Sir Orfeo as a source, yet in that poem it is Heurodis, not Orfeo, who "sleeps under the trees, and then meets knights and ladies on fine horses."

the court. His staccato response to this vision again emphasizes his stunned state of mind:

> "O happy world," thought Pelleas, "all, meseems,
> Are happy; I the happiest of them all."
> Nor slept that night for pleasure in his blood,
> And green wood-ways, and eyes among the leaves.[74]

This eerie last line, which seems to emanate from Pelleas's own duped consciousness, underscores both the active role nature has played in his delusion and the extent to which it is self-delusion: "eyes among the leaves" returns us to the pastoral frame through which Pelleas sees the world. Tennyson plays upon pastoral echoes again and again in the idyll until we realize that pastoral conventions and expectations actively participate in the downfall of Pelleas's sunny idealism like romance conventions do in *Madame Bovary*.

The pastoral genre itself mediates between Pelleas and Ettarre, preventing their liaison. On the one hand, Ettarre sees him as a walking caricature from an overused genre: "Raw, yet so stale."[75] To Ettarre, Pelleas is a "noble savage" like Spenser's Salvage Man: "O wild and of the woods, / Knowest thou not the fashion of our speech?"[76] On the other hand, Pelleas labors under what we might call "pastoralism," the expectation that all will turn out as the pastoral genre leads us to believe.[77] Having read too many pastoral romances, and enchanted by his *locus amoenus*, Pelleas expresses love for love, not for a specified object. Ettarre is doomed to be that object by her chance appearance; we can sympathize with her impatience when she speaks of his "fulsome innocence."[78]

Pelleas's downfall proceeds not from his innocence per se, but rather from his rigorous attachment to extremes of innocence and idealism. Ettarre finally realizes that she spurned him not only because of the skepticism she

---

74. *PE,* lines 129–32.

75. *PE,* line 109.

76. *PE,* lines 95–96.

77. The best examination of this process of generic imitation is by René Girard in *Deceit, Desire, and the Novel: Self and Other in Literary Structure,* translated by Yvonne Freccero (Baltimore and London: The Johns Hopkins Press, 1976 [1966]).

78. *PE,* line 258.

had imbibed in Arthur's court, but because of Pelleas's extremeness, his offering no common ground to nurture mutual love:

> Why have I pushed him from me? this man loves,
> If love there be: yet him I loved not. Why?
> I deemed him fool? yea, so? or that in him
> A something—was it nobler than myself?—
> Seemed my reproach? He is not of my kind.[79]

Here Ettarre accepts Pelleas's pastoral innocence ("fool? yea, so?") but rejects herself for not measuring up to his idealized "kind"—as if they were not both human! Once Pelleas's pastoral ideals are exploded, he too must overreact. The cynical lesson he draws from seeing Gawain's betrayal is self-reproachful and reductive: "I never loved her, I but lusted for her."[80] Turning against himself and against Arthur's order, the model for his original ideals, Pelleas denounces the specious pastoralism of the entire court:

> O noble vows!
> O great and sane and simple race of brutes
> That own no lust because they have no law![81]

This Thersites-like anger turns the pastoral and Wordsworthian ideal of instinctual health on its head: the knights are not a "great and sane and simple race," as he feels they (and he) pretend to be, but a "simple race of brutes." In the next line Pelleas's verbal ambiguity is a double-edged sword that he sinks into the heart of the pastoral ideal of harmony achieved without the force of law: the knights "own," i.e., acknowledge, but also possess "no lust because they have no law": i.e., are above the law because they follow the Arthurian code; but also, they are simply lawless. Lust is for them unacknowledged by law, hence no crime. This interpretation of the Arthurian code as cynically cavalier is borne out in fact by Gawain's response when Pelleas mentions his courtly byname, "light-of-love": "Ay,...for women be so light."[82] Tennyson's treatment of setting and of pastoral conventions stresses however that Pelleas's problems stem not so much from the failure of the court, or of Arthur,

---

79. *PE,* lines 299–303.
80. *PE,* line 475.
81. *PE,* lines 470–72.
82. *PE,* lines 353–54.

as from his own passive response—mediated by generic expectations—to the Arthurian ideal. The dark night into which Pelleas plunges was for Tennyson the ineluctable result of his "pastoralism."

In the following idyll Tristram, the woodsman, personifies the next step beyond this pastoralism: naturalism. Pastoralism in "Pelleas and Ettarre" represents the primitivist impulse implicit in naturalism: the discontent with civilization that springs from the belief that a former, simpler day was better. In the earlier idyll we witness the disastrous effects of mimicking pastoral "simplesse." To this, Tristram adds in "The Last Tournament" the argument in favor of acting upon natural instincts.

A pastoral cast to details of setting and character slowly heightens in the *Idylls* in proportion to the growth of threats to Arthur's order. These threats are the forces of nature, the skepticism of his knights, and the philosophy of naturalism of Tristram and of Arthur's enemies. The effect is ironic: as nature becomes harsher and as skepticism and naturalism burst into rampancy, the pastoral vision of nature and man obtrudes with greater insistence. It enters the *Idylls* only to be at first subtly, then violently subverted. This process begins in "Gareth and Lynette" when, as we have seen, Tennyson questions the ideal of perfect innocence. It continues in the sweet-wild ambiguities of the description of the castle in "The Marriage of Geraint." In "Geraint and Enid," the pastoral genre itself is the ironic focus. In "Balin and Balan" and in "Merlin and Vivien," the settings are negative pastorals. Finally, in "Pelleas and Ettarre," the subversion of pastoral culminates in the bitter defeat of Pelleas's sunny innocence and idealism. Pelleas's vision in the woods, so negative in its effects, follows from his "pastoralism." With Pelleas's idealism shattered, Camelot falls into the pit of naturalism.

The "pastoral sentiments" treated in the *Idylls* are wrong because they purvey a false vision of nature and of human nature. Nature and man are not harmoniously bound, at least not without man's effort. By treating this, a crucial problem in pastoral and in philosophical naturalism, Tennyson achieves his object of writing a long poem on a subject of contemporary importance while avoiding mere topicality.

From as early as 1833, when he wrote the "Morte d'Arthur," Tennyson thought of his "Epic of King Arthur" as "the chief work of his manhood." In the *Idylls* Tennyson keeps a tight rein on his fascination for "far, far away," on his "passion for the past," and on his love of nature. It is a work of personal maturity. He never lets us forget that, while we may indulge these passions— and the *Idylls* certainly do—nevertheless such passions create as many problems as they solve. He suggests the necessity of the quest for beauty, the perfect, and the ideal; but he stresses the errors that will ensue if those pursuits are simplistically conceived. He creates a world where deceit always ensnares itself in its own web, not because of the hollow illusion that the truth will out, but because, needing ideals like truth, we can approximate them only by rigorous effort. Likewise we can love nature only by helping it to evolve upward. This was the Laureate's program for Victorian England: rigorous but benevolent effort. It is an imperial program, and Tennyson shared it with Carlyle, Mill, and Arnold, with the best thinkers of his age.

CHAPTER TWELVE

"Free and Easy"?:
The Politics of Spontaneity
in the Adventures of Huckleberry Finn

1. Spontaneity and the Novel Tradition

The novel tradition, like the lyric, is shot through with the rhetoric of spontaneity. Rooted in the narratives of Menippean satire and in their heir, the carnivalesque narratives of Rabelais, the novel like other improvisations denies those generic roots. The novel by definition is innovative, not only in name, but in its overt departure from traditional *mythos*.[1] The nineteenth century novel "perfects" the formal devices of eighteenth century realism, which, according to Ian Watt, produce an aura of "immediacy and closeness" through "exhaustive presentation."[2] Lovingly detailing the minutiae of common life—Henry James's "direct impression of life"[3]—the spiritual heir of Wordsworth and of Emerson, the nineteenth century novel enforces our eternal yea and our sympathy for all of life. It seeks, in Pater's words on Wordsworth, "to open out the soul of apparently little or familiar things."[4] This heritage has roots in the Rabelaisian grotesque's embrace of lower bodily functions and in improvisation's love of life's cornucopian diversity.

Thomas Carlyle's foolish narrator in *Sartor Resartus* relates the biography of another fool, Teufelsdröckh, whose name means "devil's dung" and whose life, as yet unfinished, comes to the biographer (and to us) in fragment-

---

1. Ian Watt, *The Rise of the Novel: Studies in Defoe, Richardson and Fielding* (Berkeley and Los Angeles: University of California Press, 2001 [1957]), 13-15.

2. Ibid., 29, 30.

3. "The Art of Fiction," in *The Art of Criticism: Henry James on the Theory and the Practice of Fiction,* edited by William Veeder and Susan M. Griffin (Chicago and London: The University of Chicago Press, 1986), 198.

4. Walter Pater, *Appreciations, with an Essay on Style* (London: Macmillan, 1895), 49.

stuffed paper bags (and chapters)—like Burton's "confused company of notes." The narrator of *Wuthering Heights* is an all too urbane sophisticate who gets his story from an all too urbane servant. Their tale is one of the heights and the heart: of the spontaneous, primitive impulses of a Heathcliff and a Catherine who the sophisticated mind will never understand or adequately appreciate. Dickens's *Pickwick Papers* is related by a Swiftean hack who gets lost in his exploding periods. His subject is the encyclopedic wanderings of the naïf encyclopedist, Pickwick, who travels bodily throughout England, and, psychologically, all the way from innocence through experience to a higher innocence.

The twofold critical problem such "spontaneous" texts present is suggested, inadvertently, by this passage from Garrett Stewart's fine book on Dickens:

> Dickens's precocious masterpiece, *The Posthumous Papers of the Pickwick Club,* is like no other novel. Its vision of innocence aside, it is in another way one of the purest books of literature, pure because nothing has been refined or filtered off, pure precisely because nothing has been purified away. It is the essential, the instinctive Dickens, unhindered, eager, yet somehow miraculously mastered. By being in a sense all rough edges, it appears to have none. It is, at its finest times, full of those things Dickens does best and is to do better and better with the increase of his genius, but which he will never again do so freely. And the freedom of *Pickwick Papers* is not abandon, but discovery. It seems a freedom that has no second thoughts, that trumpets its own unimportance, yet when they come, its significances can leave us gasping.[5]

Having traced the rhetoric of spontaneity from antiquity, I should not need here to refute at length Stewart's rhetoric of uniqueness. Not only is *Pickwick Papers* like other novels in its affectation of immediacy, unmediatedness, and innovation; it also shares these qualities with other non-novel texts considered in these pages. The first critical problem, then, is that a form's claim of innovation sets the form in a tradition. Great works of art are by definition *sui generis*; in that regard Stewart's breathless appreciation is accurate.

---

5. Garrett Stewart, *Dickens and the Trials of Imagination* (Cambridge, Mass: Harvard University Press, 1974), 3.

Still, in attempting to understand how they work we must put behind us the critical tendency to privilege our favorite texts as "without precedent."

The balance of Stewart's quotation presents the second and harder critical problem. Stewart's terms—"purity," "unrefined," "essential," "instinctive," "unhindered," "eager," "rough edges," "freedom," "abandon," "no second thoughts,"—suggest that an untempered, instinctual responsiveness is the positive moral norm and standard of the novel. And yet these norms conflict with Stewart's own cogent interpretation of the novel, that Pickwick undergoes a purification by experience that leads him from his initial innocence to a higher innocence. Stewart celebrates Dickens's taking "no second thoughts" and in almost the same breath celebrates Pickwick's new-found ability to take "second thoughts." The same critical problem exists in Carlyle, where critics often fail to note the tension between the eternal yea said to intuitive experience at the center of *Sartor Resartus*, and the work ethic which crowns Diogenes Teufelsdröckh's narrative. And why is it that, while we may as moderns feel that the portraits of Heathcliff and Catherine are, as Trilling argues in his "Freud and Literature," "a plea being made on behalf of the anarchic and self-indulgent id," why are we also made to feel the relationship of Hareton and Cathy is an refinement of the earlier generation?[6] Brontë would have us admire Heathcliff but not imitate him.

These interpretations have long been debated. But the tensions, as with previous texts in this study, are often ignored. The two critical problems are one in that both reflect and focus our attentions on the near contradictions in the texts. Improvisation's legerdemain is to trick its readers into holding contradictory ideas in suspension. Although even an uninformed reader responds in some degree to these tensions, a complete articulation of how those tensions are resolved or held in suspension requires close attention. If treated at length the above examples—*Sartor Resartus, Pickwick Papers, Wuthering Heights*—would reveal the ebb and flow of the Romantic heritage. Here and there and to differing degrees Victorian artists celebrate Romantic visionary immediacy; here and there and to differing degrees Victorian artists challenge and condemn Romantic visionary immediacy; and the best

---

6. "Freud and Literature," in Lionel Trilling, *The Liberal Imagination* (New York: New York Review Books, 2008 [1948]), 37.

among them explore the inevitable tensions. Such a text is the subject of this chapter.

2. Huckleberry Finn, *Romanticism, and the Critics*

At the heart of Mark Twain's *Adventures of Huckleberry Finn* contradictory assessments of spontaneity's nature and value vie for supremacy. On the one hand, as if to prove Emerson's observation that "every surmise and vaticination of the mind is entitled to a certain respect,"[7] the novel attacks those who cannot achieve spontaneity in their lives and art; on the other, it attacks the debased Romantic notion of spontaneity, the view that unmediated behavior alone suffices us as social and moral beings. However "full of Emersonian inclinations," the novel inclines also toward Mill's almost exactly contemporaneous rationalist attack, quoted in my first chapter, on "the vein of sentiment so common in the modern world...which exalts instinct at the expense of reason."[8] Paradoxically, *Huckleberry Finn,* whose hero tells us he goes "a good deal on instinct," both affirms this consecration and, like Mill, negates it.[9] This paradox creates the novel's central expressive tension, the resolution of which is a necessary qualification of spontaneity as moral and aesthetic ideal.

What has in part blinded readers to this tension concerning the nature and value of spontaneity is the prevailing assumption that *Huckleberry Finn* is an improvised creation, like many Romantic documents before it a "spontaneous overflow of powerful feelings." Clemens himself fosters this assumption in remarks to Howells, that he is "running out of well water," and in the novel itself. But while he presents the novel in Huck's voice and in the famous first notice as improvised, he makes a counter-generic claim that also shapes our experience of the book. He introduces the novel with not one notice but two, and together they present fundamentally opposite aesthetic and moral premises. The first seems to claim that what follows will be a care-

---

7. "Nature," in *The Collected Works of Ralph Waldo Emerson,* 1: 41.

8. Richard Poirier, *A World Elsewhere: The Place of Style in American Literature* (New York: Oxford University Press, 1966), 153; Mill, "Three Essays on Religion: Nature," 392.

9. Twain, *Adventures of Huckleberry Finn,* ed. Sculley Bradley, 174.

free, improvised tale: "Persons attempting to find a motive in this narrative will be prosecuted; persons attempting to find a moral in it will be banished; persons attempting to find a plot will be shot."[10] The Notice proclaims a distrust of motive like Keats's distrust of art that "has a palpable design upon us": "motive" and "design" suggest the meddling of moralistic rationality which the Romantic artist scorns.[11] On the basis of the notice, Clemens seems to enlist in the Romantic camp. To be without motive or moral or plot is to be free of rhetoric and artifice: it is to speak from the unimpeachable heart. The basic moral and aesthetic premises critics often extract from the first notice are these: natural, spontaneous, unconniving man and his works are good; artificial, conventional, designing man and his society are corrupt. Free of these last, his notice implies, his novel will be, like Huck's life on the raft, "free and easy."[12]

And yet quite different premises are also at work in this notice. For one thing, in contrast to the "naturalness" of Huck's speech patterns in the novel proper, Clemens here creates a sentence of well-formed Ciceronian balance. Huck's normal grammatical mode of stringing clauses together by conjunctions (*polysyndeton*) here gives way to polished, elliptical asyndeton: clauses balanced upon semicolons. Where Huck achieves a spontaneous flow of speech that generates natural climaxes of image and theme, we have here an example of classical *gradatio* (arranged in climactic order), underscored by *anaphora* ("Persons...; persons...; persons...") and climactically underscored by internal masculine rhyme ("plot...shot"). While it is no doubt possible to find equally sophisticated rhetorical constructions in Huck's oft-praised "natural" style, Clemens pointedly and masterfully obscures Huck's debt to the colors of rhetoric. The first notice, by contrast, the novel's initial claim for naturalness and spontaneity, draws out attention, however subconsciously, to the artifice of the claim. No one, however he or she reads, expects to be prosecuted, banished, or shot. The tension between tenor and vehicle calls in question the assumptions and premises of the tenor, the affirmation of spontaneity and naturalness.

---

10. *Adventures of Huckleberry Finn*, 2.
11. John Keats, *Selected Letters*, 58.
12. *Adventures of Huckleberry Finn*, 96.

The second notice reinforces our doubts about these assumptions and enlists the novel in the camp of intelligent craftsmanship. For the second notice conveys more obviously the contrasting message of careful craftsmanship:

> In this book a number of dialects are used, to wit: the Missouri negro dialect; the extremest form of the backwoods South-Western dialect; the ordinary "Pike-Country" dialect; and four modified varieties of this last. The shadings have not been done in a hap-hazard fashion, or by guesswork; but pains-takingly, and with the trustworthy guidance and support of personal familiarity with these several forms of speech.
>
> I make this explanation for the reason that without it many readers would suppose that all these characters were trying to talk alike and not succeeding.[13]

We are asked to trust this not as a sport, but rather as a well-honed document ("not...in a hap-hazard fashion, [n]or by guesswork; but pains-takingly"). Now it is not the heart or the imagination, but intellect and experience ("personal familiarity") that guide us. The language of law ("to wit"), the parallel clauses, the masterful manipulation of time and phrasing in the concluding "snapper," all convey the value of intellect, reason, and care. We are invited to experience and to appreciate this narrative in terms of its thought, thoughtfulness, and craft. These premises turn the apparent celebration of naturalness of the first notice on its head and underscore its covert acknowledgment of craftsmanship.

Thus from the very beginning of *Huckleberry Finn* the premises upon which critics either praise or blame the novel—its celebration of primitive naturalness and unmediated spontaneity—are called in question by Clemens himself. Critical treatment of *Huckleberry Finn* has in large part centered upon themes associated historically with the Romantic movement: spontaneity, primitivism, unmediated experience, and the attack upon artifice and conventionality. Critics divide in their evaluation of the Romantic tendency of the whole, praising or condemning Clemens for celebrating these Romantic themes in his characterization of Huck.[14] Between these two poles

---

13. Ibid., 2.

14. William van O'Connor, for example, describes the novel as insidious because it "appeals to our desire for a condition of innocence and it is lacking in that civi-

stand those critics who examine the attack on Romanticism implicit in the book. But these critics essentially oppose such themes as Tom and Emmeline Grangerford's artificial and romantic "nonsense" to Huck's greater naturalness and spontaneity, thus substituting a "better" set of Romantic premises for a "worse," a "true" Romanticism (Huck's) for a "false" (Tom's).[15]

It is true that Clemens bases much of the satire in *Huckleberry Finn* on a Rousseauvian opposition between the Shore society's artificiality and conventionality and Huck's more fluid, natural spontaneity. Huck shows up Tom's artificial romancing, the evangelicals' rigid conventionalism in the camp-meeting episode, the Grangerfords's sophisticated feuding, and the pseudo-spontaneity of Emmeline's one-note versifying. With a writing voice "blood-warm," Huck travels down the Mississippi like an embodiment of Emerson's "Man Thinking," helping us see the "sluggish and perverted mind of the multitude."[16] In a sense Clemens does substitute his truer, purer

---

lized quality—the quality of pity," in "Why Huckleberry Finn Is Not the Great American Novel," *College English* 17, no. 1 (October 1955): 8; Henry Nash Smith, voicing the majority opinion, compares the language of the novel to that of the *Lyrical Ballads* and commends Clemens's stylistic achievement, symptomatically echoing Coleridge's *Biographia Literaria*: "The systematic elimination of conventional associations removes the cake of custom from the visible universe and fosters a completely fresh treatment of landscape. A vision not distorted by inherited modes of perception, once fresh in themselves but long since grown lifeless through over-use, can report sensory experience with supreme vividness." For Smith, Clemens's satiric target is the fact that Shore society does not "react to situations spontaneously but according to stereotyped patterns of feeling and behavior." Huck's style and character dramatize a different model, a "voice of freedom, spontaneity, autonomy of the individual," in *Adventures of Huckleberry Finn*, edited by Henry Nash Smith (Boston: Houghton Mifflin Company, 1958), xxv, xvi.

15. See, e.g., Richard P. Adams, "The Unity and Coherence of Huckleberry Finn," *Tulane Studies in English* 6 (1956): 87-103; Thomas Arthur Gullason, "The 'Fatal' Ending of Huckleberry Finn," *American Literature* 29, no. 1 (March 1957): 86-91; Gilbert M. Rubenstein, "The Moral Structure of Huckleberry Finn," *College English* 18, no. 2 (November 1956): 72-76; and Robert Penn Warren, "Mark Twain," *The Southern Review* 8 (Summer 1972): 470-72.

16. "The American Scholar," in *The Collected Works of Ralph Waldo Emerson*, 1: 53, 56.

Romanticism for the received, debased notion of that movement. He shows in effect that the Walter Scott is well sunk, the boiler of the Lally Rook well blown, and he floats Huck's innocent raft in their stead. So much is clear. But Clemens also concerns himself with the dark side of Huck's noble innocence. Huck, the naive unmasker of society's corrupt sophistications, is also to some degree unmasked. The unmasking involves Clemens in a more thorough questioning of "Romantic" premises than critics have perceived. I wish to offer a reading of *Huckleberry Finn* that does not condemn Clemens either for reneging on his celebration of a primitivist Huck in a "flawed" ending (it is flawed but not for that reason), or for the immaturity of carrying his celebration through (he does not). Clemens's treatment of primitivism and related ideas is fundamentally ambivalent.

3. *"I Go a Good Deal on Instinct"*

Although the novel's opening chapters have received far less critical attention than the closing chapters, if read carefully they reinforce the opposition between innocent spontaneity and untutored naturalness, and the value of care, craft, and thought. For most readers the opening portrays the "sivilization" from which the innocent, asocial Huck will rightly flee. But the opening is far richer than *Tom Sawyer*. Beneath its ironic portrayal of "The Enemy" Clemens sets the far more positive portrayal of the Widow Douglas, the embodiment of all the good in society.

The first paragraph still pursues the issue of authenticity we met in the notices. Like most improvisations, this work begins with an attack upon the falseness of other literary endeavors. The book *"The Adventures of Tom Sawyer,"* we hear,

> was made by Mr. Mark Twain, and he told the truth, mainly. There was things which he stretched, but mainly he told the truth. That is nothing. I never seen anybody but lied, one time or another, without it was Aunt Polly, or the widow, or maybe Mary. Aunt Polly—Tom's Aunt Polly, she is—and Mary, and the Widow Douglas, is all told about in that book; with some stretchers, as I said before.[17]

---

17. *Adventures of Huckleberry Finn*, 7.

"Made" books, Huck says, are mere fabrications. On the other hand, he implies, this spontaneous, designless, and lived account is true. With all its bad grammar—even because of its bad grammar—this is the real thing. Even so, the reader knows better than to take this opposition between Clemens and Huck at face value: behind the claim of greater naturalness and truth Clemens stands grinning. As in the notices, the humor questions the idealization of unschooled, careless spontaneity.

Embedded in Huck's attack and counterclaim is our introduction to the Widow Douglas. Mary will have no role in this adventure, and Aunt Polly only a walk-on at the conclusion. Most agree, however, that the widow symbolizes to Huck and to us civilization, conscience, and religion. But in granting her this symbolic importance, most conflate her with Miss Watson "as a double-headed symbol of familial suffocation."[18] In fact, Clemens strictly and consistently distinguishes the two women. Here, at her first entrance, the Widow Douglas is set in opposition to confirmed liars; despite Huck's subsequent reactions to her, the novel never really contradicts this positive and sympathetic portrayal.

Huck's negative assessments of the widow are always susceptible to a double reading: we first applaud his boyish rejection; then, catching ourselves, we realize that like Huck we are overreacting, responding like a naive child. Indeed, the humorous texture of his portrait insists that we read again and repeal our initial response. Huck's next statement about the widow evokes this ambivalent dynamic: "The Widow Douglas, she took me for her son, and allowed she would sivilize me; but it was rough living in the house all the time, considering how dismal regular and decent the widow was in all her ways; and so when I couldn't stand it no longer, I lit out."[19] While the child in us agrees with Huck that it is "rough living in the house all the time," the adult remembers the civilized truth that houses are handy in bad weather.

---

18. Kenneth Lynn, "Welcome Back to the Raft Huck, Honey!" *American Scholar* 46, no. 3 (Summer 1977): 345. James D. Wilson also exemplifies the conflation when he speaks of both widow and spinster under the single, opprobrious term, "Christianity" in "Adventures of Huckleberry Finn: From Abstraction to Humanity," *Southern Review* 10 (Winter 1974): 80–82.

19. *Adventures of Huckleberry Finn*, 7.

Clemens calls up in us this impulse to qualify Huck's statement by making Huck speak in excessive and categorical terms: "all the time." The same dynamic of appeal and repeal is evoked by the third phrase of Huck's portrait, "how dismal regular and decent the widow was in all her ways." Here opposite connotations evoke the child-adult swing of responses. Huck, perhaps despite himself, plays upon the etymology of "regular": according to rule. "Decent" from Huck's point of view connotes its opposite: hypocritical. Having to be "regular and decent," being acculturated, in short, is what Huck and the child within us resist. But our adult voice should interrupt with the words' opposite connotations, their more colloquial meanings: "what could you ask for, Huck, than a foster parent who is regular (consistent) and decent (fair)," indeed, as Huck says, in "all her ways." The power of Clemens's language to evoke the two voices is masterly and a key to his appeal to all ages. He makes "Mark Twains" of us all.

The humor of Huck's responses to the widow's crying over him as a "poor lost lamb" ("she never meant no harm") and to her grumbled mealtime prayers ("there warn't really anything the matter" with the food) depend upon the same kind of double, ironic readings. They also prepare us for Huck's next stroke in the widow's portrait, an especially evocative one, again despite his own understanding of it: "After supper she got out her book and learned me about Moses and the Bulrushers; and I was in a sweat to find out all about him; but by-and-by she let it out that Moses had been dead a considerable long time; so then I didn't care no more about him; because I don't take no stock in dead people."[20] This passage is usually read as but another Twainian satire of Sunday school didacticism and the "goody-goody tradition." But the widow's Sunday school lesson differs significantly from those satires: in form it lacks the pat moralism which for Clemens was the hallmark of the morally false. In substance it expresses love and acceptance, not hate and co-optation. Clemens may have had his goody-goody satires in mind, and yet he goes beyond them.

In fact, Clemens subtly turns the satire from the widow toward Huck. What Huck misses—and many readers seem to miss it too—is that in a most

---

20. Ibid., 7–8.

important way Moses still lives. According to Protestant custom, the widow has chosen her text for its application to present affairs. Like the "poor lost lamb" or prodigal son, who when found is of greater worth than all who remain in the fold, so the Moses found in the "Bulrushers" is analogous to Huck. With her Sunday school lesson the widow tells Huck how much she prizes and loves him. Huck misunderstands because of the civilization he lacks and scorns: notice the misheard "Bulrushers." To miss this message of love and acceptance, so much the goal of Huck's quest, is, it can be argued, to become inevitably lost. Huck will float down the river like Moses: the widow's image ironically looks forward to the journey. But by means of the image she hopes to say that his journey is over.

In the next paragraph Huck adds a stroke to the widow's portrait that sticks in many minds: her hypocrisy. Huck wishes to smoke and she won't let him. "And," he adds sarcastically, "she took snuff too; of course that was all right, because she done it herself." But before agreeing with Huck's assessment of the widow as hypocrite, we must note the context of his sarcastic attack:

> She said it was a mean practice and wasn't clean, and I must try to not do it any more. That is just the way with some people. They get down on a thing when they don't know nothing about it. Here she was a bothering about Moses, which was no kin to her, and no use to anybody, being gone, you see, yet finding a power of fault with me for doing a thing that had some good in it. And, she took snuff too; of course that was all right, because she done it herself.[21]

The context, along with the humor, qualifies Huck's charge of hypocrisy and all but demolishes it. Compared with Huck's blindness to the meaning and good intention behind the Moses story, the widow's fault shrinks to a mere foible. Huck's general assessment of hypocrites turns back on him in particular. "They get down on a thing when they don't know nothing about it." If Huck cannot see the purpose of her "bothering about Moses," that by analogy Moses and Huck are both "kin to her," then who is he to judge the widow's intentions? The upside-down world of ironic satire, typical of many improvisations, where the fool instructs the righteous, here turns right-side

---

21. Ibid., 8.

up: Huck's ironic mask slips as his instructions betray both the error of his ways and the Widow Douglas's essential rightness and generosity.

Let's not lose sight of Clemens's economy in portraying the widow. But her portrait, finished not by Huck but by Clemens's subtle ironies, is sharply drawn. And the succeeding contrasts with her spinsterish sister, Miss Watson, bring the widow's sympathetic character, and Huck's wrongheadedness, into still sharper focus. The contrasts between the two women further consolidate our sympathy for the widow and for the positive version of civilization she represents.

Huck introduces Miss Watson in the next paragraph. She is "a tolerable slim old maid, with goggles on," and, coming to live with her sister, she takes "a set at me now, with a spelling book" until "the widow made her ease up."[22] Here the language is too strong for us to do anything but to lend Huck all our sympathy. Appealing to the sexism of his audience with a stroke right out of fairy tale, Clemens undermines her in terms of her marital status: "old maid." And to be "set at" with a "spelling-book" is different from studying spelling, though we may doubt that Huck could distinguish the two.

The spinster is "sivilization" at its very worst—repressed and repressive, vindictive and lacking in sympathy, and very much in contrast with her sister: "the widow made her ease up."

But the point is not merely that the widow protects Huck from her sister. The opposition between the two women raises more important questions. Why does Clemens introduce Miss Watson into this narrative at all? What is her narrative agency? Could not the Widow Douglas have carried her part? There is in fact nothing in *Tom Sawyer* which would have prevented the widow from being Jim's owner, and from being as cruel as need be to set him, and Huck, on a quest for freedom. Since Tom's Aunt Sally takes over the widow's role as Huck's adopter and civilizer at the end of the tale, there is no reason why Clemens could not have killed the widow off and made her recant and set Jim free. In short, Clemens could have embodied the civilization that Jim and Huck flee in one religious, slave-holding woman. This seems to have been Clemens's plan as late as 1883 when, in interpolating the "Raft Passage" from the *Huckleberry Finn* manuscript into *Life on the Mis-*

---

22. Ibid.

sissippi, Clemens sets the scene with these significant words: Huck "has run away from his persecuting father, and from a persecuting good widow who wishes to make a nice, truth-telling, respectable boy of him; and with him a slave of the widow's has also escaped."[23] Here the "persecuting" widow is linked with "persecuting" Pap Finn; it is she who owns Jim. In the finished novel she will remain "good" in just the ambiguous way that "good widow" suggests. That is, she will retain her wish to "sivilize" Huck, but Clemens will force us to see the action from two points of view, Huck's and the "adult" reader's. The spinster Watson was added as contrast to help us see this positive side of the Widow Douglas's goodness.

The two characters exist to represent and to embody two distinct versions of civilization. Presented through the eyes of Huck, neither is immediately attractive and, under Huck's influence, the reader conflates them. But trusting the tale and not the teller, we see beyond Huck's vision of things to the fact that one is far more acceptable than the other. The Widow Douglas is even attractive—if not to Huck, at least to us. As is often the case with first-person narrations, the narrator tells us more than he knows, especially about himself. One of the first things we learn from Huck, who will do his all to evade civilization, is that civilization is not all bad. The contrast between the two women comes to a head when, after a night out with Tom's Gang, Huck gets what he deserves from both: "Well, I got a good going-over in the morning, from old Miss Watson, on account of my clothes; but the widow she didn't scold, but only cleaned off the grease and clay and looked so sorry that I thought I would behave a while if I could."[24] The widow's gentler response, pained not paining, always works better on the ever-responsive Huck, as we see later by the effect of Jim's "trash" speech. Her response is set in sharp contrast to the spinster's self-righteous castigation. The latter makes us feel for Huck; the former makes us feel for Huck's victim.

The contrast between widow and spinster continues as they respond in turn to his questions about the nature of prayer. Miss Watson calls him "a

---

23. Mark Twain, *Life on the Mississippi* (New York: Oxford University Press, 1996), 42. Many thanks to Fred W. Anderson for bringing this passage to my attention.

24. *Adventures of Huckleberry Finn*, 14.

fool" for trying to pray for fishhooks; she is blind to the fact that her own definitions of prayer are largely responsible for Huck's self-seeking misconception.[25] The widow's response, on the other hand, is warm, gentle, and pious correction:

> She said the thing a body could get by praying for it was "spiritual gifts."
> This was too many for me, but she told me what she meant—I must help
> other people, and do everything I could for other people, and look out for
> them all the time, and never think about myself. This was including Miss
> Watson, as I took it. I went out in the woods and turned it over in my
> mind a long time, but I couldn't see no advantage about it—except for the
> other people—so at last I reckoned I wouldn't worry about it any more,
> but just let it go. Sometimes the widow would take me one side and talk
> about Providence in a way to make a boy's mouth water; but maybe next
> day Miss Watson would take hold and knock it all down again. I judged I
> could see that there was two Providences, and a poor chap would stand
> considerable show with the widow's Providence, but if Miss Watson got
> him there warn't no help for him any more.[26]

A reader who insists upon Clemens's atheism and upon his horror of the hypocrisies of the "damned human race" might prefer Huck's skepticism to the widow's homespun piety. Yet the contrast between the two women is the key to our response. Like the two Providences, there are two versions of religion in the novel. Compared to her sister, the widow is unexceptionable. In seeing no advantage in Christian charity and prayer "except for other people," Huck, as so often, exaggerates her meaning and misses the point. Clemens's humor underscores Huck's mistake.

The more positive reading of the theme of religion in the novel has a bearing on our reading of the celebrated moral crisis Huck later undergoes. His basis here for deciding between "the two Providences"—on the way they feel—will be shown there to be misleading. Miss Watson, not the Widow Douglas, will be the controlling presence, a presence he finally overcomes. But he does not substitute for his "yaller dog" conscience one that empowers

---

25. Ibid.
26. Ibid., 15.

him to stop Tom's Evasions schemes.[27] And throughout the crisis he does not take responsibility for Jim's plight.

The first chapters also present Huck's alternative to these forms of civilized religion: superstition. Huck's indirect response to Miss Watson's oppressions is a passage often celebrated as an example of his unmediated, precivilized imagination. Like the primitive, he projects his feelings into the landscape:

> Miss Watson she kept pecking at me, and it got tiresome and lonesome...
> I felt so lonesome I most wished I was dead. The stars was shining, and
> the leaves rustled in the woods ever so mournful; and I heard an owl, away
> off, who-whooing about somebody that was dead, and a whippowill and a
> dog crying about somebody that was going to die.[28]

Stylistically the passage is justly celebrated: Huck achieves immediacy and naturalness in his projection of a mental landscape and wins our heart. But by emphasizing the cause and source of Huck's mythopoeic rumination—"Miss Watson she kept pecking at me"—Clemens calls attention to a moral problem. Huck may deal "directly" with nature here, but like many a child he deals not with the source of his malaise, Miss Watson, but merely with the symptoms. Avoiding the source of conflict remains ever characteristic of Huck.

In the next chapters he associates superstition by turns with Jim's dream of the devil and his hairball, with Tom's romancing, and with Pap. Later in the narrative Huck blames Jim's rattlesnake bite and all their mutual troubles not on his own behavior, but on his having touched a molted snakeskin on Jackson's Island. In the moral crisis Huck's "yaller-dog" conscience makes him feel guilty for everything but his role in getting Jim sold back into slavery. Huck's recurrent failure to assume responsibility begins here. Superstition is his way of adapting to evil in the world. But according to the terms of the novel, superstition fails as an alternative to religion because Clemens shows how, in Huck's case at least, it is used mainly as an outlet to avoid facing things too frightening to confront. Anthropologists have of course taken turns to say the same thing about superstition. At bottom Huck's superstition

---

27. Ibid., 183.
28. Ibid., 9.

is attractive for the energetic imagination it displays, and of course, however mistaken, it attracts our sympathy; but at worst superstition betrays elements of childish irresponsibility and passivity.

I do not wish to overstate the ironic undermining of Huck's in the opening chapters. To ignore his attractions is to mistake the novel's dynamics. But it is equally wrong not to acknowledge that Clemens draws the reader's attention to the negative underside of his best characteristics. To say this is in part only to remark that the opening chapters delineate the problems the protagonist will have to face in the balance of the book: he will have to grow up by becoming responsible for his actions; he will have to cast off the influence of Tom's romantic adventurism, of Pap's and Jim's superstition, and of Miss Watson's version of civilization and religion. He will have to see through society and religion's worst to their better aspects. In short, the problem the opening chapters forcibly present is this: he must see his way into society or become like Pap.

4. Clemens's Anti-Pastoral

By Chapter 4 Huck is getting so he can stand "sivilization": "the longer I went to school the easier it got to be."[29] By chapter six Huck has adapted to the horrors of cabin life:

> It was kind of lazy and jolly, laying off comfortable all day, smoking and fishing, and no books nor study. Two months or more run along, and my clothes got to be all rags and dirt, and I didn't see how I'd ever got to like it so well at the widow's, where you had to wash, and eat on a plate, and comb up, and go to bed and get up regular, and be forever bothering over a book and have old Miss Watson peeking at you all the time. I didn't want to go back no more.[30]

Typically, only the pain of Pap's "hick'ry" induces Huck to leave this questionable comfort: "I was all over welts."[31] Huck's powers of adaptation and loyalty, so often praised by critics, are called in question by such passages where the horror lies so close beneath the surface of the "lazy and jolly" life.

---

29. Ibid., 18.
30. Ibid., 24.
31. Ibid.

Huck's free-floating loyalty will attach itself to anything that passes before his ever-responsive consciousness.

Huck's passivity culminates of course in his tacit participation in Jim's belittlement in the Evasion sequence. No apology has yet succeeded in palliating the horror of his behavior there. This horror is foreshadowed in many respects: in Huck's unquestioning responsiveness to the King and Duke; in his celebration of the "free and easy" raft; indeed, in the journey south itself. These three aspects of the journey keep us unsure about Huck's ability fully to mature.

While Leo Marx reads the moment Huck and Jim pass Cairo as the moment Clemens loses control of his novel, Clemens in fact keeps the significance of passing the Ohio firmly in view.[32] Huck is continually enthralled by whatever passes before his responsive consciousness: the sunken Walter Scott, the Grangerford feud, the escapades of the King and Duke, the circus, or the river itself. Huck has a good time and expects his readers to enjoy his tale. But while part of the reader does enjoy it, another part knows better and is disturbed. The many episodes in which Huck's concern for Jim is at a low ebb are symptomatic not of Clemens's loss of control over the theme of slavery, but of Huck's over his moral responsibility to Jim. There is no room for anxiety when all drifts along so "free and easy." We see everything through Huck's eyes, yet Clemens makes it clear that continuing south is wrong and Huck's passivity is a major cause of the error.

Clemens enforces our judgment of Huck's "carefree" journey by subtle manipulation of diction, narrative context, and the dramatic irony implicit in the southward journey itself. A significant example of dramatic irony occurs just after Huck meets the King and Duke. Noting that Jim and Huck cover the raft by day, they ask if Jim is "a runaway nigger."[33] Huck's reply is ironically resonant: "Goodness sakes, would a runaway nigger run south?"[34] The reader, after enjoying Huck's quick-wittedness, asks in kind, "Indeed, would he?" This dramatic irony turns the humor, as so often, back at Huck.

---

32. Leo Marx, "Mr. Eliot, Mr. Trilling, and *Huckleberry Finn*," *American Scholar* 22, no. 4 (Autumn 1953): 432.

33. *Adventures of Huckleberry Finn*, 102.

34. Ibid., 103.

Huck's quick-witted reply gets them out of the frying pan and into the fire: the Duke responds by printing the slave bills that enable their rafting by day and that lead ultimately to Jim's being sold back into slavery. Huck's ready improvisations often have this effect: they are good for sidestepping trouble, not getting rid of it. The trouble comes back with a vengeance.

Clemens forces us to judge the southward journey by insisting, through Huck's own narration of events, upon the lengthy passage of time. The famous dawn scene begins, "Two or three days and nights went by..."[35] Huck's obliviousness to clock-time is attractive to our time-worn and time-obsessed age. Surely the timelessness contributes to the pastoral idyll that follows. But such uncertainty is misplaced when getting back to Cairo is the pressing concern and especially on a river where navigation is in part a matter of time calculations. This may well have been on the old river pilot's mind, for he breaks off the Huck manuscript at this point to turn to *Life on the Mississippi*. Clemens again makes us wonder about Huck's good faith when he has Huck elaborate: "I reckon I might say they swum by, they slid along so quiet and smooth and lovely."[36] Huck has merged with the landscape but at the expense of his union with Jim and Jim's problem. The opening of Chapter thirty-one again emphasizes the lapse of time as well as the distance traveled. For "days and days" they "kept right along down the river." Huck's description of the locale is worth close scrutiny:

> We was down south in the warm weather, now, and a mighty long ways from home. We begun to come to trees with Spanish moss on them, hanging down from the limbs like long gray beards. It was the first I ever see it growing, and it made the woods look solemn and dismal. So now the frauds reckoned they was out of danger, and they begun to work the villages again.[37]

The frauds are out of danger but Huck and Jim are clearly in pretty deep. The warm weather, the distance from home, and the Spanish moss ("the first I ever see it growing") underscore just how far they have come. The imagery further suggests that Huck himself half-recognizes the error. According to

---

35. Ibid., 96.
36. Ibid.
37. Ibid., 165.

his habitual mode of emotional transference (and avoidance), he evokes the specter of a judgmental authority figure: "moss...like long gray beards...solemn and dismal." Daunted, but taking no action, Huck and Jim passively drift ever southward.

Huck's love for the "free and easy and comfortable" raft, though a mainstay of critics' celebration of Huck, also invites our recognition of his passive trait. The context in which Huck first enunciates this creed calls the creed in question. He has just evaded the Grangerford feud. His response to the feud is often praised for its understated horror. Yet the understatement is in part not Clemens's, but Huck's, symptomatic of his failure to judge fully the nature and implications of the action. His escape to the raft enables him simply to drop the subject:

> I never felt easy till the raft was two mile below there and out in the middle of the Mississippi. Then we hung up our signal lantern, and judged that we was free and safe once more. I hadn't had a bite to eat since yesterday; so Jim he got out some corn-dodgers and buttermilk, and pork and cabbage, and greens—there ain't nothing in the world so good, when it's cooked right—and whilst I eat my supper we talked, and had a good time. I was powerful glad to get away from the feuds, and so was Jim to get away from the swamp. We said there warn't no home like a raft, after all. Other places do seem so cramped up and smothery, but a raft don't. You feel mighty free and easy and comfortable on a raft.[38]

The famous dawn scene follows. As I have argued, the reference to time ("Two or three days and nights...swum by") hints that Huck is not in control. Huck's aubade and pastoral idyll are justly celebrated, but his lingering over details again forces us to ask if this relaxation is appropriate to the narrative. What about Cairo and freedom? The juxtaposition of the Grangerford feud with Huck's pastoral enjoyment suggests that his rechristening in the river is in part mere evasion. At its worst his warm pastoral represents an improvident responsiveness to the drift of experience; like Keats's Grecian Urn's "cold pastoral," Huck's is cut off from the pressing realities of life.

At the end of the idyll passage, Huck finds the canoe that could take them to freedom but instead gets them involved with the King and Duke when

---

38. Ibid., 95-96.

Huck goes to "get some berries"[39]—even though their coffers are brimming with "corn-dodgers and buttermilk, and pork and cabbage, and greens." Huck's submissive behavior toward these con men raises disturbing questions. In chapter thirty-one we will be struck by how easily Huck skips out on the pair; but by that time it is too late: they have already sold Jim back into slavery. As early as chapter nineteen Clemens focuses the question sharply. Happy that the King and Duke had made friends, "for what you want, above all things, on a raft, is for everybody to be satisfied," Huck explains:

> It didn't take me long to make up my mind that these liars warn't no kings nor dukes, at all, but just low-down humbugs and frauds. But I never said nothing, never let on; kept it to myself; it's the best way; then you don't have no quarrels, and don't get into no trouble. If they wanted us to call them kings and dukes, I hadn't no objections, 'long as it would keep peace in the family; and it warn't no use to tell Jim, so I didn't tell him. If I never learnt nothing else out of pap, I learnt that the best way to get along with his kind of people is to let them have their own way.[40]

This is the passage, the "human credo," that Leo Marx argues "constitutes the paramount affirmation" of the novel.[41] By extension, this is the family Lionel Trilling calls "a community of saints."[42] Yet Huck's own repetitious insistence suggests how uncomfortable even he is with his decision to keep quiet: "never said nothing...never let on...kept it to my self." Huck's virtue ("keep peace in the family") is founded on a fault: avoidance. For however appealing Huck's code of the raft may be, the context of Jim's quest for freedom puts all this in question. Considering the King and Duke's potential for ruthless violence, Huck's desire to avoid confronting them is wise. But telling Jim about them need not result in "a quarrel," but only in evasion, where for once evasion is the wisest course. Even the notion of avoiding conflict is undermined in the passage by association with Pap Finn, the worst-of-all role model in the novel.

The final blow to our appreciation of this code of adapt-at-all-costs is delivered when we realize that it echoes the King, who has already said,

---

39. Ibid., 98.

40. Ibid., 102.

41. Marx, "Mr. Eliot, Mr. Trilling, and Huckleberry Finn," 431.

42. Trilling, *The Liberal Imagination,* 108.

"Make the best o' things the way you find 'em, says I—that's my motto."[43] These are indeed Pap Finn's "kind of people," always making a virtue of their vice. Huck adapts to the King and Duke at the price of the trip northward and at the moral cost of participating in their criminal schemes. Huck's behavior to the King and Duke, and toward Jim betrays the ugly side of his ready responsiveness: misplaced sympathy, undue loyalty, and the failure to judge and to act.

But beyond Huck's improvident responsiveness we finally see that the King and Duke attract him because their characters are similar to his own. Like him the King and Duke are improvisers, always ready with a tall tale or scheme or counter-scheme with which to manipulate others. Except for his Tom Sawyer-like improvising in the novel's conclusion—a *big* exception— Huck's improvising is by contrast harmless, brought to bear on others only to avoid trouble.

But the King and Duke make trouble with their lies, and one wonders if this is just what Huck will do, grown up. Situated at the novel's center, their confidence games are the dark underbelly of Tom's romancing and Huck's spontaneous improvising, and further call spontaneity and its premises into question. Through the King and Duke, improvising is associated with lying, the form of human behavior first deprecated in the novel: "Mr. Clemens…he told the truth mainly."[44]

What is troubling about lying is not just a matter of moralistic stricture. In the world of the novel we learn that lying creates habits of mind that lead ultimately to self-deception. The King and Duke have reached that point. When Huck complains that Jim was "mine," the Duke responds, "We never thought of that. Fact is, I reckon we'd come to consider him our nigger; yes, we did consider him so—goodness knows we had trouble enough for him."[45] The Duke's repetition makes the statement ring true; this is not just another lie meant to placate Huck. The final self-delusion is the Duke's believing that Jim caused them trouble, not they him. Self-delusion is the Shore's common state of mind, implicit in the Shore's hypocrisy and conventionality, and in

---

43. *Adventures of Huckleberry Finn*, 102.
44. Ibid., 7.
45. Ibid., 171.

slavery itself. Huck at his worst, like the King and Duke whose schemes he admires, is no better. Responding to the Duke, Huck complains that Jim was his "only property."[46] We are left wondering how long Huck, too, begins to believe his lies. Improvisation, free living, passivity, and misplaced sympathy together make a pretty sorry pathway to maturity. The novel makes it clear how strait is the gate through which Huck must pass.

5. *Judgment and Sympathy*

Leo Marx was surely right to say that "Huck grows in stature throughout the journey," but Huck's promising growth never comes to fruition.[47] Huck comes to appreciate more and more the "whiteness" of Jim, and he commits himself—and recommits himself—to escape from slavery. He learns that "you can't pray a lie," and that, given the general "spurious Christian morality" of the Shore, it would be better to forsake such godliness and go to hell. Important lessons. But what is finally in question in the world of the novel is not moral awareness but moral action. As Huck himself puts it earlier, "So the question was, what to do?"[48] What he is asked to do by the terms of the book is to learn to take responsibility for his actions. Clemens's deflations of Huck in the opening chapters are sustained and elaborated throughout the course of the book. Huck's moral backsliding in the Evasion sequence comes with a sad inevitability.

The novel's conclusion makes us uncomfortable, as the many attacks on the ending attest. But we must recognize that these evasions are thoroughly prepared from the beginning, and that their purpose is to culminate our uneasy responses to Huck's character. We do come more and more to value, even to love Huck, whatever negative strokes in his portrait we perceive. And perceiving his failings we do not disapprove, but sympathize, for the child-adult swing of responses has shown us that Huck's failings are our own. Like most "children's stories," *Huckleberry Finn* flatters children (and adults) in their childishness, but at the same time elicits their maturation. The novel

---

46. Ibid.

47. Marx, "Mr. Eliot, Mr. Trilling, and Huckleberry Finn," 428.

48. *Adventures of Huckleberry Finn*, 72.

is about an attractive boy's failure to grow and it makes perfectly clear what holds him back.

The final stroke in Clemens's portrait of failure is the most resonant and it has been the most debated. Marx long ago argued that Huck's decision to "light out for the territory" is his final "confession of defeat."[49] But despite Marx's suggestion, Clemens is fully in control of the confession. This is Huck's final admission that he can adapt to all the evil in the world, as we have seen, but also that he cannot see through to and adapt to the good in "sivilization." Miss Watson and Pap are gone: the worst in society and of anarchy have died a ritual death. Society is ready for Huck, and in ritual terms Huck should be ready for society. But he is not and perhaps may never be. The Widow Douglas and her delicious Providence drop from Huck's view.

In *Huckleberry Finn,* Clemens does not simply oppose a corrupt society and "depraved conscience" to the innocence of Nature and the spontaneous human heart. His moral vision embraces the difficulty of entering a society which can be corrupt, but which after all is the fruit of our fall and the condition of our prospering. To discern this implicit vision in the novel is to see the Clemens of *Huckleberry Finn* as basically Christian in his view of man and society. Through the opposition of River and Shore, the novel shows that Huck's finer qualities—spontaneity, immediacy, responsiveness—are important moral equipment if ever we are to break free of outworn conventions and artifice. But the novel makes it equally clear that they are not sufficient provisions in the journey to maturity. Clemens's narrative demonstrates how especially difficult our entrance into adult society is when we approach it with "soul-butter and hogwash" notions of an innocent, spontaneous heart. In fact he implies, like many Christians before him, that not only the "yaller-dog" conscience, but the heart itself is essentially fallen and depraved.

In effect, Clemens gives the lie to Emerson's optative trust that "if the single man plant himself indomitably on his instincts, and there abide, the huge world will come round to him."[50] Trust in our instincts, Clemens suggests, will not only fail to convert the world, but will prevent our seeing and

---

49. Ibid., 438-39.

50. "The American Scholar," in *The Collected Works of Ralph Waldo Emerson,* 1: 69.

adapting to the best in it. Huck cannot intuitively distinguish the Widow Douglas from Miss Watson, nor sense to whom he should attach his free-floating loyalty. Instinct teaches Huck that Jim, among many bad choices, is his truest father, but it cannot stick with and act upon the perception. By portraying the limitations in Huck's innocence, the novel dramatizes the necessity of adding to the spontaneous workings of the heart what care and insight the mind can provide. Through Huck's attractions Clemens tempts us to see Huck's journey as a happy fall; but Clemens makes it clear to the adult ever-nascent within us that maturity and redemption are never so easily won.

CHAPTER THIRTEEN

"Pierce[d]…with Strange Relation":
Jung, Joyce, and Mann Embrace the Back Streets

Life's nonsense pierces us with strange relation
—Wallace Stevens, "Notes Toward a Supreme Fiction"

One must have chaos if one is to give birth to a
dancing star.
—Nietzsche, *Thus Spake Zarathustra*

If one opens up chaos, magic also arises…One cannot
say what the effect of magic will be, since no one can
know in advance because the magical is lawless, which
occurs without rules and by chance so to speak.
—C.G. Jung, *Liber Novus*

Madness you may call [Dostoevsky's characters], said
Joyce, but therein may be the secret of his genius.
Hamlet was mad, hence the great drama; some of the
characters in the Greek plays were mad; Gogol was mad;
Van Gogh was mad; but I prefer the word exaltation,
exaltation which can merge into madness, perhaps.
In fact all great men have had that vein in them; it
was the source of their greatness; the reasonable man
achieves nothing.
—Arthur Power, *Conversations with James Joyce*

1. *Jung's New Gospel*

If Annie Dillard, as we saw in Chapter 1, wants to live like a weasel, Carl Jung in a crucial moment in his *The Red Book: Liber Novus* argues that modern man's problem is that "they forgot only one thing: they did not live their animal."[1] Just as for Dillard "a weasel lives as he is meant to, yielding

---

1. C.G. Jung, *The Red Book: Liber Novus—A Reader's Edition,* edited by Sonu Shamdasani, translated by Mark Kyburz, John Peck, and Sonu Shamdasani (New York and

at every moment to *the perfect freedom of single necessity"* [emphasis added], so too what appeals to Jung is the animal's constraint by instinct: "The animal does not rebel against its own kind...The animal lives fittingly and true to the life of its species, neither exceeding nor falling short of it."[2] As with Dillard, so with Jung: the challenge is how to achieve a life at one with our instincts. What faculties should we employ? Jung's answer will involve various constituents of the unconscious, all beyond our control: dreams, archetypes, the shadow, the anima or animus. All are emanations of the Self, which is partly our own, partly an articulation of all human history, and partly an expression of Nature's will—*the unus mundus.*

James Joyce, whose masterpiece of improvisation, *Ulysses,* will concern us in this chapter along with Jung's *Red Book,* had a contentious relationship with Jung, whom he knew slightly in Zurich.[3] But Joyce shared with Jung a regard for animals that was freighted with more than sentimentality. His Irish friend Arthur Power recorded these remarks in Paris:

> It always occurred to me that both the Assyrians and the Egyptians understood better than we do the mystery of animal life, a mystery which Christianity has almost ignored, preoccupied as it is with man, and only regarding animals as the servants of man...one wonders why...why the great subconscious life of Nature was ignored, a life which without effort reaches to such great perfection.[4]

The impulse to drag "the great subconscious life of Nature"—man's unconscious included—into confrontation with man's supposedly superior civilized selves motivates the crowd of improvisers who elbow one another for our attention throughout the twentieth century: surrealists, automatic writers, stream of consciousness novelists, Beats, jazz musicians, Abstract expressionists, performance artists. We saw many twentieth century instances in my opening chapters: Valéry's *Idée Fixe,* Fitzgerald's *The Great Gatsby,* Miller's

---

London: W.W. Norton, 2009), 341. All references are to page numbers in the *Reader's Edition.*

2. Ibid.

3. For an account of Joyce's consultation with Jung about his daughter Lucia's schizophrenia, see Jean Kimball, *Odyssey of the Psyche: Jungian Patterns in Joyce's* Ulysses (Carbondale and Edwardsville: Southern Illinois University Press, 1997), 22.

4. Arthur Power, *Conversations with James Joyce,* edited by Clive Hart (London: Millington, 1974), 48.

Tropic of Cancer, Ginsberg's *Howl,* the work of John Cage, Robert Irwin, and others. That there are so many is in part attributable directly to Freud and to Jung and in part indirectly to the *Zeitgeist* they all, psychologists and artists alike, expressed. As the Romantics embraced the visionary imagination to combat Newton's Rainbow and Enlightenment rationalism (Blake: "May God us keep from Single vision & Newton's sleep"[5]), so the twentieth century embraced chance and the unconscious to combat the Enlightenment's bullying heir, the scientific positivism that came of age in the nineteenth century. Freud, more accessible than Jung, probably takes the laurels for directly influencing more twentieth century artists. But it was the far more challenging Jung who not only inspired improvisers but also in his own writing more truly embraced the spirit, the tropes, and the formal concerns of improvisation. Understanding Jung's relationship to improvisation can help us approach not only his long sequestered *Liber Novus* but also one of the great masterpieces of the twentieth century, Joyce's *Ulysses.* In closing we will look at Thomas Mann's dark improvisation, *Doctor Faustus.*

What in part fuels twentieth century improvisation is Freud's (and then Jung's) revolutionary insistence that unconscious forces determine behavior and that health—if not freedom—lay in making those unconscious forces conscious. For Freud, analyzing dreams, word associations, and the process of transference in the talking cure would achieve the goal of analysis: "Where id was, there shall ego be."[6] For Freud the goal is for the unconscious to come under the control of rational consciousness.

For Jung, Freud's privileging of consciousness reflects his infection by scientific positivism, the impulse to make psychoanalysis authoritative by turning it into a scientific discipline. For Jung, by contrast, the unconscious is not the problem but the solution. There are no limits to the unconscious,

---

5. Letter to Thomas Butt, 22 November 1802, in *The Poetry and Prose of William Blake,* 693.

6. Freud writes of psycho-analysis: "Its intention is, indeed, to strengthen the ego, to make it more independent of the super-ego, to widen its field of perception and enlarge its organization, so that it can appropriate fresh portions of the id. Where id was, there shall ego be. It is the work of culture—not unlike draining the Zuider Zee." Sigmund Freud, *New Introductory Lectures on Psychoanalysis,* translated by James Strachey (New York and London: W.W. Norton, 1990 [1933]), 99-100.

a grand sea in which floated the island of mankind's ego or, in Jung's term, the "directed consciousness," in contradistinction to the unconscious, which we do not direct. As Jung writes, *"the experience of the Self is always a defeat for the ego."*[7] Furthermore, for Jung the unconscious is not just the source of the imp of the perverse and the other Freudian problems that plague us; the unconscious has a plan, a will of its own, and its purpose is fundamentally benign, to bring us to health and balance. The home of the archetypes, the complexes, the collective unconscious, and the Self, the unconscious serves a compensatory and teleological, purposeful function. Mankind is fundamentally dual, a network of antinomies—good and evil; male and female; persona and shadow; etc. Our neuroses stem from denying our duality and becoming one-sided. In an act of will independent of our conscious will, the unconscious, and, ultimately, the Self seek to reconcile our antinomies and thereby to achieve individuation, wholeness. If for Homer the source of our actions, good and ill, is the gods; if for medieval and Renaissance man, God's grace; if for the Enlightenment, rationality or enthusiasm, depending on which side of the fence we are on—then for Jung the source of our actions and our health lay beyond us and within us in a Self over which we have no conscious control. Enriched by relation with the unconscious, man's consciousness fulfills the teleology of the universe, the *unus mundus* or one world in which everything is related by becoming conscious. Thus, on the other hand, if man could open himself to his animal nature, then he could harken to the determinism of his unconscious instinctual nature—his daimon, in James Hillman's post-Jungian term—which has its roots in the collective unconscious, the historical depository of all that humanity has experienced. If he could do that, then he could achieve the freedom that comes with individuation. Determined yet free. Of such paradoxes—like improvisations through the ages—is Jung's anti-positivist system made.

Freud's vision of man is essentially tragic. Colonizing as much of the id as you can manage means you may succeed in "transforming your hysteri-

---

7. *The Collected Works of C.G. Jung,* edited and translated by Gerhard Adler and R.F.C. Hull, 20 vols. (Princeton, N.J.: Princeton University Press, 1953-79), vol. 14: *Mysterium Coniunctionis,* par. 778; emphasis in the original. All references to Jung's *Collected Works* (*CW*) will be cited by volume and paragraph number.

cal misery into everyday unhappiness."[8] Jung's vision is essentially comic. It ends in individuation, a marriage, presided over by the Self, of our antinomies. This in turn brings about our marriage with Self and Nature, the *unus mundus*. Yes, Jung's vision is cosmically comic. Like improvisation's.

For all Freud's interest in the unconscious and despite the charge from Karl Popper and others that psychoanalysis was *not* science, the elder analyst seems an unreconstructed rationalist compared to Jung. Jung's break with Freud was complex but at its center lay Freud's reductive, science-based materialism. In Freud's view all our actions were caused by and reducible to our sex drive and the Oedipal Complex. In Jung's broader concept, the libido is not just sexual energy but rather undifferentiated psychic energy that could crystallize as dreams and archetypal myths. For Jung the libido is a powerful force among many. Freud is interested in what caused complexes; Jung is open to experience that has no obvious cause, the many images, myths, archetypes, etc., mysterious and finally unexplainable, that rise unbidden from the unconscious to give shape, meaning, and direction to our lives.

The divide can be understood in Jung's own terms as the difference between the "psychological artist" and the "visionary artist." "The psychological artist," he writes in Psychology and Literature, derives his material and method from "the sphere of conscious human experience—from the psychic foreground of life."[9] He is the artist of consciousness, whose values are clarity and order and whose material comes from human experience as understood by the rational mind. For Jung the visionary artist, by contrast, draws his material from "the hinterland of man's mind, as if it had emerged from the abyss of prehuman ages." The visionary presents him/herself as the artist of the unconscious, the irrational, the obscure. His or her subject matter is not the everyday world of human life but the "primordial experience which surpasses man's understanding."[10]

---

8. Joseph Breuer and Sigmund Freud, *Studies in Hysteria,* translated by A.A. Brill (New York and Washington: Nervous and Mental Disease Publishing Company, 1936), 232.

9. *CW* 15: *Spirit in Man, Art, and Literature,* 139.

10. Ibid., 141.

Jung's opposition of psychological art to visionary art is equivalent to improvisation's dialogic opposition to craftsmanly art, which grounds its authority in, even as it privileges, rationality. "Psychological art," explains commentator Susan Rowland, "may be subtle, but its artifice is fully present to its audience."[11] By contrast, "Visionary art," writes Jung, "arises from timeless depths; glamorous, daemonic, and grotesque, it bursts asunder our human standards of values and aesthetic form, a terrifying tangle of eternal chaos." "Visionary art," Rowland writes, is more inclusive, "bringing to consciousness material consigned to 'the back streets.'"[12] Remembering our look at Lévi-Strauss and Louis Armstrong's embrace of *bricolage,* we can add that visionary art brings to consciousness the thrown-away.

Improvisation has always sought exactly that, by "burst[ing] asunder our human standards of values and aesthetic form," to challenge man's understanding, to challenge our efforts to know the world strictly through systematic, rationalist means, and thereby by going beyond rational means to know more of life, even "the back streets" and thrown-away. Though as equally committed to empirical science as Freud, beginning with his break with Freud in 1913 Jung fought unrelievedly against scientific materialism. As Jungian analyst Murray Stein points out, "The Age of Enlightenment left a legacy of facticity without meaning."[13] For encyclopedist Diderot, for example, "Facts of whatever kind, constitute the philosopher's true wealth."[14] For Jung, according to Susan Rowland, "science is...problematic textual terrain...Indeed, the struggle to define 'scientific writing' when addressed to the vagaries of the human psyche is the subject of much of Jung's unique style."[15] Jung's visionary analytic psychology embraces an empirical science that does not pursue

---

11. Rowland, *Jung as a Writer* (London: Routledge, 2005), 12.

12. Ibid., 11. Jung refers to "the man who takes to the back streets and alleys because he cannot endure the broad highway" (*CW*15: 131).

13. Murray Stein, *Jung's Map of the Soul: An Introduction* (Chicago and La Salle, Ill.: Open Court, 1998), 216.

14. Quoted in Peter France, *Diderot* (New York: Oxford University Press, 1983), 70. France writes, "Again and again in Diderot, for all his expansive elaboration of hypotheses, we see this thirst for the concrete, this taste for the particular," 71.

15. Rowland, *Jung as a Writer,* 2.

positivism's chimera of objectivity but embraces instead our inevitable subjectivity. To look at the psyche *with the psyche* is inevitably subjective. If so, says Jung, let us explore the subjectivity of dreams, archetypes, complexes, and the collective unconscious which, though subjective, have this empirical basis: in dreams and by means of what he calls the active or creative fantasy or imagination, we experience them. We need not murder to dissect them. Active imagination brings life.

Though less accessible and less well known than Freud's, what makes Jung's work nonetheless more instructive as a lens through which to view the march of improvisation into the twentieth century is that Jung not only embraces and articulates that goal but does so deploying the formal, rhetorical, and thematic strategies of improvisation. Susan Rowland argues in *Jung as a Writer,* "Jung thought that psychology writing should aspire to the greatest authenticity by including unconscious psychic creativity *within* writing, not to limit it to outside, to what psychology is *about*...[F]or Jung, a piece of writing was only truly valid if it retained a trace of the spontaneity that he believed to be integral to psychic functioning."[16] Thus, as Rowland extensively demonstrates, many of Jung's most important books and articles work not discursively, through rational argumentation, as Freud's do, but rather performatively to challenge the reasoned discursiveness of the directed conscious (the Ego, cognition). Jung fought scientific positivism not by deploying the enemy's own rationalist weaponry but by enlisting the forces of subjectivity and the Self. Meaning to show the limits of man's directed consciousness, Jung wrote in ways that forced the reader beyond his directed consciousness and into his subjectivity, his own experience of the Self and the world.

Jung developed the techniques of active imagination and creative fantasy in writing *Liber Novus* and used them throughout his career as therapist. This visionary method is mobilized when it responds to images that arise from the unconscious. Rather than interpret an image by deploying the directed consciousness or ego, the active imagination allows the image to develop through a chain of fantasies into a dramatic character one engages in dialogue. "Stick with the image" was Jung's mantra, an effort to forestall our penchant for interpretation. In an early encounter in *Liber Novus,* Elijah tells him, "Seek

---

16. Ibid.

untiringly, and above all write exactly what you see."[17] We are back to Bacon's idea that the scientist is Nature's amanuensis; only here Jung serves as the scribe of the collective unconscious. Active imagination, unlike conscious invention, can lead to the transcendent function of the Self, the collaboration of the conscious and the unconscious, which mediates opposites through the birth not of signs but of symbols.

Jung developed his idea of the active imagination/creative fantasy by writing *Liber Novus*. Though locked away in a Zurich vault until 2009 because it is so personal and because the Jung family thought it might damage his reputation, *Liber Novus* records Jung's inner response to his break with Freud. The break had many causes but was precipitated by the younger man's *Transformations and Symbols of the Libido*. Freud objected to *Transformations* for two reasons: 1) Jung shifted from Freud's emphasis on the father or Oedipal complex to the mother complex; and 2) Jung embraced a broader concept of libido, not as just sexual energy but rather as undifferentiated psychic energy. Editor of *Liber Novus* Sonu Shamdasani argues in his dialogues with James Hillman, published as *Lament of the Dead: Psychology after Jung's Red Book,* that Jung *himself* "for radically different reasons" also objected to his *Transformations*:

> He'd already written a vast study of human history, of comparative mythology, the history of religions, and in fact he'd explained it all away— all of these myths, all of these figures—as symbols of libido, but in a certain sense they bit back. It was his own rationalistic explanation that was insufficient...[H]e begins that book by contrasting two forms of thinking, rational directed thinking and undirected fantasy thinking, so while he is looking to study the interplay of these two and the persistence and perseverance and significance of fantasy thinking today, the book is written from the standpoint of direct[ed] thinking. It's a rational text on fantasy thinking...So he's finished the book but the material hasn't finished with him and he has to reapproach it from a different angle, which is the question of to what extent is this form of thinking still active and alive in himself?[18]

---

17. Jung, *The Red Book*, 198.

18. James Hillman and Sonu Shamdasani, *Lament of the Dead: Psychology after Jung's* Red Book (New York: Norton, 2013), 39-40.

"And that's where the *Red Book* begins," Hillman continues, "with the sense that he's lost his soul."[19] Jung writes in *Liber Novus,* "I had judged her [the soul] and turned her into a scientific object."[20] The problem, Shamdasani explains, is that "he's done it in a supposedly objective manner. He's left himself out of the equation."[21] By embracing subjectivity, *Liber Novus* is Jung's attempt to write his psyche's dynamics back into the effort to understand *the* psyche. While Rowland writes of Jung's anti-discursive methods before publication of the *Liber Novus,* that book is really the first of his many anti-discursive books and his *most* anti-discursive.

Those psychic dynamics and the rhetoric with which Jung presents them can be fruitfully examined through the lens of the tradition of improvisation. Like many improvisations, the form is so radically new that for many readers it is formless and perhaps an index of a psychotic break; for that reason some devout Jungians believed it should not have been published. Shamdasani and Hillman's joint rebuttal of that psychotic reading is persuasive but unnecessary to rehearse here.[22] Jung always informally referred to the manuscript as *The Red Book* because it was bound in red leather. But his actual title, *Liber Novus,* that is, *The New Book,* refers in the first instance to it being a kind of prophetic text, a new gospel, more good news. We have seen this gesture before among improvisations, which present themselves, in Rosalie Colie's term, as *nova reperta,* new-found things, something utterly new under the sun. *Repertum* derives from *reperire*—to discover, to learn, to light on—which is derived from *parire*: to give birth. A *novum repertum* is a new discovery, a new birth or rebirth. To emphasize its effort to be something new under the sun, I will call it *Liber Novus* but it will also be referred to as *The Red Book* in quotes below.

Truth be told, it *is* a mighty unique document, but unique in ways we have seen before. New-found, it nonetheless has roots in and is in Bakhtinian dialogue with, and thus shaped by, the genre of medieval dream visions and the

---

19. Ibid., 40.

20. Jung, *The Red Book,* 128.

21. Hillman and Shamdasani, *Lament of the Dead,* 40.

22. Ibid., 69–70.

Bible itself. It is about the rebirth of Jung's soul, which gives rebirth to the gods whom science has killed. The *Liber Novus*'s essential method—active imagination—sets it in dialogue with the methodology of science, reasoned and objective analysis, the quest to find meaning in the abstract or statistical rather than in the individual. Jung writes, "The statistical method shows the facts in light of the ideal average but does not give us a picture of their empirical reality...[O]ne could say that the real picture consists of nothing but exceptions to the rule, and that, in consequence, absolute reality has predominantly the character of *irregularity*."[23] Like Mandelbrot's fractals. The active imagination's rhetorical function in an age that privileges objectivity and analytic consciousness places Jung in the line of improvisers—fools, naturals, madmen, clowns, libertines, amateurs, charlatans and confidence men— who, placing themselves beyond civilization's pall, position themselves *en bas* to provide commentary on civilization's and reason's limits and to urge our getting beyond them. All these personae are versions of Trickster, the Shadow figure who dominates Jung's work and who as Hermetic *psychopompos,* guide of souls, dominates *Liber Novus* (and improvisation, as we have seen).[24] Following his fantasies in *Liber Novus* leads Jung to all sorts of marginal behaviors that invite us to look down on the Jung figure even as we bear witness to his rise, by embracing these shadows and shadow behaviors, toward rebirth. The reader's journey in *Liber Novus* is in part the dawning recognition of improvisation's power. As Rowland writes, Trickster—a mythic aspect of our Shadow—"drags audience members into experiencing their own capacity to do evil, and in this way, the trickster-art/artist fulfills its archetypal role of keeping our human potential for evil in front of consciousness."[25]

The essential premise of *Liber Novus*'s sequence of creative fantasies or acts of the active imagination is that these imagoes—his Shadow, anima, complexes, et al.—arise from his unconscious, unbidden and spontaneously. With these he enters into dialogues that go in directions he does not control. Of course the fact is, as Hillman points out, "it's worked. It's years of work.

---

23. *CW* 10: *Civilization in Transition,* 494; emphasis in original.

24. Susan Rowland, *Jung in the Humanities* (New Orleans: Spring Journal Books, 2012), 65.

25. Ibid.

Reworked and reworked."[26] Like Kerouac, whose *On the Road* was produced in a three-week-long creative burst, then edited for six years, *Liber Novus* was essentially written in a burst of two years (1913-15) then reworked in various layers and versions until 1928. Shamdasani, whose knowledge of Jung's published and unpublished work is incomparable, puts these efforts in perspective:

> He spent more time on this than on anything else, any other work. This is a person who, in terms of his major books, wrote at a furious pace. This is a man who could crank out a six-hundred-page book in one big burst of creativity. This is not particularly long, but what is exceptional is the degree with which he struggled with it.[27]

Much of that time was spent transcribing the text in the illuminated folio that has now been published, complete with laborious hand-lettered Gothic script and monastic-like illuminations. Still, the rhetoric of the text is, this is the fruit of my unconscious, watch as it unfolds. Shamdasani is right to point out the book's aesthetic roughness, a quality of immediacy it shares with many improvisations:

> There's a deeper sense in which the aesthetic is what one use[s] to convey the depth of the experience, which is the aesthetic that he himself is engaged with and which is in many ways inelegant. This is not a well-written book, nor are the paintings formally realized, but it is more effective precisely for that reason, or it is affective precisely for that reason. It jars with his own category of the aesthetic.[28]

As we've seen again and again, spontaneity's roughness authenticates and lends power. William Carlos Williams anticipates Shamdasani: "By the brokenness of his composition the poet makes himself master of a certain weapon which he could possess himself of in no other way."[29]

Perhaps the most important way that *Liber Novus* conveys the texture of improvisation is in its complete avoidance, as Hillman and Shamdasani point

---

26. Hillman and Shamdasani, *Lament of the Dead*, 142-43.

27. Ibid., 143.

28. Ibid., 194.

29. William Carlos Williams, Prologue to *Kora in Hell: Improvisations* (New York: New Directions, 1957), 19.

out, of Jung's own conceptual arsenal. *Liber Novus* presents images, dramatic dialogues, and narratives. As Shamdasani states, "this is Jung without concepts. You find Jung expressing the essence of his activities, tasks, his oeuvre, without a single conceptual term. There is no archetype. There's no unconscious, and he gets by quite fine without it. In fact, he manages to express himself in a more fitting and particular way."[30] Jung achieves what Derrida saw achieved in Alfred Jarry, "the triumph of pure mise en scène."[31] Elsewhere Jung "speaks about concepts as an attempt to tame the incomprehensible, the chaos. And in this text he tries to do away with that as much as possible, to confront the immediacy of his own experience...What he engages in is a lyrical elaboration."[32] What Jung lyrically elaborates, as Shamdasani explains, is that "he lets the chaos in. He says at one point, this was the night on which all the dams broke and he lets it in."[33]

Letting the chaos in means first and foremost dealing with aspects of himself that he would have preferred to suppress, what in his conceptual arsenal or "second level abstraction" Jung would for example call the Shadow, a term he had deployed before *Liber Novus* but here eschews. In 1909 Jung had been confronted with adulterous desires for a patient, Sabina Spielrein, that did not comport with his notion of himself. "Spiel rein" means "pure play," a synchronicity Jung, an avid reader of Schiller's *Aesthetic Letters*, cannot have missed. Out of this self-confrontation came his concept of the Shadow, our suppression of aspects of ourselves that the directed consciousness or ego does not accept. Suppressed, our Shadow grows in power and virulence. Confronted and embraced (which means acknowledging desires and aspects of ourselves, not necessarily acting upon them), the Shadow enriches our consciousness, becomes part of the dance of binaries—good/evil—that leads to individuation and to health, to richer life. This is Jung embracing his animal, instinctual side.

But all that explanation is from Jung's conceptual arsenal, some of it dating pre-*Liber Novus,* some emerging from writing that book. But in *Liber Novus*

---

30. Hillman and Shamdasani, *Lament of the Dead,* 8.
31. Derrida, *Writing and Difference,* 236.
32. Hillman and Shamdasani, *Lament of the Dead,* 8-9.
33. Ibid., 171.

the concept is not *explained*; it is *dramatized*: we see Jung in a dance with "the red one," the devil, and with Salome, who had John the Baptist beheaded, here in the role of Jung's anima; we see him engaged in cannibalism; we see him embrace a Christ figure (Abraxis) who embraces evil as part of his being. What the figures who rise from his unconscious say and ask him to do is shocking. As Shamdasani sums it up, "he's forced in his confrontation to encompass what he rejected in his life."[34]

Shamdasani and Hillman work hard in their conversation to help us understand what is meant here by "*his* life." Like most improvisations, *Liber Novus* reflects a complicated relationship with autobiography. These figures rise from Jung's personal, subjective unconscious but they are "voices of the dead." They have at least that "objective" status in the reality of human history; they exist in some narrative or myth that Jung has read. So they are not only articulations of Jung's subjectivity, personifications of aspects of himself that Jung rejected, but also of what human history has largely rejected. For Shamdasani and Hillman *Liber Novus* is Jung's "Lament of the Dead," not *for* but *of*: it gives voice to the dead. Their book so titled records this exchange:

> JH: That this collective opening the mouth of the dead is to go back through human history so that this thing always has meaning beyond for him alone.
>
> SS: Also it is an attempt to come to an affirmation of the fullness of life.
>
> JH: The fullness of life.
>
> SS: Including what is most horrific in it. It's a realization that if you rejected part of existence then you've rejected, in a way, all of it.[35]

Even "the back streets." Thus, as always with improvisation, confronting the chaos that rationality cannot deal with leads to the effort to redefine reason and to enlarge it by embracing some extra-rational faculty and means of expression. In the end this process results in embracing more of life. Some of the dead, then, that *Liber Novus* formally—through its form—unknowingly gives voice to are all those improvisers that preceded Jung in this enterprise of challenging and enlarging our rationality.

---

34. Ibid., 20.
35. Ibid., 21.

One crucial unnamed concept that Jung dramatizes in his dialogues with his personified subjective states is synchronicity, acausal coincidence that becomes meaningful to the perceiver. In fact he would not give synchronicity its name till the late 1920s, nor write about it at length until the 1950s. But synchronicity is at work in the *Liber Novus,* where, as Hillman and Shamdasani insist, all but one of the dramatic personae that rise from his unconscious have antecedents in myth and history, many from his wide reading in Gnosticism. Hillman states, "these figures are actual figures in a curious way from the literature, from history. Salome is a figure, Philemon has a background."[36] Thus Jung's narrative is lyrical, subjective, and personal and yet the meaning of his dialogues and encounters is not just in what is said and done and felt, but the correspondence between his subjective states and the historic or mythic personages that anticipate his subjective states. The paradox is that you get to the impersonal by a true, unfiltered openness to the personal. Hillman explains:

> So he is also showing that what lies in the depths of the human being—
> and he then is an example of a human being who has gone into these
> depths, which is the great classical move from Dante and so on—is what
> does not belong to him, not part of his personal life, and yet is profoundly
> personal and addressed to him. That's a paradox. And the lesson that we
> draw or that he is proposing is that this is everybody's, that there is some-
> thing universal about this. If you or I do the same thing we will encoun-
> ter figures, we will encounter scenes, we will encounter human history. I
> think that's a lesson.[37]

The images that rise up from your unconscious in active imagination are yours and not yours, a response to your experience but reverberating with the archetype, which is to say the impersonal and universal. Hillman unpacks the paradox: "It's only Jung who writes the *Red Book,* but all that material in there doesn't have his parents, doesn't have his marriage, doesn't have his tribulations, the personal isn't there, but it is intensely and deeply personal. So the idea of the personal has to be rethought."[38] Shamdasani agrees: "He

---

36. Ibid., 104.
37. Ibid., 104–5.
38. Ibid., 41.

finds that what animates his depths is the weight of human history, in the sense of the figures he encounters there, such as the mythic figures and biblical figures. His deepest conflicts are expressed in the form of the interplay between these images."[39] Jung is able to generate much of the conceptual arsenal—including the collective unconscious and its archetypes—that will become what we know as Jungian because the subjective complexes these personae embody and articulate have lived before. That conceptual arsenal is based on and drawn from subjective experience and cannot pass the scientific test of repeatability. But concepts are nonetheless empirical because *experienced*. This is the meaning of archetypes—in practice and without having to invoke the word—that we are not alone in our suffering or in our rebirth, that others have preceded us. *Liber Novus* is the more powerful because Jung does not announce "synchronicity"; we have to connect these dots ourselves.

Hillman and Shamdasani celebrate the *Liber Novus*'s strict commitment to a narrative, metaphoric, and figurative method free from conceptual nomenclature. But for them the problem with *Liber Novus* is that Jung forsook that method in his later work, using concepts as a buffer to the chaos. Shamdasani offers the metaphor that Jung's conceptual arsenal was redeployed after *Liber Novus* as "a safety [or "guard"] rail" against the chaos that it is only here confronted directly, "the face-to-face with the chaos of primal experience, primal as, in this case, *figural* experience."[40] Shamdasani explains that he sees "psychological conceptualism as fueled by psychology's will to science, the notion that, from the end of the nineteenth century onward, psychology would be the science of sciences and it would provide the key that would explain the doer of science."[41] So, for Hillman and Shamdasani, after *Liber Novus* Jung falls back into the trap of scientism that he abjured in Freud. And the problem is that devout Jungians, "the curatorium" Shamdasani dismissively calls them, have "mistaken the guard rail for the essence."[42]

There is no doubt truth in this. But while Jung's conceptual arsenal may keep us from "the face-to-face with the chaos of primal experience," Hillman

---

39. Ibid.
40. Ibid., 68.
41. Ibid., 74.
42. Ibid., 72.

and Shamdasani don't acknowledge what is implicit in Shamdasani's having to explain "primal experience" as he does: "in this case, figural experience." Clearly—"in this case"—the figural is one step removed from the primal. *Toujours déjà.* Like most improvisations, "reworked and reworked," *Liber Novus*'s "face-to-face" is rhetorical, an achieved effect. "Letting the chaos in" is an achieved effect. And they miss (or dismiss) the many ways that Jung's work after *Liber Novus* challenges discursiveness using other rhetorical effects. There are after all more ways than one to skin, or to put a skin on, chaos. Writing before publication of *Liber Novus,* Rowland explores the many anti-discursive formal and rhetorical devices Jung deploys post *Liber Novus* that work against his conceptual arsenal even as he makes use of it. As always in improvisation, the degree of immediacy, of face-to-face unmediated experience, is dialogic: it is *more* "primal"—I use the scare quotes advisedly—than Freud's. Jung's later work is less "primal" than *Liber Novus* but still far more so than the ever-discursive Freud.

Most important to us here, Hillman and Shamdasani also miss the familiar nature of Jung's retreat from radical immediacy. That they stake out their more radical posture *in a dialogue,* which privileges freedom and immediacy, is telltale. Welcome, gentlemen, to the improvisers' club. This is what improvisations always do. But having mounted a radical challenge to reason and rationality, improvisations—apart Hillman and Shamdasani—always offer in the end a both/and, not an either/or. Rather than reject reason, improvisers seek in the end to purify, to enlarge, or to enrich it. As is the pattern in improvisation, Jung's call to go beyond rationalism is in the end moderated. He writes in *The Archetypes and the Collective Unconscious* soon after the *Liber Novus* project is abandoned:

> Conscious and unconscious do not make a whole when one of them is suppressed and injured by the other. If they must contend, let it at least be a fair fight with equal rights on both sides. Both are aspects of life. Consciousness should defend its reason and protect itself, and the chaotic life of the unconscious should be given the chance of having its way too—as much of it as we can stand. This means open conflict and open collaboration at once. That, evidently, is the way human life should be. It is the old

game of hammer and anvil: between them the patient iron is forged into an indestructible whole, an "individual."[43]

This retreat may not content Hillman and Shamdasani but it has the advantage of giving voice unknowingly to another group of the dead, the many improvisers, who, caught up like Jung each in the paradigm shift of their age, have performed a like retreat from a radical embrace of irrationality, the chaos. And, looking back in order to go forward, re-embracing the rationality they had dismissed but is now enriched, enables the improviser to embrace more of life, which is always the improviser's ultimate goal. Hillman and Shamdasani agree that this is psychology's proper goal. Echoing Shamdasani echoing William James—who first described the stream of consciousness[44]—Hillman celebrates, "What's effective or what enables a person to live more fully."[45]

For Jung, as for James, it is "Man's capacity for consciousness alone [that] makes him man."[46] For Jung meaning arises *from* the unconscious—through dreams, symbols, synchronicity, etc.—but it is *made* in consciousness. To insist on the primal as the sole source or value and meaning is at the least not to take Jung on his own terms. Hillman and Shamdasani's insistence on a *psychomachia* where the right hemisphere wins is only to reverse the trend neuroscientist Iain McGilchrist describes where "the balance has swung too far—perhaps irretrievably far—toward the Apollonian left hemisphere, which now appears to believe that it can do anything, make anything, on its own."[47] *Lament of the Dead* favors the Dionysian at the expense of the Apol-

---

43. *CW* 9.1: *The Archetypes and the Collective Unconscious,* 522.

44. James writes: "Consciousness, then, does not appear to itself chopped up in bits. Such words as 'chain' or 'train' do not describe it fitly as it presents itself in the first instance. It is nothing jointed; it flows. A 'river' or a 'stream' are the metaphors by which it is most naturally described. *In talking of it hereafter, let us call it the stream of thought, of consciousness, or of subjective life.*" *Psychology: Briefer Course,* in William James, *Writings 1878–1899* (New York: The Library of America, 1992), 159.

45. Hillman and Shamdasani, *Lament of the Dead,* 16.

46. *CW* 8: *The Structure and Dynamics of the Psyche,* 412.

47. Iain McGilchrist, *The Master and the Emissary: The Divided Brain and the Making of the Western World* (New Haven and London: Yale University Press, 2009), 240.

lonian. Jung's whole point was balance and integration. Narrative and image and metaphor—symbols—might be more effective than concepts in elevating consciousness toward man's mystery, which will forever be out of reach. But concepts too are stepping stones on the path. After all, not all concepts are the same. The enemy lay in concepts born of abstraction that fail to attend to exceptions and individual cases. In a word, science. As Jung writes in a letter,

> Wherever a philosophy based upon the sciences prevails...the individual man loses his foothold and becomes "vermasst," turned into a mass particle, because as an "exception" he is valueless...I am convinced that something ought to be done about this blind and dangerous belief in the security of the scientific Trinity [time, space and causality].[48]

That something which his experience offered as an answer to "the scientific Trinity" was a fourth factor, acausality: synchronicity.

A lot in Jung invites the suspicion of an ill-informed, naive occultism. But, ever the scientist, Jung would answer that these—synchronicity, archetypes, the unconscious, the experience of the numinous—are empirical phenomena. Joyce calls them epiphanies, which the artistic sensibility is able to experience: "That is God," he says of the shouts of children on a football pitch.[49] Only an ill-informed naive scientism, with its cult of objectivity and experimentation with its insistence on repeatability, could allow us to ignore such experience. Enlisting quantum physics and his friend Wolfgang Pauli in the cause, Jung bent over backwards to give a scientific basis to such out-there—back street—ideas as synchronicity. But Jung never forswore subjectivity. From subjectivity alone way meaning comes.

Elsewhere McGilchrist writes: "In life we need the contributions of both hemispheres. As Kant memorably put it, concepts without intuitions are empty, intuitions without concepts are blind. We need the contributions of both, but for different purposes. An uncritical following of intuition can lead us astray, but so can an uncritical following of logic," in McGilchrist, *The Divided Brain and the Search for Meaning*, loc. 330-32.

48. Quoted in Roderick Main, *The Rupture of Time: Synchronicity and Jung's Critique of Modern Western Culture* (Hove and New York: Brunner-Routledge, 2004), 138.

49. James Joyce, *Ulysses* (New York: Vintage Books, 1961), 34.

2. Joyce's Long Shot

A number of the figures that rise from Jung's unconscious in *Liber Novus* have roots in Gnosticism, the early Christian sect declared heretical—back street— by the early church fathers. Jung considered the Gnostics the "first psychologists," his equal in their commitment to subjectivity. Their practice was a religion or spirituality based on experience of the numinous rather than on faith in the doctrinal authority: main street. As Jung said when asked if he believed in God, "I don't need to believe. I know."[50] It is a phrase often misunderstood as theistic and not a little hubristic. When in 1928 the translator of a Chinese alchemical text, *The Secret of the Golden Flower,* invited him to write an introduction, Jung discovered that alchemy was the missing link between his experience of the unconscious and ancient Gnosticism. Alchemists, whose quest to transmute gold was a metaphor to transmute spirit out of matter, were presumably the "second" psychologists, and the final empirical proof, in Jung's eyes, that there was a "collective unconscious." Turning to study Egyptian and medieval alchemy, Jung dropped *Liber Novus* unfinished. Jung explains in *Memories, Dreams, Reflections* that

> when I began to understand alchemy I realized that it represented the historical link with Gnosticism, and that a continuity therefore existed between past and present...[A]lchemy formed the bridge on the one hand into the past, to Gnosticism, and on the other into the future, to the modern psychology of the unconscious...
>
> The possibility of a comparison with alchemy, and the uninterrupted intellectual chain back to Gnosticism, gave substance to my psychology.[51]

Despite Stephen Dedalus's distaste for the founder of the Theosophists— "That Blavatsky woman,"[52]—James Joyce shared Jung's interest in Gnosticism and in alchemy.[53] In his first gesture toward the Dublin literary scene, Joyce

---

50. The "Face to Face Interview," in *C. G. Jung Speaking,* 428.

51. C.G. Jung, *Memories, Dreams, Reflections,* recorded and edited by Aniela Jaffé; translated by Richard and Clara Winston (New York: Vintage, 1963), 201, 205.

52. Joyce, *Ulysses,* 140.

53. See Nick De Marco, "Escaping History: Gnostic and Hermetic Trajectories in Joyce's *Ulysses,*" in *Hypermedia Joyce Studies,* Special Prague Symposium Issue (2010-2011) (online at *http://hjs.ff.cuni.cz/archives/v11_1/main/essays.php?essay=demarco*).

late one night approached poet George William Russell (pseud. Æ), whom he would satirize in *Ulysses* for his aery occult interests. In "Scylla and Charybdis" Joyce has Æ articulate the exact opposite of what Stephen and Joyce believe, that "Art has to reveal to us ideas, formless spiritual essences."[54] During Joyce's late-night visit Russell coaxes him to read his poems, and laughed long afterward with self-irony that he had responded that they had merit but, he told the young poet, future author of *Finnegans Wake*, that "You have not enough chaos in you to make a world."[55] Ha! During the evening they turned to Theosophy, and Joyce, relates his biographer, "was genuinely interested in such Theosophical themes as cycles, reincarnation, the succession of gods, and the eternal mother-faith that underlies all transitory religion."[56] Alchemy bookends Joyce's literary career. In his 1904 synopsis for his first novel, known as the 1904 *A Portrait of the Artist*, Joyce describes Stephen Dedalus, "Like an alchemist he bent upon his handiwork, bringing together the mysterious elements, separating the subtle from the gross."[57] Alchemy is a central metaphor, too, in *Finnegans Wake*, where the artist figure Shem the Penman is called "the first till last alshemist."[58] That Jung and Joyce were working simultaneously on their respective seminal texts, *Liber Novus* and *Ulysses*, and that both were suffused with Gnostic and alchemical themes and images, are among the more striking synchronicities of the literary century.

Although Jung would not give it a name until after Joyce published *Ulysses*, synchronicity is another of the key tunes on which the two visionaries harmonized. Joyce is personally and narratively utterly committed to the idea long before Jung gave it a name, so committed that years later he suggested the Irish writer James Stephens should finish *Finnegans Wake* if Joyce died first *because they shared a birthday* (or so Joyce imagined): "in the same country, in the same city, in the same year, in the same month, on the same day, at the same hour, six o'clock in the morning of the second of February."[59] Joyce scholar Sheldon Brivic has counted over one hundred instances of synchron-

---

54. Joyce, *Ulysses*, 185.

55. Richard Ellmann, *James Joyce* (New York: Oxford University Press, 1959), 103.

56. Ibid.

57. Quoted in Kimball, *Odyssey of the Psyche*, 20.

58. James Joyce, *Finnegans Wake* (New York: Penguin, 1999), 185.

59. Quoted in Kimball, *Odyssey of the Psyche*, 20.

icity in *Ulysses*.[60] Such lists don't tell us much. What matters is that much of the meaning of *Ulysses* emerges as the reader connects the many dots that litter the cityscape and the narration. Leopold Bloom and Stephen Dedalus both witness a cloud effacing the sun in each of their first chapters, "Telemachus" and "Calypso," and both think the same thought: "began to cover the sun, [wholly] slowly"[61] The exact echo first tips us to the importance of their synchronous links and introduces us to the father-son quest theme central to the novel.

The many acausal, which is to say irrational, synchronicities of the novel no doubt contributed to the experience of and the controversy about its apparent formlessness. Having characters think the same thoughts independently, for example, invites the view that the author doesn't know much about characterization. Prominent poet and critic Edmund Gosse called it "an anarchical production."[62] This apparent formlessness ensured the critical emphasis on revealing the tight formal structure of the novel. Ezra Pound leapt to Joyce's rescue: "*Ulysses* has more form than any novel of Flaubert's."[63] In time, aided by the outlines Joyce gave to his Italian translator Carlo Linati and to Stuart Gilbert, who wrote the first guide to *Ulysses*, critics trace the chapter parallels to episodes in the *Odyssey* and to the various schema that control the narrative chapter by chapter: bodily organs, historic styles, artistic types, colors, symbols, techniques. In all it gives an impression that *Ulysses* was careful laid out in advance, preconceived, which goes well with the impression both Joyce, his surrogate Stephen, and the novel itself give of a cool and distant, intellectual, not affective approach. "The artist," Stephen Dedalus argues in *A Portrait of the Artist as a Young Man*, "like the God of the creation, remains within or behind or beyond or above his handiwork, invisible, refined out of existence, indifferent, paring his fingernails."[64]

---

60. Sheldon Brivic, *Joyce the Creator* (Madison: The University of Wisconsin Press, 1985), 145–53.

61. Joyce, *Ulysses*, 9 and 61.

62. Quoted in *A Companion to James Joyce's* Ulysses, edited by Margot Norris (Boston and New York: Bedford Books, 1998), 28.

63. *Literary Essays of Ezra Pound*, edited by T.S. Eliot (New York: New Directions, 1968), 403.

64. James Joyce, *A Portrait of the Artist as a Young Man* (New York, London, and

Thus it comes as something of a surprise how much Joyce devalued conscious premeditation and control. "I suppose you would call me an intellectual writer," Joyce coyly goads his Irish friend Arthur Power in their ongoing conversations in Paris. Power responds with his admiration for the lyricism of *The Dubliners* and *A Portrait*; for him *Ulysses* was "over-conscious, and inspiration is what I admire." Joyce responds, "Depends on what you call inspiration, doesn't it? […] and it seems to me that you mistake romantic flair for inspiration. The inspiration I admire is not the temperamental one, but the steady sequence of built-up thought, such as you get in *Gulliver's Travels*, in Defoe and in Rabelais even." What he means by this is suggested by his further explanation:

> And so I have tried to write naturally, on an emotional basis as against an intellectual basis. Emotion has dictated the course and detail of my book, and in emotional writing one arrives at the unpredictable which can be of more value, since its sources are deeper, than the products of the intellectual method. In the intellectual method you plan everything beforehand. When you arrive at the description, say, of a house you try and remember that house exactly, which after all is journalism.[65]

This "journalism" after all sounds a bit like Joyce himself, who would proclaim elsewhere to his friend Budgen that he wanted "to give a picture of Dublin so complete that if the city one day suddenly disappeared from the earth it could be reconstructed out of my book."[66] "But," he adds to Power, and here gets to his real point,

> the emotionally creative writer refashions that house and creates a significant image in the only significant world, the world of our emotions. The more we are tied to fact and try to give a correct impression, the further we are from what is significant. In writing one must create an endlessly changing surface, dictated by the mood and current impulse in contrast to the fixed mood of the classical style…The important thing is not what we write, but how we write, and in my opinion the modern writer must be an adventurer above all, willing to take every risk, and

Toronto: Everyman's Library/Alfred A. Knopf, 1991), 269.

65. Power, *Conversations with James Joyce*, 95.

66. Frank Budgen, *James Joyce and the Making of* Ulysses (Bloomington and London: Indiana University Press, 1960), 67-68.

be prepared to founder in his effort if need be. In other words we must write dangerously: everything is inclined to flux and change nowadays and modern literature, to be valid, must express that flux...A book, in my opinion, should not be planned out beforehand, but as one writes it will form itself, subject, as I say, to the constant emotional promptings of one's personality.[67]

Far more than a response to Dickens's Mr. Grandgrind, Joyce's distaste for mere facts—"facticity without meaning"—is better understood as his response to the positivist spirit of his age that promised full knowledge of the world and its betterment through objective rationality. "Endlessly changing surface" and "flux and change" point toward a vision of life as "a fluid succession of presents" and "a conception of personality," as Ellmann writes, "as river rather than statue."[68] Aspiring to a narrative method that would capture such flux would fulfill Walter Pater's call in the "Conclusion" to his studies of the Renaissance, "to rouse, to startle [the human spirit] to a life of constant and eager observation," for

> Every moment some form grows perfect in hand or face; some tone of the hills or the sea is choicer than the rest; some mood of passion or insight or intellectual excitement is irresistibly real and attractive to us,—for that moment only. Not the fruit of experience but experience itself is the end...
>
> To burn always with this hard gemlike flame, to maintain this ecstasy, is success in life.[69]

Joyce's first narrative answer to Pater's call to alertness was his secularized and aestheticized idea of the epiphany. Doctrinally a revelation of a god, for Joyce an epiphany is the sudden "revelation of the whatness of a thing," moments when "the soul of the commonest object...seems to us radiant."[70] Early in the century he writes a series of short prose poems, some of which will find their way into *Portrait* and into *Ulysses*. "The initial and determining act of judgment in [Joyce's] work," writes Ellmann, "is the justification of the

---

67. Power, *Conversations with James Joyce*, 95.
68. Ellmann, *James Joyce*, 150.
69. Pater, *The Renaissance*, 249-50.
70. James Joyce, *Stephen Hero* (New York: New Directions, 1963), 213.

commonplace."[71] We can now add, of the back streets and the thrown away. "The constant emotional promptings of one's personality" can be understood too in light of Jung's embrace of subjectivity. And it's not just a matter of how Joyce composes but how his characters compose their lives, how they live their stories which we get to witness. *Ulysses* works not simply by inviting us to observe the carefully drawn, naturalistic details of Dublin and its inhabitants—which is as far as Jung's mostly hostile reading of *Ulysses* took him in his review of the novel[72]—but rather by displaying how characters make meaning of such details, and inviting us to do the same.

Joyce's encyclopedic bricolage of narrative methods is an immense and complicated subject that we need not fully undertake here. But through his narrative method's most salient feature, stream of consciousness, the narrative "forms itself" by "the constant emotional promptings of" his *characters'* "personalit[ies]." It is not merely that we are inside the characters' heads time and again but that what is in their heads—their personal idioms—often shape the narrative voice, our surrogate. "*Stately* plump Buck Mulligan..."— the famous first words of *Ulysses*—is the language Buck Mulligan would have used. Stephen Dedalus "suffers" Mulligan to remove his handkerchief not because as Wyndham Lewis objects, that there was "something old-fashioned in Mr. Joyce's method" but because this is how Stephen feels, something of a supercilious prig himself, and feeling put upon by the "usurper" Mulligan.[73] Eminent Joyce scholar Hugh Kenner writes, "The narrative idiom is bent by a person's proximity as a star defined by Einstein will bend passing light"[74]—a metaphor Jung, who pressed quantum physics into service to support his idea on synchronicity, would have appreciated. "This," Kenner writes, "is something apparently new in fiction, the normally neutral narrative vocabulary pervaded by a little cloud of idioms which the character might use if he were

---

71. Ellmann, *James Joyce*, 3.

72. "'Ulysses': A Monologue." He writes, for example, "This utterly hopeless emptiness is the dominant note of the whole book" (*CW* 15: 164).

73. I rely here on the details Hugh Kenner adduces in his argument in *Joyce's Voices* (Berkeley, Los Angeles, and London: University of California Press, 1978), 15-38.

74. Kenner, *Joyce's Voices*, 71.

managing the narrative."[75] We are in the characters' streams of consciousness before Joyce's stream of consciousness method really kicks in.[76] Apart from Stephen, their flames are not always gemlike, but the stream of consciousness narrative method is Joyce's second, stunningly brilliant answer to the Paterian injunction.

We don't have to wait long to witness the stream of consciousness not just trickling into the narrative voice but bursting forth in full. On the novel's first page, Stephen's interior monologue intrudes upon the narration in response to Mulligan's "even white teeth glistening here and there with gold points."[77] On our own, if attentive, we might respond to these gold points as canine or lupine enough to anticipate the theme by which the chapter will end, Mulligan as "Usurper."[78] Seeing the gold points of the glistening teeth, Stephen thinks, "Chrysostomos," Greek for "golden-mouthed." We are inside his head hearing it. With the help of Joyce's annotators, we know what a bundle of associations this epithet evokes, anticipating by contrast Stephen's rotten teeth, and alluding to Greek rhetorician Dion Chrysostomos, to patriarch of Constantinople St. John Chrysostomos, and to the Roman pope, Gregory Goldenmouth, who sent St. Patrick to convert Ireland—all feeding into Stephen's concerns and animadversions toward Mulligan as usurper.[79] "Chrys-

---

75. Ibid., 17. Ellmann anticipates Kenner in his discussion of the 1904 *A Portrait of the Artist*. Ellman writes of the short treatment for the novel, "the prose has been infected by the hero's mind" and "[t]his magnetization of style and vocabulary by the context of person, place, and time, has its humble origin in the few pages Joyce wrote" in 1904. Ellmann, *James Joyce,* 151.

76. The grand, stately "S" of the Random House edition, chosen by book designer Ernst Reichl, helps to convey Buck Mulligan's aplomb but it also has this ill effect: it gives the impression that the author's voice is commenting on Buck and steers us away from recognizing Mulligan's gravitational pull on the word choice. According to Reichl's daughter Ruth, former editor of *Gourmet,* Joyce had no involvement in the design. Personal email with Ruth Reichl, 9 August 2013.

77. Joyce, *Ulysses,* 3

78. Ibid., 23.

79. Don Gifford, Ulysses *Annotated: Notes for James Joyce's* Ulysses, 2nd ed. (Berkeley, Los Angeles, and London: University of California Press, 1988), 14 (s.v. "Chrysostomos").

ostomos" is not part of the "cloud of idioms" that trails behind Stephen. It is his interior voice we hear. Joyce has moved us seamlessly—without narrative direction—from an alertness to how characters move the atmosphere around them to an alertness to shifting centers of consciousness. *Ulysses* makes us alert. Who can experience *Ulysses*'s stream of consciousness and not become more alert to his or her own passing thoughts? Usually unregistered, such thoughts are mere throw always.

Or perhaps Stephen's intrusion into the narrative should be called a stream of *unconsciousness* or at least of liminal consciousness, the kind of liminality or intrusion of the unconscious into consciousness that Jung will spend a career exploring and championing. Such intrusions are the source of the "transcendent function" which reconciles our antinomies through symbols created in the alembic of the conjunction. Seeming to describe Joyce's stream of consciousness method, Stein writes of Jung:

> The intuitions and thoughts that appear from the unconscious are not the products of deliberate efforts to think but are inner objects, bits of the unconscious that land on the surface of the ego occasionally. (Jung sometimes liked to say that thoughts are like birds: They come and nest in the trees of consciousness for a little while and then they fly away. They are forgotten and disappear.)[80]

Forgotten, thrown away, or even flown away, unless you are Joyce, who tucks them away for later use in his art. "[C]lassical literature represents the daylight of human personality," Joyce tells Power, "while modern literature is concerned with the twilight, the passive rather than the active mind."[81] Joyce calls it "passive," intending not "passivity" but rather the opposite of the *actively* "directed consciousness" Jung will oppose to the unconscious. Elsewhere Joyce speaks, in terms Jung would recognize, of "the subterranean forces, those hidden tides which govern everything and run humanity counter to the apparent flood."[82] This is the part of *Ulysses* that Jung got right in his review: "An earnest endeavor to rub the noses of our contemporaries in the

---

80. Stein, *Jung's Map of the Soul*, 208.
81. Power, *Conversations with James Joyce*, 74.
82. Ibid., 54.

Shadow-side of reality."[83] Whether Joyce means us to read Stephens's manifold associations on goldenmouth as conscious or unconscious, what is clear
is that Stephen's intrusive interior voice creates an image whose unconscious
associations go beyond the feral narrative detail of "white teeth glistening...
with gold points." One can imagine "Chrysostomos" popping into Stephen's
conscious mind, trailing energetic roots from his unconscious—exactly what
Jung meant by symbol. As Murray Stein points out, for Jung

> often synchronicity occurs...when a person is psychically in an *abaisse-*
> *ment du niveau mental* (a lower level of conscious awareness, a sort of
> dimming of consciousness) and the level of consciousness has dropped
> into what is today called an alpha state. This means also that the uncon-
> scious is more energized than consciousness, and complexes and arche-
> types are aroused into a more activated state and can push over the
> threshold into consciousness.[84]

One function of Joyce's stream of consciousness is to portray this *abaisse-*
ment du niveau mental where, per Joyce, "the subterranean forces, those hidden tides" are, per Jung, "aroused into a more activated state and can push
over the threshold into consciousness."

Another function of stream of consciousness is to induce it. Witnessing
such liminal states in the characters and narration prepares us to do the same.
Within the reading experience of the novel, the synchronicities invited by the
alpha state Joyce produces are both objective and subjective. They are objective in that we bear witness to characters' experiencing synchronicity—like
Jung, an empiricism of the subjective. They are subjective in that, under the
aegis of Hermes the connection-maker, connecting the narrative's dots, we
make meaning ourselves.

For Jung, not living our animal in part means not living our Shadow. The
Shadow is that part of ourselves that our conscious selves deny. For Jean
Kimball, in her rich and wise Jungian reading of the novel, "*Ulysses* is the
Book of the Shadow" where Bloom represents the Shadow to Stephen's Ego or
directed consciousness.[85] From her Jungian point of view, behind the narra-

---

83. *CW* 15: 180.

84. Stein, *Jung's Map of the Soul*, 211.

85. Kimball, *Odyssey of the Psyche*, 71.

tive's central father-son quest lies the even deeper Jungian quest for the Ego to "realize" the Shadow. The challenge the Ego faces is to become aware of this part of itself it has denied; in Stephen's case, because he lives so much in his head, he must become aware of his animal, bodily self, which offal-eating, masturbating, sexually obsessed Bloom represents in full. Bloom's stream of consciousness is the example *par excellence* of Jung's idea of the *abaissement du niveau mental*. As Kimball argues, "Steven discovers in the course of the novel what Jung says the Ego discovers during the realization of the Shadow: that he cannot 'settle everything and do everything by the force of [his] will.'"[86] Bloom, as earthbound Body, represents the constraining limits—like the animals' instinctual natures that Jung prized—that Stephen's high-flying Spirit must acknowledge and embrace to become a true artist. Though incomplete by the end of the novel, Stephen's encounter with Bloom hints at a resolution of opposites, the two sides of the developing artist, hence an act of individuation that makes possible the mature Joyce who writes *Ulysses*. Kimball adds, "With the advent of Bloom in Stephen's life, the fiction faces up to the unconscious as an integral part of the portrait of the artist."[87] Kimball's case for the correspondence between Jung and Joyce's vision of the psyche's development is luminous and full of deep insights.

Kimball points out that Joyce's "portrait of Bloom is suggestively congruent with the 'trickster,' a 'collective shadow figure,' as Jung comments in 'The Psychology of the Trickster-Figure.'"[88] That other Bloom, the Yale Trickster Harold, dismisses Leopold Bloom's role as Trickster: "Joyce's endlessly amiable Leopold Bloom...is a sport in the annals of *Ulysses*."[89] Yet Leopold Bloom casts a Shadow dark enough to undergo sadomasochism, transgendering, and childbirth in Nighttown—polymorphous perverse enough for any Trickster. Now working the shadowy craft of advertising, as a modern Odysseus—whose great grandfather in myth is Hermes—Bloom displays the *metis*, the wiles, characteristic of *polytropos* Trickster: the "ability to deal with whatever comes up, drawing on certain intellectual qualities: forethought[,] perspicac-

---

86. Ibid., 146.

87. Ibid., 71.

88. Ibid.

89. *Bloom's Literary Themes: The Trickster*, edited by Harold Bloom (New York: Bloom's Literary Criticism, 2010), xv.

ity, quickness and acuteness of understanding, trickery, and even deceit."[90] In Greek culture any happy coincidence would inspire the remark, "Hermes is present." Bloom, like Hermes a connection-maker, serves as catalyst for many of the synchronicities of *Ulysses*.

Like Jung's mythic and historic Gnostic interlocutors in *Liber Novus*, who synchronize acausally with Jung's unconscious states, the largest synchronicity bodied forth in *Ulysses* lies in the correspondences between Dublin and Ithaca, Bloom and Odysseus, Stephen and Telemachus, in sum, the *Odyssey* and *Ulysses*. Joyce intends, as Ellmann cleverly writes, "to blend the two ends of the Western tradition like a multitemporal, multiterritorial pun."[91]

Examining "T/throwaway," both the horse that wins the Ascot Gold Cup and the metaphor, will clarify how synchronicity works on a smaller scale in Joyce's masterpiece of bricolage. Joyce had many reasons for choosing June 16, 1904 as Bloomsday—not the least being the emotionally charged fact that it was the day Joyce and his future wife Nora Barnacle sealed their fate together when Nora masturbated James on the strand, an event that gets tinkered into *Ulysses* when Leopold Bloom pleasures himself on the strand as he watches Gerty McDowall, a cripple and thus in our culture another throwaway (as we will see). A chambermaid at Finn's Hotel, Nora's family name suggests she too is a throwaway. Yet one can imagine Joyce's joy when, having chosen the day for personal reasons, he perused the many newspapers that were piled high in his writing room and saw that there really was a horse *Throwaway* that won the Ascot Gold Cup on that day, paying 20-to-1 odds and beating the favorite *Sceptre*—just as Joyce would have liked his thrown-away, extra-metropolitan nation to outdistance the scepter of London and Rome (and Irish sentimentality, if we can for a moment substitute the Irish harp for the scepter). The many linkages surrounding "T/throwaway" throughout the novel create a web of acausal connections—again, the special province of Trickster/Hermes—that invite the reader to create emotion-charged meaning. None of it makes rational sense, but sense is there for the making, which is just the point.

---

90. Detienne and Vernant, *Cunning Intelligence,* 44.
91. Ellmann, *James Joyce,* 2.

"Throwaway" as metaphor is introduced in "Lestrygonians"—the canni-
bal eaters—when a Y.M.C.A. evangelist hands Bloom a "throwaway" pamphlet announcing the coming of the revivalist John Alexander Dowie, who
proclaimed himself "Elijah the Restorer."[92] When Bloom first sees the pamphlet's reference to "Blood of the Lamb," he mistakes the first letters for his
own name—"Bloo...Me? No"[93]—thus linking him not only to Elijah but to
Christ the Redeemer. Bloom—"ben Bloom Elijah" he is called at the end of
"Cyclops"—will be associated again and again with Elijah, the prophet who
warns King Ahab against worshiping pagan gods, and whose career echoes
Moses when God parts the Jordan for him and when he is elevated to heaven
in a chariot before death. Most importantly in both Judaic and Christian
traditions, he is the herald of Christ's second coming and thus a herald and
avatar, like Bloom, of love. As Marilyn French remarks, Bloom is "a walking
exemplar of caritas."[94]

As metaphor, "throwaway" pops up again in "Lotus-Eaters" when Bantam
Lyons, an unsympathetic man with "yellow blacknailed fingers," misunderstands Bloom's offer of the paper Lyons wants to peruse for the racing news.
Willing to sacrifice the paper to be "shut of him," Bloom tells him, "I was just
going to throw it away."[95] Lyons, who can't be bothered to listen attentively to
such a marginal, unimportant person as Bloom, nor to fold the paper he has
borrowed when he returns it, mistakes it for a tip on the long-shot horse:

> Bantam Lyons doubted an instant, leering: then thrust the
> outspread sheets back on Mr. Bloom's arms.
> —I'll risk it, he said. Here, thanks.[96]

Lyons's "outspread sheets" exemplifies the "impersonal," nail-paring nature
of Joyce's narrative method. Presenting a purely naturalistic image without
authorial judgment—a wedding of Wordsworth's "presentational style" (see
above, Chapter 9) with the non-kinetic art Joyce learned from Aristotle and
from Flaubert—the narrator gives us plenty of information to judge for our-

---

92. Gifford, Ulysses *Annotated*, 157.

93. Joyce, *Ulysses*, 151.

94. Marilyn French, *The Book as World: James Joyce's* Ulysses, (Cambridge, Mass.:
Harvard University Press, 1976), 42.

95. Joyce, *Ulysses*, 85.

96. Ibid., 86.

selves. Clearly Lyons hasn't embraced Wordsworth's message of "that best portion of a good man's life, / His little, nameless, unremembered, acts / Of kindness and of love."[97]

But that is just a sidebar. The main point lies in the acausal connections: Lyons's mistaken idea that Bloom has a tip on the dark horse that wins at long odds will feed into the anti-Semitic theme that haunts him throughout the day and comes to a head in "Cyclops" with its theme of one-sided, one-eyed prejudice. Lenehan, who will later falsely claim to have had an affair with Molly and who puts Lyons off the tip, blames not himself for Lyons's loss but rather scapegoats Bloom, who

> had a few bob on *Throwaway* and he's gone to gather his shekels...
> Bet you what you like he has a hundred shillings to five on. He's the only man in Dublin has it. A dark horse.
> —He's a bloody dark horse himself, says Joe.[98]

Thus, by this point, Joyce has woven a skein of associations around the horse Throwaway: marginality, anti-Semitism, prophecy and false prophecy, and the promise of redemption.

The next metaphoric "throwaway" is the skiff that Bloom sees on the river Liffey:

> a crumpled throwaway, Elijah is coming, rode lightly down the Liffey, under Loopline bridge, shooting the rapids where water chafed around the bridgepiers, sailing eastward past hulls and anchorchains, between the Customhouse old dock and George's quay.[99]

How a skiff is a "crumpled throwaway" I don't exactly know; it must be an unimpressive craft at best, all the more unimpressive in contrast to the lilting prose, "the *fin de siècle* beauty" with which the narrator describes it. In any case, it reminds Bloom of the earlier crumpled throwaway, the pamphlet about Elijah. "Elijah is coming" is Bloom's stream of consciousness interjection when he sees the skiff. But the real import of this passage is the scene from which it is the jump-cut (this is "Wandering Rocks" which works by

---

97. Wordsworth and Coleridge, *Lyrical Ballads,* lines 34-35.
98. Joyce, *Ulysses,* 335.
99. Ibid., 227.

jump-cuts, all enforcing the isolation and purposelessness of the many characters): the pathetic scene in the Dedalus "closesteaming kitchen" where
Katey, Boody, and Maggy, Stephen's sisters, discuss their fruitless effort to
pawn Stephens's books to get the wherewithal to eat. They've gotten nothing
from M'Guiness's Pawn Shop but nonetheless they settle in to eat the yellow
pea soup that they've been charitably given by Sister Mary Patrick. "Boody,
breaking big chunks of bread into the yellow soup," indulges in sacrilegious
parody—"Our father who art not in heaven"[100]—that comments bitterly
on their father's feckless absence and looks ahead to the scene a few pages
later when Simon Dedalus abuses his other daughter Dilly. Joyce's attitude
to pea soup is made perfectly clear in *Finnegans Wake*: "He even ran away
with himself and became a farsoonerite, saying he would far sooner muddle
through the hash of lentils in Europe than meddle with Ireland's split pea
soup."[101] Stuck eternally in Ireland, the Dedalus girls are more throwaways
at the hands of their father, of Irish society in general, and of the Catholic
Church in particular, whose charity is best understood through the lens of
Blake's "Holy Thursday":

> Is this a holy thing to see
> In a rich and fruitful land,
> Babes reduced to misery,
> Fed with cold and usurous hand?[102]

Blake's *Songs of Experience* are a frequent presence in Stephen's allusive mind.
Stephen's charitable sympathy for his sisters is good-spirited and yet constitutes one of the nets that he must overfly if he is not to become lost, thrown-
away, himself.

Although the word is not employed, clearly Joyce meant us to see the lame
Gerty MacDowall in the "Nausicaa" chapter as another "throwaway." Hardly
the equal of the princess in the *Odyssey*, Gerty shares the Phaeacian princess's
romantic nature but to the point of parody. The chapter's narrative voice
appropriates Gerty's manner, or rather it is her "cloud of idioms" that appropriates the narrative voice. Like Emma Bovary, Gerty has been too influenced

---

100. Ibid.
101. Quoted in Ellmann, *James Joyce*, 78.
102. *The Poetry and Prose of William Blake*, 19.

by sentimental romances and songs. But she is not totally naïve. When Bloom begins to masturbate behind the rock on the strand, Gerty is aware of it, loosens her hair, and lifts her dress. She will have a role in Bloom's masochistic dreamscape in Nighttown.

How we are to respond to Joyce's satiric portrait of Gerty is challenging. Clearly we are invited to look down on her as a banal victim of the sentimentality that is another of the Irish nets Stephen must escape. But the Emma Bovary parallel is telling. Gerty is not only a version of the temptress on the strand to which Stephen wrote his villanelle in *A Portrait*. She is also a version of Joyce and of Stephen, who both love Irish sentimental songs as much as they hate the harp as symbol of Irish sentimentality. *Gerty, c'est moi.*

Jung, surely Stephen's equal as haughty intellectual, has a similar encounter with the banal in *Liber Novus*. In "The Castle in the Forest," he meets a scholar and then his daughter:

> She: I am the old man's daughter. He holds me here in unbearable captivity, not out of envy or hate, but out of love, since I am his only child and the image of my mother who died young.
> I scratched my head: is this some kind of hellish banality?
> Word for word, pulp fiction from the lending library![103]

Nonetheless Jung manages to recognize that she is "real." Once recognized, not denied, she is transformed before his eyes. Jung learns from her that he should not "stumble now over the fabulous, since the fairy tale is the great mother of the novel, and has even more universal validity than the most-avidly read novel of your time."[104] We should not miss the high praise for the novel implicit here: for Jung the novel through its use of fairy tale has done much to unveil the workings of the psyche.

We look down on the banal and common—as on the shadowy back streets— at our peril. Jung had learned earlier and more abstractly from the spirit of the depths, that is, his soul, that he had to conquer his arrogance, "and I had to swallow the small as a means of healing the immortal in me…But the small, narrow and banal is not nonsense, but one of both of the essences of the

---

103. Jung, *The Red Book*, 223.
104. Ibid., 224.

Godhead."[105] Joyce had contempt for the Irish fairy tales and common folk that Yeats and the Irish Renaissance lionized. But like Jung, he embraces the ordinary, the everyday. Both men needed their haughty, intellectual persona chastened and *Liber Novus* and *Ulysses* perform that function.

16 June 1904 was a Thursday. Joyce was born on a Thursday, the day named for Thor, the god of thunder. As it will in *Finnegans Wake,* thunder will play a crucial (and synchronistic) role in *Ulysses* after the prostitute Zoe (=life) reads his palm and calls him "Thursday's child [who] has far to go."[106] Just as the thunder claps and the life-renewing rain begins, Stephen, experiencing a guilt-ridden vision of his dead mother, smashes the chandelier in Nighttown with his ashplant or walking stick, named *Nothung*—Needful—for the redemptive sword wielded by Siegfried in Wagner's *Ring.* Stephen is finally freed from the maternal guilt and mother complex that has haunted him.[107] This Thursday theme is how Joyce's mind worked, finding personal meaning in acausal connections. But one need not have recourse to Joyce's personal associations; the naturalistic images and the network of allusions invite us to connect the dots, to appreciate the breakthrough Thursday's child has just had. The breakthrough offers hope that Stephen himself will not be thrown away, that he will find his way. After a day of crossed purposes, Stephen is free finally to engage with Bloom, his surrogate father.

Many of these allusions to "throwaway" are drawn together in "Ithaca," the chapter where Stephen and Bloom commune. The catechist who serves as narrator asks, "Where had previous intimations of the [Gold Cup race] result, effected or projected, been received by him?" In answer, Bloom's day is summarized, each address and incident itemized:

> In Bernard Kiernan's licensed premises 8, 9 and 10 Little Britain street: in David Byrne's licensed premises, 14 Duke street: in O'Connell street lower, outside Graham Lemon's when a dark man had placed in his hand

---

105. Ibid., 121.

106. Joyce, *Ulysses,* 562.

107. According to Kimball, Joyce's reading of Jung's *Transformations and Symbols of the Libido* helped him develop the mother complex in *Ulysses,* 22. So, synchronistically, *Transformations* inspired both *Liber Novus* and *Ulysses.*

a throwaway (subsequently thrown away), advertising Elijah, restorer of the church in Zion: in Lincoln place outside the premises of F. W. Sweny and Co (Limited), dispensing chemists, when, when Frederick M. (Bantam) Lyons had rapidly and successively requested, perused and restituted the copy of the current issue of the *Freeman's Journal and National Press* which he had been about to throw away (subsequently thrown away), he had proceeded towards the oriental edifice of the Turkish and Warm Baths, 11 Leinster street, *with the light of inspiration shining in his countenance and bearing in his arms the secret of the race, graven in the language of prediction.*[108]

The clause that I have emphasized echoes MacHugh's windy recitation of Taylor's speech in "Aeolus": "He would never have spoken with the Eternal amid lightnings on Sinai's mountaintop nor ever have come down with the light of inspiration shining in his countenance and bearing in his arms the tables of the law, graven in the language of the outlaw."[109] The echo enforces the pun in "race": Gold Cup/Throwaway/Moses/Jews. All, we could say, are led by more or less metaphoric throwaways: "the tables of the law" are thrown away when Moses descends from the mountain; Moses doesn't cross the Jordan; Bloom doesn't get the tip on the Gold Cup "graven in the language of prediction." Yet all are redeemed: Throwaway leads at the finishing line.

Thus Joyce weaves this tightly woven skein of connections around "Throwaway": the dark horse that beat Sceptre, a manifold symbol of the Irish nation and its beleaguered Catholicism and colonial status; the promise of prophecy (Elijah) and redemption and love (Christ) represented by the most significant throwaway of the novel, the Hungarian Jew who cannot find his place in Irish life. All this points symbolically to the larger meanings of his novel. "T/throwaway"—horse, men, and metaphor—is the simplest yet most profound example of what his great biographer Richard Ellmann writes of Joyce's "larger plan": "to make irrelevance relevant," that is, to show the value of the apparently meaningless, the marginal, the back streets; to give form to the epiphanic moments when the divine shows through the commonplace.

But my active verbs here—to show, to express, to give form to—are misleading. Joyce creates the network of connections, and the biographers and

---

108. Joyce, *Ulysses,* 676; emphasis added.
109. Ibid., 143.

annotators have persuaded us that they meant those things to him. But the way *Ulysses* works as we read it is that Joyce stands back, paring his nails. Joyce, we are schooled in *A Portrait,* seeks to achieve a static, non-kinetic art, an art that has no design upon you, whose only purpose is to inspire aesthetic arrest, the invitation to be "the hard gemlike flame" that lights the epiphanic beauty of the world around us, seeking only, as Conrad admitted was his task as novelist, "by the power of the written word to make you hear, to make you feel—it is, before all, to make you *see.*"[110] Like Jung, Joyce is in the equation but not in the equation, a subjective presence who creates an objective text that invites our subjective presence. Impersonal, the text is static; it does not actively guide our response. But the effect on us is kinetic. "The object of any work of art," Joyce told Arthur Power, "is the transference of emotion; talent is the gift of conveying that emotion."[111] It is we who must connect the dots for these meanings and emotions to emerge. Joyce's talent is to set up the warp and woof but to make *us* the weavers, no less so than Penelope.

What we weave out of Joyce's overdetermined naturalistic and allusive details is not a shroud but something with the texture and vitality of life, and shot through with love, represented objectively not only by Bloom but also experienced subjectively as we are incited to shower our alertness on the narrative even as he schools us how to. *Ulysses* enforces that definition of love: paying attention. What we weave into the connections are not Joyce's subjective emotions—which may be the first cause—but our own, which are the final cause, as we respond to the affective details of a nation and its men, women, and children who are being abused by the one-sidedness of preju-dice and paternalism, and by a culture of sentimentality. "In synchronistic events," Rowland suggests, "we are part of what we observe. Moreover, we change what we observe by the act of observing it."[112] The meanings of the synchronicities that saturate *Ulysses* don't emerge deductively from Joyce's mind but inductively from ours. The way *Ulysses* works, in other words, answers the patriarchal authority of London and Rome *and* of scientific pos-

---

110. "Preface," in Joseph Conrad, *The Nigger of the "Narcissus,"* edited by Richard Kimbrough (New York: W.W. Norton, 1979), 147.

111. Power, *Conversations with James Joyce,* 98.

112. Rowland, *Jung in the Humanities,* 115.

itivism: top down, deductive. *Ulysses* works bottom up, inductively. Where his Modernist colleagues flirt with fascism and anti-Semitism, Joyce saturates *Ulysses* in the spirit of democracy even as it recreates (or participates in) the open-ended spirit of improvisation.[113]

A Gnostic and alchemical text, *Ulysses* gives us the opportunity to experience the numinous in the everyday. Though a sendup of scientific positivism and literary naturalism's "myth of mythlessness," the flaw in the novel, if there is a flaw, is in its title. "Ulysses"—not the use of myth but the pointing to it—demystifies. The title tells us that we are to respond to the narrative through the lens of the *Odyssey*. It is as if Jung had stooped in *Liber Novus* to using his conceptual vocabulary. But, despite this lapse, Joyce creates a world, a microcosmos—Dublin, Bloom/Dedalus—that reflects the visionary experience of the macrocosmos, the way life works complete with its irrational synchronicities. Joyce explained that he made sure that not everything could be explained in *Ulysses* because not everything can be explained in life. The man in the McIntosh is a famous example. "Ulysses" explains too much.

But it's the only thing Joyce explains. All the other explanations, right or wrong, are our doing. Their accuracy, like Bloom's pseudo-science, is less important than the spirit in which they are alchemized. The alertness *that* requires prepares us to appreciate the portrait, in Kenner's words, of "Bloom's unflagging alertness."[114] Though Bloom is not universally embraced, I think there is cause to love Bloom for the openness and alertness to life he embodies. Stephen wants to find epiphanies in the everyday world, but it is Bloom, *homme moyen sensuel,* who spends much of his time in an *abaissement du niveau mental* that invites, according to Jung, the connection making that the experience of the noumenal demand. Stephen needs to reconcile himself to the dead, but it is Bloom who travels to the underworld. Stephen wants to go to Nighttown, but it is Bloom who, tagging along, displays an openness to his Shadow that Nighttown elicits. Needing an enemy to fuel his art, Stephen rouses himself at every opportunity to fight the "Usurper," but it is Bloom

---

113. Terry Eagleton describes the author of *Ulysses* as "that rare creature, an avant-garde artist who is also a genuine democrat. Hardly any other modernist writer is at once so esoteric and down to earth…He also lacks the mandarin tone of so many of his modernist colleagues," in *The English Novel*, 284-85.

114. Kenner, *Joyce's Voices*, 62

who makes a separate peace with his many imagined usurpers, including the one true usurper, Blazes Boylan. Stephen sees the divine in the sound of boys on a pitch, but in "Hades" as they ride by carriage to the graveyard, Bloom's great-souled empathy extends even to a workhorse whose feelings he tries to imagine:

> A team of horses passed from Finglas with toiling plodding tread, dragging through the funereal silence a creaking waggon on which lay a granite block. The waggoner marching at their head saluted.
>
> Coffin now. Got here before us, dead as he is. Horse looking round at it with his plume skeowways. Dull eye: collar tight on his neck, pressing on a bloodvessel or something. Do they know what they cart out here every day? Must be twenty or thirty funerals every day.[115]

Here Bloom reaches out to what Joyce prized in the Egyptians, "the great subconscious life of Nature [that civilization has] ignored, a life which without effort reaches to such great perfection."

Narrated, as Joyce explained to Budgen, "in the form of a mathematical catechism," the "Ithaca" chapter is *Ulysses's* most impersonal, a parody at once of scientific rationalism, literary naturalism, and Catholicism. But it is the novel's big emotional payoff. As Joyce continues in his description to Budgen: "All events are resolved into their cosmic, physical, psychical, etc. equivalents...but Bloom and Stephen thereby become heavenly bodies, wanderers like the stars at which they gaze"[116]—an heroic riposte to Deasy's anti-Semitic slur in "Nestor": "They sinned against the light, Mr Deasy said gravely. And you can see the darkness in their eyes. And that is why they are wanderers on the earth to this day.[117]

"Ithaca's" many catalogues' presentational style is one of the chapter's dominant characteristics and Bloom's big heart looms large. When asked "What spectacle confronted them when they, first the host, then the guest, emerged silently, doubly dark, from obscurity by a passage from the rere of

---

115. Joyce, *Ulysses*, 101.

116. *Letters of James Joyce*, edited by Stuart Gilbert and Richard Ellmann, 3 vols. (London: Faber and Faber, 1957-66), 1:159-60.

117. Joyce, *Ulysses*, 34.

the house into the penumbra of the garden?"[118]—in the narrator's reply, perhaps bent by Stephen's poetic idiom, we are meant to hear an echo of the closing lines of Dante's *Inferno*: "The heaventree of stars hung with humid nightblue fruit."[119] The lunar "nightblue fruit" anticipates Bloom's kissing Molly's "plump mellow yellow smellow melons of her rump, on each plump melonous hemisphere, in their mellow yellow furrow, with obscure prolonged provocative melonsmellonous osculation."[120] Synchronicities converge apace. Bloom's kiss (as well as his pandering offer of Molly to Stephen) was anticipated in "Proteus" when Stephen recalled his dream of the generous Haroun al Raschid: "The melon he had he held against my face. Smiled: creamfruit smell"[121]—a promise of the woman Stephen needs. Now, having left the kitchen where they have communed as close to father and son as they will manage, Bloom, long Stephen's Shadow, becomes his Hermetic *psychopompos*, offering "meditations…[to] accompany his demonstration to his companion of various constellations?"[122] His catalogue, filled with the scientific inaccuracies we have come to expect from Bloom, nonetheless lovingly embraces the macrocosmos, "a wanderer…like the star at which [he] gazes":

> Meditations of evolution increasingly vaster: of the moon invisible in incipient lunation, approaching perigee: of the infinite lattiginous scintillating uncondensed milky way, discernible by daylight by an observer placed at the lower end of a cylindrical vertical shaft 5000 ft deep sunk from the surface towards the centre of the earth: of Sirius (alpha in Canis Maior) 10 lightyears (57,000,000,000,000 miles) distant and in volume 900 times the dimension of our planet: of Arcturus: of the precession of equinoxes: of Orion with belt and sextuple sun theta and nebula in which 100 of our solar systems could be contained: of moribund and of

---

118. Ibid., 698.

119. Ibid. Gifford offers this gloss from Dante: "The Guide [Virgil] and I entered by that hidden road to return into the bright world; and without caring for any rest, we mounted up, he first and I second, so far that I distinguished through a round opening the beauteous things which Heaven bears; and then we issued out, again to see the Stars." Ulysses *Annotated*, 581.

120. Joyce, *Ulysses*, 734-35.

121. Ibid., 47.

122. Ibid., 698.

nascent new stars such as Nova in 1901: of our system plunging towards the constellation of Hercules: of the parallax or parallactic drift of socalled fixed stars, in reality evermoving wanderers from immeasurably remote eons to infinitely remote futures in comparison with which the years, threescore and ten, of allotted human life formed a parenthesis of infinitesimal brevity.[123]

Another catalogue follows where Bloom embraces teeming microcosmic life. But Bloom's invocation here of "parallax" is another synchronous climax to the novel. Associated with metempsychosis and Molly's "Met him pike hoses" in "Lestrygonians," parallax is a way of getting to the real by taking more than one sighting and adjusting for subjective point of view, just as transmigration of souls gives us more than one opportunity to work out who we are. *Ulysses*'s manifold narrative points of view are an extended essay in parallax. Neither Buck nor Blazes Boylan nor Buck Mulligan are the villains of the novel. Mulligan's real first name Malachi, messenger of the gods, suggests he is at worst another Trickster psychopompos to Stephen, only a negative one, who tries to lead him where he should not go. Joyce's true villains are the one-eyed Cyclopes of prejudice, anti-Semitism, nationalism, blind facts, and single-minded styles: those who cannot achieve parallax.

One-sidedness, too, takes center stage in Jung's line-up of evils. One-sidedness is the source of our neuroses, which the Self tries to heal by forcing us to see and experience the other parts of our being. Jung writes, "The idea of synchronicity with its inherent quality of meaning produces a picture of the world so irrepresentable as to be completely baffling. The advantage, however, of adding this concept is that it makes possible a view which includes the psychoid [i.e., subjective, unconscious] factor in our description and knowledge of nature."[124] Synchronicity is one of his anti-discursive gestures. However you explain it, fundamentally acausal in a post-Enlightenment world that only accepts cause as explanation, synchronicity is transgressive. Baffled, we embrace not just the world our left-brained, analytic, directed consciousness can experience, but also other ways of knowing the world: the unconscious, intuition, dreams, synchronicities. In a word, parallax.

---

123. Ibid.
124. *CW*8: 962.

And another: *bricolage.* Synchronicity tinkers together apparently unrelated and meaningless events and phenomena to make meaning. The chapter's "mathematico-astronomico-physico-mechanico-geometrico-chemico sublimation of Bloom and Stephen" performs as alchemical parallax. As S.L. Goldberg writes:

> [T]he point of the chapter is the difference between what the mask represents and its actual dramatic *effect.* The mask proceeds with its ruthless vivisection of the "scientific" facts of modern society and of the sensibility characteristic of that society—a sensibility, of course, that Blooms shares. This vivisection, however is not the final comment on Bloomsworld; it is only one term in the dialectic of the chapter, for its effect is...not to demolish Bloom and Stephen into scattered, fragmentary "facts," but rather to show their ultimate invulnerability to this view of them...the "scientific" perspective only heightens our sense of an imperishable dignity and vitality in the two characters.[125]

How does one get from "facticity without meaning" to "imperishable dignity and vitality"? Magic. Alchemy.

Such double consciousness is the hero of *Liber Novus* and of *Ulysses.* Murray Stein articulates what is at stake in Jung embrace of synchronicity:

> For Jung, the unconscious defies the Kantian categories of knowledge [time and space] and surpasses consciousness in the range of possible knowing. In other words, in the unconscious we know many things that we do not know that we know. These could be called unthought thoughts or unconscious *a priori* knowledge. It is this notion that takes Jung into the furthest reaches of his speculations about the unity of psyche and world.[126]

With "unthought thoughts or unconscious *a priori* knowledge" we approach the dream of improvisation, unmediated experience of the world.

For both Jung and Joyce, experiencing the other parts of our being—"the subterranean forces, those hidden tides," the "back streets"—opens the cornucopian world to us. In the climax of the "Aeolus" chapter, after all his pyrotechnic display misreading *Hamlet,* Stephen is taken aback when one of the

---

125. S.L. Goldberg, *The Classical Temper: A Study of James Joyce's* Ulysses (London: Chatto and Windus, 1961), 189-90.

126. Stein, *Jung's Map of the Soul,* 212.

journalists alludes to a passage, which, as Kimball notes, is "Augustine's great affirmation of the inherent goodness of everything that exists in this world": "It was revealed to me that those things are good which yet are corrupted which neither if they were supremely good not unless they were good could be corrupted."[127] For James Hillman the "dream of psychology" is

> this great romantic dream of the restoration of the Gods, the return of the romantic vision of Shelley, of Heine in a way, of Nietzsche in a way, of a world in which everything is psychological because everything is meta-phorical and mythical. There's no split-off fallen world, in other words, this is a redemptive fantasy. It probably moves me, despite my skepticism. I think it's, as you say, aspirational. In a way it's more than aspirational, it's a very enlivening fantasy. It's like D.H. Lawrence, seeing how alive the world can be, even *is*.[128]

No two writers perhaps ever detested one another more than Joyce and Lawrence but in this they are on the same page, the aspirational celebration of alertness. *Liber Novus* and *Ulysses* are both masterpieces in performatively engendering greater degrees of alertness in the reader.

Jung and Joyce too were contentious toward one another in life. Jung mostly hated *Ulysses*. Joyce's response to Edith Rockefeller McCormick's offer to pay for analysis with Jung is memorialized in *Finnegans Wake* where the command "Get yourself psychoanolised!" meets with "I can psoakoona-loose myself any time I want."[129] But on the page they were extensively at one. Gnostics, alchemists, and kabbalists,[130] Jung and Joyce both celebrate the essentially comic, if aspirational, Terentian injunction that lies at the heart of improvisation, that "nothing human is alien to me." Embracing the way that our subjectivity brings meaning to the world, they both go Terence one better. By embracing the Other we perceive the cornucopian *unus mundus*, which, by

---

127. Kimball, *Odyssey of the Psyche*, 108.

128. Hillman and Shamdasani, *Lament of the Dead*, 208.

129. Joyce, *Finnegans Wake*, 522. Noted in Kimball, *Odyssey of the Psyche*, 21.

130. On Jung and Kabbalah, see Sanford L. Drob, *Kabbalistic Visions: C. G. Jung and Jewish Mysticism* (New Orleans: Spring Journal Books, 2010). On Joyce and Kabbalah, see, e.g., Jackson I. Cope, "Ulysses: Joyce's Kabbalah," *James Joyce Quarterly* 7, No. 2 (Winter, 1970): 93-113.

perceiving, we bring to birth and the cosmic dance that Milton describes in his improvisation, *The Nativity Ode,* which I must invoke again:

> For if such holy Song
> Enwrap our fancy long,
>   Time will run back and fetch the age of gold,
> And speckl'd vanity
> Will sicken soon and die,
>   And lep'rous sin will melt from earthly mold,
> And Hell itself will pass away,
> And leave her dolorous mansions to the peering day.[131]

At the center of the vision, Mercy, which is to say, Bloom's Love, holds sway:

> Yea Truth, and Justice then
> Will down return to men,
>   Orbed in a rainbow; an dlike glories wearing
> And Mercy will sit between,
> Throned in celestial sheen,
>   With radiant feet the tissued clouds down steering,
> And heaven as at some festival
> Will open wide the gates of her high palace hall.[132]

3. Mann's Dark Breakthrough

The tensions ever at the heart of improvisation come to a kind of fulfillment in the crisis of the modern novel. Joyce offers his articulation of the crisis, the novel tradition's exhaustion, and his way through: a wedding of the objective and subjective through a narrative method characterized by synchronicity, myth, shifting points of view, and symbol, all challenges to the scientific positivism that prizes objective fact. Thomas Mann offers his vision of this crisis and his answer in *Doctor Faustus: The Life of the German Composer Adrian Leverkühn As Told by a Friend.* A look at Mann's monumental portrait and answer to this crisis can help us see the darkest side of improvisation, implicit in the form from the beginning: not Odysseus's redemptive impro-

---

131. "On the Morning of Christ's Nativity," *The Poems of John Milton,* edited by John Carey and Alastair Fowler (London: Longmans, 1968), 107, lines 133–40.

132. Ibid., 107–8, lines 141–48.

visations but those that end in the death of all his men; not the Ancient Mariner's spontaneously blessing the water snakes, which leads to redemption, but his killing the albatross spontaneously, which leads to human and ecological holocaust.

Mann's sense of the crisis is not unlike Joyce's, a correspondence that Mann recognized.[133] The modern age is critical, intellective, rational. Mann and his ironic stand-in, the composer Adrian Leverkühn, accept the challenge of finding a breakthrough from the coldness of modern critical sensibility to the warmth of spontaneous creativity and expressiveness. Both Joyce and Mann seek to go beyond the mere facticity of the realist or naturalist tradition. Mann critic Gunilla Bergsten explains: "One reason for the special method Mann uses in *Doctor Faustus* is that he felt the crisis in art had shown the need for new methods that would have more bearing on reality than was possible within the self-sufficient world of illusion provided by the art forms of the past."[134] Like Duchamp, Mann wants, as it were, to get beyond "retinal art" that appeals merely to the eye, as illusion does. Mann explains in *The Story of a Novel*, his account of writing *Doctor Faustus*, that "my book would have to become what it dealt with: namely constructivist music."[135] His great meditation on this problem is utterly constructivist, a tissue of quotation tinkered together from the medieval Faustbuch, from the biographies of Nietzsche and Mann and his family, and from German history. It is what Bergsten calls an example of "total, rational structuring...determined absolutely by a series of themes or leitmotifs."[136] While the artist's powers of invention (*inventio* in Quintilian) have been central to rhetor's art, and preeminent in improvisation, Mann "demonstrates," writes Bergsten, "that free invention is certainly no prerequisite of great art."[137]

---

133. Gunilla Bergsten, *Thomas Mann's Doctor Faustus: The Sources and Structure of the Novel*, translated by Krishna Winston (Chicago and London: The University of Chicago Press, 1969), 111.

134. Ibid., 168.

135. Quoted in ibid., 166.

136. Ibid., 177–78.

137. Ibid., 180.

Nonetheless, *Doctor Faustus* presents itself as an artless improvisation in the voice of a foolish persona Serenus Zeitblom (="Serene Flowering—or metaphor—of the Age"). Zeitblom relates the tale of his virtuoso composer friend Leverkühn (="living audaciously"), a belated master of the forms that make up the Western musical canon. Like improvisation the novel is encyclopedic, though doubly so: a history of Western music perverted into craftsmanly formalism, and a history of German culture and nationalism perverted into fascism. Zeitblom claims his tale is formless, digressive and uncrafted, but behind him Mann pulls the strings that make every word a crafted leitmotif, the whole parallel to the constructivist method employed by the composer Leverkühn. The conflict between freedom and determinism lies at its center. Longing for a breakthrough from mastery back into emotion and free expressivity, Leverkühn contracts with the devil by contracting syphilis, binding himself to the course of the disease. Through this constraint he is freed to experience the madness that brings him the breakthrough into warmth, humanity, and expressiveness. In the end the warmth is hellish and the humanity demonic.

All this in Mann's hands becomes not just an account of the consequences of art's exhaustion but at the same time a dark allegory about Germany's march to fascism and war. The idea of National Socialism's roots in Romanticism, Wagner especially, is by now commonplace,[138] but Mann's subtle and dense portrait, written while the war progressed, is anything but cliché. Just as Jung read Hitler as a man who "listens intently to a stream of suggestions from a whispered source and then *acts upon them,*" so, too, Mann portrays fascism as the very darkest version, point by point, of the inspired art of improvisation. The milieu from which Leverkühn springs, for example, embraces the cult of youth. We can almost see improvisation's *puer* preparing to don the brown shirts of the Hitler Youth when one of Leverkühn's university classmates makes the case that

> The concept of youth is a prerogative and privilege of our nation, of us Germans—others hardly know it. Youth as its own self-conception is as

---

138. See, for example, Jacques Barzun, "To the Rescue of Romanticism," *The American Scholar* 9, no. 2 (Spring 1940): 147-58.

good as unknown to them; they are amazed at the demeanor of German youth, so emphatically itself and endorsed by those of more advanced years—are even amazing at its garb, its disregard for bourgeois dress. Well, let them. German youth represents, as youth, the spirit of the people, the German spirit itself, which is young and full of the future...[139]

This cult of youth is part of the German Romantic impulse wish to "plunge back into what is elemental."[140] They dismiss

Enlightenment...rationalism, which still has never been grasped by the powerful forces beyond and beneath reason...

The demonic, in German, that means the instinctual. And that's precisely the case nowadays when the instincts are used in propaganda offering all sorts of commitments—the instincts are incorporated, too, you see, and the old idealism is decked out with a psychology of the instincts, creating the alluring impression of a greater concentration of reality.[141]

"The powerful forces beyond and beneath reason" and "a greater concentration of reality": exactly what improvisation promises. So too they are pulled toward philosophic naturalism, that philosophy with the potential, John Stuart Mill warned long before, for self-serving and self-righteous absolutism. Leverkühn's circle believes that "only being that is direct and unreflective could enjoy true existence."[142] For Mann the ultimate perversion of German civilization is the rejection of the greatest strengths of German civilization and soulfulness.

Such ideas float in Leverkühn's circle but he is cut off from them by his cold, intellectual spirit. His perversion of German culture will take another form. His early art is motivated not by inspiration or the like but by a "work-idea" that creates the artwork's

unity and organic wholeness, plastering over cracks, plugging holes, establishing the "natural flow" that was not there originally, and so is not natural at all, but rather a product of art—in short, it is only after the

---

139. Thomas Mann, *Doctor Faustus: The Life of the German Composer Adrian Leverkühn As Told by a Friend,* translated by John E. Woods (New York: Vintage, 1997), 126.

140. Ibid., 127.

141. Ibid., 129, 133.

142. Ibid., 124.

fact and as a mediator that this manager creates an impression of immediacy and organic wholeness...Its ambition is to make others believe that
it was not made but rather simply arose, burst forth from Jupiter's head
like Pallas Athena fully adorned in enchased armor. But that is only a
pretense. No work has ever come into being that way. It is indeed work,
artistic labor for the purpose of illusion—and now the question arises
whether, given the current state of our consciousness, our comprehen-
sion, and our sense of truth, the game is still permissible, still intellectual
possible, can still be taken seriously.[143]

This is artlessness as artifact, a danger that improvisation has always courted.
Leverkühn will later write a cantata meant as "a formal negation of the
Ninth [Symphony]."[144] Here he offers a formal negation of the tradition of
improvisation.

But Leverkühn is not done. Like his schoolmates, he seeks art and life that
is "direct and unreflective," but he cannot deny the self-reflective consciousness of his character or his age. The solution is a breakthrough that employs
self-consciousness but in such a manner to get beyond it. Like Mann himself
and like Joyce given to irony and to parody, Leverkühn next creates a music
that is cold, mathematical, and crafted out of the past. His opera based
on Shakespeare's most mannered play, the courtly and euphuistic *Love's
Labour's Lost,*

> is a filigree handiwork, a clever grotesquery of notes, humorous and inge-
> nious in its combinations and rich with the inventions of a refined play-
> fulness; any lover of music who, weary of Romantic democracy and popu-
> lar moralistic harangues, might have demanded an art for art's sake, or for
> artists' and experts' sake, art with no ambitions or rather with only the
> most exclusive ambitions, would have had to be enraptured by this self-
> centered and perfectly cool esotericism—which in the esoteric spirit of
> the piece, however at every turn mocked and exaggerated itself as parody,
> mixing a drop of sadness, a grain of hopelessness into the rapture.[145]

In sum, the opera is free of what the play's most affected courtier Lord Ber-
owne "calls 'barbarism'—that is, whatever is spontaneous and natural—cel-

---

143. Ibid., 192.
144. Ibid., 514.
145. Ibid., 233.

ebrates no triumphs in this music."[146] Instead, what triumphs is the dialectic of freedom so central to improvisation. The narrator Zeitblom describes Leverkühn's artistic process as

> a kind of composing prior to composing. The entire disposition and organization of the material would have to be finished before the actual work could begin, and so the question then is: Which is the actual work? For the preparation of the material would consist of variation, and the productive process of variation, which one could call the actual composing, would then be transferred back to the material itself—along with the composer's freedom. When he set to work he would no longer be free.[147]

Leverkühn agrees, anticipating Annie Dillard's paradox of freedom and constraint when confronting the weasel: "Bound by the self-imposed constraint of order, which means free."[148] As Bergsten argues, "In *Doctor Faustus* the opposition of obligation and freedom is all-pervasive."[149]

This "learned refinement that profoundly despises life and nature, which indeed sees barbarism in life and nature, in immediacy, humanity, feeling" is all Leverkühn is capable of before he courts madness by contracting syphilis, as in legend Nietzsche had, to achieve the Dionysian breakthrough he seeks. The syphilis, "that illumination, the aphrodisiac of the brain," functions in the novel as the naturalistic correlate of Leverkühn's pact with the devil. As in Goethe's *Faust,* the Devil visits Leverkühn in a blast of cold air, part of which blows across the notions of inspiration and enthusiasm that improvisation through the centuries has worked so hard to promote and privilege. The Devil takes those prized values of improvisation as his own:

> Who knows still today, who knew even in classic times, what inspiration, what genuine ancient, primal enthusiasm is, enthusiasm ne'er sicklied o'er with criticism, lame prudence, and the deadly reins of reason—what holy rapture is? The Devil, I believe, is held to be the man of ravaging criticism? Slander—once again my friend! God's bodykins! If there be

---

146. Ibid.
147. Ibid., 207.
148. Ibid.
149. Bergsten, *Thomas Mann's Doctor Faustus,* 209.

something he hate, something most contrary in all the world, it is ravaging criticism. What he wishes and spends, that is verily the triumph beyond such, *the shining want of thought!*[150]

"The shining want of thought": what improviser has said it better? But since Eden the devil has always had a way with words. Mann's translator aptly puts Hamlet's "sicklied o'er with the pale cast of thought" in the Devil's mouth. Like Hamlet, Leverkühn yearns to break out of the paralysis brought on by "the pale cast of thought." Here, "ravaging criticism" is Leverkühn's own exhausted self-consciousness. He makes a pact with the Devil who sees himself as "the true Lord of Enthusiasm."[151]

Leverkühn's longing for breakthrough as always is allegorically interwoven with Germany's similar longing. Germany longs to "break...out into the world" through its colonial aspirations that led to World War I. Leverkühn finds this aspiration anticipated by Kleist's *On the Marionette Theatre* from the Romantic period:

> "How does one break through? How does one reach free and open air? How does one burst the cocoon and become a butterfly? The whole situation is governed by that question. Here, too," he said, tugging at the red ribbon in the volume of Kleist lying on the table, "the issue of breakthrough is dealt with, in the splendid essay on marionettes, to be precise, where it is specifically called 'the last chapter of world history.' Although it speaks only about aesthetics, about charm, about the free grace that in actuality is reserved solely for the puppet and for God—that is for the unconscious and for the endlessly conscious—whereas every reflection between zero and infinity kills such grace. Consciousness, so this writer suggests, must pass through an infinity in order for grace to reappear, and Adam must eat again of the Tree of Knowledge in order to fall back into the state of innocence."[152]

This is what improvisation has always finally promoted, a widening of consciousness so that it includes the unconscious, which results in the "glorious affirmation of vitality" characteristic of improvisation. But in Leverkühn's

---

150. Mann, *Doctor Faustus*, 252-53; emphasis added.
151. Ibid., 253.
152. Ibid., 325.

hands the breakthrough, *The Lamentation of Dr. Faustus,* will seek to take back the affirmation of life. Leverkühn tells Zeitblom:

> "I have discovered it ought not be."
>
> "What ought not be, Adrian?"
>
> "The good and the noble," he replied, "what people call human, even though it is good and noble. What people have fought for, have stormed citadels for, and what people filled to overflowing have announced with jubilation—it ought not to be. It will be taken back. I shall take it back...The Ninth Symphony."[153]

Leverkühn achieves this breakthrough by means of cold intellection: "a style in which there is nothing that is not thematic, nothing that could not qualify as a variation of something forever the same. This style, this technique as it was called, permitted no note, not one that did not fulfill its thematic function within the overarching structure—free notes would no longer exist."[154] His breakthrough is to use his freedom to make everything determined: "Working uninhibitedly within the preorganized material and unconcerned about its preexistent construction, the creator of the *Lamentation of Dr. Faustus* can abandon himself to subjectivity. Therefore, this, his strictest work, a work of utmost calculation, is simultaneously purely expressive."[155] This would seem a far cry from the loose freedom of improvisation, and yet, since we have found that improvisations are in key ways predictable, Leverkühn's "work of utmost calculation" merely pushes the determinism implicit in improvisation to its furthest extreme.

Mann's novel is itself exactly what he portrays in Leverkühn's constructivist music, a bricolage of utmost calculation, quotation, strictness, and "simultaneously purely expressive," an account of his deep feelings about the twentieth century German catastrophe. The ultimate paradox is one Mann shares with Joseph Conrad, as Leverkühn does with Kurtz in the *Heart of Darkness,* that, as Bergsten writes, "the best qualities of the German people would also be the basis of the German catastrophe...Mann interprets the process as one of 'demonization,' analogous to the process whereby Adrian's noblest features

---

153. Ibid., 501.
154. Ibid., 510.
155. Ibid., 512.

make him a victim of the powers of darkness."[156] The same can be said of Mann's demonic improvisation, that it is a negation of improvisation and at the same time an affirmation, if muted, because only a twisted demonization of the form's historic nobility. Like Goethe's *Faust* and perhaps Mann's, for Leverkühn's end is ambiguous, improvisation's affirmation of life is finally, if narrowly, apotheosized. Understanding how an affirmation of life can be demonically perverted, perhaps we can rescue it from future perversions.

Insofar as the improviser presents himself as an epistemological adventurer, rejecting the status quo of knowledge, the figure of Faust, not only in Mann's hands but throughout Faust's long history, is in important ways the ultimate improviser. Goethe's Faust is characteristic: he declares inadequate all received, systematic approaches to knowledge: "philosophy,/ Jurisprudence, and medicine,/And, help me God, theology."[157] Faust says, I have learned everything these received modalities of knowing can teach; I need another way to know the world. He embraces instead magic, the alchemical, and the irrational, and is visited by the hermetic Mephistopheles who becomes his guide. Inspiration, the unconscious, and knowledge beyond what the rational and systematic can yield are all a Faustian bargain, which is to say a bargain with the devil, remembering of course that in this case the devil is Trickster.

The *sine qua non*, the enabler of improvisation is that alertness to the moment that prepares improviser and his audience to respond to life as it happens. Faust paradoxically embodies both the form's forward-looking perspective and its embrace of the present moment. Goethe's Faust loses his bargain if he forsakes his ever-questing, ever-aggressive, and ever-penetrating attitude toward the world. At the end of *Faust II*, in helping the Dutch farmers reclaim the sea, Faust forsakes the global quest in favor of the local, choosing not all knowledge in all time, but practical knowledge here and now. But this failure to keep the devil's bargain in Goethe's *Faust II* leads to his apotheosis. Enter angels from the fly. Having made a pact not to love, Leverkühn breaks his bargain by loving his nephew Nepomuk, nicknamed

---

156. Bergsten, *Thomas Mann's Doctor Faustus*, 209.

157. Johann Wolfgang von Goethe, *Faust: A Tragedy*, translated by Walter Arnt (New York: Norton Critical, 2001), 12.

Echo, an act of embracing the present moment, but as his nickname suggests perhaps just an act of narcissism. As I've said, Leverkühn's spiritual fate is ambiguous.

Presenting Leverkühn as a modern Faust exemplifies Mann's belief in the "tendency to repetition in the structure of Germany's intellectual development."[158] *Doctor Faustus* portrays the pattern of rebellion against objective form by subjective feeling in both musical and theological history. As Bergsten argues, "one may justifiably speak of a sort of cyclical interpretation of history."[159] Eternal recurrence functions as Mann's acausal synchronicity. Like Jung and Joyce, he found a like mind in Vico[160] So, too, improvisation fits a Viconian vision of cycles.

Improvisation is recurrent and cyclic because it touches fundamental polarities of our humanity. As in Jung and Joyce, so in Mann: rethinking the personal, if you go deep enough into the subjective you arrive at the objective bedrock of our abiding humanity, the longing for a breakthrough into unmediated experience.

---

158. Bergsten, *Thomas Mann's Doctor Faustus,* 150.
159. Ibid.
160. Ibid., 152.

CHAPTER FOURTEEN

"Dreaming the Myth Onwards":
Saturn vs. Hermes in Ian McEwan's Saturday

> Not for a moment dare we succumb to the illusion that
> an archetype can be finally explained and disposed of.
> Even the best attempts at explanation are only more or
> less successful translations into another metaphorical
> language. (Indeed, language itself is only an image.) The
> most we can do is to dream the myth onwards and give
> it a modern dress
>
> —C.G. Jung, "The Psychology of the Child Archetype"

I t should come as no surprise, the issues improvisation explores were not settled by the improvisations of the twentieth century, even Joyce's thunder-wielding masterpiece. Nor is the form terminated by Mann's improvisation-to-end-all-improvisations. As Leverkühn's first mentor Kretzschmar says of music in *Doctor Faustus,* "It lay in the nature of this singular art that at every moment it was able to begin all over again, out of nothing, absent any knowledge of the cultural history through which it had already passed, of its achievements over the centuries—to rediscover itself, to regenerate."[1] Ian McEwan's novel *Saturday* reinvents improvisation as it has been reinvented as if *de novo,* without precedent, again and again in paradigm shift after paradigm shift. McEwan seems to take Jung's advice "to dream the myth onwards and give it a modern dress."[2]

Hardly associated with improvisation, McEwan has a well-deserved reputation as craftsman; for the *New York Times,* McEwan "is the master clockmaker of novelists, piecing together the cogs and wheels of his plots with

---

1. Thomas Mann, *Doctor Faustus: The Life of the German Composer Adrian Leverkühn As Told by a Friend,* translated by John E. Woods (New York: Vintage, 1997), 71.

2. *CW* 9.1: *The Archetypes and the Collective Unconscious,* 271.

unerring meticulousness."[3] Nonetheless, McEwan quickly situates *Saturday* in the tradition of improvisation with a cascade of tropes and figures of immediacy. The novel's epigraph invokes the voice of the great wildman protagonist of Saul Bellow's *Herzog,* who improvises unsent letters and who "characteristically...was determined to act without clearly knowing what to do, and even recognizing that he had no power over his impulses."[4] *Saturday* opens "some hours before dawn," when "Henry Perowne, a neurosurgeon, wakes to find himself," like Hermes of the Homeric hymn, "already in motion, pushing back the covers from a sitting position, and then rising to his feet."[5] Perowne is awake but still in a liminal state: "It's not clear to him when exactly he became conscious, nor does it seem relevant."[6] Perowne is an accomplished neurosurgeon, a "master clockmaker" in his own right who likes to take charge of his usually quite regimented day. "It's not possible to be an unassertive brain surgeon,"[7] we will learn later, but right now everything is new, easy, naked, unmediated, and Perowne is a passive receptor of fleeting impressions:

> He's never done such a thing before, but he isn't alarmed or even faintly surprised, for the movement is *easy,* and pleasurable in his limbs, and his back and legs feel unusually strong. He stands there, *naked* by the bed—*he always sleeps naked*—feeling his full height, aware of his wife's patient breathing and of the wintry bedroom air on his skin. That too is a pleasurable sensation. His bedside clock shows three forty. He has no idea what he's doing out of bed: he has no need to relieve himself, nor is he disturbed by a dream or some element of the day before, or even by the state of the world. It's as if, standing there in the darkness, he's *materialised out of nothing, fully formed, unencumbered.*[8]

Like Athene, burst from the forehead of Zeus—a birth, it will be remembered, midwifed by Hermes. We hear that Perowne's "vision—always good—seems

---

3. Zoe Heller, "'Saturday': One Day in the Life," *New York Times,* March 20, 2005, Sunday Book Review.

4. Saul Bellow, *Herzog* (Harmondsworth, Middlesex: Penguin, 1964), 248.

5. Ian McEwan, *Saturday* (New York: Doubleday, 2006), 1.

6. Ibid.

7. Ibid., 21.

8. Ibid., 1. Emphasis added.

to have sharpened." This is a man with the alertness and the grace of newborn Hermes himself:

> In fact, he's *alert* and *empty-headed* and *inexplicably elated.* With no decision made, *no motivation at all,* he begins to move towards the nearest of the three bedroom windows and experiences *such ease and lightness in his tread that he suspects at once he's dreaming or sleepwalking.* If it is the case, he'll be disappointed. *Dreams don't interest him; that this should be real is a richer possibility. And he's entirely himself, he is certain of it, and he knows that sleep is behind him: to know the difference between it and waking, to know the boundaries, is the essence of sanity.*[9]

But while Hermes is always about liminality, man of science Henry Perowne is a man almost wholly committed to Jung's directed consciousness and not a little uncomfortable with encroachments thereupon. There's no reason to believe McEwan has Jung's nomenclature in mind, but "directed consciousness" is a helpful concept to describe Perowne's comfort zone. Perowne likes control but he has been attentive enough to the life of the mind to know there are limits, that his control is ephemeral. He knows that "the second-by-second wash of his thoughts is only partially his to control—the drift, the white noise of solitary thought is driven by his emotional state."[10] Perowne is a post-Freudian, post-Jungian, post-Bloomian man: he knows that unconscious forces determine behavior.

Committed nonetheless to and shaped by a life in science, Perowne's vision sometimes suffers from *deformation professionelle.* Like many surgeons, he cannot "deny the egotistical joy in his own skills, or the pleasure he still takes in the relief of the relatives when he comes down from the operating room like a god, an angel with the glad tidings—life, not death."[11] We hear his Cartesian description of some nurses he sees from his godlike, early morning perch at the window:

> With his advantage of height and in his curious mood, he not only watches them, but watches over them, supervising their progress with the remote possessiveness of a god. In the lifeless cold, they pass through the

---

9. Ibid., 1-2. Emphasis added.
10. Ibid., 78.
11. Ibid., 23.

night, hot little biological engines with bipedal skills suited to any terrain, endowed with innumerable branching neural networks sunk deep in a knob of bone casing, buried fibres, warm filaments with their invisible glow of consciousness—these engines devise their own tracks.[12]

An Enlightenment clock with free will: the antinomy between determinism and free will is much in Perowne's thoughts. Here the "lifeless cold" seems to be not only the night's but his own. What he will learn in the course of the day is that another part of sanity is to know that boundaries aren't so easy to know and that, after all, as Trickster teaches us, they can and should be porous.[13] Henry will spend a lot of his Saturday—Saturn's day—fending off the back streets. For the alchemists *"prima materia* is 'saturnine,' and the malefic Saturn is the abode of the devil, or again it is the most despised and rejected thing, 'thrown out into the street,' 'cast on the dung-hill,' 'found in filth.'"[14] Perowne is about to experience the shadowy Trickster, who will throw a spanner wrench in his clockworks. *Saturday* is about a partisan of Saturn—in astrology associated with limitation, restriction, boundaries, structures, and practicality—forced to accommodate ever-fluid, impractical Hermes. Like novelist Italo Calvino, Perowne is "a Saturn who dreams of being a Mercury."[15] The arc of the novel challenges Perowne to transmute Saturn—lead—by a confrontation with Trickster/Mercury/Hermes into the gold of well-being of self and family.

Trickster will have far worse matters in store for Perowne, but he intrudes even here. In his just-risen, liminal state Perowne witnesses a crippled airliner limping into Heathrow. Trickster first messes with perspective. Initially Perowne "assumes proportions on a planetary scale: it's a meteor burning out in the London sky, traversing left to right, low on the horizon, though well clear of the taller buildings."[16] But no, it moves too slowly: "It's a comet, tinged with yellow, with the familiar bright core trailing its fiery envelope."

---

12. Ibid., 12.

13. Cf. Lewis Hyde on Trickster's opportunism, a word that stems from *porta,* entrance, passageway, in *Trickster Makes This World,* 46.

14. *CW* 13: *Alchemical Studies,* 10.

15. "Quickness," in Italo Calvino, *Six Memos for the Next Millennium* (Cambridge, Mass.: Harvard University Press, 1988), 52.

16. McEwan, *Saturday,* 12.

Then he hears "a low rumbling sound, gentle thunder gathering in volume."[17] Now that he knows it's a plane with an engine afire, the hermeneutic problem becomes, what caused it? This is post 9/11. Is it jihadists on their way to attack London?

This is not the only troubling thought Trickster introduces. Perowne is tempted to read his waking just in time to see the crippled airliner as a synchronicity, an acausal and meaningful connection that puts him at the center of events:

> If Perowne were inclined to religious feeling, to supernatural explanations, he could play with the idea that he's been summoned; that having woken in an unusual state of mind, and gone to the window for no reason, he should acknowledge a hidden order, an external intelligence which wants to show or tell him something of significance.[18]

But, ever the man of reason, he rejects such a notion; there are causal explanations, Occam's razors which he uses to shred the occult, supernatural explanation:

> But a city of its nature cultivates insomniacs;...That it should be him and not someone else is an arbitrary matter. A simple anthropic principle is involved. The primitive thinking of the supernaturally inclined amounts to what his psychiatric colleagues call a problem, or an idea, of reference. An excess of the subjective, the ordering of the world in line with your needs, an inability to contemplate your own unimportance. In Henry's view such reasoning belongs on a spectrum at whose far end, rearing like an abandoned temple, lies psychosis.[19]

For Perowne such thinking is not just crazy but dangerous. Imagining the plane the victim of 9/11 style jihadists, Perowne associates synchronicity with the magical thinking of ideologues: "And such reasoning may have caused the fire on the plane. A man of sound faith with a bomb in the heel of his shoe."[20] A man, Perowne might add, driven by "an excess of the subjective" to believe that he knows God's wishes through unmediated experience.

---

17. Ibid., 13.
18. Ibid., 16.
19. Ibid., 16-17.
20. Ibid., 17.

Unlike the terrorist he imagines, Perowne is an exquisitely trained scientist who needs causal explanations for things. He has matters conceptually squared away. But life won't let him off so easy. Later that day, he goes to hear his son Theo in rehearsal. Theo [=god] is a blues guitarist who "plays like an angel" and represents to Perowne an artistic freedom and grace that go beyond Perowne's professional *techné*: "There's nothing in his own life that contains this inventiveness, this style of being free. The music speaks to unexpressed longing or frustration, a sense that he's denied himself an open road, the life of the heart celebrated in the songs."[21] If Theo is a god, then he is Hermes: inventor of the lyre, lord of freedom and the open road. Perowne knows "he ought to learn from Theo how to let go."[22] When Perowne recounts his morning witnessing the crippled airliner, Theo, coming at things as an artist, is prepared to accept synchronicity's appeal to read meaning into coincidence:

> "But uh, so what were you doing at the window?"
> "I told you. I couldn't sleep."
> "Some coincidence."
> "Exactly that."
> Their eyes meet—a moment of potential challenge—then Theo looks away and shrugs...As Henry understands it, Theo's world-view accommodates a hunch that somehow everything is connected, interestingly connected, and that certain authorities, notably the U.S. government, with privileged access to extra-terrestrial intelligence, is excluding the rest of the world from such wondrous knowledge as contemporary science, dull and strait-laced, cannot begin to comprehend.[23]

So Perowne manages to wedge synchronicity momentarily back into its comfortable cubbyhole: it's a little nuts and he hopes his artsy son will grow out of it. Facts is facts. Unlike Jung and Joyce and unlike Bellow's Herzog, who is troubled because *"in ancient days, the genius of man went largely into metaphors. But now into facts,"*[24] Perowne is uncomfortable with metaphor. When he ventures the metaphor that "the quality of silence in the house is thick-

---

21. Ibid., 28.
22. Ibid., 56.
23. Ibid., 30.
24. Bellow, *Herzog,* 266.

ened...by the fact of Theo deeply asleep on the third floor," he has to back off parenthetically: "Perowne can't help unscientifically thinking."[25] For his poet daughter Daisy, who is trying to school him in the arts, Perowne is a "Gradgrind" who should "look at your Mme Bovary again...[Flaubert] was warning the world against people *just like you.*"[26]

But Perowne is no Philistine. He wonders with awe at human achievement and thinks science offers a better record of those wonders than does fiction: "Daisy's reading lists have persuaded him that fiction is too humanly flawed, too sprawling and hit-and-miss to inspire uncomplicated wonder at the magnificence of human ingenuity, of the impossible dazzlingly achieved."[27] Embracing one of improvisation's highest values, for Perowne "the impossible [is] dazzlingly achieved" through alertness.

As in *Ulysses* we are front-and-center witnesses to Perowne's alertness by means of the formal device of center-of-consciousness narration and interior monologue. While his narrative method may lack Joyce's pyrotechnics, in his choice of central consciousness McEwan does Joyce's intellectual, failed medical student Stephen one better. Perowne is not just, like Stephen, "an habitual observer of his own moods"[28] and thoughts, but also of the brain and other bodily systems that make the machine tick. Unlike Bloom, who shares his interest in the body's functions, Perowne is extremely competent and professional; his running commentary on how the world and body work is far better than Bloom's often-mangled guesswork. In *Saturday* we witness a neurosurgeon's thoughts, informed by a century of scientific progress since Jung and Joyce.

This is a man who can explain his pre-verbal, image-based thoughts, Shamdasani's "primal" figures, as he responds to a demonstration in the London streets against the impending first Gulf War:

> A second can be a long time in introspection. Long enough for Henry to make a start on the negative features, certainly enough time for him to think, or sense, without unwrapping the thought into syntax and words,

---

25. McEwan, *Saturday,* 64.
26. Ibid., 67. Emphasis in text.
27. Ibid.
28. Ibid., 4.

that it is in fact the state of the world that troubles him most, and the marchers [in the demonstration] are there to remind him of it...The assertions and the questions don't spell themselves out. *He experiences them more as a mental shrug followed by an interrogative pulse. This is the pre-verbal language that linguists call mentalese. Hardly a language, more a matrix of shifting patterns, consolidating and compressing meaning in fractions of a second, and blending it inseparably with its distinctive emotional hue, which itself is rather like a colour.* A sickly yellow. Even with a poet's gift of compression, it could take hundreds of words and many minutes to describe.[29]

Perowne seems to be describing the mind's output somewhere between primal and when figure emerges.

Wherever they stem from, Perowne is having these thoughts, "driving with unconscious expertise," just as a key plot point is about to come bursting in upon his complacent life—a car accident: "So that when a flash of red streaks in across his left peripheral vision, like a shape on his retina in a bout of insomnia, it already has the quality of an idea, a new idea, unexpected and dangerous, but entirely his, and not of the world beyond himself."[30] Just like the events at dawn when he awoke, this event is saturated in immediacy:

He's driving with unconscious expertise into the narrow column of space framed on the right by a kerb-flanked cycle path, and on the left by a line of parked cars. It's from this line that the rings, and with it, the snap of a wing mirror cleanly sheared and the whine of sheet-steel surfaces sliding under pressure as two cars pour into a gap wide enough for one. Perowne's instant decision at the moment of impact is to accelerate as he swerves right.[31]

The Shadow/Trickster at the wheel of the red car is more a malignant Buck Mulligan than a benign Leopold Bloom: a thug, Baxter, complete with goons, Nark and Nigel.

Baxter has a neurological condition that makes him subject to wild mood swings: an emotional improviser. He exemplifies the dark side of improv, improv gone wrong: "Here is the signature of so many neurodegenerative diseases—the swift transition from one mood to another, without awareness or

29. Ibid., 80–81. Emphasis added.
30. Ibid., 81.
31. Ibid.

memory, or understanding of how it seems to others."[32] Perowne's mother, suffering from Alzheimer's, offers another image of immediacy gone wrong: for her "everything belongs in the present."[33]

Perowne, confronted by these thugs, deploys the quick thinking—the *metis*[34]—of a diagnostician to use as leverage against this dangerous adversary, first to make his escape from the accident scene where they threaten to bloody him badly and later when they invade his elegant eighteenth century central London townhouse to menace his family. The symbol of medicine, the rod of Asclepius, which has one coiled snake, is often confused with Hermes's caduceus, which has two, perhaps not without reason. Medicine is both *techné* and *ars*. Perowne is a master technician, but in watching Perowne formulate his diagnosis of Baxter, we experience the polytropic hermetic *metis* of the *art*, not *craft*, of medicine:

> Baxter's fixed regard is on [the crowd] as it passes, his features faintly distorted, strained by pity. A textbook phrase comes to Henry in much the same way as the cantata melody—a modest rise in his adrenaline level is making him unusually associative. Or the pressures of the past week won't release him from the habits, the intellectual game of diagnosis. The phrase is, *a false sense of superiority.* Yes, it can be down to a slight alteration in character, preceding the first tremors, somewhat short of, a little less disabling than, those other neurological conditions—grandiosity, delusions of grandeur. But he may be mis-remembering. Neurology is not his field. As Baxter stares at the marchers, he makes tiny movements with his head, little nods and shakes. Watching him unobserved for a few seconds, Perowne suddenly understands—Baxter is unable to initiate or make saccades, those flickering changes of eye position from one fixation to another. To scan the crowd, he is having to move his head.[35]

There is an element here of the ratiocinative, the deductive, of concepts being applied to shape evidence. But the "modest rise in [Perowne's] adrenaline level" which makes "him unusually associative" suggests that a Jungian *abaissement du niveau mental* is involved, conceptual categories emerging

---

32. Ibid., 96.
33. Ibid., 168.
34. Detienne and Vernant, *Cunning Intelligence,* 44.
35. McEwan, *Saturday,* 91.

from empirical induction: "The textbook phrase comes to Henry in much the same way as the cantata melody [which a trumpet among the marchers has just evoked in him]." We don't hear Perowne's conceptual diagnosis—Huntington's disease—for some pages on. As usual with improv, what is promoted is alertness: this is Perowne at his most alert, Man Thinking.

The car accident throws Perowne into the turbulent world of Chaotics, a world overseen by Hermes/Trickster where events are both unpredictable and determined, a paradox Perowne is alert to. Perowne thinks about the "pure artifice" of "the urban drama" in their confrontation over the car accident:

> Someone is going to have to impose his will and win, and the other is going to give way. Popular culture has worn this matter smooth with reiteration, this ancient genetic patrimony that also oils the machinations of bullfrogs and cockerels and stags. And despite the varied and casual dress code, there are rules as elaborate as the *politesse* of the Versailles court that no set of genes can express. For a start, it is not permitted as they stand there to acknowledge the self-consciousness of the event, or its overbearing irony: from just up the street, they can hear the tramping and tribal drums of the peace mongers. Furthermore, nothing can be predicted, but everything, as soon as it happens, will seem to fit.
> "Cigarette?"
> Exactly so. This is how it's bound to start.[36]

Understanding that events are both fractally fated and subject to free will prepares Perowne to ride the crest of the present moment, both inevitable and a surprise.

Perowne's broad sympathies also commend him. Though he manipulates Baxter with his diagnosis to get himself out of a street fight in which he will surely be the loser, he feels guilty for doing so, taking the Hippocratic Oath further than most of his readers would. He does not condescend to Baxter and has a sincere interest in helping him deal with his inevitable diminishment of function. After Baxter invades the Perowne townhouse and holds a knife to Perowne's wife's throat and forces Daisy to undress, and after Theo throws Baxter down the stairs, breaking his neck, Perowne performs the

---

36. Ibid., 87.

needed surgery. In a way that recalls Bloom's sympathy for the horse in the "Hades" chapter of *Ulysses*, Perowne, shopping for the ingredients for a fish stew he will serve to his family, finds sympathy for the fish he is about to cook:

> Naturally, Perowne the fly-fisherman has seen the recent literature: scores of polymodal nociceptor sites just like ours in the head and neck of rainbow trout. It was once convenient to think biblically, to believe we're surrounded for our benefit by edible automata on land and sea. Now it turns out that even fish feel pain. This is the growing complication of the modern condition, the expanding circle of moral sympathy. Not only distant peoples are our brothers and sisters, but foxes too, and laboratory mice, and now the fish. Perowne goes on catching and eating them, and though he'd never drop a live lobster into boiling water, he's prepared to order one in a restaurant. The trick, as always, the key to human success and domination, is to be selective in your mercies.[37]

No tree- (or fish-) hugger, here Perowne embraces mankind's inexorable shadow, that we must kill to survive.

Perowne's sympathy for fish is an act less of the heart than of directed consciousness, his ego's attempt to inhabit the world with a good conscience. But the novel also provides the darkest possible portraits of "inhabiting the narrowest slice of the present."

The present moment is where chance lives. Chance may be the fount of John Cage's art, but it can be the source of much modern misery. Chance is a crucial issue in a novel hinging on car accidents and in which the protagonist is reading a biography of Darwin, who brought chance genetic mutation to the center of the conversation of the nineteenth century. For Perowne chance can mean freedom: "Even as a child, and especially after Aberfan, [a 1966 Welsh mining disaster that killed many adults and many more children] he never believed in fate or providence, or the future being made by someone in the sky. Instead, at every instant, a trillion trillion possible futures; the pickiness of pure chance and physical laws seemed like freedom." But Perowne is aware that chance can lead to constraint and determinism. Baxter's Huntington's disease was brought on by a chance, spontaneous genetic mutation: "The misfortune lies within a single gene, in an excessive repeat of a single

---

37. Ibid., 127–28.

sequence—CAG. Here's biological determinism in its purest form. More than forty repeats of that one little codon, and you're doomed. Your future is fixed and easily foretold."[38] Baxter is "that unpickable knot of affliction."[39] *Saturday* may not pick nor cut the Gordian knot of affliction, but if offers images and figures that with Keatsian Negative Capability hold knotted antinomies in suspension.

As with most improvisations, *Saturday* privileges immediacy—in this case first of all through its narrative method—even as it figures this overabundance of examples of immediacy and careful craftsmanship that complicate that privileging and invite us to see and experience spontaneity and immediacy from different angles. That narrative method—moment-by-moment interior monologue/center of consciousness—is set implicitly in contrast (and dialogue) with traditionally crafted biography, as Sterne had done in *Tristram Shandy,* the received notion of how to know a life, an example of which Perowne is reading: "At times this biography [of Darwin] made him comfortably nostalgic for a verdant, horse-drawn, affectionate England; at others he was faintly depressed by the way a whole life could be contained by a few hundred pages—bottled, like homemade chutney."[40]

Like *Ulysses* or *Mrs. Dalloway,* this moment-by-moment account will capture "a whole life" not by offering more than "a few hundred pages—bottled, like homemade chutney" but instead by being alert to just one day's lived life. The novel's setting contrasts to the immediacies that will play out there. Perowne's townhouse is situated on elegant eighteenth-century Fitzroy Square "enclosing a perfect circle of garden—an eighteenth-century dream bathed and embraced by modernity."[41] Yet their square is situated in a London that Perowne sees as a masterpiece of self-emergent order: "Henry thinks the city is a success, a brilliant invention, a biological masterpiece—millions teeming around the accumulated and layered achievements of the centuries, as though around a coral reef, sleeping, working, entertaining themselves, har-

---

38. Ibid., 94.
39. Ibid., 282.
40. Ibid., 5.
41. Ibid., 3.

monious for the most part, nearly everyone wanting it to work."[42] That's how spontaneity can work positively at a macrocosmic level.

There are also a number of positive figurations of spontaneous behavior on a microcosmic level. On the squash court Perowne experiences the *"gracious* freedom" we saw Paul Ricoeur celebrate, "bodily spontaneity allied with the initiative which moves it without resistance"[43]; just so for Perowne, "It's possible in a long rally to become a virtually unconscious being, inhabiting the narrowest slice of the present, merely reacting, taking one shot at a time, existing only to keep going."[44]

As neurosurgeon, Perowne is the professional embodiment of thoughtful craft with a taste for order who experiences

> the pleasure of knowing precisely what he's doing, of seeing the instruments arrayed on the trolley, of being with his firm in the muffled quiet of the theatre, the murmur of the air filtration, the sharper hiss of oxygen passing into the mask taped to Baxter's face out of sight under the drapes, the clarity of the overhead lights. It's a reminder from childhood of the closed fascination of a board game.[45]

He is very aware that he stands on the shoulders of craftsmen/scientists/technicians who carefully developed the procedures he employs: "Almost a century of failure and partial success lay behind this one procedure, of other routes tried and rejected, and decades of fresh invention to make it possible, including this microscope and the fibre-optic lighting."[46] This is the progress the Enlightenment promised.

But Perowne is a man of many parts. Doing his Friday paperwork the day before, Perowne displays his own chops as improviser: "Long after his secretary went home he typed in his overheated box of an office on the hospital's third floor…He prides himself on speed and a sleek, wry style. It never needs much forethought—typing and composing are one."[47] And though we hear a lot in the course of his day about the craft of surgery and the careful trial-

---

42. Ibid.
43. Ricoeur, *Freedom and Nature*, 485.
44. McEwan, *Saturday*, 111.
45. Ibid., 258.
46. Ibid., 46.
47. Ibid., 10.

and-error history behind every procedure, even surgery offers blissed-out immediacy when he, as on the squash court, "inhabit[s] the narrowest slice of the present":

> For the past two hours he's been in a dream of absorption that has dis-
> solved all sense of time, and all awareness of the other parts of his life.
> Even his awareness of his own existence has vanished. He's been deliv-
> ered into a pure present, free of the weight of the past or any anxieties
> about the future. In retrospect, though never at the time, it feels like pro-
> found happiness. It's a little like sex, in that he feels himself in another
> medium, but it's less obviously pleasurable, and clearly not sensual. This
> state of mind brings a contentment he never finds with any passive form
> of entertainment. Books, cinema, even music can't bring him to this…He
> feels calm, and spacious, fully qualified to exist. It's a feeling of clarified
> emptiness, of deep, muted joy.[48]

Music may not usually bring him this joy, but his son Theo's blues guitar brings joy and for Perowne the experience of "aesthetic arrest" worthy of Stephen Dedalus's aspirations:

> He lets ["the great engine of sound"] engulf him. There are these rare
> moments when musicians together touch something sweeter than they've
> ever found before in rehearsals or performance, beyond the merely col-
> laborative or technically proficient, when their expression becomes as
> easy and graceful as friendship or love. This is when they give us a glimpse
> of what we might be, of our best selves, and of an impossible world in
> which you give everything you have to others, but lose nothing of your-
> self. Out in the real world there exist detailed plans, visionary projects
> for peaceable realms, all conflicts resolved, happiness for everyone, for
> ever—mirages for which people are prepared to die and kill. Christ's king-
> dom on earth, the workers' paradise, the ideal Islamic state. But only in
> music, and only on rare occasions, does the curtain actually lift on this
> dream of community, and it's tantalisingly conjured, before fading away
> with the last notes…And here it is now, a coherent world, everything fit-
> ting at last.[49]

Unmediated experience can produce this sense of community, "fetch," in Milton's words "the age of gold." So we imagine.

---

48. Ibid., 266.
49. Ibid., 175–76, 178.

Theo's lyric "fetches" "a coherent world, everything fitting at last" by lovingly invoking the family home on Fitzroy Square:

> Baby, you can choose despair,
> Or you can be happy if you dare.
> So let me take you there,
> My city square, city square.[50]

A constant touchstone of the narrative—*Saturday* begins and ends with Perowne contemplating it—Fitzroy Square figures a circle within a square or squared circle, the mathematical impossibility long the dream of rationalists, like the square's Enlightenment era architect Robert Adam: "And the Perownes's own corner, a triumph of congruent proportion; the perfect square laid out by Robert Adam enclosing a perfect circle of garden—an eighteenth-century dream bathed and embraced by modernity."[51]

All that Enlightenment perfection is now troubled in the light of day and dark of night by the druggies and ticket scalpers who use it to transact illicit business, and by Nark and Nigel, who use it as a staging area to invade the Perowne's elegant townhouse. Theo's embrace of the square as *locus amoenus* is at once an act of will and the directed consciousness—"you can choose despair,/Or you can be happy *if you dare*./So *let me take you* there." I also serves as mandala image, figure, and symbol, an act of the transcendent imagination reconciling opposites that can't rationally be reconciled.

Something must be working because Theo's visionary utopia isn't all aery poetry: the Perowne family gives the lie to Tolstoy's chestnut that "happy families are all alike." The Perowne family's happiness is ample and its members are individuated to a striking degree. Everyone has their way and boundaries are respected. The Perowne family may not inhabit the age of gold and the Fitzroy Square may be no *locus amoenus,* but the Perownes do seem to have created a high functioning little commonwealth, a little nugget of transmuted gold.

Jung's interest in the squared circle mandala was confirmed by a dream he had just after receiving the Chinese alchemical text, which confirmed for

---

50. Ibid., 175.
51. Ibid., 3.

him the existence of archetypes and led to his dropping the *Liber Novus*. He records the dream in *Memories, Dreams, Reflections*:

> When we reached the plateau, we found a broad square dimly illuminated by street lights, into which many streets converged. The various quarters of the city were arranged radially around the square. In the center was a round pool, and in the middle of it a small island...On it stood a single tree, a magnolia, in a shower of reddish blossoms. It was as though the tree stood in the sunlight and were [sic] at the same time the source of light.[52]

"Through this dream," Jung comments, "I understood that the self is the principle and archetype of orientation and meaning...For me, this insight signified an approach to the center and therefore to the goal. Out of it emerged the first inkling of my personal myth." "It was the *prima materia*," he adds, "for a lifetime's work."[53]

Like many heirs to the Enlightenment, Perowne operates under the myth of mythlessness, that we can know the real and know ourselves without the mediation of story and figure. He doesn't have or need a personal myth. He reflects, "This notion of Daisy's, that people can't 'live' without stories, is simply not true. He is living proof." Perowne thinks he doesn't need story but brain surgeon that he is, he knows the real point is not brain but mind, the central mystery of how a bunch of cells and its neural network can produce mind, consciousness, spirit. He wishes "that penetrating the skull [brought] into view not the brain but the mind."[54] He responds to Daisy's attempt to educate him to the findings of literature that

> A man who attempts to ease the miseries of failing minds by repairing brains is bound to respect the material world, its limits, and what it can sustain—consciousness, no less. It isn't an article of faith with him, he knows it for a quotidian fact, the mind is what the brain, mere matter, performs. If that's worthy of awe, it also deserves curiosity; the actual, not the magical, should be the challenge. This reading list persuaded Perowne

---

52. Jung, *Memories, Dreams, Reflections*, 198.
53. Ibid., 199.
54. McEwan, *Saturday*, 249.

that the supernatural was the recourse of an insufficient imagination, a dereliction of duty, a childish evasion of the difficulties and wonders of the real, of the demanding re-enactment of the plausible.

When anything can happen, nothing much matters. It's all kitsch to me.[55]

The fantasy imagination will not get you there. Reason can. To which Daisy responds, "You ninny…you Gradgrind. It's literature, not physics!"[56]

Perowne's problem—and McEwan's challenge to the reader—is that he isn't in fact the kind of scientific ninny C.P. Snow described in *The Two Cultures,* able to restrict himself to physics and the merely material. His response to his daughter's favorite poet Philip Larkin's "If I were called in/To construct a religion/I should make use of water" is to substitute "evolution" for Larkin's "water":

If he ever got the call, he'd make use of evolution. What better creation myth? An unimaginable sweep of time, numberless generations spawning by infinitesimal steps complex living beauty out of inert matter, driven on by the blind furies of random mutation, natural selection and environmental change, with the tragedy of forms continually dying, and lately the wonder of minds emerging and with them morality, love, art, cities—and the unprecedented bonus of this story happening to be demonstrably true.[57]

No wonder Daisy hasn't given up on this Gradgrind. Larkin's image is congruent with Jung's pool at the center of the mandala. The poem's last stanza,

I should raise in the east
A glass of water
Where any-angled light
Would congregate endlessly,[58]

suggests Jung's antinomies which the Self contains and which thereby lead, like Larkin's poem, to the suggestion of rebirth ("I should raise in the east…").

---

55. Ibid., 66.

56. Ibid., 67.

57. Ibid., 54.

58. "Water," in Philip Larkin, *Collected Poems,* edited by Anthony Thwaite (New York: Farrar, Straus, Giroux, 1989), 93.

Perowne's embrace of evolution alludes to the Darwin biography Daisy put in his hands. He wakes (for the second time) on Saturday with a memory of Darwin's peroration at the end of *Origin of Species* that haunts him intermittently throughout the day: *"There is grandeur in this view of life."*[59] For Perowne,

> to soften the message, [Darwin] also summoned up the Creator, but his heart wasn't in it and he ditched Him in later editions. Those five hundred pages deserved only one conclusion: endless and beautiful forms of life, such as you see in a common hedgerow, including exalted beings like ourselves, arose from physical laws, from war of nature, famine and death. This is the grandeur. And a bracing kind of consolation in the brief privilege of consciousness.[60]

The source of both freedom and determinism, the laws of chance and mutation are Perowne's (and Darwin's) God. For Perowne, with a century of study of the brain to draw upon and the exciting new developments in neuroscience, those laws are ultimately knowable, but the mystery will remain:

> For all the recent advances, it's still not known how this well-protected one kilogram or so of cells actually encodes information, how it holds experiences, memories, dreams and intentions. He doesn't doubt that in years to come, the coding mechanism will be known, though it might not be in his lifetime. Just like the digital codes of replicating life held within DNA, the brain's fundamental secret will be laid open one day. But even when it has, the wonder will remain, that mere wet stuff can make this bright inward cinema of thought, of sight and sound and touch bound into a vivid illusion of an instantaneous present, with a self, another brightly wrought illusion, hovering like a ghost at its centre. Could it ever be explained, how matter becomes conscious? He can't begin to imagine a satisfactory account, but he knows it will come, the secret will be revealed—over decades, as long as the scientists and the institutions remain in place, the explanations will refine themselves into an irrefutable truth about consciousness. It's already happening, the work is being done in laboratories not far from this theatre, and the journey will be completed, Henry's certain of it. That's the only kind of faith he has. There's grandeur in this view of life.[61]

---

59. McEwan, *Saturday,* 53. Emphasis in text.

60. Ibid., 54.

61. Ibid., 262-63.

Perowne thinks he doesn't need story, but the teeming brain with its "ghost at its center" is one of his stories, the irreconcilable consubstantial, simultaneous presence of matter and spirit. His lifetime of exploring that story is the "open road" he thought his professional life had denied him.

Fitzroy Square and the teeming city of which it is the center also images Perowne's personal story and myth: the irreconcilable impulses in him to rationality and to an openness to experience that rationality neither allows nor explains. Above the square looms the London Post Office Tower with its garish 1960s optimism:

> It rises above the plane trees in the central gardens, behind the reconstructed façade on the southern side; set high on the glass-paned stalk, six stacked circular terraces bearing their giant dishes, and above them, a set of fat wheels or sleeves within which is bound the geometry of fluorescent lights. At night, the dancing Mercury is a playful touch.[62]

British Telecom's logo, "dancing Mercury," rightful symbol of communications and commerce, may be dancing with joy as Trickster often does at the pretense of rationalism the square was meant to figure. Perhaps the Post Office Tower with its "dancing Mercury" is a stand-in for Jung's dream's tree of life at the pond's center with its "shower of reddish blossoms" which at once "stood in the sunlight and [was] the source of light."

Perowne's Fitzroy Square as mandala balances his love of order and his love of teeming chaos. British Telecom's "dancing Mercury" holds his caduceus out and above him in such a manner as to offer a second reading, that it figures not Mercury but Pan with his flute (another of Hermes's inventions; in some genealogies, Hermes is Pan's father and his mother, the nymph Dryope, is sometimes conflated with Penelope). Perowne's myth combines those two aspects of Shadow—Hermes and Pan—that counter his conscious embrace of Apollonian order.

In this, Perowne's mandala points to the mandala that Joyce uses to end the "Ithaca" chapter of *Ulysses*. As Bloom drifts off to sleep he thinks of Sinbad the Sailor: "Going to dark bed there was a square round Sinbad the Sailor

---

62. Ibid., 202.

roc's auk's eggs in the night of the bed of all the auks of the rocs of Darkinbad the Brightdayler."[63] The roc's egg is the circle within the square, envisioning a "wholeness," Kimball argues, that synchronistically repeats Jung's vision of "the hypothetical summation of an indescribable totality...bright and dark and yet neither."[64] So, too, Fitzroy Square and Perowne's vision of it: "bright and dark and yet neither." McEwan offers us not a choice of Hermes or Saturn but rather an image that reconciles Hermes and Saturn.

63. Joyce, *Ulysses*, 737.
64. *CW* 14: 129n. 66.

> To study an art form is to explore a sensibility.
> —Clifford Geertz, *Local Knowledge*

The conflict—and reconciliation— between Hermes and Saturn in Ian McEwan's *Saturday,* between the flexible and inflexible, the irrational and rational, matter and spirit is at the heart of the sensibility to which improvisation gives form and expression. Limning that conflict, improvisation consistently differentiates itself from the mainstream where the status quo, bolstered by the cultural moment's version of rationality, otherwise serenely reigns. In the ecology of ideas, improvisation inhabits the edge, a locale of turbulence in which a new order emerges or is resisted.

Our approach to the sensibility of improvisation has inevitably been multidisciplinary, an approach this book seeks to encourage. Like the form itself I have overstepped many boundaries. To infringe boundaries is inevitable: the gesture of spontaneity puts in question the entire edifice of authority offering outside-the-mainstream ways to make and judge value, to determine what is good and bad, and in sum to know the world.

Through the lens of literary criticism, the first of the many disciplines deployed here, we have seen that improvisation scorns constraint. Besides stretching beyond what the literary canon constrains as fit material or appropriate form, improvisation also scorns the disciplinary and period cubbyholes literary criticism itself relies on to know the canon. Literary criticism, based on some privileged, systematic rationality *du jour,* offers a monolithic approach to texts and to life. It offers readings that are comprehensive or absolute: totalizing explanations or metanarratives. By contrast, the multi- or interdisciplinary approach that improvisation invites offers explanations from many angles—intuitive, symbolic, mythic, historical, to name a few.

Such multivalent explanations do not pretend to authoritative completeness but rather are self-consciously and avowedly contingent on the point of view adopted. None pretend to completeness. Explanations of a text that are polytropic—*many turning*—do not come to identical conclusions yet such explanations need not contradict one another. Privileging no reading above another, they are complementary and syncretic. Such explanations are both/ and rather than either/or. Like the Zen master who circles the Tao and sees it from many angles, this multidisciplinary approach adds up to more than any single reading. Depending on the questions you ask, light is both particle and wave. Rabelais is both conservative Christian and libertine Rabelaisian insofar as he urges us to embrace more of life. Wordsworth both abjures the dizzy raptures of youth and, for his sister's sake, embraces them. And so on. The reconciliation is often partial and sometimes purposefully obscure. Often we do not penetrate the obscurity or misread the ironies because of our "uncritical absorption in Romanticism's own self-representations" our cultural assumption that the natural and spontaneous are the unalloyed values the improvised text embraces.[1]

If we pictured improvisation's edge space as a Janus figure, on the analogy to Bruno Latour's Janus-faced science, we might see a backward looking Themis, Zeus's second wife who represents things as they should be. Themis uses her scales of justice to declare what is right based on received canonical law, custom, and rationality. The other side of the improvisation's Janus

Ready Made Science

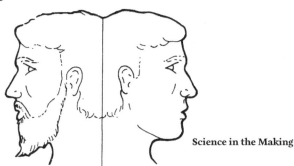

Science in the Making

Bruno Latour's Janus-faced science[2]

figure is a forward looking Metis, Zeus's first wife, whose nature it is to point past Themis's scales to the fecund variety of life that Themis can't fit

---

1. McGann, *The Romantic Ideology*, 1.

2. From Bruno Latour, *Science in Action: How to Follow Scientists and Engineers through Society* (Cambridge, Mass.: Harvard University Press, 1987), 4.

on her balance. Metis sees not just things as they should be but also things as they are.

Improvisation manages to skate on the moment's razor's edge by implementing an approach to experience characterized by the kind of intelligence Metis inspires, "which operates in the world of becoming, in circumstances of conflict—[and] takes the form of an ability to deal with whatever comes up."[3] Such an approach to experience is in dialogue with or denies the *themic,* moral law approach that operates in a world of being, categorical and definitive. *Metis* relies on mental faculties too quick to be rational acting on events too rapid to be susceptible to reason: a mind that comes to meet life as it unfolds.

Inhabiting the edge, the great majority of improvisations lean toward the forward verge, toward emergent new orders: Janus's forward looking face. But exceptional examples—Homer's efforts to define and promulgate Hellenism, Pindar's Orphic rhapsodies, or Swift's ironies—defend the ramparts rather than affect to tear them down. But all, both *arrière*-and *avant-gardists*, address conflict between more-or-less traditional and more-or-less modern, that is to say, emerging standards of value and ways of knowing. Improvisation is the mode of discourse for advancing or resisting a paradigm shift.

Diverse commentators define "Modernism" as a paradigm shift that historically/diachronically begins diversely with Renaissance humanism, the founding of modern science, the rediscovery of Lucretius, the Enlightenment, the Romantic watershed, or the so-called Modernist period itself. Yet improvisation is, as we have seen, an element in each of those. Representing itself as a break (or fortification) of the past, embracing (or denying) creative destruction, improvisation articulates the spirit of modernism, or the resistance to modernism, no matter what the period, synchronically. "Breaking with the past," said to be a definitive idea in Modernism, is an intrinsic element in improvisation's mythos or narrative—*in any age* (Homer, Pindar, and Swift limn the *dangers* of breaking with the past).

Improvisations have been following (or denying) Pound's injunction to "make it new" since mankind experienced the promise (or threat) of change.

---

3. Detienne and Vernant, *Cunning Intelligence,* 44.

As Valéry said, "Everything changes but the *avant-garde.*"[4] Improvisation expresses our response to change: trying to bring it about, resisting it, or at least trying to make sense of it. Improvisation is the leading edge of modernity and, paradoxically, *always has been.* The Modernist Period in the last century—with its masterpieces of improvisation like *Ulysses, Mrs. Dalloway, The Waste Land,* and Pound's *Cantos*—begins to seem the climactic triumph of the perennial improvisational space where the nature and value of our rational and craftsmanly tools are always in question and the artist's ultimate expression is the "glorious affirmation of vitality" characteristic of improvisation that Stephen Greenblatt finds in Lucretius.[5] But there is no triumph, no endpoint or culmination, just more of the same, where different definitions of rationality are challenged through the agency of various non-rational, disruptive faculties or methods. Always finding something to disrupt, improvisations over time embrace more and more of life. What is constant is not some particular aspect of life to be embraced but rather the act of embracing *more* (or to fend off those who would embrace more).

Modernism shares this glorious affirmation of vitality with Romanticism, the historic period. But insofar as Romanticism is thought to be the perennial and cyclic partner of classicism, it is largely improvisation's chaotic vitality that defines it in opposition to classicism's orderly restraint. It is in that sense that improvisation pulses at the heart of Romanticism, not in the period's or in improvisation's supposed unalloyed embrace of spontaneity as a value.

Seeing improvisers as inhabiting a conceptual space that persists over time makes nonsense of our tendency to understand literary history in terms of distinct periods. Study of this perennial space drives us to embrace instead a sense of recurrent cycles, the kind of eternal return that Jung, Joyce, and Mann amongst modern improvisers take to be a primary source of meaning. Periods cycle and spiral around poles defined by attitudes toward how we know ourselves and the world. The pendulum swings between an emphasis on reason or unreason. Each return is culturally determined, shaped in part by time and place. Improvisers on the cutting edge of a paradigm shift

---

4. Quoted in Bernard Sahlins, *Days and Nights in the Second City: A Memoir, with Notes on Staging Review Theatre* (Chicago: Ivan R. Dee, 2001), 11.

5. Greenblatt, *The Swerve,* 9.

develop a right-brained approach to knowing that embraces some irrational faculty that the left-brain dismisses. This shift then becomes congealed into a craftsmanly, more rational style that is mostly left-brained. Then the pendulum swings back. I say *spiral* because each return is culturally determined, shaped in part by time and place, and there is some sense of an incremental or progressive nature to the return: more and more of life is embraced using more and more non-rational means.

Thus, seen through a wide-angled intellectual history lens, improvisation is woven into the emergence of both modernity *and* romanticism, the concepts not the periods. But looking at intellectual history with a more narrowly focused lens, improvisation is built upon perennial ideas deeply rooted in Western culture and characterized by their disruptiveness, their challenge to the mainstream: primitivism (simpler is better); antinomianism (rational, moral law is of no consequence beside the power of nonrational faith); Gnosticism (the necessity of unmediated revelation); synchronicity (acausal coincidence that produces meaning). Through its disruptions of the mainstream, improvisation embraces more and more of the "back streets" or "throwaways"—that we saw embraced by Jung and Joyce—from whatever marginalized precinct the cultural moment is *least* ready to embrace.

Seen through the lens of genre studies, improvisation inhabits that edge where the received canon of genres, which presents itself as embodying all forms of knowledge and all kinds of experience, is shown wanting. Uncanonical by denying genre or by hybridizing or mixing genres, improvisation demonstrates that the canon comes up short-handed before the cornucopian experience of life. Scorning the canon but ever in dialogue with it, improvisation is the canon's double or secret sharer, underscoring and embracing what the canon denies. Improvisation is both anti-genre and a metagenre unto itself, subsuming the many genres that through dialogic interplay it gobbles up: lyric, epic, essay, dialogue, Menippean satire, novel, and so on.

Improvisation is often concerned with how we know the world. Seen through the lens of science or philosophy, improvisation inhabits that edge where new ways of knowing confront received ways of knowing. The *arrière-gardists* like Homer and Swift defend received knowledge against the *avant-gardists* who would promulgate new knowledge. The Renaissance with its new science and openness to experience, for example, turns its back on scholasticism with its dogmatic, system-mongering adherence to Aristotle and Aquinas, what Alfred North Whitehead calls "the rationalistic orgy of the Middle Ages."[6] The Romantics turn their backs on the new physics that "murders to dissect." And so on. Through this lens we see the progress of science figured by Bruno Latour as Janus-faced, where "Science in the Making" turns its back on "Ready Made Science," and vice versa. I take this as the same opposition we have found in improvisation: the choice between *Man Having Thought* and *Man Thinking*. I like that Latour has pictured his backward-looking Janus as bearded (as Janus sometimes is): I imagine gray-bearded. I take his forward-looking figure as the fresh-faced new man, like Dryden's Neander from the "Essay of Dramatick Poesy." Their expressions are mirror images, but for me the pursed lips of Ready Made Science express disapproval at the new-fangled ideas of Science in the Making, whose pursed lips instead express awe at the new world his new science makes visible. Latour's figure also captures the paradox of improvisation, that it must look backward through dialogue with the past in order to see forward and to embrace the present moment: *retrocedens accedit,* "look[ing] back to see forward,...advancing by retreating."[7]

Seen through the more narrowly focused lens of Chaos science, which of course provides my edge and turbulence metaphors, improvisation inhabits that edge where new order emerges from apparent chaos. Improvisation in formal and thematic ways mimetically embodies the emergence in nature of order from apparent chaos. The analogous edge in cultural studies goes by the name "creolization," the mixing of races and cultures from which emerges, for example, the richness and vibrancy of New Orleans culture and New Orleans jazz. Chaotic and pointedly uncraftsmanly (in the culturally dominant way), improvisation allows us to witness the emergence of a new, broader, or richer order, fuzzy and yet more complete than systematic rationality allows. Like Chaos science, improvisation explores the conundrum of freedom and determinism. Tristram Shandy's *libertine* voice recounts the fortuitous events—the misnamed baptism, the falling of the sash—that *determine* his life and opinions. We never know where Tristram's desultory mind will next take us.

---

6. Whitehead, *Science and the Modern World,* 16.

7. "Hermetic Intoxication," in *Uniform Edition of the Writings of James Hillman,* vol. 6: *Mythic Figures* (Putnam, Conn.: Spring Publications, 2007), 273.

But we know, as with Chaos science's fractals, it will be within the scope of the non-linear equation that delineates his sensibility.

Seen through the wider-angled lens of the history of science, improvisation inhabits that edge where paradigms shift. The drive of Western civilization has been toward an increasing commitment to knowing and mastering the world through reason, will, craft, and scientific objectivity—left-brain. But appropriating Melville's words again, we can add that civilization "spins *against* the way it drives."[8] Or, to shift to Joyce's metaphor, improvisation represents "those hidden tides which govern everything and run humanity counter to the apparent flood."[9] The countercurrent that drives beneath or through the dominant tide is the suggestion at the heart of improvisation that we can know more of the world through non-rational means. As the tide of positivistic, rationalist science has mounted, this strong riptide has run through it—no minor eddy, but a strong countercurrent articulated by some of the strongest minds of the western tradition. Neuroscientist Iain McGilchrist's vision of a constant and ongoing cultural conflict resulting from the hemispheres' conflict suggests that this countercurrent is an expression of the right hemisphere, and that the conflict is perennial, that it always has been and always will be with us, not only Janus-faced but Protean, ever changing.

Seen through the lens of myth, improvisation is shepherded and overseen by Hermes (or some iteration of mythic Trickster), perennial lord of boundaries, the border between spirit and commerce, the living and dead, good and evil, rational and irrational, compassionate and greedy, communitarian and individualistic. Hermes is an outsider and latecomer, his mythos essentially analogous to or touching upon the mythos of the fool or natural who instructs the righteous insider. A *metic* spirit, he thumbs his nose at the *themic* moral order. The mainstream may believe that things *should* be a certain way, but Trickster comes to remind us that everything is contingent, nothing necessarily ought to be. Improvisation invites us to experience the green world, less orderly and more dangerous than the world of civilization, and, in Folly's words, *"all the truer for that."* Improvisers participate in the myth of the

---

8. "The Conflict of Convictions," in *The Poems of Herman Melville*, 55.

9. Power, *Conversations with James Joyce*, 54.

hero who, often guided by Trickster, experiences a wounding in the chaotic, green world beyond civilization's pale but transforms it into a boon that he offers as a gift to the society to which he returns. He is *puer,* the eternal youth whose spirit informs *senex* when the old man is at his best, not the pedant of Menippean satire, not "my father" in *Tristram Shandy,* but the vibrant, life-and-death-embracing Pastor Yorick. The improviser says, *you believe you can best know the world through mastery; but by accepting the wound of your limitations, especially reason's limitations, you can know more of the world.* Hermes (or Trickster), then, is the archetypal embodiment of this perennial conceptual space; improvisation is the artistic form that expresses Trickster.

Seen through the lens of psychology, improvisation gives voice to the lower faculties in the traditional hierarchy of faculties. The Great Chain of Being, the pre-modern vision of the orderly hierarchies that characterize all aspects of man and the universe, sees will, reason, and judgment as our highest and most divine faculties; through them we achieve a god-like objective knowledge that enables our mastery over the world.[10] Improvisation explores the proposition, by contrast, that through our lesser faculties—instinct, emotion, and subjectivity—we can achieve our full humanity, which paradoxically may better reflect the divine in us. Improvisation scorns mastery. It explores instead the value of submission to things larger than or beyond than the rational self. Improvisation embraces mystery.

With the rare exceptions of Annie Dillard, Sappho, and, in passing, Marianne Moore, my examples have been mostly male. But the work of Virginia Woolf—*Mrs. Dalloway* and *Orlando* especially—makes clear that improvisation is not necessarily or intrinsically a masculine form. Indeed, in vital ways improvisation's is a feminine voice. The faculties improvisation privileges are linked with the feminine—intuition, emotion, subjectivity, irrationality—while making nonsense of those links. By giving voice to unvoiced faculties improvisation anticipates the women's movement's (and other movements') effort to affranchise. No one could imagine Rabelais's list of *torche-culs* emanating from a feminine persona, and yet improvisers, ever dialogic, are always about difference, the marginalized, and the vulnerable. Though Trickster is usually male and for that matter often priapic, Hermes by bedding Aphrodite

---

10. E.M.W. Tillyard, *The Elizabethan World Picture* (New York: Vintage, 1959).

produces the hermaphrodite who, as a reflection of their union, suggests that Hermes himself is the male god with the closest affinity to the feminine.[11] Tiresias, the bisexual Trickster/guide figure in Odysseus's descent into Hades, embodies the disruption of gender categories: he knows *more,* he knows the future. Improvisation functions in the patriarchal Western tradition as its anima figure and its shadow. What the mainstream would like to dismiss or not to acknowledge, improvisation forces upon our consciousness.

Improvisation is preeminently a mode of discourse that addresses the problem of knowledge, how we can most accurately and fully know the world and the complexities of our own humanity. As science historians Shapin and Schaffer write, "Solutions to the problem of knowledge are solutions to the problem of social order."[12] One way, then, to integrate these polytropic, interdisciplinary approaches, perhaps the nearest thing we can come to an overarching approach to improvisation, is through the lens of politics, how this intellectual space or sensibility fits in the relationship of human beings to power.

The affirmation of vitality ultimately tends to level hierarchies, which makes improvisation throb with a democratic impulse. While Homer's epics are the affairs of noblemen and the gods, the *Iliad* and *Odyssey*'s digressive epic similes introduce in loving detail the everyday events of commoners and the natural world. Homer's long description of Achilles's shield, the product of Hephaestus's *metic* hand, depicts the world of nature and men, war and conflict, but also the world beyond war: feasts and dances, marketplaces and crops at harvest, artisans at their labors, laborers in their fields, and children dancing, all the things worth fighting to preserve and all the things that make war tragic even before the bloodletting starts. Rabelais's "Do what thou wilt" is, as we saw, not only less libertine but also less democratic than it sounds. His careless monks are honorable gentlemen—a class marker—whose values by definition won't lead them astray. Some improvisations resist the democratic mob: Pindar and Swift are in effect royalists embracing the spirit of hierarchies, whether aristocratic or meritocratic. *Utopia* may have done

---

11. See Hyde's appendix on Trickster's mostly male gender in his *Trickster Makes This World,* 335–46.

12. Shapin and Schaffer, *Leviathan and the Air-Pump,* 332.

"more to make William Morris a Socialist than ever Karl Marx did," but only because we miss More's ironies.[13]

Historically, then, improvisation will have to grow into its progressive spirit. Wordsworth's celebration of the common and low, in part inspired by the French Revolution—is an important juncture in this development. Whitman's catalogues—and Ginsberg's—complete what is implicit in Wordsworth's presentational style ("this...this...this") and, as Hyde argues, "put hierarchy to sleep."[14] *Ulysses*, with its celebration of throwaways, is a kind of culmination of this impulse, the most brilliant articulation and embodiment formally and thematically of this democratic, egalitarian spirit. Louis Armstrong, a throwaway himself had his horn not saved him, gives Joyce a run for his money. Improvisers show us the way to our all becoming improvisers, which according to the sensibility of improvisation is our native birthright.

Although subject to perversion, as Mann's *Doctor Faustus* makes clear, improvisation perhaps finds its ultimate expression in the spirit of American democracy with its dual vision of man's frailty and his perfectibility. Like improvisation, democracy believes every voice, however marginal or foolish, should be heard, every vote counted in the "'jam session'" which, as jazz historian and commentator Albert Murray argues, is "the representative anecdote for life in the United States."[15] Along with his catalogues, Whitman's louche carelessness, his directness, his openness to the power of chance and found objects, his overarching commitment to intimacy and to pastoral express democracy's commitment to embracing the thrum of commerce and exchange as a manifestation of spirit. All these are Whitman's way of finding "a way through the world," which according to Wallace Stevens "is more difficult to find than the way beyond it."[16] All these at once articulate Whitman's commitment to improvisation and to democracy. As Stanley Crouch argues:

---

13. R.W. Chambers, "The Meaning of *Utopia*," in Sir Thomas More, *Utopia*, translated and edited by Robert M. Adams (New York: W.W. Norton, 1975), 149.

14. Hyde, *Trickster Makes This World*, 163.

15. Albert Murray, "Improvisation and the Creative Process," in *The Jazz Cadence of American Culture*, edited by Robert G. O'Meally (New York: Columbia University Press, 1998), 112.

16. "Reply to Rapini," in Stevens, *Collected Poetry and Prose*, 382.

In essence, then, the Constitution is a document that functions like the blues-based music of jazz: it values improvisation, the freedom to constantly reinterpret the meanings of our documents. It casts a cold eye on human beings and on the laws they make; it assumes that evil will not forever be allowed to pass by. Yet the Constitution, like the blues singer willing to publicly take apart his own shortcomings, perceives human beings as neither demons nor angels but some mysterious combination of both.[17]

Improvisation, like democracy, makes room for our dualities, our "demons and angels," negating neither, holding them in suspension.

Summing up the spirit of Theatresports, the improvisational theatre he invented, Keith Johnstone remarks, "There are people who prefer to say 'Yes,' and there are people who prefer to say 'No.' Those who say 'Yes' are rewarded by the adventures they have, and those that say 'No' are rewarded by the safety they attain."[18] So too, the metagenre I call improvisation, never interested in safety, is bathed in the adventure of affirmation. But its affirmations are not cheaply won. No pushover, improvisation is always in critical dialogue with some form or sensibility that comes up short and merits refutation. Nor is improvisation rosy-visioned. Like Robert Burton and Tristram Shandy in their anatomies of melancholy, the blues and jazz musician has experienced tragedy but sings or plays his way to happiness. Haunted by the ultimate negation, death, improvisation nonetheless affirms life in its unfolding. As Karl Kerényi points out with regard to improvisation's tutelary deity Hermes, "Life's most obvious alternative course—its overflowing in generation and productivity, its fruitfulness and multiplication—appears...as something incalculable, as purest accident."[19] Improvisation, like Hermes, doesn't need to negate death because it is adept at embracing—indeed, gobbling up—life's polarities. Sterne's Pastor Yorick, the closest thing *Tristram Shandy* offers to a model for living, is named for Hamlet's *momento mori*. Haunted by death,

---

17. Stanley Crouch, "Blues to Be Constitutional: A Long Look at the Wild Wherefores of Our Democratic Lives as Symbolized in the Making of Rhythm and Tune," in *The Jazz Cadence of American Culture*, 159.

18. Johnstone, *Impro: Improvisation and the Theatre*, 92.

19. Kerényi, *Hermes*, 26.

improv has the last word, managing to embrace death as part of life, seizing not only life—*vitam*—but also death: *mortem*. The *ars moriendi*, Montaigne's victory over death in the *Essais*, is the *ars vivendi*: the art of dying well is living well. In its buoyancy, in its profuse sympathy for all the life it alertly surveys, presents, and gobbles up, improvisation demonstrates how we might live better as it presents to us why life is worth living: the "wonderful world" that Satchelmouth freely offers us with his cornucopian horn.

While the epic hero is "timely" only at the moment of death when he fulfills his heroic destiny,[20] the improviser defeats death by being timely during life. The improviser momentously rides the crest of the present. Thoreau seeks "to stand on the meeting of two eternities, the past and the future, which is precisely the present moment; to toe that line."[21] The improviser employs, as jazz commentator Albert Murray puts it, his "consummate skill at producing [an] instantaneous response to life." This presentness, related to the digression so common in improvisation, is also expressed by the jazz "'break,'...the disruption of the normal cadence of a piece of music." Murray adds, "It is precisely this disjuncture, which is the moment of truth. It is on the break that you 'do your thing.' The moment of greatest jeopardy is your moment of greatest opportunity. This is the heroic moment."[22] His protégé Stanley Crouch continues the thought:

> Part of the emotion of jazz results from the excitement and the satisfaction of making the most of the present...Jazzmen supplied a new perspective on time, a sense of how freedom and discipline could coexist within the demands of ensemble improvisation, where the moment was bulldogged, tied, and given shape. As with the Italian artists of the Renaissance, their art was collective and focused by a common body of themes, but for jazzmen, the human imagination in motion was the measure of all things.[23]

"The human imagination in motion [as] the measure of all things" is another good summation of improvisation.

---

20. Nagy, *The Ancient Greek Hero in 24 Hours*, 32.
21. Thoreau, *Walden, Civil Disobedience, and Other Writings*, 14.
22. Murray, "Improvisation and the Creative Process," 112.
23. Crouch, "Blues to Be Constitutional," 162-63.

In his discussion of swing music and dance in the machine age, Joel Dinerstein adds that "improvisation puts audiences on alert: you must be prepared
to follow the band wherever it goes. In other words, such rhythmically sophisticated music, by its very nature, puts audiences literally and figuratively on
their toes."[24] Urging that to be on our toes is the most fruitful attitude to life,
improvisation's essential lesson is to promote that alertness that makes the
improviser's momentous ride possible. Spontaneity is a call to attention, but
a certain kind of attention: not the rigor, inflexibility, and discursiveness of
logic and rationality—logic requires attention too, but an attention always
looking over its shoulder. Spontaneity urges instead an attitude that is open,
fluid, immethodical, *metic,* intuitive, with a penchant for metaphor and symbol, for connotation rather than denotation, for play and, of course, for narrative and for myth. In the political sphere, the idea often attributed to Thomas
Jefferson that "the price of liberty is eternal vigilance," here applies. Alertness
is essential to democracy too.

Improvisation often seems to insist that we find our way back to the innocent alertness of childhood. But usually in the end what it promotes is an
alertness that doesn't sacrifice self-consciousness, the fruit of our fall into
adulthood, a fall that it considers fortunate if we can just wed consciousness
and unconsciousness into a post-rational higher innocence. For Thomas
Mann's Leverkühn, "Consciousness…must pass through an infinity in
order for grace to reappear, and Adam must eat again of the Tree of Knowledge in order to fall back into the state of innocence."[25] Not all eurekas in
the shower are sound or lead to truth but we must be alert in order to glean
those that might prove out. How many insights get away because we aren't
taking notes? Innocents don't take notes; adults who know their frailty and
limitations do.

---

24. Joel Dinerstein, *Swinging the Machine: Modernity, Technology, and African American Culture between the World Wars* (Amherst and Boston: University of Massachusetts Press, 2003), 24. Dinerstein finds in 1930s music and dance a discourse analogous to what we have found in improvisation since Homer, a discourse where reason
and unreason clash: "Big-band swing music and dance humanized the cold, rational
machine-world created and fetishized by technical, corporate, and even artistic elites
in the early twentieth century," 28.

25. Mann, *Doctor Faustus,* 325.

For French theologian Nicolas Malebranche, "Attentiveness is the natural prayer of the soul."[26] The improviser agrees. Improvisation's attentiveness constantly demonstrates that, perceived with the proper attitude—Stephen Dedalus's—every shout on the football pitch is god. In such hierophantic moments the divine is objectively immanent because it is subjectively experienced. "The mortal world is enough," in Auden's phrase, not because of the facticity without meaning the left hemisphere thinks is the whole picture. Divinity, or meaning, is in the world because the improviser alertly and subjectively embraces the intuitive, gestalt vision of the right hemisphere, which posits meaning that may be all we know of the divine. With that Dionysian vision the improviser is able to bear witness to the Apollonian event with which Thoreau concludes *Walden*: "Only that day dawns to which we are awake."

_____

26. *Treatise on Nature and Grace* II, sect. XXXVII.

Abraham, Ralph. *Chaos, Gaia, Eros: A Chaos Pioneer Uncovers the Three Great Streams of History* (New York: HarperCollins, 1994)

Abrams, M.H. *Natural Supernaturalism: Tradition and Revolution in Romantic Literature* (New York: W.W. Norton, 1971)

———. "Structure and Style of the Greater Romantic Lyric," in *From Sensibility to Romanticism: Essays Presented to Frederick A. Pottle,* edited by Frederick W. Hilles and Harold Bloom (New York: Oxford University Press, 1965)

Adams, Richard P. "The Unity and Coherence of Huckleberry Finn," *Tulane Studies in English* 6 (1956): 87-103

Adorno, Theodor W. *Essays on Music,* edited by Richard Leppert; translated by Susan H. Gillespie (Berkeley, Los Angeles, and London: University of California Press, 2002)

———. *Prisms: Essays on Veblen, Huxley, Benjamin, Bach, Proust, Schoenberg, Spengler, Jazz, Kafka,* translated by Samuel and Shierry Weber (Cambridge, Mass.: The MIT Press, 1983)

Alter, Robert. *Partial Magic: The Novel as a Self-Conscious Genre* (Berkeley, Los Angeles and London: University of California Press, 1975)

Argyros, Alexander J. *Blessed Rage for Order: Deconstruction, Evolution, and Chaos* (Ann Arbor: University of Michigan Press, 1991)

Aristotle. *The Basic Works of Aristotle,* edited by Richard McKeon (New York: Random House, 1941)

Armstrong, Louis. *Louis Armstrong in his Own Words: Selected Writings,* edited by Thomas Brothers (New York: Oxford University Press, 1999)

Arnold, Matthew. *The Complete Prose Works of Matthew Arnold,* 13 vols., edited by R.H. Super (Ann Arbor: The University of Michigan Press, 1973)

Auden, W.H. *Collected Poems,* edited by Edward Mendelson (New York: Random House, 1976)

Bacon, Francis. *The Works of Francis Bacon,* translated by James Spedding, Robert Leslie Ellis, and Douglas Denon Heath, 14 vols. (London: Longman, 1857-74).

Bailey, Derek. *Improvisation: Its Nature and Practice in Music* (Boston: Da Capo Press, 1993 [1980])

Bakhtin, Mikhail. *Rabelais and his World,* translated by Hélène Iswolsky, (Bloomington: Indiana University Press, 1984).

——. *Speech Genres and Other Late Essays,* translated by Caryl Emerson and Michael Holquist (Austin: University of Texas Press, 1986)

Balliett, Whitney. *Improvising: Sixteen Musicians and Their Art* (New York: Oxford University Press, 1977)

——. "Monk" (online at *http://www.monkzone.com/Balliet%20Obit.htm*)

Barrett, Joshua. "Louis Armstrong and Opera," *The Musical Quarterly* 76, no. 2 (Summer 1992): 216-41

Barzun, Jacques. "To the Rescue of Romanticism," *The American Scholar* 9, no. 2 (Spring 1940): 147-58

Bateson, F.W. *Wordsworth: A Re-Interpretation* (London: Longmans, 1956 [1954])

Baym, Nina, ed. *The Norton Anthology of American Literature,* shorter 8th ed. (New York and London: W.W. Norton, 1998)

Beatty, Arthur. *William Wordsworth: His Doctrine and Art in Their Historical Relations* (Madison: University of Wisconsin Press, 1960 [1922])

Beer, J.B. *Coleridge's Poems* (London: Dent; New York: Dutton, 1963)

Belgrad, Daniel. *The Culture of Spontaneity: Improvisation and the Arts in Postwar America* (Chicago: The University of Chicago Press, 1999)

Bellow, Saul. *Herzog* (Harmondsworth, Middlesex: Penguin, 1964)

Benjamin, Walter. *Reflections: Essays, Aphorisms, Autobiographical Writings,* translated by Edmund Jephcott, edited by Peter Demetz (New York: Harcourt Brace Jovanovich, 1978)

Berger, John. *The Success and Failure of Picasso* (New York: Pantheon, 1989)

Bergsten, Gunilla. Thomas Mann's *Doctor Faustus: The Sources and Structure of the Novel,* translated by Krishna Winston (Chicago and London: The University of Chicago Press, 1969)

Blake, William. *The Poetry and Prose of William Blake,* edited by David Erdman (Garden City, N.Y.: Doubleday, 1970)

Blanchard, W. Scott. *Scholars Bedlam: Menippean Satire in the Renaissance* (Lewisburg: Bucknell University Press, 1995)

Bloom, Harold. *Bloom's Literary Themes: The Trickster, edited by Harold Bloom* (New York: Bloom's Literary Criticism, 2010)

—. *The Visionary Company: A Reading of English Romantic Poetry* (Ithaca and London: Cornell University Press, 1971)

Boudreau, Gordon V. *The Roots of Walden and the Tree of Life* (Nashville: Vanderbilt University Press, 1991)

Brantley, Richard E. *Wordsworth's "Natural Methodism"* (New Haven: Yale University Press, 1975)

Branch, Lori. *Rituals of Spontaneity: Sentiment and Secularism from Free Prayer to Wordsworth* (Waco, Texas: Baylor University Press, 2006)

Brody, Richard. "Norman Mailer at the Movies," *The New Yorker,* October 30, 2013 (online at *https://www.newyorker.com/culture/richard-brody/norman-mailer-at-the-movies*)

Brothers, Thomas. *Louis Armstrong's New Orleans* (New York: Norton, 2007)

Brown, Norman O. *Apocalypse and/or Metamorphosis* (Berkeley and Los Angeles: University of California Press, 1991)

Browne, Thomas. *The Prose of Sir Thomas Browne,* edited by Norman J. Endicott (New York: New York University Press, 1968)

Bruner, Jerome. *On Knowing: Essays for the Left Hand,* exp. ed. (Cambridge, Mass. and London: The Belknap Press of Harvard University Press, 1979)

Buckley, Jerome Hamilton. *Tennyson: The Growth of the Poet* (Cambridge, Mass.: Harvard University Press, 1960)

—. *The Victorian Temper: A Study in Literary Culture* (New York: Vintage, 1964 [1951])

Budgen, Frank. *James Joyce and the Making of* Ulysses (Bloomington and London: Indiana University Press, 1960)

Buford, Bill. *Among the Thugs* (New York: Vintage Books, 1991)

Burke, Kenneth. *Language as Symbolic Action: Essays on Life, Literature, and Method* (Berkeley and Los Angeles: University of California Press, 1966)

—. *Permanence and Change: An Anatomy of Purpose* (Los Altos, California: Hermes, 1954)

Burton, Robert. *The Anatomy of Melancholy* (East Lansing: Michigan State University Press, 1965)

Campbell, Joseph. *Creative Mythology: The Masks of God* (New York: Viking, 1968)

—. *The Hero with a Thousand Faces* (New York: Pantheon, 1949)

Carlyle, Thomas. *Sartor Resartus,* edited by Archibald MacMechan (Boston and London: The Atheneum Press, 1902)

Cassirer, Ernst. *An Essay on Man: An Introduction to a Philosophy of Human Culture* (New Haven: Yale University Press, 2021 [1944])

Cave, Terence. *The Cornucopian Text: Problems of Writing in the French Renaissance* (Oxford: Clarendon Press, 1979)

Cheng, François. *Chinese Poetic Writing: With an Anthology of T'ang Poetry,* translated by Donald A. Riggs and Jerome Seaton (Bloomington: University of Indiana Press, 1982)

Coleridge, Samuel Taylor. *Biographia Literaria, or Biographical Sketches of My Literary Life and Opinions,* edited by J. Shawcross, 2 vols. (London: Oxford University Press, 1907)

—. *Collected Letters of Samuel Taylor Coleridge,* edited by Earl Leslie Griggs, 6 vols. (Oxford: Clarendon Press, 1956-71)

Colie, Rosalie. *Paradoxia Epidemica: The Renaissance Tradition of Paradox* (Princeton, N.J.: Princeton University Press, 1966)

Conrad, Joseph. *Heart of Darkness,* edited by Richard Kimbrough (New York: W.W. Norton, 1988)

—. *The Nigger of the "Narcissus,"* edited by Richard Kimbrough (New York: W.W. Norton, 1979)

Croll, Morris W. *"Attic" and Baroque Prose Style: The Anti-Ciceronian Movement. Essays by Morris W. Croll,* edited by J. Max Patrick and Robert O. Evans, with John M. Wallace (Princeton, N.J.: Princeton University Press, 1996)

Crouch, Stanley, "Blues to Be Constitutional: A Long Look at the Wild Wherefores of Our Democratic Lives as Symbolized in the Making of Rhythm and Tune," in *The Jazz Cadence of American Culture,* edited by Robert G. O'Meally (New York: Columbia University Press, 1998)

Csikszentmihalyi, Mihaly. *Flow: The Psychology of Optimal Experience* (New York: Harper & Row, 1990)

—. *Creativity: Flow and the Psychology of Discovery and Invention* (New York: Harper Collins, 1996)

Culler, A. Dwight. *The Poetry of Tennyson* (New Haven: Yale University Press, 1977)

Cunnell, Howard. "Fast this Time: Jack Kerouac and the Writing of On the Road," in Jack Kerouac, *On the Road: The Original Scroll* (New York: Penguin, 2008)

Curtius, Ernst Robert. *European Literature and the Latin Middle Ages,* translated by Willard R. Trask (Princeton, N.J.: Princeton University Press, 1973 [1953])

De Marco, Nick. "Escaping History: Gnostic and Hermetic Trajectories in Joyce's *Ulysses,*" in *Hypermedia Joyce Studies,* Special Prague Symposium Issue (2010–2011), *online at http://hjs.ff.cuni.cz/archives/v11_1/main/essays.php?essay=demarco*

Derrida, Jacques. *Dissemination,* translated by Barbara Johnson (Chicago: The University of Chicago Press, 1981)

—. *Writing and Difference,* translated by Alan Bass (Chicago: The University of Chicago Press, 1978)

—. *Margins of Philosophy,* translated, with additional notes, by Alan Bass (Chicago: The University of Chicago Press, 1985)

Detienne, Marcel, and Jean-Pierre Vernant. *Cunning Intelligence in Greek Culture and Society,* translated by Janet Lloyd (Chicago: The University of Chicago Press, 1991)

Diderot, Denis. *Rameau's Nephew and First Satire,* translated by Margaret Mauldon (New York: Oxford World's Classics, 2006)

Dillard, Annie. *Teaching a Stone to Talk* (New York: Harper Perennial, 1988)

Dinerstein, Joel. *Swinging the Machine: Modernity, Technology, and African American Culture between the World Wars* (Amherst and Boston: University of Massachusetts Press, 2003)

Donne, John. *The Sermons of John Donne,* 10 vols., edited by George R. Potter and Evelyn Simpson (Berkeley: University of California Press, 1962)

Drob, Sanford L. *Kabbalistic Visions: C. G. Jung and Jewish Mysticism* (New Orleans: Spring Journal Books, 2010)

Dryden, John. *The Works of John Dryden,* vol. 17: *Prose, 1668–1691, An Essay of Dramatick Poesie and Shorter Works,* edited by Samuel Holt Monk and A. E. Wallace Maurer (Berkeley, Los Angeles, and London: University of California Press, 1971)

Eagleton, Terry. *The English Novel: An Introduction* (London: Wiley-Blackwell, 2013)

—. *Literary Theory: An Introduction* (Minneapolis and London: University of Minnesota Press, 1993 [1983])

Ehrhart, W. D. "Hunting," in *Winning Hearts and Minds: War Poems by Vietnam Vets,* edited by Larry Rottman, et al. (New York: McGraw-Hill, 1972)

Eliot, T. S. *Selected Essays* (London: Faber and Faber, 1932)

—. *The Waste Land: A Facsimile and Transcript of the Original Drafts Including the Annotations of Ezra Pound,* edited by Valerie Eliot (New York: Harcourt, 1974)

Ellman, Richard. *James Joyce* (New York: Oxford University Press, 1959)

Emerson, Ralph Waldo. *The Collected Works of Ralph Waldo Emerson,* 5 vols., edited by Robert E. Spiller (Cambridge, Mass.: The Belknap Press of Harvard University Press, 1971)

—. *Essays, First and Second Series* (New York: Macmillan, 1926)

Empson, William. *Some Versions of Pastoral* (New York: New Directions, 1960)

Entzminger, Robert L. *Divine Word: Milton and the Redemption of Language* (Pittsburgh: Duquesne University Press, 1985)

Erasmus, Desiderius. Adagia, in *Opera Omnia,* vol. 20 (North-Holland: Elsevier, 1993 [1703-6])

—. *The Praise of Folly,* translated by Clarence H. Miller (New Haven: Yale University Press, 1979)

Fadem, Richard. "Dorothy Wordsworth: A View from 'Tintern Abbey,' " *The Wordsworth Circle* 9, no. 1 (Winter 1978): 17-32

Farrell, William J. "Nature versus Art as a Comic Pattern in Tristram Shandy," *English Literature History* 30, no. 1 (March 1963): 16-35.

Feder, Lilian. *Madness in Literature* (Princeton, N.J.: Princeton University Press, 1980)

Ferguson, Frances. *Wordsworth: Language as Counter-Spirit* (New Haven and London: Yale University Press, 1977)

Ferry, David. *The Limits of Mortality: An Essay on Wordsworth's Major Poems* (Middletown, Conn.: Wesleyan University Press, 1959)

Fertel, R. J. "The Wye's 'Sweet Inland Murmur,' " *The Wordsworth Circle* 16, no. 3 (Summer 1985): 134-35

Fichter, Andrew. "Ode and Elegy: Idea and Form in Tennyson's Early Poetry," *English Literature History* 40, no. 3 (Autumn 1973)

Fish, Stanley E. *Self-Consuming Artifacts: The Experience of Seventeenth Century Literature* (Berkeley and Los Angeles: University of California Press, 1972)

——. *Seventeenth-Century Prose: Modern Essays in Criticism* (New York: Oxford University Press, 1971)

——. *Surprised by Sin: The Reader in Paradise Lost* (Berkeley, Los Angeles, and London: University of California Press, 1971)

——. "With Mortal Voice: Milton Defends against the Muse," *English Literature History* 62, no. 3 (Fall 1995): 509-27

Fitzgerald, F. Scott. *The Great Gatsby* (New York: Charles Scribner's Sons, 1925)

Foley, John Miles. *The Theory of Oral Composition: History and Methodology* (Bloomington: Indiana University Press, 1988)

Foucault, Michel. *Madness and Civilization: A History of Insanity in the Age of Reason* (New York: Vintage, 1973 [1965])

Fox, Ruth A. *The Tangled Chain: The Structure of Disorder in the* Anatomy of Melancholy (Berkeley, Los Angeles, and London: University of California Press, 1976)

Freud, Sigmund. *A General Introduction to Psychoanalysis,* translated by Joan Riviere (Garden City, N.Y.: Garden City Publishing, 1943)

——. *New Introductory Lectures on Psychoanalysis,* translated by James Strachey (New York and London: W.W. Norton, 1990 [1933])

Fry, Paul H. *The Poet's Calling in the English Ode* (New Haven and London: Yale University Press, 1980)

Frye, Northrop. *Anatomy of Criticism: Four Essays* (Princeton, N.J.: Princeton University Press, 1957)

Garrod, H.W. *Wordsworth: Lectures and Essays* (Oxford: Clarendon Press, 1927)

Gasché, Rodolphe. *Inventions of Difference: On Jacques Derrida* (Cambridge, Mass.: Harvard University Press, 1994)

Geertz, Clifford. *Local Knowledge: Further Essays in Interpretive Anthropology* (New York: Basic Books, 1983).

Gérard, Albert S. *English Romantic Poetry: Ethos, Structure, and Symbol in Coleridge, Wordsworth, Shelley, and Keats* (Berkeley and Los Angeles: University of California Press, 1968)

Gibson, William. "Back From the Future," *The New York Times Magazine,* August 2007

Gifford, Don. *Ulysses Annotated: Notes for James Joyce's* Ulysses, 2nd ed. (Berkeley, Los Angeles, and London: University of California Press, 1988)

Ginsberg, Allen. *Composed on the Tongue* (Mechanicsville, Virginia: Grey Fox Press, 2001).

—. *Deliberate Prose* (New York: Harper Perennial, 2001)

—. *Howl and Other Poems* (San Francisco: City Lights, 1956)

—. *Howl: Original Draft Facsimile,* edited by Barry Miles (New York: Harper Perennial, 1995)

—. *Spontaneous Mind: Selected Interviews 1958-1996* (New York: Perennial, 2002)

Gladwell, Malcolm. *Blink: The Power of Thinking without Thinking* (New York: Little, Brown and Company, 2005)

Gleick, James. *Chaos: Making a New Science* (New York: Viking, 1987)

Goethe, Johann Wolfgang von. *Faust: A Tragedy,* translated by Walter Arnt (New York: Norton Critical, 2001)

Gombrich, E.H. *Art and Illusion: A Study in the Psychology of Pictorial Representation* (Princeton, N.J.: Princeton University Press, 1961)

Goodman, Nelson. *Languages of Art* (Indianapolis: Bobbs-Merrill, 1968)

Lord Byron. *Byron's Don Juan: A Variorum Edition,* 5 vols., edited by Truman Guy Steffan and William W. Pratt (Austin: University of Texas Press, 1957-71)

Gordon, Ken. "Improvisers and Revisers: An Experiment in Spontaneity," *Poets & Writers* (May/June 2006) (online at *https://www.pw.org/content/improvisers_and_revisers_experiment_spontaneity*)

Gourevitch, Philip. "Mr. Brown," in *The New Yorker* (29 July 2002)

Graham, A.C. *Reason and Spontaneity: A New Solution to the Problem of Fact and Value* (London and Dublin: Curzon Press; Totowa, N.J.: Barnes & Noble Books, 1985)

Graves, Robert. *The Greek Myths: Complete Edition* (New York: Penguin, 1993)

Gregory, E.R. *Milton and the Muses* (Tuscaloosa: University of Alabama Press, 1989)

Greenblatt, Stephen. *Renaissance Self-Fashioning: From More to Shakespeare* (Chicago: The University of Chicago Press, 1980)

—. *The Swerve: How the World Became Modern* (New York: W.W. Norton, 2012)

Grob, Alan. *The Philosophical Mind: A Study of Wordsworth's Poetry and Thought, 1797-1805* (Columbus: Ohio State University Press, 1973)

Gullason, Thomas Arthur. "The 'Fatal' Ending of Huckleberry Finn," *American Literature* 29, no. 1 (March 1957): 86-91

Hampton, Timothy. "'Turkish Dogs': Rabelais, Erasmus, and the Rhetoric of Alterity," *Representations* 41 (Winter 1993): 58-82.

Hartman, Charles O. *Jazz Text: Voice and Improvisation in Poetry, Jazz and Song* (Princeton, N.J.: Princeton University Press, 1991)

Hartman, Geoffrey. *The Unmediated Vision: An Interpretation of Wordsworth, Hopkins, Rilke, and Valéry* (New York: Harcourt, Brace & World, 1966 [1954])

Havelock, Eric A. *The Muse Learns to Write: Reflections on Orality and Literacy from Antiquity to the Present* (New Haven: Yale University Press, 1986)

—. *Preface to Plato* (Cambridge, Mass.: Harvard University Press, 1963)

Havens, Raymond Dexter. *The Mind of the Poet,* vol. 1: *A Study of Wordsworth's Thought* (Baltimore: The John Hopkins Press, 1941)

Hayles, N. Katherine, ed. *Chaos and Order: Complex Dynamics in Literature and Science* (Chicago: The University of Chicago Press, 1991)

—. *Chaos Bound: Orderly Disorder in Contemporary Literature and Science* (Chicago: The University of Chicago Press, 1990)

Hazlitt, William. *The Complete Works of William Hazlitt,* edited by P.P. Howe, 21 vols. (London: J.M. Dent and Sons, 1932)

Heller, Zoe. "'Saturday': One Day in the Life," *New York Times,* March 20, 2005, Sunday Book Review

Henke, Robert. *Performance and Literature in the Commedia dell'Arte* (New York: Cambridge University Press, 2002)

Herbert, George. *The Works of George Herbert,* edited by F.E. Hutchinson (Oxford: Clarendon Press, 1941)

Herr, Michael. *Kubrick* (New York: Grove Press, 2000)

Hillman, James. *Uniform Edition of the Writings of James Hillman,* vol. 6: *Mythic Figures* (Thonmpson, Conn.: Spring Publications, 2021 [2007]

—. *Pan and the Nightmare* (Thompson, Conn.: Spring Publications, 2020 [1972])

—, and Sonu Shamdasani. *Lament of the Dead: Psychology after Jung's* Red Book (New York: Norton, 2013)

Hirsch, Edward. *How to Read a Poem: And Fall in Love with Poetry* (New York: Harvest, 1999)

Hofstadter, Douglas R. *Gödel, Escher, Bach: An Eternal Golden Braid* (New York: Basic Books, 1979)

Homer. *The Iliad,* translated by Richard Lattimore (Chicago: The University of Chicago Press, 1951)

——. *The Odyssey,* translated by Robert Fagles (New York: Viking, 1996).

——. *The Homeric Hymns,* translated by Apostolos N. Athanassakis (Baltimore: The Johns Hopkins University Press, 2004 [1976])

——. *The Homeric Hymns,* translated by Charles Boer (Chicago: The Swallow Press, 1972 [1970])

——, and Hesiod. *Works of Hesiod and the Homeric Hymns,* translated by Daryl Hine (Chicago and London: The University of Chicago Press, 2005 [1972])

Howe, Irving. *William Faulkner: A Critical Study* (Chicago: The University of Chicago Press, 1975)

Huizinga, Johan. *Homo Ludens: A Study of the Play Element in Culture* (Boston: Beacon Press, 1955 [1950])

Hulme, T. E. *Speculations: Essays on Humanism and the Philosophy of Art* (London: Routledge, 2010)

Hyde, Lewis. *The Gift: Imagination and the Erotic Life of Property* (New York: Random House, 1983)

Hyde, Lewis. *Trickster Makes This World: Mischief, Myth and Art* (New York: Farrar, Straus and Giroux, 1997)

Iser, Wolfgang. *The Act of Reading: A Theory of Aesthetic Response* (Baltimore: The Johns Hopkins University Press, 1978)

Jacobus, Mary. *Tradition and Experiment in Wordsworth's Lyrical Ballads (1798)* (Oxford: Clarendon Press, 1976)

James, Henry. *The Art of Criticism: Henry James on the Theory and the Practice of Fiction,* edited by William Veeder and Susan M. Griffin (Chicago and London: The University of Chicago Press, 1986)

James, William. *Essays in Psychology* (Cambridge, Mass. and London: Harvard University Press, 1983)

——. *The Principles of Psychology*, 2 vols. (New York: Henry Holt and Co., 1890)

——. *Writings 1878-1899* (New York: The Library of America, 1992)

Jarry, Alfred. *Selected Works of Alfred Jarry*, edited by Roger Shattuck and Simon Watson Taylor (New York: Grove Press, 1980)

Johnson, Monte Ransome. "Nature, Spontaneity and Voluntary Action in Lucretius," in *Lucretius: Poetry, Philosophy, Science*, edited by Daryn Lehoux, A. D. Morrison, and Alison Sharrock (Oxford: Oxford University Press, 2013)

Johnson, Samuel. *Lives of the English Poets*, edited by George Birkbeck Hill, 3 vols. (Oxford: Clarendon Press, 1905)

Johnson, W. R. *The Idea of the Lyric: Lyric Modes in Ancient and Modern Poetry* (Berkeley and Los Angeles: University of California Press, 1982)

Johnstone, Keith. *Impro for Storytellers: Theatresports and the Art of Making Things Happen* (New York: Routledge, 1999)

——. *Impro: Improvisation and the Theatre* (New York: Routledge, 1987)

Joyce, James. *Ulysses* (New York: Vintage Books, 1961)

——. *A Portrait of the Artist as a Young Man* (New York, London, and Toronto: Everyman's Library/Alfred A. Knopf, 1991)

——. *Stephen Hero* (New York: New Directions, 1963)

——. *Letters of James Joyce*, edited by Stuart Gilbert and Richard Ellmann, 3 vols. (London: Faber and Faber, 1957-66)

Jung, Carl Gustav. *The Collected Works of C. G. Jung*, edited and translated by Gerhard Adler and R. F. C. Hull, 20 vols. (Princeton, N.J.: Princeton University Press, 1953-79)

——. *C. G. Jung Speaking: Interviews and Encounters*, edited by William McGuire and R. F. C. Hull (Princeton, N.J.: Princeton University Press, 1977)

——. *The Red Book: Liber Novus—A Reader's Edition*, edited by Sonu Shamdasani, translated by Mark Kyburz, John Peck, and Sonu Shamdasani (New York and London: W.W. Norton, 2009)

——. *Memories, Dreams, Reflections*, recorded and edited by Aniela Jaffé; translated by Richard and Clara Winston (New York: Vintage, 1963)

Kahneman, Daniel. *Thinking, Fast and Slow* (New York: Farrar Straus and Giroux, 2011)

Kaiser, Walter. *Praisers of Folly: Erasmus, Rabelais, Shakespeare* (Cambridge, Mass.: Harvard University Press, 1963)

Kamoche, Ken N., Miguel Pina e Cunha, and João Vieiri da Cunha, eds. *Organizational Improvisation* (London and New York: Routledge, 2005 [2002]).

Kant, Immanuel. *Critique of Judgment,* translated by J. H. Bernard (New York: Hafner Press, 1951)

Kauffman, Stuart. *At Home in the Universe: The Search for the Laws of Self-Organization and Complexity* (New York and Oxford: Oxford University Press, 1995).

Keats, John. *Selected Letters,* edited by Robert Gittings (Oxford: Oxford University Press, 2002)

Keller, Karl. "The Example of Edward Taylor," in *The American Puritan Imagination: Essays in Revaluation,* edited by Sacvan Bercovitch (New York: Cambridge University Press, 1974)

Kenner, Hugh. *Joyce's Voices* (Berkeley, Los Angeles, and London: University of California Press, 1978)

Kerényi, Karl. *Hermes: Guide of Souls* (Thompson, Conn.: Spring Publications, 2020 [1976])

Kerouac, Jack. *On the Road* (New York: Penguin, 1976)

—. *On the Road: The Original Scroll* (New York: Penguin, 2008)

—. *Visions of Cody* (New York: Penguin, 1993)

Kharpertian, Theodore D. *A Hand to Turn the Time: The Menippean Satires of Thomas Pynchon* (Rutherford: Fairleigh Dickinson University Press; London and Toronto: Associated University Presses, 1990)

Kimball, Jean. *Odyssey of the Psyche: Jungian Patterns in Joyce's* Ulysses (Carbondale and Edwardsville: Southern Illinois University Press, 1997)

Koren, Leonard. *Wabi-Sabi for Artists, Designers, Poets & Philosophers* (Point Reyes, California: Imperfect Publishing, 2008)

Kugel, James L. *Poetry and Prophecy: The Beginning of a Literary Tradition* (Ithaca: Cornell University Press, 1990)

Kuhn, Thomas S. *The Structure of Scientific Revolutions,* 4th ed. (Chicago and London: The University of Chicago Press, 2012 [1962])

Kundera, Milan. *The Unbearable Lightness of Being* (New York: Harper and Row, 1987 [1984])

Kurke, Leslie. *The Traffic in Praise: Pindar and the Poetics of Social Economy* (Berkeley: California Classical Studies, 2013 [1991])

Lanham, Richard. *A Handlist of Rhetorical Terms: A Guide for Students of English Literature* (Berkeley, Los Angeles, and London: University of California Press, 1991)

—. *The Motives of Eloquence* (New Haven: Yale University Press, 1976)

—. *Tristram Shandy: The Games of Pleasure* (Berkeley and Los Angeles: University of California Press, 1973)

Lawrence, D. H. *The Complete Poems of D. H. Lawrence,* edited by Vivian de Sola Pinto and F. Warren Roberts, 2 vols. (New York: The Viking Press, 1964)

Lehrer, Jonah. *How We Decide* (New York: Houghton Mifflin, 2009)

—. "The Eureka Hunt," *The New Yorker* (28 July 2008)

—. *Proust was a Neuroscientist* (New York: Houghton Mifflin, 2007)

Lentricchia, Frank. *After the New Criticism* (Chicago: The University of Chicago Press, 1981)

Lévi-Strauss, Claude. *The Savage Mind* (Chicago: The University of Chicago Press, 1966)

Levinson, Marjorie. *The Romantic Fragment Poem: A Critique of a Form* (Chapel Hill: University of North Carolina, 1986)

Lewalski, Barbara. Paradise Lost *and the Rhetoric of Literary Forms* (Princeton, N.J.: Princeton University Press, 1985)

Lewis, C. S. *Studies in Words,* 2nd ed. (London: Cambridge University Press, 1967)

Locke, John. *An Essay Concerning Human Understanding,* edited by Peter H. Nidditch (Oxford: Oxford University Press, 1975)

Loevinger, Jane, and Augusto Blasi. *Ego Development* (San Francisco: Jossey-Bass, 1977)

López-Pedraza, Raphael. *Hermes and His Children* (Einsiedeln: Daimon, 1989)

Lord, Albert. *The Singer of Tales* (New York: Atheneum, 1970 [1960])

Lovejoy, Arthur O., and George Boas. *Primitivism and Related Ideas in Antiquity* (New York: Octagon Books, 1965 [1935])

Lowes, John Livingston. *The Road to Xanadu: A Study in the Ways of Imagination* (New York: Vintage Books, 1959 [1927])

Lowth, Robert. *Lectures on the Sacred Poetry of the Hebrews,* translated from the Latin by G. Gregory; edited by Calvin E. Stowe (Boston: Crocker & Brewster; Boston: J. Leavitt, 1829 [1787])

Lynn, Kenneth. "Welcome Back to the Raft Huck, Honey!" *American Scholar* 46, no. 3 (Summer 1977): 338-47

MacCaffrey, Isabel Gamble. Paradise Lost *as "Myth"* (Cambridge, Mass.: Harvard University Press, 1959)

Mailer, Norman. *Advertisements for Myself and Other Writings* (New York: Putnam, 1959)

Main, Roderick. *The Rupture of Time: Synchronicity and Jung's Critique of Modern Western Culture* (Hove and New York: Brunner-Routledge, 2004)

Mandelbrot, Benoît B. *The Fractal Geometry of Nature* (New York: W.H. Freeman, 1983)

—. "How Long is the Coast of Britain: Statistical Self-similarity and Fractional Dimension." *Science* 156, no. 3775 (5 May 1967): 636-38.

Mann, Thomas. *Doctor Faustus: The Life of the German Composer Adrian Leverkühn As Told by a Friend,* translated by John E. Woods (New York: Vintage, 1997)

—. *Thomas Mann's Addresses Delivered at the Library of Congress, 1942-1949* (Rockville, Maryland: Wildside Press, 2008)

Martial. *Epigrams,* 2 vols., translated by Walter C.A. Ker (London: William Heinemann; New York: G.P. Putnam's Sons)

Marx, Leo. "Mr. Eliot, Mr. Trilling, and *Huckleberry Finn,*" *American Scholar* 22, no. 4 (Autumn 1953): 423-40

Maslow, Abraham. *Toward a Psychology of Being* (Princeton, N.J.: Van Nostrand, 1968)

McEwan, Ian. *Saturday* (New York: Doubleday, 2006)

McGann, Jerome. *The Romantic Ideology: A Critical Introduction* (Chicago: The University of Chicago Press, 1983)

McGilchrist, Iain. *The Master and the Emissary: The Divided Brain and the Making of the Western World* (New Haven and London: Yale University Press, 2009)

——. *The Divided Brain and the Search for Meaning: Why Are We So Unhappy?* (New Haven: Yale University Press, 2012). Kindle Edition.

McNeill, Daniel, and Paul Freiberger. *Fuzzy Logic: The Revolutionary Computer Technology That Is Changing Our World* (New York: Touchstone, 1993)

McNulty, Bard J. "Self-Awareness in the Making of 'Tintern Abbey,'" *The Wordsworth Circle* 12, no. 2 (1981): 97-100

Mellor, Anne Kostelanetz. *Blake's Human Form Divine* (Berkeley, Los Angeles, and London: University of California Press, 1974)

Melville, Herman. *The Poems of Herman Melville,* edited by Douglas Robillard (Kent, Ohio, and London: The Kent State University Press, 2000)

Mill, John Stuart. *The Collected Works of John Stuart Mill,* vol. 10: *Essays on Ethics, Religion, and Society,* edited by J.M. Robson (Toronto: University of Toronto Press and Routledge & Kegan Paul, 1969 [1833)]

Miller, Henry. *Tropic of Cancer* (New York: Grove Press, 1961)

Miller, James. *Examined Lives: From Socrates to Nietzsche* (New York: Farrar Straus and Giroux, 2011)

Milton, John. *The Poems of John Milton,* edited by John Carey and Alastair Fowler (New York: W.W. Norton, 1972)

——. *Complete Poems and Major Prose,* edited by Merritt Y. Hughes (New York: The Odyssey Press, 1957)

Montaigne, Michel de. *The Complete Essays of Montaigne,* translated by Donald M. Frame (Stanford: Stanford University Press, 1958)

Moore, Marianne. *The Poems of Marianne Moore,* edited by Grace Schulman (New York: Viking, 2003)

Moorman, Mary. *William Wordsworth: A Biography,* vol. 1: *The Early Years, 1770-1805* (London, Oxford, and New York: Oxford University Press, 1968)

More, Sir Thomas. *The Yale Edition of The Complete Works of St. Thomas More,* vol. 4: *Utopia,* edited by Edward Surtz S.J. and J.H. Hexter (New Haven: Yale University Press, 1965)

——. *Utopia,* edited and translated by Robert M. Adams (New York: W.W. Norton, 1992)

Nabholtz, John R. "The Integrity of Wordsworth's 'Tintern Abbey,'" *The Journal of English and Germanic Philology* 73, no. 2 (April 1974): 227-38

Nachmanovitch, Stephen. *Free Play: The Power of Improvisation in Life and Art* (New York: Penguin Putnam, 1990)

Nagler, Michel N. *Spontaneity and Tradition: A Study in the Oral Art of Homer* (Berkeley and Los Angeles: University of California Press, 1974)

Nagy, Gregory. *The Ancient Greek Hero in 24 Hours* (Cambridge, Mass., and London, England: The Belknap Press of Harvard University Press, 2013)

Nagy, Gregory. *Poetry as Performance: Homer and Beyond* (London: Cambridge University Press, 1996)

Nashe, Thomas. *The Works of Thomas Nashe,* 3 vols., edited by Ronald B. McKerrow (London: A.H. Bullen, 1904)

Nettl, Bruno, and Melinda Russell. *In the Course of Performance: Studies in the World of Musical Improvisation* (Chicago: The University of Chicago Press, 1998)

New, Melvyn. *Tristram Shandy: A Book for Free Spirits* (New York: Twayne Publishers, 1994)

Nicolas of Cusa. *On Learned Ignorance,* translated by Jasper Hopkins (Minneapolis: Banning Press, 1981)

Nietzsche, Friedrich. *The Birth of Tragedy* and *The Genealogy of Morals,* translated by Francis Golffing (Garden City, N.Y.: Doubleday, 1956)

Norris, Margot, ed. *A Companion to James Joyce's* Ulysses (Boston and New York: Bedford Books, 1998)

O'Connor, William Van. "Why Huckleberry Finn Is Not the Great American Novel," *College English* 17, no. 1 (October 1955): 6-10.

Olshin, Toby A. "Genre and Tristram Shandy: the Novel of Quickness," *Genre* 4 (December 1971): 360-75

Ong, Walter J. *Orality and Literacy: The Technologizing of the Word* (New York: Routledge, 2000 [1982])

Otto, W.F. *The Homeric Gods: The Spiritual Significance of Greek Religion,* translated by Moses Hadas (London: Thames and Hudson, 1954)

Ovid. *Metamorphoses,* translated by Stanley Lombardo (Indianapolis and Cambridge: Hackett Publishing, 2010).

Owen, Wilfred. *The Collected Poems of Wilfred Owen,* edited by Cecil Day Lewis and Edmund Blunden (New York: New Directions, 1965)

Oxford Anthology of English Literature, The, edited by Frank Kermode and John Hollander, 2 vols. (New York: Oxford University Press, 1973)

Parry, Milman. *The Making of Homeric Verse: The Collected Papers,* edited by Adam Parry (New York: Oxford University Press, 1987)

Pater, Walter. *Appreciations, with an Essay on Style* (London: Macmillan, 1895)

—. *The Renaissance: Studies in Art and Poetry* (London: Macmillan and Co., 1917 [1873])

Pattison, Robert. *Tennyson and Tradition* (Cambridge, Mass.: Harvard University Press, 1979)

Perkins, David. *Wordsworth and the Poetry of Sincerity* (Cambridge, Mass.: Harvard University Press, 1964)

Perloff, Marjorie. *Poetic License: Essays on Modernist and Postmodernist Lyric* (Evanston, Ill.: Northwestern University Press, 1990)

—. *Unoriginal Genius: Poetry by Other Means in the New Century* (Chicago: The University of Chicago Press, 2012)

Petrie, Graham. "Rhetoric as Fictional Technique in *Tristram Shandy,*" *Philological Quarterly* 48, no. 4 (October 1969): 479-94

Peters, Gary. *The Philosophy of Improvisation* (Chicago: The University of Chicago Press, 2009)

Piaget, Jean. *Play, Dreams, and Imitation in Childhood* (New York: W.W. Norton, 1962)

Pinsky, Robert. *The Situation of Poetry: Contemporary Poetry and its Traditions* (Princeton, N.J.: Princeton University Press, 1976)

Poe, Edgar Allan. *The Selected Writings of Edgar Allan Poe: Authoritative Texts, Backgrounds and Contexts, Criticism,* edited by G.R. Thompson (New York and London: W.W. Norton, 2004)

Poggioli, Renato. *The Oaten Flute: Essays on Pastoral Poetry and the Pastoral Ideal* (Cambridge, Mass: Harvard University Press, 1975)

Poirier, Richard. *A World Elsewhere: The Place of Style in American Literature* (New York: Oxford University Press, 1966)

Pound, Ezra. *Literary Essays of Ezra Pound,* edited by T.S. Eliot (New York: New Directions, 1968)

Power, Arthur. *Conversations with James Joyce,* edited by Clive Hart (London: Millington, 1974)

Price, Martin. *To the Palace of Wisdom: Studies in Order and Energy from Dryden to Blake* (New York: Doubleday, 1964)

Prigogine, Ilya. *From Being to Becoming: Time and Complexity in the Physical Sciences* (New York: W.H. Freeman & Co., 1981)

Quintilian. *Institutio Oratoria,* translated by Donald A. Russell (Cambridge, Mass.: Harvard University Press, 2001)

Rabelais, François. *The Five Books of Gargantua and Pantagruel,* translated by Jacques Le Clercq (New York: The Modern Library, 1936)

Rader, Melvin. *Wordsworth: A Philosophical Approach* (Oxford: Clarendon Press, 1967)

Ricoeur, Paul. *Freedom and Nature: The Voluntary and the Involuntary,* translated by Erazim V. Kohák (Evanston, Ill.: Northwestern University Press, 1966)

——. *The Symbolism of Evil,* translated by Emerson Buchanan (New York: Harper and Row, 1967),

Robinson, J. Bradford. "The Jazz Essays of Theodor Adorno: Some Thoughts on Jazz Reception in Weimar Germany," *Popular Music* 13, no. 1 (January 1994): 1-25

Rosenberg, John D. *The Fall of Camelot: A Study of Tennyson's* Idylls of the King (Cambridge, Mass.: Harvard University Press, 1973).

Rowland, Susan. *Jung as a Writer* (London: Routledge, 2005)

——. *Jung in the Humanities* (New Orleans: Spring Journal Books, 2012)

Rubenstein, Gilbert M. "The Moral Structure of Huckleberry Finn," *College English* 18, no. 2 (November 1956): 72-76

Ruskin, John. *The Elements of Drawing; in Three Letters to Beginners* (London: Smith, Elder, 1856-57)

Sahlins, Bernard. *Days and Nights in the Second City: A Memoir, with Notes on Staging Review Theatre* (Chicago: Ivan R. Dee, 2001)

Said, Edward W. *Reflections on Exile and Other Essays* (Cambridge, Mass.: Harvard University Press, 2002)

Sappho. *Lyrics in the Original Greek with Translations by Willis Barnstone* (Garden City, N.Y.: Anchor Books, 1965)

Schiller, Friedrich. *The Aesthetic Letters, Essays, and the Philosophical Letters,* translated by John Weiss (Boston: Little and Brown, 1845)

Schindler, Walter. *Voice and Crisis: Invocation in Miltons's Poetry* (Hamden, Conn.: Archon Books, 1984)

Schopenhauer, Arthur. *World as Will and Representation,* translated by Judith Norman and Alistair Welchman; edited by Christopher Janaway (Cambridge: Cambridge University Press, 2010)

Scholes, Robert, and Robert Kellogg. *The Nature of Narrative* (New York: Oxford University Press, 1966)

Schuller, Gunther. *Early Jazz: Its Roots and Musical Development* (New York: Oxford University Press, 1968).

Screech, M.A. *Rabelais* (London: Gerald Duckworth & Co., 1979)

Shaffer, E. S. *"Kubla Khan" and the Fall of Jerusalem: The Mythological School in Biblical Criticism and Secular Literature, 1770-1880* (Cambridge: Cambridge University Press, 1975)

Shaffer, Paul. *We'll Be Here for the Rest of Our Lives* (New York: Doubleday, 2009).

Shahn, Bernarda Bryson. *Ben Shahn* (New York: Abrams, 1972)

Shapin, Steven, and Simon Shaffer. *Leviathan and the Air-Pump: Hobbes, Boyle, and the Experimental Life* (Princeton, N.J.: Princeton University Press, 2011)

Shay, Jonathan. *Odysseus in America: Combat Trauma and the Trials of Homecoming* (New York: Scribner, 2002)

Sheats, Paul D. *The Making of Wordsworth's Poetry, 1785-1798* (Cambridge, Mass.: Harvard University Press, 1973)

Slingerland, Edward. *Effortless Action: Wu-Wei as Conceptual Metaphor and Spiritual Ideal in Early China* (New York: Oxford University Press, 2003)

Spenser, Edmund. *Spenser's Minor Poems,* vol. 1 of *The Poetical Works of Edmund Spenser,* edited by Ernest de Sélincourt (Oxford: Clarendon Press, 1909)

Stein, Murray. *Jung's Map of the Soul: An Introduction* (Chicago and La Salle, Ill.: Open Court, 1998)

Sterne, Laurence. *Tristram Shandy: An Authoritative Text,* edited by Howard Anderson (New York and London: W.W. Norton, 1980)

—. *The Life and Opinions of Tristram Shandy, Gentleman,* edited by James Aiken Work (New York: The Odyssey Press, 1940).

—. *The Florida Edition of the Works of Laurence Sterne,* edited by Melvyn New and Joan New (Gainesville: University of Florida Press, 1978-84)

Stevens, Wallace. *Collected Poetry and Prose* (New York: Library of America, 1997)

Stewart, Garrett. *Dickens and the Trials of Imagination* (Cambridge, Mass: Harvard University Press, 1974)

Swearingen, James E. *Reflexivity in* Tristram Shandy: *An Essay in Phenomenological Criticism* (New Haven and London: Yale University Press, 1977).

Swift, Jonathan. *The Writings of Jonathan Swift: Authoritative Texts, Backgrounds, Criticism,* edited by Robert A. Greenberg and William Bowman Piper (New York: W.W. Norton, 1973).

Thompson, Robert Farris. *Flash of the Spirit: African and Afro-American Art and Philosophy* (New York: Vintage, 1984)

—. *Aesthetics of the Cool: Afro-Atlantic Art and Music* (Pittsburgh and New York: Periscope, 2011)

Thoreau, Henry David. *The Heart of Thoreau's Journals,* edited by Odell Shepard (New York: Dover, 1961)

—. *A Writer's Journal,* edited by Laurence Stapleton (London: Heinemann, 1961)

—. *Walden, Civil Disobedience, and Other Writings,* edited by William Rossi (New York and London: W.W. Norton, 2008)

Tillyard, E.M.W. *The Elizabethan World Picture* (New York: Vintage, 1959)

Toulmin, Stephen. *Cosmopolis: The Hidden Agenda of Modernity* (Chicago: The University of Chicago Press, 1990)

Trilling, Lionel. *The Liberal Imagination* (New York: New York Review Books, 2008 [1948])

Tufail, Burhan. "Oulipian Grammatology: *La règle du jeu,*" in *The French Connections of Jacques Derrida,* edited by Julian Wolfreys, John Brannigan, and Ruth Robbins (Albany: State University of New York, 1999)

Twain, Mark (Samuel Clemens). *Adventures of Huckleberry Finn,* edited by Sculley Bradley, 2nd ed. (New York: W.W. Norton, 1977)

—. *Adventures of Huckleberry Finn,* edited by Henry Nash Smith (Boston: Houghton Mifflin Company, 1958)

—. *Life on the Mississippi* (New York: Oxford University Press, 1996)

Ulmer, Gregory L. "The Object of Post-Criticism," in *The Anti-Aesthetic: Essays on Postmodern Culture,* edited by Hal Foster (Seattle: Bay Press, 1983)

Valéry, Paul. *The Collected Works of Paul Valéry,* vol. 5: *Idée Fixe,* translated by David Paul (Princeton, N.J.: Princeton University Press, 1971)

Venturi, Robert, Dennis Scott Brown. and Steven Izenour, *Learning from Las Vegas* (Cambridge, Mass., and London: The MIT Press, 1972)

Warren, Robert Penn. "Mark Twain," *The Southern Review* 8 (Summer 1972): 470-72

Watt, Ian. "The Comic Syntax of *Tristram Shandy*," in *Studies in Ciriticsm and Aesthetics, 1660-1800,* edited by Howard Anderson and John S. Shea (Minneapolis: University of Minnesota Press, 1967),

—. *The Rise of the Novel: Studies in Defoe, Richardson and Fielding* (Berkeley and Los Angeles: University of California Press, 2001 [1957])

Watts, Isaac. *Horae Lyricae and Divine Songs* (Boston: Little, Brown and Company, 1854 [1706])

Weinbrot, Howard D. *Menippean Satire Reconsidered: From Antiquity to the Eighteenth Century* (Baltimore: The Johns Hopkins University Press, 2005).

Wells, Samuel. *Improvisation: The Drama of Christian Ethics* (Ada, Mich.: Brazos Press, 2004).

Weschler, Lawrence. *Seeing is Forgetting the Name of the Thing One Sees: A Life of Contemporary Artist Robert Irwin* (Berkeley and Los Angeles: University of California Press, 1982).

—. *Seeing Is Forgetting the Name of the Thing One Sees: Over Thirty Years of Conversations with Robert Irwin,* exp. ed. (Berkeley and Los Angeles: University of California Press, 2008)

White, Hayden. *The Wildman Within: An Image in Western Thought from the Renaissance to Romanticism,* edited by Edward Dudley and Maximilian Novak (Pittsburgh: University of Pittsburgh Press, 1972)

Whitehead, Alfred North. *Science and the Modern World: Lowell Lectures, 1925* (New York: The Free Press, 1967)

Whitman, Walt. *Leaves of Grass: Comprehensive Reader's Edition,* edited by H.W. Blodgett and Sculley Bradley (New York: W.W. Norton, 1965)

Wilcken, Patrick. *Claude Lévi-Strauss: The Poet in the Laboratory* (New York: Penguin, 2010)

William Carlos Williams, *The Collected Poems of William Carlos Williams,* vol 1: 1909-1939, edited by A. Walton Litz and Christopher MacGowan (New York: New Directions, 1986)

——. *Kora in Hell: Improvisations* (New York: New Directions, 1957)

——. *Paterson,* rev. ed., prepared by Christopher MacGowan (New York: New Directions, 1992)

Williams, Meg Harris. *Inspiration in Milton and Keats* (Totowa, N.J.: Barnes & Noble Books, 1982)

Williamson, George. *The Senecan Amble: A Study in Prose Form from Bacon to Collier* (Chicago: The University of Chicago Press, 1951)

Wilson, A.N. *The Life of John Milton* (Oxford: Oxford University Press, 1983)

Wilson, James D. "Adventures of Huckleberry Finn: From Abstraction to Humanity," *Southern Review* 10 (Winter 1974): 80–82

Witt, Ronald. *In the Footsteps of the Ancients: The Origins of Humanism from Lovato to Bruni. Studies in Medieval and Reformation Thought* (Leiden: Brill Academic Publishers, 2003)

Wittreich, Joseph Anthony, ed. *Milton and the Line of Vision* (Madison: The University of Wisconsin Press, 1975)

Wordsworth, William. *The Poetical Works of William Wordsworth,* edited by Ernest De Selincourt, 5 vols. (Oxford: Clarendon Press, 1940–49)

——. *The Prelude, or Growth of a Poet's Mind,* edited by Ernest de Selincourt and Stephen Gill (Oxford: Oxford University Press, 1970)

Wordsworth, William, and S.T. Coleridge. *Lyrical Ballads, 1798,* edited by W.J.B. Owen (London: Oxford University Press, 1967)

Yeats, William Butler. *Yeats's Poetry, Drama, and Prose,* edited by James Pethica (New York and London: W.W. Norton, 2000)

Young, David C. "Pindaric Criticism," in *Pindaros und Bakchylides,* edited by William Calder and Jacob Stern (Darmstadt: Wissenschaftliche Buchgesellschaft, 1970)

Young, Edward. *The Poetical Works of Edward Young,* 2 vols. (Boston: Little, Brown, and Company, 1859)

Zeki, Semir. *Splendours and Miseries of the Brain* (London: Wiley-Blackwell, 2009)

FILMOGRAPHY

Bennett, Stephanie, producer. *Let the Good Times Role: A Film about the Roots of American Music,* Delilah Music Pictures in Association with Island Visual Arts, 1992.

Dick, Kirby, and Amy Ziering Kofman, directors. *Derrida,* Jane Doe Films, 2002.

Murrow, Edward R., and Fred W. Friendly, producers. *Satchmo the Great,* CBS-TV with United Artists, 1957.

Made in the USA
Las Vegas, NV
10 October 2024

96603060R00291